KT-524-755

Contents

Finnish design
colour section
following p.88

Sauna
colour section
following p.248

◀◀ A summertime post-sauna dip in the Lake District ◀ Inarin Porofarmi reindeer farm, Inari

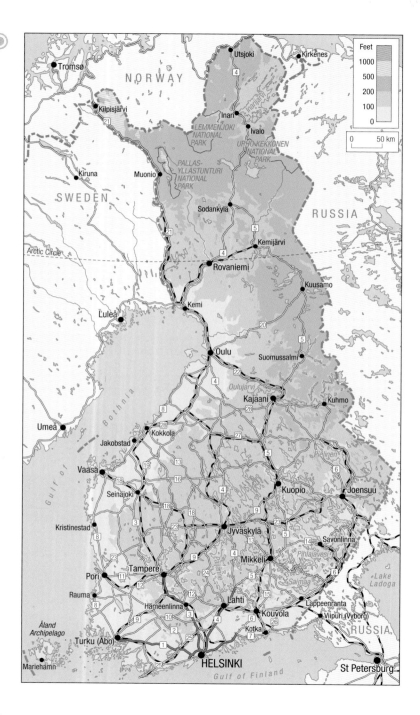

The Rough Guide to

Finland

written and researched by

Roger Norum and James Proctor

ROUGH
GUIDES

www.roughguides.com

Introduction to
Finland

Undoubtedly one of Europe's least understood countries, Finland is also one of the continent's most enigmatic and intriguing places to visit. Scrunched into the eastern pocket of Scandinavia and flanked to the east by the lengthy Russian border nearly all the way to the Arctic Sea, this captivating cultural anomaly remains the most unique of all the Scandinavian nations, having long cultivated a strong and distinctive sense of identity. Finland offers its citizens one of the world's most enviable standards of living, to say nothing of a stellar transport system, cradle-to-grave infrastructure and extremely safe cities and towns. Tack on to this a hip, happening and ridiculously walkable capital, and an enviable collection of national parks, birch forests and immaculate waterways – rivers that empty out into the Baltic and Bothnian seas as well as nearly 200,000 inland lakes – and you can see why Finns have kept their fabulous country a secret.

Finland was long a pawn played between the rulers of the Swedish and Russian empires, but since its independence in 1917, the country has fully come into its own. That Finns speak a **language** unrelated to most European tongues hasn't made being accepted any easier, of course – though their near-native fluency in English certainly has.

However the Finns' ties to their own history and traditions should not be underestimated. This is by far the most ethnically homogenous nation

Fact file

• Finland is one of the five Nordic nations and, with a total land area of 338,145 square kilometres, one of the largest (it's slightly smaller than Germany). The population is 5.35 million – with an average of seventeen people per square kilometre, this is the least densely populated country in the EU. A mere 2.2 percent of the population is made up of foreign-born citizens and their descendants. Unemployment averages 6.8 percent, above the European average.

• The standard of living in Finland is one of the highest in the world – income tax hovers around 31.5 percent (lower than the other Nordic countries), and 22 percent VAT is levied on most goods. In return Finns receive free, comprehensive social welfare.

• Finland is not called "the land of a thousand lakes" for nothing; in fact there are 187,880 of them, more lakes than any other country in the world. Lakes make up ten percent of the country's land mass; forests cover nearly seventy percent of what's left.

• The human population of Finnish Lapland is 188,000. The reindeer population is 210,000.

• According to a recent study, Finland is the least corrupt, most competitive and most democratic country in the world – and it's near the top of the list for environmental sustainability and technological innovation, too.

• Finland has nearly one sauna for every two people.

• Finns are the world's highest per-capita consumers of coffee, drinking some 5.7 cups a day, or 10kg per year.

▲ Lutheran Cathedral, Helsinki

in the EU, with very little foreign **immigration** – though the countenance of the country is changing, especially in the capital. Since Finland was part of both Sweden and Russia for eons, it has only recently had the opportunity to play any decisive role in European affairs – and it has risen to the occasion with strong social democratic principles, an excellent welfare and social services system and an interest in the environment and sustainable industry that is decades ahead of many other nations. Though on the whole Finns tend to be more taciturn, introverted and reserved than other Nordic peoples, once they invite you into their homes – and their saunas – you'll find them to be extremely welcoming, good humoured and great fun.

Although Finland is one of Europe's largest countries geographically, it maintains a dependable **railway system** that stretches from the far south all the way up to Rovaniemi in the Arctic north, covering most all major cities in between – and when trains don't go to some of the smaller settlements, buses generally will. The many islands that make up Finland's archipelagoes, meanwhile, are linked by regular (and often free) ferries. The bulk of visitors are drawn to the major **cities** of Helsinki, Turku and Tampere – all sizable settlements with a striking small-town charm. Still, it would be a shame to miss some of the more pastoral areas of the country – many of them gorgeous, Arcadian little settlements – especially as Finland's sense of place in the modern world is strongly tied to the past of its rural villages. After the sauna and monster-mask heavy metal bands, Finland is perhaps best known for its **great outdoors**: millions of acres of forests, plains, meadows, rivers, lakes, islands and beaches.

Where to go

Nearly all visitors get their first glimpse of Finland through dynamic, spirited **Helsinki**, the country's largest transport gateway and an absolute must see, given that it is one of Europe's most culturally vibrant and exciting cities – and fundamental to understanding what Finns are really about. Handsome and historic, Helsinki offers visitors a clutch of interesting museums, intriguing architecture, cutting-edge design shops, an

▲ The harbour, Helsinki

enviable café and restaurant scene and a simmering nightlife. In summer the entire city is overtaken with concerts, performances and festivals – many of which are free.

Outside Helsinki are a number of coastal destinations easily reached by a short bus or train ride, including riverside **Porvoo** with its distinctive crimson buildings, the one-time spa resort town of **Hanko** and the maritime centre **Kotka**. If your interest lies in things nautical, you'll definitely want to get to know Finland's southwestern pocket, where the main settlement is **Turku**, a relaxing spot that is much more sleepy town than second city, whose collection of likeable museums and active student life make it great for a few days of cultural (and hedonistic) exploration.

Immediately north of here are the towns of **Rauma** and **Pori**, the former known for its well-preserved, centuries-old wooden buildings, the latter for hosting one of the best annual jazz festivals in Europe. Splayed off the southwestern coast is an archipelago of some 20,000 islands and skerries, easily accessible from Turku thanks to a series of free ferry connections – and perfect for a few days' seaside cycle. Still further off into the Baltic are 6500 more specks of land that make up the autonomous province of **Åland**, a place that is – culturally, linguistically and geographically – much closer to Sweden than Finland. Its laidback capital of **Mariehamn** is a great place to hole up for a few days as you gear up for a jaunt around any number of seriously idyllic islands.

Along the country's eastern fringes fronting the Russian border stretches the region known as **Karelia**, a place of slender lakes, Russian Orthodox churches and old wooden summer homes. The very name Karelia evokes

Fox fires and midnight suns

One of the Northern Hemisphere's most spectacular visual experiences is the Aurora Borealis, or Northern Lights – bright, fiery tapestries of hazel and amber that flicker and stretch across the heavens. Known in Finnish as *revontulet* (lit. "fires of the fox"), the country's northern reaches are some of the best places in the world to see them. The 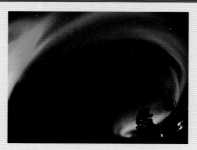 lights are best seen on clear nights in rural areas from February to March and September to October. The further north you are the better: in some parts of northern Lapland there are as many as 200 displays per year. If you're hoping to take snapshots of the aurora sky, remember to use long exposures – between 5 and 60 seconds – and bring a tripod. In the summertime, meanwhile, the midnight sun – 24 hours of daylight – is visible from anywhere north of the Arctic Circle during high summer.

▲ Snowtime rally racing, Kuhmo

strong emotions for both Finns and Russians alike, and the entire area became symbolic of Finnish independence and national identity after years of having its eastern fringes consistently shaved off and handed over to the Russians. The rural landscape here was the inspiration for the national epic *Kalevala*, and its strategic location for years made it both a target and a line of defence; the world's longest man-made bunker, the 1200-kilometre Salpa Line built during World War II, slices through the region's heart. Some aspects of the Karelian past can be found in the fortresses of towns such as **Lappeenranta** and the historical museums of cities such as **Joensuu**. North of here is the region of **Kainuu**, a thickly forested spot whose pines once produced the bulk of Finland's tar export and are now extremely popular among trekkers (and brown bears), especially along the well-known UKK hiking route fronting the Russian border.

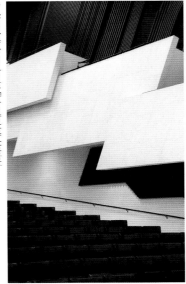

▲ Alvar Aalto's modernist Finlandia Hall, Helsinki

West of Karelia is Finland's **Lake District**, a sprawling chunk of land smack in the middle of the country that is characterized by thousands of water-ways, the largest of which, Lake Saimaa, is Europe's fifth largest and runs into Lake Ladoga and Vyborg in Russia. This is an ideal part of the country to get to know the great outdoors, with lakeside settlements that run the gamut from sleepy, quaint **Savonlinna** – which is sleepy and quaint only outside of its world-renowned month-long summer opera festival – to lively, industrial **Tampere**, the perfect port of call for an afternoon or evening lake cruise. West of here along the Bothnian coast lie a series of towns that hold the lion's share of the country's Swedish-speaking popula-tion. The central settlement here is bilingual **Vaasa**, a

▲ Neoclassical onion-domed building, Vaasa

marine and arts centre named after the Swedish king of the same name, while north near the Swedish border is **Oulu**, a somewhat livelier place and certainly more urbane in sensibility, but also a great jumping off point for exploring Finland's more exotic pastures further north.

By far Finland's most dramatic landscape is found in the northernmost reaches of the country, where the sprawling landmass of barren tundra and dense forests known as **Finnish Lapland** covers nearly half the country and provides a home to the region's indigenous people, the Sámi. Far up here, away from the cares (and many of the facilities) of the modern world, the region's few main settlements – Rovaniemi, Muonio and Inari – serve as adequate introductions to the ways of the North, with more than enough to occupy you for a day or two. But to really get to know how magical Lapland can be – at any time of the year – you'll want to suit up, arm your pack with provisions and venture into the wilds, where Finland really shows her true colours.

When to go

ention the very word "Finland," and most people will shiver at the very notion of the place, with images that involve frozen tundra and thickly iced lakes. Despite sitting fairly far north, Finland maintains a relatively mild **climate**, thanks to its many lakes and the warming Gulf Stream that flows in off the Norwegian coast – though the weather can change quite quickly, especially during the winter. Rainfall levels

▶ Late summer, Hanko

are moderate and more or less constant throughout the year, with an annual average of 65cm; the coast and the northern stretches tend to rain less than in the south and in the interior.

In the south, **spring** usually begins around mid-April, though it can remain chilly in a number of places until May, especially in Lapland, where it's not unheard of to find snow hanging around until nearly the beginning of summer.

Definitively the best time to visit Finland is during the **summer** months of June, July and August, when the climate is warmest, the days are longest and the blossoming landscape at its prettiest, and when tourist facilities and transport services operate at full steam. Remember though that August is holiday month for Finns, who tend to head en masse to the countryside or the coast just after midsummer – though even then, only the most popular areas are uncomfortably crowded. Summer is almost always sunny and clear, with temperatures rarely stifling: the warmest month is July, which averages 17°C (62°F), though highs of 26°C (32°F) are not uncommon, especially in the interior. The best times to visit Helsinki are May, early June and September – though you'll find plenty going on throughout the year.

Visually speaking, **autumn** is a superb time to visit the country, especially in Lapland during *ruska-aika* (russeting): the lower fells become bathed in

▼ A lakeside sauna log cabin outside Mikkeli

golds and oranges, bracken and beech glow bronze, poplars cloak the hills in yellow and the higher hills turn a deep crimson. Bear in mind though that the coastal waters can be fairly nippy as early as September, and that most sights and attractions have reduced hours outside of high season, from mid-September onwards.

Long, dark and cold, Finnish **winters** are nevertheless far from inordinately severe or intolerable. Although temperatures can drop as low as minus 7°C (19°F) – and at times colder – things generally tend to hover just below freezing. The best part about the chillier months is the amazing variety of outdoor activities, which include cross-country skiing, snowmobiling, ice diving, jumping off an ice breaker into freezing cold waters and – of course – that most quintessentially Finnish of pastimes: broiling in a rural sauna, then cooling off in the frigid waters of a nearby lake. During the darkest months, when daylight is in short supply, pints of beer and slugs of national

▲ Swedish-speaking Finns at tea time, Mariehamn (Åland)

13

drinks such as *salmari* and *fisu* – admittedly extremely acquired tastes – help
to keep the cold at bay, and Finns muster up no small amount of charm and
hospitality, especially if it involves passing on their quirky traditions and wry
humour to the unsuspecting visitor.

Average daytime temperatures and rainfall

	Jan	Feb	Mar	Apr	May	Jun	Jul	Aug	Sep	Oct	Nov	Dec
Helsinki												
°C	−7	−7	−3	3	10	15	17	15	10	6	0	−4
°F	20	20	27	37	50	59	62	59	50	42	32	25
mm	40.6	30.5	33	38.1	35.6	43.2	73.7	81.3	73.7	73.7	71.1	58.4
Turku												
°C	−6	−6	−3	3	10	15	17	15	11	6	1	−3
°F	21	21	27	37	50	59	62	59	51	42	33	26
mm	45.7	33	33	38.1	35.6	43.2	78.7	83.8	71.1	68.6	71.1	58.4
Jyväskylä												
°C	−10	−9	−4	1	9	14	16	14	8	3	−2	−7
°F	14	15	24	34	48	57	60	57	47	38	28	19
mm	43.2	30.5	35.6	38.1	40.6	55.9	78.7	91.4	66.0	55.9	58.4	48.3
Rovaniemi												
°C	−10	−11	−6	−1	4	12	15	12	7	1	−5	−10
°F	13	11	20	30	40	55	59	54	45	34	22	14
mm	42.1	33.6	35.6	30.9	35.9	59.1	69.1	71.7	54.0	54.6	48.6	41.7

things not to miss

It's not possible to see everything that Finland has to offer in a single trip – and it would be foolish to suggest you try. What follows is a selective taste of the country's highlights (in no particular order), from imposing castles and fine museums to vast rural landscapes and scattered islands. They're arranged in five colour-coded categories with a page reference to take you straight into the guide, where you can find out more.

01 **Jugendstil architecture, Helsinki** Page **68** • The distinctly Finnish interpretation of Art Nouveau is found throughout the capital in façades, interiors, sculptures – even entire railway stations.

02 **Husky safari, Muonio** Page **297** • Grab the reins and head out on an unforgettable adventure through a winter wonderland, led by a pack of sled dogs across the tundra plains and through the dense boreal forests of Lapland's most intimidating wilderness.

04 **Nightlife, Helsinki** Page **91** • The Finnish capital presents an enviable collection of chic lounges, speakeasies, bars and clubs, a handful of which offer tempting newfangled cocktails. Birch root or sea buckthorn martinis, anyone?

03 **Cathedral, Turku** Page **135** • Finland's first capital is home to the country's largest church, rebuilt several times over but standing tall and elegant, and holding the ornate marble tomb of Catharine Månsdotter, Queen of Sweden.

05 **Summer cycling, Åland** Page **168** • Hop on a bike, board a gratis ferry and head off to explore Åland's 6500 islands: idyllic, hushed spots perfect for pedaling through at your own pace.

06 **Glass igloos, Kakslauttanen** Page **286** • These modern, transparent-roofed steel cabins give you near-perfect views of the Arctic heavens, allowing you to drift off to sleep below the Northern Lights, the midnight sun or simply the twinkling stars – all the while basking in Lappish chic.

07 **Festivals** Page **40** • The Finns' quirky, off-beat sense of humour has spawned some of the world's most unique festivals, including a high-heel race, a mosquito-swatting contest and a wife-throwing competition.

08 **Dining out** Pages **36–39** • Put away your inhibitions and preconceptions: Finnish cuisine these days is some of the most inventive, daring and tempting anywhere, with wunderkind chefs and the freshest of locally sourced ingredients.

09 **Pihlajasaari, Helsinki** Page **82** • Island-hopping off the capital's coast is as easy as a fifteen-minute ferry ride to this narrow isle of wild flowers and pine trees, perfect for sunning, swimming and – if you're so inclined – going au natural on the best of Finland's best nude beaches.

10 Designer shopping, Helsinki Pages **94–95** • Jostling with Copenhagen as Europe's reigning polestar for picking up gorgeously designed housewares, clothing and objets d'art, Helsinki has hundreds of great shops.

11 Snow Castle, Kemi Page **265** • Every winter, cold-blooded architects butt heads with frosty sculptors to build a functioning castle (and snow hotel, restaurant, chapel and ice bar) entirely out of frozen H$_2$O.

12 Sand Castle, Lappeenranta Page 182 •

Every summer, this Karelian fortress town gathers some 3 million kilos of sand at the marina to erect a colossal, near life-size sand castle – the largest in the country.

13 Santa Claus, Rovaniemi

Page **280** • Good old Saint Nick resides far up in the Finnish Arctic, where he accepts visitors year-round into his workshop – and multiple souvenir shops.

14 Sámi Culture, Inari Page 289 •

The indigenous inhabitants of Lapland have managed to forge a complicated – but largely prosperous – relationship between old and new, fusing their traditions with modern technological innovation.

15 **Opera Festival, Savonlinna** Page **205** • There can be no better venue for a glorious aria than the enormous forecourt that graces the medieval lakeside Olavinlinna castle, site of one of Europe's most revered opera festivals for an entire month during the summer.

16 **Arctic icebreaker, Kemi** Page **265** • Explore the confluence of steel, ice and sea on a day aboard the Sampo icebreaker, where you can don a drysuit and dive into the icy waters at the gateway to Finnish Lapland.

17 **Midnight sun, Finnish Lapland** Page **8** • There's little more magical than staying up late on a summer's eve to gaze out at the sun flirting with the horizon at 1am, a defining characteristic of the Arctic firmament.

18 **Kiasma, Helsinki** Page **70** • A stand-out modern art museum, Kiasma shows off regular cutting-edge installation, sculptural, video and print works inside a mountainous slab of titanium smack in the city centre.

19 **Valamo Monastery, Lake District** Page **214** • Set deep in the forests where the lakeland meets the Karelian countryside, this uncharacteristically lively Orthodox cloister is best arrived at by boat to the monks' private mooring – and best experienced on an overnight stay in one of their lodgings.

21 **Lake cruise, Savonlinna** Page **208** • A lake cruise in the Finnish summertime offers the opportunity to take in the country's most enviable scenery at a leisurely pace – and maybe dine on smoked herring and hear some foot-stomping Dixieland jazz.

20 **Bothnian beaches, Kalajoki** Page **257** • Images of Finland may not exactly scream sun, sand and surf, but that doesn't stop the crowds of Finns who flock to this coastal town to take in the long summer days, warm waters and great beach scene.

22 **The Old Town, Rauma** Page **148** • Day trippers in the southwest flock to the cobblestone lanes of this eighteenth-century hamlet, filled to the brim with charismatic old wooden buildings.

23 **Hiking, Kainuu** Page **200** • The trails that run along the Russian border in the northern reaches of Kainuu offer the chance to explore one of the world's most remote regions.

Basics

Basics

Getting there

Given the extremely long distances and journey times involved in reaching Finland overland, flying will not only save you considerable amounts of time – but money, too. The main gateways are Helsinki and Tampere, though in winter destinations in Finnish Lapland such as Rovaniemi and Kittilä are also served by a number of direct charter flights from abroad. Air fares are generally cheaper when booked as far in advance as possible. Midweek travel is less expensive than weekend departures.

Flights from the US and Canada

Only one airline operates **from the US** to Finland: Finnair flies from New York (JFK) to Helsinki once daily all year round. During the summer months, Finnair also operates from Toronto to Helsinki, though departures are not daily. Less expensive tickets can sometimes be found on European airlines routing via their home hub, for example British Airways via London Heathrow or Icelandair via Keflavík, or on American carriers who operate via various European cities such as Paris, London or Stockholm. From **New York** a return midweek fare to Helsinki (8hr) will cost around US$950 in high season, US$750 in low season. From the **West Coast** (journey time at least 16hr), you'll pay around US$200–300 more. From **Canada**, fares from **Toronto** (journey time 10–14hr depending on connections) are Can$1100–1300 in high season, Can$850–1050 in low season. From Vancouver, they're around Can$500 higher.

Flights from the UK and Ireland

Flights for Helsinki and Tampere leave from several **UK airports**. Flying to Finland with Ryanair to Tampere or easyJet to Helsinki is usually the cheapest way of getting there. Single fares can be as low as £20 and

sometimes less than that, though in the case of Ryanair it is rare for flights to Tampere to be discounted to rock-bottom prices, unlike many other destinations in the network. In peak season, a return price of around £100 is more realistic, depending on how early the booking is made and the choice of departure dates.

The other main airlines serving Finland are British Airways, Finnair and Blue1, who offer return tickets to Finland starting around £150. The Latvian airline, Air Baltic, can also be useful in reaching provincial cities in Finland via its hub in Riga, though it only operates from London Gatwick in the UK and Dublin in Ireland. **From Ireland**, Finnair and Ryanair also operate direct services to Finland. In the wintertime, there are direct charter flights – including a number of "Santa Special" day-trips – from the UK to Lapland; Rovaniemi, Kittilä and Ivalo are the most popular destinations.

Flights from Australia, New Zealand and South Africa

There are no direct flights to Finland from Australia, New Zealand or South Africa and by far the cheapest option is to find a discounted fare to **London** and arrange a **flight to Finland** from there. All air fares

roughguides.com

Find everything you need to plan your next trip at ⓦ www.roughguides.com. Read in-depth information on destinations worldwide, make use of our unique trip-planner, book transport and accommodation, check out other travellers' recommendations and share your own experiences.

from Australian east-coast gateways are similarly priced, with the cheapest deals via Asia starting around Aus\$1800. From Perth or Darwin, flights are around Aus\$100 less. From New Zealand reckon on NZ\$2500 as a starting point from Auckland, NZ\$250 more from Wellington. From South Africa, count on around ZAR7300 from the cheapest return from Cape Town.

Trains

Getting to Finland by **train** is much more expensive than flying. There are no through tickets and the total cost of all the tickets you'll need, including the final ferry crossing from Stockholm to either, Mariehamn or Helsinki, is likely to cost around £400–500. Hence, it's worth buying a rail pass instead; a global InterRail pass (from £240) or Eurail pass (from US\$511) are the best options. **From London** trains go via Brussels, Cologne, Hamburg and Copenhagen to Stockholm, from where you catch a ferry to Finland. A typical journey will involve changing trains four or five times, plus the transfer to the ferry, and takes around 36–40 hours.

Ferries

The following companies operate daily departures between Stockholm and **Helsinki**, allowing rail passengers to make the final connection of a land/sea journey to Finland: Silja Line (ⓛwww.tallinksilja .com; 16hr; €31 obligatory cabin, €52 car) and Viking Line (ⓛwww.vikingline.fi; 16hr; €36 deck passenger, €42 car). Frequent discounts are offered by both throughout the year and you can occasionally land a bed in a four-person **cabin** for around €20.

Both companies have a year-round overnight service, leaving at 5pm and arriving at 9.30am, and both also run a twice-daily service from Stockholm to **Turku**, which takes ten or eleven hours (Silja cabin €15.50, €21 day, €42 night; Viking Line foot passenger €10). Quicker still (4hr) are the daily services between Stockholm and **Mariehamn**, run by Viking (passengers €11, car €11). Prices for all the routes are usually cheapest on daylight trips outside of the summer months and during the week.

Airlines, agents and operators

Airlines

Air Baltic ⓛwww.airbaltic.com.
Air Berlin ⓛwww.airberlin.com.
American Airlines ⓛwww.aa.com.
Blue1 ⓛwww.blue1.com.
British Airways ⓛwww.ba.com.
Continental Airlines ⓛwww.continental.com.
Delta ⓛwww.delta.com.
easyJet ⓛwww.easyjet.com.
Finnair ⓛwww.finnair.com.
Icelandair ⓛwww.icelandair.com.
KLM (Royal Dutch Airlines) ⓛwww.klm.com.
Lufthansa ⓛwww.lufthansa.com.
Ryanair ⓛwww.ryanair.com.
SAS (Scandinavian Airlines) ⓛwww.flysas.com.
United Airlines ⓛwww.united.com.

Rail contacts

European Rail UK ☎020/7619 1083, ⓛwww .europeanrail.com.
Europrail International Canada ☎1-888/667-9734, ⓛwww.europrail.net.
Eurostar UK ☎0870/518 6186, ⓛwww.eurostar .com.
Rail Europe US ☎1-888/382-7245, Canada ☎1-800/361-7245, UK ☎0844/848 4064, Australia ☎03/9642 8644, South Africa ☎11/628 2319; ⓛwww.raileurope.com.

Ferry contacts

Tallink Silja ⓛwww.tallinksilja.com.
Viking ⓛwww.vikingline.fi.

Agents and operators

Don't be put off by the idea of an inclusive **package**, as it can sometimes be the cheapest way of doing things, and a much easier way of reaching the remote areas of northern Finland in winter. City breaks are invariably less expensive than if you arrange the same trip independently. There are also an increasing number of operators offering specialist-interest holidays to Finland, particularly Arctic expeditions.
5 Stars of Scandinavia ☎1-800/722 4146, ⓛ5stars-of-scandinavia.com. The American specialist in holidays to Finland including city tours to Helsinki, Turku and Naantali, as well as excursions to Finnish Lapland and the Lake region.

Six steps to a better kind of travel

At Rough Guides we are passionately committed to travel. We feel strongly that only through travelling do we truly come to understand the world we live in and the people we share it with – plus tourism has brought a great deal of **benefit** to developing economies around the world over the last few decades. But the extraordinary growth in tourism has also damaged some places irreparably, and of course **climate change** is exacerbated by most forms of transport, especially flying. This means that now more than ever it's important to **travel thoughtfully and responsibly**, with respect for the cultures you're visiting – not only to derive the most benefit from your trip but also to preserve the best bits of the planet for everyone to enjoy. At Rough Guides we feel there are six main areas in which you can make a difference:

• Consider what you're contributing to the **local economy**, and how much the services you use do the same, whether it's through employing local workers and guides or sourcing locally grown produce and local services.

• Consider the **environment** on holiday as well as at home. Water is scarce in many developing destinations, and the biodiversity of local flora and fauna can be adversely affected by tourism. Try to patronize businesses that take account of this.

• Travel with a purpose, not just to tick off experiences. Consider **spending longer** in a place, and getting to know it and its people.

• Give thought to how often you **fly**. Try to avoid short hops by air and more harmful night flights.

• Consider **alternatives to flying**, travelling instead by bus, train, boat and even by bike or on foot where possible.

• Make your trips **"climate neutral"** via a reputable carbon offset scheme. All Rough Guide flights are offset, and every year we donate money to a variety of charities devoted to combating the effects of climate change.

Canterbury Travel ☎01923/457017, ⊛www.laplandmagic.com. The market leaders in short trips to see Santa Claus on the Arctic Circle with an impressive range of departures from most UK regional airports.

Discover the World ☎01737/218800, ⊛www.discover-the-world.co.uk. Experienced and well-respected specialist UK operator with years of experience in arranging holidays to Finnish Lapland including everything from bear-watching in Kuhmo to skiing inside the Arctic Circle.

MyBentours ☎02/9241 1353, ⊛www.myplanet australia.com.au. The leading Australian specialist to Finland offering air, rail and ferry tickets as well as dogsledding tours in Finnish Lapland.

North South Travel UK ☎01245/608 291, ⊛www.northsouthtravel.co.uk. Friendly, competitive travel agency, offering discounted fares worldwide. Profits are used to support projects in the developing world, especially the promotion of sustainable tourism.

Scantours ☎020/7554 3530, ⊛www.scantours .co.uk. A wide range of holidays to Finland from this London-based tour operator, including skiing in Ylläs, visits to Lake Inari and dogsledding at Harriniva near Muonio.

STA Travel US ☎1-800/781-4040, UK ☎0871/2300 040, Australia ☎134 782, New Zealand ☎0800/474 400, South Africa ☎0861/781 781; ⊛www.statravel .com. Worldwide specialists in independent travel; also student IDs, travel insurance, car rental, rail passes, and more. Good discounts for students and under-26s.

Trailfinders UK ☎0845/058 5858, Ireland ☎01/677 7888, Australia ☎1300/780 212; ⊛www.trailfinders.com. One of the best-informed and most efficient agents for independent travellers.

Travel CUTS Canada ☎1-866/246-9762, US ☎1-800/592-2887; ⊛www.travelcuts.com. Canadian youth and student travel firm.

USIT Ireland ☎01/602 1906, Northern Ireland ☎028/9032 7111; ⊛www.usit.ie. Ireland's main student and youth travel specialists.

Getting around

Save for the fact that traffic tends to follow a north–south pattern, you'll have few headaches getting around the more populated parts of Finland. The chief form of public transport is the train, backed up, particularly on east–west journeys, by long-distance coaches. For the most part trains and buses integrate well, and you'll only need to plan with care when travelling through sparsely inhabited areas such as the far north and east. Feasible and often affordable variations come in the form of ferries, planes, bikes, and even hitching – car rental is strictly for the wealthy.

The complete **timetable** (*Suomen Kulku-neuvot*) for train, bus, ferry and air travel within the country is published every four months; it's sold primarily at large bookshops for €30. This is essential for plotting complex routes; for simplified details of the major train services, pick up the *Rail Pocket Guide* booklet, available at most train stations for around €1 (or downloadable as a PDF for free from ⓦwww.vr.fi).

Trains

The swiftest land link between Finland's major cities is invariably the reliable **train service**, operated by the state railway company, Valtan Rautatie (VR). Large, comfortable *pikajuna* ("express" trains, though often quite slow), super-smooth IC (inter-city trains) and an increasing number of state-of-the-art tilting *pendolino* trains serve the principal **north–south** routes several times a day, reaching as far north as Rovaniemi on the Arctic Circle, although occasional services penetrate as far north as Kemijärvi. Elsewhere, especially on east–west hauls through sparsely populated regions, rail services tend to be skeletal and trains are often tiny two-carriage affairs. The Arctic North has a very limited network of services. More details on Finnish Railways can be found at ⓦwww.vr.fi.

InterRail, BIJ and ScanRail **passes** are valid on all trains; if you don't have one of these and are planning a lot of travelling, get a **Finnrail Pass** before arriving in Finland (you can't buy it in Finland itself) from a travel agent or Finnish Tourist Office (for addresses, see p.47). This costs €129 for three days' unlimited travel within a month, €131 for three days, €175 for five days or

€237 for ten days. Otherwise, train **fares** are surprisingly reasonable. As a guide, a one-way, second-class ticket from Helsinki to Turku (a trip of around 200km) costs around €28; Helsinki to Kuopio (465km) €56; and Helsinki to Rovaniemi (900km) €81.

Tickets are purchased for specific dates and times, though there is no fee if you want to change the date or routing. Some journeys also allow you to break your journey en route – check when you purchase. You should **buy tickets** from station ticket offices (*lippumyymälä*), although you can also pay the inspector on the train. If there are three or more of you travelling together, **group tickets**, available from a train station or travel agent, can cut the regular fares on journeys over 80km by at least 15 percent (20 percent for parties of 11 or more). **Senior citizens**, those over 65 with valid identification, are entitled to a 50 percent discount on regular tickets; pensioners under 65 must purchase a Finnish Senior Citizens railcard (€9). The cost of **seat reservations** depends on the distance travelled but is generally around €5 – remember that although they are not necessary on express trains, reservations can be a good idea if you're travelling over a holiday period or on Fridays or Sundays.

Buses

Run by local private companies but with a common ticket system, **buses** cover the whole country, and are often quicker and more frequent than trains over the shorter east–west hops, and essential for getting around the remoter regions; they are not necessarily cheaper than trains, however. In the Arctic North there is a very limited railway network, so almost all public transport is by road, hence it's here that you'll find buses most useful. The main operators are Gold Line (☎016/334 5500, ⓦwww.goldline.fi) and Eskelisen Lapin Linjat (☎016/342 2160, ⓦwww.eskelisen-lapinlinjat.com).

The free bus **timetable**, *Suomen Pikavuorot*, lists all the routes in the country and can be picked up at most long-distance bus stations but is not very user-friendly, especially if you're not fluent in Finnish. Schedules and detailed information in English on travel in Finland by coach and bus can also be found at ⓦwww.matkahuolto.fi/en. South of the Arctic Circle, you're more likely to use the excellent network of rail services than endure the hassle of buses.

All **fares** are calculated according to the distance travelled: Helsinki to Turku (160km) costs around €28, Helsinki to Kuopio (400km) around €58. Express buses charge a supplement of approximately €3 per journey and are worth it for the correspondingly faster journey times. All types of **ticket** can be purchased at bus stations or at most travel agents; only ordinary one-way tickets can be bought on board the bus, though on journeys of 80km or less there's no saving in buying a return anyway. On return trips of over 80km, there is a reduction of ten percent.

Ferries

As **lake travel** is aimed more at holidaying families than the budget-conscious traveller, **prices** are high considering the distances, and progress is slow as the vessels chug along the great lake chains. One exception is the southern archipelagos – the islands off Turku (see p.139) and Åland (p.161) – where ferry travel is an essential (and thus markedly inexpensive) mode of transport. Still, even in other regions, if you have the time, money and inclination, it can be worth taking one of the shorter trips simply for the experience. There are numerous routes and details can be checked at any tourist office in the country and at Finnish Tourist Offices abroad; we've detailed some of the more scenic routes in the Guide.

Planes

When bought in advance, domestic **flights** can be comparatively cheap as well as time-saving if you want to cover long distances, such as from Helsinki to the Arctic North. That said, travelling by air means you'll miss many interesting parts of the country. Finnair (ⓦwww.finnair.com), Blue1 (ⓦwww.blue1.com) and Finncomm (ⓦwww.fc.fi), which operates the biggest domestic network in Finland, offer a variety of advance-purchase low fares which can be checked and purchased online. Youth **fares** are available for 17–24-year-olds and offer a fifty percent discount on the normal fare, though it's usually cheaper to book a regular single ticket well in advance. Flights operate daily between most large cities, and one-way fares start at €38 including taxes, though to ensure seats this cheap you must book several weeks in advance.

Driving and hitching

Renting a car is extremely expensive in Finland (as is petrol), and with such a good public-transport network, it's only worth considering if you're travelling in a group. The big international companies have offices in most Finnish towns and at international arrival points. If you're in Helsinki it's also worth checking the local company Transvell (☎08000/7000, ⓦwww.transvell.fi), a subsidiary of SIXT. They all accept major credit cards; if paying by cash, you'll need to leave a substantial deposit. You'll also need a valid driving licence, at least a year's driving experience, and to be a minimum of 19–24 years old, depending on the company you rent from.

Rates for a medium-sized car start at around €50 per day, with reductions for longer periods – you'll pay upwards of €300 for a week's use. On top of this, there can be a surcharge of up to 75 cents per kilometre (which may be waived on long-term rentals) and a drop-off fee of around €150 if you leave the car somewhere other than the place from which it was rented. For more details on car rental before arriving in Finland, visit the website of one of the international companies mentioned below, or ask at a Finnish Tourist Board office.

If you **bring your own car** to Finland, it's advisable (though not compulsory) to have a Green Card as proof that you are comprehensively insured in the event of an accident.

Some insurers in EU countries will offer you a Green Card for free as part of your insurance package, whilst others will charge a premium. Further **information** about driving in Finland can be obtained from Autoliitto, the Automobile and Touring Club of Finland, Hämeentie 105A, 00550 Helsinki (℡09/7258 4400, ⓦwww.autoliitto.fi).

Once underway, you'll find the next financial drain is **fuel**, which costs around €1.40 a litre (unleaded), though bear in mind that in rural areas, especially in Lapland, fuel is considerably more expensive than in Helsinki. Except in the far north, **service stations** are plentiful and usually open from 7am to 9pm between Monday and Saturday, and are often closed on Sunday – although in busy holiday areas many stay open round the clock during the summer. Larger towns will also have automatic pumps which function round-the-clock and accept cash and credit cards, though many of these machines do not recognize foreign cards. Though fuel prices may well impoverish you, take some consolation in the fact that you can drive on all Finnish motorways for free, as there are no tolls.

Though **roads** are generally in good condition there can be problems with melting snows, usually during April and May in the south and occasionally early June in the far north. Finnish **road signs** are similar to those throughout Europe, but be aware of bilingual place names; one useful sign to watch for is *Keskusta*, which means "town centre". **Speed limits** vary, though generally the legal limit is between 30kph and 40kph in towns, and from 80kph to 100kph on major roads – if it's not signposted, the basic limit is always 80kph. On motorways the maximum speed is 120kph in summer, 100kph in winter.

Other **rules of the road** include using headlights all the time when driving outside built-up areas, as well as in fog and in poor light, and the compulsory wearing of seatbelts by drivers and all passengers. Penalties for drink-driving are severe – the police may stop and breathalize you if they think you've been driving erratically. In some areas in the north of the country, reindeer and elk are liable to take a stroll across a road, especially around dusk. These are sizeable creatures and damage (to the car) is likely to be serious; all such collisions should be reported at the nearest police station and the Finnish Motor Insurers' Centre (*Liikennevaku-utuskeskus*), Bulevardi 28, 00120 Helsinki (℡09/680 401, ⓦwww.lvk.fi), which can also help with local breakdown companies.

Hitching is generally easy, and sometimes the quickest means of transport between two spots. Make sure you have a decent road map and emergency provisions/shelter if you're passing through isolated regions. While many Finns speak English, it's still handy to memorize the Finnish equivalent of "let me out here" (*jään pois tässä*).

Car rental agencies

Auto Europe ⓦ www.autoeurope.com.
Avis ⓦ www.avis.com.
Budget ⓦ www.budget.com.
Easy Car ⓦ www.easycar.com.
Europcar ⓦ www.europcar.com.
Hertz ⓦ www.hertz.com.
Holiday Autos ⓦ www.holidayautos.co.uk (part of the LastMinute.com group).
SIXT ⓦ www.sixt.com.

Cycling

Thanks to the enlightened attitude to visiting the great outdoors, Finland's broad-minded dogma of **jokamiehenoikeus** (Every Man's Right) makes the country one of the best in the world for **cycling**, allowing anyone to bike anywhere in the countryside.

Villages and towns may be separated by several hours' pedalling, however, and the scenery can get monotonous. The only appreciable hills are in the far north and extreme east. You can take your bike along with you on an InterCity **train** for a €10 fee – as this isn't too common a practice you shouldn't need to reserve a spot ahead of time. Finnish **roads** are of high quality in the south and around the large towns, but are much rougher in the north and in isolated areas; beware the springtime thaw when the winter snows melt and sometimes cover roads with water and mud. All major towns have bike shops selling spares – Finland is one of the few places in the world where you can buy bicycle snow tyres with tungsten-steel studs. Most youth hostels, campsites and some hotels and tourist offices offer **bike rental** from €10–15 per day, €50–60 per week; there may also be a deposit of around €30.

Accommodation

Whether you're at the end of one of Finland's long-distance hiking trails or in the centre of a city, you'll find some kind of accommodation to suit your needs. You will, however, have to pay dearly for it: prices are high, and only by staying in a youth hostel, making use of special offers or travelling during low season will you be able to sleep well on a budget.

Hotels

A Finnish **hotel** (*hotelli*) is rarely other than polished and pampering: TV, phone and private bathroom are standard fixtures, a breakfast buffet is invariably included in the price, and there's generally free use of the sauna and swimming pool, too. Chain hotels dominate mid- to upper-level accommodation in most cities, and many of the rooms follow a very strict, homogenous layout. Costs can be formidable – frequently in excess of €120 for a double – but planning ahead and taking advantage of various discount schemes and seasonal reductions can cut prices, often to as little as €50.

One trend that's catching on in Finland is that of the unmanned **concept hotel**, in which guests book over the internet or by toll phone call, receive a password to enter their room and carry out their entire stay with zero interaction with on-site hotel staff – who, incidentally, don't exist. Rooms are sleekly designed with many environmentally aware considerations, and while they might feel very Ikea-furnished, they are nevertheless a welcome change from the predictable furnishings of so many large Finnish hotels. The best aspect is the price: as low as €39 or so per night in some cases, though to get these rates you need to book several weeks in advance. *Omena Hotel* was the pioneer of this idea – they have seven such hotels in southern Finland (and over a dozen more planned for the rest of the country. Other companies such as *GreenStar* have since added their own hotels to the mix. Note that booking a room in these hotels via the internet is free, while phone bookings incur a hefty surcharge – often as much as €9 – which explains why we only print the website for such hotels.

Room rates vary depending on the season and whether there is a town festival being staged; on the whole, though, accommodation is much more expensive on weekdays and in winter. This is especially the case at the larger, business-oriented hotel chains (*Cumulus, Scandic, Sokos* and *Best Western*) in major cities, when winter weekday prices can frequently be double that of a weekend in the summer; there are frequent bargains at such hotels during July and August, and on Fridays, Saturdays and Sundays throughout the year. Exact details of these change frequently, but it's worth checking the current situation online or at a local tourist office. Reductions are also available to holders of Helsinki Cards and the similar cards issued for Tampere.

Otherwise, between July and August you're unlikely to find anything under €50 by turning up on spec, except of course in a youth hostel. Hotels in country areas are no less comfortable than those in cities, and often a touch less costly, typically €50–70. However, space is again limited during summer. Expense can be trimmed a little by using the **Finncheque** (Ⓦ www.finncheque.fi) system: you buy an unlimited number of €41 or €50 vouchers, each valid for a night's accommodation for one person (double occupancy), plus breakfast, in any of the 110 participating hotels from June to September (weekends-only the rest of the year). The two price categories correspond to the quality of room. There's a full list of places to buy the cheques and the addresses of all the hotels included in the scheme are on the website. Don't worry about buying more vouchers than you might need – they are refundable at the place of purchase.

In many towns you'll also find **tourist hotels** (*matkustajakotit*) or **guesthouses** (*majatalot*),

Accommodation price codes

The hotels and guesthouses listed in the Guide have been graded according to the following price bands, based on the cost of the **least expensive double room in summer**, usually mid-June to mid-August. However, many hotels offer summer and/or weekend discounts, and in these instances we've given two grades, covering both the discounted and the regular rate (eg ❸/❺).

❶ €25 and under
❷ €26–50
❸ €51–75

❹ €76–100
❺ €101–125
❻ €126–150

❼ €151–200
❽ €201–300
❾ €301 and over

more basic types of family-run hotels, though the qualitative difference between these and standard hotels may only be that they're not owned by a chain. They charge €30–45 per double room and sometimes have cheaper wood cabins out back, but may well be full throughout the summer. The facilities of **summer hotels** (*kesähotelli*), too, are more basic than regular hotels, since the accommodation is in student blocks which are vacated from June to the end of August: there are universities in all the major cities and in an impressive number of the larger towns. Reservable with any Finnish travel agent, summer hotel prices are around €35 per person. Bear in mind that identical accommodation – minus the bed linen and breakfast – comes a lot cheaper in the guise of a youth hostel.

Youth hostels

The easiest and cheapest place to rest your head is often a **youth hostel** (*retkeilymaja*). There are seventy such hostels throughout the country, in major cities (which will have at least one) and isolated country areas. They are run by the Finnish Youth Hotel Association, Suomen Retkeilymajajärjestö (SRM). It's always a good idea to phone ahead and reserve a place, which many hostel wardens will do for you, or book online at the address below. If you're arriving on a late bus or train, say so when booking and your bed will be kept for you; otherwise bookings are only held until 6pm and reception often closes around 8pm, though you can usually check in later, provided you let staff know in advance. Hostels are busiest during the peak Finnish holiday period, roughly mid-June to mid-August. Things are quieter after mid-August, although a large number

of hostels close soon after this date – check that the one you're aiming for doesn't. Similarly, many hostels don't open until June.

Overnight **charges** are generally around €20 per person (though can be as little as €10 and as much as €50), depending on the type of accommodation, with hostels ranging from the basic dormitory type to those with two- and four-bed rooms and at least one bathroom for every three rooms. Bed linen, if not already included, can be rented for an extra €3–7. With a Hostelling International Card (not obligatory) you can get a €2.50 reduction per person per night. The SRM publishes a useful free guide, *Hostels in Finland*, available directly from them at Suomen Retkeilymajajärjestö, Yrjönkatu 38B, 00100 Helsinki (☎09/565 7150, ⓦwww.hostellit.fi), listing all Finnish hostels, and the very helpful staff there can also provide a free map showing locations.

All youth hostels have wardens to provide general assistance and arrange **meals**: most hostels offer breakfast, usually for €4–6, and some serve dinner as well (around €7.50). Hostel breakfasts, especially those in busy city hostels, can be rationed affairs and – hunger permitting – you'll generally be better off waiting until you can find a cheapish lunch somewhere else (see "Food and drink", p.36). The only hostel breakfasts really worth taking advantage of are those offered at summer hotels, where hostellers can mingle with the hotel guests and, for €5–7, partake of the help-yourself spread.

Campsites and holiday villages

There are some 200 official **campsites** (*leirintäalue*) in Finland, and several hundred more operating on a less formal basis. Most open from May to September, although around seventy stay open all year. The approved sites, marked with a blue and white tent sign in a letter C, are classified by a star system: one-star sites are in rural areas and usually pretty basic, while on a five-star site you can expect excellent cooking and laundry facilities and sometimes a well-stocked shop.

The cost for two people sharing is €18–22 per pitch, depending on the site's star rating. Where prices for campsites fall within this range, we haven't given prices within the text (when less expensive, though, we have). Campsites outside major towns are frequently very big (a 2000-tent capacity isn't uncommon), and they're very busy at weekends during July and August. Smaller and more remote sites (except those serving popular hiking routes) are, as you'd imagine, much less crowded.

Holiday villages (*lomakylä*) have been sprouting up throughout Finland in the last few years and there are now over 200 of them. Standards vary considerably, with accommodation ranging from basic cabins to luxurious bungalows. All provide fuel, cooking facilities, bed linen and often a sauna – but you'll need to bring your own towels. Costs range from €115 to €510 per week for a cabin sleeping up to four people, though for a luxury bungalow you might well pay upwards of €1100.

To camp in Finland, you'll need a Camping Card Scandinavia, available at every site for €7 and valid for a year. The card is valid across Scandinavia and offers discounts on many campsites all over Finland. If you're considering **camping rough**, remember it's illegal without the landowner's permission – though in practice, provided you're out of sight of local communities, there shouldn't be any problems.

Hiking accommodation

Hiking routes invariably start and finish close to a campsite or a youth hostel, and along the way there will usually be several types of basic accommodation. Of these, a *päivätupa* is a cabin with cooking facilities which is opened during the day for free use; an *autiotupa* is an unlocked hut which can be used by hikers to sleep in for one night only – there's no fee but often no space either during the busiest months. A *varaustupa* is a locked hut for which you can obtain a key at the Tourist Centre at the start of the hike – there's a smallish fee and you'll almost certainly be sharing. Some routes have a few *kämppä* – cabins originally erected for forest workers but now used mainly by hikers; check their exact location with the nearest tourist centre. On most hikes there are also marked spots for pitching your own tent and building fires.

Food and drink

Finnish food is full of surprises and demands investigation, especially now that Nordic cuisine is in the middle of a Renaissance. Food is pricey, but you can keep a grip on the expenses by using markets and Finland's many down-to-earth dining places, saving restaurant blowouts for special occasions. Though tempered by many regulations, alcohol is widely available and is less expensive than in neighbouring Norway and Sweden.

Food

Though it may at first seem a stodgy, rather unsophisticated cuisine, **Finnish food** is an interesting mix of Western and Eastern

influences. Firm favourites include an enticing array of delicately prepared fish (herring, whitefish, salmon and crayfish), together with some unusual meats like reindeer and elk – while others bear the stamp of Russian cooking: solid pastries and casseroles, strong on cabbage, pork and mutton.

All Finnish and Scando-European fusion restaurants will leave a severe dent in your budget, as will the foreign places, although the country's innumerable pizzerias are relatively cheap by comparison. The golden money-saving rule is to have your main meal at **lunch** (*lounas*, usually served 11am–2pm, sometimes until 3pm) rather than the much dearer **dinner** (*päivällinen or illallinen*, usually from 6pm). Also, eke out your funds with stand-up snacks and by selective buying in supermarkets. If you're staying in a hotel, don't forget to load up on the inclusive **breakfast** (*aamiainen*) – more often than not a generous buffet table laden with herring, eggs, cereals, porridge, cheese, salami and bread.

Snacks, fast food and self-catering

Economical **snacks** are best found in market halls (*kauppahalli*), where you can get basic foodstuffs along with local and national specialities. Adjoining these halls are cafeterias, where you're charged by the weight of food on your plate. Look out for *karjalan piirakka* – oval-shaped Karelian rye pastries containing rice cooked in milk (sometimes mashed potato), served hot with a mixture of finely chopped hard-boiled egg and butter for around €2.

Also worth trying is *kalakukko*, a chunk of bread with pork and whitefish baked inside it – legendary around Kuopio but available almost everywhere. Expect to spend around €4 for a chunk big enough for two. Slightly cheaper but just as filling, *lihapiirakka* are envelopes of pastry filled with rice and meat – ask for them with mustard (*sinappi*) and/or ketchup (*ketsuppi*). Most train stations and the larger bus stations and supermarkets also have cafeterias proffering a selection of the above and other, greasier, nibbles.

Less exotically, the big **burger** franchises are widely found, as are the often ubiquitous roadside fast-food stands, known as *grilli* in Finnish, turning out burgers, frankfurters and hot dogs for around €3; they're always busiest when the pubs shut.

Finnish **supermarkets** – Sokos, K-Kaupat, Pukeva and Centrum are widespread names – are fairly standard affairs. In general,

a substantial oval loaf of dark rye bread (*ruisleipä*) costs €2, eight *karjalan piirakka* €2.50, a litre of milk €1, and a packet of biscuits around €2. A usually flavoursome option containing hunks of meat and vegetables, Finnish tinned **soup** (*keitto*) can be an excellent investment if you're self-catering.

Coffee (*kahvi*) is widely drunk – per capita, more than anywhere else in the world, in fact – and costs €1.50 per cup; in a *baari* or *kahvila* (bar or coffee shop) it's sometimes consumed with a *pulla* – a kind of doughy bun. It's normally drunk black, although milk (*maito*) is always available if you want it; you'll also commonly find espresso and cappuccino, although these are more expensive. **Tea** (*tee*) costs around €1, depending on where you are and whether you want to indulge in some exotic brew. In rural areas, though, drinking it is considered a bit effete. When ordering tea, it's a good idea to insist that the water is boiling before the teabag is added – and that the bag is left in for more than two seconds.

Lunch and dinner

If you're in a university town, the campus cafeteria or **student mensa** is the cheapest place to get a hot dish. Theoretically you have to be a student, but outside of Helsinki you are unlikely to be asked for ID. There's a choice of three meals: *Kevytlounas* (KL), the "light menu", which usually comprises soup and bread; *Lounas* (L), the "ordinary menu", which consists of a smallish fish or meat dish with dessert; and *Herkkulounas* (HL), the "delicious menu" – a substantial and usually meat-based plateful. All three come with bread and coffee, and each costs €5–6. Prices can be cut by half if you borrow a Finnish student ID card from a friendly diner. The busiest period is lunchtime (11.30am–12.30pm); later in the day (usually 4–6pm) many *mensas* offer price reductions. Most universities also have cafeterias where a small cup of coffee can cost as little as 60 cents.

If funds stretch to it, you should sample at least once a **ravintola**, or restaurant, offering a lunchtime buffet table (*voileipäpöytä* or *seisova pöytä*), which will be stacked with tasty traditional goodies that you can feast on to your heart's content for a set price of around €10. Less costly Finnish food can be found in a **baari**. These are designed for working people, generally close at 5pm or 6pm, and serve a range of Finnish dishes and snacks (and often the weaker beers; see "Drink", below). A good day for traditional Finnish food is Thursday, when every *baari* in the country dishes up *hernekeitto ja pannukakut*, thick pea soup with black rye bread, followed by oven-baked pancakes with strawberry jam, and buttermilk to wash it down – all for around €6. You'll get much the same fare from a *kahvila*, though a few of these, especially in the big cities, fancy themselves as being fashionable and may charge a few euro extra.

Although *ravintola* and *baaris* are plentiful, they are often outnumbered by **pizzerias**. They're as varied in quality here as they are in any other country, but especially worthwhile for their lunch specials, when a set price of around €9 buys a pizza, coffee and everything you can carry from the bread and salad bar. Many of the bigger pizza chains offer discounts for super-indulgence – such as a second pizza for half-price and a third for free if you can polish off the first two.

Vegetarians are likely to become well acquainted with pizzerias – specific vegetarian restaurants are thin on the ground, even in major cities. Now that Finland has opened its doors to immigration, kebab restaurants are found in a number of cities. This isn't necessarily a cheap option though: most kebab plates or sandwiches will cost upwards of €8.

Drink

Finland's repressive **alcohol** laws are designed to reduce the nation's boozing, which, as in Norway and Sweden, amounts to a serious social problem. Some Finns, men in particular, drink with the sole intention of getting paralytic; younger people these days are on the whole more inclined to regard the practice simply as an enjoyable social activity, though spend a few nights in any town and you're sure to witness your share of plastered, stumbling Finnish youth – boys and girls alike.

What to drink

Finnish spirits are much the same as you'd find in any country. **Beer** (*olut*), on the other hand, falls into three categories: "light beer"

(*I-Olut*) – more like a soft drink; "medium-strength beer" (*Keskiolut*, *III-Olut*) – more perceptibly alcoholic and sold in many food shops and cafés; and "strong beer" (*A-Olut* or *IV-Olut*), which, at 5.2 percent, is well on a par with the stronger international beers, and can only be bought at the ALKO shops and fully licensed (Grade A) restaurants and nightclubs.

The main – and cheapest – outlet for alcohol of any kind is the state-run **ALKO** shop (Mon–Thurs 9am–6/8pm, Fri 9am–8pm, Sat 9am–4pm/6pm). Even the smallest town will have one of these, and prices don't vary. In these shops, strong beers like Lapin Kulta Export – an Arctic-originated mind blower – and the equally potent Karjala, Lahden A, Olvi Export, and Koff porter, cost from €1.26 for a 33cl bottle. Imported beers such as Stella Artois go for around €2.50 a bottle. As for **spirits**, Finlandia vodka and Jameson's Irish Whiskey are €19 and €26.50 respectively per 75cl bottle. There's also a very popular rough vodka called Koskenkorva, ideal for assessing the strength of your stomach lining, which costs €14.70 for 75cl. The best **wine** bargains are usually Hungarian or Bulgarian, and cost around €15 per bottle in a restaurant, though you can buy bottles in ALKO for under €6. One particularly Finnish drink worth a try is Salmari, a pre-mixed vodka cocktail of Koskenkorva vodka and salty liquorice.

Where to drink

Continental-style **brasseries** or British-influenced **pubs** are the most pleasant places to have a drink. Frequented by both men and women of all ages, you're most likely to feel more at home in these familiar environments than in the dingy, generally all-male bars which proliferate in many of the small towns away from Helsinki, especially in the north – these charmless drinking dens are nothing more than places to get seriously hammered.

Most **restaurants** have a full licence, and some are actually frequented more for drinking than eating; it's these that we've listed under "Drinking" throughout the text. They're often also called bars or pubs by Finns simply for convenience. Just to add to the confusion, some so-called "pubs" are not licensed; neither are *baari*.

Along with ordinary restaurants, there are also **dance restaurants** (*tanssiravintola*). As the name suggests, these are places to dance rather than dine, although most do serve food as well as drink. They're popular with the over-40s, and before the advent of discos were the main places for people of opposite sex to meet. Even if you're under 40, dropping into one during the (usually early) evening sessions can be quite an eye-opener. Expect to pay a €3–5 admission charge.

Once you've found somewhere to drink, there's a fairly rigid set of **customs** to contend with. Sometimes you have to queue outside the most popular bars, since entry is permitted only if a seat is free – there's no standing. Only one drink per person is allowed on the table at any one time except in the case of porter (a stout which most Finns mix with regular beer). There's always either a doorman (*portsari or järjestuksenvalvoja*) or a cloakroom into which you must check your coat (and bag, if you have one) upon arrival

(again around €2). Bars are usually open until midnight or 1am, though a handful may stay open till 2am or, in the case of discos and clubs, 4am. Last call is announced half an hour before the place shuts by a winking of the lights – the *valomerkki*.

Some bars and clubs have **waitress/waiter service**, whereby you order, and pay when your drinks are brought to you. A common order is *iso tuoppi* – a half-litre glass of draught beer, which costs €3–4 (up to €6 in some nightclubs). This might come slightly cheaper in **self-service** bars, where you select your tipple and queue up to pay at the till. Though saying "beer" and pointing to the tap will generally work, you might get a more friendly response by offering up *Yks pist olut, kiitos*: Finnish for "A pint, please".

Wherever you buy alcohol, you'll have to be of **legal age**: at least 18 to buy beer and wine, and 20 or over to have a go at the spirits. ID will be checked if you look too young – or if the doorman's in a bad mood.

The media

The biggest-selling Finnish newspaper, and the only one to be distributed all over the country, is the daily Helsingin Sanomat (€2), whose online edition (ⓦ www.hs.fi) also includes a small section in English. Most other papers are locally based and sponsored by a political party; however, all carry entertainment listings – only the cinema listings (where the film titles are translated into Finnish) present problems for non-Finnish speakers. A better bet may be the Swedish-language tongue-twister, Hufvudstadsbladet (ⓦ www.hbl.fi), a quality daily that can be found in Helsinki. The best information about what's on, if you're in Helsinki, Tampere or Turku, is the free City (appearing fortnightly in Helsinki, monthly in Turku and Tampere), which carries regional news, features and entertainment details in Finnish and English; it's available at tourist offices.

Overseas newspapers, including most British and some US titles, can be found, often on the day of issue, at the Academic Bookstore, Pohjoisesplanadi 39, Helsinki. Elsewhere, foreign papers are harder to find and less up-to-date, though they often turn up at the bigger newsagents and train stations in Helsinki, Turku, Tampere and, to a lesser extent, Oulu.

Finnish **television**, despite its four channels (one of which is called MTV, but is unrelated to the music station), isn't exactly inspiring and usually goes off the air at midnight. Moderately more interesting is the fact that, depending on where you are, you might be able to watch Swedish and other Scandinavian programming. A few youth hostels have TV rooms, and most hotel-room TVs have the regular channels plus a feast of cable and satellite alternatives. As with films shown in the cinema, all TV programmes are broadcast in their original language with Finnish subtitles.

The only **radio station** that non-Finnish speakers are likely to find interesting and useful is YLE Mondo (@www.yle.fi /ylemondo), a multi-language channel which relays programmes from foreign broadcasters including the BBC and NPR. Broadcast on 97.5FM in Helsinki, the channel also transmits a short English-language news summary (Mon–Fri 7.30am, 8.55am & 4.29pm) put together by the Finnish national broadcaster YLE. This bulletin can also be heard at the same time in Lahti on 90.3FM, Jyväskylä 87.6FM, Kuopio 88.1FM, Tampere 88.3FM and in Turku on 96.7FM.

Holidays and festivals

Finnish holidays are for the most part organized around the seasons. Most celebrations are lively events, as Finns are great party people – especially once the vodka begins to flow. The highlight of the year is the Midsummer festival, when the whole country gets involved, and wild parties last well into the early hours. The date of Midsummer's Day varies from year to year but it is the Saturday closest to the actual summer solstice.

Major holiday festivals

Runeberg Day (February 5). People eat special Runeberg cakes, available in all bakeries, to commemorate Finland's national poet, Johan Ludvig Runeberg.

Vappu (April 30). One of the most important festivals in Finland, heralding the beginning of spring, with plenty of partying and boozing. The official celebration begins at 6pm in Esplanadi Park in Helsinki where one of the statues is crowned with a white cap.

Quirky festivals

Some of the world's most iconic and quirky festivals take place in Finland, primarily in the summer months. We've selected some of our favourites below:

Festival of Twangy Guitar Music Nastola. Late June. @www.rautalankaa.com.

Sex Festival Kutemajärvi. Late June. @www.seksifestivaalit.com.

Wife Carrying World Championships Sonkajärvi. Early July. @www.sonkajarvi.fi.

Hay-mowing World Championships Liminka. Early July. @www.liminka.fi.

Swamp Soccer World Championships Hyrynsalmi. Mid-July. @www.suopotkupallo.fi.

Finnish Pea Eating Championships Metsäkansa. Mid-July. @www.juva.fi.

Sauna World Championships Heinola. Early August. @www.heinola.fi.

World Championships in Crowbar Walking Tammela. Mid-August. @www .forssanseutu.fi.

World Mobile Phone Throwing Championships Savonlinna. Late August. @www .savonlinnafestivals.com.

Air Guitar World Championships Oulu. Late August. @www.airguitarworldchampion ships.com.

Finnish Championships in Berry Picking Suomussalmi. Early September. @www .arctic-flavours.fi.

Juhannus (late June). Midsummer is the event in the Finnish festive calendar. People leave the towns and head out to their summer cottages in the countryside where they light lakeside bonfires, have a sauna, swim and go rowing – and consume much alcohol. Juhannus is celebrated on the Saturday between June 20 and 26, though the main party takes place on the Friday night.

Crayfish parties (throughout August). Held in the August moonlight across the country to say a wistful farewell to the short Finnish summer.

Independence Day (December 6). Known as Itsenäisyyspäivä in Finnish, the day is marked by processions of people across the country carrying burning torches, church concerts and a visit to the President's residence by the rich and famous, relayed on national television.

Pikkujoulu (throughout December). In the run-up to the festive season, "Little Christmas" is a collection of private parties, sometimes held in public restaurants, where there's much eating, drinking and merrymaking at this very dark time of year.

Christmas (December 24). Finnish joulu is second only to Midsummer in importance in the Finnish year. At midday in Turku, the former capital, Christmas Peace is declared whilst later in the evening it's traditional for families to visit the graves of their deceased relatives by candlelight. The traditional Christmas fare is salted ham, which is eaten on December 25 to an accompaniment of pickled beetroot and carrot.

New Year (December 31). Fireworks light up the night skies above Finland as people prepare to usher in the New Year – with much alcohol and dancing in the wee small hours.

Shopping

Though Finland is hardly the most affordable place to shop, you can find some unique products that make great gift items. Obvious choices for purchases include any number of design-related goods (see pp.94–95), including glassware, ceramics, housewares, textiles and fashionable clothing.

Finland is also known for its artisan **handicrafts**, which include wooden curios (often with a reindeer theme), knives and handwoven *ryijy* rugs. In **Lapland** you'll come across a great number of Sámi handicraft items made of wool (such as colourful mittens or handknitted jumpers) and silver (traditional jewellery is a popular seller). Keep an eye out for the Duodji label, marked on authentic Sámi handicrafts.

Remember, too, that the indoor **markets** (*kauppahalli*) in a number of Finnish cities are excellent spots to pick up local foods, some of which you can taste right then and there. Most shops are open Monday to Friday from 9am to 6pm, and Saturday from 9am–3pm. Department stores are often open later and, occasionally, on Sunday.

Sports and outdoor activities

Finland is a wonderful place if you love the great outdoors, with fantastic hiking, fishing and, of course, winter-sports opportunities. Best of all you won't find the countryside overcrowded – there's plenty of space to get away from it all, especially in the north. Finnish lakes and beaches are clean and inviting: perfect for rowing, swimming or simply catching a few rays.

Canoeing

With many lakes and rivers, Finland offers challenges to every type of **canoe** enthusiast, expert or beginner. There's plenty of easy-going paddling on the long lake systems, innumerable thrashing rapids to be shot, and abundant sea canoeing around the archi-pelagos of the south and southwest coast. Canoe rental (available wherever there are suitable waters) costs around €3 per hour, €8–20 per day, or €60 per week, with prices dependent on the type of canoe. Many tourist offices have plans of local canoeing routes, and you can get general information from the Finnish Canoe Federation, Olympiastadion, Eteläkaarre, 00250 Helsinki (℡09/494 965, ⓦwww.kanoottiliitto.fi).

Fishing

Although **angling** and **ice-fishing** are consi-dered public rights in Finland and require no permit, non-Scandinavians do need a General Fishing Licence if they intend to fish with a lure in Finland's waterways; this costs €6 for a seven-day period from post offices. In certain parts of the Arctic North and the Åland Archipelago you'll need an additional licence costing between €5–10 per day and obtain-able locally. Throughout the country you'll also need the permission of the owner of the particular stretch of water, usually obtained by buying a permit on the spot. The nearest campsite or tourist office will have details of this, and advise on the regional variations on national fishing laws.

Hiking

Finland's **Right of Public Access**, *jokamie-henoikeus*, means you can walk freely right across the entire country (See box below). A network of long-distance paths covers the whole of Finland, with overnight accom-modation available in mountain stations and huts. The best known of all the trails is undoubtedly the **Karhunkierros**, which tracks through a deep river valley and canyon, north of Kuusamo, covering a distance of 80km.

Public access to the Finnish countryside

In Finland, your right to walk, ski, cycle and ride on other people's land is enshrined in law, the **jokamiehenoikeus** or Everyman's Right. In common with similar legisla-tion in the other Nordic countries, it also allows you to pick wild berries, mushrooms, and unprotected wild flowers, as well as to swim and fish in lakes right across the country. The main exception is the immediate vicinity of people's homes and gardens where the law does not apply.

However, in true Scandinavian fashion, this freedom brings with it a raft of responsi-bilities: you must not damage crops, forest plantations or fences, nor may you pitch a tent on land used for farming. The law also obliges you to seek permission from the landowner should you plan to camp for a prolonged period on someone's land. Driving off-road, lighting fires and disturbing wildlife are also prohibited. Full details on Everyman's Right can be found on the Finnish Environment Ministry's website, ⓦwww.environment.fi.

The nation's longest trail, the **UKK route**, is one of the most popular, stretching 240km through pristine scenery from its start point at Koli, north of Joensuu. However, throughout the north of the country walking trails are plentiful: particularly enjoyable hikes can be found within the Lemmenjoki and Kevo national parks near Utsjoki in the far north, as well as in the Pallas-Yllästunturi national park which stretches between Ylläs and Hetta (Enontekiö).

Nude bathing

Despite their predilection for taking saunas in the **nude**, Finns are rather uptight and very un-Scandinavian in their attitude to public nudity outdoors. Hence, sections of some Finnish beaches are designated nude bathing areas, more often than not sex-segregated and occasionally have an admission charge of around €1.50. The local tourist office or campsite will part with the facts – albeit in a rather embarrassed fashion. However, you should encounter no problem sunbathing naked by a secluded lake or in the forest.

Saunas

These are cheapest at a public swimming pool, where you'll pay €2–3 for a session. Hotel **saunas**, which are sometimes better equipped than public ones, are more expensive (€5–7) but free to guests. Many

Finnish people have saunas built into their homes and it's common for visitors to be invited to share one, though men and women are expected to bathe separately. Note that the sauna – and subsequent bathing in the nearest lake – is the one locale where nudity is commonly and publicly practised; it's fine to take along a towel or bathing suit, but bear in mind that your Finnish host will probably remain *au natural* (see *Sauna* colour section).

Skiing and winter pursuits

During the winter months, **skiing** is incredibly popular and in the north of Finland it's not unheard of for people to ski to work. The most popular ski resorts are Levi, Ylläs and Ruka; these and many others are packed out during the snow season when prices hit the roof. If you do intend to come to ski, it's essential to book accommodation well in advance or take a package holiday. In northern Finland you can ski from the end of October well into April. Lapland, in general, is the best place to base yourself if you're looking for winter activities, whether you fancy **dogsledding**, snowmobile riding, a trip on an icebreaker or a reindeer safari. Bear in mind though that temperatures in Finnish Lapland regularly plummet to -30°C and below, making cold-weather gear an absolute must.

Travel essentials

Costs and banks

Though the **cost** of a meal or the bill for an evening's drinks can occasionally come as a shock, prices in Finland are generally comparable with those in most European capitals, and there is no shortage of places catering for those on tighter budgets, even in the more far-flung locales. Bargain lunchtime "specials" are common and travelling costs, in particular, can come as a pleasant

surprise – travel by plane, for example, is exceptionally good value in Finland when tickets are bought in advance.

There are ways to **cut costs**, which we've detailed where relevant, but as a general rule you'll need £25–35/US$45–65 a day even to live fairly modestly – staying mostly at youth hostels or campsites, eating out every other day and supplementing your diet with food from supermarkets, visiting only a

Emergencies

For police, ambulance and fire service, dial ☏ 112.

few selected museums and socializing fairly rarely. To live well and see more, you'll be spending closer to £50/US$100. Banks are open from Monday to Friday 9am to 4.15pm.

Crime and personal safety

Finland is one of the safest countries in Europe in which to travel. Violent **crime** is extremely rare though, as in other countries, you should always be aware of petty crime such as pickpocketing. The one exception to this is when alcohol plays a role and some men in particular can become aggressive after an evening's drinking. However, take the normal precautions you would at home and steer clear of any potential troublemakers.

Electricity

The **current** in Finland is 220 volts AC, with standard European-style two-pin plugs. British equipment needs only a plug adaptor; American apparatus requires a transformer and an adaptor.

Entry requirements

EU, US, Canadian, Australian and New Zealand citizens need only a valid passport to enter Finland for up to three months. All other nationals should consult the relevant embassy about **visa requirements**. For longer stays, EU nationals can apply for a residence permit while in the country, which, if it's granted, may be valid for several years. Non-EU nationals can only apply for residence permits before leaving home and must be able to prove they can support themselves without working. Contact the relevant embassy in your country of origin. In spite of the lack of restrictions, checks are frequently made on travellers at the major points of entry. If you're young and are carrying a rucksack, be prepared to prove that you have enough money to support yourself during your stay. You may also be asked how long you intend to stay and why.

There are few, if any, **border formalities** when entering Finland from neighbouring Norway or Sweden by land; many of the old customs booths and checkpoints are these days largely abandoned, ramshackle edifices. The same applies when crossing by sea; only by air do you usually need to show your passport. Much more of a headache are crossings into Russia, still full-on bureaucratic nightmares with rubber stamps, scrupulous passport checks and askance eyes cast towards your baggage. In any event you'll need to plan well ahead to obtain the visa paperwork for a visit – the one exception being the cruises along the Saimaa canal into Karelian Russia (see p.183 for details).

Finnish embassies

Australia and New Zealand Embassy in Canberra ☏ 02/6273 3800, ⓦ www.finland.org.au. There is also a consulate in Sydney.
Canada Embassy in Ottawa ☏ 613/288-2233, ⓦ www.finland.ca.
Ireland Embassy in Dublin ☏ 01/478 1344, ⓦ www.finland.ie.
South Africa Embassy in Pretoria ☏ 12/343 0275, ⓦ www.finland.org.za. There are also honorary consulates in Cape Town and Johannesburg.
UK Embassy in London ☏ 020/7838 6200, ⓦ www.finemb.org.uk.
US Embassy in Washington, DC ☏ 202/298-5800, ⓦ www.finland.org. There are also consulates in Los Angeles and New York.

Gay and lesbian travellers

For **gays and lesbians**, Finland is one of the most liberated and tolerant countries in Europe. Discrimination against gay men and women is a criminal offence and the age of consent is the same as for heterosexuals at 16. Registered partnerships became legal in 2002 giving Finnish same-sex couples the same rights as straight couples in all areas except adoption, and the Helsinki municipality has been campaigning to certify many local establishments as "gay friendly". Nevertheless, and perhaps as a result of this very tolerance, there is not much of a scene outside Helsinki. SETA, the Organization for Sexual Equality in Finland (ⓦ www.seta.fi), is a good starting point for information on bars and clubs in the Finnish capital.

Health and insurance

Under reciprocal **health arrangements** involving members of the European Union, nationals of all EU countries are entitled to free or discounted medical treatment within the public health care system of Finland. Non-EU nationals have to pay for medical attention in full and should take out their own medical insurance to travel to Finland. EU citizens may want to consider private health insurance too, as it will cover the cost of items not within the EU's scheme, such as dental treatment and repatriation on medical grounds. That said, most private insurance policies don't cover prescription charges – their excesses are usually greater than the cost of the medicines. The more worthwhile policies promise to sort matters out before you pay (rather than after) in the case of major expense; if you have to pay upfront, get and keep the receipts. For more on insurance, see below.

Across Finland, the local pharmacy should be able to provide the address of an English-speaking doctor or dentist, though bear in mind in remote districts this could be some distance away. If you're seeking treatment under the EU reciprocal public health agreement, double-check that the doctor/dentist is working within the system. This being the case, you'll receive free or reduced-cost/government-subsidized treatment just as the locals do; any fees must be paid upfront, or at least at the end of your treatment, and are non-refundable – a good reason to have a private insurance policy.

You may be asked to produce documentation to prove you are eligible for EU health care and it's therefore wise to have your passport and your **European Health Insurance Card** (EHIC) to hand. If you have a travel insurance policy covering medical expenses, you can seek treatment in either the public or private health sectors, the main issue being whether – at least in major cases – you have to pay the costs upfront and then wait for reimbursement, or not.

Internet

Finland comes second only to the US in terms of per-person home **internet** use, a fact made clear by the near absence of public internet points in many towns, which can come as quite a shock to many travellers to the country. For web and email access, the most reliable option should be your hotel. Free wi-fi connections are offered (having to pay for an internet connection in a Finnish hotel is very rare) which should suit if you have a laptop. Otherwise, many hotels (and even some bars) have a computer terminal or two available for guest use; these are also often free.

Outside of your hotel, another source of internet access is tourist offices, where wi-fi is always free and terminals are either free or very inexpensive to use. Larger towns will have cafés with free wi-fi access for customers, and finally there are public-library terminals, which are always free. Most short-use terminals, but for anything longer than ten minutes or so you will probably have to book a spot (possibly the day before). As a last resort, you could try to find an internet café, where you'll usually pay €3–5 per hour.

Mail

In general, **communications** in Finland are dependable and quick, although in the far north, and in some sections of the east, minor delays arise due simply to geographical remoteness.

Unless you're on a hiking trek through the back of beyond, you can rest assured your letter or postcard will arrive at its destination fairly speedily. The cost of mailing anything weighing under 50g internationally is 65 cents second class, or 80 cents first class. You can buy **stamps** from **post offices** (Mon–Fri 9am–5pm; longer hours at the main post office in Helsinki), street stands or R-Kiosks, and at some hotels. **Poste restante** is available at the main post office in every large town.

Maps

The maps in this book should be adequate for most purposes, but drivers, cyclists and hikers will require something more precise. Tourist offices often give out reasonably useful local road maps and town plans, but anything more detailed will require a trip to a bookshop. Freytag & Berndt's (ⓦwww .freytagberndt.com) *Finland* map (1:500,000) is an excellent general-purpose resource, though for more detailed coverage you should resort to the superbly detailed regional maps (1:250,000) produced by Genimap which can be bought in most branches of the national bookstore chain, Suomalainen Kirjakauppa. Akateeminen Kirjakauppa, Pohjoisesplanadi 39, in Helsinki, has a very large travel and maps section, while the Helsinki city tourist office sells a great map and walking guide, *See Helsinki On Foot* (€2).

Money

The Finnish **currency** is the **euro** (€), which comes in coins of 5 to 50 cents, €1 and €2, and notes of €5 to €500. Note that Finland no longer circulates 1- and 2-cent coins as the government considered them too low a value. The **exchange rate** at the time of writing was €1.10 to £1, €0.67 to US$1, €0.64 to Can$1, €0.62 to Aus$1 and €0.48 to NZ$1. For up-to-date rates, visit the web site ⓦwww.oanda.com.

Credit cards are one of the best ways to pay for goods – in addition to being easy to carry around securely, they offer the most competitive exchange rates and few Finnish establishments will charge any over-and-above commission for you to use one. Major credit and charge cards – Amex, MasterCard, Visa, Diner's Club – are usually accepted by hotels, car rental offices, department stores, restaurants and sometimes even by taxis. However, it's still advisable to check beforehand.

For **cash**, your best bet is withdrawing money from ATMs using your home bank **debit card**. Nearly all foreign bank cards will work in a Finnish ATM/cash machine (known as a *pankkiautomaatti*), and banks usually give good exchange rates and charge 1–3 percent commission for foreign cash withdrawals. Note that there may be a minimum charge, so it could be worth taking out a larger amount when you use the machine; check with your bank for the charges they apply.

Travellers' cheques can be changed at most **banks**, which open Monday to Friday from 9.15am to 4.15pm; the charge is usually €2 (though several people changing money together need only pay the commission once). You can also change money at hotels, though normally at a much worse rate than at the banks. In a country where every cent counts, it's worth looking around for a better deal: in rural areas some banks and hotels are known not to charge any commission at all.

Outside normal banking hours, the best bets for changing money are the **currency-exchange desks** at transport terminals which open to meet international arrivals, where commission is likely to be €3–5, roughly the same as at banks, though airport exchange rates are often a little more generous. There are no restrictions on the amount of money you can take into or out of Finland.

Opening hours and public holidays

On the following days, shops and banks close and most public transport operates a Sunday schedule; museum opening hours may also be affected. **Holidays** are:

January 1, May 1, December 6, December 24, 25 and 26; variable dates are Epiphany (between Jan 6 and 12), Good Friday and Easter Weekend, the Saturday before Whit Sunday, Midsummer's Eve, and All Saint's Day (the Saturday between Oct 31 and Nov 6).

Supermarkets are usually open Monday to Friday 9am to 8pm, Saturday 9am to 6pm. Some in cities keep longer hours, for example 8am to 10pm. In Helsinki the shops in Tunneli are open until 10pm. In the weeks leading up to Christmas some stores and markets are open on Sunday too.

In larger towns, **markets** usually take place every day except Sunday from 7am to 2pm. There'll also be a market hall (*kauppahalli*) open weekdays 8am to 5pm. Smaller places have a market once or twice a week, usually including Saturday.

Phones

Due to Finland's ridiculously quick adoption of mobile-phone technology, Finland is no longer building any landline infrastructure, and the once-ubiquitous Finnish **public telephones** are rapidly on the decline. This decommissioning stems from a deal between Nokia and the Finnish government – one which will install Finns as the world's foremost users of mobile technology. As the bill for using a hotel phone is often unfathomably expensive, the best bet for making calls is to use your **mobile phone or your laptop**. If you plan to make a lot of calls while in Finland, you'd be wise to invest in a Finnish SIM card for use in your phone. For around €20 you get a Finnish number plus about sixty minutes of domestic calling time or a few hundred domestic text messages; SIMs are available at R-Kioski newsagents; Sonera and DNA are two reliable companies with good networks and inexpensive rates.

Finland's international country code is ☏358 and to ring abroad from Finland you dial ☏00. Operator numbers are ☏118 for domestic calls and ☏92020 for reverse-charge international calls.

Tax

A **sales tax** (MOMS) of 22 percent is added to almost everything you buy – but it's always included in the price. Non-EU citizens can claim a refund at the airport, provided you fill out a Global Refund Cheque at the point of purchase.

Time

Finland is **two hours ahead** of the UK and seven to ten hours ahead of the continental US. Clocks go forward by one hour in late March and back one hour in late October (on the same days as in Britain and Ireland).

Tourist information

Before you leave, it may be worth checking out the Finnish national **tourist information** website, ⓦwww.visitfinland.com, for accommodation listings, bookings and timetables, though much of this information will be readily available in tourist offices once you're in Finland. Most Finnish towns have a tourist office where you can pick up free town plans and information, brochures and other bumph. During summer, they're open daily until late evening; out of high season, shop hours are more usual, and in winter they're sometimes closed at weekends. You'll find full details of individual offices throughout the Guide.

Travellers with disabilities

As you might expect of a Scandinavian country, Finland has adopted a progressive and thoughtful approach to the issues surrounding **disability** and, as a result, there are decent facilities for travellers with disabilities across the country.

An increasing number of hotels, hostels and campsites are equipped for disabled visitors and are credited as such in tourist literature. Furthermore, most mainline Finnish trains have special carriages with wheelchair space, hydraulic lifts and toilets for the disabled; domestic flights either cater for or provide assistance to disabled customers; and ships on ferry routes have lifts and cabins designed for disabled people. In the cities and larger towns, many restaurants and most museums and public places are **wheelchair accessible**. Although facilities are often not so advanced in the countryside, things are improving rapidly. Many of the larger car-rental companies have modified vehicles available. On a less positive note, city pavements can be uneven and difficult to negotiate, particularly in winter when snow and ice make things worse. For more information contact the Finnish Association of People with Physical Disabilities (Invalidiliitto) at Mannerheiminitie 107, 00280 Helsinki (☎09/613 191, ⓦwww .invalidiliitto.fi).

Guide

Guide

www.roughguides.com

Helsinki and around

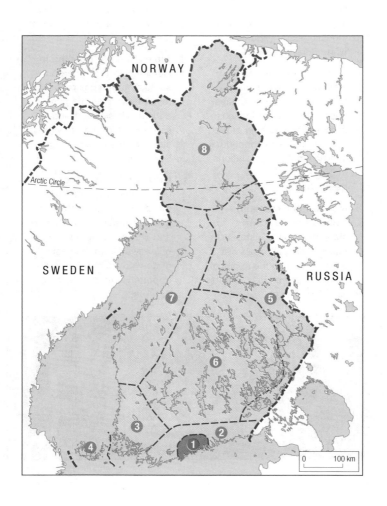

NORWAY

Arctic Circle

SWEDEN

RUSSIA

0   100 km

CHAPTER 1 # Highlights

* **Jugendstil architecture** The city centre – especially the Central Railway Station and the Katajanokka district – is a showcase for this unique style of building design, featuring elaborate decorative mouldings and expert stone-work. See p.68 & p.66

* **Kiasma** This stunning modern design museum, a breathtaking swathe of steel and glass, is a destination in itself – to say nothing of the cutting-edge and conceptual international art installations that grace the interior. See p.70

* **Mannerheim Museum** Finland's best known statesman, Carl Gustaf Mannerheim, filled his villa to the brim with the spoils of empire – and medals from his illustrious career. See p.75

* **Suomenlinna** The best known of the capital's offshore ports of call, this former Swedish stronghold makes the perfect summer getaway to catch some rays, sprawl out for a picnic and let the good times roll. See p.80

* **Dining and bar hopping in Helsinki** Having undergone something of a gastronomic renaissance over the past decade, Helsinki's dining scene is now on a par with its stellar café and bar offerings. See pp.83–91

* **Hvitträsk** Eliel Saarinen and his architect buddies built this beautiful rural retreat to find inspiration among nature and bask in some peace and quiet away from the hustle of downtown; don't miss the opportunity to do the same. See p.99

▲ Drinking in Helsinki

Helsinki and around

Positioned on a rocky headland cradling the Baltic Sea, **HELSINKI** is one of Europe's most handsome, idiosyncratic and captivating capital cities. The city maintains a personality that is markedly different from that of other Scandinavian capitals, and in many ways is closer in temperament – and certainly in looks – to the major cities of Eastern Europe. For years an outpost of the Russian empire, its very shape and style was originally modelled on its powerful neighbour's former capital, St Petersburg, with buildings extant today that are virtual carbon copies of pre-communist structures from the former Russian Empire. Yet throughout the twentieth century Helsinki was also a showcase for the design ideals of an independent Finland, with much of its impressive **architecture** drawing inspiration from the rise of Finnish nationalism and the growth of the republic. Equally the city's **museums**, especially the Ateneum Art Museum and the National Museum, reveal the country's growing awareness of its own folklore and culture.

Much of central Helsinki is a succession of compact granite blocks, interspersed with more characterful buildings, alongside waterways, green spaces and the glass-fronted office blocks and shopping centres you'll find in any European capital. The city is hemmed in on three sides by water, and all the things you might want to see are within walking distance of one another – and certainly no more than a few minutes apart by tram or bus. There are stretches of green throughout, including several parks right in the centre, as well as a dozen or so idyllic offshore islands (accessible via regular ferry transport in the warmer months) that are excellent spots for escape. In the city itself, the streets maintain a youthful buzz – particularly during the short summer season, when Finns break out of their shells and take to strolling its boulevards, cruising its shopping arcades and mingling (and drinking to no small extent) in its outdoor cafés and restaurants; everywhere there's prolific street entertainment. Come night-time the pace picks up significantly, with a prodigious selection of bars and clubs, free rock concerts among the numerous parks, and an impressive quota of fringe events and festivals. The **Helsinki Festival** (W www .helsinginjuhlaviikot.fi), a huge cultural and arts celebration that takes place during the last two weeks of August, is the biggest of these, with performances and activities all around the capital.

Some history

The dream of Helsinki was born in 1550, when the Swedish King Gustav Vasa was inspired to found a city on the Gulf of Finland's northern coast in order to catch up with Russia's expansion of its Baltic trade routes. Vasa's initial valiant attempts ultimately failed, however, and it would take another century before the city was settled with any success. The choice of sites was moved from the initial location

What is in a name?

The Swedish title **Helsingfors** is the original name of the Finnish capital city, an amalgamation of *Helsinge*, the title of a parish along the Vantaa River, and the Swedish word for the rapids (*fors*) that once trickled through the town's original settlement. Though Helsingfors still remains the city's official Swedish name, it is best known by its Finnish version, **Helsinki**, with the stress on the first syllable. Over the years, Helsinki has acquired a number of different monikers: it is known in downtown argot as *stadi* (from the Swedish for "city", *stad*); by those who live outside the city centre as *hesa*; and by people who live in rather posher Espoo as *kaupunki* ("the city"). And given their sympathies for the droll, the disaffected and the disestablishmentarian, local heavy-metal aficionados have tenderly renamed the city *Hellsinki*.

on the Vantaa River a few kilometres south to Vironniemi (its current position of Kruununhaka), but in its early years Helsinki languished, growing erratically on account of the craggy ground of its position and harsh coastal climate. Things only really began to take off after the construction of **Suomenlinna fortress** off Helsinki's coast in 1748, which brought thousands of builders and soldiers and their families to the city. And then, in 1808, during the Russian occupation, the entire place was levelled by fire, forcing a rebuilding of the city from scratch – but not before Tsar Alexander I had moved the Grand Duchy's capital here from Turku.

The plans conceived by statesman Johan Ehrenström for the city's reconstruction only began in 1817 – once Swedish Finland had become property of the Russian empire – but Helsinki would have been nothing were it not for the ideas and inspiration of German-born architect **Carl Ludwig Engel**. Engel based his city planning directly on St Petersburg, and with materials no more eminent than brick and wood (marble was unavailable at the time), he built a capital that was remarkably Hellenic in look and feel: a terraced cathedral with Doric columns atop a prodigious staircase; broad buildings with three-storey columned facades; and square, symmetrical blocks for stately residences. When Engel came to town, the city had a population of 4000; when he died, it had grown to nearly five times that.

Towards the end of the nineteenth century, vast areas of the city were rebuilt and expanded in the forward-looking Art Nouveau and Jugend styles and, later, under the influence of National Romanticism, made manifest by a trio of locally born architects – Herman Gesellius, Armas Lindgren and Eliel Saarinen (as well as a fourth, Lars Sonck), whose approach formed the basis of the work of the mastermind designer **Alvar Aalto** (see box, p.225). Aalto, of course, brought worldwide fame to Finland through his architecture, in addition to a small number of memorable buildings to Helsinki. But more importantly, he moved a generation (or three) of architects to look in their back yards for inspiration, seeking construction based around organic forms and utilizing natural materials – ideas which have brought Helsinki well into the modern world.

Arrival and information

Helsinki's **airport**, Vantaa, 20km to the north of the city, is a clean and efficient affair. The airport's official tourist information bureau (look for signs saying "Neuvonta") is open 24 hours a day and run by a very helpful lot of ladies who hand out maps and sell Helsinki Cards (see p.58) and phone cards for use in booths all over Finland. There are three Travelex branches open daily from 5.30am to 11.30pm; these take a €4 commission for all travellers' cheques, cash and credit card exchanges. Airpro is a private airport tourist service that occasionally has good deals with city hotels, which can make their €10 commission for reservations less of a sting. Downstairs are a number of small lockers for storage (€3 per day).

Unfortunately, Vantaa airport has yet to build any direct train connection to the city centre, but a few **bus routes** do the job just fine. Quickest are the frequent Finnair airport buses (35min; €5.90 or €3.80 with a tourist ticket, see p.58, or Helsinki Card) that stop at the Finnair terminal behind the *Scandic Hotel Continental*, halfway between the city centre and the Olympic Stadium, before continuing to the railway station; on the return journey they depart from lane 30 just behind the *Vltava* restaurant at the west entrance of the station. A cheaper if slightly slower (45min) airport connection is city bus #615; this costs €3.80 and runs roughly every fifteen minutes from the airport to the city bus terminal beside the train station, though if you ask the driver you can get off beforehand at any of various fixed stops. The fare includes just over an hour on all Helsinki transport, which can make the end sum of getting to your destination somewhat cheaper. There's an assigned **taxi** rank just outside the terminal, from which a taxi to the centre should cost about €35.

The Viking and Tallink Silja **ferry** lines have their terminals on opposite sides of the South Harbour or Eteläsatama (at docks known respectively as Katajanokan and Olympia), and disembarking passengers from either have a walk of less than 1km to the centre. Eckerö Lines boats from Tallinn arrive at West Terminal (Länsisatama), reached from the end of Kalevankatu by following Hietasaarenkuja; bus #15A goes to the central railway station, and bus #15 to the Ruoholahti metro station.

The **central train station** (Rautatieasema), equipped with luggage lockers (€3), is set smack in the heart of the city on Kaivokatu, next to Rautatientori, where local buses terminate. All trams stop immediately outside or around the corner along Mannerheimintie, across from which, between Simonkatu and Salomonkatu, is the modern Kamppi shopping centre, whose basement houses the modern and efficient **long-distance bus terminal** (Linja-autoasema).

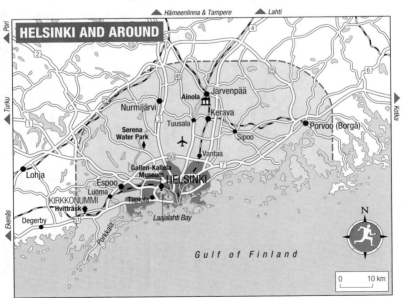

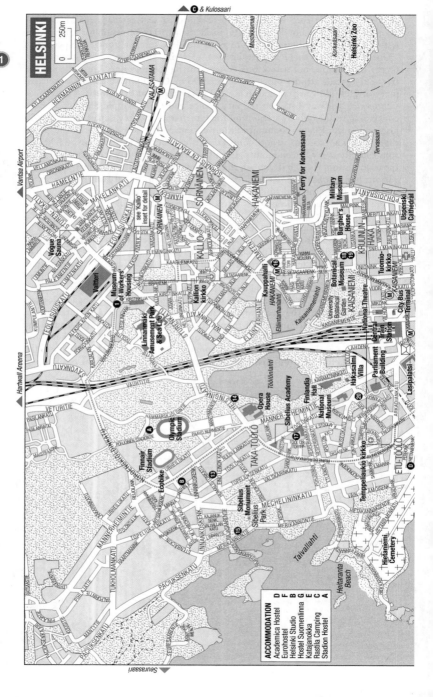

HELSINKI

0   250m

& Kulosaari

Vantaa Airport

Hartwall Areena

Seurasaari

ACCOMMODATION
Academica Hostel   D
Eurohostel   F
Helsinki Studio   B
Hostel Suomenlinna   G
Katajanokka   E
Rastila Camping   C
Stadion Hostel   A

Mustikkamaa

Korkeasaari

Helsinki Zoo

Tervasaari

Ferry for Korkeasaari

Military Museum

Burgher's House

Uspenski Cathedral

Kruununhaka

Tuomio-kirkko

Botanical Museum

Kauppahalli

University Botanical Garden

National Theatre

City Bus Terminal

Central Train Station

Parliament Building

Hakasalmi Villa

Lasipalatsi

Finlandia Hall

Opera House

Sibelius Academy

National Museum

Temppeliaukio kirkko

Taka-Töölö

Olympic Stadium

Finnair Stadium

Ecobike

Sibelius Monument

Sibelius Park

Hietaniemi Cemetery

Hietaranta Beach

Etu-Töölö

Taivallahti

Töölönlahti

Kallio

Kallion kirkko

Museum of Workers' Housing

Linnanmäki Amusement Park & Sea Life

Vogue Sauna

Valtteri

see 'Kallio' inset for detail

Sörnäinen

Hakaniemi

Kaisaniemi

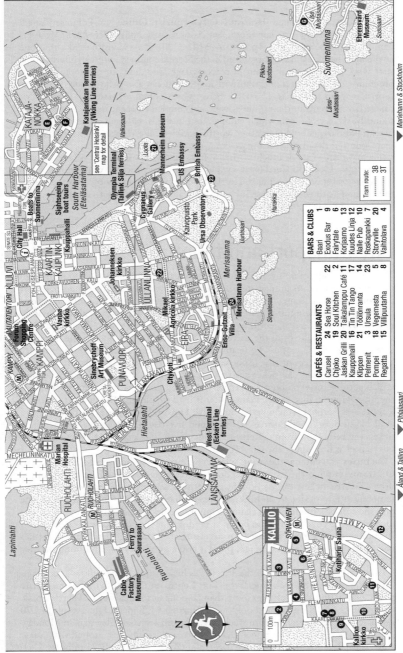

Suomenlinna museums ▲

Mariehamn & Stockholm ▼

▼ Åland & Tallinn   ▼ Pihlajasaari

CAFÉS & RESTAURANTS

Carusel	24
Chioko	19
Jaskan Grilli	20
Kauppahalli	16
Klippan	21
Pelmeni	3
Pompei	18
Regatta	15

Sea Horse	22
Soul Kitchen	2
Taikalamppu Café	11
Tin Tin Tango	17
Töölöinranta	14
Ursula	23
Vegemesta	5
Villipuutarha	8

BARS & CLUBS

Baari	1
Exodus Bar	9
Fairytale	6
Korjaamo	13
Kuudes Linja	12
Nalle Pub	10
Roskapankki	7
Storyville	20
Vahtolava	4

Tram route:
——— 3B
········· 3T

Information

The newly re-envisioned **Helsinki City Tourist Office**, at Pohjoisesplanadi 19 (May–Sept Mon–Fri 9am–8pm, Sat & Sun 9am–6pm; Oct–April Mon–Fri 9am–6pm, Sat & Sun 10am–4pm; ☏09/3101 3300, ⓦwww.visithelsinki.fi), is one of the most helpful and well organized in the Nordic countries, with an international staff who, together, speak about fifteen languages and dole out recommendations, brochures and free street and transport maps. You can also pick up the useful free tourist magazine *Helsinki This Week* here, which contains masses of **listings** for forthcoming events in the capital as well as a couple of decent maps, as well as the monthly *We Are Helsinki*, which enumerates hip shops, bars and restaurants. While here, try also to get hold of another worthy booklet, *See Helsinki On Foot* (€2), which maps out and details interesting walking tours of the city. If you're staying for a while and plan to see as much of the capital and its museums as possible, consider purchasing a **Helsinki Card** (ⓦwww.helsinkicard.fi), which gives unlimited travel on public transport, including the ferry to Suomenlinna, and entry to around fifty museums. The three-day card (€55) is the best value, although there are also two-day (€45) and one-day (€34) versions.

City transport and tours

Thanks to its agreeable size, much of Helsinki is easily covered on foot, though the central area and its immediate surrounds are covered by an integrated transport network of buses, trams, ferries and a limited metro system. A **single-journey ticket** on any of these costs €2.50, and is valid for unlimited transfers allowed within one hour. A tram ticket, entitling you to one single journey without changing, costs €2.50 if bought from the driver, or €2 if bought in advance at the machines located at many tram stops. You can also buy a **Tourist Ticket** covering the city and surrounding areas such as Espoo and Vantaa (for the airport), valid from one to seven days. The first day ticket costs €12; each additional day tacks on €6 to this, which permits travel on buses and trams displaying double arrows (effectively all of them); obviously, this is only a cost-cutter if used frequently. If you don't intend to leave the city proper, you're better off with a **Helsinki-only Tourist Ticket**, again available in one- (€6.80), three- (€13.60) and five-day (€20.40) versions. All these tickets can be bought from drivers or conductors, R-kiosk stands, the long-distance bus station at Kamppi or the City Tourist Office.

On **buses** you enter at the front, where you must either buy or show your ticket. On **trams**, enter at the front if you don't have a ticket and purchase one from the driver. **Metro** tickets can be bought from the machines in the stations. If you're tempted to fare-dodge in Helsinki, be aware that there's an €80 on-the-spot fine plus the cost of a single ticket; claiming ignorance upon being caught by any of the inconspicuous conductors who board at random for spot checks will rarely work. In summertime, **ferries** are used for accessing the outlying islands off Helsinki's coast (see p.80), while **cycling** (see p.33) is also a good way to get around the city in the warmer months.

Taxis can either be hailed in the street (a vehicle is free if the yellow "taxi" sign is illuminated) or pre-booked: call the Taxi Centre on ☏0100/0700 for immediate travel, or ☏0100/0600 for trips more than an hour or so in advance. There's a basic charge of €5 (or €6 if you pre-book), with a further €1.30 per kilometre, plus €2.70 surcharge between 8pm and 6am weekdays and from 4pm Saturday to 6am Monday. A trip to the airport if you ring ahead to order will usually cost around €40 (a few euros cheaper if you hail one on the street) and take approximately 35 minutes.

City tours

Together **trams #3T** and **#3B** follow a figure-of-eight route around the city, carrying you past the most obvious attractions (though you'll need to change at the end of either line to connect and make a full circle of the city). For a more leisurely exploration, join one of the two-hour guided **bus tours** (€26) run by Helsinki Expert (☎09/2288 1600, ⓦwww.helsinkiexpert.fi), who can be visited at the City Tourist Office. They also offer **walking tours** of the Design District (see box, pp.94–95; June–Aug Mon & Fri 1.30pm; €15). There are also numerous **boat sightseeing tours** on offer along Eteläsatama at the South Harbour, costing around €35 for three hours, and including a bus tour. These run daily from around 11am to 7pm between May and September, and brochures are available at the tourist office or from touts at the harbour itself. Less-traditional-style tours of the city include those run by Helsinki City Ride (☎44/955 8720, ⓦwww.helsinkicityride.com; from €29), which offers **Nordic walking** tours of various neighbourhoods. This combines active walking with elements of cross-country skiing, using ski poles specially modified for use on the streets. In the wintertime, they lead **cross–country ski tours** across the iced-over harbour to Seurasaari (€45), and throughout the year even organize a **tango tour**, on which you learn to dance your way through the streets of Helsinki.

Accommodation

While Helsinki has long had its share of bland Scandinavian chain accommodation, designed mainly to appeal to business travellers, there is now a cluster of **boutique hotels**, though staying in these comes at a cost. Less bling are the ubiquitous "Scandinavian modern" rooms in a number of **chain hotels**, most of which retain some degree of charm (in contrast to similar chain places in other Finnish cities). The city does have a small handful of moderately priced, non-chain hotels, and while they lack some luxuries they can be a good-value alternative. Most have en-suite bathrooms and some offer inexpensive meals. There are also half a dozen **hostels** spread all about the city, offering excellent facilities and free wi-fi. All but one have no evening curfew, and all are open all year.

Note that many of the more long-standing hotels drop their rates dramatically in the summer tourist season, while nearly everywhere will offer some sort of reduction at weekends. To take advantage of any bargains, it's essential to book as early as possible – either online, by phoning the hotel directly or by making a reservation through a travel agent or the very helpful **Hotel Booking Centre** in the main hall of the train station (June–Aug Mon–Fri 9am–6pm, Sat & Sun 10am–6pm; Sept–May Mon–Fri 9am–6pm, Sat 10am–5pm; ☎09/2288 1400, ⓦwww.helsinkiexpert.fi); they will book you a hotel or hostel room for a fee of €5 in person, though there is no charge if you phone them. However much you pay, it's unlikely that you'll leave any Helsinki hotel feeling ripped off: service and amenities – such as the inclusive help-yourself breakfast which is generally included in the price of the room – are usually excellent.

If you're planning on staying in town for more than just a few days, you'd do well to consider a short-term **apartment rental**. Apart from Helsinki Studio, listed on p.61, other pricier options for furnished flats include Domin, Uudenmaankatu 4–6 (☎09/687 7940, ⓦwww.dominrental.com), and Citykoti, Telakkakatu 1C (☎050/555 0058, ⓦwww.citykoti.com).

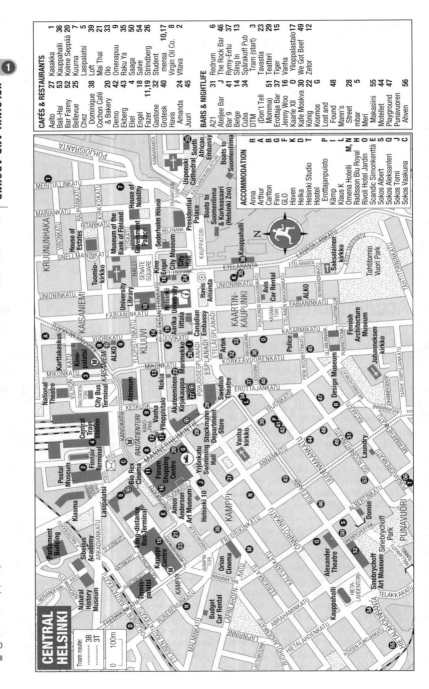

Finally, of Helsinki's **campsites**, only one makes a reasonable base if you're planning to spend time in the city. This is *Rastila* (☎09/3107 8517, ⓦwww.rastilacamping.fi), 12km to the east and conveniently on the metro line (Rastila station, an 18min ride) and also served by buses #90, #90A, #965 and #98 from Mannerheimintie. Open year-round with a lush, wooded site for tents (€20), an array of cottages (€45–187 per night) as well as a beach, restaurant, saunas, wi-fi access and bicycle and kayak rentals, it's one of the most popular camping spots in all of Finland. If you stay here in the wintertime, be sure to head out for a memorable afternoon of ice swimming.

Places listed below are marked on the "Central Helsinki" map on p.60, except where noted.

Hotels

Anna Annankatu 1 ☎09/616 621, ⓦwww.hotel anna.com. Small, central place set in a former Christian mission building dating from 1926. Despite the fairly run-of-the-mill rooms – some of which are so small you can stretch your hands and touch both walls at the same time – the overall atmosphere is much more cosy than a chain hotel. Excellent breakfasts. ❼

Arthur Vuorikatu 19 ☎09/173 441, ⓦwww .hotelarthur.fi. One of the few places in the city centre where the rooms haven't yet been rescued from early 1980s hotel decor purgatory, the *Arthur* is close to the railway but only a good option in a real pinch. Occasional last-minute discounts can knock 40 percent off the room rates. ❹/❺

Carlton Kaisaniemenkatu 3 ☎09/684 1320, ⓦwww.carlton.fi. In a lovely old 1930s building, this classy boutique business choice has 19 rooms in shades of cream, beige and light brown that sport dim mood lighting and designer sheets. It's a two-minute walk from the train station, and there's a *Robert's Coffee* just downstairs. ❻

Finn Kalevankatu 3B ☎09/684 4360, ⓦwww .hotellifinn.fi. Compact and rather down-at-heel hotel in an anonymous office building near Stockmann, though the slightly cramped rooms (the cheapest ones have shared baths) are still very good value considering the central location. If you press them, you can often get a better deal, especially if it's last minute. ❹

🏃 **GLO** Kluuvikatu 4 ☎09/675 111, ⓦwww .palacekamp.fi. This wonderful boutique hotel offers exposed pine, gorgeous black-marble baths and huge plush beds, as well as a very good on-site Basque restaurant. You can order anything you want to your room – gym equipment, bright-light lamps and even spa treatments. Surprisingly affordable too, with weekend rates that can rival those of the chains. The street below, however, can get noisy at weekends. Popular with the design-conscious businessperson. ❼

🏃 **Haven** Unioninkatu 17 ☎09/6128 5850, ⓦwww.hotelhaven.fi. Opened in 2009, this wonderfully lavish, smack-in-the-centre luxury hotel – Finland's first member of the Small Luxury Hotels of the World collection – takes the trophy for the city's best five-star. Stylish rooms feature everything you could want, really, including full-service Nespresso machines, Iittala glassware and massive Bose flatscreens – ask for a room with views of the harbour and Uspenski Cathedral. A downstairs honesty bar is set around a plush living room, with leather couches, a fireplace and a library of bound coffee-table books. Check the website, as they occasionally have stupendous offers that can bring double-room prices to under €100. The only anomaly: no sauna. ❽

🏃 **Helka** Pohjoinen Rautatiekatu 23 ☎09/613 580, ⓦwww.helka.fi. Ignore the unassuming exterior and settle down in one of the city's newest boutique(-ish) hotels, with super-comfortable beds, black-tiled bathrooms and quirky features such as life-size photographs of farming scenes on the ceiling. One of the more affordable design-minded places in the city, it's set a few paces west of the Kamppi centre. Regular promotions, and also has several sleek apartments, too, if you're staying a bit longer. ❺/❼

🏃 **Helsinki Studio** Punavuorenkatu 16D & Minna Canthinkatu 5 (see map opposite) ☎050/343 8774 or 040 771 7034, ⓦwww.helsinki studio.fi. Though technically not a hotel, these two stunningly designed apartments are nicer (and much more affordable) than most of the city's top-notch boutique hotels. They're also much more intimate (each features a roof terrace, one has a private sauna), offering the sense that you've taken over a good friend's plush pad for a few days. Designed by a local architect with Scandinavian minimalist flair, both are outfitted with classic pieces of Finnish furniture, lofted beds and bright living spaces. ❹

Kämp Pohjoisesplanadi 29 ☎09/675 111, ⓦwww .hotelkamp.fi. Opened in 1887, this *belle-époque* affair was Scandinavia's first luxury hotel – it played host to the secret meetings of the underground Kagel movement in the early 1900s, and Sibelius and Gallen-Kallela were regular guests. Today, marble bathrooms, polished stonework and lavish rooms make for decadent glamour. ❽

Katajanokka Vyökatu 1 ☏ 09/686 450, ⓦ www .bwkatajanokka.fi. This nineteenth-century jail has been retrofitted as a sleek luxury hotel whose small-ish rooms feature comfy beds, silk cushions and striped brown and orange carpeting that make them feel less, well, imprisoning. Tram #6 lets you off right on the doorstep. See map, pp.56–57. ❻

🏃 **Klaus K** Bulevardi 2 ☏ 020/770 4700, ⓦ www.klauskhotel.com. Taking the organic themes of the national epic Kalevala as inspiration, this superb choice is the capital's reigning house of style. It features a sleek white/off-white lobby, beautiful reception staff and velvet wallpapered rooms that serve as studies in cutting-edge interior design; if there's a celebrity in town, they're almost guaranteed to be staying here. Also has a trendy bar, and two great restaurants. ❼

🏃 **Omena Hotelli** Eerikinkatu 24 and Lönnrotinkatu 13 ⓦ www.omena.com. Travellers watching their purse strings should log on and book a room at either of these two receptionless concept hotels. Enter a code to get access to your snazzy room, sporting a microwave, small fridge, coffee machine and flat-screen TV with WebTV. Internet connection in the rooms for an extra charge. Booking far in advance gets the best prices. ❷

Radisson Blu Royal Runeberginkatu 2 ☏ 020/1234 701, ⓦ www.radisson.com. White-tiled, glamorous hotel that calls to mind buildings like the Opera House and Finlandia Hall. Rooms are well kitted out with sleek designs and large, very comfy beds; most of those on the higher floors have city views. Rates are cut by half in the summer. ❹/❼

Rivoli Hotel Jardin Kasarmikatu 40 ☏ 09/681 500, ⓦ www.rivoli.fi. Though mistakenly labelled a "boutique" hotel, this recently renovated place does offer some style (as well as great showers) and is a breath of fresh air from the predictable chains. It's a two-minute jaunt to Esplanadi, meaning you're never very far from a great shot of espresso. Booking online can get some smoking discounts. ❺/❻

🏃 **Scandic Simonkenttä** Simonkatu 9 ☏ 09/68 380, ⓦ www.scandichotels.com. A steel-and-glass facade and efficiently designed standard rooms that are the greenest in the city: parquet floors are made from specially cultivated Nordic trees, rubbish bins are recycled rubber and 97 percent of the rest of the materials are recyclable. Some rooms have balconies, others a terrace and sauna. An excellent choice for business – or for clubbing, as it's within reaching distance of half a dozen dance-all-night discos. ❹/❼

Sokos Albert Albertinkatu 30 ☏ 020/123 4638, ⓦ www.sokoshotels.fi. Not your ordinary chain hotel, this is Sokos' first foray into the world of boutique hotelerie, opened in 2007. An unremarkable facade leads to smallish rooms featuring very modern decor with a vague 1970s theme, which easily have the most atmosphere of any of the city's chain options. Avoid those on the second floor, which get no small amount of noise from the restaurant's kitchen. For best rates book directly through the Sokos website. ❹/❻

Sokos Aleksanteri Albertinkatu 34 ☏ 020/1234 643, ⓦ www.sokoshotels.fi. This glamorous hotel features a maze of stairways and a sprawling lobby with a bar and restaurant, though the rooms don't offer anything you haven't seen before. Best of all is the location – a refreshingly residential, quiet street in Punavuori. ❹/❻

🏃 **Sokos Torni** Yrjönkatu 26 ☏ 09/43 360, ⓦ www.sokoshotels.fi. Across from the classic sauna and pools on Yrjönkatu, this sophisticated hotel is an Art Nouveau-styled masterpiece and a business favourite. On a clear day, the thirteenth-floor bar's patio gives views all the way to Estonia, but the drinks are pricey, as are the rooms – though weekend rates can drop dramatically, especially last-minute. ❹/❼

Sokos Vaakuna Asema-Aukio 2 ☏ 09/43 370, ⓦ www.sokoshotels.fi. Flanking the train station, this smart hotel was built for the Olympic Games and retains many of its original, quintessentially Finnish architectural features. The lobby is a grand, semicircular sitting-room reminiscent of a Soviet legislation chamber, while the restaurant on the top floor – where the lavish breakfast spread is served – has grand views of city rooftops. ❺/❼

Hostels

Academica Hostel Hietaniemenkatu 14 ☏ 09/1311 4334, ⓦ www.hostelacademica.fi. The grim 1960s exterior of 2008's Finnish Hostel of the Year leads to a significantly cheerier and sociable scene inside. Offering a morning sauna and pool (at other times you must pay), this fairly central spot offers spotless doubles (❸) and four-person dorms (€24) as well as wi-fi and very good cooking facilities. Open June–Aug. See map, pp.56–57.

Eurohostel Linnankatu 9 ☏ 09/622 0470, ⓦ www .eurohostel.fi. Comfortable place in a clean modern building with free morning sauna and a restaurant. It's in the quiet Katajanokka area, close to the Viking Line arrival point; take tram #4. Dorm beds (€23) are set in double rooms, and there are private doubles (❸) as well, though those with shared bath are the cheapest. See map, pp.56–57.

Hostel Erottajanpuisto Uudenmaankatu 9
☎09/642 169, ⓦ www.erottajanpuisto.com. Small
and homely place on the second floor of a residential office building offering simply furnished dorms
(€25) and some doubles (❸), as well as friendly
staff and a large salon with worn leather couches,
often abuzz with travellers trading war stories.
Perfect for party types as it's near some great bars
(though there is a strict policy of no noise inside
after 11pm).

🏃 **Hostel Suomenlinna** Suomenlinna
☎09/684 7471, ⓦ www.snk.fi/suomenlinna.
While hardly central, this year-round hostel with
dorms (€22) and doubles (❸) boasts possibly the

most idyllic location of any hostel in Europe: a
remote island connected to the city only by boat. It
gets eerily quiet here – even in the summer – and
if you arrive in the winter you can bank on having
the place to yourself. Last ferry is at 2am, first one
at 6am. See map, pp.56–57.

Stadion Hostel Olympic Stadium ☎09/477 8480,
ⓦ www.stadionhostel.fi. An efficient, if dated setup
2km from the city centre, with private doubles (❷)
and dormitories (€20) sleeping up to twelve and
offering large shower rooms. Trams #3T, #4, #7A
and #10 from Mannerheimintie stop outside, as
does the Finnair bus from the airport (ask to get off
at "Opera"). See map, pp.56–57.

The City

Following a devastating fire in 1808, and the city's elevation to capital in 1812,
Helsinki was totally rebuilt in a style commensurate with its status: a grid of wide
streets and Neoclassical, Empire-style brick buildings, modelled on the then Russian
capital, St Petersburg. This grid forms the basis of the modern city, and it's a tribute
to the vision of planner Johan Ehrenström and architect Carl Engel that in and
around **Senate Square** the grandeur has endured, often quite dramatically. The
square itself, overlooked by the gleaming Lutheran Cathedral, is still the city's single
most eye-catching feature, while just a few blocks away, past the South Harbour and
the waterside market square, is the handsome tree-lined avenue of the **Esplanadi**,
with a narrow strip of greenery along the centre.

The city effectively branches out from Eliel Saarinen's Central Railway Station,
off which branches the great artery of **Mannerheimintie** – the main route into
the centre from the suburbs – carrying traffic and trams past Kiasma, the Finlandia
Hall and the Olympic Stadium on one side, and the National Museum and the
streets leading to Sibelius Park on the other. The bulge of land that extends
south of Esplanadi has long been one of the most affluent sections of town, and
embraces the hip, youthful areas of **Punavuori** and **Kaartinkaupunki**. Dotted by
palatial embassies and wealthy dwellings, these neighbourhoods feed into the rocky
Kaivopuisto Park, where the peace is disturbed only by the rumble of the trams
and a handful of summer rock concerts, while west of Kaivopuisto are the narrow
streets of the equally exclusive **Eira** quarter.

Heading north of the city centre and divided by the waters of Kaisaniemen-
lahti, the districts of **Kruununhaka** and **Hakaniemi** contain what little is left
of pre-seventeenth-century Helsinki, in the small area up the hill behind the
cathedral, compressed between the botanical gardens and the bay; over the bridge
is a large marketplace and the hill leading past the formidable **Kallio church**
towards the modern housing districts further north. Helsinki also has innumerable
offshore islands, the biggest of which are **Suomenlinna** and **Seurasaari**. Both of
these, despite their location close to the city centre, offer untrammelled nature and
a rewarding crop of museums.

Senate Square and along the Esplanadi

The heart of Helsinki lies in and around **Senate Square** (Senaatintori), a compact area
known officially as Kruununhaka containing broad bustling streets, grand buildings,
famous (to Finns) shops, and, in **Esplanadi**, the most popular promenading spot in

the entire country. Though the residents here have historically been comprised of primarily city and state officials, most of the streets leading into Senate Square are fairly narrow and unremarkable – a fact that serves to increase the impact as the square comes into view. From here you can easily access the city's two most spectacular churches, half a dozen museums and decorative buildings whose facades and details recall the Helsinki of over a century ago.

Tuomiokirkko

Step onto Senate Square and you're struck by the sudden burst of space, the graceful symmetry of the buildings, and most of all by the exquisite form of the **Tuomi-okirkko**, or Lutheran Cathedral (daily: June–Aug 9am–midnight; Sept–May 9am–6pm), raised on granite steps that support it like a pedestal. Designed, like most of the other buildings on the square, by Engel, its construction was begun in 1830 and overseen by him until his death in 1840, before being finally completed, with a few variations, in 1852. E.B. Lohrmann added to Engel's plans four small towers on the sides of the church, two pavilions on the Senate Square side of the terrace and the statues of the twelve apostles that line the roof. The last of these changes may seem familiar if you've visited Copenhagen: they're copies of Thorvaldsen's sculptures for Vor Frue Kirke. After the Neoclassical extravagances of the exterior, the spartan Lutheran interior comes as a disappointment; better is the gloomily atmospheric **crypt**, which is now used as a café (June–Aug Mon–Sat 11am–5pm, Sun 1–5pm; entrance on Kirkkokatu).

Government Palace and Helsinki University

The buildings around the square contribute to the pervading sense of harmony, and although none is open to the public, some are of great historical significance. The **Government Palace** (Valtioneuvosto), known as the Senate House until independence, consumes the entire eastern side at Snellmaninkatu 1. Constructed in 1822, it was Engel's first building on the square, a colossal Corinthian-columned structure 110m in length with a domed central projection

▲ Tuomiokirkko

and side projections at each end of the facade. It was here that an angry Finnish civil servant, Eugen Schauman, became a national hero by assassinating the much-hated Russian governor-general Bobrikov in 1904. The entire building underwent a renovation in the 1980s, bringing its staircase and presidential chamber back to their original lustre.

On the opposite end of the square stand the Ionic columns of **Helsinki University** (Helsingin Yliopisto), constructed in symmetry with the palace. The building was completely renovated in the 1990s, though its dark corridors and staircases still retain a decidedly olde-worlde feel to them. In theory you need to be a member of the university to enter the university buildings, though in practice you'll rarely get carded. A block north is the **University Library** (Yliopiston Kirjasto), consisting of a necked dome flanked by barrel-vaulted halls awash in natural light. It's considered by many to be Engel's finest single building, but unfortunately only students and bona fide researchers are allowed access.

The House of Estates and House of Nobility

Just northeast of the square between Kirkkokatu and Rauhankatu is the **House of Estates** (Säätytalo), the most striking nineteenth-century public building in Finland. It served as the assembly hall and seat of the Diet of clergy, burgesses and peasantry that governed the country until 1906, when the three estates were abolished in favour of a single-chamber parliament elected by universal suffrage (at the time, Europe's most radical parliamentary reform). The building sports a titanic entrance hall, towered over by a massive staircase (note the coloured skylight above), with grand assembly rooms illustrated by depictions of the quotidian lives of members of the Diet. In the small park just to the east of the Government Palace is the **House of Nobility** (Ritarihuone), where the upper crust of Helsinki society rubbed shoulders a hundred years ago. It is the city's most striking example of neo-Gothic architecture. Today it's the main office of the university's Department of Architectural History, while the auditorium is often used as a venue for popular chamber-music concerts.

Museums around the square

On the eastern side of the cathedral's pedestal at Snellmaninkatu 2 is the entrance to the **Museum of the Bank of Finland** (Suomen Pankin Rahamuseo; Tues–Fri 11am–5pm, Sat & Sun 11am–4pm; free; www.rahamuseo.fi), which features examples of the pre-euro Finnish currency, the markkaa, as well as an interesting exhibition on shortlisted designs for euro notes. Catty-corner to the square at Aleksanterinkatu 18 is Helsinki's oldest stone building, **Sederholm House** (Sederholmin Talo; Wed & Fri–Sun 11am–5pm, Thurs 11am–7pm; free), dating from 1757. Commissioned by industrialist Johan Sederholm, a member of parliament and Helsinki's most prominent shipping magnate, the two-storey building consists of a mansard roof of tarred board and second-floor windows festooned with wooden balustrades. It now houses a small **museum** of eighteenth-century life in the city, with exhibitions on trade, education and construction, though what makes it most enjoyable is perhaps the eighteenth-century music collection – you can ask to choose from a range of classical CDs while you wander around.

One block southwest of the Sederholm House, past City Hall, the **City Museum**, Sofiankatu 4 (Kaupunginmuseo; Mon–Fri 9am–5pm, Sat & Sun 11am–5pm; free; www.helsinkicitymuseum.fi), is a more high-tech record of Helsinki life, where the permanent "Time" exhibition gives glimpses of Helsinki from its origins as a country village right up to the present day. It's an impressive show, with photographs and films, though the disjointed chronology can be a bit hard to follow.

Uspenski Cathedral and Katajanokka

Follow Aleksanterinkatu to its eastern end and you'll be face to face with the red-and-green onion-shaped domes of the Russian Orthodox **Uspenski Cathedral** (Uspenskin katedraali; Mon–Fri 9.30am–4pm, Sat 9.30am–2pm, Sun noon–3pm, closed Mon Oct–April, Tues in summer till 6pm; Ⓦ www.ort.fi/helsinki), Helsinki's Church of the Holy Trinity, surmounting an outcrop separated from the mainland by a small canal. The present-day church rests on the site of the city's first Orthodox temple, and was consecrated in 1868. With its gilded onion domes and pavilion roof, the church poses a striking Byzantine contrast to its Lutheran counterpart – visible from the front steps – with Russian elements complementing Romanesque motifs. As the largest Orthodox church in Western Europe, it houses a rich display of icons and other sumptuous adornments, including an impressive array of chandeliers dangling from the vaulted ceiling.

Behind the cathedral the triangular-shaped islet known as **Katajanokka** extends out to sea. City planning for the wedge of land was carried out in the early 1890s, after which a railway line was installed to the island and it became used as a depot for maritime transport of goods. It now demarcates the borders of a long-term dockland development programme that is slowly converting the area's old warehouses into pricey new apartments. Though there is little in terms of traditional sights here, the area's Jugend-style buildings remain the city's best preserved.

Esplanadi

Several blocks west of the cathedral past the passenger harbour and a mishmashed confluence of tram lines stretch the twin thoroughfares of Pohjoisesplanadi and Eteläesplanadi, together known as **Esplanadi**. It was along this neat boulevard that opposing factions demonstrated their allegiance during the Swedish–Finnish language conflict that divided the nation during the mid-nineteenth century – Finns walking on the south side and Swedes on the north. Nowadays it's dominated in the morning by hobos and Nordic walkers (see p.59), at lunchtime by office workers escaping the grind, later in the afternoon by buskers and tourists, and at night by strolling couples and inebriated skateboarding teens. Musical accompaniment is provided free on summer evenings and weekends from the hut at the eastern edge of the walk – expect anything from Peruvian pan flutes to hardcore rock.

At the far eastern end of the Esplanadi is the **Havis Amanda**, an Art Nouveau mermaid sculpture by Ville Vallgren to symbolize the rebirth of the city at the end of the nineteenth century. Since its erection in 1908, it has become one of the symbols of the city. Every year on Vappu (1 May), Manta, as she is known colloquially, is a focal point for city celebrations and is capped with a white sailor hat in a drawn-out, drunken ceremony.

Kauppatori and kauppahalli

Though not quite the centre of local consumerist activity it once was in days gone by, there's still a good amount of colour and liveliness along the waterfront among the stalls of the **kauppatori**, or central market square (Mon–Thurs 8am–5.30pm, Fri 8am–6pm, Sat 8am–3pm). During the early morning, the square is laden with fresh fruit and vegetable stalls and several tented cafés selling coffee and breakfast treats; you can also pick up fresh fish directly from the boats moored around the edge of the harbour. Later in the day, the tourist stalls arrive to set up shop, with T-shirts, mittens, sundry reindeer trinkets and – if your principles allow it – a not-half-bad selection of mink and fox hats and coats (cheaper here than in the city's dwindling number of fur salons). Owners of classic American cars – Finland's fetish for them is legendary, with thousands of mint examples around the country – gather to show them off on the square the first Friday of each month. Towards the southern end of the square is the Old Market Hall or **Wanha Kauppahalli** (Mon–Fri 8am–6pm, Sat 8am–4pm), a piebald, brick building from 1888 boasting an original interior of carved mahogany, and a good place for snacks such as reindeer kebab and open salmon sandwiches, and with excellent cheeses on display too.

Presidential Palace and City Hall

Immediately opposite the market square along Pohjoisesplanadi stands the modest **Presidential Palace** (Presidentinlinna), conspicuous today only for its uniformed guard out front. The building was originally planned as a burgher's residence, modelled on Paris's noble palaces, with two wings reaching the street and the main building set back around a forecourt. This three-storeyed section features Ionic columns, and a gable – the first of its kind in the city. After the city purchased the building in 1837, Engel and his son Carl Alexander converted it into an imperial palace with a chapel, Gothic hall, mirrored hall and grand dining room.

Known today as **City Hall** (Kaupungintalo), the Engel-built pastel-blue hunk that sits two blocks west at Pohjoisesplanadi 11–13, originally functioned as a hotel, and until an architecture competition for a new City Hall building failed to bring any workable entries, and it took over as seat of the municipality in 1913. Its grandiose auditorium was designed by Carl Albert Edelfelt in 1862 after Engel died, and is today used primarily to host municipal functions.

The Swedish Theatre, Stockmann and around

At the opposite end of Esplanadi is the off-white **Swedish Theatre** building (Svenska Teatern; main entrance on Mannerheimintie), a well-funded national theatre that puts on regular performances of original Swedish plays as well as international hit shows in translation. If you think Esplanadi is crowded, wait until you venture across from the theatre and step inside **Stockmann**, the brick Constructivist department store just to the north. Scandinavia's largest department store, this is the place to buy everything from bubble gum to Persian rugs, and is a very popular city meeting point. Also part of Stockmann's (though it has its own entrance on Aleksanterinkatu), the Academic Bookstore, or **Akateeminen Kirjakauppa**, is a prodigious space holding many English-language paperbacks and a sizeable stock of foreign newspapers, magazines and stationery supplies. A popular afternoon activity for lunching ladies and retired men is to sit upstairs in the Alvar Aalto-designed café (see p.225). Directly across Mannerheimintie is the massive **Forum shopping mall** which, along with the Kamppi centre, has helped put a dent in Stockmann's profits.

Vanha Ylioppilastalo and Kaivopiha

Opposite Stockmann's main entrance at the western edge of Aleksanterinkatu is the eye-catching *Three Smiths* statue by Felix Nylund; a trio of naked men swinging hammers in unison around a centrally positioned anvil, it commemorates the workers of Finland who raised money to erect the **Vanha Ylioppistalo**, or Old Students' House, whose main doors face the statue and the small triangular square known as **Kaivopiha**. The Finnish Students' Union is based here, owning what is now some of the most expensive land in Finland and renting it out at considerable profit. In the Vanha, as it's usually known, is the Vanhan Galleria (during exhibitions usually 10am–6pm; free), a small gallery with frequent displays of modern art. The building also contains a handful of lively bars worthy of an evening visit.

Taking a few strides further along Mannerheimintie brings you to the Bio Rex cinema; beside it, steps lead down into a little modern courtyard framed by burger joints and pizzerias, off which runs the entrance to Tunneli, an underground complex containing shops, the central metro station and a pedestrian subway to one of the city's most striking structures – the railway station.

Railway station area and Kluuvi

Just north of Kaivopiha is the commercial district of **Kluuvi**, which centres around Helsinki's main railway station. The entire area was once a wet and boggy marshland that had to be drained in the late nineteenth century in order to allow the city to expand, after which it became a residential area for artisans and their patrons. Today, the area contains one of Helsinki's best museums, the largest working theatre in the country and the city's largest and most central stretch of garden and parkland.

Rautatieasema (central train station)

Located in what is today the very centre of Helsinki, the unmistakably Art Nouveau **central train station**, or Rautatieasema, ranks among architect Eliel Saarinen's greatest achievements. Helsinki's first railway station was built on this spot in 1860, once the country's first rail line (to Hämeenlinna) was completed, but as more lines were added the original station was deemed too small. Saarinen won the subsequent competition in 1904 with ease, and the building was eventually completed in 1919.

Standing in front of the huge doors (so sturdy they often give the impression of being locked), it's hard to deny the sense of strength and solidity the building exudes. Yet this power is tempered by gentleness, a feeling symbolized by four muscular figures on the facade, each clasping a spherical glass lamp above the heads of passers-by. Designed by Emil Wikström and known as *lyhdynkantajat* (lantern bearers) or *kivimiehet* (stone men), they have become unofficial mascots of Helsinki, and are often parodied in Finland on billboards and in print, appearing as animated figures in a 2009 TV advertising campaign for Finland's government-owned railway operator, Valtionrautatie (VR). Saarinen travelled around Europe to study various stations, and the interior, with its Art Deco chandeliers, large arched windows and elephantine granite entranceways, shows it; make for either one of the two restaurants (see p.84) to admire the interior further. One of the station's most unique features is a private 50m waiting room designated for the exclusive use of the President of Finland. The lounge, which has entrances to the Rautatientori square and the main station hall, was originally built for the private use of the tsar and is the only one of its kind in the world.

Postal Museum

Immediately opposite the train station is a large, monolithic building that holds the city's main post office and the surprisingly enjoyable and newly renovated **Postal Museum** (Posti Museo; Mon–Fri 10am–6pm, Sat & Sun noon–5pm; €6; ⓦ www.posti.fi), a remarkably innovative collection displaying some unlikely looking items covering some 370 years of Finnish postal history – be sure to have a look at the display of mid-nineteenth-century ten-kopek stamps – along with multiscreen displays, special areas for children and a 3D CGI computer game that lets you deliver mail in Helsinki from a genuine Posti delivery bike.

Lasipalatsi and Kamppi shopping centre

Opposite the Postal Museum is the renovated **Lasipalatsi** (ⓦ www.lasipalatsi.fi), built for the 1940 Olympics as the main transit and entertainment building. After falling into disrepair for many years, a restoration in 1998 brought back its late 1930s Art Nouveau glamour – including a string of fetching period neon signs on the roof – and the complex now contains shops, galleries, exhibition sites, cafés and a one-screen cinema. Behind the Lasipalatsi stands the sleek, aluminium-and-glass-framed **Kamppi** shopping and apartment complex; built in 2005, its six floors contain more than 150 shops and restaurants, while the basement houses the long-distance bus terminal.

National Theatre

Just northeast of the station is the imposing granite Jugend form of the **National Theatre** (Suomen Kansallisteatteri), home of Finnish drama since 1872 when it was relocated here from Turku. Under the country's then governing Swedish-speaking elite, "Finnish culture" was considered simply a contradiction in terms, while later under the tsars it was felt (quite rightly) to pose a nationalist, anti-Russian threat – Finnish theatre during the Russification process became so politically charged that it had to be staged away from the capital in the southwest coastal town of Pori. At the forefront of Finnish drama during its early years was **Aleksis Kivi** (1834–1872), who died insane and impoverished before being acknowledged as Finland's greatest playwright. He's remembered here by Wäinö Aaltonen's bronze sculpture. Interestingly, nobody knows for sure what Kivi actually looked like, and this imagined likeness, finished in 1939, has come to be regarded as the true one. Today, the theatre divides its performances between a main and a smaller stage, and about half of its repertoire is original Finnish-language stage plays.

University Botanical Garden

Just north of the National Theatre, spreading east to Unioninkatu in Kaisaniemi district is the University of Helsinki-run **Botanical Garden** (Kaisaniemen kasviti- eteellinen puutarha; daily 9am–8pm), a lovely place for a stroll on a sunny day. The park – like just about everything else in the city – was designed by Carl Engel, who had originally split the grounds into a symmetrical, tree-lined preserve and a separate landscaped garden with undulating paths, though this was later pared back. Of the park's current buildings, constructed by architect Gustaf Nyström, the most notable are the large wrought-iron, glass-roofed Palm House, built in 1889, and the main institute building from 1903, which is now home to the **Botanical Museum** (Tues– Sun 10am–5pm; €6). A trio of bombs during the Continuation War damaged most of the buildings – and killed nearly all of the plants. The grounds now hold more than 2800 plants of different origins, and the on-site greenhouse some 800 more.

Ateneum Art Museum

Just southeast of the train station is the elephantine **Ateneum Art Museum** (Tues & Fri 10am–6pm, Wed & Thurs 10am–8pm, Sat & Sun 11am–5pm; €6, €8 or more for special exhibitions; ⓦ www.ateneum.fi). Held in a grand old building, the museum is effectively Finland's National Gallery, holding a large collection of Finnish paintings, including a stirring selection of works from the late nineteenth century – the so-called Golden Age of Finnish painting, when the spirit of nationalism was surging through the country and the movement towards independence gaining strength; indeed, the art of the period was a contributing factor in the growing awareness of Finnish culture, both inside and outside the country.

Among the prime names of the Golden Age were **Akseli Gallen-Kallela** (1865–1931) and **Albert Edelfelt** (1854–1905), particularly the former, who translated many of the mythic scenes of the Kalevala onto canvas. A half-dozen of these are on display here – have a look at *Lemmenkäinen's Mother* (1897), *Swan of Tuomeli* (1905) and *Kullervo Cursing* (1899), the protagonist of which bears a striking resemblance to a young David Bowie wearing an Andy Warhol wig. Slightly later came **Juho Rissanen** (1873–1950) with his moody and evocative studies of peasant life, and **Hugo Simberg** (1873–1917), responsible for the eerie *Death and the Peasant* and the powerful nude triptych *Boy Carrying a Garland*. Cast an eye, too, over the works of **Helene Schjerfbeck** (1862–1946), for a long time one of the country's most underrated artists but now enjoying an upsurge in popularity – and collect- ability. She is given several rooms here, one of which contains a string of grotesque portraits of various humours and demeanours.

Among the best examples of pure Finnish landscape are the works of **Pekka Halonen** (1865–1933) – *Pioneers in Karelia* is typical, with soft curves expressively denoting natural scenes – and **Ferdinand von Wright** (1822–1906), whose larger-than-life-size *Fighting Capercaillies* was finished after the artist ended a lengthy bout of illness and puttering around. The painting, in which a male wood grouse is vying for the favour of a female, reinstated the ageing Ferdinand as a seminal figure in early Finnish art, and is today one of the most popular images in Finland, copies in various forms having made their way into thousands of homes. Also of particular note are the works of **I.K. Inha** (1865–1930), an early photographer who travelled throughout Finnish and Russian Karelia during the late nineteenth century, documenting the peoples and landscapes evoked in the Kalevala. Inha was a founding member of the Karelianists, a group of young Finnish artists who saw the Kalevala as the foundation of Finnish culture, and the vistas and portraits of his early but masterful photographs have become permanently etched in the Finnish Kalevalaic consciousness.

Though temporary exhibitions tend to take over several floors at a time, the permanent collection's best Finnish art is assembled on the higher floors: be sure to visit the museum's Golden Age works, as well as spend some time admiring the provocative Expressionism of **Tyko Sallinen** (1879–1955) and the November Group, an association of Finnish Expressionists formed just before Finland's declaration of independence from Russia. There are also some token **foreign masters** – a Van Gogh, two Gaugins, a Chagall and a few Cézannes. Before you leave, check out the excellent art bookshop on the ground floor.

North along Mannerheimintie

The logical route for exploring north of the city centre, the wide thoroughfare of **Mannerheimintie** is named after the military commander and statesman C.G.E. Mannerheim, who wielded considerable influence on Finnish affairs in the first half of the twentieth century. A great lover of horses, he's commemorated by an equestrian statue in front of Kiasma near the busy junction with Arkadiankatu, a structure on which the city's bird population has left its mark.

Natural History Museum

Reopened in 2008 after a floor-to-ceiling renovation, the country's premier **Natural History Museum** (Luonnontieteellinen museo; Tues, Wed & Fri 9am–4pm, Thurs 9am–6pm, Sat & Sun 10am–4pm; €6) is at Pohjoinen Rautatiekatu 13. Housed in a building originally constructed as a Russian school for boys in the later days of the Grand Duchy, the zoological museum's four permanent exhibits take visitors through the ins and outs of Finnish fauna. In addition to a lobby with the requisite collection of dinosaur skeletons, the museum has interesting exhibits that cover each of Finland's geographic regions and present several well-curated exhibits on wildlife in the far northern reaches of the country. The building itself is compelling for the arched doors, period windows and original tile and herringbone oak parquet floors uncovered during the restoration.

Kiasma Museum of Contemporary Art

Just beyond the Lasipalatsi at Mannerheiminaukio 2 is the **Kiasma Museum of Contemporary Art** (Tues 10am–5pm, Wed–Fri 10am–8.30pm, Sat & Sun 10am–6pm; €7, free first Wed eve of every month; ⓦ www.kiasma.fi), a slightly forbidding, steel-clad and tube-like structure that looks from the side like a mix of the Sydney Opera House and the Guggenheim in Bilbao – a vaguely pretentious building for the usually functionalist Finns. Inside the catacomb-like interior are sweeping curves and well-lit hallways; on the ground floor natural light pours in from a variety of angles onto a brilliant-white interior that looks like it gets a new coat of paint on a weekly basis. Entry to this floor is free, and there's a decent café, internet access, one of the best art bookshops in Finland and an interactive children's playroom.

Kiasma draws its **exhibition** material from an archive of thousands of pieces of contemporary art, as well as works by visiting artists, although as you explore you begin to feel that it's the building itself – with its play on space, light and technology – that is the principal exhibit. Various touchscreen terminals built into the walls at strategic points tell you all you need to know about the works on show. Nothing is permanently on display, and exhibitions change every two to three months, but on account of the sheer space available the museum tends to put on extremely large scale installations of cutting-edge international artists, many of whom produce conceptual works. Check the museum's website for details, and keep an eye out, too for performances, workshops, seminars, lectures and film screenings staged at the museum's small theatre.

Parliament Building

The section of Mannerheimintie north from Kiasma passes a number of outstanding buildings, the first of which is the **Parliament Building** on the left (Eduskuntatalo; guided hour-long tours July & Aug daily 11am & 1pm, Sept–June Sat 11am & 12.30pm, first Sun of each month noon & 1pm; when in session, access is to the public galleries only; free; ⓦwww.eduskunta.fi). The work of J.S. Sirén, the porridge-coloured building, with its fourteen pompous Corinthian columns and choking air of solemnity, was completed in 1931. Intended to celebrate the new republic, its style was drawn from the revolutionary Neoclassicism that dominated public buildings from Fascist Italy to Nazi Germany – albeit accented with a touch of Art Deco and functionalism – and its authoritarian features can appear wildly out of place in Helsinki, though it's worth a look nonetheless. The guided tours of the building and its 200-seat plenary session hall are well worth joining, not least because they help explain the history of Finnish government and how the modern political system functions.

National Museum

Just north of here is the **National Museum** (Suomen Kansallismuseo; Tues & Wed 11am–8pm, Thurs–Sun 11am–6pm; €7; ⓦwww.nba.fi), whose design was the result of an early twentieth-century competition won by the three Young Turks of early twentieth-century Finnish architecture – Armas Lindgren, Herman Gesellius and Eliel Saarinen. With National Romanticism at its zenith, they steeped their plan in Finnish history, drawing on the country's legacy of medieval churches and granite castles (even though many of these were built under Swedish domination), culminating in a weighty but slender tower that gives the place a cathedral-like profile. The entrance is guarded by Emil Wikström's sculptured bear and the interior ceilings are decorated by Gallen-Kallela with scenes from the Kalevala.

The museum may seem the obvious place to discover what Finland is all about but you might well find the **collections** rather disappointing. Being dominated by other nations for many centuries, Finland had little more than the prerequisites of peasant life to call its own up until the mid-1800s (when moves towards Finnish nationalism got off the ground), and the rows of farming and hunting tools alongside endless displays of bowls and spoons from the early times do little to fire the imagination. The most interesting section is an exhibition entitled **The Past Century**, which relates to the rise of Finnish self-determination and the early years of the republic. Large photographs show the enormous crowds that massed in Helsinki's streets to sing the Finnish anthem in defiance of their (then) Russian rulers, and there are cabinets packed with curios and memorabilia that give a sense of the left–right struggles that marked the early decades of independence and the immediate postwar years – periods when Finland's political future teetered precariously in the balance, a long way from the stability and prosperity enjoyed in more recent times.

Finlandia Hall and around

Stylistically a far cry from the National Museum building but equally affecting, **Finlandia Hall** (Finlandia Talo; guided tours at 3pm when not in use, though dates vary; €7; ring ⓣ 09/40 241 or check at the City Tourist Office) stands directly across Mannerheimintie, partially hidden by the roadside foliage. Designed by Alvar Aalto a few years before his death in 1976, Finlandia Hall was conceived as part of a grand plan to rearrange the entire centre of Helsinki. The plan, which involved the removal of the rail-freight yards and placed the hall at the centre of the city, never saw the light of day, but arrive in the evening to admire the hall's light reflected softly off of Töölönlahti and you'll get some sense of the potential beauty of the greater concept. Inside the hall, Aalto's characteristic wave pattern (the architect's surname, as it happened, meant "wave" in Finnish, which many believed predestined him to create the type of forms he did) and asymmetry are much in evidence. Aalto based the main auditorium on a classical Greek theatre, and while the structure has not proven to be the best in terms of acoustics, it does feature Aalto's distinctive marble balconies and cobalt-blue walls adorned with undulating swathes of wood. From the walls and ceilings through to the lamps and vases, the place has a quiet and graceful air – though the view from the foyer still looks down to the dilapidated rail-freight yards.

Next door is **Hakasalmi Villa** (Hakasalmen huvila; Wed–Sun 11am–5pm, closed mid-June to mid-Sept; free), an Italian Neoclassical construction built in the 1840s by a councillor and patron of the arts whose collection inspired the founding of the museum. It houses engaging, long-term temporary exhibitions, often strikingly designed; a recent show looked at the life of the Roma people in Finland. The construction work taking place next door to the villa will in time become the **Music Hall** (Musiikkitalo), an all new, state-of-the-art concert centre consisting of a 1700-seat main hall, as well as five smaller stages that will be used by the Sibelius Academy, the Helsinki Philharmonic and the Finnish Radio Symphony Orchestra. The complex is due to open in 2011.

Opera House

Finland's **Opera House** (Ooppera; Mon–Fri 9am–6pm, Sat 3–6pm, Sun open 2hr before performances; guided tours early May to Aug Wed 3pm, €8), a little way beyond Finlandia, is, like so many contemporary Finnish buildings, a Lego-like expanse of white-tiled facade. Its light-flooded interior is enlivened by displays of colourful costumes though, and its grounds and entrance spiked with minimalist black-granite sculptures.

Kamppi to Punavuori

Head east of the massive Kamppi centre and you'll find narrow cobblestone (and pedestrian-only) streets buzzing with young locals and families patronizing small boutiques and casual eateries. In the late 1990s, Punavuori rose to become the hippest place to hang in Helsinki, and while it's lost some of its edge to the northern district of Kallio, there's still plenty to do here – it's the densest concentration of shops, restaurants and venues in the capital, in fact.

Yrjönkatu

The **Yrjönkatu Swimming Hall** (Yrjönkadun Uimahalli; Mon & Sun noon–9pm, Tues–Fri 6.30am–9pm, Sat 8am–9pm; €4.40; ⓦ www.hel.fi/sport), Yrjönkatu 21B, is a gorgeous example of 1920s Classicism. The oldest pool in Scandinavia

– and "Europe's third-best indoor swimming experience", according to *Wallpaper** magazine – these open-air baths are one of the most evocative public spaces in Scandinavia. Because clothing is optional – and rarely worn – entrance days are separate for men (Tues, Thurs & Sat) and women (Mon, Wed, Fri & Sun). Prices include bathrobes, towels and sauna access, and upstairs is a small café and large cabanas (€12) where you can kick back and hang loose.

Immediately next door at no. 27 is the quirky **Amos Anderson Art Museum** (Mon, Tues, Thurs & Fri 10am–6pm, Wed 10am–8pm, Sat & Sun 11am–5pm; €8; Ⓦwww.amosanderson.fi), the one-time home of devotee of sacred and choral music, Amos Anderson. Most of what you see is given over to rotating exhibitions on modern art and graphic design though the museum's permanent collection, set among floors 4½ to 6, include a number of excellent mid-twentieth-century works including stark self-portraits by Vilho Lampi (1933), Martti Ranttila (1930) and William Lönnberg (1929). Anderson's chapel, which he consecrated in 1926, makes up the museum's fifth floor.

Two blocks south of here at the corner of Yrjönkatu and Lönnrotinkatu is a grassy square containing the **Vanha kirkko** (Old Church; Mon–Fri noon–3pm). This humble wooden structure, another example of Engel's work, isn't just old: it's Helsinki's oldest, and was the first Lutheran church to be erected after Helsinki became the Finnish capital, predating the one in Senate Square by some years but occupying a far less glamorous plot – a mass grave dating from 1710 holding the bodies of some one thousand plague victims from the Northern War.

Bulevardi

The southern edge of the church square is flanked by **Bulevardi**, a broad, leafy road that runs on all the way from Mannerheimintie in the northeast to Hietalahdentori in the southwest. Bulevardi's stately nineteenth- and twentieth-century stone buildings were originally private homes, though at no. 9 is **Ekberg**, Helsinki's oldest café (see p.84), while the decorative building straddling nos. 23–27 is the **Alexander Theatre** (Aleksanterin Teatteri). Originally built in the 1870s as a Russian garrison theatre, it was taken over by the Finnish National Opera after independence in 1918, and given its current name once the opera moved to its modern home in Töölö in the 1990s. Today, the theatre puts on regular Finnish-language productions of international plays, as well as the occasional opera and ballet.

Sinebrychoff Art Museum

A little further down off the southern side of Bulevardi is a large park grounds known as **Sinebrychoff Park** (Sinebrychoffin puisto), an English-style gardens designed by Russian merchant Nikolai Sinebrychoff that is now dominated by the **Sinebrychoff Art Museum** (Sinebrychoffin Taidemuseo; Tues & Fri 10am–6pm, Wed–Thurs 10am–8pm, Sat & Sun 11am–5pm; €5, €7.50 for special exhibitions; Ⓦwww.fng.fi) at no. 40. This precious museum occupies a three-storey stone structure originally built as Nikolai's office in 1842, before becoming the family home of the merchant's son Paul and his wife, Swedish Theatre actress Fanny Grahn, in the 1880s. The couple began amassing an unrivalled (for Finland) art collection of some seven hundred works, which they donated to the Finnish state in 1921. The museum houses mostly sixteenth- and seventeenth-century Flemish, Dutch and Swedish paintings and portraits, along with some excellent miniatures, delicately painted porcelain, dainty *objets d'art* and refined period furniture.

The first floor consists of rotating temporary exhibitions of foreign art, while upstairs holds the bulk of the family's art collection and period rooms. **Paintings** of particular note here include Franchoys Wouters' dazzling *Cupid and his Bow*, as well as a number of watercolour and gouache portraits of various soldiers and royalty painted on vellum and ivory and into copper lockets. The standout of the couple's ornate living spaces is the **Gustavian Room**, a Louis XVI-style salon used for gatherings that today features an intarsiate parquet floor, rose-tinted divans and settees with gold brocade fabric, with drapes made of the same. Further on is the **Empire Room**, bathed in gold – a popular style in early nineteenth-century Scandinavia. Note the mahogany sofa, re-covered in gorgeous gilded silk upholstery. Incidentally, the family rented out four of the museum's most opulent rooms to a local school that had been destroyed during World War II. Once it took over the premises, the school whitewashed over the rooms' ornate ceilings – since uncovered – ostensibly to prevent the pupils from zoning out on its intricate patterns.

Hietalahdentori and around

Just opposite the waterfront is the wide **Hietalahdentori**, a concrete square that perks up with a daily morning flea market and, in summer, an evening market (3.30–8pm). The *kauppahalli* (Mon–Fri 10am–5pm, Sat 10am–3pm), with a wooden ceiling, has a permanent collection of stalls and a café. Flanking the western side of Hietalahdentori stand the 1870s-era buildings that formerly housed Finland's oldest **brewery**, Sinebrychoff. Nikolai Sinebrychoff won the exclusive rights to manufacture and sell beer in Helsinki at an auction in 1819, though beer was never a huge money-maker for the family, which built its fortune mainly from large-scale construction projects in Russia and Poland. These days, rent from these original brewery buildings helps to support the family's art museum.

Kaartinkaupunki

To the southeast of Esplanadi along Kasarmikatu is the compact district of **Kaartinkaupunki**. Demarcated, roughly, by the Esplanadi and the Tähtitornin Vuori park, the area was named after an old Russian barracks and is now known for several small, offbeat museums.

Museum of Finnish Architecture

The first of these is the **Museum of Finnish Architecture** (Suomen Rakennu-staiteen Museo; Tues, Thurs & Fri 10am–4pm, Wed 10am–8pm, Sat & Sun 11am–4pm; €3.50–5 depending upon exhibitions, free on Fri; ⓦwww.mfa.fi) at Kasarmikatu 24, which is aimed at the serious fan: while a useful resource for a nation with an important architectural heritage, it's primarily visited for its archives and library. Small rotating exhibitions, however, are always on and architectural tours of less accessible buildings both in Helsinki and around the country can be arranged here. The neo-Renaissance building itself, designed by Magnus Schjerfbeck in 1899, is worth popping into to see its elegant wrought-iron banisters and broad stairwells.

Design Museum

A block from Kasarmikatu is Korkeavuorenkatu, holding the well-curated **Design Museum** at no. 23 (Designmuseo; June–Aug daily 11am–6pm; Sept–May Tues–Sun 11am–6pm, Tues until 8pm; €7; ⓦwww.designmuseum.fi), which traces the relationship between art and industry in Finnish history. Though for a museum about design it feels terribly outmoded, there are full English-language explanatory texts that cover the period exhibits, which stretch from Karelianism – the representations of nature and peasant life from the Karelia region in eastern Finland that dominated Finnish art and design in the years just before and after independence – to the modern movements, along with the postwar shift towards the more familiar, and less interesting, pan-Scandinavian styles. Some pieces of note include: Eero Saarinen's oak and wool armchair, its back shaped like a bishop's helmet; Birger Kärpianen's sgraffito wall plaque of an oblong-shaped woman holding a rose (1950s); Richard Lindh's turquoise and white moped (1960); Harbie Kurtemaa's *Laku-Pekka* ("Liquorice Pete") blackface poster (famously banned); and, finally, Eero Aarnio's *nojatuoli* fibreglass chair from 1966, a replica of which can be picked up two blocks away at Aero, Yrjönkatu 8, for several thousand euros.

Kaartinkaupunki's churches

At the far end of Yrjönkatu on the corner of Unioninkatu is the twin-spired Gothic Revival **Johanneksenkirkko** (St John's Church), whose 74-metre-high towers are a handy navigation aid; it's worth popping into for a gander at the altarpiece, *A Divine Revelation*, painted by Eero Järnefelt, brother-in-law to Jean Sibelius. A second church, the oblong neo-Gothic **Saksalainen Kirkko** (German Church), is located several blocks east at the intersection of Bernhardinkatu and Unioninkatu. Its name derives from its use in the latter half of the nineteenth century by Helsinki's small German community. Today it is one of the city's most popular choices for weddings.

Ullanlinna, Eira and Kaivopuisto

Running parallel to the southern edge of Helsinki's central peninsula is **Tehtaankatu** ("Factory Street"), a mostly nondescript cobblestone road embedded with rails that carry the #3T tram and connecting the residential **Ullanlinna** district with equally residential **Eira**. Both districts contain a number of prominent buildings, including the fenced-in Neoclassical Russian embassy – for many years, the very name of the street was invoked to reference the influence of the Soviet Union in Finnish politics.

Kaivopuisto Park

Immediately south of Tehtaankatu is the large, hilly park known as **Kaivopuisto** ("Kaivari" in local slang), one of Helsinki's most visited spots. In the 1830s this land was developed as a health resort, with a spa house that drew Russian nobility from St Petersburg to sample its waters (the springs and sea baths were destroyed in 1944). Today, what was once bare cliffs has now been turned into swathes of green with lookouts, carpet bedding and natural rocky outcrops, in the middle of which is the park's central avenue and the tiny **Ursa Observatory** (℡09/653 505, ⓦ www.ursa .fi). Operated by a local astronomy club, the newly renovated Jugendstil observatory slides open its roof and extends its telescope for both star shows (mid-Jan to mid-March & mid-Oct to mid-Dec Tues–Sun 7–9pm; €2) and solar screenings (mid-March to mid-June, Aug & Sept Sun 1–3pm; €2). The hill it sits on offers splendid views of the harbour, as well as a summertime restaurant in the white pavilion next door. Each summer, locals splay out across the greens of Kaivopuisto to sunbathe, picnic and hang out (in the winter, it's a great sledding spot) and there are occasional rock, pop and classical **concerts** in the park, too. The park is the site of the citywide hangover that follows the Dionysian celebrations of Vappu (1 May), when it's overcrowded with fancy dress, blaring music and no small amount of sheer intoxication. For a listing of concerts, check with the city tourist office.

Mannerheim Museum

From the southern end of the park, follow the perimeter road (Ehrenströmintie) around to the South Harbour, then double back along short Porrastie onto Kalliolin-nantie. At no. 14, you'll find the house where military leader and former president Carl Gustaf Mannerheim spent much of his later life. The building is now maintained as the fascinating **Mannerheim Museum** (Mannerheim Museo; Fri–Sun 11am–4pm,

Finland's greatest statesman: Carl Gustaf Emil Mannerheim

To the manor born, Baron Carl Gustaf Emil Mannerheim (1867–1951) was the son of a Finnish noble family from Louhisaari Manor near Turku; though originally German, the family had emigrated to Finland from Sweden. Mannerheim embarked on a military career at an early age, serving in the Russian army (Finland was part of Russia at this time) for nearly two decades before returning home to Finland and entering politics. He was made chairman of Finland's Defence Council in 1931 with a promise of becoming Commander-in-Chief in the event of war. After the Soviet attack on Finland of November 30, 1939, Mannerheim took up his new role and established his wartime headquarters in Mikkeli (see p.216). During the Winter War, he exerted a significant influence on Finnish politics, though did not actively participate in government affairs. Finland's resistance against superior Russian forces gained Mannerheim great respect amongst the Finnish people and politicians alike; this distinction ultimately led Parliament to elect him as President in August 1944, though he held the post for less than two years, citing failing health as the reason for his resignation. Moving to a sanatorium in Montreux to recover after an ulcer operation, Mannerheim lived out the rest of his life in Switzerland, though he regularly returned to Finland, passing away in January 1951. He is buried in Hietaniemi Cemetery in Helsinki.

other times by appointment, call ℡09/635 443; €8 including guided tour; ⓦwww .mannerheim-museo.fi), easily one of the city's best museums. The interior is left much as it was when the man died in 1951, and the clutter is astounding. During his travels – which reached as far as Siberia – Mannerheim raided flea markets and bazaars at every opportunity, collecting a remarkable array of plunder that comprises assorted furniture, antiques, ornaments and books from all over the globe. Upstairs is the camp-bed which Mannerheim found too comfortable ever to change, and in the wall is the vent inserted to keep the bedroom as airy as a field-tent.

Cygnaeus Gallery

If he had lived a few decades earlier, one of Mannerheim's Kallionlinnantie neighbours would have been Frederik Cygnaeus (1807–1881), art patron and Professor of Aesthetics at Helsinki University. In 1860 Cygnaeus built a summer house at no. 8, a lovely yellow-turreted affair, and filled it with an outstanding collection of art. Later he donated the lot to the nation and today it's displayed as the **Cygnaeus Gallery** (Wed 11am–7pm, Thurs–Sun 11am–4pm; €4; ⓦwww.nba.fi). Everything is beautifully laid out in the tiny rooms of the house, with whole walls of work by the most influential of his contemporaries. The von Wright brothers (Ferdinand, Magnus and Wilhelm) are responsible for the most touching pieces – the bird and nature studies. Look out, too, for a strange portrait of Cygnaeus by Ekman, showing the man sprouting sinister wings from under his chin.

Eira

The edge of Kaivopuisto looks out across a sprinkling of little islands and the Suomenlinna fortress. You can follow one of the pathways down into **Merikatu**, along which lie several of the Art Nouveau villas lived in by the big cheeses of Finnish industry during the early part of the twentieth century. Easily the most extreme is no. 25, the **Enso-Gutzeit villa**, now portioned off into offices and with a lingering air of decay hanging over its decorative facade. Inland from Merikatu, the curving alleys and tall, elegant buildings of the **Eira** district are landmarked by the 106-metre-high steel needle rising from the roof of **Mikael Agricola Church** (Mikael Agricolan Kirkko) named after the man who codified the modern Finnish language and translated the first Finnish Bible, but making no demands on your time.

North to Kallio

Head north along Unioninkatu into the northern reaches of the **Kruununhaka** district, where there are a couple of interesting museums and some good university bars and you'll find things start to slow down a good deal. Across the three-arched granite Hakaniemensilta bridge straddling slender Kaisaniemi Bay, the commercial **Hakaniemi** neighbourhood was until the nineteenth century a full-fledged island, and the bridge, dating from 1912, long demarcated the middle- and working-class city districts. In the late nineteenth century, a fledging factory-workers' community called **Kallio** (literally, "stone") began to form several blocks north of the bridge. Traditionally, Kallio has had some of the lowest rents in Helsinki, attracting artists and students (and, in the 1990s, prostitutes and sex shops). In recent years, though, rents have been on the up, as has the area's reputation as an extremely hip place to live, work and hang out.

Burgher's House

East of Unioninkatu at Kristianinkatu 12, the single-storey wooden **Burgher's House** (Ruiskumestarin Talo; Wed–Sun: June–Aug 11am–6pm; Sept–May 11am–5pm; free; ⓦwww.hel.fi/kaumuseo) stands in vivid contrast to the tall granite dwellings around it – and gives an indication of how Helsinki looked when wood was still the predominant building material. Also known as the Pumpmaster's House, it is the oldest original standing wooden structure in the city – built in 1818, just after the great fire – and was privately owned until 1974, when it was purchased by the municipality. Its interior has been kitted out with a mishmash of middle-class furnishings from the mid-nineteenth century, and rooms include a vestibule, living room, kitchen and two bedrooms.

Military Museum

A short walk along Kristianinkatu towards where it meets with Maurinkatu brings you to the recently renovated **Military Museum** (Sotamuseo; Tues–Thurs 11am–5pm, Fri–Sun 11am–4pm; €4), a rather formless selection of weapons, medals and glorifications of armed-forces life, but with some excellent documentary photos of the Winter and Continuation wars. Finland was drawn into World War II through necessity rather than choice. When Soviet troops invaded eastern Finnish territories in November 1939 under the guise of protecting Leningrad, they were repelled by technically inferior but far more committed Finns (the Winter War) – the legend of the "heroes in white" (Finnish soldiers camouflaged in the winter snows) was born then. Soon after, however, faced with possible starvation and a fresh Soviet advance, Finland joined the war on the Nazi side (the Continuation War), mainly in order to continue resisting the threat from the east. For this reason, it's rare to find World War II spoken of as such in Finland: much more commonly it's divided into these separate conflicts.

Hakaniementori kauppahalli

Traditionally working-class **Hakaniemi** is a district chiefly visited for its indoor market or **kauppahalli** (Mon–Fri 8am–5pm, Sat 8am–2pm), about the liveliest in the city, by the busy traffic interchange of Hakaniementori. The market hall not only houses an excellent array of fresh fruit, vegetables, meats and fish, but also makes a great stop for quick, cheap eats. On Sundays, the square hosts one of the best **flea markets** in the city.

Kallionkirkko and Kotiharju Sauna

Peek out north up Siltasaarenkatu – the longest straight road in the city – from the square and you'll be able to see right up the hill to the impressive Art Deco brickwork of **Kallionkirkko** (Kallio church), designed by Lars Sonck in 1912 and containing two organs – one Baroque, one French Romantic. Jean Sibelius composed a melody specifically for its seven bells. A five-minute walk east of the church is the **Kotiharju Sauna** (Tues–Fri 2–8pm, Sat 1–7pm; €10; Ⓦwww .kotiharjunsauna.fi), Helsinki's only wood-burning sauna, at Harjutorinkatu 1.

Museum of Workers' Housing and Linnanmäki

Half a kilometre west of the sauna beyond the busy Sturenkatu is the **Museum of Workers' Housing** at Kirstinkuja 4 (Työväenasuntomuseo; June–Aug Mon–Thurs & Sun 11am–4pm; €3; Ⓦwww.hel.fi/kaumuseo). This series of renovated wooden buildings makes up one of the country's better ethnographic open-air museums and is a great place to brush up on your Finnish social history. The buildings were constructed during the early 1900s to provide housing for the impoverished country folk who moved to the growing, increasingly industrialized city to work as street cleaners and refuse collectors. Six of the one-room homes have been re-created with period furnishings, and a biography on the door describes each flat's occupants – woeful tales of overcrowding, overwork, and sons who left for America and never returned.

West of the museum in the same open green area – there'll be no mistaking the towering, undulating roller coaster – is the hundred-year-old **Linnanmäki amusement park** (late April to mid-Sept; adults €8, under-15s €15; Ⓦwww .linnanmaki.fi), Finland's most popular theme park after Naantali's Moomin-world. Known to children all over the country as "Lintsi", the place is filled with rides, towers, carousels, puppet shows and the like, making it a good break from the museum route if you've kids in tow. One definite stop for kids of all ages is Panoraama, a 53-metre observation tower (free with entry) that gives great views of the city (though it's not quite as high as the Olympic Stadium tower a few minutes' walk west). The adjacent **Sea Life park** (Sept–April Mon, Tues & Thurs–Sun 10am–5pm, Wed 10am–8pm; €14.50; Ⓦwww.sealife.fi), Tivolitie 10, holds some fifty tanks in which you can observe up close sharks, piranhas, seahorses and hundreds of other creatures.

The Olympic Stadium and Sibelius Park

Immediately west of Linnanmäki across the railway tracks – but most commonly reached from Mannerheimintie – is the Olympic Stadium, Finland's first and largest arena. Nearly a kilometre west of here is the Sibelius Park, an uneven spot of grass that commemorates Finland's greatest composer.

Olympic Stadium and Sports Museum

Originally intended for the 1940 games, the **Olympic Stadium** eventually staged the second postwar Olympic Games in 1952. From the 72m-high **Stadium Tower** (Mon–Fri 9am–8pm, Sat & Sun 9am–6pm; €2) there's an unsurpassed view over the city and a chunk of the southern coast. If you're a stopwatch-and-spikes freak, ask at the tower's ticket office for directions to the **Sports Museum** (Mon–Fri 11am–5pm, Sat & Sun noon–4pm; €3.50; Ⓦwww.urheilumuseo.org), whose mind-numbing collection of track officials' shoes and swimming caps overshadows a worthy attempt to present sport as an integral part of Finnish culture. The nation's heroes, among them racing driver Keke Rosberg and athlete Lasse Virén, are lauded to the skies. Outside, Wäinö Aaltonen's sculpture of Paavo Nurmi is a beautiful depiction of Finland's most famous sportsman, mid-run and fully naked – this atypically Finnish expression of public nudity caused quite a stir when the sculpture was unveiled in 1952.

Sibelius Park

There is little of note north of the stadium, so you are best off crossing Mannerheimintie and following the streets off it leading to the shady and pleasant **Sibelius Park** (Sibeliuksen Puisto). Here you'll find Eila Hiltunen's **monument** to the composer, made from 24 tons of steel tubes. Resembling a large silver Surrealist organ, it's a dead ringer for a set piece from the film *Brazil*; next to it, there's an irrefutably horrid sculpture of Sibelius's dismembered head.

West of the Centre: Hiehtaniemi and Ruoholahti

Head a kilometre or so due west from the Kiasma centre along Arkadiankatu into the neighbourhood of Etu-Töölö and you'll arrive at two of the city's star attractions: the Temppeliaukio church and, just beyond, the cemetery at **Hietaniemi** – both definitely worth taking part of an afternoon. Southwest of here is **Ruoholahti**, an area that came into being at a time when Nokia still manufactured rubber tyres, rain boots and electric cables – provenance for the honorific affixed to the main building here, The Cable Factory. Today the district is a centre for new technology companies, while serving as the main link between the city centre and the suburbs of Espoo that lie west of downtown.

Temppeliaukio kirkko

A few hundred metres south of the Sibelius Park towards the city centre brings you to Lutherinkatu 3, just off Runeberginkatu, where you'll find the breathtaking **Temppeliaukion kirkko** (Rock Church; mid-May to mid-Sept Mon, Tues, Thurs & Fri 10am–8pm, Wed 10am–6.30pm, Sat 10am–6pm, Sun noon–1.45pm & 3.30–6pm; closed Tues in winter and during services). Brilliantly conceived by Timo and Tuomo Suomalainen and finished in 1969, the underground, stone-hewn church is built inside a massive block of natural granite in the middle of an otherwise ordinary residential square – effectively, the brothers picked a jagged outcrop of solid rock that rose 12m above street level and blasted out the walls from the inside. Whilst here, try and see it from above if you can: the copper dome that pokes through the rock makes the thing look like a forgotten flying saucer.

The building's granite facade is otherwise much less interesting than its innards, where circular, serrated rock walls run up to the massive concave ceiling made of copper wire, and light streams above through 180 slabs of glass – this a seriously Finnish construction. The odd combination of man-made and natural materials has made it a fixture on the guided tour bus circuit, but even when crowded it's a thrill to be inside. Classical concerts frequently take place here, the raw rock walls making for excellent acoustics, and in the summer you can watch the blue skies turn from purple to midnight blue during the performances. Check the noticeboard at the entrance for details or visit ⓦ taivallahti.helsinginseurakunnat.fi. There are also English-language worship services every Sunday at 2pm.

Hietaniemi Cemetery

Some 200m west of the church you first pass through the small Islamic, Jewish and Orthodox – Helsinki's oldest – cemeteries, and then arrive at the expanse of tombs comprising **Hietaniemi Cemetery** (Hietaniemen Hautausmaa; usually open until 10pm). A prowl among the gravestones is like a stroll through a "Who was Who" of Finland's last 150 years: Engel, Snellman, Waltari, Jansson and a host of former presidents (including Mannerheim and Kekkonen) are buried here, and you'll also find the Sinebrychoffs' surprisingly austere family plot too (on site No. 3). Just inside the main entrance, lined with several handsome rows of linden trees, lies

Alvar Aalto, his witty little tombstone consisting partly of a chopped Neoclassical column; behind it is the larger marker of Gallen-Kallela, his initials woven around a painter's palette. Local schoolkids head to the cemetery when skipping off lessons during warm weather, not for a smoke behind the gravestones but to reach the **beaches** that line the bay just beyond its western walls. From these you can enjoy the best sunset view in the city.

Cable factory museums

Situated immediately west of the city centre in Ruoholahti (tram #8 or Metro: Ruoholahti), the former cable factory or **Kaapelitehdas** (Ⓦ www.kaapelitehdas .fi), Tallberginkatu 1F, puts on a series of cultural events year round. It's also home to dance and theatre companies and, accessed via the "G" entrance to the factory, a clutch of moderately interesting museums (all open Tues–Sun 11am–6pm). The most interesting is the **Finnish Museum of Photography** (€6; Ⓦ www.fmp .fi), which puts on excellent and diverse temporary exhibitions of international and Finnish photography, both modern and historical. Be sure to check exactly what's on beforehand, however, since the museum's permanent collection (which occupies the space in between exhibitions) – effectively a shabby closet-full of old cameras – suggests that Finnish photography never really progressed beyond the watch-the-birdie stage.

Up one floor is the **Theatre Museum** (€6; Ⓦ www.teatterimuseo.fi), whose very large permanent collection of costumes, stage sets, lights and several hundred puppets and marionettes make it one of the best places in Helsinki to take kids: many of the exhibits are intended to be interactive, and you can dress up in costumes, play with the puppets, work stage lights and sound controls and film your own performance. Temporary exhibitions, which tend to focus on different aspects behind the scenes in Finnish theatre, are however more or less lost on non-Finnish or -Swedish speakers, since there is no translation.

Finally, the entirety of the fourth floor is taken up by the moderately inter-esting **Hotel and Restaurant Museum** (€2; Ⓦ www.hotellijaravintolamuseo.fi), essentially designed for die-hard aficionados of the catering trade, although the photos on the walls of its two rooms reveal a somewhat unique social history of Helsinki, showing hotel and restaurant life from both sides of the table, alongside a staggering selection of matchboxes, beer mats emblazoned with the emblems of their establishments and a collection of handwritten menus (in Finnish and Swedish) dating back to the 1800s.

The islands

The coast off Helsinki is filled with some 330 islands, some of which make for great escapes during the warmer months. Among them, you'll find many peaceful, relaxing spots offering bathing huts, grassy parks, picnic areas, jetties, beaches, villa restaurants and gardens for sprawling out and enjoying Helsinki's often surprisingly warm summers. Many of the more popular islands are connected (in the summer) by regular launch service from the market square.

Suomenlinna

Helsinki's – in fact Finland's – most popular island is located a few kilometres off the coast of Kaivopuisto district, reached by regular ferry from the South Harbour. Set across five interconnected islands and built by the Swedes to protect Helsinki from seaborne attack, the eighteenth-century fortress of **Suomenlinna** (Ⓦ www.suomenlinna.fi) makes a rewarding break from the city centre – even if you only want to laze around on the dunes. Though there are a couple of museums spread about the island, the main joy here lies in exploring its craggy headlands and quiet bays; in the summertime, the whole place is crammed with locals drinking, swimming and enjoying the sun. You'd be wise to have a torch with you, though, if you want to explore some of the island's tunnels and caves.

Originally used by Helsinki residents as grazing ground for sheep and cattle – and by passing sailors for its tavern – Suomenlinna had its role in Finnish history solidified when construction began in 1748 on Sveaborg ("Fortress of Sweden"), a bastion intended to defend against the maritime routes of the Swedish empire. The fortress only existed under Swedish rule for a few years, though: a short, decisive battle in 1808 saw it surrendered to Russian forces. In 1855, the Russian-held bulwark was bombed by the French and the British, and in the years following Finnish independence, the military buildings on the island were employed as a prison camp for some 12,000 Red Guard troops. A few prison inmates still reside on the island, involved in construction and restoration projects as part of their sentences, but joining them as island residents are some 850 inhabitants, including residents of the Pikku Mustasaari Naval Academy, who kick back in the world's largest sauna, seating one hundred. The only invaders nowadays, meanwhile, are the thousands of tourists and locals who flock here in the summertime who take to the rocks and dunes with their picnic baskets and cases of Lapin Kulta.

A few minutes' walk from the ferry terminal is the one-time naval store that now houses the **Suomenlinna Museum** (Suomenlinna museo; daily: Oct–April 10.30am–4.30pm; May–Sept 10am–6pm; €5). This excellent museum covers the entire history of the island through well-lit, expertly documented displays that help flesh out the lives of the eighteenth- and nineteenth-century officers and soldiers who resided here during Swedish and Russian rule; the 25-minute *The Suomenlinna Experience* film, screened every half-hour, is also worth catching.

None of Suomenlinna's other museums are particularly riveting, although the **Ehrensvärd Museum** (daily: late May 10am–4pm; June–Aug 11am–6pm; Sept 11am–4pm; €3) is worth a look. The museum occupies the residence of the first commander of the fortress, Augustin Ehrensvärd, who oversaw the building of the fortress and now lies in the elaborate tomb in the grounds; his personal effects remain inside the house alongside displays on the fort's construction. Other museums include a **Toy Museum** (Suomenlinnan Lelumuseo; April & Sept Sat & Sun 11am–4pm; May, June & Aug daily 11am–4pm; July daily 11am–6pm; €5), which has a number of pretty examples of dolls and dollhouse miniatures dating back to 1800, and the **Manege Military Museum** (Sotamuseon Maneesinäyttely; mid-May to Aug daily 11am–6pm; €4), which records Suomenlinna's defensive actions, and where, for an extra €3.50, you can clamber around the darkly claustrophobic World War II submarine *Vesikko*.

Ferries to Suomenlinna depart the market square year-round roughly every half hour between 6am and 2.20am.

Korkeasaari and Helsinki Zoo

Set out on the craggy, 22-acre island of Korkeasaari just northeast of Katajanokka, Helsinki's city **zoo** (Korkeasaaren eläintarha; daily: April & Sept 10am–6pm; May–Aug 10am–8pm; Oct–March 10am–4pm; €7, or €12 with ferry; €4/6 for kids aged 6–17, free for kids under 6; ⓦwww.korkeasaari.fi) contains a decent collection of some 150 species of domestic and non-native creatures, including a particularly fetching collection of snow leopards, though there aren't many large mammals on show. Ferries depart for the zoo every half hour from both the *kauppatori* (daily May–Sept) and from Hakaniemi pier just east of the Hakaniemen-silta bridge (June–Aug daily; May Sat & Sun); you can also reach it by taking bus #16 or the metro to Kulosaari, then walking 2km through the Mustikkamaa park.

Seurasaari and around

Fifteen minutes northwest of the city centre is **Seurasaari**, a small wooded island delightfully set in a sheltered bay. Linked since 1892 by bridge to the centre, the island rivals Suomenlinna as a popular weekend spot to picnic and sun. You can also catch a glimpse of some of the traditional Finnish cottages and manor homes that, before World War II, lined much of the Finnish countryside.

The three contrasting museums on or close by Seurasaari fill a well-spent day. Just across the bridge to the island from the southern end of Tamminiementie you'll come to the **Open-Air Museum** (Seurasaaren ulkomuseo; late May & early Sept Mon–Fri 9am–3pm, Sat & Sun 11am–5pm; June–Aug daily 11am–5pm; €6), a collection of vernacular buildings assembled from all over Finland, speckled about the island and connected by various pathways. There are better examples of traditional Finnish life elsewhere in the country, but if you're only visiting Helsinki this will give a good insight into how the country folk lived until surprisingly recently. The museum's 87 buildings also include a country shop, and its old-style church is a popular spot for city couples' weddings. Aside from exploring the island's 46 wooded hectares of hills, wetlands and forests, people also come to Seurasaari to strip off at the sex-segregated **nudist beaches** lining part of the island's western coast – also a popular offshore stop for the city's weekend yachtsmen, armed with the latest in binocular technology.

Leaving the island, on the other side of the bridge is a long driveway leading to the **Urho Kekkonen Museum** (Urho Kekkosen Museo Tamminiemi; ⓦwww .nba.fi), the villa where the esteemed president lived until his death in 1986. Whether they love him or loathe him, few Finns would deny the vital role Urho Kekkonen played in Finnish history, most significantly by continuing the work of his predecessor, Paasikivi, in the establishment of postwar Finnish neutrality. He accomplished this largely through delicate negotiations with Soviet leaders – whose favour he would gain, so legend has it, by taking them to his sauna (open for viewing in summer only) – that narrowly averted major crises and saw off the threat of a Soviet invasion on two separate occasions. Kekkonen preferred to conduct official business here rather than at the Presidential Palace in the city, yet the feel of the place is far from institutional: filled with birchwood furniture, its large windows giving peaceful views of surrounding trees, water and wildlife, it has a light and very Finnish character. The museum was in the middle of a massive renovation at the time of writing and was due to reopen in 2011; check with the tourist office or ⓦwww.seurasaarisaatio.fi for the latest details.

Slightly further north along Tamminiemientie is the **Meilahti Art Museum** (Taidemuseo Meilahti; Tues–Sun 11am–6.30pm; €8; ⓦwww.taidemuseo.fi). The museum contains one of the city's best collections of modern Finnish art, and is primarily made up of twentieth-century Finnish paintings, though there are also several works by French artists from the 1930s. Regular temporary exhibitions, during which the permanent collection is put into storage, show off various works of pictorial art, industrial art and photography.

Tram #4 and bus #24 run near to Seurasaari; get off one stop after the big hospital on the left, from where it's a one-kilometre walk.

Pihlajasaari

Pihlajasaari is one of Helsinki's most enjoyable day-trip destinations. The two small islands here, linked by a narrow isthmus and footbridge, are a summer haven of wild flowers, long grasses and swaying pine and rowan trees (*pihlaja* is Finnish for "rowan") vying for space between outcrops of smooth bare rock that are perfect for catching a few rays. The main island, itself no more than 500m in length, consists of a network of walking paths leading through the forest to a series of **beaches** – sandy to the north, rocky to the south – while near the southwestern tip a **café** is a pleasant place to sit and watch the enormous superferries glide towards Helsinki en route from Sweden. The smaller of the two islands, reached by turning left from the boat jetty and crossing the small footbridge, is home to Helsinki's best **nudist beach**, which even has its own gay section. Follow the signs for the *naturistiranta* and note that the outer limits of the area are obsessively marked by signposts so as not to offend the Finns' rather un-Scandinavian unease with public nudity.

Pihlajasaari is a fifteen-minute boat ride from the Merisatama small-boat harbour by the southwestern entrance to Kaivopuisto Park in the south of the city. Creaking, thirty-year-old wooden pleasure boats depart here every hour on the half hour (mid-May to Aug; €5 return) for the short trip across to the island; the last boat back leaves the island at 9pm. There is also a service from Ruoholahti in western Helsinki (from which you can catch a metro to the centre), though this is somewhat less regular and has been known to cease service entirely at certain times.

Eating

Eating well in Helsinki has never come cheap, but these days there is now thankfully ample choice – both for top-notch dining and, with careful planning, some spots that go easier on your purse-strings. Remember that most hotels offer a decent all-you-can-eat **breakfast** buffet – and the city's top stays, especially the chain hotels, tend to lay out proper gourmet feasts – which means if you stock up early on you can often last on just a midday snack through until dinner (hostel breakfasts, though, tend to be rationed). Otherwise, it's best to hold out until **lunch**, when many restaurants offer a reduced fixed-price menu, or a help-yourself buffet (both often under €10). With all of the quiet green spots in the city,

---

Eating on a budget

Given how eye-wateringly expensive Helsinki can be, it will help to know that there are affordable places to eat, and you don't have to choose between either paying for your hotel or sating your hunger. If you're really looking to save cash, **pizzerias** and **kebab** joints are always a good bet. The central and popular Kamppi and Forum shopping centres (see p.68) both offer a number of popular, inexpensive eating places on two floors, while all-night party streets such as Iso Roobertinkatu or the area right around the train station contain a handful of decent kebab and fast-food joints, or, elsewhere, the slightly more unusual **grilli** roadside stands, which sell hot dogs, hamburgers and plenty of other greasy goodies. One of the best known and most patronised of these is *Jaskan Grilli*, just behind the Parliament building at Dagmarinkatu 2. This well-known late-night grill spot serves some of the most rewarding greasy comfort food in the city, including burgers (from €2.90) named after local politicians and regulars. It is open until midnight during the week, 3am on weekends. For **self-caterers**, there are several supermarkets in Tunneli by the train station that stay open until 10pm.

Hands down the best choices for the hungry and impoverished though, are the numerous **student mensas**, or university-run, cafeteria-type eateries located in various parts of the city. Anyone can eat in these (€7.30), though they are slightly cheaper (€4.20) if you can produce a student ID. The largest of them are centrally located in the main university buildings at **Fabianinkatu 33**, and at **Mannerheimintie 3** (entry at Kaivopiha 10C, the triangular, cobbled plaza to the side of the Vanha Ylioppilastalo). Both are open during the summer, and a dozen more are open during term time. The *mensas* can be cheaper still in the late afternoon, from 4pm to 6pm, and are also usually open on Saturdays from 9am to 1pm.

picnic food, too, is a viable option; visit the markets and **market halls** (*kauppahalli*) at the South Harbour or – somewhat less touristy – Hakaniementori for fresh vegetables, meat and fish. The *kauppahallit* also house a collection of food stalls that are great for sandwiches and the like and tend to be quite affordable. For more on eating on a budget, see the box on p.83.

Cafés and bakeries

Finns proudly consume more coffee per capita than anyone else in the world – ten cups a day, if the statistics are to be believed – and Helsinki's many classically styled **cafés** intend to keep it that way. There's not a *Starbucks* in sight (though the city does have its own chain, *Roberts*, which serves an excellent brew). Across the city, café coffee tends to be very good, though quite a bit stronger then elsewhere – *niin vahva että lusikka jää pystyyn*, as the Finns put it, or "so strong the spoon stands on end". The best cafés are stylish, atmospheric affairs dating from the beginning of the twentieth century, where throughout the day, up until 5pm or 6pm, you can get a coffee and pastry for around €5; many also function as de facto **bakeries**.

Places listed here are shown on the "Central Helsinki" map on p.60, except where noted.

Aalto Akateeminen Kirjakauppa, Pohjoisesplanadi 39. Designed by the world-famous Finnish architect whose name it bears, and well worth a visit after a morning's book-browsing. Sandwich prices hover around the €10 mark, but you can always soak up the atmosphere over just a coffee. Free wi-fi.

Bar Fanny Bulevardi 40. Named after the wife of Paul Sinebrychoff, this excellent glass-walled bar and café overlooks the Sinebrychoff Park, and is perfect after a visit to the Sinebrychoff Museum. Try the excellent *korvapuusti*, cinnamon buns. Weekend brunch 11am–3pm €13.50.

Carusel Merisatamanranta 10. The queues outside for breakfast at this bright seaside café are packed with everyone from giddy teens to lunching ladies, motorcyclists to mommies-in-waiting, who come here to enjoy the views and the heaping portions of food (presented self-service style). Great pastries. Occasional music in the evenings. See map, pp.56–57.

Chjoko Liisankatu 9. This new corner spot is more chocolate producer than café, but the premises have a few seats where you can try out their perfectly divine *praliinit*, little sugary chocolate balls filled with various flavours (€1.20 each). The *karpolovodka*, with berry vodka, is out of this world. See map, pp.56–57.

Cochon Café and Bakery Mannerheimintie 14. Run by the Välimäki family of *Chez Dominique* fame, this ground-floor patisserie does some of the best fresh breads and pastries in the city. Great for a morning croissant and coffee (opens at 8am), and they also do solid set lunches with veggie specials, as well as the odd burger and chicken dish.

Ekberg Bulevardi 9. Opened in 1852, this landmark café retains nineteenth-century fixtures and a *fin-de-siècle* atmosphere, with starched waitresses bringing the most delicate of open sandwiches and pastries to green-marble tables. Order one of their classics: the Napoleon pastry.

Eliel Ground floor, Central train station. You wouldn't expect to get great meals at a railway station restaurant – and you don't, really (though the self-service breakfasts are good value). What you do get are an airy, vaulted Art Nouveau interior that is one of the most fetching places you'll ever wait for a train, and a roulette table. Open daily until 11pm (10pm on Sun).

Engel Aleksanterinkatu 26. Named after the Berlin-born designer of all the buildings you can see from its window, this is a haven of gourmet coffee, pastries, cakes and intellectual chitchat, just across from Senate Square. Try the smoked-fish salad, or the French breakfast for €11. Breakfast served daily 8am–2pm.

Fazer Kluuvikatu 3 & the Forum Shopping Centre. Pronounced "FAH-tzer" in Finnish, this is Helsinki's best-known bakery, justly celebrated for its lighter-than-air pastries, cakes, sweets and chocolates. Try the speciality, "Bebe", a praline-cream-filled pastry for €3, any of the excellent bite-sized chocolates or the Resis-sumies Kana (€7.30), a grilled open chicken sandwich topped with a sweet sauce. Breakfast buffet €8.50. The main Kluuvikatu branch is a whirlwind of Art Deco meets Art Nouveau decor where, reportedly, the acoustics are such that you can hear someone whispering from the other side of the room.

Regatta Merikannontie 10, immediately northwest of the Sibelius Park. A lovely little seaside place to watch the kayakers go by as you munch on home-made cakes. Friendly staff and – a real rarity in Finland – free refills of coffee. See map, pp.56–57.

Strindberg Pohjoisesplanadi 33. Stylish outdoor coffee-sipping in the morning sun – though it's a good deal more pricey if you want to eat, with the upstairs restaurant serving such items as smoked reindeer with Lapland cheese followed by slow-fried grayling and arctic cloudberry. More familiar items like roast beef sandwiches are sizeable and cost under €10.

Taikalamppu Café Torkkelinkatu 21. One of the most colourful, characterful cafés in the city, "The Magic Lantern" is a corner Kallio spot that gets all the morning sunshine you'd want for enjoying your coffee and pastry. Coffee and ice cream for €3.50. See map, pp.56–57.

Tin Tin Tango Töölöntorinkatu 7 ☎09/2709 0972. It could only exist in Finland: a retro café that allows you to sip on a pint of Arctic lager as you sweat it up in a sauna and wait for a load of laundry to dry. Set a short tram ride from the city centre, this irreverent spot is done up in original and derivative Tintin art and is very popular with local music students from the nearby Sibelius Academy (classic Argentine tango is pumped in round-the-clock). They serve a range of breakfasts (from €5.60–9.60) all day. Sauna costs €22 per hour and on-site self-service laundry €7.20 for a wash and dry with soap; both require reservations. See map, pp.56–57.

Ursula Ehrenströmintie 3. On the beach at the edge of the Kaivopuisto Park, this is an outdoor terrace that offers views straight out to sea, this has long been one of Helsinki's most beloved spots for a coffee or Karhu. Decent cakes, sandwiches and light lunches (around €10), and all profits go to charity. Open till midnight in the summer, during which it catches the sun as it (just) sets. See map, pp.56–57.

Villipuutarha Kaarlenkatu 13 ⓦ www.villipuutarha .fi. The menu, decor and ethos at this divine little place, fairly new to Kallio, do its name ("Wild Garden") proud. Veggie soups, fresh green salads and larger dishes such as roast lamb with mint sauce are served in an irreverent setting of stuffed pets and oddball statues (think Lenins, squirrels and Virgin Marys). A range of cool evening events includes knitting parties, philosophy talks and impromptu acoustic concerts. Closed Sun & Mon. See map, pp.56–57.

Restaurants

In the good ol' days, the phrase "Helsinki kitchen" would have easily conjured up images of robust, kerchiefed Soviet-esque women ladling out cauldrons of boggy potato stew to cigar-smoking, moustachioed Finns, many of them possibly already very well sauced themselves. While you can still find such places in the city if you scour some of the outlying working-class districts, much of central Helsinki has been colonized since the early Noughties by a *nouvelle vague* of edgy gastro-conscious restaurants, turning it into a spectacular place for experiencing both exciting **fusion** cooking as well as back-to-basics Nordic dishes where fresh local ingredients take pride of place. Indeed, many restaurants serve such eclectic menus that it's hard to tell whether the cuisine is Finnish, Scandinavian, French, Asian, "continental" or a complete twist on everything at once.

While at most of these *nouveau* places you can spend anywhere from €30 to €70 per person – and easily twice that at the city's Michelin-starred spots – you can still find a great meal for under €15 if you're willing to compromise on either location or setting. The city also presents a great collection of tried-and-true **Finnish** and **Russian** standbys which have been around for decades, though they serve food at prices that have well exceeded the rate of inflation (mains often start at well over €20). There is also a growing handful of **vegetarian**-only restaurants, and for **non-European** cuisines, there is a good share of pan-Asian food places and a bizarrely large number of Nepali restaurants.

Many restaurants are open daily until around 1am, though the majority of kitchens close by 11pm (and often 9pm on Sun); Monday is the most common day for closing. Note that we've given phone numbers only for restaurants where booking is essential. *Hyvää ruokahaluaa!* (Bon appetit!)

Budget and mid-range

Bali-Hai Iso Roobertinkatu 35. One of the city's coolest little restaurants, with a spartan, almost Hopper-esque interior and a solid menu of Finnish updates of diner standbys such as salads, pastas, steaks and burgers (try the amply-sized *rödburger*, €14). A popular stop for young Finnish actors, musicians and other celebs.

Gastone Korkeavuorenkatu 45. This snazzy but simple Italian spot off Eteläesplanadi could use a few more wines, but the mains – oven-cooked shin of lamb, for example – are excellent, and remain well under €20. In the summer, dine out on the small courtyard terrace. You'll often encounter Finns here speaking in Italian to the waiters – it's that kind of place.

Juuri Korkeavuorenkatu 27. This precious little spot distinguishes itself with its range of *sapas*, their self-styled Finnish tapas (€4.50 each). These succulent bite-sized dishes are miniature reinventions of Scandinavian standbys, and include crispy mustard crayfish, cottage-cheese-filled cabbage leaves and – the real winner here – smoked reindeer heart (don't tell the kids). Traditional Finnish mains, too, from €24.50. Great wine list.

Mai Thai Annankatu 32 ☏09/685 6850. The least expensive and at the top of the city's crop of Thai restaurants, seating here is for fifteen – so get here early. Mains from €12, full lunches for under €10. Soups and appetisers are very, very spicy so watch out. Reservations not required, but not a bad idea.

Omenapuu Keskuskatu 6. Directly opposite the railway station, this otherwise run-of-the-mill restaurant is a superb place to come for the great weekday lunch buffets (€6.70–10.90). Especially good on Sundays from noon to 4pm, when a jazz band plays to brunching locals. See map, p.60.

Pelmenit Kustaankatu 7. This hole in the wall of a Russo-Judeo-Finnish restaurant serves some of the best (and best-priced) home-cooked meals in the city. They specialize in Eastern European dishes such as *pelmeni* (dumplings), blini and thick, saucy borscht. There's very little that costs over €6. See map, pp.56–57.

Pompei Snellmaninkatu 16. Run by a Neopolitan transplant to Helsinki, this simple Italian place does the best pizzas (from €7) in the city, period. Also has several dozen pastas, salads and larger dishes. See map, pp.56–57.

Salve Hietalahdenranta 11. This excellent, inconspicuous sailor's pub down by the harbour is one of the city's oldest restaurants, adorned with kitschy maritime memorabilia, drenched in nostalgic Finnish music and resembling a drunken sailor's tavern more than the great dining spot it's become. Memorable dishes

here include the Scandinavian hash and the fried herring, which arrives straight from the boats just across the street and comes with towering heaps of mashed potatoes (€14.90).

Sea Horse Kapteeninkatu 11. *Wallpaper** magazine magnate Tyler Brûlé called his meal at this cavernous Helsinki classic one of his ten best, though it's been wowing visitors for nearly a century. Featuring dim lighting and plain walls, it's refreshingly one of the few restaurants left in the capital that doesn't feel like a design museum. Especially renowned for its various fish dishes, which start at €10, and great for people-watching. See map, pp.56–57.

Soul Kitchen Fleminginkatu 26–28. A sizeable American-style restaurant serving southern specialities such as gumbo soup (€9.50), grilled chicken (€16), and macaroni and cheese (€16), though the best choice is the succulent BBQ ribs (€16). The soul theme is most notable in the music, which tends to be a constant stream of Aretha, Ray and their contemporaries. See map, pp.56–57.

Vegemesta Vaasankatu 6. This basic, vegetarian fast-food joint serves half a dozen burgers, including tofu, soy, seitan and hemp versions (from €4.50) and several other veg options, including falafel. It's on a street known for cheap bars, so makes a great late-night munchies option. See map, pp.56–57.

Virgin Oil Co. Mannerheimintie 5 ⊛www.virginoil.fi. With barrel-bottom tables and deep, dark woods, this American-style brasserie presents a terrific, large Mediterranean menu, including many tasty, thin-crust pizzas. There is also a solid lunch buffet (11am–3pm). Once you're done, you only need to head upstairs to catch the latest Finnish pop group rocking out on stage.

Vltava Elielinaukio 2. Pronounced "VAHL-tava" and ideally located next to the train station in one of Saarinen's buildings, this Czech restaurant effectively functions as a railway or airport lounge, filled with commuters, business travellers and office workers filling up on a beer or nine before heading off. Its marketing campaign around the city consists of far too many puns on the word "Czech", but there are several dozen Czech and international lagers and ales on offer, plus Bavarian dishes such as bratwurst, schnitzel, pork ribs and knuckle – follow any of these with the finger-licking apple strudel.

Expensive

Bellevue Rahapajankatu 3, behind the Uspenski Cathedral ☏09/179 560. A superb Russian restaurant opened, ironically, in 1917, the year Finland won independence from Russia. Polished samovars create a period ambience for the expensive, gourmet Russian food, considered some of Europe's best. Try Marshal Mannerheim's favourite starter of minced lamb flavoured with herring (served with schnapps) for €16.50; for the more adventurous, there's also a pot-roasted bear steak (€69). Closed Sat & Sun lunchtime.

Chez Dominique Rikhardinkatu 4 ☎09/612 7393. For ten years running Finland's two-starred gastronomic darling, this white-hued, minimalist place still widens Finnish eyes. Chef-to-the-stars Hans Välimäki changes his heralded four-, six- and nine-course Franco-Scandinavian menus on a weekly basis, but perennial showings are made by Anjou pigeon filled with duck foie gras, roasted pikeperch and boiled lobster. The €29 three-course lunch is, perhaps unequivocally, the best bargain in Finland. Closed Tues & Sat lunch, and Sun & Mon.

Demo Uudenmaankatu 9–11 ☎09/2289 0840. Though it has the facade of a fairly casual eating place, Michelin-starred *Demo* has served to help pull Helsinki restaurants out of the dark ages. Extremely innovative dishes include roasted breast of goose, goose gizzards with kumquat sauce, and prawn bisque flavoured with fennel, apple and aioli crab salad. Four-course menu €58.

Grotesk Ludviginkatu 10 ☎010/470 2001. A fusion spot opened in 2007 by the chefs from *Demo* (including a former national cook of the year) whose name derives from the menu's font. Interior is done up in black-and-red Gothic decor, while every dish is perfectly matched to a vintage from the extensive wine list. Excellent *focaccia* arrives at your table; follow it with either the baked salmon or roast duck. The restaurant's bar (next door) is one of the city's perennial *it* drinking spots.

Havis Amanda Unioninkatu 23. The oldest and best seafood restaurant in the city, albeit pricey and a tad staid. The decor is heavily nautical: brass fittings, ship-in-a-bottle scale models and lithographs of marine life. Most mains, such as gratinated Baltic herring in a tasty tartar sauce, around €25. Superb service.

Kasakka Meritullinkatu 13. One of the city's first Russian restaurants and probably its best, decked out in authentic tsarist paraphernalia. It's the cooking though that draws Russkies in the know (the ambassador to Russia is a regular). Try the blini with vendace roe (€23), followed by a Russo-Finnish speciality: reindeer filet sashlik with cranberry sauce and bulgur (€35).

Klippan Luoto island, just off the coast across from Kaivopuisto. Gorgeous wooden Empire-style villa from 1898 with a red-spired roof. Evening meals are heavy on archipelago seafood recipes; try to make it for one of the summertime pavilion crayfish parties. Expect to pay way over €100 for dinner for two, especially with wine. Regular ferry service departs from the Olympia terminal. See map, pp.56–57.

Kolme Seppää Mannerheimintie 14 ☎020/761 9888. This upscale second-floor eatery does a solid selection of continental meals that taste much better taken with some of the best views of the city: straight onto Mannerheimintie and the railway station.

Kuurna Meritullinkatu 6. This tiny (22 covers), charming spot behind the Presidential Palace does grunge chic very well and takes its food very seriously: some locals reckon the chefs here are in the running for a Michelin star. In true cutting-edge gastronomic form, the avant-Finnish menu changes once a week, but if you see either the beetroot served with ricotta cheese or the steak tartare (with a distinct taste of mushroom), order them straight away. Remarkably affordable selection of wines.

Lasipalatsi Mannerheimintie 22–24. This large, central, functionalist restaurant attracts Finns of all shapes and sizes. Upscale Finnish dishes (most under €25) are tasty enough, though the casual atmosphere and views up and down Mannerheimintie are what draw the crowds. The chef's specialities of lamb Vorschmack and pikeperch à la Mannerheim are both excellent; other favourites include sautéed reindeer and blinis. The more informal café downstairs dishes out pastries, pastas, salads, soups and sandwiches.

Loft Yrjönkatu 18. Done up in a minimalist decor of muslin curtains and dark woods, with moody lounge music that aims in part to draw your attention away from the equally minimalist portions. Still, the Nordic dishes are outstanding – with exclusively local products that include whitefish, reindeer, wild mushrooms and wild buckthorn berries – and the generous wine list provides dozens of 75cl-sized excuses for extended afternoon or evening dining. Lunches not a bad bargain.

Olo Kasarmikatu 44 ☎09/665 565. Given that its chef has worked in many of the city's best restaurants, it shouldn't come as a surprise that this casual-meets-mod spot was named Finland's restaurant of the year in 2009. Meals are primarily Finnish spins on pan-Nordic dishes, and include lemon herring, veal and breast of pigeon. For dessert, the cardamom doughnut with sea buckthorn has probably never disappointed anyone. Expect to shell out a good €100 for a meal for two, exclusive of wine, but lunches at the bar – just as good – can be had for less than a tenner.

Raku Ya Eteläranta 14 ☎09/675 449. Helsinki's finest Japanese restaurant opened in 2008 right across from the *kauppahalli*. Unique sushi, sashimi and fish dishes include sashimi rakuya, seared with hot sesame oil and yuzu soy sauce and served with scallop (€13.90), and tuna with avocado and garlic mayonnaise (€16.90). If you can't decide, try the Omakase (€55), which gives you a wide selection of the restaurant's offerings. Hushed – but not pretentiously so – premises. Tues–Sat dinner only.

Saaga Bulevardi 34B ☎09/7425 5544. With an interior that is all pelts, moccasins and wooden chandeliers resembling reindeer antlers, this is one of the best places in the capital to taste Arctic delicacies such as snow grouse, reindeer and bear. Start with the Saagin Jumpura cranberry house cocktail before moving onto Fish of the Four Winds, a collection of uniquely prepared bites that includes char-grilled whitefish and vendace roe, and follow it up with flambéed bear meatballs. Go on a (very) empty stomach, but bring a full wallet.

Töölönranta Helsinginkatu 56. This modern, white-tablecloth affair is set smack overlooking the Töölö bay. They serve a sprawling Mediterranean Sunday brunch (noon–2.30pm & 3–5.30pm; €28.50) with garlic-marinated mushrooms, roasted beetroot, vendace, shrimp, hummus, merguez, bubbly and much more. See map, pp.56–57.

Drinking

Drinking in Finland is something of a national sport, and nowhere is Finns' penchant for the drink as visible as in Helsinki – be it 2pm or 2am. Although never cheap, alcohol is far from a dirty word in Finland, and first-time visitors to the country will be astounded at how readily many of the capital's otherwise upstanding, respectable citizens – everyone from boppy teen girls to investment bankers – get completely blotto long before midnight; it's a veritable weekly rite of passage for many *Helsinkilaiset*. Still, going out need not be a binge affair for everyone, and drinking, especially beer, can be enjoyed in pubs, bars and lounges all across the city, which are where most Helsinki folk go to socialize – you'll find one on virtually every corner.

Traditionally, the neighbourhood of **Punavuori**, southwest of the train station, has maintained the highest concentration of hip bars – have a wander along Uudenmaankatu or Iso Roobertinkatu to get a sense for what's on – but with gentrification in full force here, those in the know are these days opting for the cheaper, hole-in-the-wall dives in the working-class **Kallio** district; you can reach these by taking the metro to Sörnäinen or the #1 or #3B trams to Kallio. Only a few places in the city have a dress code, and you may find these too elitist – or expensive – to be worth bothering with anyway.

Most bars are open from the afternoon until 1 or 2am, though a few of the more popular ones will keep the juices flowing until 3 or 4am, especially on the weekends. On the whole, Monday to Thursday is normally quiet, though Wednesday, known to many locals as *pikkulauantai* ("little Saturday"), can be a popular clubbing night; on Fridays and Saturdays on the other hand, it's best to arrive as early as possible – around 10ish, say – to get a seat without having to queue. Sundays though are extremely sedate, and many areas of the city won't have a single establishment open for a tipple after 10pm. A number of drinking dives will also serve food, although the grub is seldom at its best in the evening (where it's good earlier in the day, we've included it under "Restaurants"). In recent years, however, a number of local bars have also started to serve breakfast.

Popular local **drinks** include Sahti, a yeasty farmhouse ale flavoured with juniper berries; and Salmari, a Finnish speciality and one of the most acquired tastes on the planet – Koskenkorva vodka and salty liquorice. Fisu, meanwhile, is grain alcohol mixed with Fisherman's Friend. Yum.

If you want a drink but are feeling antisocial, or just very hard-up, the cheapest method, as ever, is to buy from the appropriately named **ALKO shop**: there are self-service ones at Fabianinkatu 7 and Vuorikatu 7.

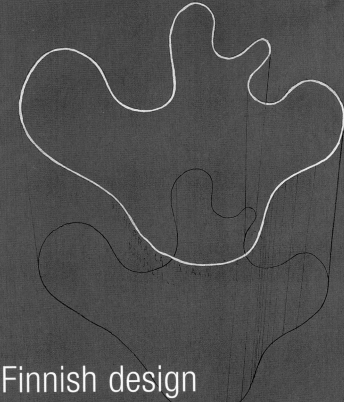

Finnish design

When it comes to modern design and style, Finns have been raising the bar for well over a century. From the early, undulating creations of Alvar Aalto to the bright mid-century textiles of Marimekko and the new-millennium bespoke urban fashion of Hanna Sarén, the work of Finnish designers has always pushed boundaries, while remaining respectful of tradition and natural forms and materials. Finnish designers make use of organic ingredients, simple lines and subtle touches that manage to be bold without screaming for attention. Whether in a museum restroom or hotel lobby, you'll be reminded of the nation's keen aesthetic sensibilities and high standards of craftsmanship.

Finland is well known for its sleek glassware ▲

Mid-century Finnish modern decor ▲

Forward-thinking Finnish houseware design ▼

History

Finnish design, like the country's culture, language and history, has always stood apart from the mainstream. Though known for its architects as early as the 1800s, Finland didn't land on the design map until Alvar Aalto unveiled his now-iconic Savoy vase at the Paris World's Fair in 1937. A revolutionary designer and architect, Aalto used muted, matte materials in smooth, understated motifs that evoked nature herself – it's thought he modelled his vase on the shape of a lake in central Finland.

Aalto admired the forward-thinking aesthetic of Bauhaus, but disagreed with the modernists' reliance on alloys and other synthetic materials, which he deemed inappropriate for residential use. Designs had to look good and be extremely practical – hardly surprising given a harsh climate that means a lot of time spent indoors – while remaining simple and free of frill, an aesthetic that makes perfect sense in a region where standing out in a crowd is a social gaffe. Long before "eco-friendly" became a buzzword, Finnish designers were applying form-meets-function ideals across the board to housewares and the applied arts, and the rest of the world swiftly took notice. Tapio Wirkkala's laminated-wood leaf platter by Iittala was hailed by *House Beautiful* magazine as the "most beautiful object of 1951," and his Ultima Thule glassware showed up on Finnair's first flights to New York. Jackie Kennedy, meanwhile, purchased eight Marimekko cotton dresses during the Kennedy–Nixon campaign, professing her admiration for the exuberant patterns and vivid colours and stealing the headlines during her husband's presidential campaign.

By the 1970s, Finland's woodwork, glassmaking, metalwork, ceramics and fashion had begun to influence designers well outside the Nordic countries. Today, the country's standout brands — Aarikka, Arabia and Artek, for example (and that's just the As) — have succeeded in melding Finland's heritage of classic design with the innovation of young design talent.

▲ Bright, sprightly Finnish kitchenware

▼ Janne Kyttänen's stackable Monarch stools

Who's who

The traditions laid down by Alvar Aalto, Finland's Frank Lloyd Wright, were followed by generations of young Finns working at the drafting tables, kilns and lathes of the country's best known design houses. Iittala (pronounced EAT-tallah), for example, has been producing extremely successful housewares since 1909, and along with other Finnish design houses — Marimekko, Tonfisk, and Verso to name a few — has helped make the careers of many designers over the years, including Kaj Franck, Maija Isola, Klaus Haapaniemi and Harri Koskinen.

▼ Block prints are a Finnish fashion standby

Franck sought beauty and harmony in his Teema tableware (1952), kitchen sets that now grace the cupboards of millions of European families, while Isola designed well over 500 different patterns for Marimekko, such as her unique Unikko (poppy) pattern, introduced in 1964. Other important work today includes the birch and cherry houseware creations of Maria Jauhiainen and Jani Martikainen, ergonomic benches and lamps by Janne Kyttänen and unique furniture by Sari Anttonen and the two Mikkos — Laakkonen and Paakkanen — to say nothing of Nokia's mobile phone prototypes.

Finnish fashion, meanwhile, had a boost with an early, memorable appearance on *Sex and the City* by Hanna Sarén's handbags

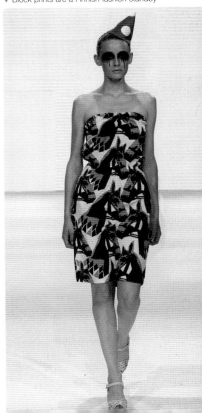

Handknit Sámi mittens at the Sámi Duodji shop ▲

and clogs. Since then, the retro prints, rustic crochet work and hand-striped embroidery of Paola Suhonen's IVANAHelsinki line have graced the figures of thousands of Finns; other stars include Tia Vanhatapio, Minna Parikka and Julia Lundsten, whose quirky, sculptural FINSK line of hand-carved pumps and boots has earned her the moniker "The Eames of Footwear".

Moomin mugs produced by Arabia ▼

Marimekko's Unikko boots walk the runway ▼

Top five spots for Finnish design

Helsinki is an obvious choice to buy Finnish design creations, especially since the city is World Design Capital for 2012 (Ⓦwww.wdc2012helsinki.fi), but there are other options too:

▶▶ **Artek Shop (Jyväskylä)** The store inside the Alvar Aalto Museum purveys classics objects and furniture by Aino and Alvar, as well as books on architecture, style and design. See p.225.

▶▶ **Esplanadi (Helsinki)** A central, grassy thoroughfare holding the flagship stores of half a dozen classic Finnish design houses, including Iittala, Marimekko and Aarikka, just paces from the Design District. See pp.94–95.

▶▶ **SALT (Mariehamn)** This maritime-quarter crafts house is perfect for unique textiles, ceramics, wood and metalwork produced by archipelago artisans and designers, many of whom convey the islands' sense of warmth – and isolation – in their work. See p.166.

▶▶ **Sámi Duodji (Inari)** Traditional handicrafts have a strong symbolic value for the Sámi; this collective purveys knives, containers and clothing made out of everything from birch bark to reindeer antlers. See p.289.

▶▶ **Taito Shop (Ⓦwww.taitoshop.fi)** These 26 shops around the country are run by a national arts and crafts association and sell splendid utensils and decorative items created by local artisans.

The Pub Tram

For a unique way to imbibe, hop on the **Spårakoff Pub Tram** (mid-May to late Aug; €9 including one beer), a bright red streetcar that's well known for the hordes of Finns that hop on to get tanked. The moving pub-crawl departs hourly from 2pm to 9pm, beginning from the Mikonkatu tram stop. It holds thirty passengers, takes approximately forty minutes to circumnavigate Helsinki and is a great way to see the city (sober or otherwise), since the route takes in most major downtown sights, including Linnanmäki, Töölö Bay and the Olympic Stadium. There's also a toilet on board.

Places listed here are shown on the "Central Helsinki" map on p.60, except where noted.

A21 Annankatu 21. Named Best Bar in Finland several years running by the epicures at foodie mag *Viisi Tähtea*, this posh, beau-monde spot, housed in a former brothel, is great for its bold, inventive cocktails. The designer seating, cushioned booths with lacquered tables and cliques of clientele who spend way too much time in front of the mirror are a good backdrop for the locally inspired, upscale drinks menu, which includes ingredients such as birch, buckthorn, basil and cloudberry jam. Try, for example, the Rhuba Martini: Koskenkorva, rhubarb, honey and basil leaves. Press the doorbell just outside and if the bartendress likes the way you look, you might actually be let in. Closed Mon.

Ateljee Bar Yrjönkatu 26. This compact spot, on the thirteenth floor of the glitzy *Sokos Torni* hotel, takes the prize for rums with a view, with outstanding balcony vistas as far as Estonia on a clear day. It's a good setting for some good people-watching and a respectable selection of cocktails (mojitos are a speciality) – bar manager Mika wrote a book on the best bartenders in Finland, so he knows a thing or two. Women should make sure they visit the toilet to take advantage of the best seat in the city. Perfect at midsummer.

Baari Porvoonkatu 19. A great selection of board games means that the scene at this low-key bar – which, incidentally, has no official name other than "bar" – is often refreshingly tame. Plush shag carpeting, comfy leather seats and bar food that includes toasted sandwiches and peanuts. Free wi-fi. See map, pp.56–57.

Bar 9 Uudenmaankatu 9. This unpretentious neighbourhood bar – called *ysibaari* if you're from around these parts – has been a standby for Helsinki's artists and hipsters for over a decade, and shows little sign of losing its edge. Good food, too, including massive grilled ham and cheese sandwiches and spicy pastas, and occasional live music.

Belge Kluuvikatu 5 ⓦ www.belge.fi. Filled to the gills with domestic and international yuppies, this is nevertheless a good place to get your fill of Belgian lagers and lambics, including draughts of Hoegaarden and Het Kapittel Pater or bottles of 8.5% Gouden Carolus Classic (€6.90). Snag a seat upstairs in the "library", with large sofas and an open fire. If you need something to absorb all that alcohol, try the *moules* or the Talon Sandwich – chicken, tomato and cheese on toasted bread sided with Dijon mustard mayonnaise *friet* (€11.90).

Cuba Erottajankatu 4. They play more than just salsa at this brightly coloured bar, with themed evenings that include everything from hip-hop to jazz. In fact, the only thing vaguely Cuban here is the twelve different types of mojitos (blueberry, for example) on the drinks menu.

Erottaja Bar Erottajankatu 15–17. Very central semi-basement bar a block from the Swedish theatre with a definite underground feel to it. Inside you'll find small wooden tables with comfy chairs, and in summer there are tables fronting the street. Popular with students from Helsinki's art and design school who come for the atmosphere and inexpensive *tuoppi* (draught beers), it starts to fill up around 6pm or so most days of the week.

Exodus Bar Kaarlenkatu 10. This Kallio original is populated almost exclusively by members of the neighbourhood's large African immigrant population, with lots of loud reggae and beers for €2.80. The clockwork drug raids from the district fuzz don't seem to deter the tufts of smoke from reappearing. See map, pp.56–57.

Kaarle XII Kasarmikatu 40 ⓦwww.kaarle.com. Thursday- and Friday-night queuing to get in to this very casual bar and dance space (known familiarly as "Kaale") is a regular pastime for hundreds of working *Helsinkilaiset*. Inside are six separate battered, old-wood bars, including two inside a large Art Nouveau dance hall with red-granite walls and one with a rather good beer selection. Show up before 10pm or you might well be waiting outside for hours.

Kafe Moskva Eerikinkatu 11. Like the Cold War never happened. An anonymous-looking entrance gives way to this quirky, intimate and cool Soviet-themed bar, done out in retro decor and playing Russian music on dusty vinyls. They serve Russian vodka, *champanskoe* and very cheap beer.

Kosmos Kalevankatu 3. This is where the big media cats – TV producers, PR people, well-connected authors – hang out and engage in loud conversation as the night wears on. The wonderful interior is unchanged since the 1920s, though you'll have to get past the officious doorman to see it.

🏃 **Lost and Found** Annankatu 6 ⓦwww .lostandfound.fi. Better known locally as *lostari*, this late-night spot is best well after midnight on weekends – though try to come before 1am to avoid the queue that often forms around the block. Downstairs is a very popular and very sweaty dance club, *Hideaway*, that doesn't feel too Euro-trashy. Very gay friendly.

mbar Mannerheimintie 22–24 ⓦwww.mbar.fi. This hip designer place, offering internet terminals, electronica DJs and the occasional live band, has become a second living-room to many travellers and freelancers. The 200-seat terrace, out back, is packed during the summer.

Meri Makasiini Hietalahdenranta 4. Slightly out of the way, on a street running off Hietalahdentori towards the waterfront, but worth a visit on a Friday or Saturday night when the restaurant customers spill onto the terrace to drink while gazing at the cranes of the city's cargo harbour. Closes at midnight.

Motellet Annankatu 10. You'll know what you're getting at this vaguely chichi Punavuori bar from the massive bay windows that front the street. Come late and you might have some trouble talking your way in past the bouncer if you don't know the right people; come early (before 7.30pm) and you can have the entire place to yourself, lounging out on comfy tweed couches and enjoying cheap beers. Happy hour 8–10pm. Free wi-fi.

Punavuoren Ahven Punavuorenkatu 12. One of Helsinki's best *olutravintolat* ("beer restaurants"), this tranquil dive is the perfect Punavuori spot to wind up an evening out if you're past the age of clubbing and grinding. It's very, very local, with Finns of all ages sporting berets, moustaches, pipes and various other retro accoutrements. True to its name, they serve nearly a hundred international beers.

The Rock Bar Bulevardi 28 ⓦwww.therock-bar.fi. True grunge ambience with Anthrax and Megadeth on the tubes, but not so loud that you can't hear yourself ordering. Your fellow drinkers may well be dressed head to toe in black grunge clothing, with piercings and tattoos.

Roskapankki Helsinginkatu 20. You're likely to have a tough time leaving this ever-popular Kallio dive bar for one of two reasons: either the cheap beer prices (€2.50), or you're leaving past 9pm, when the floor is sticky enough to make a rapid departure rather problematic. See map, pp.56–57.

Rymy-Eetu Erottajankatu 15–17 ⓦwww .rymy-eetu.fi. This recent addition to the local bar scene – named after a long-running wartime Finnish comic strip – just about pulls off the Bavarian-beer-hall look it's going for. The layout couldn't be less Finnish: long wooden benches require you to sit next, and possibly even speak, to people you don't actually know. Does a weekday "retro lunch" buffet (€9.20) from 11am to 2pm; at other times the à la carte Teutonic standards include sauerbraten, jägerschnitzel and a meatball and mashed potatoes dish that could feed a family of eleven. Most evenings feature regular live music groups – from Soviet-era big band to Finnish nostalgia rock (€2–4 cover).

Sling In Mikonkatu 8. It's very simple: this central bar makes the best – and best-priced – cocktails in Helsinki. The fanatically knowledgable bartenders make all the classics to perfection, but also do their own inventive concoctions. Awkwardly located on the second floor of a shopping mall across from the train station, but undoubtedly worth trying to find. Enter on Kaivokatu.

Teatteri Pohjoisesplanadi 2. Spend a few hours in this indoor/outdoor complex – casual and relaxed early, later rowdy and inebriated – and you'll encounter a cross-section of Helsinki characters, some of whom you may have to help get up off the ground. After drinks, head just next door for a good sit-down meal at *Teatterin Grilli*.

🏃 **We Got Beef** Iso Roobertinkatu 21.
Helsinkilaiset know this modish, pre-dancing watering hole as "Beeffi," and after several years it still reigns as one of the coolest places around. The lighting and decor call to mind a well-lit diner, and it's forever popular with students, schmoozers, skateboarders and their arm-candy. DJs spin slamming beats in a back room.

🏃 **Zetor** Kaivopiha, Mannerheimintie 3 ⓦ www.zetor.net. A true Finnish classic, the name for this irreverent and loud country-themed bar – in true non-sequitur form – comes from a popular make of Czech agricultural machinery. Filled with old rusty tractors (with seats arranged around them), it was designed in the Nineties by the people behind the irreverent Leningrad Cowboys rock group. An older crowd typically gets down to hard rock and 1980s tunes, and there is food served all day and all night (with a limited meatballs-and-potatoes menu from midnight until 3.30am). A good place to try *sahti* – Finnish home-brewed ale.

Nightlife and entertainment

Considering its diminutive size, Helsinki probably has more ways to spend an evening out – per capita – than any other European city. For up-to-the-minute details of what's on, read *NYT*, the Friday supplement to *Helsingin Sanomat* or the free papers *SixDegrees* (ⓦ www.6d.fi) or *City* – the latter two are found in record shops, bookshops and the tourist office – which all offer listings in English covering **rock and classical music**, **clubs**, **cinema**, **theatre** and **opera**. The Lasipalatsi (see p.68) has a youth service centre with information on **festivals**, concerts and events, or else simply watch out for posters on the streets.

Live music and clubs

Aside from the always-growing number of bars and late-night cafés, the city dishes out a steady diet of **live music**. Much Finnish rock and pop might seem an acquired taste for some – bands are certainly not helped by the awkward metre of the Finnish language – but a night out catching a couple of bands shouldn't cost more than €10 for entry (sometimes free). The best gigs are on during term-time, but summers are also host to a spate of free events and festivals all over the city – the biggest of these takes place almost every Sunday in Kaivopuisto Park. For tickets to a variety of music events, contact Tiketti, Yrjönkatu 29C on the third floor of Forum shopping centre (Mon–Fri 10am–7pm, Sat 10am–4pm; toll call ☏0600/11 616, ⓦ www.tiketti.fi), which charges a small commission.

Meanwhile, Helsinki does have its share of beautiful-people **clubs** – generally massive, several-floor affairs with the requisite dismissive beefy doormen and dress codes. Clubs almost as a rule change ownership, style, format and name with baffling rapidity – three years is considered to be *very* old – and our listings are only a pointer to what may be on offer: you're best to check out the city's listings magazines, or just head for the disco-laden streets around Fredrikinkatu in Kamppi. Most clubs operate Wednesday to Saturday from 10pm until 4am, though some occasionally will open a bit earlier; when there is a cover charge, it shouldn't ever be more than €10, and quite possibly half that. Many city nightclubs have a minimum age requirement of 24, but some will admit 18- or 20-year-olds. In addition to the places listed on p.92, note that Kaapelitehdas (see p.80) occasionally organizes mammoth, deafening raves.

Places listed here are shown on the "Central Helsinki" map on p.60, except where noted.

Jenny Woo Simonkatu 6 Ⓦ www.jennywoo.fi. This dark nightclub is best known for a guerilla marketing campaign that culminated in English-language expletives plastered all over the city. Today, it's most recognizable by the teeny-boppers who linger out front hoping to sneak their way in.

König Mikonkatu 4. This super central spot is great for a romantic candlelit dinner – they specialize in great steaks – but it's better known as one of the most happening places in the city for respectable professionals to come boogie on the (admittedly small) dancefloor. During the summertime, the alleyway out back fills up with a hoard of heavily inebriated businesspeople letting down their hair. Occasional live music on Wed evenings.

🏃 **Korjaamo** Töölönkatu 51B Ⓦ www .korjaamo.fi. A tram depot – especially one still in use – may not sound like the kind of place you'd hang out in at night, but this excellent cultural centre puts on a series of superb concerts throughout the year. Headliners run the gamut from pop and indie rock to electronica and seriously avant-garde. See map, pp.56–57.

Kuudes Linja Hämeentie 13 Ⓦ www.kuudeslinja .com. This smallish music club is a fairly hip place to hear live bands and DJs – the perfect warmer-upper before heading out to explore the bars of nearby Kallio. See map, pp.56–57.

🏃 **Redrum** Vuorikatu 2 Ⓦ www.redrum.fi. This downstairs dance club regularly invites a solid collection of DJs who hypnotize the crowd from their central throne. Younger clientele often able to slip their way in despite the over-21 stipulation.

Playground Iso Roobertinkatu 10 Ⓦ www .clubrosegarden.com. Large, labyrinthine basement club with DJs playing in various themed rooms. It can get pretty hot in here after midnight when it packs in the weekend crowds.

Storyville Museokatu 8 Ⓦ www.storyville.fi. Though it's something of a hike from the centre, this buzzing jazz joint puts on live Dixieland, swing or bebop every night of the week. In the summer, there's music outside on the idyllic garden terrace until 9pm. Cover is always under €10, and you can eat a pricey and filling Finnish dinner at your table. Kitchen open until 3.30am. See map, pp.56–57.

Tavastia Urho Kekkosenkatu 4–6 Ⓦ www .tavastiaklubi.fi. The country's premier rock club, and a major showcase for Finnish and Swedish bands. Downstairs holds the stage and bar; the balcony is waitress service.

🏃 **Tiger** 1A Urho Kekkosenkatu Ⓦ www .thetiger.fi. Sprawling across several cavernous floors, this extremely popular nightclub features multiple black-marble dancefloors, large terrace lounges and a couple of VIP rooms you won't ever set foot in. Located in the penthouse of the Kamppi shopping centre. Don't be surprised if the name changes several times during your stay in the city.

Vaihtolava Fleminginkatu 21 Ⓦ vaihtolava.info. A small corner arts space in Kallio that puts on regular theatre, music and performing arts events. See map, pp.56–57.

Vanha Ylioppilastalo Mannerheimintie 3 Ⓦ www.vanha.fi. A leading venue for indie rock groups from around the country and around the world, just next to Stockmann's department store.

Classical music, opera, theatre and cinema

In terms of high culture, Helsinki can lag a bit when compared to its Nordic neighbours. But this doesn't stop city residents from heading out most nights of the week to take advantage of everything their city does offer. In terms of **classical music**, Helsinki is home to two symphony orchestras: the Finnish Radio Symphony (Ⓦ www.yle.fi/rso) and the Helsinki Philharmonic (Ⓦ www .hel.fi/filharmonia) – the latter the Nordic countries' first permanent orchestra – which for now put on performances at the Finlandia Hall (see p.72; Ⓦ www .finlandiatalo.fi); from 2011 the new Musiikkitalo (see p.72; Ⓦ www.musiikkitalo .fi) will host most orchestral performances, after which Finlandia Hall will focus mostly on conferences, congresses and corporate events. The Finnish National Opera (see p.72; Ⓦ www.operafin.fi), meanwhile, has its dedicated building in Töölö. To see classical music on the cheap, try to catch one of the performances at the Sibelius Academy (Ⓣ 020/75390, Ⓦ www.siba.fi), spread across three different buildings in Töölö.

Theatre in the city, meanwhile, is based at the National Theatre (Ⓦwww .nationaltheatre.fi), the Alexander Theatre (Ⓦwww.aleksanterinteatteri.fi) and the Swedish Theatre (Ⓦwww.svenskateatern.fi); performances at the former two are nearly always in Finnish. Tickets for most events can be bought at the venue or, for a small commission, at Tiketti (see p.91).

Helsinki **cinema** is presided over almost exclusively by Finnkino, a theatre conglomerate offering both the latest blockbusters and a halfway decent selection of fringe films. Seats usually cost €9–11.50, although some places do a €6.80 matinee show. Check the listings in *City* (see p.91) or pick up a copy of *Elokuva-Viikko*, a free weekly leaflet that lists the cinemas and their programmes; it's available at the cinemas themselves. English-language films are shown with Finnish (and often Swedish) subtitles – there's no overdubbing to speak of. For Hollywood blockbusters and Finnish films, the megaplexes to head for are Tennispalatsi, Salomonkatu 15, and Kinopalatsi, just east of the train station at Kaisaniemenkatu 2 (both ☎0600/007 007, Ⓦwww.finnkino.fi). The single screen at Bio Rex (☎020/7424 220, Ⓦwww.biorex.fi), in the Lasipalatsi complex, shows similar fare international films, so if you're looking for something more independent, try the Finnish Film Archive's theatre, Orion, Eerikinkatu 15 (☎09/685 2546, Ⓦwww.kava.fi/esitykset), which screens art-house films several times daily, or Kino Engel, Sofiankatu 4 (☎0201/555 801, Ⓦwww.cinemamondo.fi), which screens indies throughout the year – including showings in an outdoor courtyard during the summer.

Gay Helsinki

Always the slowest of the Scandinavian countries to reform sexuality laws, Finland finally decriminalized homosexuality in 1971 and passed partnership laws in 2002. These days, public displays of affection are accepted, while the **gay scene** in Helsinki has flourished in recent years: today there's a gay choir, an annual pride parade in late June, an LBT culture festival in mid-September and a fair number of exclusively gay and gay-friendly establishments, the latter clustered around **Eerikinkatu** and the southern end of **Mannerheimintie**. In recent years, the city has embarked on a campaign to get a number of local establishments to become certified as "gay friendly," though exactly what this means in this day and age is anyone's guess. For the latest details on what's going on, visit the online gay guide and forum QLife (Ⓦwww.qlife.fi), which details listings and events, and offers gay-targeted tours of Helsinki and other cities. Otherwise, contact the state-supported gay and lesbian organization SETA (☎09/681 2580, Ⓦwww.seta.fi). Mäntymäki Park, between Mäntymäentie and Helsinginkatu, is known as a popular **cruising** location, and Pihlajasaari island is good for **nude bathing**. Helsinki Pride Parade is in late June (Ⓦwww .helsinkipride.fi).

Bars, clubs and saunas

DTM (Don't Tell Mamma) Iso Roobertinkatu 28 Ⓦwww.dtm.fi. Known to regulars as *Mama* or *Mummola*, this legendary gay and lesbian nightclub is the largest in Scandinavia and well known further afield. The disco was completely renovated in 2007, and it is still *the* place to go, with great house music most nights and regular drag shows and special events. During the day, the downstairs café offers breakfasts, pastries, snacks, coffee and free wi-fi.

Fairytale Helsinginkatu 7 Ⓦwww.fairytale.fi. Dark and intimate little bar primarily frequented by older men. Pints €2.90 until 8pm. Ring the doorbell to get in. See map, pp.56–57.

Mann's Street Mannerheimintie 12 (upstairs) Ⓦwww.mannsstreet.com. You'll find generous helpings of karaoke, Finnish music and older gay men at this very friendly bar.

Nalle Pub Kaarlenkatu 3–5 (upstairs). A relaxing Kallio bar that feels a bit like a living room. While you're sipping on a bottle of Bud you can watch

Shopping in Helsinki

Whether for clothing, design objects, music or handicrafts, Helsinki is without a doubt the best place in the country to pick up goodies for yourself or people back home. The best downtown shopping streets include **Aleksanterinkatu** (Aleksi for short) and **Esplanadi** (known locally as Espa), and there's even a specially demarcated **Design District**, where you can find well over a hundred shops within a kilometre radius selling thousands of classic and one-off creations; visit ⓦwww .designdistrict.fi for a complete listing of establishments. Here are some of our favourite places to shop:

Books
Akateeminen Kirjakauppa Pohjoisesplanadi 39. The city's largest selection of books – some 8km of them – stocking nearly 200,000 titles, many of which are in English.

Antikvar Hagelstans Fredrikinkatu 35. One of Scandinavia's best antiquarian booksellers; you can pick up a lot here for a euro or two.

Suomalainen Kirjakauppa Aleksanterinkatu 23. Though selling fewer titles than Akateeminen, they do offer regular discounts, especially on phrasebooks and dictionaries.

Department stores and shopping malls
Kamppi Centre Urho Kekkosenkatu 1. With 150 shops, this shopping centre opened in 2006 and is the capital's most chic (and also has the best selection and prices of any of the malls).

Stockmann Aleksanterinkatu 52. Scandinavia's largest single shop (see p.67) has pretty much everything under the midnight sun, including a good number of Sámi handicrafts.

Tunneli This underground complex by the train station is useful for its late hours, open till 10pm every day.

Fashion and jewellery
Cloth Gallery Fredrikinkatu 31. Leena Ikonen's collection of flowing silk dresses, beaded vests and unadorned wool coats.

The Greendress Laivurinkatu 41. Hip young fashion shop that sells their own couture line and also offers personal shoppers for the day.

Helsinki 10 Eerikinkatu 3. Billing itself as a "lifestyle warehouse", this sizeable boutique deals in the latest streetwear and vintage clothing.

Kalevala Koru Unioninkatu 25. High-minded designer jewellery that takes Finland's mythology as its inspiration.

Kiseloffin Talo Aleksanterinkatu 28F. Small indoor bazaar with over a dozen shops purveying handmade, one-off clothing items such as wool sweaters (from €159) as well as candles, quilts and jewellery.

Marimekko Pohjoisesplanadi 31. This is the classic Finnish designer's flagship shop and the best place to catch the next season's lines.

Nina's Bulevardi 13. Designer shoes, bags and accessories, from Miu Miu to Marc Jacobs, plus Finnish brands such as Jasmin Santanen.

UFF Fredrikinkatu 36. Great secondhand clothing. Four times a year they put on a massive sale where each item in the shop gets reduced to under seven euros.

Flea markets

Valtteri (Aleksis Kivenkatu 17) is the city's best flea market, a massive indoor bazaar held in an old industrial brick building on Teollisuuskatu, just north of Kallio. It's most vibrant on weekends, but there are also a few permanent stalls there open during the week. It's not the kind of place you can bargain though, as all products have price tags and are paid for at a central till. On weekends, the outdoor markets at the **Hietalahdentori** and, to a lesser extent, **Hakaniementori** are good bets too.

Food

The best place for culinary browsing is Helsinki's open-air **harbourside market**, where you can pick up bags of chanterelle mushrooms for cheap and fishermen sell produce right off the back of their boats. Try, too, the *kauppahallit*, or **market halls**, at the main market square and at Hakaniementori, where specialist stalls sell fish, meat, cheese, cakes and sweets.

Housewares, handicrafts and knick-knacks

Aarikka Pohjoisesplanadi 27. Super collection of design gifts, as well as jewellery, toys and unique household utensils – much of it made from natural woods.

Arabia Hämeentie 135. Located in northern Helsinki, this factory outlet is the best spot for deals on remainders, irregulars and discounted glassware and ceramics from the Arabia, Iittala and Hackmann brands. Tram #6.

Artek Eteläesplanadi 18. Alvar Aalto's collective has the best selection of the wunderkind's original household *objet* creations.

Iittala Pohjoisesplanadi 25. Form and function merge perfectly at this concept store, with a wide selection of glass- and tableware.

Kitsch Kalevankatu 13. Pretty much what it says on the tin: everything as kitschy as you'd ever want it to be.

Myymälä2 Uudenmaankatu 23. Independent art gallery that also sells posters, jewellery and clothes.

Secco Fredrikinkatu 33. Unique collective selling retro-urban purses, over-dyed tees and general boho paraphernelia, much of it recycled from such things as old car tires and laptop keys.

Sin City Annankatu 21. Devilish little place with oils, condoms and books.

Taito Shop Helsky Eteläesplanadi 4. Handicrafts that range from wool socks to liquorice. Great for gifts.

Music

The best collection of music shops is found at Viiskulma, the intersection of five streets at the eastern end of Albertinkatu. Try:

Digelius Laivurinrinne 2. Finland's best music shop for world, folk and jazz music (and some classical, too), with a terrific selection of both vinyl and CDs.

Eronen also at Laivurinrinne 2. Great for reggae, Latin and African music.

Stupido Iso Roobertinkatu 20–22. The best selection of rock music in the country.

Other

Karttakeskus Vuorikatu 14. Maps of regions and national parks.

Nokia Aleksanterinkatu 46. Even if you can't possibly afford a several-thousand-euro phone, the flagship Nokia store is a must-see for the latest in mobile innovation.

Trips to Estonia

Estonia and Finland have similar languages, a common ancestry, and histories which had largely run parallel up until the Soviet Union's annexation of Estonia in 1940. Today, though geographically and politically miles away – it's slowly catching up economically – Estonia is one of the most popular day-trip destinations for visitors to Finland, and a good number of passenger vessels now ply the 85-kilometre route across the Baltic between Helsinki and the Estonian capital, **Tallinn**. Furthermore, as Turku is sharing its crown of European Capital of Culture 2011 with Tallinn, the city has much planned in terms of entertainment from late 2010 onwards. For more on Tallinn, see *The Rough Guide to the Baltic States*.

Crossings (1hr 30min–3hr 15min) depart from the South and West harbours and are offered by Tallink Silja (☎09/228 311, ⓦwww.tallinksilja.com; Olympia Terminal; trams #1A, #3B & #3T); Viking Line (☎09/123 5300, ⓦwww.vikingline.fi; Katajanokka Terminal; tram #4T), Eckerö Line (☎09/2288 544, ⓦwww.eckeroline.fi; West Harbour; bus #15A) and Linda Line (☎09/668 97060, ⓦwww.lindaline.fi; Makasiini Terminal; trams #3B & #3T). Expect to pay from €19 and up to €72 for a deck seat depending on time, day of week and season; cars can range from €19 to €67. Buying in advance gets you the cheapest tickets, but look out for last-minute bargains in travel agency windows and on the front page of *Helsingin Sanomat*; you can find day returns for under €40, and during seasonal promotions at half that. There are left-luggage facilities at the ferry terminal in Tallinn.

TV, pop a euro in for a song on the jukebox or read a paper. Happy hour 3–6pm daily. Popular with bears and, on the weekend, lesbians. See map, pp.56–57.

Vogue Sturenkatu 27A ☎09/728 2008. Finland's only gay sauna, with a bar, steamroom, terrace and masseur. €16 entry. Open Sun–Thurs 3pm–11pm, Fri & Sat 3pm–midnight.

Listings

Airlines British Airways, Vantaa Airport ☎09/6937 9538; Finnair, Finnair City Terminal, Elielin Aukio (next to the train station) ☎09/818 800; SAS, Vantaa Airport ☎06/0002 5831; Blue1, as SAS.

Airport Enquiries ☎09/8277 3103.

Banks and exchange As well as the banks dotted all around the city (Mon–Fri 9.15am–4.15pm), the bank at the airport opens long hours (daily 6am–10pm), and there's an exchange counter at Katajanokka harbour, where Viking and Finnjet ferries dock (Mon–Sat 10–11.30am, 4–5.30pm & 7.30–9.15pm, Sun 10–11.30am, 4–5.30pm & 6.30–8pm). The Forex desk in the central train station (daily 8am–9pm) and Otto, opposite the station (Mon–Fri 8am–8pm, Sat 10am–6pm), handle cash advances on all major cards.

Bike rental Ecobike, Savilankatu 1B (☎0400/844358, ⓦwww.ecobike.fi); GreenBike (☎050/550 1020, ⓦwww.greenbike.fi). Both hire cycles for €15 per day.

Bus enquiries Long-distance buses ☎09/682 701 or 0200/4000; city buses ☎09/310 1071.

Car rental Avis, Pohjoinen Malminkatu 24 ☎09/441 155; Budget, Malminkatu 24 ☎020/746 6600; Europcar, Elielinaukio, by the station ☎09/4780 2220.

Doctor ☎09/3106 3231.

Embassies Canada, Pohjoisesplanadi 25B ☎09/228 530; South Africa, Rahapajankatu 1A5 ☎09/6860 3100; UK, Itäinen Puistotie 17 ☎09/2286 5100; USA, Itäinen Puistotie 14A ☎09/616 250. Citizens of Australia and New Zealand should contact the Australian Embassy in Stockholm.

Emergencies Ambulance and police ☎112. For non-urgent ambulance, ring ☎09/394 600; non-urgent police matters ring ☎09/1891.

Ferries Reservations and information: Tallink Silja Line ☎09/18 041, ⓦwww.tallinksilja.fi; Viking Line ☎09/123 51, ⓦwww.vikingline.fi.

Hospital Marian Hospital (Marian sairaala), Lapinlahdenkatu 16 ☎4711 or 09/4716 3339.

Internet cafés Café Aalto, 2nd floor, Akateeminen kirjapauppa, Pohjoisesplanadi 39; Telecenter, Vuorikatu 8; Netcup, Aleksanterinkatu 52; mbar, in the Lasipalatsi, Mannerheimintie 22–24. Helsinki's tourist office and the main post office each have several free terminals.

Laundry Rööperin pesulapalvelut, Punavuorenkatu 3 (Mon–Thurs 8am–8pm, Fri 8am–6pm, Sat 10am–3pm, Sun noon–4pm); *Café Tin Tin Tango*, Töölöntorinkatu 7 (Mon–Thurs 7am–midnight, Fri & Sat 9am–2am, Sun 10am–midnight; ring ☎09/2709 0972 to reserve).

Left luggage There are lockers (from €3) in the long-distance bus station (Mon–Thurs & Sat 9am–6pm, Fri 8am–6pm), and in the train station (Mon–Fri 7am–10pm).

Lost property (*löytötavaratoimisto*) 3rd floor, Päijänteentie 12A (Mon–Fri 10am–2pm; ☎09/189 3180).

Pharmacy Yliopiston Apteekki (☎0300/20 200, toll call), Mannerheimintie 96, is open 24hr; its branch at Mannerheimintie 5/Kaivopiha, is open daily 7am–midnight.

Police Pieni Roobertinkatu 1–3 ☎112 (emergencies), ☎09/1891 (non-emergencies).

Post office The main office is at Elielinaukio 1A (Mon–Fri 8am–8pm, Sat & Sun 9am–2pm); poste restante at the rear door (Mon–Sat 8am–10pm, Sun 11am–10pm). Stamps are available from post offices or the yellow machines in shops.

Saunas Kotiharju (see p.78); Rastila (see p.61); Yrjönkatu Swimming Hall (see p.72).

Sport Ice hockey, Hartwall Arena (☎060/010 800, ⓦ www.hartwall-areena.com), or Helsingin Jäähalli at Olympic Stadium (☎09/477 7110, ⓦ www.helsinginjaahalli.fi). Football, Finnair Stadium next to Olympic Stadium (☎060/010 800, ⓦ www.lippupalvelu.fi).

Telephone enquiries ☎118 or 020202.

Train enquiries ☎0600/41 902 (toll call) or 09/2319 2902.

Travel agents Kilroy Travels, Kaivokatu 10D, Kaivopiha (☎02/0354 5769, ⓦ www.kilroytravels.fi), is the Scandinavian youth travel agent, specializing in discounted tickets for students and young people. Suomen Matkatoimisto (SMT), the Finland Travel Bureau, Kaivokatu 10A (☎010/8261, ⓦ www.smt.fi), organizes trips to Russia and the necessary visas.

Around Helsinki

Compelling as the capital is – you could easily occupy a week exploring the sights, attractions and range of entertainment options in downtown Helsinki – you'd definitely be missing out if you were to disregard some of its outlying regions. To the west and north sprawl a series of leafy suburbs that developed and expanded in the mid-twentieth century, after Helsinki had become a thriving enough metropolis to encourage the growth of a commuter culture. Immediately due west of Helsinki are the well-plotted landscaped towns that comprise **Espoo** and **Kirkkonummi**, offering a couple of museums worth a visit, including one crackerjack architectural museum that feels as though it has been dormant for a hundred years. North of the city, meanwhile, is rural **Järvenpää**, where you can visit the homes of the composer Sibelius and artist Pekka Halonen. A bit further east are the evocative old riverfront buildings of **Porvoo**, a preserved river town that also serves as the perfect access point for exploring the much under-rated southeastern pocket of the country (see p.117). And given the availability of excellent and efficient transportation options, almost all of these places can be visited rather easily and quickly on a day-trip from the city that will have you back in the capital in time for dinner and a drink.

Espoo and around

Some 10km west out of Helsinki, the suburban area of **Espoo** (Esbo in Swedish) comprises several separate districts, the nearest and most famous of which, located directly across the Laajahalti (Bredviken) Bay from Helsinki, is the "garden city" of **Tapiola**, by far Espoo's most compelling place to visit. This leafy area holds a few museums that are perfect for an afternoon outside the city centre. Tapiola also holds the region's **tourist office** (Mon–Fri 9am–5pm; ☎09/8164 7230, ⓦ www .visitespoo.com), Tapiontori 3A next to the Kulttuurikeskus cultural centre, which handles enquiries about the whole Espoo area.

Tapiola

In the 1950s, many an organically minded Finnish urban planner attempted to blend new modernist housing schemes with the lush surrounding forests and hills – most of these efforts resulted in compromises that turned ugly and cumbersome as expansion occurred. **Tapiola** was the sole exception, built by leading artists Ervi, Blomstedt and Rewell, among others, as a self-contained living area rather than a dormitory town, with alternating high and low buildings, abundant open areas, gardens, parks, fountains and pools; in 1968, Finland's first shopping centre was opened here. Much praised on its completion by the architectural world, it's still refreshing to wander through and admire the idea and its execution.

The town's primary attractions are set within the former Welin & Göös printing works at Ahertajantie 5, known as the **WeeGee** (pronounced VAY-gay; Ⓦ weegee.espoo.fi) building. Once printing operations were shut in the late 1990s, the reinforced-concrete-and-glass constructivist structure was turned into a rough-hewn, multifunction museum and art centre. The premier site here is the spectacular **Espoo Museum of Modern Art** (EMMA; Tues & Fri–Sun 11am–6pm, Wed & Thurs 11am–8pm; €10; Ⓦ www.emma.museum). Opened in 2006, it is the largest museum in the country, and comprises the biggest and oldest private collection of Finnish art in the world. The City of Espoo began collecting art in the 1950s for use in primary schools and its 2500-piece-strong collection of paintings, sculptures, etchings, photographs and installations covers the entire oeuvre of Finnish art, stemming from its roots in the nineteenth century to contemporary, modern (and often quite conceptual) works. In the same building are five other museums, including the **Espoo City Museum** (Espoon kaupunginmuseo; €10; Ⓦ www.espoonkaupunginmuseo.fi), which houses an interesting permanent exhibition on the city, "A Trip through Time in Espoo".

Frequent buses run throughout the day from Helsinki's long-distance bus station at Kamppi to Tapiola – try either #105, #106 or #109 (tell the driver that you want to get off at "Tapiolan keskus").

Gallen-Kallela Museum

On the northern shores of the Laajalahti Bay opposite the peninsula of central Helsinki, the **Gallen-Kallela Museum** (Gallen-Kallela Museo; mid-May to Aug daily 11am–6pm; Sept to mid-May Tues–Sat 11am–4pm, Sun 11am–5pm; €8; Ⓦ www.gallen-kallela.fi), Gallen-Kallelantie 27, is housed inside the Art Nouveau studio of the influential painter Akseli Gallen-Kallela (1865–1931), who lived and worked here from 1913. It's something of an anticlimax though, lacking either atmosphere or any particularly decent display of the artist's work. Meanwhile, in an upstairs room are the pickled remains of reptiles and frog-like animals collected by Gallen-Kallela's family, and, inscribed into the floor, a declaration by the artist: "I Shall Return". Consider yourself warned.

The museum is poorly signposted; to get there from Helsinki, take tram #4 to the end of its route (on Saunalahdentie), then walk 2km along Munkkiniemi on the bay's edge to a footbridge over the water and towards it. Alternatively, bus #33 runs from the tram stop to the footbridge about every twenty minutes.

Serena Water Park

Some 27km north of here along the E12 road is **Serena Water Park** (daily June to mid-Aug 11am–8pm, at other times schedule varies wildly; ☎09/887 0550, Ⓦ www.serena.fi; €22), Tornimäentie 10 in Nurmijärvi. Here is Scandinavia's largest water theme park, offering giddy youngsters more slides, chutes, flumes, wave pools, whirlpools, roaring rapids and artificial beaches than they know what to do with – it is Finnish hedonism at its best. In the wintertime they operate a small ski centre – the closest skiing you'll find near Helsinki. To reach Serena Water Park from Helsinki take bus #339; from Tapiola, take bus #82.

Kirkkonummi: Hvitträsk

Southwest of Espoo, **Kirkkonummi** is a quiet, pleasant region where things begin to feel less suburban and more like the sticks. It's also home to one of the best architectural museums in the country – the hugely absorbing **Hvitträsk** (May–Sept daily 11am–5pm; Oct–April Wed–Sun 11am–5pm; €5). This lakeside studio-home was built and shared by architects Eliel Saarinen, Armas Lindgren and Herman Gesellius, three men who had established their partnership at the turn of the century shortly before their graduation in Helsinki. Hvitträsk was built to consolidate their practice, escape city life and seek inspiration in nature for their artistic works – a move rather in line with National Romantic ideals. The complex includes a shared studio and homes for each of their families, arranged around a central garden courtyard. Externally, the whole place is an extended and romanticized version of a traditional Karelian log cabin – more National Romanticism – the leafy branches that creep around making the structure look like a mutant growth emerging from the forest. Inside, the house, spanning several floors, contains a number of curiosities: frescos by Gallen-Kallela; a fridge from the early 1900s – the architects would take ice straight from the lake; and a fireplace, whose columns are adorned with several "whisky rings", ostensibly installed by Saarinen, who would dare guests at his many dinner parties to stand up on one leg while holding onto a ring. If they succeeded, they were promptly given another drink; fail, and they'd be sent off to bed. Upstairs are several bedrooms, each with rather stout doorways and diminutive beds – Saarinen and his wife were both quite short – as well as several chairs inspired by Scottish designer Rennie Mackintosh. There is also an original linoleum floor, quite rare at that time – and clearly a design choice of Saarinen, who was always keen to try out new materials.

The architects lived here until 1904, when their partnership dissolved amid the acrimony caused by Saarinen's independent (and winning) design for Helsinki's train station, though any work-related group tension surely wasn't alleviated by their bizarre marriage patterns. As the story goes, Saarinen's Helsinki-born, upper-class wife, Matilda, would regularly wander around the gardens in search of entertainment. This eventually came in the form of Herman Gesellius, whom she married in 1904 – but not before Saarinen could ask for the hand of Gesellius's sister. After the amicable double wedding, the women effectively just swapped houses and life went on as usual – though gossip on the lot of them spread around Helsinki faster than a city conflagration, and Gesellius and Lindgren eventually moved out. Saarinen lived here until the 1920s, after which he moved to the US – though he kept the building as a summer house until his death in 1950. The Saarinens had two children, both born here; Eero, their son, became a famous architect who designed the TWA terminal in New York and the St Louis Gateway Arch. The interior of Hvitträsk can only be seen by guided tours, which are offered throughout the day. There is an excellent, elegant café and **restaurant** on the grounds, as well as a small cemetery, where Saarinen and his wife are buried.

To get from central Helsinki to Hvitträsk, take the local (line L or U) train to Louma (37min) and follow the signs for 3km, or take bus #166 from Helsinki (45min).

Jean Sibelius

Now regarded as one of the twentieth century's greatest composers, **Jean Sibelius** was also – before the Moomins at least – Finland's finest musician. Born in Hämeenlinna in 1865, Sibelius had no musical background to speak of, and by the age of nineteen was enrolled on a law course at Helsinki University. He had, however, developed a youthful passion for the violin and took a class at the capital's Institute of Music. Law was soon forgotten as Sibelius's real talents were recognized, and his musical studies took him to the cultural hotbeds of the day, Berlin and Vienna. Returning to Finland to teach at the Institute, Sibelius soon won a government grant, which enabled him to begin composing full time, the first concert of his works being performed in 1892.

Sibelius profited from impeccable timing, becoming established in the 1890s, when the Finnish people were tiring of Russia's yoke and the intelligentsia starting to get antsy feet. His early works capitalized on the wave of nationalism, drawing much inspiration from the Finnish folk epic, the Kalevala, and in 1899 the country's Russian rulers banned performances of his rousing *Finlandia* under any name that suggested its patriotic sentiment – it was instead published simply as "Opus 26 No. 7". While the overtly nationalistic elements in Sibelius's work mellowed in later years, his music continued to reflect a very Finnish obsession with nature: "Other composers offer their public a cocktail," he said, "I offer mine pure spring water."

Notorious for his bouts of heavy drinking, however, in 1926 Sibelius was hit with self-criticism and a destructive quest for perfection – an angst-ridden bout of self-imposed musical exile known as "the silence from Järvenpää" – during which no new work appeared; it's widely suspected that he had completed, and destroyed, two symphonies during his final thirty years. Sibelius died in 1957, his best-known symphonies having set a standard younger Finnish composers have only just begun to approach.

Järvenpää

Around 40km north of Helsinki and easily reached by either bus or train, **JÄRVENPÄÄ** is a lively commercial town largely set along the shores of Lake Tuusulanjärvi. A lively community of artists flourished here at the start of the twentieth century, carried by the nationally famous author Juhani Aho and his painter wife Venny Soldan-Brofeldt, as well as Eino Leino, Eero Järnefelt, Pekka Halonen and Finland's most famous export, Jean Sibelius. The latter two have museums dedicated to them here, which comprise the town's main sights.

On the northeast banks of the lake, the wood-filled grounds of **Ainola** (May–Sept Tues–Sun 10am–5pm; €5.50) mark the residence where Jean Sibelius lived for 53 years with his wife, Aino (Järnefelt's sister), after whom the place is named. Sibelius built Ainola in 1904 to be, in his words, "sufficiently far from the temptations of Helsinki", and the tranquil house, set within whistling distance of lakes and forests, is just the kind of home you'd expect for a man who included representations of flapping swans' wings in his music. The wood-filled grounds are as atmospheric as the building, which is a place of pilgrimage for devotees, although books, furnishings and a few paintings are all there is to see. His grave is in the grounds, marked by a marble stone inscribed simply with his name. For more tangible Sibelius memories, and more of his music, visit the Sibelius Museum in Turku (see p.136).

A few minutes' walk away is the compelling **Halosenniemi Museum** (Halosen-niemi Museo; Tues–Sun: May–Aug 10am–6pm; Sept–April noon–5pm; €5.50), set south of Ainola on the Tuusula lakeside road. A beautifully serene place, this is the rustic home of Pekka Halonen, one of Finland's most renowned artists, and its National Romantic decor has been painstakingly restored, housing some of Halonen's pictures and painting materials in their original setting.

Porvoo

Some 50km northeast of Helsinki, **PORVOO** (Borgå in Swedish) is one of the oldest towns lining the southern Finnish coast. The town's narrow cobblestone streets, lined with small, two-storey wooden buildings, offer a strong sense of the Finland that predated the bold squares and Neoclassical grandeur of Helsinki and the bland structures and modern geometry of most other Finnish cities and towns. With its elegant riverside setting – the town's originally Swedish name means "castle river" – and unhurried mood, Porvoo has some real rustic flavour, though word of these peaceful time-locked qualities has spread and, in the summer at least, you're hardly likely to be alone.

Arrival, information and accommodation

During the summertime, you can reach Porvoo from Helsinki by **boat** (see box, p.102), but **buses** run all day throughout the year from the bus station at Kamppi (€9.20–11.90). Your stop should be the **tourist office** at Rihkamakatu 4 (early June to Aug Mon–Fri 9am–6pm, Sat & Sun 10am–4pm; Sept to early June Mon–Fri 9am–4.30pm, Sat 10am–2pm; ☎019/520 2316, ⓦtourism.porvoo.fi) for a free map of the town.

Although Helsinki has the country's best (and best priced) collection of hotels and hostels, spending the night in Porvoo leaves you quite well placed to continue into Finland's southeastern corner. Most inexpensive of all is the town's year-round **youth hostel** (☎019/523 0012, ⓦwww.porvoohostel.cjb.net; dorms €18,

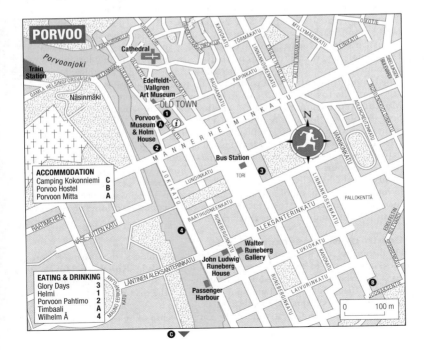

> ## Porvoo by boat
>
> You can reach Porvoo by water from Helsinki on the **M/S Katarina** (late June to mid-Aug Tues–Sun 10.20am; €39 return, €28 one way; ☎020/711 8333, ⓦwww .royalline.fi) or the **M/S J.L. Runeberg** (mid-May to early Sept daily except Thurs 10am; €35 return, €24 one way; ☎019/524 3331, ⓦwww.msjlruneberg.fi), both of which depart Helsinki's *kauppatori* and ply the archipelago towards Porvoo. The trip takes roughly 3hr 15min and both boats have food available on board. Return trips to Helsinki depart at 4pm. Tickets for both boats can be bought from their respective ticket offices in the *kauppatori* in Helsinki. The quay for boats is located on the eastern side of the river just south of Aleksanterinkatu.

rooms ❷), Linnankoskenkatu 1–3, a comfy red wooden building with three dozen beds spread across ten rooms. Much more plush is *Porvoon Mitta* (☎019/580 131, ⓦwww.hotelporvoonmitta.fi; ❻), Jokikatu 43, a perfectly gorgeous family-run guesthouse with ten classically designed rooms: decor ranges from eighteenth-century Gustavian to early twentieth-century elegant modern. *Camping Kokoniemi* (☎019/581 967, ⓦwww.fontana.fi/camping; early June to late Aug) is located 2km south of the centre on the river at Uddaksentie 17, and offers tidy and clean grassy grounds; they also have ten cabins (from €59).

The old town

The marvellously rustic, fire-engine red ochre warehouses that line Porvoo's river form the bulk of buildings that make up the **old town** (follow the signs for "Vanha Porvoo"), built around the hill on the north side of Mannerheiminkatu and the town's main attraction. To explore, start at the top of the old town, where the fifteenth-century **Tuomiokirkko** (Cathedral; May–Sept Mon–Fri 10am–6pm, Sat 10am–2pm, Sun 2–5pm; Oct–April Tues–Sat 10am–2pm, Sun 2–4pm) marks the place where in 1809 Alexander I proclaimed Finland a Russian Grand Duchy, himself Grand Duke, and convened the first Finnish Diet. Tragically, the church was partially destroyed in a fire in 2006 started by three local teens, though a two-year renovation project has brought most of it – including its evocative wall paintings – up to scratch again. Along with other aspects of the town's past, the church can be further explored in the **Porvoo Museum** (Porvoonmuseo; May–Aug Tues–Sat 10am–4pm, Sun 11am–4pm; Sept–April Wed–Sun noon–4pm; €5) at the foot of the hill in the old town's main square. There are no singularly outstanding exhibits here, just a diverting selection of furnishings, musical instruments and general oddities, largely dating from the years of Russian rule; next door, the **Holm House** (Holmin talo; same hours and price) gives an idea of how a wealthy Porvoo merchant family would have lived at the end of the eighteenth century, with period living room, salon, smoking and laundry rooms. The warehouse buildings themselves – or at least their facades – are easily enough explored by walking about Jokikatu and the streets that branch off of it.

South of Mannerheiminkatu

Head south of the museum along the water for five blocks, then turn left onto Aleksanterinkatu to reach the preserved **Johan Ludvig Runeberg House** at no. 3 (Runebergin koti; May–Aug daily 10am–4pm, Sun 11am–5pm; Sept–April Wed–Sat 10am–4pm, Sun 11am–5pm; €5), where the man regarded as Finland's national poet lived from 1852 while a teacher at the town school. Despite writing in Swedish, Runeberg greatly aided the nation's sense of self-esteem, especially with *Fänrik Ståls sägner* ("Tales of Ensign Ståhl"), which recounted the people's struggles with Russia in the 1808–09 conflict. The first poem in his collection *Our Land* later provided the lyrics for the national anthem. Runeberg's Empire-style home remains as it was during the last thirteen bedridden years of his life until his death in 1877. The building includes various works of art, hunting weapons and pretty examples of porcelain; his wife Fredrika's well-watered plants still bloom in the house. Also have a look at the bust of Runerberg sculpted by his third son, Walter, in 1860.

You can find more family art at the **Walter Runeberg Gallery** (same hours as Runeberg House; ticket valid for both), just across the road, where there is a sizeable collection of works by Walter, one of Finland's more celebrated sculptors. Among many acclaimed works, he's responsible for the statue of his father that stands in the centre of Helsinki's Esplanadi.

Eating and drinking

Porvoo has a couple of dainty **cafés** that are wonderful spots to tarry on a summer afternoon. Try, for example, *Helmi*, Välikatu 7, housed in a nineteenth-century upper-class home and specializing in Russian teas and the local pastry speciality, the Runeberg tart. A block south of here on the water at Mannerheiminkatu 2 is *Porvoon Pahtimo*, a beautiful red-tiled warehouse that dates from 1902. They create an excellent four-bean espresso blend from the on-site roastery, and you can sit and have a beer and a sandwich out on their retro-fitted barge floating out on the river.

During the summertime, the modern riverside *Wilhelm Å* on Jokikatu is a superb place to come for a filling **meal** – soups, salads and pastas are mostly what they trade in – and a drink at sunset out on their floating terrace. Just behind the town hall in the old town is *Timbaali*, Välikatu 8/Jokikatu 43, a modern white-tablecloth eatery that specializes in snails. Try the escargots Roquefort (€11), the Dijon-seasoned escargot stew (€20) or the filet of lamb, served with shoulder terrine and goat's cheese gnocchi (€23).

After hours, pop in for a **drink** at the check-floored, American-themed *Glory Days*, Rauhankatu 27, by the market square.

Travel details

Trains

Helsinki to: Ekenäs (hourly; 1hr 20min–1hr 50min); Espoo (every 10min; 18–25min); Hämeenlinna (hourly; 1hr–1hr 20min); Hanko (hourly; 2hr); Jyväskylä (every 30min; 3hr 10min–4hr 20min); Järvenpää (every 30min; 30min); Kajaani (9 daily; 5hr 40min–7hr 40min); Kotka (6 daily; 2hr 20min–3hr); Kuopio (9 daily; 4hr–5hr 20min); Lahti (every 30min; 50min–1hr 30min); Mikkeli (7 daily; 2hr 25min–2hr 45min); Oulu (17 daily; 5hr 45min–9hr 40min); Rovaniemi (8 daily; 9hr–12hr 30min); Tampere (every 30min; 1hr 25min–2hr); Turku (hourly; 2hr 5min–4hr 30min).

Buses

Helsinki to: Fiskars (7 daily; 1hr 50min–3hr); Hanko (10 daily; 2hr 5min–3hr 20min); Järvenpää (every 30min; 50min–1hr 5min); Joensuu (10 daily; 6hr 55min–9hr 10min); Jyväskylä (every 30min; 4hr–6hr 25min); Kotka (every 30min; 2hr–3hr 10min); Lohja (several hourly; 1hr 5min–2hr); Loviisa (1hr 30min–2hr 15min); Mikkeli (hourly; 3hr 20min–4hr 20min); Porvoo (every 15min; 1hr); Pyhtää (6–13 daily; 2hr–2hr 45min); Tampere (every 30min; 2hr 15min–4hr 5min); Turku (every 30min; 2hr 10min–2hr 45min); Virojoki (8 daily; 3hr 10min–4hr 35min).

Porvoo to: Helsinki (frequent; 55min–1hr 10min); Kotka (hourly; 1hr 20min–1hr 55min); Loviisa (every half-hour; 30min–50min).
Tapiola to: Helsinki (frequent; 20min).

Ferries

Helsinki to: Mariehamn (3 daily; 10hr–11hr 15min).

International trains

Helsinki to: Moscow/Moskova (1 daily; 13hr); St Petersburg/Pietari (2 daily; 5hr 50min–6hr 30min, though under 3hr from 2011).

International buses

Helsinki to: St Petersburg/Pietari (3 daily; 8hr 10min–9hr 30min); Vyborg/Viipuri (3 daily; 5hr 25min–6hr 10min).

International ferries

Helsinki to: Stockholm (3 daily; 16hr); Tallinn (every 2hr; 1hr 30min–3hr 30min).

THE SOUTH COAST

2

The south coast

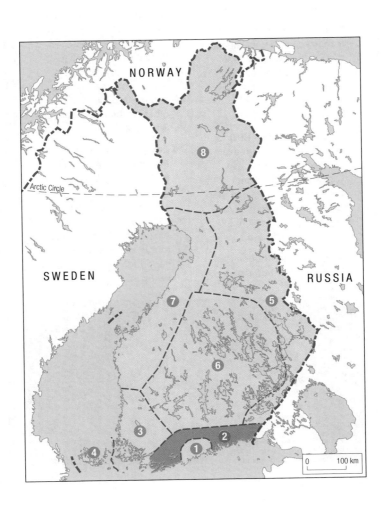

CHAPTER 2 # Highlights

* **Raseborg Castle** The ruins of this fourteenth-century fortress are best visited in the summer, when the area livens up with medieval markets and theatre performances. See p.112

* **Fiskars** Better known for the orange scissors your mum used to have in the kitchen, this sleepy artisan town offers more rustic charm than you'll know what to do with. See p.113

* **Lace villas, Hanko** Built for wealthy Russians in the late nineteenth century, these wooden gems are some of the most prepossessing summer homes in the country – you can even spend a night at some of them. See p.115

* **Bengtskär Lighthouse** Set out a good few hours away in the middle of the Baltic, this brick structure has been restored to tiptop shape, and even outfitted with a café and a hotel. See p.116

* **Maritime Centre Vellamo, Kotka** This modern nautical museum offers some real insight into the maritime past of Finland's coastal settlements, as well as the chance to explore the world's oldest icebreaker out back. See p.122

* **Langinkoski Imperial Fishing Lodge** Explore the surprisingly austere rooms of this large wooden structure – a one-time summer residence of Tsar Alexander III – then take a tour in the river to try your hand at fly-fishing for pike. See p.123

▲ Bengtskär Lighthouse, Hanko

2

The south coast

Travel a few dozen kilometres west or east of Helsinki and you may well feel like you've arrived in a different country entirely. Taken as a whole, Finland's **south coast** is the most populated and industrialized part of the country, but it also comprises some gorgeous backwater spots, too. As the more remote areas rest some way from the major centres, foreign tourists tend to neglect this area. In-the-know Finns, however, rate it highly, and have been flocking here for generations to head out on boat trips around its archipelago and to explore the area's many small coastal communities, offering the quickest path from Helsinki to experiencing some real Finnish rustic flavour. Several centuries ago, kings and tsars – and the bishops, burghers, armies and tradesmen who followed them – would plod through these parts along a route that stretched from western Norway into Russia, linking the more remote quarters of the Swedish kingdom with one another. Known as **The King's Road**, or Kuninkaantie (Kungsvägen in Swedish), the route today is indicated by chestnut-coloured roadside signs embossed with golden crowns, and is made up of highways and byways that wend their way through birch and pine woods. A fair number of farmsteads and churches – the rural whistle-stops that once accommodated the travelling hordes of yore – still exist today.

With regular, frequent trains and buses from Helsinki, getting to the region is very simple, but to reach some of the more rural (and coastal) areas, having your own transport would be handy – although local municipalities are making plans to beef up bus routes to some of the smaller, more visited destinations.

West of Helsinki

Some 30km due west of Helsinki past the fields and meadows of Kirkkonummi province, lies the charming region of **Western Uusimaa**, with its wooden villa towns, sandy beaches and remote islands. Despite its proximity to the capital, this has remained the region least visited by foreigners though facilities and infrastructure are improving. The first main town is **Lohja**, with impressive Lakeland scenery, and to the south, **Ingå**, whose outskirts are filled with a number of engaging museums, manors and guesthouses. Further on is **Ekenäs**, a fairly modern, commercial place but with a medieval-style old quarter that slows things down a bit. Just outside of Ekenäs lie the small villages of **Snappertuna**, which holds the ruins of the fourteenth-century **Raseborg Castle**, and **Fiskars**, an industrial-turned-artisan forge town famous for its namesake orange scissors. Finally, at Finland's most southerly point is **Hanko**, a beguiling resort town of romantic wooden villas and laconic beaches.

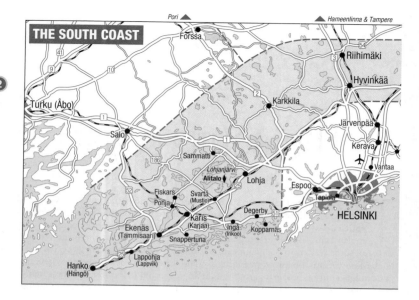

As this region is the furthest south of anywhere in the country, the summer season lasts longer than in other places, and the lush landscape produces vegetables and fruit until late in the season; inspired by this, a growing **Slow Food** movement has been taken up by many regional chefs to serve up healthier, more organic cuisine. It's also a region heavily populated by **Swedish** speakers, meaning a respite for visitors struggling with the knotty Finnish language.

While Uusimaa's largest municipalities are connected to the capital by frequent train service, inter-town **transportation** within the region is spotty at best. And since the region only really gets interesting once you get well off the beaten (that is, railway) track to explore the countryside, having your own transport is well advised. For more information on travel in the region, contact **Visit Southpoint Finland** (T040/779 8969, Wwww.visitsouthpointfinland.fi) in Ekenäs, a knowledgeable group that can help organize tours in and around the region, including out to islands in the archipelago.

Lohja and around

Set on the banks of the large **Lake Lohja**, **Lohja** offers visitors the closest Lakeland scenery to Helsinki. At the town's centre is the rustic, stone **Church of St Lawrence** (Pyhän Laurin kirkko; May to mid-Aug daily 9am–4pm; mid-Aug to April daily 10am–3pm), which features alluring, folksy sixteenth-century wall paintings in *a secco* style (in which the paint is applied directly to a dry wall, allowing for a longer painting period). You'll find more adventure 1km north of the centre along Tytyrinkatu, where you can descend 110m in an old mining car to an underground **mining museum** (Tytyrin kaivosmuseo; June–Aug daily 11am–6pm; Sept–May Sat & Sun noon–4pm; €10), located within an actual shaft of the Tytyri Mine (claustrophobes beware). The 90-minute guided tour, which includes a sound and light show at the main quarry, offers a realistic impression of a miner's working day, though as the temperature rarely rises above 8°C, be sure to bring warm clothes. Once you're back

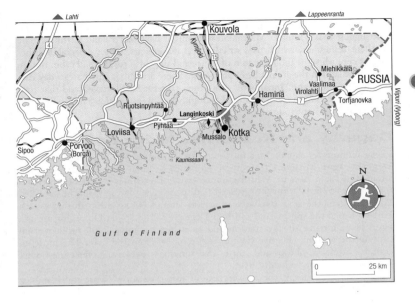

above ground, opt for an afternoon spent tasting cider at **Alitalo** (mid-May to mid-Aug daily noon–5pm; Ⓦ www.ciderberg.fi), Pietiläntie 138, on Lohjansaari island, several kilometres west of town. Lohja is known across Finland for its profuse apple production, and Alitalo maintains some thirteen thousand apple trees; it also has a great **café** serving fresh juices. The lake can be taken by kayak or canoe, too, with Melontapooli (Ⓣ044 584 9122, Ⓦ www.melontapooli.fi; from €35 per day, or €40 for a tandem), though you should try to reserve a few days in advance.

Buses to Lohja arrive on Laurinkatu in the city centre, though as there's little going on in the town proper, you're best arriving with your own transport to facilitate getting out into the countryside.

Ingå and around

The flatlining town of **INGÅ** (Inkoo in Finnish) made headlines in 2007 for being home to Finland's first and only all-wooden shopping centre, opened by champion rally driver Marcus Grönholm. Otherwise, though, the town is really only worth visiting for its thirteenth-century grey-stone **St Nicholas Church** (Mon–Fri 8am–4pm, plus May–Aug Sat & Sun 9am–4pm), holding a unique *Death Dance* mural, in which various incarnations of Death are seen waltzing with recent arrivals to the afterlife. The region's **archipelago** can be explored by three-hour boat tours (€15) departing Ingå harbour on Sundays in July at 12.30pm (other times by arrangement on Ⓣ040/502 6836), while the town's forested environs offer some of Finland's best **horseriding** territory. Aktiivitalli (€25 per hr; Ⓣ044/588 7764, Ⓦ www.aktiivitalli.fi), 6km east of Ingå at Gunnarsvägen 47, obliges with a stable of Finnhorses, one of the most versatile coldbloods and Finland's only native horse breed, for riding tours.

Ingå, reachable by regular bus from Helsinki, has itself little in the way of **accommodation**, but a few kilometres east at Västerbyvägen 95 is ⚜ *Westerby Gård* (Ⓣ09/295 2589, Ⓦ www.westerby.fi; ❻), an immaculately restored farmhouse with check curtains, large matte-white dining tables and large oak-plank flooring that suggest that a Finnish Martha Stewart might have had a hand in things. The excellent restaurant, which uses strictly local ingredients, serves delectable dishes such as crayfish soup and roast loin of lamb, and they also run a small cabin out on a remote island in the archipelago, *Torrharun*. There are only a few buses a day that pass by (get off at the "Innanbäck" stop, then take the small gravel road that runs from there for 2km to reach the farm), though you can easily catch a bus to Ingå and then a quick taxi out to the farm.

Degerby and Kopparnäs hiking area

Eleven kilometres east of Ingå in the village of **Degerby**, the small, homespun **Degerby Igor Museum** (Degerbyn Igor-museo; June to mid-Aug Tues–Sat 11am–4pm; late Aug to May Sat noon–4pm; other times by appointment on ☎040/541 8526; €2), Furuborgsvägen 6, displays relics dating from the so-called Porkkala Parenthesis, a twelve-year period from 1944 to 1956 during which Finland leased the spit of land south of Degerby to the Soviet Union for use as a naval base, forcing the evacuation and resettling of some 7200 residents and causing the region's effective (temporary) removal from the map. The museum contains artefacts, photos and stories that movingly evoke the effect the Soviet occupation took on residents' lives.

Just south of Degerby, the 800 hectares of forest, meadow, shore and islands at **KOPPARNÄS**, a de facto nature reserve, have been earmarked as excellent spots for hiking, swimming and clambering across the rocks hunting for discarded Soviet shells – the area was a popular spot for artillery exercises during the Porkkala Parenthesis. Facilities are basic, but the gorgeous scenery is one spot in Finland where you definitely get to try out Finland's tenet of *jokamiehenoikeudet* ("Everyman's Right"; see p.42), for which you should not forget *jokamiehenvelvollisuudet* ("Leave only footprints", essentially). The *Kopparnäsin Kestikievari* (☎040/070 1159, ⓦwww .kupariniemi.fi; ❹), Kopparnäsvägen 428, near the entrance to the area, offers **accommodation** in basic rooms with shared facilities. Use of the rustic hot tub and sauna is included in the rate and the restaurant serves good, down-home Finnish meals.

Ekenäs

Roughly 100km west of Helsinki, the seaside town of **EKENÄS** (Tammisaari in Finnish) is a majority Swedish-speaking settlement with a couple of worthy sights which makes a good base for getting your bearings before heading off to the more inspirational destinations of the surrounding Raseborg region (in order to do away with the superfluous duplication of administrative functions – a trend befalling many areas of the country these days – the municipality of Ekenäs, along with nearby Karis and Pohja, were consolidated into the single township of Raseborg – Raasepori in Finnish – in 2009). The name Raseborg was borrowed from the castle ruins just outside Ekenäs.

Swedish King Gustav Wasa had big plans to turn the town into an important centre for trade, but it never got much beyond the one-horse-town stage. Today, however, one-horse serves visitors to this small settlement just fine, with its quaint collection of diminutive eighteenth- and nineteenth-century wooden houses, narrow cobbled roads, oak trees (Ekenäs means "Oak Peninsula" in Swedish) and stately apple orchards.

Arrival, information and accommodation

Hanko-bound trains from Karis (Finnish: Karjaa), which connect from Helsinki, stop at Ekenäs's **train and bus station**, a ten-minute walk northeast of the

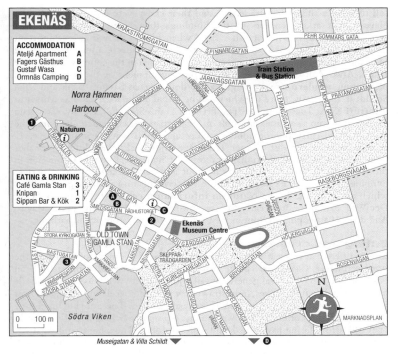

EKENÄS

ACCOMMODATION
Ateljé Apartment	A
Fagers Gästhus	B
Gustaf Wasa	C
Ormnäs Camping	D

EATING & DRINKING
Café Gamla Stan	3
Knipan	1
Sippan Bar & Kök	2

Museigatan & Villa Schildt ▼   ▼ **D**

town centre. The local **tourist office** (May–Aug Mon–Fri 8.30am–6pm, Sat 10am–2pm; Sept–April Mon–Fri 8.30am–4pm; ☎019/289 2010, �www .raseborg.fi), located on the main square, Rådhustorget, offers information on the entire Raseborg region.

Overnighting in Ekenäs offers a welcome change from the chain hotel experience, with a number of great bed-and-breakfast and cottage-type options, at the top of which list is *Ateljé Apartment* (☎040/715 0448, �www.design4you.fi /hosting/gwg; ❸), Gustav Wasas gata 3. This old whitewashed inn features quaint rooms with kitchenettes and a tiny, well-tended garden out back. On the same road at no.10 is the alluring *Gustaf Wasa* (☎019/241 3020, �www.gustaf-wasa .nu), with a modern apartment (€120) and a more rustic cottage (€140), a few metres from the main shopping street, Kungsgatan – though as they're rather popular, booking far in advance is well advised. Just as close to the water is *Fagers Gästhus* (☎050/351 0015, �www.fagers.fi; from €100), Smedsgatan 6–10, five cosy self-catering apartments; ask for the 1775-era Gustavian flat, with wide plank flooring and pretty period furniture. Ekenäs's **campsite**, *Ormnäs Camping* (☎019/241 4434, �www.ek-camping.com) is set 1km from the town centre by the seashore. They also have some minuscule cabins (from €31) for rent, as well as cycle and rowboat hire.

The Town

Ekenäs's topography betrays its strong artisan history, visible most recognizably in the irregularly patterned **Old Town** (Gamla Stan), where roads such as Hattmagaregatan (Milliner's Street) and Linvävaregatan (Linen Weaver's Street) call to mind a time when tradesmen and their crafts were the hub of city life. Have a look at the corners of the buildings themselves, painted with tiny emblems of various types of fish – from when Ekenäs thrived as an important fishing settlement – and at the town's piebald stone **church**, a fetching example of Scandinavian Baroque and the second oldest church in the country, built in the 1680s. Alvar Aalto had a small hand in the development of the somewhat less picturesque **modern town**, designing the dour Ekenäs Savings Bank and Villa Schildt in the 1960s, more on which can be found at the local **Ekenäs Museum Centre** (EKTA; Tues–Thurs 4–7pm, Fri–Sun 11am–5pm; €2), Gustav Wasas gata 11. The museum also has exhibitions on local artists and craftsmen, including the innards of an early photographer's studio, and holds three paintings by early twentieth-century realist painter **Helene Schjerfbeck**; well known for her deeply melancholic self-portraits, local resident Schjerfbeck sought inspiration in the winter bleakness of the town's harbour and parks. Ekenäs is also a perfect jumping-off point for exploration of the Western Uusimaa archipelago, details of which can be found in the **Naturum information centre** (Feb–April & Sept–Dec Wed–Sat 10am–3pm; early May to mid-May daily 10am–3pm; mid-May to Aug daily 10am–6pm, till 8pm in July, set in an old salt store at the harbour.

Eating and drinking

Ekenäs offers a few great **eating** joints, the most welcoming of which is the summertime ☂ *Café Gamla Stan*, Bastugatan 5 (ⓦ www.cafegamlastan.fi), an outdoor café run by several generations of a jovial family who do a roaring trade in lush chocolate fudge cakes, light strawberry tarts and excellent coffee, and host popular live music performances on Tuesday afternoons. There are big lunchtime specials (€8.50) on offer at the town square's *Sippan Bar & Kök*, a spiffy, recently opened bistro offering pasta, steak and seafood dishes. The same friendly gastronomes also run *Knipan*, Ekenäs's best-known restaurant, set in a smashing, early twentieth-century wooden building on sea stilts at the dockside at Strandallén. The chef – a strong proponent of the Slow Food movement – prepares a number of good Finnish dishes, including a great fried pikeperch with lemon sauce and potatoes (€23), and after hours it becomes the town's most popular **bar**.

Around Ekenäs

Outside of Ekenäs are a few spots that give the town a run for its money in terms of appeal, not least of all the intact ruins of **Raseborg Castle**, whose large courtyards and bastion towers give a great sense of the strategic importance of this area in days gone by. A short ride away is **Fiskars**, about as sleepy and idyllic an artisan town as you're going to find anywhere in the Nordic countries, while **Svartå Manor**, to the northeast of Ekenäs, makes a winning spot for traditional, white-tablecloth Finnish dining and to hole up for a night along the banks of this one-time iron forge settlement.

Snappertuna and Raseborg Castle

Seventeen kilometres due east of Ekenäs, south of Route 25, is the one-horse town of **SNAPPERTUNA**, a handful of old wooden buildings that include an ochre-coloured, cruciform **church** dating from 1688 and a more compelling folklore **museum** (June–Aug Tues–Sun noon–5pm) showcasing what life was like for rural folk a few centuries ago. The village's name unfortunately has nothing do with the fish: *tuna* is an Old Norse word meaning "enclosed yard", etymologically related to the English word "town".

Today, the place is best known for the nearby (intact) ruins of the towering **Raseborg Castle** (May & mid- to late Aug daily 10am–5pm; June to mid-Aug daily 10am–8pm; Sept Sat & Sun 10am–5pm; €1; @ www.raseborg.org) accessed by a 300-metre wooded path. The namesake for the newly minted municipality, the horseshoe-shaped Raseborg (Finnish Raasepori) was built in the 1370s atop an outcrop of glaciated rock on what was then an island, then added to and amended several times over the next few centuries. Raseborg borrowed its name from Ratzenburg in northern Germany, where Swedish kings once owned land, and was established to manage the growing Baltic trade between Tallinn and the Finnish coast. The settlement it produced thrived as an import-export administrative centre, defending on numerous occasions Swedish interests from the incursions of Hanseatic pirates. Though it fell into disrepair once King Gustav Wasa seized power and moved local rule to Ekenäs in 1546, the castle's large round tower, bailey and two forecourts are intact enough to explore, and the entire grounds come alive during the summer, with medieval markets and outdoor performances by a renowned Swedish-language theatre. Guided **tours** of the castle are also offered (3pm: May–Aug Sat & Sun plus Wed & Fri in July). Snappertuna holds a small travellers' **hostel** (☎019/234 180, @ www.vnur.org /vandrarhem), Kyrkvägen 129, with dorms (€15), doubles (❶) and bargain-basement single rooms (€20).

Fiskars

Like many of the hamlets within the Raseborg region – once the centre of Finnish iron manufacturing on account of its plentiful water and timber supply – endearing **FISKARS** grew up as a *bruk* (ironworks), founded in 1649 by Dutchman Peter Thorwöste. For centuries Fiskars the town (@www .fiskarsvillage.fi) has effectively been owned and managed by Fiskars the company (@www.fiskars.fi), which made small fortunes in industrial machinery manufacturing and streamlined agricultural products. The company struck it rich after launching their iconic and astronomically popular ergonomic **orange-handled scissors** in 1967 (they have since sold over one billion of them), and when manufacturing was moved elsewhere in the late 1980s, the company re-envisioned its birth town as a live-work environment for craftspeople and artists – a hermitic crowd of ceramicists, jewellery makers and other industrial designers ply and sell their wares in the town's shops.

Fiskars is a lovely, compact place to wander around and explore, beginning at the **Fiskars Wärdshus** (see below) and moving east along the river, past old brick **artisan workshops** (where you can try your hand at forging your own pig-iron nails at an ironsmiths), a large **granary** holding temporary art exhibitions, and the Engel-esque **clock tower** building with a large exhibition on the company's history and a shop of Fiskars products. Continue past various and sundry boutiques to end up, roughly 1km on, at the **Fiskars Museum** (Jan–April Sat 1–4pm; May–Sept daily 1–4pm; Oct–Dec Sat & Sun 1–4pm; €2.50), once the forge canteen and now holding no small amount of information on the history of iron production and the people who played a role in it. The Orvis shop, located in the ground floor of the old granary, can organize half-day and day-long guided river and lake **fishing tours**.

Practicalities

Buses to town make two stops along Fiskarsvägen, the town's principal road, the first of which is just outside the excellent, modern **hotel**, ⚜ *Fiskars Wärdshus* (☎019/276 6510, @www.wardshus.fi; ❺), Fiskarsvägen 14, a renovated coaching inn with fifteen gorgeously designed doubles sporting locally designed elm furnishings and wrought-iron railings. A less expensive option is the *Vanha Meijari* (☎044/594 1959, @www.kahvilavanhameijeri.fi; ❹), Suutarinmäki 7, a darling year-round **B&B** whose two rooms have exposed beams and pastel decor. **Eating** options are simply enumerated: the *Wärdshus* runs a smashing restaurant, with great seafood mains – try the fresh whitefish fillet – served on a sunny terrace. Just across in the old copper forge is *Kuparipaja*, which serves buffet lunches on a veranda overlooking the river, while *Café Antique*, in the clock tower building, is a small bookstore-meets-café that serves the best cinnamon buns in town.

Svartå Manor

Some 30km northeast of Ekenäs, just off Route 186 towards Salo, is the dazzling canary-yellow **Svartå Manor** (Svartå Slott; May–Aug Tues–Sun 11am–5pm; €8), at Hållnäsvägen 89 in **Svartå** (Finnish: Mustio). The manor, once a *bruk*, was built in the late eighteenth century just as Rococo was being replaced by Neoclassical as the architectural style of the day. A handsome three-storey structure, surrounded by a lake and gardened grounds, it's now a **museum** displaying the personal effects of the Linder family, nobles who regularly entertained kings and tsars, with decor that is spot-on Gustavian. The forge's five workers' homes have been converted into rustic-chic ☂ **rooms** (☏019/36231, ⓦwww.mustionlinna.fi; ❼), some fairly run of the mill, some offering much more personality; try to book the Merlin's Tower, the forge's old transformer and now a captivating two-storey, terraced suite (€190 week/€230 weekends) with burnt-sienna walls and oak flooring. The manor's attached **restaurant**, *Slottskrogen*, in a grand old neo-Gothic brick coach house, serves modern-day hearty dishes such as venison with turnips and a yummy duck casserole that would awaken even the most ferric of miner's palates.

Hanko and around

Known to some daydreamers as the Finnish Riviera, **HANKO** (Swedish: Hangö) thrived in its heyday in the late 1800s as a trendy resort of spas and casinos that served the Grand Duchy's *beau monde* – or at least those lucky enough to escape Russia after the tsar banned foreign travel for Russians. Those with the means stayed and built portly two- and three-story neo-Renaissance estates, many of which still stand today and whose fairytale towers and gables call to mind something out of the Moomins. Hanko was also known for being the final point of departure for Finnish emigrants for the New World; some 250,000 passed through the town's harbour between 1880 and 1930. Today, with some 30km of beachfront and pretty, tree-lined streets, the town remains a popular destination for Finns on the hunt for Baltic sun and surf, especially during the annual **Regatta** (ⓦwww.hrw.fi) in early July, which has garnered something of a reputation for wild, all-night beach parties. Outside of high season, though, you'll have the place much to yourself.

Arrival, information and accommodation

The **bus and train stations** are a ten-minute walk from the **tourist office** at Raatihuoneentori 5 (June–Aug Mon–Fri 9am–5pm, Sat & Sun 10am–4pm; Sept–May Mon–Fri 9am–4pm; ☏019/220 3411, ⓦtourism.hanko.fi), which runs a number of guided organized **tours** in the summertime – including the fascinating Emigrant's Footsteps historical tour that visits the rock where many emigrants had a final dance before making the long journey to America – though not all are offered in English.

There is a decent variety of **places to stay** in town, including half a dozen villa properties, though only one really stands out – *Villa Maija* (see opposite). Hanko also has the largest number of **private accommodation** in Finland; enquire at the tourist office. If you're arriving during the Regatta, you'll definitely want to reserve in advance; at other times you should be able to show up to most places unannounced – though it never hurts to book ahead.

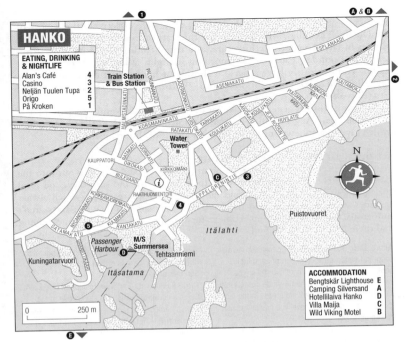

HANKO

EATING, DRINKING & NIGHTLIFE

Alan's Café	4
Casino	3
Neljän Tuulen Tupa	2
Origo	5
På Kroken	1

Train Station & Bus Station

Water Tower

Puistovuoret

Itälahti

KAUPPATORI

KIRKKOMÄKI

RAATIHUONEENTORI

Passenger Harbour

M/S Summersea

Tehtaanniemi

Kuningatarvuori

Itäsatama

0   250 m

ACCOMMODATION

Bengtskär Lighthouse	E
Camping Silversand	A
Hotellilaiva Hanko	D
Villa Maija	C
Wild Viking Motel	B

Bengtskär Lighthouse ☎02/466 7227, ⓦwww.bengtskar.fi. It doesn't get more off the beaten path than this: a towering brick lighthouse 25km off the Finnish coast, with windswept brush, jagged rocks and plenty of littoral charm. The several rustic rooms have been restored and furnished much to how they would have looked when the keeper's family lived here in the early 1900s. May–Sept only. ❹

Camping Silversand Lahdentie 1 ☎019/248 7540, ⓦwww.silversand.fi. The town's best camping option is set out 4km northeast of the centre in a wooded spot smack on the Baltic. They also have basic cottages (from €78) for six as well as more motel-like accommodation (❺/❹), and rent windsurfing equipment, rowboats, canoes and bicycles. Open year-round.

Hotellilaiva Hanko Itäsatama harbour ☎050/061 0113, ⓦwww.hotellilaivahanko.fi. This well-kept purpose-built hotel boat moored at the harbour wins the prize for most unique stay. The tiny, tidy rooms feature en-suite baths and flat-screen TVs. May–Oct only. ❸

Villa Maija Appelgrenintie 7 ☎050/505 2103, ⓦwww.villamaija.fi. This *fin-de-siècle* hotel is the best kept of all of the town's lace villas, and also one of the few spots open year-round. Set across three wooden buildings 100m from the beach, the charming rooms vary in shape, size, price and amenities, but most have quaint floral wallpaper and striped or checked duvets and pillowcases, and several have small terraces. ❺

Wild Viking Motel Lasitehtaankatu 6 ☎040/834 5091, ⓦwww.wildvikingmotel.fi. This quirky, Viking-themed place is a welcome respite from the pastel-is-precious nature of the town's villas. Yes, rooms are brown-beige with linoleum flooring, but at least they present some personality, with tiny radios built into the headboards and Viking headdresses adorning the walls, and the staff are fun. Breakfast €7. Open year-round. ❸

The Town

Hanko itself is handsome enough that you could easily spend much of your day just lazing about and taking in the town's numerous decorative **lace villas**, referred to locally as "the old ladies" on account of the Russian women's names bestowed upon them by their owners: originally built for the Russian aristocrats of the late nineteenth-century, they were effectively the dachas of the Duchy. The villas, which today line the seafront road **Appelgrenintie**, are studies in late Romantic architecture, and many feature wood-burning stoves and glass verandas that catch the morning sunlight. While most are in private hands, you can easily have a peek at those that have been turned into hotels, including villas *Doris* (no. 23), *Maija* (no. 7), *Tellina* (no. 2), *Thalatta* (no. 1) and *Eva* (Kaivokatu 2).

Otherwise, visitors generally make for the **water tower** (Vesitorni; daily June & July noon–6pm, Aug 1–3pm; €1), located immediately north of the tourist office, which gives great views out to the inlets and islets of the archipelago.

Eating, drinking and nightlife

As you'd expect from its setting – a pointy needle of land shooting out into the Baltic Sea – Hanko's **restaurants** tend to focus on fish and seafood; good local specialities include salmon soup and the archipelago smörgåsbord, which always includes smoked whitefish and Baltic herring in a variety of sauces. **Bars** aren't numerous, though in the summertime hang out around the beaches come evening and there'll be plenty going on.

Alan's Café Rådhustorget. This seaside bohemian soup-and-sandwich shop is part of an antique bookshop and handicrafts boutique. Take your coffee along with a great home-made dessert and kick back in the fresh maritime breeze in the large garden, reading that old novel you couldn't resist buying next door.

Casino Appelgrenintie 10. This large hall was the hub of Hanko social life a century ago and as such maintains a distinct air of past grandeur, serving popular traditional Finnish lunch buffets and à la carte dinners, sometimes with live music. No casino to speak of though, sadly.

Neljän Tuulen Tupa Pieni Mäntysaari, about 2km east of the harbour. Once a boisterous sailors' club during the Finnish prohibition era, this joint's impropriety so perturbed General Mannerheim (who lived next door) that he purchased it in 1926 and turned it into a dainty teahouse, which it has remained to this day. Jutting out onto the rocks alongside a small

sunning beach, it's perfect for afternoon pastries (the strawberry cake is divine) and coffee. Summer only.

Origo Satamakatu 7 Ⓦ www.restaurant-origo.com. Set in a converted waterside storehouse at the town's harbour, this terrace restaurant has a wildly popular fish buffet with fresh Baltic herring and salmon; the chef is a well-respected town foodie and is an adherent of the farm-to-plate dogma. Upstairs, *Bar Origo* has some great music nights and, for the linguistically inclined, occasional stand-up comics (who sometimes even do English-language sets).

På Kroken Hangonkylä harbour ☎ 040/358 1815. Owned and run by local fisherman Magnus Ekström, this excellent seafood restaurant is in Hanko's northern harbour a 2km walk from the centre. The fish and seafood dishes – grilled lobster or zander in white wine sauce, say – couldn't be fresher. Daily in summer; weekends only the rest of the year.

Trips to Bengtskär

From mid-June to late August the M/S *Summersea* departs Hanko's passenger harbour daily at 11am for the trip out to the 52m-high granite **Bengtskär** (€46 including lunch; Ⓦ www.marinelines.fi), Scandinavia's tallest **lighthouse**, 25km off Hanko on the outermost rocky islet of the archipelago. The 1906-built lighthouse sustained major damage during a vicious World War II skirmish with the Russians, and has now been renovated by a pair of charming local social historians. The tippity top of its 252-step tower gives some excellent views, and the current charming keepers keep a great café and several dainty rooms (June–Aug 10am–7pm; ⑦) in the main building, whose deep grey bricks and boxy shape lend it some real industrial-age flavour. You can also arrive by boat from Kasnäs and Rosala, in the far southwest of the Turku archipelago (see pp.138–139).

Lappohja: The Front Museum

Hanko was lucky enough to escape bombing during World War II, largely on account of its occupation by Soviet forces for several years. This history is attended to at the **Front Museum** (Rintamamuseo; late May to early Sept daily 11.30am–6.30pm; mid-Sept to late Sept Sat & Sun 11.30am–6.30pm; Ⓦ www.frontmuseum.fi), 19km out of town just off Route 25 in **Lappohja**; the Hanko–Ekenäs train stops nearby. The motley collection of artillery vehicles, communications equipment, besuited mannequins and wartime memorabilia gives visitors some insight into this stormy period for local residents.

East of Helsinki

East of Helsinki, the splintered lands that line the country's southeastern coast offer a string of handsome little towns that stretches all the way to the Russian border. This part of the Finnish seaboard sees few tourists as most people avoid a coastal detour on their way to the lakes or Karelia. And if you're looking for activity in the traditional sense, none of these destinations is necessarily going to blow your socks off – least of all in the colder months. But it's an intriguing area, especially if you hold any interest in military or maritime history, and definitely worth two or three days of travel – most of which will be by bus, since rail lines are almost nonexistent; if you can visit by car, you'll be able to cover much more ground.

Loviisa, the first settlement of note, is a great place to start exploring the collection of islands strewn about the coast. Beyond here is **Ruotsinpyhtää**, an old iron-forge town whose gorgeous wooden buildings make it one of the most atmospheric places hereabouts, and further on, **Pyhtää**, a good spot for catching a boat out to explore some remote islands or heading off into the woods on some invigorating hikes. The only community of significant size and importance between Helsinki and the Russian border is the shipping port of **Kotka**, site of the biggest naval defeat in Nordic history and, these days, a super-modern maritime centre. Lastly, the fortress town of **Hamina** is compelling for its Renaissance-inspired centre and a series of preserved ramparts.

For several centuries, these lands were playgrounds (and frequently cemeteries) for the Russian and Swedish militias – one bloody 1790 battle took the lives of some ten thousand soldiers and civilians – and at times the border dividing the two empires seems to have changed demarcation every couple of weeks. Even for modern Finns, the region definitely stirs memories: its proximity to the Soviet border means it saw countless battles during the Winter and Continuation wars in the last century.

Loviisa

Some 87km east of Helsinki, **LOVIISA** is a goods port and fishing village that became popular in the nineteenth century as a spa town, and whose population of 7500 is divided more or less into equal numbers of Finnish and Swedish speakers. Named after Lovisa Ulrika, the wife of Swedish King Adolf Frederik, this town of wooden homes and cobbled streets is today pleasantly free from crowds of Helsinki day-trippers, unlike nearby Porvoo (see p.101).

Arrival, information and accommodation

Buses arrive hourly from Helsinki (and from destinations further east) at the small **bus station**, a three-minute walk from the central *kauppatori* at Mannerheimintie. During July, the M/S *J.L. Runeberg* makes the six-hour **sail** between Helsinki and

Loviisa on Thursdays (€33 one way, €61 return including lunch buffet; Ⓦwww
.msjlruneberg.fi). The **tourist office** (Mon–Fri 9am–4pm, plus June–Aug Sat
10am–3pm; Ⓣ019/555 234, Ⓦwww.loviisa.fi) is at Mannerheiminkatu 4, near
the bus station. Loviisa is not a bad base for a **night** if you're headed further east,
the best option being *Hotel Degerby* (Ⓣ019/50561, Ⓦwww.degerby.com; ❹/❺),
a block away from the tourist office at Brandensteininkatu 17, with fifty largish
if somewhat bland rooms, and a decent restaurant (see p.119). Otherwise, try the
more affordable *Majatalo Loviisa* (Ⓣ040/835 7997, Ⓦwww.majatalolovisa.fi; ❸),
four blocks away at Sibeliuksenkatu 3, with a handful of tiny, cute rooms and a
small pool.

The Town

Dating from the eighteenth century, Loviisa was the first town in Finland to be
founded on strict Classical architectural principles – simple foundations, proportion
and symmetry. While most of the town's buildings visible today date from after the
fire in 1855 – the town was burnt to a crisp during the Crimean War – a few **Old
Town** buildings survived, most notably along the streets of Linnankuja, Mariankatu
and Aleksanterinkatu, which now house artisan ateliers, and the *Degerby Gille* (see
p.119). Just north of the main square, a row of prettily preserved houses points the
way east towards the Rosen and Ungern **bastion ruins** and the **Town Museum**,
Puistokatu 2 (Loviisan kaupungin museo; May–Aug Tues–Fri 11am–5pm, Sat &
Sun 11am–4pm; Sept–April Tues–Fri & Sun noon–4pm; €4), once home to the
local officer in charge. It contains a fine stock of Gustavian furniture, Romantic
postcards and other items from Loviisa's nineteenth-century heyday, as well as a
display on Jean Sibelius, who summered here as a child (an annual **music festival** in
mid-June commemorates this relationship; for information contact Ⓣ044/055
5499 or Ⓔsirpa.flinck@loviisa.fi).

A few minutes' walk south of the town centre is the town's marina, **Laivasilta**,
where a cobblestone row of old log-cabin salt granaries houses the town's
Maritime Museum (Loviisan Merenkulkumuseo; mid-May to Aug Tues–Sun
10am–6pm; €3), a modest collection of model ships, seamen's chests and maritime
paraphernalia. After the town's founding in 1745, its shipyards built some two
hundred sailing ships that exported (mostly) timber to – and imported salt from
– various ports around the Mediterranean and Portugal. Outside is moored the
recently rebuilt **Österstjernan** (Ⓦwww.osterstjernan.fi), a replica nineteenth-
century sailing ship that once functioned as a regular passenger and cargo vessel
plying between Loviisa and Stockholm.

Svartholm Fortress

Set out 10km at the mouth of the Loviisa bay is the **Svartholm Fortress**
(Svartholman merilinnoitus), constructed in the 1750s by the Swedes to (again)
beef up Finland's eastern frontier following the redefinition of the border with
Russia at the Treaty of Åbo. In the event, Svartholm was handed over to the
Russians shortly thereafter, and the majority of island residents ended up
consisting of Finnish petty-crime convicts and Russian political prisoners. The
fortress, which had hitherto never seen any real action, was fire-bombed and
heavily damaged by the English during the Crimean War but it's since been
(partially) restored and it's possible to walk around an intact section of walls and
view a small exhibition on its history. The site can be visited on English-
language **guided tours** (on request; €5; enquire at the museum shop), and
there's also a **restaurant**. Svartholm can be accessed via daily summertime ferries
from Laivasilta marina (June to mid-Aug 10am, noon & 2pm; €10; Ⓦwww
.saaristolinja.com); it's a 45-minute journey.

Nuclear power in Finland

Some 13km off Loviisa's bay towers a sight that can turn the stomach of many who value Finland's intimate relationship with Mother Nature: the oldest of the country's nuclear power plants. Finland's Cold War balancing act between East and West led to the country purchasing its nuclear hardware – unconventionally – from both power blocs: these two towers spent several decades producing plutonium for (allegedly) Soviet nuclear weapons, with the plant's run-off nuclear waste exported to Russia for disposal – a practice now illegal. The country's other trio of Western-backed plants were built on Olkiluoto island off the coast of Rauma. At the centre of the power debate these days is the construction of a fifth nuclear reactor, **Olkiluoto 3** – Europe's first in fifteen years and the world's most powerful to date – which, after years of delays and budgetary overruns is scheduled to be up and running by 2012.

Finland as a nation is divided over the merits of nuclear power, a debate stirred up in 2009 when Finland's economy minister declared that the country might require a sixth reactor by 2020 (a survey in 2008 showed that 34 percent of Finns would approve such a project). With demand for electricity growing at a rate faster than in other Nordic countries, Finland currently derives around 25 percent of its energy needs from nuclear power, importing nearly everything else – a constraint that is threatening both its energy independence and economic balance.

Eating

Styrbord, the **restaurant** at the *Hotel Degerby*, serves tasty Finnish meals such as trumpet chanterelle soup (€7), grilled arctic char (€21) and a big fat pepper steak (€33), though much more atmospheric for a meal is the *Degerby Gille*, Sepänkuja 4, the town's oldest building and its most important historical sight. Originally a large cavalry estate, the *Gille* later served as a home for nobles, a hospital, a school and, for most of the twentieth century, a private gentleman's club. While it's generally only open to group reservations, enquire at the reception of the *Hotel Degerby* whether one of their public dining events is on, as they do tasty smoked salmon and reindeer filets (€21) and the wonderfully maintained collection of pastel sitting rooms are well worth a gander. For **drinks**, try *Aleksi*, a new pub on Aleksanterinkatu, just around the corner from the *Hotel Degerby*.

Ruotsinpyhtää and Pyhtää

Venture east of Loviisa – regular, reliable buses serve most towns – and you'll find that things get very rural very fast, with a handful of the tinier settlements along the coast and just inland well worth a day or two of exploration.

Ruotsinpyhtää

The colourful former iron-forging settlement of **RUOTSINPYHTÄÄ**, some 20km on from Loviisa, is an enjoyable retreat for a summer's day. The village's name dates back to the Treaty of Åbo of 1743, which bisected the town of Pyhtää – the eastern half going to Russia (see p.305), the western to Sweden and thus being renamed (unimaginatively) "Swedish Pyhtää". The village, which is set along the banks of the barely flowing Kymijoki River, had already been churning out bar iron for several decades when the split occurred, and its main attraction remains the fire-engine-red **ironworks** (Strömfors; June to mid-Aug 10am–6pm), which dates from 1711 and functioned as a nail forge until 1950. The cottage buildings and brick factories, surrounded by lovely thick foliage, are now home to a fair number of artisans and craftspeople who carve out a livelihood here and draw a good number of visitors in the summertime, providing the otherwise daisy-pushing town with some animation. The main surviving building is a red-brick water-powered forge, with the sawmill next door dating from 1887 and two dozen other forge buildings from the same era. During the summer there are demonstrations of carpet weaving, jewellery making and painting – though beware that the town effectively shuts down in the off season. While here, take a moment to visit the oddly octagonal-shaped **wooden church** (mid-June to mid-Aug daily 11am–6pm), built in the early 1770s, to admire the beautiful Resurrection altarpiece, designed by Helene Schjerfbeck in 1898.

Ruotsinpyhtää is accessible by **bus** from Loviisa. The local **information centre** (June–Aug daily 8am–4pm; ☏044/363 6616, ⓦwww.ruotsinpyhtaa.fi) is housed within a café on the bridge over the inlet that once divided the two feuding empires. To spend a night in town is to experience Finland's oldest clay-walled building, built in 1805 as a boarding house for mill workers and now one of its most atmospheric **hostels**, ⚐ *Krouvinmäki* (☏050/586 7215; dorms €30, ❸), with eight old-fashioned rooms, a common kitchen and shared bathrooms. There's great local **food** to be had at *Ruukinmylly*, Ruukintie 15, and come mid-June, the town is the site of one of the better **bluegrass festivals** in Finland, the well-named Rootsinpyhtaa (ⓦwww.rootsinpyhtaa.fi).

Pyhtää and Kaunissaari

Twenty minutes by bus further east from Ruotsinpyhtää is the original village of **PYHTÄÄ**, a good deal less captivating but offering access to some delightful islands that make up the archipelagic coastline. Ferry services depart the quay during the summer to the nearby islands, including **Kaunissaari**, a small island of four square kilometres, from which you can connect with an evening motorboat straight on to Kotka (see box below). Kaunissaari is home to a quiet and well-preserved fishing port with a lone lighthouse from the 1880s on its northern shore, and a sheltered marina on its southern tip; and the island's southern coast also features a collection of fenced-in plots, gardens, landing stages and boat sheds, with diversions that include a small beach, cemetery, watchtower, art gallery, shop, decent **museum** (daily June–Sept 9am–8pm; €5.50) and nature information hut (June–Aug daily 10am–6pm), with brochures on the **Eastern Gulf of Finland National Park** archipelago, of which the island is part. There's even an **inn** to hole up in for the night, the *Metsäranta* (☏05/215 467; ❷), as well as a **restaurant** – though you're best off buying fresh smoked fish from the seaside storehouses. The municipality office in Pyhtää at Siltakyläntie 175 can provide limited **tourist information** (Mon–Fri 8am–3.45pm; ☏020/721 1600, ⓦwww.pyhtaa.fi).

Kotka and around

After the smattering of tiny communities that run east of Porvoo, **KOTKA**, built on an island extending into the Gulf of Finland about 130km east of Helsinki, feels

---

Boats to Kaunissaari

Small boats to Kaunissaari depart **Pyhtää** (late June–Aug Wed & Sun 10am; €10 one way, €17 return) from a small jetty 500m west of the town centre along the Siltakylänjoki River. The trip takes two and a half hours, departing the island for the return journey at 3.30pm. There is also regular transport (€8) between **Kotka** and Kaunissaari between June and August several times a day most days of the week; many visitors choose to arrive from **Pyhtää** on the early boat, spend the day exploring the island, then continue on to Kotka on the last boat, usually leaving the island at either 6 or 7pm.

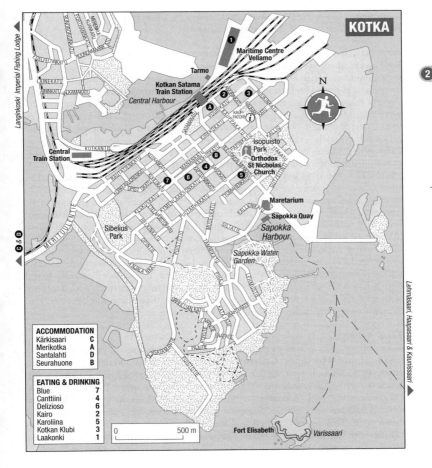

ACCOMMODATION

Kärkisaari	C
Merikotka	A
Santalahti	D
Seurahuone	B

EATING & DRINKING

Blue	7
Canttiini	4
Delizioso	6
Kairo	2
Karoliina	5
Kotkan Klubi	3
Laakonki	1

0   500 m

positively immense. Named after the white-tailed eagles (*merikotka* in Finnish) that once nested here, Kotka's tumultuous past reflects its proximity to the sea. Numerous battles have been fought off its shores, among them the Sweden–Russia confrontation of 1790, the largest military engagement ever seen in Nordic waters, in which nearly ten thousand soldiers and civilians lost their lives, and an incursion during the Crimean War, when the British fleet effectively reduced Kotka to rubble. More recently, though, water has been fundamental to the town's prosperity: Kotka was one of the largest centres in Finland for paper-making thanks to the once-thrashing Kymi River, which served as a power source and portage trail for timber during the last century, and the delta's deep-water harbour made it into an ideal transit point for cargo – and the country's largest export port. In 1949, Alvar Aalto designed the red brick buildings of the massive Ahlström Sunila paper mill at the mouth of the Kymi that dominates views of Kotka; wunderkind and polymath that he was, he also designed many of the company's glass objects. Today the town is a super destination for its many maritime activities, though you're probably not going to need much more than a day here – unless you're tempted by a fishing or rafting tour of the Kymi, for which you should tack on an extra day.

Arrival, information and accommodation

Rail and road connections from the mainland (you must change trains in Kouvala if coming from Helsinki) bring you right into Kotka's compact centre. It's best to disembark at the second, terminus station at the harbour (Kotkan Satama), as it is slightly more proximate to the city centre and to the **tourist office** (late June to early Aug Mon–Fri 9am–6pm, Sun 10am–2pm; early Aug to late June Mon–Fri 9am–5pm; ☏05/234 4424, ⓦwww.kotka.fi), Keskuskatu 6, which will fill you in on local bus details – essential for continuing around the southeast.

If you're planning on **staying overnight** here, there are only two options in the centre of town, the best of which is the chain standby *Seurahuone*, Keskuskatu 21 (☏020/123 4666, ⓦwww.sokoshotels.fi; ❹/❻), with spacious if predictable rooms. Somewhat simpler is the pleasant *Merikotka*, Satamakatu 9 (☏05/215 222, ⓦwww.hotellimerikotka.fi; ❹), which offers bright, well-decorated rooms. If neither of these suit, head 5km south of Kotka to the seaside town of **Mussalo** (bus #13 and #27), where you'll find a personable guesthouse, *Kärkisaari* (☏05/260 4804, ⓦwww.villakarkisaari.com; mid-May to mid-Sept; ❸), overlooking a spectacular bay. The rooms here are comfortable enough, though the 1970s decor may grate on some. There is also a more modern beachside holiday village, *Santalahti* (☏05/260 5055, ⓦwww.santalahti.fi; late April to early Oct), with a very well outfitted, five-star **camping** ground in a beautiful wooded setting with a beach just a few metres away. Their cabins (€66) have kitchenettes; the cheapest ones share bathroom facilities with the campsite.

The Town

Kotka offers a few places to help while away an afternoon, the most obvious of which is the **Maritime Centre Vellamo** (Merikeskus Vellamo; Tues–Sun 10am–6pm, Wed till 8pm; €8 for access to all museums, Wed eves free admission; ⓦwww.merikeskusvellamo.fi), Tornatorintie 99A at the port. It's held within a gorgeous, ultra modern triangular building, worth a look in itself, which feels more than a tad out of place alongside the greasy transport cranes that front the cargo port. This prized cultural and historical centre was opened in 2008 and contains the **Maritime Museum of Finland** (Suomen Merimuseo), presenting an excellently curated overview of Finnish maritime history and underwater archeology. The collection's maps, drawings, photographs, manuscripts and sundry marine paraphernalia successfully communicate the nation's profound historical dependence on sea trade and commerce – particularly during the brutal Finnish winters. In the same complex is the moderately less interesting **Kymenlaakso Provincial Museum** (Kymenlaakson Museo), where you'll learn a bit about Kotkan history through a hotchpotch of weapons, ropes and spyglasses found on a sunken Russian frigate off the coast. Parked just out behind the building is the **Tarmo**, the oldest intact and functioning icebreaker in the world, built in England in 1907, every bit of which you can explore, from bridge to engine room.

After Vellamo, Kotka's **Maretarium** (daily: mid-May to mid-Aug 10am–8pm; mid-Aug to mid-May 10am–5pm; €10.50; ⓦwww.maretarium.fi), Sapokankatu 2, is markedly less spectacular, though interesting for its fifty indigenous fish species across 22 different aquariums. The town is also notable for its eighteenth-century **Orthodox Church of St Nicholas** (Pyhän Nikolaoksen ortodoksinen kirkko; June–Aug Tues–Fri noon–3pm, Sat & Sun noon–6pm), a sizeable structure which has been kept in pristine condition after surviving the British bombardment – it is easily the most astounding example of Russian Neoclassicism in Finland. Designed by a Russian architect in 1801, the interior exhibits floral embellishments and a number of well-preserved icons, including the exquisite image of *St Nicholas on Kotka Island*, gilded and brooding in the afternoon ruska light.

During the summer, there is regular **boat** service from Kotka's Sapokka quay to several islands just off the coast, whose imposing cliffs and brackish waters make them havens for families of migratory water birds. These include the **Varissaari**, site in 1790 of the largest naval battle in northern Europe and now holding the ruins of Fort Elisabeth (Ruotsinsalmi); **Lehmäsaari**, offering a beckoning beach and ambling paths; **Haapasaari**, with a shop, church and nature information point; and **Kaunissaari** (see p.120).

Eating and drinking

Grumbling stomachs at lunchtime can be easily sated at *Kotkan Klubi*, Kirkkokatu 2, which has an excellent lunchtime buffet (€11.50). Otherwise, try the town's newest food offering, *Laakonki*, a great **café–restaurant** inside the Maritime Centre Vellamo which does a more ample two-course salad-bar lunch for €8.50. Elsewhere is *Delizioso*, Keskuskatu 29, a Slow-Food Italian place and *Canttiini*, Kaivokatu 15, a surprisingly well-run Tex-Mex restaurant that also serves up Finnish dishes, pastas and steaks; specialities include mixed fajitas (€17), pork chipotle (€15) and reindeer pasta (€10.90). Although Kotka is no longer popular with drunken sailors due to shorter onshore times, there is still a lively **bar** scene – try the music bar *Blue*, Kotkankatu 9, the maritime-themed *Kairo*, Satamakatu 7, or the Irish watering hole *Karoliina*, Puutarhakatu 1.

Langinkoski Imperial Fishing Lodge

The Kymijoki is one of Finland's largest rivers and one of its best for salmon, sea trout and whitefish fishing. Kotka holds three of the river's five estuaries, Siikakoski, Korkeakoski and Langinkoski, the last of which is presided over by a

▲ Fishing at Langinkoski Imperial Lodge

devil of a fishing lodge, **Langinkoski** (May daily 10am–4pm; June–Aug daily 10am–6pm; Sept & Oct Sat & Sun 10am–4pm; €5; Ⓦwww.langinkoskimuseo .com), about 5km north of the town centre (bus #12). Here, Tsar Alexander III would relax while in transit between Helsinki and St Petersburg, foraging for wood or fishing for salmon while his Danish-born wife would prepare food for him and their children. The simply built Swiss-style wooden building, set deep in the woods right by the fast-flowing Kymi River, was a gift to the tsar from the Finnish government and is the only surviving structure outside of Russia once owned by the Imperium. All the rooms – from the well-stocked kitchen to the Empress's dressing room upstairs – are kept more or less as they were a century ago, with their original (often Finnish-made) furnishings, fittings and house-wares, the most notable of which are the axe used by the tsar for chopping wood and the royal waffle iron, which emblazoned tsar family breakfasts with the two-headed eagle, emblem of the Russian Empire. To try your hand at **fly-fishing** – pike and asp fish are easiest to catch – contact Fishventures (Ⓣ050/354 8595, Ⓦwww.fishventures.fi), who run full-day tours from April to October for up to five people starting at €400, including licences, equipment and a guide. They also do year-round **rafting tours** along the Kymijoki starting at €420; rafts take up to nine people.

Hamina

Twenty-six kilometres east of Kotka is **HAMINA**, the easternmost port in the mainland EU and a compelling place to visit thanks to its Renaissance fortress bastions. Originally founded by Per Brahe in 1653 as Vekhalahti, the town has been a busy node of overland and waterway trade routes since the Middle Ages but is today best known for its magnificently bizarre town plan: eight inter-secting streets that radiate outwards towards the town ramparts, forming a perfect octagon encircling the central Raatihuoneentori, or town hall square. The centre of Hamina was constructed this way to allow the incumbent Swedish forces to withstand attack – the town being the site of many Swedish–Russian battles.

Arrival, information and accommodation

Buses to Hamina arrive a few blocks west of the *kauppatori* on Rautatienkatu. Additionally, buses from Helsinki to Viipuri, the formerly Finnish town now on the Russian side of the border (see p.183), pass through Hamina several times a day; check details at the tourist office. Hamina's **tourist office**, Raatihuoneentori 16 (Mon–Fri 9am–4pm; Ⓣ05/749 2641, Ⓦwww.hamina.fi), hands out informa-tion on walking tours and sea cruises and can also assist with **accommodation** in a pinch. If you're hoping to spend the night, there are only a handful of options in the town centre, plushest of which is the hundred-year-old, just-renovated *Haminan Seurahuone*, Pikkuympyräkatu 5 (Ⓣ05/350 0263; ❺), with sparkling rooms and a good weekday lunch buffet at its restaurant, *Cactus*. Even if you're not staying here, do have a peek into the upstairs Marski Room, which presents a series of wall paintings by Tove Jansson, author of the Moomin books, depicting historic Hamina. A step down in price is the central *Best Western Hamina*, Sibeliuskatu 32 (Ⓣ05/353 5555, Ⓦwww.hotellihamina.fi; ❹), whose three dozen rooms are fairly run of the mill but offer pleasant views to the sea. Cheapest of all – and most atmospheric – is the *Pormestarintalon Pihakammari* (Ⓣ044/056 8332; ❹), Manner-heimintie 7, an idyllic room for two set around a courtyard with Empire-style decor, a wrought-iron bed and a small veranda; the name translates as "Mayor's Little Chamber".

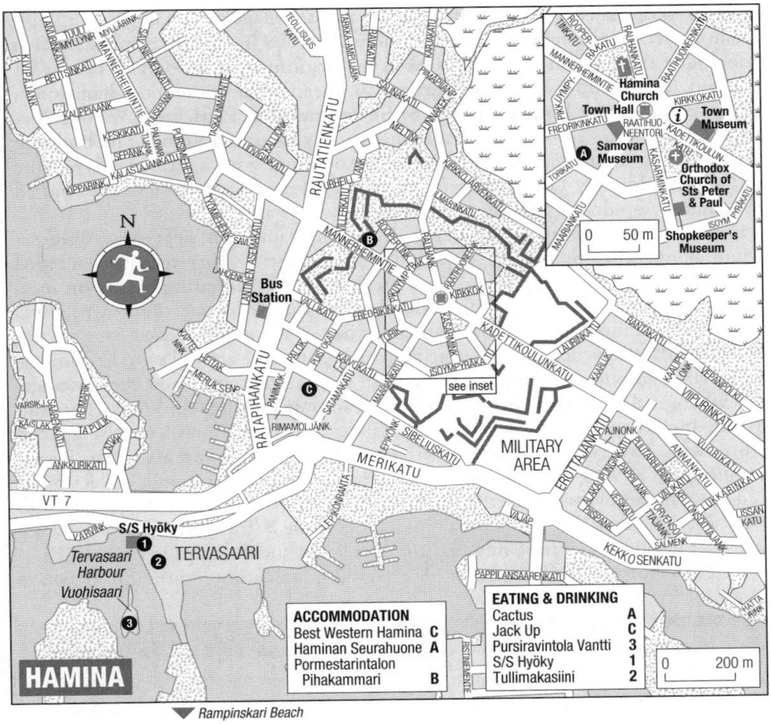
HAMINA
Hamina Church
Town Hall
Town Museum
Samovar Museum
Orthodox Church of Sts Peter & Paul
Shopkeeper's Museum
0 50 m
Bus Station
see inset
MILITARY AREA
TERVASAARI
S/S Hyöky
Tervasaari Harbour
Vuohisaari
RAUTATIENKATU
MANNERHEIMINTIE
KADETTIKOULUNKATU
MERIKATU
SIBELIUSKATU
RATAPIHANKATU
KEKKOSENKATU
VIIPURINKATU
VT 7
ACCOMMODATION
Best Western Hamina C
Haminan Seurahuone A
Pormestarintalon Pihakammari B
EATING & DRINKING
Cactus A
Jack Up C
Pursiravintola Vantti 3
S/S Hyöky 1
Tullimakasiini 2
0 200 m
Rampinskari Beach

The Town

The **fortress** – one of a half-dozen such concentric defensive constructions in Europe – was based on a sixteenth-century Renaissance design, with two squares aligned symmetrically so as to form a star-shaped blockhouse, the corners of each square forming the six bastions, each of which is named after a Finnish town. You can still amble around the base of the original defending wall, preserved and restored in various parts, or follow the **Rampart Trail** (pick up the free historical guide *Walking in Old Hamina* from the tourist office, then follow signs to the "bastoni"), a signposted route following 4.5km of fortress and garrison walls around Hamina's centre. The central bastion, or **keskusbastioni**, was constructed in the early nineteenth century with 58 masoned casemates intended to serve as bombproof quarters, though in the end they mostly functioned as a store for provisions and weapons. The vaulting has been recently reinforced and the bastions are now employed as a regular events venue for horse festivals, concerts, exhibitions and private parties (Ⓦ www.haminabastioni.fi) – "Europe's largest canopy" is one superlative locals seem to enjoy throwing around.

Elsewhere in Hamina are a number of old **wooden buildings**, churches of various styles and the stone homes of wealthy nineteenth-century merchants, all of which remain in quite good nick. Smack dab at the centre of the concentric circles is Hamina's Baroque-meets-Neoclassical German-designed **town hall**. After various tenures as a bank, shop, jail, constabulary and guard post, the building now houses municipal administration offices; an hourly chime emanates from the bell tower perched atop. Immediately north of here is

Engel's Neoclassical **town church**, built in the image of a Greek temple; a memorial cornerstone here commemorates the 1809 Treaty of Hamina, which concluded the Finnish War and marked the beginning of the Grand Duchy of Finland. To the south side of the town hall, meanwhile, is the more handsome, peach-coloured **Orthodox Church of St Peter and St Paul**, an 1837 construction with a detached bell tower and Russian-styled onion dome. The building represents an interesting take on Neoclassical design with a series of Byzantine influences added by Louis Visconti, the Italian-French architect who designed the famous sepulchral monument to Napoleon in Paris.

Hamina's **town museum** (June–Aug Tues–Sun 10am–4pm; Sept–May Wed–Sat 11am–3pm, Sun noon–5pm; €2), Kadettikoulunkatu 2, has recently emerged from a thorough renovation and now presents a few interesting rooms on local history. Originally built in 1760, the building has a noble history of its own: it was once used as a meeting point for Catherine the Great and her second cousin King Gustavus III of Sweden in 1783, during which Catherine arrived with her notoriously large entourage, filling the town with unexpected pomp and circumstance. Elsewhere is the **Shopkeeper's Museum**, Kasarminkatu 6 (June–Aug Tues–Sun 10am–4pm; Sept–May Wed–Sat 11am–3pm, Sun noon–5pm), once a general store owned by a Finno-Russian merchant, and the **Samovar Museum**, Raatihuoneentori 8 (Wed–Sat 11am–3pm, Sun 11am–5pm; €5), housing a collection of old Russian samovars and Orthodox religious artefacts, some of which date from the 1700s. Moored out in Hamina's small port is the **S/S Hyöky** (Ⓦ www.hyoky .net), a café and museum selling maritime artefacts, such as ships in a bottle. Built in St Petersburg in 1912, the ship once served as a floating lighthouse. If you're

Finland's Russian frontier

The 1340km-long Finnish–Russian border maunders its way from Virolahti in the southerly reaches of the country snaking its way through bogs, meadows and birch forests, and around the shores of umpteen lakes, rivers and waterways, before hurtling up to the tundra plains of Muotkavaara in northern Lapland. For centuries, the border between Finland and Russia was drawn and redrawn – often willy-nilly – by various international treaties, peaces and agreements. The borderlands were kept fortified and heavily guarded, with zero tolerance for contact between people residing on either side – even if they may have lived within shouting distance of each other. During the Cold War, this border was emblematic of West–East relations, and marked the widest economic-prosperity gap between two bordering nations of anywhere in the world.

Today, things have changed, and cross-border trade between Finland and Russia is flourishing. In 2007, one million lorries (to say nothing of Russian tourists) made the journey across the Vaalimaa–Torfjanovka border post alone, transporting raw timber and wood products, construction materials, farm machinery and consumer goods – a third of which were transported to Finnish sea ports and destined for export to other countries. Russia makes such regular use of the Finland crossing because the Baltic harbours that line St Petersburg have remained ill-equipped to deploy, receive and store goods.

The physical boundary, while still patrolled, is but a thin strip of land resting between naturally placed stones and man-made poles, with thirteen official permanent crossings between the two countries. Because it delimits the Schengen area, controlling the land border is considered a matter of pan-European security, which explains the presence of three thousand Finnish border guards – along with the assistance of aeroplanes, helicopters, SUVs, camera, radar, boat tracking systems and a fleet of trained skiing canines.

interested in **swimming**, make for the small **Rampsinkari beach**, located at the southern tip of Tervasaari, 1km southwest of the centre.

Eating and drinking

Apart from *Cactus* (see p.124), Hamina's best **food** options are down by the Tervasaari harbour: *Tullimakasiini* serves good Finnish lunches (May–Sept) in what was once the town's toll house, while *Pursiravintola Vantti* is a great seafood restaurant set on tiny Vuohisaari island 50m from the harbour, accessible via a small shuttle ferry. For something quicker, try the café on board the *S/S Hyöky* (see p.126). In the summer, try any of the town's terrace **pubs**, the best of which is *Jack Up*, Sibeliuskatu 32, offering a remarkably good selection of beers.

Virolahti and the Salpalinjan bunkers

Finland's most southeastern municipality, **Virolahti**, is a densely wooded area that makes up the last Finnish stretch of the King's Road. For two centuries, the quarries that line the shores of the Virolahti bay provided granite for canals, bridges, roads and buildings in St Petersburg. The region's main town of **Virojoki**, located 31km east of Hamina is on a popular migratory route for black woodpeckers, goosanders and Caspian terns, and is thus a popular stop for twitterers – but the real reason to visit is to see the museums of the **Salpalinjan bunkers**, a massive line of World War II defensive fortifications along the Finnish–Russian border built to defend Finland's eastern border from Soviet attack. The 1200km-long defence consists of 3000 wooden field fortifications, 728 massive reinforced concrete bunkers and scores of anti-tank barricades stretching from the Gulf of Finland along the eastern Finnish border up to Savuksoski, northeast of Rovaniemi, then continuing in a fortified line all the way to the Arctic Ocean. Built by some 35,000 men (and 2000 female members of Finland's auxiliary defence services, the Salpalinja (Salpa Line; Ⓦwww .salpakeskus.fi) was never actually employed in battle, but it was the most comprehensive defence line of any single country during the war, greatly boosted Finnish morale and may have influenced Stalin's decision to cease the barrage of attacks on the Finnish front. The region has two points of historical interest related to the line: several well-indicated miles west of Virojoki along Route 7 is the **Bunker Museum** (daily June–Aug 10am–6pm; €4), where military enthusiasts are eager to show off the outdoor base fortifications, bunkers' nooks and crannies, anti-tank obstacles and trenches and lead visitors to the seats of ageing stationary guns. Twelve kilometres north in **Miehikkälä** is the **Salpa Line Museum** (Salpakeskus; same hours and price), a more comprehensive indoor affair, with some interesting displays as well as several short films on the trials and tribulations of constructing the line.

For an overnight sojourn in these parts, you might as well go all out and stay as close to Russia as you possibly can without actually crossing the border. The collection of creaky **cabins** at ⚒ *Hurpun Tila*, Hurpuntie 362A (Ⓣ040/701 8056, Ⓦwww.hurpuntila.fi; from €30), reached by taking the road leaving Virojoki to the south, offers the opportunity to rent rowing boats for a comradely paddle out to Russo–Finnish No Man's Land. Otherwise, the modern Vaalimaa Shopping Centre, which will consist of several dozen shops, a day spa and a hotel, is due to open in 2011.

Travel details

Train

Ekenäs to: Hanko (hourly; 30min); Helsinki (hourly; 1hr 20min–1hr 50min).
Hanko to: Ekenäs (hourly; 30min); Helsinki (hourly; 2hr).
Kotka to: Helsinki (6 daily; 2hr 20min–3hr); Kouvola (6 daily; 45min).

Bus

Ekenäs to: Degerby (1 daily; 15min); Fiskars (12 daily; 45min); Ingå (8 daily; 55min); Lohja (6 daily; 55min–1hr 35min); Snappertuna (4 daily; 35min); Svartå (7 daily; 40min–1hr).
Fiskars to: Ekenäs (12 daily; 45min); Ingå (4 daily; 50min); Helsinki (7 daily; 1hr 50min–3hr).
Hanko to: Ekenäs (hourly; 40min); Helsinki (10 daily; 2hr 5min–3hr 20min).

Ingå to: Degerby (1 daily; 15min).
Kotka to: Hamina (hourly; 35min); Helsinki (frequent; 2hr–3hr 10min); Kouvola (3–10 daily; 1hr 10min); Pyhtää (frequent; 25–40min); Virojoki (11 daily; 1hr 20min–2hr 5min).
Lohja to: Ekenäs (6 daily; 55min–1hr 35min); Helsinki (frequent; 1hr 5min–2hr), Ingå (3 daily; 40–50min) Svartå (hourly; 20–30min).
Loviisa to: Helsinki (1hr 30min–2hr 15min); Kotka (frequent; 45min–1hr); Porvoo (frequent; 35–55min); Pyhtää (frequent; 15min); Ruotsinpyhtää (3–6 daily; 15–30min); Virojoki (10 daily; 1hr 35min–2hr 30min).
Pyhtää to: Helsinki (6–13 daily; 2hr–2hr 45min); Loviisa (frequent; 15min); Ruotsinpyhtää (1 daily; 15min).
Virojoki to: Helsinki (8 daily; 3hr 10min–4hr 35min).

3

The southwest

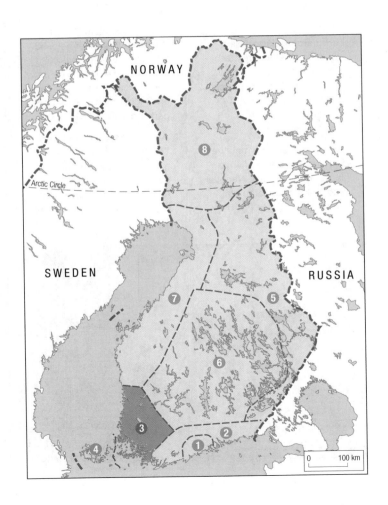

CHAPTER 3 # Highlights

✳ **Aboa Vetus Ars Nova, Turku** The cultural capital of Swedish-speaking Finland is home to this gem of a museum, guaranteed to pique the interest of kids of all ages. See p.136

✳ **Turku archipelago** This lush – and well-connected – collection of islands and coastal headlands is perfect for experiencing Finland's many maritime charms. See pp.138–139

✳ **Naantali** Best known as the summertime home of Tove Jansson's Moomins, Naantali also holds a winsome old town. See pp.142–146

✳ **Old Rauma** Finland's finest wooden structures are the six hundred soft-hued Renaissance homes on view in this lovely old town, a few minutes from the coast. See pp.148–149

✳ **Pori jazz festival** One of Scandinavia's most beloved (and most visited) music festivals is set on the banks of this riverside town: nine days and nights of jazz, rock and partying. See p.151

✳ **Juselius Mausoleum, Pori** This moving memorial to a little girl's life, with half a dozen mammoth frescos by Akseli Gallen-Kallela, is just a short walk from Pori's centre. See p.154

▲ Aboa Vetus Ars Nova, Turku

The southwest

Venture west for a few hours through the endless stretches of forest and lakes that characterize Finland's bread basket and you'll eventually arrive in the delightful southwestern pocket of the country. The jagged shoreline here is made up of thousands of islands and inlets, with a spectacular archipelago stretching halfway to Sweden. Many of the coastline's welcoming, easy-going towns meanwhile are home to distinctive Finnish-Swedish coastal communities, and offer more than their share of rural charm among quiet streets.

Finland's **southwest** has always been heavily dominated by **Turku**, the country's oldest city. Today it's also one of its most vivacious, offering genuinely absorbing museums and churches, an intact medieval castle and a crackerjack of a cultural scene abetted, in part, by two large universities and a strong and proud Swedish-speaking population. A quick bus-ride away is **Naantali**, home to a theme park based around Tove Jansson's Moomin characters and a strip of pretty nineteenth-century homes, while a short boat-ride away is one of Finland's most enjoyable **archipelagos**, perfect for some day- or weekend-tripping by bike. North of Turku, the towns turn Finnish-speaking again: first on is the waterside hamlet of **Uusikaupunki**, which despite its epithet ("New Town") is seriously old and seriously sleepy. A bit further north is laconic **Rauma**, whose traditions of lace making are well maintained among the old town's six hundred UNESCO-protected wooden buildings, few of which have changed an inch in centuries. And lastly, agreeable **Pori**, another short ride up the coast and best known today for its annual jazz festival, which draws big names and even bigger numbers of visitors who come to stomp their feet and tap their fingers against their beers late into the night.

Although transport between Helsinki and Turku is made quick and easy thanks to fast, regular **train** connections, there's little coastal railway to speak of. **Bus** connections, however, are rather good, both to the major towns and smaller settlements in the region, and there's a good transport network further out to the archipelago.

Turku and around

As Finland's oldest city, its capital for a brief time and with the vaunted accolade of European Capital of Culture for 2011, the inhabitants of **TURKU** (or **Åbo** as it's known in Swedish) have plenty of reason to be proud of their modestly sized city. Turku ruled as Finland's principal city when the country was a Swedish province, losing its status to Helsinki in 1812 when Alexander I decided that it was too closely aligned with Sweden and too far from Russia to serve as an effective capital of the Grand Duchy. Most of its buildings were lost in a ferocious fire fifteen years hence, following which the city was reconfigured and rebuilt by Finland's favourite architect,

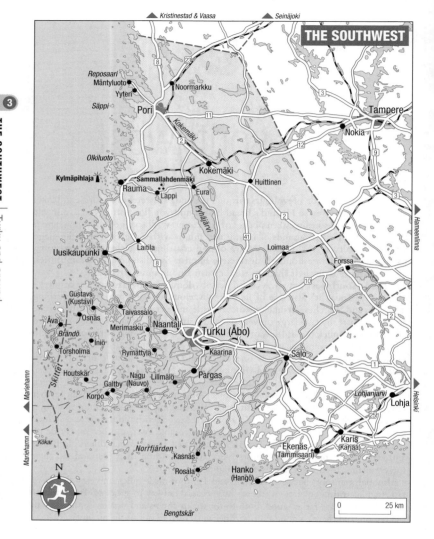

Carl Ludvig Engel. These days Turku is easy to navigate and highly sociable, and thanks to the boom years under Swedish rule and the students from its two universities – many of them Swedish-speaking – it's bristling with history and culture. You'll just about be able to take in everything worth seeing in a day, although two days is more sensible if you want to have energy left for Turku's sparkling nightlife.

Arrival and information

Frequent, fast trains from Helsinki arrive at the **train station**, from which it's a five-minute walk downhill to the city centre; direct buses from Rauma and Pori arrive at the **bus station** a few blocks east. Turku's **harbour**, which receives regular passenger ferries from its archipelago, as well as daily cruise ships from Åland and Sweden, lies 3km from the city centre. Bus #1 covers the route frequently, as do trains timed to meet most ferry arrivals at a small harbour depot (*satama* in Finnish). The *Ukkopekka* **steamer** from nearby Naantali, meanwhile, arrives at a dock along the Aura River by Martinsilta bridge.

You'll find the **tourist office** at Aurakatu 4 close to the river (April–Sept Mon–Fri 8.30am–6pm, Sat & Sun 9am–4pm; Oct–March Mon–Fri 8.30am–6pm; ☎02/262 7444, ⓦ www.turku.fi); it stocks plenty of maps and leaflets, and also rents 7-speed **bicycles** (€15 per day). They also sell the **Turku Card** (1-day €21, 2-day €28), which offers free entry to nearly every museum in the city, as well as free rides on city transport and on most guided bus **tours**. Enquire at the tourist office too about all-inclusive tours to Moominworld (see p.145) on the wonderfully named Muumibussi (€10 return), departing from various hotels in town. If you need **internet**, try the tourist office (€3.60 per hr).

Accommodation

Turku has one of the best selections of accommodation of any city in Finland, with an excellent **hostel** and several mid-range **hotels**, and finding a place to stay here is rarely a problem – even in the height of summer. In addition to the main *Hostel Turku*, a second (unaffiliated) hostel, the *Interpoint YWCA*, Hämeenkatu 12A, opens some summers; contact the tourist office for details.

Hesehotelli Läntinen Pitkäkatu 1 ☎045/634 3443, ⓦ www.hesburger.fi/hesehotelli. Although "reception" for this modern three-star is the tills at the burger joint downstairs, the rates are some of the lowest you'll find, especially considering the free internet connection and satellite TV in the rooms. Located close to the bus station, a five-minute walk from the city centre. ❷

Hostel Turku Linnankatu 39 ☎02/262 7680, ⓦ www.turku.fi /hostelturku. The town's excellent official youth hostel is one of the best in the country, located off a quiet central courtyard by the river and open year-round. Inside, pine floors and comfy sofas lead to amply sized doubles and dorms, as well as plenteous cooking and laundry facilities. There's also bicycle hire to boot. Bus #30 from the train station drops you off right in front. Dorms €18, doubles ❷

Omena Hotelli Humalistonkatu 7 ⓦ www.omena.com. Placed one block from the *kauppatori*, this simple, central, automated hotel has no reception but features scores of clean, efficient rooms that can sleep up to four people and feature satellite TV and instant coffee makers. Book online or at the automated kiosk in the lobby. ❷

Park Rauhankatu 1 ☎02/273 2555, ⓦ www.parkhotelturku.fi. A three-minute walk from the train station, this 1902 hotel still oozes *fin-de-siècle* Art Nouveau charm, with each room individually done in a mélange of styles, shapes and sizes. It is Turku's best hotel and a welcome respite from the chaindom gloom of most mid-level hotels, with prices that are rarely much higher. ❻

Ruissalo Camping Ruissalo Island ☎02/262 5100, ⓦ www.turku.fi/ruissalocamping. Turku's most easily

---

European Capital of Culture 2011

Throughout 2011, Turku will share the crown of European Capital of Culture (ⓦ www .turku2011.fi) with Tallinn. Since winning the title in 2007, the city has funded scores of cultural and artistic projects, many of them showcasing the creative innovation for which Finns have become renowned. Highlights of the programme – many of which will continue after 2011 has passed – include aerial acrobatics over the Aura River, a folk opera based on Turku's role during the days of witch-hunting and public stake burnings, a series of *in situ* artworks and events splayed out across the archipelago, as well as circus performances, plays, talks, concerts, digital media exhibitions, and plenty of interesting cultural surprises all over the city.

accessible campsite is located on the small island of Ruissalo near a patch of meadow and a handsome harbour. The campsite offers basic rooms, and the island's sandy beaches, lush botanical garden and panoramic lookouts to the archipelago are just paces away. Open June–Aug. Take bus #8 from the city centre (15min). Rooms ❷

Sokos Hamburger Börs Kauppiaskatu 6 ☎02/337 381, ⓦwww.sokoshotels.fi. Smart, elegant Scandinavian design features such as sheeny fabrics and dim, recessed lighting adorn this *kauppatori* hotel.

Rooms range from gorgeous suites to cosy, smaller rooms that look out onto the square and catch great sunsets. Summer and weekend bargains make it an especially good choice out of season. ❹/❺

Tuure Tuureporinkatu 17C ☎02/233 0230, ⓦwww.tuure.fi. Located two blocks south of the train station, this bare-bones B&B sports fifteen teeny rooms that house from one to four persons, though they offer only a slight upgrade in charm from the local hostels. Friendly owners with an even friendlier cat. ❸

The City

The city is bisected by the Aura, whose tree-lined banks form a natural promenade and a moorage for small tour boats, as well as a useful orientation point. Turku's central grid is on the north side of the river, home to gleaming department stores, banks and offices; the cathedral and castle stand at opposite ends of the river, with the main museums found along its banks in between – walking along the water visiting these sights, snacking in any of the museum cafés and enjoying the riverbank can easily take up the better part of a day. Though less-than-inspired redevelopment across the city during the 1970s and 1980s resulted in a number of really hideous buildings (and a new national catchphrase, *Turun tauti* – "Turku Disease"), streets of intricately carved wooden houses still survive around the **Port Arthur** (or **Portsa**, colloquially) area immediately north of the castle, a lovely part of the city for simply strolling around.

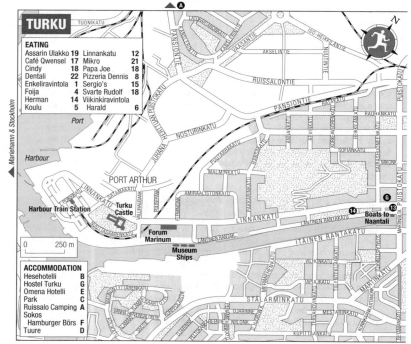

TURKU

EATING
Assarin Ulakko	19	Linnankatu	12
Café Qwensel	17	Mikro	21
Cindy	18	Papa Joe	18
Dentali	22	Pizzeria Dennis	8
Enkeliravintola	1	Sergio's	15
Foija	4	Svarte Rudolf	18
Herman	14	Viikinkiravintola	
Koulu	5	Harald	6

ACCOMMODATION
Hesehotelli	B
Hostel Turku	G
Omena Hotelli	E
Park	C
Ruissalo Camping	A
Sokos Hamburger Börs	F
Tuure	D

Turku Art Museum

The **Turku Art Museum** (Turun taidemuseo; Tues–Fri 11am–7pm, Sat & Sun 11am–5pm; €7 or €8 including special exhibitions; Ⓦ www.turuntaidemuseo.fi), housed in a purpose-built Art Nouveau structure close to the train station at the northern end of Torninkatu, is one of the better collections of Finnish art in the country. Built in the early twentieth century, the museum's rustic granite facade and palatial exterior of columns and turrets were originally far more of an attraction than the actual art it once held – not least of all because most of the surrounding terrain was farmland. The museum is now a grand repository for works by every great name to come out of the country's Golden Age – Gallen-Kallela, Pekka Halonen, Edelfelt, Simberg and others – as well as a commendable stock of moderns. Not least among these are the wood sculptures of Kain Tapper and Mauno Hartman, which stirred up heated "But is it art?" debate on the merits of carefully shaped bits of wood being presented as art when they were first shown during the 1970s. The collection also consists of nearly a hundred self-portraits by Finnish painters from the past century, including several deeply melancholic ones by Juhani Vikainen, Hannes Siivonen, Merja Parikka and Aimo Kanerva.

Turku cathedral

Before the great fire that befell the city in 1827, the tree-framed space just across the river and east of the modern city centre was the bustling heart of the community, an area still overlooked by the **Tuomiokirkko** (daily mid-April to mid-Sept 9am–8pm; rest of the year until 7pm). The cathedral, erected in the thirteenth century on "Sheep's Knoll", a pagan worship ground, was at the centre of the Christianization process inflicted by the crusading Swedes on the pagan

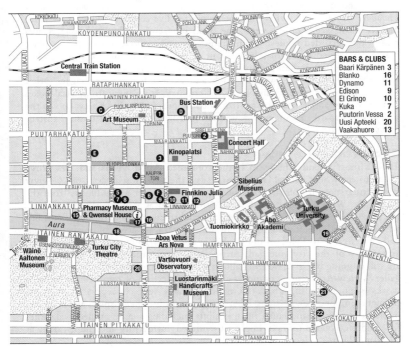

Finns, and grew larger over the centuries as the new religion became stronger and Swedish involvement in Finland escalated. The building, still the heart and soul of the Finnish Church, has been repeatedly ravaged by fire, although the thickness of the walls enabled many of its medieval features to survive. Of these, one **tomb** in particular catches the eye: that of Catharine Månsdotter, commoner wife of the Swedish king Erik XIV, with whom she was imprisoned in Turku Castle in the mid-sixteenth century. As the only queen Finland ever produced, Catharine is as popular in death as she reputedly was in life, judging by the numbers who file past her simple black-marble sarcophagus. You can also visit the **cathedral museum** upstairs (same times as cathedral; €2), where an assortment of ancient jugs, goblets, plates and spoons provides more insight into the cathedral's past – though most absorbing up here are the collections of church textiles.

Immediately outside the cathedral is a statue to **Per Brahe**, who founded the country's first university, housed in the nearby yellow Empire-style buildings (the actual seat of learning was moved to Helsinki during Russian rule). Next to these are the oldest portions of the **Åbo Akademi** – one of only three Swedish-language universities in Finland – while the modern, Finnish-language **Turku University** is at the other end of Henrikinkatu: these days both are more notable as places for eating, at their student *mensas* (see p.140), rather than sightseeing.

Sibelius Museum

Back past the cathedral and across Piispankatu is the sleek low form of the **Sibelius Museum** (Tues–Sun 11am–4pm, Wed also 6–8pm; €3; ⓦ www.sibeliusmuseum .abo.fi). Although Jean Sibelius had no direct connection with Turku, this museum is a fitting tribute to him and his contribution to the emergence of an independent Finland. You're likely to be greeted by the recorded strains of *Finlandia* as you enter: when not the venue for live concerts (which take place nightly most weeks of the year), the small but acoustically ideal concert area pumps out recorded requests from the great man's oeuvre; just take your place beside dewy-eyed Finns for a lunch hour of Scandinavia's finest composer. The Sibelius collection gathers family photo albums and original manuscripts along with the old man's hat, walking stick and even a half-smoked cigar. Other exhibits cover the musical history of the country, from intricate musical boxes and the frail wooden *kantele* – as strummed by peasants in the Kalevala – to the weighty keyboard instruments downstairs; all in all some 350 musical instruments are on display.

Aboa Vetus Ars Nova

Turku's most splendid museum is the combined **Aboa Vetus** and **Ars Nova** (April to early Sept daily 11am–7pm; rest of the year closed Mon; €8; ⓦ www .aboavetusarsnova.fi), on the bank of the Aurajoki River a few blocks from the university. With a name that translates from Latin as "Old Turku, New Art", the place was originally intended to be a straightforward modern art gallery, but when the building's foundations were dug in 1995 a warren of medieval lanes and cellars came to light, an unmissable opportunity to present the history and archeology of the city emerged. Archeological excavations under the museum are still ongoing but glass flooring allows a near-perfect view of the remains. The gallery's New Art section comprises a striking collection of hundreds of modern works – some Finnish, others international, many very conceptual – alongside frequent temporary exhibitions. There are also various other displays and activities interspaced with the museums' main exhibits, including a series of medieval games for children. Guided tours in English are offered during July and August daily at 11.30am. There's a decent café, too.

Vartiovuori Observatory and Luostarinmäki Handicrafts Museum

Opposite the cathedral from the Sibelius Museum is a small hill, a one-time Viking outlook point, topped by the wooden dome of the **Vartiovuori Observatory**. It was designed to serve the first Turku University by Carl Engel, who had arrived in Turku seeking work in the days before his great plan for Helsinki made him famous. Disputes between Engel and his assistants and a misunderstanding of scientific requirements rendered the place useless for its intended purpose, however, and today it's little more than a pretty silhouette against the evening sky, noticeable when the Vartiovuori Park's **summer theatre** puts on its outdoor performances.

From the observatory, head directly down the side of the hill to the more engrossing **Luostarinmäki Handicrafts Museum** (early May to late Sept Tues–Sun 10am–6pm; €7.50) on Luostarinkatu (Cloister Hill), one of the best – and certainly the most authentic – open-air museums in Finland; even the youngest buildings here are over two hundred years old. Following a severe fire in 1775, rigorous restrictions were imposed on the construction of new city buildings, but due to a legal technicality they didn't apply in this district. The single-storey wooden houses that you see here today were thus built by local working people in traditional style and occupied until the 1930s. Highlights among the various buildings include a violin-maker's studio, a plank-carrier's home (check out the cool wallpaper made from newspapers – avant-garde these days but a common fashion back then), saddle-makers' and furriers' workshops and a working printing press from 1642, demonstrations of which are provided in the summertime. Unpaved streets now run across the large site between tiny wooden houses, some of which once had goats tethered to their chimneys to keep the turfed roofs cropped. The chief inhabitants now are the museum volunteers who dress up in period attire and demonstrate the old handicrafts.

Wäinö Aaltonen Museum

A short walk from the handicrafts museum further along the riverbank is another worthwhile indoor collection: the **Wäinö Aaltonen Museum** (Tues–Sun 11am–7pm; €7; Ⓦwww.wam.fi), dedicated to the famous Finnish sculptor (see box below). Visitors are greeted in the lobby by one of the collection's larger works,

---

Wäinö Aaltonen

Unquestionably the best-known modern Finnish sculptor, **Wäinö Aaltonen** (1894–1966) grew up close to Turku and studied for a time at the local art school. His first public show, in 1916, marked a turning point in the development of Finnish sculpture, introducing a freer, more individual style to a genre struggling to break from the constraints of the Neoclassical tradition and French Realism. Aaltonen went on to dominate his field throughout the 1920s and 1930s and his influence is still felt today; the man's work turns up in every major town throughout the country – Turku itself has eleven of his sculptures on outdoor display – and even the parliament building in Helsinki was designed with special niches to hold some of his pieces.

Much of Aaltonen's output celebrates the individuals who contributed to the growth of the Finnish republic, typically representing them with enormous heads, or as immense Social Realist statues. His public sculptures thus became particularly important during the early years of Finland's independence, when he forged several original, imaginative works of long-lasting national value. His sculpture of Paavo Nurmi, located outside Helsinki's Sports Museum, captures the champion runner of the 1920s in full stride, while his bronze 1939 likeness of Aleksis Kivi outside the National Theatre has become the accepted image of the great Finnish writer – no one actually knows for sure what Kivi looked like.

Cycling the Turku archipelago

With tens of thousands of islands splayed out in the Baltic Sea, the **Turku archipelago** (Finnish: Turun Saaristo; Swedish: Åbo Skärgård) is a perfect destination for a couple of days' adventure. The largest archipelago in the Baltic region, it contains some 6000 islands extending as much as 100km out into the sea, and encompasses the entire range of maritime topography, from tiny bald skerries barely big enough for a few water-birds to large, verdant isles holding lighthouses, beaches and hotel complexes. With extensive bridges and regular, gratis ferries, you certainly don't need a boat to get out here. You don't even need a car, and while you could, in theory, drive most of the route in a day (though some of the smaller ferries will not accept automobiles), this would be missing the point. Infrastructure for getting around seems to have been designed, in large part, for cyclists alone.

The Archipelago Trail

The most common journey tackled by bike – the oft-touted **Archipelago Trail** – covers a circuit of some 250km that begins and ends in Turku, following a well-indicated route (the Skärgårdens Ringväg, or Saariston Rengastie in Finnish) through some of the most picturesque islands accessible by boat and bridge. You should allow at least a week to fully enjoy the route – which takes in some ten archipelago municipalities, twelve bridges and nine ferry crossings – though it's possible to do it in less time if need be, making use of shortcuts and alternate ferry routes.

Beginning in Turku, it's 27km to the market town of **Pargas**, the capital of the archipelago, where you can pay a visit to the Turunmaan Seutu (see opposite) for any specific information you might need for your journey. From here you'll ride 17km southwest to Lillmälö for the short ferry ride over to the island of **Nagu**, from which it's a 10km cycle to the island's main town – be sure to stop to admire the stupendous views from the Norrströmmen bridge on the way. The small, industrious town has a great collection of seafood restaurants, a dignified wooden church set up when the island served as a leper colony and the last available ATM before reaching Gustavs. From here, head to Pärnäs for the ferry to **Korpo**, after which it's a 7km ride to the

---

the four-metre-long *Suomen Neito* ("Maiden of Finland"), a *zaftig* nude holding her Medusa-like hair, rich with detail and sentiment. Elsewhere, the diversity, originality and sensitivity of Aaltonen's oeuvre is fully explored, spanning several floors and rooms of the museum, though one roomful of his paintings shows why he perhaps chose to concentrate on sculpture.

Pharmacy Museum and Qwensel House

Across the river from the Aaltonen Museum, immediately behind a floral display in the grass that spells out TURKU:ÅBO, a wooden staircase runs up to the front door of the **Pharmacy Museum and Qwensel House** (Apteekkimuseo ja Qwenselin Talo; early April to late Sept daily 10am–6pm; €7.50), site of the oldest standing bourgeois residence in Turku. Built in the late 1600s for court judge Wilhelm Johan Qwensel, it later became a working apothecary and the home of Professor Josef Gustaf Pipping – the "father of Finnish medicine", who filled it with all and sundry medicinal and chemists' implements, among them some memorable devices for drawing blood. The museum features period rooms from the apothecary days, including two laboratories filled with beakers, burners and pipettes for measuring out doses, and a herb room, where plants from the garden out back were dried and sorted. The grandest room of all, however, is the apothecary's front office, filled with jars, canisters and bottles, many with their original labeling. Period Rococo and Gustavian furnishings remain throughout the house, attesting to just how wealthy and stylish the life of the eighteenth-century

small town centre. If you have some extra time, you can catch ferries out to smaller, westerly islands such as Bergham, Storpensar and Elvsö – though these lie off the main archipelago route.

From Korpo centre ride north to **Galtby**, where you can catch ferries to **Houtskär**'s southern port of Kittius. Galtby also offers connections further west to Åland (see pp.159–176). It's a 27-kilometre ride through Houtskär, passing through a collection of forested islands that make up the only unilingual municipality in the archipelago (Swedish, naturally). After two mini-ferries through Kivimo and Björkö, Mossalo on the northern tip is the point of departure for the hour-long journey to teensy **Iniö**, a nevertheless well-appointed hamlet good for fishing tours and nature hikes. From here there's another ferry to **Gustavs**, another springboard for Åland and a veritable megalopolis after what you've just been through. At **Taivassalo**, just east, a ferry whisks you to Teersalo, then past the ports of Askainen, Merimaski and Rymättylä, and finally on towards Naantali and Turku.

Practicalities

Specific timings of all archipelago **ferries** can be found at Ⓦwww.lautat.fi; there are usually several sailings a day. **Accommodation** across the islands largely comprises small, independently run cottages, but there are plenty of beachside campgrounds as well, some with more than adequate facilities, others completely wild. In addition, every village will have B&B accommodation of some sort, but you should consider planning ahead – Archipelago Booking Finland (Ⓣ02/410 6600, Ⓦwww.archipelagobooking.fi) will be able to advise. Turku's tourist office offers a free, detailed *Archipelago Travel Map*, which features accommodation listings and activities in the region, as well as up-to-date ferry and bus schedules. They also hire out 7-speed **bicycles** (€15 per day, €75 per week, including helmet), and even run a number of guided cycling **tours**, the shortest of which covers 160km and costs €210 per person. For more detailed **information** on exploring the archipelago – on cycle or on foot – contact the Turunmaan Seutu (Ⓣ02/458 5942, Ⓦwww.saaristo.org), which has an office at Uurnalehdontie 4 in Pargas.

bourgeoisie actually was. In the summertime, a small café (see p.140) serves coffee and cakes out on a courtyard terrace.

Forum Marinum

A glance at the undulating repository of ships that line the Aura River is as good a clue as any to the pivotal place of seafaring in Turku's history. The **Forum Marinum** (May–Sept daily 11am–7pm; Oct–April Tues–Sun 11am–6pm; €7, €12 including museum ships), Linnankatu 72, houses a compelling permanent exhibition focusing on the region's maritime history, with exhibits on merchant societies, rural seafaring shipwrecks and the Finnish Navy, plus regular rotating temporary exhibitions covering themes such as archipelago wildlife and sport boating. Moored out back at the banks of the Aura float a fleet of **museum ships** (entrance included with €12 museum ticket, otherwise €5 per boat), including: the *Suomen Joutsen*, a fully rigged frigate that was once a depot for submarines and a hospital; the *Keihässalmi*, the first minelayer and minesweeper to be constructed in Finland after World War II; and, several blocks east, the *Sigyn*, a black three-masted wooden vessel built in 1887 in Gothenburg that transported timber all over the Baltic. Needless to say, each of these ships is a guaranteed cure for any kid bored to tears with Finnish museums.

Turku Castle

The city's museums, and its cathedral and universities, are all symbols of Turku's elevated position in Finnish life, but by far the major marker to its many years of

Though walking in the city is a pleasure, the small *Pikkuföri* **river ferry** (🌐www.forum
-marinum.fi) is a great way to get from one end of the river to the other, with several daily
sailings from early June to mid-August between the Forum Marinum and the Lilja statue
just east of the university. For boat trips by steamship to **Naantali**, see the box on p.144.

importance stands at the western end of Linnankatu. Follow the signs for "Turun
Linna", or take bus #1 from the harbour, and you'll eventually see, appearing
somewhat anachronistic among the present-day ferry terminals, the relatively feature-
less, piebald exterior of **Turku Castle** (early May to late Sept Tues–Sun 10am–6pm;
late Sept to mid-April Tues & Thurs–Sun 10am–6pm, Wed noon–8pm; €7.50). Fight
any dismay, though, since the compact cobbled courtyards, maze-like corridors and
darkened staircases of the interior provide a great place to wander and wonder – and
to dwell on the fact that this was the seat of Finland's government for centuries. It's
well worth buying one of the small guidebooks (€5) at the entrance to help figure
out the importance of everything that's here; even better is to join one of the guided
tours (€2.50), often led by some knowledgeable local history student dressed up in
medieval burlap vestments.

The castle went up sometime around 1280, when the first bishop arrived from
Sweden, intending it as a military fortress. Gradual expansion over the next two
centuries accounts for the patchwork effect of its architecture – and the bewildering
and often labyrinthine array of rooms. The majority of the fortification took place
during the turbulent sixteenth century, instigated by Swedish ruler Gustavus Vasa
for the protection of his son, whom he crowned Duke Johan, the first duke of
Finland. Johan was sentenced to death after exceeding his powers, but reclaimed
the crown of Finland in a mini-coup, and the somewhat unstable Erik XIV, who
had arrested him, ended up himself imprisoned in the castle. His bare cell is one of
the more compelling rooms on view, and contains a gloomy nineteenth-century
painting by Erik Johan Löfgren, of Erik with his head on the lap of his queen
(Catharine Månsdotter, deposed and also imprisoned here), while the lady's eyes
look askance to heaven. The castle, which after ongoing renovation is now one of
the most well-looked-after castle structures in Finland, provides a backdrop for
numerous medieval re-enactment events every year.

Eating

You'd have to be very fussy – or allergic to everything – not to find somewhere
to your liking to eat in Turku. Many places offer complete lunchtime meals for
under €10, and while traditional Finnish restaurants make up most of the city's
offerings, a small number of fusion and ethnic places spice things up. A half-dozen
or so summer **floating restaurants** – *Papa Joe*, *Svarte Rudolf* and *Cindy*, to name the
perennial favourites – are often chock-full in the evenings with locals and visitors.
All serve reliably good continental-style meals and occasionally put on live music;
Cindy even sticks around in the winter months. If you're saving your pennies, visit
any of the half-dozen **student cafeterias** spread about the Åbo Akademi grounds
– aside from *Assarin Ulakko* (see below), there's also *Dentali*, Lemminkäisenkatu 2,
and *Mikro*, Kiinamyllynkatu 13.

Assarin Ulakko Rehtorinpellonkatu 4A. You'll find rock-bottom-priced meals and a lively student atmosphere at this student *mensa* just off Hämeentie. It's easily the cheapest option in town (€5.50 for lunch). Closed Sun.

Café Qwensel Läntinen Rantakatu 13. Fabulous cakes in atmospheric eighteenth-century surroundings in the courtyard between the Pharmacy Museum and the tourist office.

Enkeliravintola Kauppiaskatu 16 ☏02/231 8088. A stylishly old-fashioned restaurant with a fairytale decor of candelabra, statuettes and fantastical wall paintings. They offer a standard but scrumptious à la carte menu that includes mushroom soup (€9), beef tenderloin (€26), and the *kauppahalli's* catch of the day (€24). Just next to the Art Museum, though it's a bit of an uphill walk from the centre.

Foija Aurakatu 10. Busy cellar restaurant with vaulted ceilings opposite the *kauppatori*, with good-value and delicious pastas, salads and pizzas from €6.50, and great service. It's been around for over 150 years and is still popular with the city's younger set.

Herman Läntinen Rantakatu 37 ☏02/230 3333. Set in a bright and airy 1850s-era storehouse right on the Aura (ask for the table for two overlooking the river). The fantastic traditional meals here tend towards the higher end of things (€25 or so). Lunch, however, is tremendous value at €8.60.

Koulu Eerikinkatu 18. Occupying a grand old late-1880s school building, this is the largest restaurant-brewery in Finland, with a huge selection of beers and wines. The bargain lunch menu (€8.90) is the best deal, while à la carte specials include parsley root soup with mushroom ravioli (€8.40) and warm roast beef sandwich with cheddar sauce and tomato sauce (€11). Dinner served until 11.30pm.

Linnankatu 3 Linnankatu 3 ☏02/233 9279. Set just at the Aura River, this somewhat upscale restaurant has a casual-meets-formal interior done in adobe tile with white-tablecloth settings. Some of the more interesting mains include breast of goose with raspberry sauce (€24) and reindeer liver with cranberry sauce (€32). Perfect for lunch (€8.70).

Pizzeria Dennis Linnankatu 17. Although this pizza joint might look a bit tatty on the outside, don't be put off. It's renowned for its range of decent, well-priced pizzas and pastas, most around €11. Soup lunch platter for €8.20.

Sergio's Läntinen Rantakatu 27 ☏02/233 0033. Superb, new-ish Italian-run restaurant with wonderful river views serving very authentic dishes, such as Sardinian *gnocchetti* with smoked *scamorza* cheese and veggies (€14.50), *garganelli* in crayfish bisque sauce (€15.50), and excellent *tiramisú*. You should be able to get out for under €20, with wine and coffee. Extremely attentive staff.

Viikinkiravintola Harald Aurakatu 3 ☏02/276 5050. Cashing in on the little Finland actually has to do with the Vikings, this fun dining spot effectively employs whittled furnishings, earthenware plates and heads of game mounted on the walls to win most atmospheric restaurant in town. The food is somewhat hearty, with dishes including King Canute the Great's Shield (€31.20): massive cuts of lamb, deer and ox skewered on a sword, served with root vegetables. The €8.70 fish and vegetable buffet lunch, served until 3pm, is a great bargain. And don't miss the sweet and smoky tar ice cream.

Drinking and nightlife

Owing to its lively student population and constant stream of tourists and visitors, nights out in Turku are a blast, with something for everyone. A **drink** at one of the many boats moored along the Aura has become *de rigueur* for many locals, but if you want to fill your nights with something more energetic than sunset beers, there are several lively **bars** and livelier **discos** (and karaoke joints) open till 2am or so.

Baari Kärpänen Kauppiaskatu 8 🌐www .baarikarpanen.fi. "Fly Bar" (or Barfly, perhaps) is an excellent, unconventional watering hole: a hard rock bar with embroidered red velvet seating and a cobblestone terrace. Though seemingly rough at first blush, the locals are some of Turku's most sociable and chatty.

Blanko Aurakatu 1 🌐www.blanko.net. Once voted Scandinavia's trendiest bar, this down-to-earth hipster lounge is still just as hip, with pillowed couches in the back, tables out front, DJs spinning electronica at weekends and tasty fusion lunches and dinners (give the spaghetti with mushroom, provolone and rucola a whirl).

Dynamo Linnankatu 7 🌐www.dynamo klubi.com. A rocking two-floor dance bar with a chic-meets-alternative interior of red velour designy chairs and olive leather couches. Only gets going after midnight, and a good place to end the night. Thursdays are the ever-popular YouTube nights, when everyone picks a favourite internet clip to screen on the wall.

Edison Kauppiaskatu 4. Fairly standard, carpeted, modern pub, extremely popular with exchange students and the twentysomething after-work crowd who come to let their hair down a bit. It's most happening from 6 to 7pm, and definitely slows down after 10pm.

El Gringo Kauppiaskatu 6. Grungy decor with sombreros and Santana posters, and inexpensive beers (€2.50 Lapin Kulta half-litres), draw a diverse crowd, with music that ranges from reggae to gangsta rap and R&B.

Kuka Linnankatu 17. This irreverent style-bar has eclectic fixtures such as a barber's chair, pod-like seats, popcorn machines as tables and a dilapidated Vespa hanging over the door. Tuesday's bingo night brings out the tragically hip in droves. Several tables out front if you can't stand the heat.

Puutorin Vessa Puutori. Quirky circular bar housed in a former public toilet on a small square just north of the *kauppatori*. Locals are often found with beer in hand shouting comments at Finnish television serials. Definitely worth a peek in, if not *yks tuoppi* ("a pint").

Uusi Apteekki Kaskenkatu 1. Allegedly predating Damien Hirst's famous *Pharmacy* London bar-restaurant, this smoky, laid-back drinking hole is housed in an old chemist's shop, with drug and pill bottles scattered about the place. Popular with cigar aficionados, bikers, and fans of multiple piercings.

Vaakahuone Linnankatu 38 ⓦwww.vaakahuone.fi. A very lively place set in a winter garden down by the waterside, buzzing with Finns of all ages. An established house band plays jazz of all sorts every night during the summer, and they serve reasonably priced salads, soups and pizzas, too.

Entertainment

During August, the **Turku Music Festival** (ⓣ02/262 0814, ⓦwww.tmj.fi) packs thousands of visitors into a number of venues for performances across a wide range of musical genres. If your tastes tend towards the classical, take in a performance of one of the oldest symphony orchestras in Europe, the **Turku Philharmonic**, founded in 1790 and currently based in Turku Concert Hall at Aninkaistenkatu 9. The box office (ⓣ02/262 0030, ⓦwww.tfo.fi; Tues–Sat noon–7pm) is located in the Turku City Theatre at Itäinen Rantakatu 14 and generally opens in mid-August; the concert season begins in mid-September. Another option is one of Turku's several **cinemas**, the largest of which, Kinopalatsi, Kauppiaskatu 11, has nine screens. Finnkino Julia, Eerikinkatu 4, has five. Visit ⓦwww.finnkino.fi for latest showtimes.

Naantali

Some 16km northwest of Turku, **NAANTALI** has become famous all over the world as the home of **Moominworld**, an island theme-park dedicated to Tove Jansson's famous creations and a must-see if you're here in the summer with children. But the rest of Naantali, an otherwise quiet old convent town of wooden homes and forested outskirts, is also well worth visiting, and a rather less frantic spot to spend an afternoon, especially once the kids have worn themselves out running around with the likes of Moominpappa, Moomin-mamma and Lilla My.

The original town of Nådendal (Swedish for "Valley of Grace"), from which the Finnish name is derived, was first established in 1442 as a convent by the St Birgitta nuns. The convent was shut down a century later by King Gustav Vasa and its lands subsequently confiscated by the Swedish crown. For the following three centuries, the town earned its keep as a major sock exporter – those nuns had been wizard heel-makers, from which knitting socks was a natural extension – until a spa and health resort was built along its shores in 1863, drawing the pleasure-seeking and the infirm from around the grand duchy.

Arrival, information and accommodation

Frequent municipal **buses** from Turku arrive at Naantali's small *kauppatori* in the modern town centre. From here, it's a ten-minute walk along some leafy,

A family of white, round trolls whose cute ears and large snouts lend them the likeness of a baby hippo crossed with a rabbit, **the Moomins** are well in the running for the most famous Finns. They were the fantasy of **Tove Jansson** (1914–2001), a Finlandssvenska dreamer born in Helsinki who spent much of her life on the tiny island of Klovharu, off Finland's southern coast. Jansson sketched her first Moomin in the 1930s after a

▲ A Finnish child embracing a Moomin

dare from her brother to draw the ugliest creature she could think of. Over the years, the Moomins developed more affable snouts, appearing in print for the first time in 1945 in *The Moomins and the Great Flood*. Depressed by the war, Jansson wanted to write something innocent, naïve and uplifting for kids of all ages. Though her first book received nary a mention, sales of the subsequent tomes – *Comet in Moominland* and *Finn Family Moomintroll* – skyrocketed, securing Jansson's fame. Only nine Moomin books were ever released – in addition to five picture books and a comic strip – but they became huge successes, eventually resulting in syndication in sixty languages across some forty countries. After the Kalevala, the Moomin books are the most widely translated works of Finnish literature.

The Moomin and friends live in Moominvalley, an idyllic spot deep in the Finnish forest, experiencing adventures that constantly test their steadfastness and goodwill. Throughout their lives, the valley's inhabitants, while socially conscious and tolerant of difference, are plagued by a distinct sense of mischief and knavery as they try to adapt to uncertainty and ponder the problems of friendship, solitude and freedom. The Moomins themselves are ostensibly reflective of Jansson's family: austere, bohemian, close to nature and extremely tolerant (Jansson herself was a lesbian, open at least to her family, during a time when homosexuality in Finland was far from tolerated – least of all from children's authors). Peripheral characters, meanwhile, display varying degrees of prototypically Finnish melancholic characteristics. Even the landscape – the black, hill-shaped Groke that freezes whatever ground she sits upon and kills everything she touches – reflects Scandinavian gloominess. Jansson, for her part, always claimed that she never intended to philosophize or preach to anyone: the Moomins were an escape.

These days, a Moomin merchandizing empire exists in Finland and abroad rivalling that of America's Disney World, with a **muumibuumi** ("Moomin boom") of rampant commercialization in the 1990s, consummated with a 78-part television series in Japan and the subsequent opening of Moominworld. These days, the characters' likenesses are printed on everything from T-shirts to coffee mugs, store signs (they are the official mascots of the Japanese Daiei shopping-centre chain) to airports (Helsinki's Vantaa airport was once plastered in Moomin imagery). Though the Jansson family has vowed never to sell out to the likes of Disney, Moominworld is now one of the biggest tourist destinations in Finland.

residential streets to the old town, where most activity for visitors is concentrated and where you can find the **tourist office** (early June to Aug Mon–Fri 9am–6pm, Sat & Sun 10am–4pm; Sept to early June Mon 9am–5pm, Tues–Fri 9am–4.30pm;

Naantali by steamship

The most interesting way to reach Naantali from Turku is on the last working passenger steamship in Finland, the **S/S Ukkopekka** (early June to mid-Aug; €22 return; ⓦwww.ukkopekka.fi), which departs Turku at 9.30am and 2pm, arriving at Naantali's old town around two hours later. The return journey begins two hours after each arrival – just enough time for a quick jaunt through Moominworld and a bite to eat at the marina.

☏02/435 9800, ⓦwww.naantalinmatkailu.fi), Kaivotori 2, which rents out a few cycles (€10 per day). Staying **overnight** in the old town is a great way to break up the trip between bustling Turku and its back-of-beyond archipelago, though prices can often soar in the height of the summer.

Amandis Nunnakatu 5 ☏02/430 8774, ⓦwww.hotelamandis.com. Six cutesy rooms in bright colours with exposed oak floors and plenty of rustic allure. A great terrace café downstairs looks out to the water. ❺

Harriet Katinhäntä 3 ☏040/910 3333 or 910 4444, ⓦwww.harriethomes.com. Rooms in this small guesthouse range from spot-on red-checked rustic to nineteenth-century grandmother's parlour (old furniture pieces, wrought-iron-framed beds). They also let out a sleekly designed flat (€60; see ⓦwww.harriet.fi) in the centre ideal for groups and families. ❸

Naantali Camping Kuparivuori ☏02/435 0855 or 045/110 4828, ⓦwww.naantalinmatkailu.fi/camping. Half a kilometre south of the marina in a picture-perfect seaside setting. They hire out a long list of recently renovated cottages (€40–140), some of which have their own sauna (€25 per hr).

Naantalin Kylpylä Matkailijantie 2 ☏02/44 550, ⓦwww.naantalispa.fi. Out of the 390 rooms at this

highly luxurious spa hotel, located 1km northeast of the centre, most manage to feel pretty chainy (though some have small balconies), but the decor in the suites has a bit more pizzazz. Large outdoor/indoor pool, plus day-spa. Also operates a titanic-sized luxury liner yacht hotel, the *Sunborn Princess*, out back with 140 modern rooms (❼). ❸/❹

Villa Antonius Mannerheiminkatu 9 ☏02/435 1938, ⓦwww.cafeantonius.fi. Drenched in deep, resonant colours, the half-dozen rooms in this memorable guesthouse beckon the dramaturge in us all, with heavy silk brocade, upholstered settees and quilted, frilly bedspreads. Enter at your own peril: you might never return from the nineteenth century. ❷

Villa Saksa Rantakatu 6 ☏040/761 8384, ⓦwww.villasaksa.doldrums.fi. Set just on the water in the old town. The rooms themselves are more or less unremarkable, but the decor throughout the rest of the place is classic 1950s styling. Cheery, welcoming service. ❻

The Town

Naantali today consists of a fairly sleepy modern centre and a much more atmospheric old town, which could body double for a New England seaside village. You can explore the remnants of the town's religious past at the **Naantali Convent Church** (Naantalin luostarikirkko; May daily 10am–6pm; June–Aug daily 10am–8pm; Sept–April Wed noon–2pm & Sun 11am–3pm). Inside is a large altar of St Birgitta, with the nuns' chancel gallery columns above it, fronted by a German-style wooden altar screen depicting the coronation of the Virgin Mary. Every June, the Naantali Music Festival (ⓦwww.naantalimusic.com) fills the church with chamber music during evening concerts.

A few blocks south of the church, the **Naantali Museum** (Naantalin museo; mid-May to Aug Tues–Sun 11am–6pm), Katinhäntä 1, is housed across several eighteenth-century merchants' and craftsmen's homes set around a rose garden courtyard. Exhibits cover the history of the convent and town, along with various archeological findings unearthed over the years. Just opposite Naantali is the island of Luonnonmaa, home to the granite manor of **Kultaranta** ("Golden Beach"), the official summer residence of the Finnish president (whose schoolmarmish looks

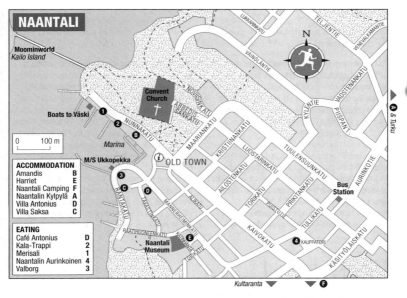

NAANTALI

Moominworld
Kailo Island

Convent
Church

Boats to Väski

0   100 m

Marina

M/S Ukkopekka

OLD TOWN

ACCOMMODATION
Amandis   B
Harriet   E
Naantali Camping F
Naantalin Kylpylä A
Villa Antonius   D
Villa Saksa   C

EATING
Café Antonius   D
Kala-Trappi   2
Merisali   1
Naantalin Aurinkoinen 4
Valborg   3

Naantali
Museum

Bus
Station

KAUPPATORI

Kultaranta

make for frequent comparisons to Moominmamma). Designed by architect Lars
Sonck, the palace is surrounded by 560,000 square metres of parks and gardens,
one of the latter containing a display of nearly 4000 roses. Guided tours of the
manor's exterior and parks leave from the tourist office (late June to mid-Aug
Tues–Sun 1.40pm; €13); tickets are also available at the gates (€9).

Moominworld and Väski Adventure Island

A few hundred metres north of Naantali's old town, over an arched wooden
bridge, lies **Moominworld** (Muumimaailma; early June to late Aug daily
10am–6pm; €20; Ⓦwww.muumimaailma.fi), the essential destination for families
visiting Finland, Santa Claus notwithstanding. The place is less Disney-like than
you might think, and often feels a bit homespun, surely adding to its charm.

Moominworld's central attraction is the five-storey, robin's-egg-blue Moomin
House, while elsewhere are attractions such as Hemulen's yellow house, Moomin-
mamma's kitchen, Snufkin's camp, Moominpappa's boat and the Hattifatteners'
cave; if you know the books you'll recognize everything you see here. There are
also regular theatre performances in a large, covered amphitheatre, and smaller,
more impromptu music concerts both inside and outside the various buildings.
Moominworld prides itself on realizing the Moomin philosophy, promoting safety
and environmental consciousness. Unfortunately, they also hold dear the vaunted
tenet that theme-park food must be inordinately highly priced, so expect to pay
through the roof for anything you consume here.

Children also love being taken to the nearby **Väski Adventure Island** (Väski
Seikkailujen Saari; early June to mid-Aug daily 11am–7pm; €16; Ⓦwww.vaski.fi),
an outgrowth of Moominworld aimed at older children, with archery, gold panning
and a bouncy castle, as well as theatre performances and a "fisherman's village"
featuring livestock and Finns garbed in rural get-up. The *Rosita* ketch (price included
in park entrance) ferries passengers regularly from Old Naantali to Väski.

Eating and drinking

Naantali has a handful of very good (and a few very mediocre) **restaurants**, most of them located at the old town's marina just by the gates to Moominworld.

Café Antonius Mannerheiminkatu 9. Decent coffee and a catalogue of cakes are served in a likeable salon off a cobbled street. Decor perfectly melds the old days with the chintzy, with random family portraits adorning the walls in a living room that calls to mind a Finnish folkloric museum. Forgivably crotchety staff.

Kala-Trappi Nunnakatu 3. Next door to the *Merisali*, this "gourmet" restaurant has a fairly run-of-the-mill interior, but the menu holds a few pleasant surprises, including pepper steak with truffle sauce and potato croquettes (€22.90) and fried salmon with lobster sauce and crayfish mousse (€18.90).

Merisali Nunnakatu 1. The first worthwhile place you hit on the walk from Moominworld to the marina, this large pavilion-style hall, drowning in maritime paraphernalia and looking right out onto the harbour, serves fresh fish, affordable salads and a good smorgasbord for €12. Also occasional evening live music events.

Naantalin Aurinkoinen Tullikatu 11. Cakes, breads and pastries right by the *kauppatori*, so it's perfect for a quick bite upon bus arrival/departure.

Valborg Mannerheiminkatu 1. This seriously cosy, casual lounge restaurant-café has modern, fuzzy grey couches and art-gallery-style halogen lighting, plus a courtyard terrace. They do pizzas and salads (most around €11) but it's better as a place to unwind with a drink after a long day with the Moomins.

Uusikaupunki

Were it not for the handful of decidedly Finnish modernist buildings visible on the approach to **UUSIKAUPUNKI**, 70km northwest of Turku along the coast, this captivating little hamlet might well be a town spanning the banks of, say, the Garonne River in central France. Despite the literal-mindedness of its honorific, "New Town", the place feels very old, with a great collection of beautifully decorated nineteenth-century wooden homes and a decidedly unhurried feel.

The town is best known for its annual July **woodwind festival** (ⓦ www.crusell.fi) and for the **Bonk Centre** (late June to Aug daily 10am–6pm; ⓦ www.bonkcentre .fi; €6), Siltakatu 2, a local artist's astonishing collection of non-functioning machines and artefacts, each presented deadpan with its own concomitant mythology. It's the sort of thing you might find in a Python outtake, and has quintessential Finnish why-be-normal humour written all over it. More serious are the local **Museum of Cultural History** (Kulttuurihistoriallinen Museo; early June to Aug Mon–Fri 10am–5pm, Sat & Sun noon–3pm; rest of year Tues–Fri noon–5pm; €2), Ylinenkatu 11, with a motley collection of ethnographic artefacts from the nineteenth century, and the **Pyhämaa Votive Church** (Pyhämaan uhrikirkko; June–Aug Mon–Sat 11am–5pm), a simple red wooden structure built out of logs by Franciscan monks in the 1640s and holding a good number of floral, Baroque-style paintings.

The territory of Uusikaupunki was long known as Pahamaa ("badlands") by local sailors on account of the treacherous waters hereabouts. Today, Uusikaupunki is still home to an active maritime life, with several day-long **cruises** (€35) each week out to the striped Isokari Lighthouse and the tsarist Katanpää Fortress, or quicker passages (€15) direct to **Gustavs** (Kustavi), a perfect jumping-off point for exploration of the Åland archipelago (see box, p.161). Enquire at the tourist office for the latest schedules.

Practicalities

Buses arrive at the *kauppatori*, across from the **tourist office** (late June to early Aug Mon–Fri 9am–5pm, Sat 9am–3pm; rest of year Mon–Fri 9am–4pm;

ⓉⒿ02/8451 5443, ⓌⒿwww.uusikaupunki.fi), which will rent you a bicycle for the day. **Accommodation** options are severely limited here, but the best bet (and most endearingly named) is right at the main square: *Gästhaus Pooki* (ⓉⒿ02/847 7100, ⓌⒿwww.gasthauspooki.com; ❹), Ylinenkatu 21, with rooms that emit no small amount of maritime charm. The nearest **camping** spot is *Santtioranta* (ⓉⒿ02/842 3862; June–Aug), some 2km northwest of town at Kalaluokkikuja 14, with a great seaside location and sporting several log cabins (❷). Otherwise, ask at the tourist office for information on local B&Bs.

Fine dining has never been Uusikaupunki's forté, but things are looking up: The *Pooki* has a great terrace **restaurant** with inexpensive à la carte meals and €14 buffet lunches next door at *Juhla*. The riverbank along Aittaranta is lined with a handful of one-time salt stores recently re-imagined as handicrafts boutiques, antique shops and fetching restaurants that now draw the bulk of locals in the summertime. For lunch try *Sualaspuar* at no. 8, while *Captain's Makasiini* at no. 12 is a great dinner choice, with a wide selection of Finnish dishes; it's also a popular spot where diners stay long after the kitchen closes to nurse their beers (and themselves into oblivion).

Rauma and around

Some 92km north of Turku set just inland from the Bothnian coast, **RAUMA** may be best known to older Finns for its antiquated Finnish dialect and its high-quality lacework, but its principal draw is its charming and elegant wooden old town, the most complete and best preserved in Scandinavia, which has remained virtually unchanged for three centuries. Now a UNESCO World Heritage Site, Rauma had both a Catholic church and Franciscan monastery even before gaining town status as a trading centre in 1442; the latter are thought by some to have brought the tradition of bobbin lace-making to the town before being exiled by Lutheran reformers in 1538. Nearly the entire town was devastated in the great fires of 1640 and 1682, though remarkably, the layout of the narrow winding streets and curiously shaped gardens and allotments has little changed since then. By the mid-1800s, it had become a popular seaport, and by 1897 the town had the largest fleet of sailing boats in the country – some 57 vessels. Today, Rauma's core is gracelessly encircled by a commercial – if just as sleepy – modern town, but the undisturbed medieval centre remains the real draw.

Arrival, information and accommodation

From the **bus station**, just northwest of the old town, it's a five-minute walk to the **tourist office** in the old town hall at Kauppakatu 13 (June–Aug daily 10am–6pm; Sept–May Mon–Fri 9am–5pm; ⓉⒿ02/834 3512, ⓌⒿwww.visitrauma.fi), where

---

Lace making in Rauma

Lace making in Rauma became big in the late 1500s, around the time that ladies' bonnets came into fashion, and local women were often trained from the age of 5 in the Rauman art of weaving with extremely thin thread, producing Baroque- and Rococo-styled lace and lattice weavings that were exported to Russia and the rest of Scandinavia. A number of local societies are keeping the tradition alive, and it's a pastime celebrated in the lively annual **Pitsiviiko** (Lace Week) at the end of July. The tourist office can recommend some excellent local shops.

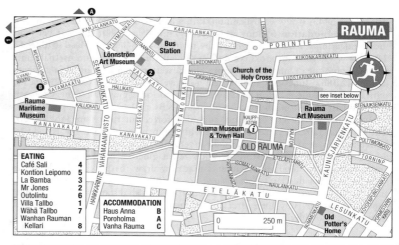

you can pick up leaflets on local history and walking tours. There are a few solid options for **places to stay**, though only one is located in the old town. The ⚓ *Vanha Rauma* (☎02/8376 2200, ⓦwww.hotelvanharauma.fi; ❻), Vanhankirkonkatu 26, is a beautiful modern hotel on the edge of Kalatori with an Art Deco theme and delightful rooms, though old-town style doesn't come cheap. A fifteen-minute walk due west is *Haus Anna* (☎050/551 1222, ⓦwww.hausanna.fi; ❸), Satamakatu 7, a simply designed guesthouse with basic but comfortable rooms on two floors and effusive staff. Two kilometres northwest along Valtakatu from the old town centre is *Poroholma*, the combined **youth hostel** and **campsite** (☎02/533 5522, ⓦwww .poroholma.fi; mid-May to Aug), Poroholmantie 8, with pitches, €14 dorms, basic double rooms (❷) and more comfortable wooden cottages (from €60).

The Town

Despite the large number of tourists it attracts, the medieval core of **Old Rauma** (Vanha Rauma), held within a narrow triangle of land bordered on two sides by the trickling Raumanjoki River, holds enough quiet lanes, paths and alleyways – a total of six hundred individual buildings across a thirty-hectare area – to allow you to explore almost undisturbed.

Old Rauma

Old Rauma's rich past is documented in the **Rauma Museum**, in the Baroque eighteenth-century town hall at Kauppakatu 13 (late June to early Sept daily

10am–5pm; early Sept to mid-May Tues–Fri noon–5pm, Sat 10am–2pm, Sun 11am–5pm; summer €6, winter €5). Here you'll find a couple of scale models of the sailing ships that once brought vast wealth into the town and a diminutive collection of displays of **bobbin lace-making**, with live demonstrations on Tuesdays, Thursdays and Fridays during the summer.

From the museum, hang a right and stroll along **Kauppakatu**, which soon merges with **Kuninkaankatu**. These two unevenly cobbled streets, the old town's main thoroughfares, and the lanes that branch off them, are lined with houses painted in a riot of pastel shades, most clad principally in decorative neo-Renaissance style. Two have been turned into living museums: **Marela** (same times as Rauma Museum; €3, or free with Rauma Museum ticket), at Kauppakatu 24, a preserved ship-owner's residence from the seventeenth century; and **Kirsti**, a block north over a small footbridge at Pohjankatu 3 (late June to early Sept daily 10am–5pm, closed Mon rest of the year; €3, or free with Rauma Museum ticket), a group of brookside homestead buildings with a similar history.

East of here is the **Rauma Art Museum** (Rauman taidemuseo; Tues–Thurs 10am–6pm, Fri 10am–4pm, Sat & Sun 11am–4pm; €5; Ⓦwww.raumantaidemuseo .fi), Kuninkaankatu 37, with interesting displays on folk art. West down Pohjankatu and across Isopoikkikatu is the **Church of the Holy Cross** (Pyhän Ristin kirkko; May–Sept 8am–5pm), which has served as Rauma's main church since the Franciscans were exiled in 1538. The aisled interior features a carved altar cabinet from the 1440s and a 1625 Renaissance-style pulpit, adorned with carvings of saints and apostles.

Once you've taken in enough of the old town *in situ*, pay a visit to the **Old Rauma Restoration Centre** (Korjausrakentamiskeskus Tammela; June–Aug noon–6pm), around the corner from the town hall at Eteläpitkäkatu 17, an exhibition centre with displays on how the old wooden buildings are restored and maintained – all explained in very clear English.

Museums outside the old town

Rauma has a pair of worthwhile sights just outside the old town. The **Lönnström Art Museum** (Lönnströmin taidemuseo; May–Aug Tues–Thurs 10am–6pm, Fri–Mon noon–4pm; Sept–April daily except Mon 11am–4pm, Thurs till 8pm; €5; Ⓦwww.lonnstromintaidemuseo.fi), a few hundred metres northwest of the old town at Valtakatu 7, displays the Lönnström family's private art collection – Golden Age paintings, silver, porcelain, glass and sculpture work – and holds rotating exhibitions on contemporary Finnish art and design. Occasional music performances are put on in the upstairs loft.

A few minutes' walk from here along Satamakatu brings you to the **Rauma Maritime Museum**, Kalliokatu 34 (Rauman merimuseo; early June to early Aug daily 11am–5pm; May and mid-Aug to late Aug Tues–Fri & Sun noon–4pm; €7), with extensive displays on local maritime history, though the real draw is the navigation simulator, a fascinating contraption that allows would-be mariners the chance to man their own open-sea voyage. It offers a choice of over a hundred sailing routes, including New York harbour and the English Channel, and the computer-generated visuals are projected onto a huge screen in front of the ship's bridge, allowing you to plot a course, navigate obstacles and bring your ship safely into port.

Eating and drinking

Rauma doesn't throw up a multitude of **eating** options, and despite the large stream of daytime visitors, night-time entertainment is also extremely sedate; the town doesn't hold a candle to other regional towns – Pori, for example – when it comes to a **bar** scene.

Café Sali Kuninkaankatu 22. Great place for a morning coffee and pastries before a jaunt around the old town, with bright, spiffy Art Deco decor. Salads and sandwiches served all day long.

Kontion Leipomo Kuninkaankatu 9. Rauma's best bakery is much beloved for its *pitsileivos* (sweet tart with dainty lace icing), though it's also good for a hot chocolate and *korvapuusti*.

La Bamba Posellinkatu 6. One of the town's simplest eating options, with an extensive choice of pizzas, burgers and pasta dishes from around €10. Lunch €8.20. If It's sunny, try to snag a table at the small, leafy terrace out back.

Mr Jones Valtakatu 5. Though set in the town's *Best Western* with a standard modern pub aesthetic, this is the best place in town to go out drinking; you can even book a spot in the on-site sauna (€10 per person).

Outolintu Kauppakatu 16. "The Strange Bird" can be a pretty dire spot, especially once the karaoke machine is hauled out, but it's good for local gossip, with a coterie of octogenarian locals often found talking timber preservation and lace technique at the bar.

Villa Tallbo Petäjäksentie 178. Housed in a ship-owner's restored *fin-de-siècle* summer villa near the sea, this darling spot vies for the best setting in town to linger over almond trout (€14.60) or grilled salmon remoulade (€14.40).

Wähä Tallbo Vanhankirkonkatu 3. An appetizing old-town lunch option, with heaping lunch plates for under €10.

Wanhan Rauman Kellari Anundilankatu 8. Around the corner from *Wähä Tallbo*, this vaulted brick basement joint serves extremely large plates of Finnish dishes (€13–29). Perfect for a late evening meal.

Around Rauma

A fifteen-minute drive from Rauma in **LAPPI** is the UNESCO World Heritage Site **Sammallahdenmäki**, thirty-six Bronze Age burial cairns set in a dense forest. As transportation to the poorly indicated site is limited, though, contact the region's expert on the site, Ulla Antola (☏044 387 2136, @ulla.antola@eritys .fi), if you'd like to go out and explore, or ask at the Rauma tourist office. Lappi is also now known for its **"Polar Honey"** (@www.lappi-hunaja.fi), a toothsome product that comes in dozens of flavours, with imagery and marketing that deftly capitalizes on the fact that the town shares the name with the Finnish word for Lapland. You can test out the product's various forms at Lappi's country store at Sahamäentie 1, which also doubles as an **information** point.

Rauma also offers access to a small **archipelago** that stretches out for around 10km from the shore, though it's somewhat overshadowed by the nuclear-plant island of Olkiluoto (see box, p.119), visible off the coast. By far the most enticing spot on the archipelago is the working **Kylmäpihlaja Lighthouse**, 15km from Rauma. It may not be the most attractive lighthouse in Finland – its boxy, modernist construction gives it a slight resemblance to a prison watchtower – but it is a great place to hang out for a few hours in the breeze and visit the island's café and handicrafts shop, or sit down for the fresh seafood lunch buffet (€14.50) or dinner at the superb **restaurant**. It also doubles as a small **hotel**, whose rooms have breathtaking views of the sea (☏044/082 2964, @www.kylmapihlaja.com; June–Aug; ❺). Canoes and rowboats are available for rent, and there's regular boat transport from Rauma's harbour (ring ☏0400/775 875).

Pori and around

Upon arrival at **PORI** in 1901 with her husband, the painter Akseli, Mary Gallen-Kallela penned to a friend, "Here we are in the city of bears. It's big and empty, absolutely amazingly empty, but fun with its low houses." Such a characterization would not be out of place a hundred-plus years later: Pori, whose coat of arms is flanked by a grizzly bear (Pori's name derives from the town's Swedish name, Björneborg, or "bear city"), is still as sleepy a Finnish town as you'll find anywhere. Still, today, most Finns would readily free associate Pori with another four-letter word: **jazz**. On account of its yearly festival – now increasingly less jazz- and more rock- and pop-oriented as it approaches its fiftieth birthday – this sizeable settlement of some 70,000 has become one of the most visited towns in Finland. For one week each July, its pavements and squares are filled with buzzing saxophones, wailing guitars, simmering snare drums and the fêting of the 150,000 people who come to listen to it all – for more on the event, see below. The town has also branched out into other genres of festival, hosting two other summer extravaganzas, **Pori Folk** (Ⓦwww.pori.fi/kulttuuri/porifolk) and **Sonisphere** (Ⓦfi.sonispherefestivals .com), but throughout the rest of the year it reverts to normality as a small, quiet industrial town with a worthy art museum and a handful of architectural and historical oddities. It's also a centre for **ice hockey**, and while its team, Porin Ässät ("The Aces"), doesn't quite retain the glory it once held, it still manages to bring Pori's residents together during their Saturday-night games from September to March.

Though hard to believe, present-day downtown Pori was once completely underwater – which explains why it is so flat. It reigned as Finland's leading shipping port in the mid-1800s, when vast quantities of whitefish, salmon, spices and fine wines made their way in and out of its waters, but it was to prove a short-lived crown: a devastating fire in 1852 burned the entire city to cinders in a single day. After the fire, Finnish architects re-envisioned a safer new town with broad boulevards and brick buildings. Combined with the extremely slow nature of life here, these give Pori a distinct sense of remove.

Pori Jazz

Pori's annual **jazz festival** (Ⓦwww.porijazz.com) is one of Finland's most popular festivals, drawing some 150,000 people over nine days to 160 concerts – of which nearly two-thirds are free. The festival is mainly spread along the southern banks of the Kokemäki River, with the two largest venues set on nearby Kirjurinluoto Island – it's worth having a bike to cycle between venues. **Tickets** for the world-class weekend concerts at *Café Jazz* are always sold out many months in advance (buy online at Ⓦwww.porijazz.com, or via the tourist office), though the late-night jam sessions can usually be crashed quite easily. If you're going to stay the whole week it's best to buy a pass (around €200; on sale from 1 April). Individual tickets range from €50 to €60 for the bigger-name acts – in the past these have included Raphael Saadiq, Erykah Badu, Gilberto Gil, Duffy and everyone's European festival favourites, Herbie Hancock and Chick Corea – while concerts from smaller acts are significantly cheaper, and often free. There is a **Jazz Festival Office** (Ⓣ02/626 2200) in an old cotton mill at Pohjoisranta 11 where you can buy any tickets that haven't already been sold and pick up festival programmes and informa-tion. **Accommodation** is best fixed up at least six to nine months in advance – hotels, hostel and campsite fill up very quickly (despite nearly doubling their prices), although the tourist and jazz festival offices endeavour to house as much of the overspill as possible in private homes (€100 per night for double room; minimum two nights) or on mattresses in local schools (€10–20 per person). A local campsite, *Isomäki*, also operates during the festival, 2km south of the centre in the Isomäki Sports Centre (call the festival office for details) and linked to the centre by frequent shuttle buses. You'll even come across more unconventional places to stay – such as a disused train carriage in the station – though such spots are never advertised.

Arrival, information and accommodation

Trains arrive just southwest of downtown, from which it's a ten-minute walk along Rautatienpuistokatu; arrive by **bus** and you'll be a tad more central, a short walk along Isolinnankatu to the central crisscross of cobblestone streets overrun with indoor shopping centres that marks Finland's first pedestrian walkway. One of these malls, the Promenadi Centre at Yrjönkatu 17, contains the helpful **tourist office** (June to mid-Aug Mon–Fri 9am–6pm, Sat 10am–3pm; mid-Aug to May Mon–Fri 9am–4.30pm; ☎02/621 7900, ⓦwww.pori.fi), where you can get information on the town and surrounding region and book accommodation and tickets to local events. There's free **internet** access both here as well as at the library, Gallen-Kallelankatu 12 (Mon–Fri 10am–7pm, Sat 10am–3pm). Free hired **bicycles** (free; €20 deposit) are available from Arkki, Pohjoispuisto 7.

Accommodation, it must be said, is extremely difficult to come by if you're here during the jazz festival (see box, p.151), though at other times, you should have your pick of options fitting various budgets. Alternatively, stay 20km outside of town in **Yyteri** (see p.155), close to one of the best beaches in the country and accessible on bus #32.

Pori

Amado Keskusaukio 2 ☎02/631 0100,
ⓦwww.amado.fi. A welcome change from the chains, this family-run place by the bus station may feel a mite tired and old, but the rooms here are bigger than you tend to find elsewhere, and there is a decent on-site restaurant. ❹
Buisto Itäpuisto 13 ☎02/633 0647 or 044/333 0646, ⓦwww.hostelbuisto.net. This unofficial guesthouse is the city's cheapest place to crash, with tidy, colourful rooms featuring Marimekko-patterned curtains. Popular with youth groups (though without dorm beds), it's just around the corner from a pair of thrumming disco-bars. ❷

🏃 **Sokos Vaakuna** Gallen-Kallelankatu 7
☎02/528 100, ⓦwww.sokoshotels.fi.
The town's spiffiest hotel is this sleek, business-oriented place, offering immediate access to the market square. An upstairs disco is the place to be seen for the post-thirty crowd on weekends. Great weekend discounts. ❹/❺

Yyteri

Top Camping Yyteri ☎02/634 5700, ⓦwww .pori.fi/camping. This is Pori's nearest non-festival campsite, offering pitches, a shop, café, sauna and many types of cabin (❷).
Yyteri Spa Hotel Sipintie 1 ☎02/628 5300, ⓦwww.yyterinkylpylahotelli.fi. This massive, modern silver building looks like it might have been used in the film *Brazil*, but the interiors are much less exotic, epitomes of the Finnish hotel-room style of *blandi*. Still, nearly all sport seafront views and the rates include spa access. More atmospheric – and pricey – are the large wooden timeshare cottages outside, though availability is hard to come by. ❻

The Town

The central section of Pori, from the train station in the south to the riverbank just north of Hallituskatu, can be crossed on foot in about fifteen minutes despite the town's wide, grid-style streets.

Along Hallituskatu

The town's architectural pride and joy is a block of late nineteenth-century buildings on the broad asphalt Hallituskatu, immediately south of the Kokemäki River. Most striking of these is the **old courthouse**, designed by architect C.L. Engel in 1831 and best admired from the leafy, manicured park that flanks it from below. The building facade bears the city's ursine coat of arms; Pori's original (Swedish) name is Björneborg, meaning "Bear Castle". Several buildings away at no. 12 is the **Junnelius Palace**, the Venetian-style neo-Renaissance town hall from 1895. Architect August Krook was commissioned to come up with the design, and subsequently took a trip to Italy expressly to map out the style for

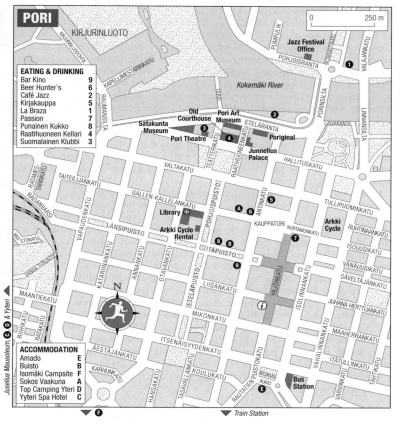

the clearly derivative facade. Just next door at no. 14 stands the renovated **Pori Theatre** (Mon–Fri 11am–6pm; free), the oldest Finnish-language theatre building in the country, and Finnish drama's temporary home during the Russification period when it was considered too provocative to appear in a larger centre like Turku or Helsinki. Built in 1884, it has a striking neo-Renaissance facade, and the tiny interior – seating just 300 – is heavy with opulent frescos and sculptured chandeliers (enquire at the tourist office for a visit inside).

Towards the end of Hallituskatu at no. 11 is the **Satakunta Museum** (Satakunnan museo; Tues–Sun 11am–5pm, Wed till 8pm; €4), where three well-stocked floors trace the story of Pori and the surrounding Satakunta region, displaying some 70,000 medieval findings, late nineteenth-century photos and shop signs, and typical house interiors; there's also some interesting memorabilia from the powerful labour movement of the 1930s and a scale model of Pori as it stood before the 1852 fire. Immediately north of here on Eteläranta is the **Pori Art Museum** (Pori taidemuseo; Tues–Sun 11am–6pm, Wed till 8pm; €5), actually one of the most important in Finland. Set in a large ex-warehouse, the museum now puts on displays of primarily Finnish abstract art from the 1900s to the 1980s as well as temporary exhibitions of international modern art – often large installations. Just next door is a great modern art gallery with the corny name, **Poriginal** (Tues–Sun 11am–6pm; free).

Juselius Mausoleum

Pori's most extraordinary sight is found in the sprawling **Käppärä Cemetery** (Käppärän hautausmaa), a good twenty-minute walk west along Maantiekatu. Towering over the cemetery's several thousand gravestones are two structures: a small red neo-Gothic wooden chapel and, next to it, the Gothic-arched **Juselius Mausoleum** (May–Aug daily noon–3pm; Sept–April Sun noon–2pm; free), an octagonal vaulted structure of steeples and towering cathedralesque windows that looks like it might have well been a study for a section of Notre Dame's roof. The building was commissioned in 1899 by local timber magnate F.A. Juselius as a memorial to his daughter, Sigrid, who died aged 11 of tuberculosis. Juselius called on the leading Finnish church architect of the time, Josef Steinbäck, to manage the design along with his colleague and contemporary Gallen-Kallela, who decorated the interior with some of his best large-scale paintings. A fire destroyed the interior in 1931; what you see today are re-paintings by the Gallen-Kallelas' son, Jorma, from his father's sketches.

Enter the building through the chased copper double doors, their entryway adorned above with frescos, to the main chamber. Below here you can see the tomb: resting on a marble floor is a granite catafalque holding Sigrid's white marble sarcophagus. The walls above are plastered with Gallen-Kallela's six glorious landscape-sized frescos, two of which stand out in particular. *Building* depicts a couple putting together a log cabin at the seaside. Though they are blind to the fact, Death himself, dressed in a periwinkle frock and a sailor's cap, smiles wryly in the background as he helps out with a hand drill. Adjacent is the even more poignant *At Tuonela River*, in which a hardy-looking man and his sobbing wife set out in a rowing boat towards a black river, the red swan of death conspicuously perched in the corner, as a crowd of glum onlookers look on. The artist himself is in the painting, too, as the weathered, moustachioed man on the far right – the only bystander glancing away from the scene. In his own words, the frescos represented "the sweeping journey of our people along the crest of life into the lap of the Underworld", ideas and themes that the artist had been developing since his own daughter's death from diphtheria at age 4 several years earlier.

Eating, drinking and entertainment

Pori still has its fair share of kebab-pizza and *grilli* joints, though recent years have seen the advent of a number of fairly good (if fairly pricey) **restaurants** proper. If you must go for **fast food**, be sure to try the local speciality *porilainen*, a large, thick slice of grilled sausage served hamburger-style in a roll with pickles, ketchup and chopped onion. Come evening most locals gravitate to the town centre, where you'll find a good selection of smallish **bars**. There are several open-air drinking spots at the Eteläranta riverbank – *Barco*, *Lautta* and *Pub Charlotte* among them – perfect for sipping a pint in the setting sun.

Restaurants

Kirjakauppa Antinkatu 10. Opened in 2009, this cheery, sizeable lunch, dinner and snack spot serves a limited menu of small salads, sandwiches and tapas plates, most for under €10. Decor is dark fleur-de-lis wallpaper and polished, pale oak flooring with white-leather designer seating; clientele tends towards fortysomethings. Popular among locals late in the evening for a pint of Karhu or shot of Koskenkorva.

La Braza Siltapuistokatu 1. Though awkwardly located just across the river on a roundabout edge, this excellent casual-meets-upscale spot serves superb Finnish seafood and steak dishes with Asian and South American flair in a red brick interior with rattan seating. Try the scrumptious *kokoos-porkkanakeitto*, a lightly spiced coconut and carrot soup (€7.50), followed by the sirloin steak with spicy morel sauce (€22.50). Lunch buffet €9.50.

Raatihuoneen Kellari Hallituskatu 9 ℡ 02/633 4804. This classy vaulted brick spot, set into the basement of the old courthouse, is one of Pori's best restaurants. The scene is usually fairly besuited and upscale, and it is popular with local bureaucrats and often the local choice for wedding parties. The changing spreads of various Finnish-style meat and fish dishes range from €16 to €31 – the lemony sea salmon is a speciality here – and they do a great all-you-can-eat lunch buffet for €13.

🍴 **Suomalainen Klubbi** Eteläranta 10. This great dinner choice sports white tablecloths, but it's informal enough for the odd beshorted traveller. They do a whirling trade in group dinners for seniors groups, which often lead to some pretty slow outdoor pavilion-style dancing on weekends during the summer. Their à la carte menu is a tad pricier than similar spots, but it's the waterside setting you're paying for.

Bars

Bar Kino Itäpuisto 10A ⊛ www.barkino.com. Set in an old cinema, this bar-club attracts students and young professionals with regular live music on Thursday nights and DJs on Wednesdays and at the weekend, though beware of the occasional themed evenings aimed strictly at 18–20-year-olds. €5 cover most nights.

Beer Hunter's Antinkatu 11. Poor punnery has done nothing to halt the flocks of Finns who descend on this pub once work lets out. They brew their own stouts and lagers and serve over two hundred other bottled beers, the names of which are scribbled in chalk on a large blackboard. Try a pint of the supple, dark Mufloni lager, named after the wild mouflon sheep on nearby Säppi Island.

🍴 **Café Jazz** Eteläranta 6. This all-year spin-off from the jazz festival sits right on the banks of the Kokemäki River. Standard Finnish fare is served both indoors and out, but most people take to the terrace if the weather's right. Loud rock cover-bands often take over the stage, so don't come necessarily expecting Ella and Louis.

Passion Yrjönkatu 10. One of the city's more popular venues for twentysomethings, this indoor-outdoor bar is also big with the post-teenybopper set gearing up for a night of clubbing. Looks right onto the market square and within shouting distance of the town's other main watering holes. €2.90 bottles of Karhu.

🍴 **Punainen Kukko** Itäpuisto 13 ⊛ www .punainenkukko.fi. Long Pori's most popular venues, this labyrinthine place contains several floors divided up into a lounge, karaoke bar, dance club and live rock venue. It's aimed at a more mature crowd, and anyone who doesn't look to make the age limit of 24 is sent straight across the road to *Bar Kino* – though this doesn't prevent some serious drinking and concomitant drunken behaviour from finding its way here.

Around Pori

The region surrounding Pori, known as **Satakunta**, offers access to a pair of peninsulas, one beachy and resorty, the other more rural and rustic. If you can't stand the hustle and bustle of downtown Pori, take to the holiday resort of **YYTERI** (from the Swedish *Ytterö*, or "outer island"), 17km northwest. Yyteri is best known for its six-kilometre stretch of **beachfront**, fronted by a shallow bay that's great for wading and backed by distinctive natural dunes that offer some shelter from the wind. The beach's main resort is the *Yyteri Spa Hotel* (see p.152) but a block has thankfully been put on further beachfront construction due to feared dune erosion. Yyteri also has a small unisex nudist area, one of two official spots in the country. The recently renovated 63m-high observation tower offers dreamy views of the sea and the forests that front it, as well as a summertime café.

Much less resorty is the three-kilometre-long island of **Reposaari**, 6km on and connected to the mainland via a causeway lined with four windmills that power Finland's largest wind-power plant. Once the largest fishing port along Finland's Bothnian coast, its deep, sheltered harbour became crucial once the outlet of the Kokemäka River silted up at the beginning of the nineteenth century. The town boasts a fetching maritime scene of old wooden houses and a harbourside **park** of exotic summer flowers – ballast soil carried by ships to the island contained seeds from far-flung destinations. Nearby **Reposaari Church** (May–Aug daily 9am–3pm) was built by Norwegian sailors in 1876, with detailed ceiling paintings added half a century later by nature artist Lennart Segerstrale; in front of it is a

sculpture by Wäinö Aaltonen, a memorial to the 53 crew members killed when the *S2* torpedo ship sank off the Reposaari shore in 1925. There are a few places to stay around Yyteri (see p.155), while for a fine meal on Reposaari head to *Ravintola Reposaari*, just across from the harbour at Satamapuisto 34, an ochre-slatted wooden building that serves great herring and other fresh fish dishes. You can reach Yyteri via bus #32 (or Reposaari via #40M) from Pori's bus station; alternatively, there's a nice wooded 18km cycling route.

Fifteen kilometres north of Pori outside the village of **NOORMARKKU** is **Villa Mairea** (ⓦwww.villamairea.fi; visits only by appointment, €20 per person, call ⓣ010/888 4460 to reserve, minimum four people), one of Alvar Aalto's most accomplished works. The house, commissioned by a wealthy Finlandssvenska couple, is a beautiful boxy building richly accentuated with wood, stone and brick in its facade and calls to mind a Japanese temple; it was allegedly inspired by Frank Lloyd Wright's Fallingwater. Aalto was active in this region between the late 1930s and early 1950s, drafting plans for some twenty buildings, nearly all of which saw the light of day. Regular buses leave from Pori to Noormarkku, from which it's a short walk to the villa.

Travel details

Train

Pori to: Tampere (4–6 daily; 1hr 30min).
Turku to: Helsinki (hourly; 2hr); Tampere (7–9 daily; 1hr 55min).

Bus

Pori to: Helsinki (frequent; 3hr 45min–5hr 15min); Noormarkku (frequent; 20min); Rauma (hourly; 45min–1hr 10min); Reposaari (frequent; 50min); Turku (frequent; 2hr 10min–2hr 55min); Uusikaupunki (hourly; 1hr 10min–1hr 30min); Yyteri (frequent; 45min).
Rauma to: Pori (hourly; 45min–1hr 5min); Turku (hourly; 1hr 30min); Uusikaupunki (hourly; 1hr).

Turku to: Helsinki (every 30min; 2hr 10min–2hr 45min); Gustavs (9 daily; 1hr 40min); Naantali (frequent; 30min); Uusikaupunki (hourly; 1hr 10min–1hr 30min).

Domestic ferries

Turku to: Mariehamn (4 daily; 5hr); Naantali (2 daily; 2hr).

International ferries

Turku to: Kapellskär (2 daily; 7hr); Stockholm (4 daily; 9hr 45min).

4

Åland

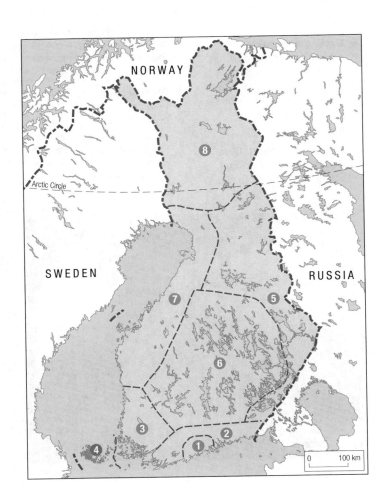

NORWAY

8

Arctic Circle

SWEDEN

RUSSIA

7   **5**

6

3   **2**

4   **1**

0   100 km

CHAPTER 4 # Highlights

✳ **Kobba Klintar** Take a day-trip to this once-abandoned island for a great seafood buffet, impromptu theatre performances and cracking views of the open sea. See p.167

✳ **Cycling the islands** With seemingly endless stretches of forested road and sun-drenched coast – and easy access by ferry – biking has never been better. See p.168

✳ **Havsviddan Resort, Geta** Bet you've never had five-star luxury this remote: a minimalist-chic resort set smack at the sea with a sumptuous world-class restaurant plus a smoke sauna. See p.170

✳ **Kastelholm Castle** This grand, granite fourteenth-century stronghold is one of the most striking fortresses in Finland. See pp.170–171

✳ **St Anna's Church, Kökar** Set in an umber wheatfield fronting the craggy edge of the archipelago, this one-time Franciscan monastery has the most spectacular position of any church in Finland. See p.175

▲ Kastelholm Castle

4

Åland

The flat and thickly forested archipelago of **ÅLAND** (pronounced "AWE-lahnd" and known as Ahvenanmaa in Finnish) is very much its own little world. Geographically positioned in the Bothnian Gulf between Finland and Sweden, these 6000-plus islands and their inhabitants are politically Finnish but culturally Swedish, clinging to a unique form of independence with their own parliament and flag (a red and yellow cross on a blue background), their own postal system, automobile number plates and country code top-level domain (Ⓦ.ax). And while they may carry Finnish passports and pay in euros, Ålänningar – Ålanders – are themselves confidently a breed apart from mainland Finns; most in fact prefer to think of themselves as Swedes through and through. Nearly ninety percent speak Swedish as their native language – most even with fairly heavy Stockholm accents – and probably the only Finnish you'll hear spoken while here will be from the mouths of vacationing Finns, which helps explain why nearly all towns have Swedish-only forms of their names. As Swedish is mercifully closer to English, a visit here can make a welcome break from the perpetual battle with the Finnish language.

There's plenty here to appeal too. For one, these are some of the quietest and most remote islands that you'll find in all of Scandinavia, maintaining a distinct sense of tranquillity throughout the year – even in the high season. It is easily the best region of the country – possibly the best in Scandinavia – for **cycling**, while efficient, regular ferries run throughout the archipelago that remain free to foot passengers. In contrast to the Finlandssvenska gentry who reside on the mainland, Ålanders have survived with more simple livelihoods such as farming, forestry, fishing and shipping – an aspect that's certainly part of the islands' appeal – and which accounts for the propensity of maritime museums and artefacts spread across the archipelago. **Beaches** here, too, are rather good, and almost all of them filled with soft, ochre sands; while those in and around Mariehamn tend to get the busiest in the high season, head out to the more remote islands and you'll often have entire stretches of strand to yourself. The islands are also known for a number of **festivals** throughout the summertime (see box, p.163), and you'll also find a number of handsome **guesthouses** – a handful actually fairly upmarket – though the winning choice is clearly to **camp**: there are plentiful organized sites, and in isolated areas you should be able to camp rough with no problems.

Some history

The Åland archipelago has a documented history that stretches back to 4200 BC or so, when the first inhabitants arrived. By 900 AD, the thriving population was trading with places as far away as the Arabian Gulf, while Viking communities set up shop in places all over the islands – several of their intact burial mounds are still

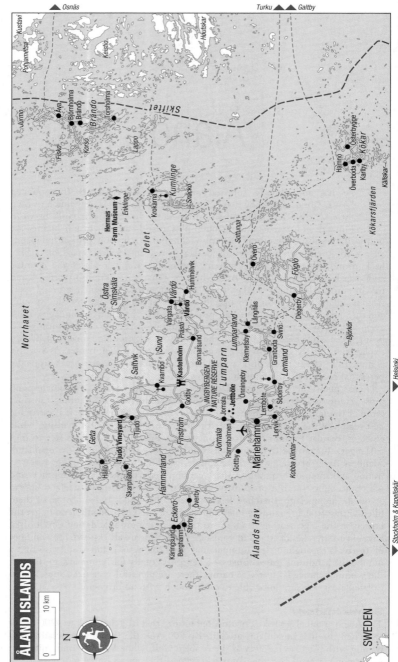

ÅLAND ISLANDS

Osnäs

Turku ▲▲ Galtby

Kustavi

Pohjanmetsä

K-hto

Houtskär

Vurmo

Åva

Björnholma

Brändö

Korsö

Torsholma

Fiskö

Brändö

Lappo

Skitttet

Österbygge

Kökar

Hamnö

Överboda

Karlby

Kökarsfjärden

Källskär

Hermas
Farm Museum

Krokarna

Kumlinge

Snäckö

Enklinge

Delet

Seglinge

Överö

Föglö

Norrhavet

Östra
Simskäla

Vårdö

Humnelvik

Vargata

Vårdö

Prästö

Långnäs

Degerby

Björkör

Sund

Bomarsund

Kastelholm

Kvarnbo

Lumparn

Klemetsby

Svinö

Granboda

Lumparland

Saltvik

Godby

Lemland

INGBYBERGEN
NATURE RESERVE

Jettböle

Lemböte

Söderby

Lemland

Geta

Tjudö Vineyard

Tjudö

Finström

Jomala

Önningeby

Lervik

Helsinki

Hällö

Skarpnätö

Ramsholmen

Mariehamn

Kobba Klintar

Hammarland

Gottby

Eckerö

Överby

Käringsund

Storby

Bergham

Ålands Hav

N

0   10 km

SWEDEN

Stockholm & Kapellskär

Grisslehamn

visible today. In Swedish hands throughout the Middle Ages – from which period a number of handsome red-granite churches across the islands date – the archipelago was coveted by the Russians on account of their strategic location in the Baltic, and the islands became part of the Russian Grand Duchy of Finland in 1807. When Finland gained independence, the future of Åland was referred to the League of Nations (though not before several Åland leaders had been imprisoned in Helsinki on a charge of high treason). Although the islanders had hoped to belong to Sweden, Finland won out when in arbitration and Finnish sovereignty was

Åland transport

Ferries to Åland

Getting to Åland is straightforward. Daily **ferries** to Åland from mainland Finland and Sweden (as well as Estonia) are operated by several companies: **Tallink Silja Lines** (Torggatan 14; ☎018/16711, ⓦwww.tallinksilja.com), **Viking Line** (☎018/26011, ⓦwww.vikingline.fi), **Eckerö Linjen** (☎018/28000, ⓦwww.eckerolinjen.fi) and **Birka Line** (☎018/27027, ⓦwww.birkaline.com). The largest Tallink Silja, Viking and Birka Line (Stockholm only) cruise ships, coming from Helsinki (10hr) or Stockholm (5hr 30min–6hr 45min), arrive at **Mariehamn**'s Västerhamn (West Harbour), while night-time arrivals on the Turku–Kapellskär or Turku–Stockholm routes (5hr 30min from Turku) dock at **Långnäs**, 45 minutes east; you need to book a shared taxi (€14) when you buy your ferry ticket to get from Långnäs to Mariehamn. Eckerö operates a small ferry from Grisselhamn, Sweden (3hr), that arrives at **Eckerö** (see p.169), 45 minutes northwest of Mariehamn.

    Fares for deck passengers from Helsinki to Åland range from €18–€41 in the summer – around half that in low season – and they're cheaper from Turku (about half) and Sweden. Cabins in high season range from €72 up to several hundred euros, depending on the cabin size, while transporting a car from Helsinki costs €72 – and again, half that from Turku. Fares are somewhat lower in low season. Bicycles can be taken on board for a nominal fee of around €5.

    Åland lies outside the EU system when it comes to indirect taxation, thereby heavily incentivizing Baltic ferries to stop here, which explains the armies of Scandinavians wheeling trolleys full of booze upon disembarking.

Flights to Åland

If you're in a real rush to get out here, **Air Åland** (☎018/17110, ⓦwww.airaland.com) operates flights from Helsinki and Stockholm, while **Turku Air** (☎0207/218 800, ⓦwww.turkuair.fi) runs from Turku. Both airlines depart the island's small airport (☎018/634 411), a few kilometres northwest of Mariehamn. These are mostly used by business travellers, but you can usually find a seat to Helsinki from €79, even last minute. Turku flights are pricier, running upwards of €225 each way.

Transport around the archipelago

Once on dry land, there's a fairly thorough and inexpensive **bus service** (☎018/525 100, ⓦwww.alandstrafiken.ax) covering mainland Åland; the maximum fare for any bus trip is €4. **Cycling** is a super alternative (see box, p.168). Archipelago **ferry** transport, on which you'll need to rely to get to many of Åland's most winsome spots, is operated by the efficient, always-on-time Ålandstrafiken, who link all of the major islands and a number of the smaller ones. Passengers (and their bicycles) always travel for free on all ferries – it's subsidized by all those astronomically high taxes paid by local residents – but vehicles cost €10–23 per route. If you're desperate to be on x island by y o'clock, you can always hire an expensive **taxibåt** with Ålands Båtar (☎040/506 1299). **Cars**, meanwhile, can be rented from Rundbergs Biluthyrning (☎018/525 505, ⓦwww.rundbergs.com), Strandgatan 1B.

established, in return for autonomy and complete demilitarization: the Ålanders now regard themselves as a shining example of Nordic cooperation, and living proof that a small state can run its own affairs while being part of a larger one. The islanders, for their part, much prefer to be called Ålänningar than Finns; theirs is an independence to be especially proud of.

Mariehamn

A laid-back – if at times quite lively – seaside resort home to nearly half of Åland's population, **Mariehamn** (Finnish: Maarianhamina), Åland's capital, is a wonderful place to kick back for a couple of days, though it's really best used as a place to gear up for an exploration of the more remote parts of the archipelago. Its status dates back to 1861, when Tsar Alexander II swooped in on the rinky-dink fishing village of Övernäs (pop. 33, then), renamed it after his wife Maria Alexandrovna and brought on board Hilda Hongell, Finland's first female architectural engineer, to build up the settlement following the tradition of Swedish urban planning. This involved the construction of houses adjacent to one another with American-style porches, large lawns and rows of trees separating them from the street, these elegant specimens that line virtually every street giving Mariehamn its nickname of the "town of a thousand linden trees".

Arrival and information

The **airport** is located 3km from Mariehamn, and while there's no public transport, the taxi fare to the town centre is negligible. **Ferries** arrive at one of two terminals in Mariehamn's Västerhamn (West Harbour), a fifteen-minute walk away from the islands' excellent principal **tourist office** at Storagatan 8 (April, May & Sept 9am–4pm, Sat 10am–3pm; early to mid-June & mid- to late Aug Mon–Fri 9am–5pm, Sat 9am–4pm; mid-June to early Aug daily 9am–6pm; Oct–March Mon–Fri 9am–4pm; ☎018/24 000, ⓦwww.visitaland .com), which can provide the latest details regarding travel and accommodation and also sells detailed cycling and hiking maps and guides. They also have an inexpensive **internet** terminal (the library, Strandgatan 29, has some for free, though you may have to book a slot if you need to do more than check your mail). You can pick up **maps** as well as English-language books and periodicals at Lisco, Skarpansvägen 25 (☎018/17177). If you need **laundry** services while in Åland, most of the archipelago's guest harbours offer washers and dryers for about €7 per load.

Accommodation

Mariehamn holds several enticing accommodation options, though if you turn up in summer on spec you'll have a tough time finding something: there are just three official youth **hostels** across the islands and, though a handful of cheapish **guesthouses** offer hostel-type facilities in town, these fill up rather quickly. In a pinch, you're likely to find space in one of the three- or four-star chain **hotels**, though you'll pay for the privilege. Alternatively, enquire with the Viking Lines office, which often cuts good deals with local hotels.

Arkipelag Strandgatan 31 ☎018/24020, ⓦwww.hotellarkipelag.com. Åland's smartest hotel is this nonetheless fairly predictable four-star, with all 84 rooms and suites featuring the same light floral duvets, walnut-finish headboards and brass lamps that scream chain conformity. But a good number have small terraces, the operation is well run and you're

Come summertime, Åland – as with many places in Finland – likes to let a little bit loose, the main island putting on over a dozen large festivals throughout the warmer months that draw folks from all over the archipelago and further afield. The largest is the rocking **Rockoff Festival** (mid-July; ⓦ www.rockoff.nu), basically an excuse to party hard for ten days and listen to loud Finnish and Swedish rock bands. Slightly less sybaritic is the **Ålandia Jazz Festival** (mid-July; ⓦ www .alandiajazz.aland.fi), held over a long weekend and featuring thrumming concerts primarily by celebrated Scandinavian musicians. Later in the month, Saltvik puts on the **Viking Market Festival** (late July; ⓦ www.aland-vikingar.com), in which hippies, washouts and "Vikings" from all over Europe come to bustle about in thick burlap dress and savour the finer points of jousting and lance-to-shield combat; there are also chain dancing, marionette theatre shows and plenty of good-time medieval music concerts. The PAF Open (mid-Aug 2010 and 2011; ⓦ www.pafopen.com), meanwhile, is an annual, week-long international **beach volleyball championship** during which Mariehamn is overtaken by tall, bronze Adonises and Amazons who come to serve, volley and slam right on the town's shores; there are parties throughout the week. Finally, the **Harvest Festival** (mid-Sept; ⓦ www.jomala.aland .fi) takes place in Jomala's Ålands Landsbygdscentrum, and is good for picking up local products and enjoying the brief (but very beautiful) autumn that befalls the archipelago before the cold months set in.

only a lift ride away from the city's most happening (and only) nightclub, *Arken*. ⓺
Gröna Udden Östernäsvägen ⓣ018/21121, ⓦ www.gronaudden.com. This well-sized camping area, set south of town on a large beach with a bathing jetty, also features cute cherry-red cabins (€90) and more guesthouse-like rooms (⓷), both of which share facilities in a separate building. Breakfast €7. Open May to mid-Sept.
Hotel Adlon/Kaptensgårdarna Hamngatan 7 ⓣ018/15300, ⓦ www.alandhotels.fi. Immediately next to the ferry terminal, this place offers very standard rooms and a large pool downstairs. If that doesn't suit, they also run the next-door *Kaptensgårdarna* inn (ⓣ018/15400), whose more rustic rooms are set about a couple of old captains' villas. *Adlon* ⓹; *Kaptensgårdarna* ⓷
Hotell Pommern Norragatan 8–10 ⓣ018/15555, ⓦ www.hotellpommern.aland.fi. Though parts of it feel a bit dated, this central spot on the esplanade has an air of sophistication about it, with 54 smart rooms and a classy bar (and restaurant) downstairs good for an evening drink. ⓹
🏃 **Övernäsgården** Östernäsvägen ⓣ018/12525, ⓦ www.overnasgarden.ax. Two kilometres south of the centre along a quiet wooded path, this superb spot offers standard

rooms in the main guesthouse, as well as several dozen chalets (⓸) spread out on a hilly stretch of land fronting a tiny sandy beach. The real bombshell is their motorized, self-propelled sauna boat which you can take for a spin out into the middle of the bay. Convivial staff. Open May–Sept. ⓷
Park Alandia Norra Esplanadgatan 3 ⓣ018/14130, ⓦ www.vikingline.fi/parkalandiahotel. Owned and operated by Viking Line, this great mid-level option often has combo deals with ferry tickets. Some rooms are a bit aged, while others feel brand spanking new – ask to be put in one of the latter. There's an indoor pool, as well as a very popular resto-pub downstairs. ⓹
Pensionat Solhem Lökskärsvägen ⓣ018/16322, ⓦ www.visitaland.com/solhem. Though a few kilometres south of the centre and the ferries, this fairly basic villa is set on sprawling lawns just opposite the water, with rowboats available for free. Open May–Oct. ⓷
Strandbergs Stugor Varvsvägen L183 ⓣ018/22855, ⓦ www.strandbergsstugor.net. A dozen cottages and apartments set northwest of the city centre in green grounds fronting the water. There is a large outdoor pool, and kayaks and bicycles are available for hire. Linen €5 extra. No breakfasts. Cottages from ⓷; apartments ⓹

The Town

Mariehamn is spread out on a small peninsula that runs north to south, with two harbours lining its western and eastern banks – the former for cruise ferries, the latter for sailing boats and dinghies. The town's few sights are set at either end of the leafy esplanade that bisects the town, towards the eastern end of which lies Torggatan, the town's sole shopping street with boutiques, cafés and most of the island's local business and services. The eastern coastal road provides access to the rest of mainland Åland further north, as well as ferry terminals further east onto more remote islands, while south of the centre are a few tiny marinas with access to the islands directly off the coast of Mariehamn.

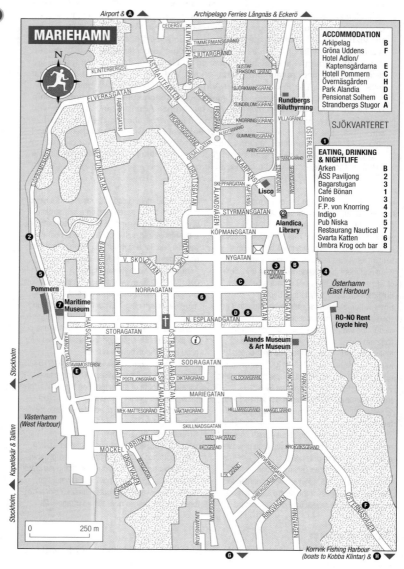

▲ Ship's prow in Mariehamn's maritime quarter

Maritime Museum and Pommern

At the far western end of Storagatan is the **Åland Maritime Museum** (Ålands Sjöfartsmuseum; June & first two weeks Aug daily 9am–5pm; July daily 9am–7pm; mid-Aug to May Mon–Fri 10am–4pm, Sat & Sun noon–4pm; €5, combined ticket with the *Pommern* €8; Ⓦ www.sjofartsmuseum.aland.fi), Hamngatan 2, which celebrates the fact that, despite their insignificant size, the Åland islands once maintained the largest fleet of sailing ships in the world. The museum, whose collection includes sculpted bowsprit figureheads from old ships, scale models of sailing and military yachts and a reconstructed captain's saloon, is undergoing a major renovation and expansion that will last until 2011. Out back is the **Pommern** (daily: May, June & Aug 9am–5pm; July 9am–7pm; Sept 10am–4pm; €5, combined ticket with Maritime Museum €8), a four-masted steel bark ship built in Glasgow in 1903 that set a world record in the 1930s' Great Grain Race, sailing from Australia to England around Cape Horn in 86 days. Every bit of the 310-foot barque is now in tip-top shape – it's one of the best museum ships in Scandinavia.

Ålands Museum

The excellent **Ålands Museum** (June–Aug daily 10am–5pm; Sept–May Tues & Thurs 10am–8pm, Wed & Fri 10am–4pm, Sat & Sun noon–4pm; May–Sept €4, Oct–April free; Ⓦ www.museum.ax), at the far eastern end of Storagatan, is, as far as Finnish city history museums go, one of the best. The exhibits cover the entire Åland story, from Stone Age Bothnian prehistory all the way through to the islands' modern autonomous place under the Finnish flag, going into detail about the geology and ecology of the archipelago and the communities and societies that have settled here. In the same building, the **Åland Art Museum** (Ålands konstmuseum; same hours; €4) has a large collection of paintings that traces the development in Ålands landscape since the nineteenth century, spicing it up with exhibits on modern Swedish and Finnish artists and designers. Most of the locally produced paintings here deal with landscape: *Village Road* by Joel Petterson (1935) and *Longing* by Guy Frisk (1975) are a pair of the most evocative, with dim, muted colours that speak somewhat of the archipelago's winter hues. The museum also holds the archipelago's most famous painting, *Ålands Peasant Bride* by Karl Emanuel Jansson, who painted the portrait when he was just 23 years old.

Sjökvarteret

Resting on the eastern edge of town several blocks north of Alandica (see p.164) is **Sjökvarteret**, Mariehamn's traditional maritime quarter, where the small collection of crimson seaside buildings and old boats make for a good hour or two's ambling. The enclave houses a silver- and goldsmith's workshop, several wooden boat shipyards with a few works in progress, two great handicrafts boutiques – SALT and Guldviva – as well as a café (see opposite) and **museum** (daily: mid-June to mid-Aug 10am–6pm; mid-Aug to mid-June Mon–Fri 9–11am; €4; W www.sjokvarteret.com) whose sawdust-on-the-floor collection holds examples of the various types of hand-built boats that have played a role in Åland's development over the years. Outside the museum are moored several old traditional **ships** built here, including the *Albanus*, a galley ship, and the *Linden*, a replica of an early twentieth-century fore-and-aft schooner whose completion required 40,000 man hours and a thousand pine trees. The *Linden* sails out on lunch and dinner cruises around Marihamn during the Åland Sea Day in July and at other times (W www.linden.aland.fi).

Eating, drinking and nightlife

Eating in Åland is not cheap, and many **restaurants** jack up their prices during the summer months to make a killing from the Swedish tourist traffic, but there are quite a few places in Mariehamn where you can try some fresh local seafood. A Mariehamn meal is best had on a terrace at sunset; after a day's hard cycling or archipelago exploration, any one of the town's outdoor spots are ideal for sipping a beer and watching the sun sink slowly towards the horizon. Many town restaurants turn into lively **bars** once their kitchens close, too, so you'll rarely have to go far to find some libation, especially since most places are located within a few blocks of each other. In terms of proper **nightlife**, Mariehamn offers remarkably little variety considering that it's the largest town for hundreds of miles. For more cultural **entertainment**, make for Alandica, Strandgatan 29 (T 018/24570, W www.alandica.ax), whose frightfully uninspiring exterior hides a large hall for concerts, musicals and drama.

Arken *Hotel Arkipelag*, Strandgaten 31. Åland's party scene turns in for the night when the doors shut at *Arken*, a club with casino and dancefloor and music provided by both DJs and live bands. The sheer numbers here make the hotel backdrop less dire than it might otherwise be. Generally starts going after midnight; closes at 4am.

Ålandskt Svartbröd

Åland is well known around Finland for its soft, moist *svartbröd*, or **black bread**, a traditional side dish to breakfast, lunch and dinner. Made from buttermilk, molasses, brown sugar and malt, the round, flat bread's sweetish taste is best experienced served in leaf-thin slices with a layer of real butter or a slice of creamy cheese. It's also excellent as an hors d'oeuvre topped with cured salmon, pickled herring, Kastelholm cheese or something else salty. The bread is served in restaurants all over the archipelago, but you can also pick some up at local shops or on ferries – Birka Svartbröd and ÅCA brands are the best.

ÅSS Paviljong Sjöpromenadan. One of Åland's classiest restaurants is this sailing pavilion ship designed by National Romantic architect Lars Sonck. The crayfish soup is a winner, as is the *glad gris*, a marinated fillet of pork served with potatoes. Open April–Sept.

Bagarstugan 7 Hantverkare. An adorable salon done up in Gustavian furniture, this is Mariehamn's best place for coffee and snacks through the day. Delightful staff serve a number of just-made pastries and the town's best *ålandpann-kaka* – a semolina pancake served with stewed plums or jam and a dollop of whipped cream – as well as tasty *kinuskitårta*.

Café Bönan Sjökvarteret. Vegan-friendly lunch spot serving fair-trade coffee and local organic snacks and vegetarian lunches that include bean salads and falafel. If it's sunny, pick up a takeaway box and enjoy it out on the docks of the maritime quarter. May–Aug only.

Dino's Strandgatan 12. This evening rock resto-bar showcases regular live cover bands, and serves a good menu of pizzas and burgers, most of which are enjoyed on the outside terrace. Weekends can get quite busy, and most locals usually make it a requisite stop before heading to dance the night away at *Arken*.

F.P. von Knorring Österhamn ☎018/16500. Åland's most atmospheric place to eat is moored in Österhamn harbour immediately south of the *Arkipelag*. This Dutch-built ship – once used to smuggle Jews out of Germany during the war – serves fish and steak dishes starting at €22 (a nice alternative is the €12.80 blini starter, filled with whitefish roe, onion and sour cream). In summer, pull up a table on the aft deck at sunset and order a salad or club sandwich off the more reasonable pub menu.

Indigo Nygatan 1 ☎018/16550. Mariehamn's most popular place to eat and drink. Downstairs is a casual dining spot with granite walls and recessed lighting offering standard Scandinavian dishes for around €20, and bottles of Stallhagen, Åland's own micro-brewed lager, with a terrace café in the summer. Upstairs is Åland's trendiest bar, replete with mood lighting, white leather couches and can't-really-be-bothered bar staff.

Pub Niska Sjöpromenadan. Just in front of the *ÅSS Paviljong* restaurant, this casual new pub-restaurant is named after a well-known smuggler. It serves unique, tasty *plåtbröd* (lit. "bread plate", the restaurant's speciality pizzas, filled and topped with goodies such as smoked salmon, red onion and horseradish cream. One of the best places for lunch on the islands.

Restaurang Nautical Hamngatan 2. Regally outfitted island spot above the Maritime Museum with views on the *Pommern*. Their Brändö Archipelago board (€13) is an excellent introduction to local cuisine with lightly salted herring, roe and other seafood plus *svaårt-bröd*, while some of the best à la carte mains include aioli bouillabaisse (€21) and island lamb with baked garlic (€26). There's also a €9.80 set lunch menu.

Svarta Katten Norragatan 15. With wrought-iron accents in a centuries-old wooden house, "The Black Cat" is a great place to try the archipelago's famous local pancakes. Open summer only.

Umbra Krog och Bar Norra Esplanadgatan 2. ☎018/51550 Run by the guys who own *Indigo*, this modern European restaurant serves excellent traditional Italian dishes prepared with all local ingredients. They do a weekday buffet lunch (11am–3pm) for a recession-busting €9.90.

Kobba Klintar

Ten kilometres off the coast of Mariehamn is **Kobba Klintar**, a rocky skerry dominated by an old pilot's house that contains the oldest original foghorn in Scandinavia, both now renovated following neglect and disrepair. An afternoon visit to Kobba Klintar involves little more than stomping about the rocks and admiring the views out to the sea, but the foghorn rings out on a shimmering summer day and the place feels perfectly magical. Regular **boats** depart for the island from Mariehamn's Korrvik fishing harbour from 11am (early July to mid-Aug daily; late Aug to late Sept Fri & Sun only; €35 including transport and lunch, €18 transport only; ☎040/552 8572); after lunch a local group of artists puts on a Swedish-language play before the return journey to Mariehamn. Invigorating **kayak** trips (€70 per person) can also be arranged out to the island from Lervik, 2km south of Mariehamn; contact Friluftsentreprenörerna SGU (☎018/14757, ⊛www.sgu.nu).

Mainland Åland

North of Mariehamn sprawls the landmass commonly known as Fasta, or "Mainland" Åland, a collection of nine municipalities – which correspond to how we have divided up this chapter. Easily the most visited of these is **Eckerö**, arrival point for a few ferries from Sweden and once the main receiving end of the postal route to Russia. East of here are humdrum **Hammarland**, then **Jomala**, a popular colony for painters around the turn of the century, and finally **Finström**, whose brandy vineyards are well worth an afternoon (assuming you have brought an accompanying designated biker). Approaching the northern tip of the island is **Saltvik**, which holds a pleasant old church that was the meeting point for Åland's first self-run government. Still further north and facing the open sea are the stunning hills, hummocks and forests of **Geta**, where you have some superb hiking trails – one of which dips down to a small cave fronting a laconic bay – complemented by a classy waterfront resort. Just east is **Sund**, site of two massive island defences that served the archipelago well in darker times – the medieval castle of Kastelholm Slott and ruined Bomarsund fortress. **Vårdö**, an island just east of here connected by cable ferry, doesn't have too much more than a small church to hold your attention before you head off by ferry to the northeastern archipelago (see pp.172–174). South of here, meanwhile – and easily accessible from Mariehamn – are **Lemland** and **Lumparland**, mostly unremarkable but for a handful of churches but either makes a sterling stop before heading out by boat to explore the handful of islands in the archipelago's southeast (see pp.174–176).

Exploring the archipelago

Thanks to its extensive, well-paved road system, meagre automobile traffic, few hilly areas and excellent inter-island ferry connections, Åland is one of the best places in Finland to **cycle**. In addition to a whole lot more freedom – several bicycle-only ferries (€9 per bike) make some of the more remote places less hard to reach – Åland also offers slightly cheaper rental rates than on the mainland; reckon on €10 per day for a bike with gears. In Mariehamn, RO-NO Rent (June to mid-Aug daily 9am–6pm; Ⓦ www.visitaland.com/rono) is the best bet, with outlets at Hamngatan (Ⓣ 018/12821) right opposite the ferry terminal and on the waterside at Österhamn (East Harbour; Ⓣ 018/12820) in the town proper, and is a good source of cycling information; they also maintain a smaller branch (Ⓣ 0400/529 315) in Berghamn in Eckerö. Note that bikes can also be carried on island buses for a fee of €6 (and on all island ferries, except the cycle-specific ones mentioned above, for free).

In addition to cycling, there are a number of other ways to explore Åland's varied landscape, with a range of providers. RO-NO Rent's Österhamn branch also rents out Vespa-like 50cc **scooters** (€80 per day), **beach buggies** (€60), **canoes** (€80) and **boats** with outboard motors (€100). For **kayaking** try Friluftsentreprenörerna SGU (Ⓣ 018/14757, Ⓦ www.sgu.nu; €70 full-day guided kayak tour, including lunch) or Nimix Kajakuthyrning (Ⓣ 050/66716, Ⓦ www.nimix.ax; kayak rental €15 per day; €25 for a tandem; the latter will deliver the kayak to and pick it up from wherever you are). For **watersports** such as parasailing, wakeboarding and waterskiing, contact Larssons Vattensport (Ⓣ 0457/524 4072, Ⓦ larssonsvattensport.tripod.com; introduction to kiteboarding €50), while **fishing** tours are run by Ulf Rundberg (Ⓣ 0457/313 4664) and Ålands Turist & Konferens (Ⓣ 018/15349, Ⓦ www.turist-konferens.aland.fi; three-day tour €445 per person), and Alandia Adventures (Ⓣ 040/541 7413 or 0457/313 5202, Ⓦ www.alandia-adventures.com), who also offer **hunting** trips. For underwater wreck **diving**, meanwhile, try Oceanic Tech Åland (Ⓣ 018/21010, Ⓦ www.divealand.com; wreck dive €111, including equipment rental) or Hagge (Ⓣ 040/552 8572, Ⓦ www.hagge.nu; two wreck dives €145, including equipment rental).

Eckerö

Immediately fronting Åland's west coast, the region known as **Eckerö** marks the beginnings of the old post road, the only mail link from Stockholm to what was then tsarist St Petersburg, passing through the bread belt of Finland and through much of Åland proper. To their long-lasting chagrin, the people of Åland were charged with ensuring the safe passage of the mail, which included transporting it across the frozen winter sea – and quite a few died in the process. At the island's western extremity in the main town of **Storby** is the nineteenth-century, Carl Engel-designed **Post House**, easily the most anachronistic building in the archipelago. Standing on the coast facing Sweden, the U-shaped, Empire-style building was intended to instil fresh arrivals with awe at their first sight of the mighty Russian empire – Finland had only become a grand duchy of Russia in 1809. The small **Mail Boat Museum** (Postrotemuseet; mid-June to mid-Aug Tues–Sun 10am–3pm; €2) offers some history of mail transport in days of yore, though it's best known for its original 1860s ice boat. Elsewhere in town, Eckerö's rectangular **medieval church** dates from the early 1200s and houses the oldest church bell in Finland, though you can get much more of a sense of the islands' local traditions at the **Åland Hunting and Fishing Museum** (Ålands Jakt och Fiskemuseum; May to mid-Sept daily 10am–5pm, open until 6pm mid-June to mid-Aug; €4.20), 3km north of Storby at the Käringsund fishing harbour, which displays examples of herring drift and drum nets from way back when. Around 3km east of the harbour off the main road between Överby and Storby is *Andersson's Gästhem* (☎018/38668, ⓦwww.anderssons.ax; April–Oct; ➌), Marholmsvägen 4, a bright B&B in a converted *bagarstuga* (bakehouse) featuring lots of wood and four renovated double rooms whose shared facilities also share a sauna. **Kayaks** can be rented with Nimix (☎018/38284 or 050/66716, ⓦwww.nimix.ax; €30 per day); they will bring the kayak to anywhere you want in Eckerö.

Hammarland, Jomala and Finström

Head immediately east of Eckerö and you'll pass through the swathes of open pastures that typify **Hammarland**, a landscape abloom with groves of yellow wood anemones and enormous juniper berry bushes, but little else of real note. Further on from here, the rather flat but very colourful landscape that borders Mariehamn to the north, **Jomala**, is best known for its Stone Age grounds at Jettböle. The island's main towns of Jomala and Gottby hold most of the municipality's facilities, but more interesting is the hamlet of **Prästgården by**, which holds what is likely Åland's oldest stone church (June to mid-Aug Tues–Sat 9.30am–3.30pm, Sun 1–3.30pm), **St Olaf's**. The church's 52-metre tower looks out to a large Viking burial ground, while inside is Gothic artworks (the oldest date from 1280) of animals and humans – particularly memorable is a Romanesque limestone sculpture of a lion eating a man. Just south of here, set in an old stone cowshed in **Önningeby**, an **art history museum** (Önningebymuseet; June Tues–Fri 11am–4pm; July to mid-Aug Fri–Sun 11am–4pm; free) covers the artist colony run here in the late nineteenth century by landscape painter Victor Westerholm, founder of Finland's Impressionist movement. The museum displays some of the paintings from this time and describes how the landscape and setting influenced the painters. Elsewhere, there is good **hiking** to be had along the indicated trails at Ramsholmen and in the Ingbybergen nature reserve.

Further north is **Finström**, proud home to the **Tjudö Vineyard** (late June to mid-Aug daily 11am–5pm; tours 11am & 2pm €17; ⓦwww.visitaland.com /tjudovingard), a local family-run enterprise that produces wine and spirits from its ten thousand apple and cherry trees – the largest orchard in Finland, set in lush grounds settled by a family of ostriches. Åland is known for its strong drink, and a few shots of Tjudö's 42 percent Ålvados apple brandy should be enough to knock you out for the afternoon. A comprehensive **tour** goes into the distillation and wine-making process in detail and offers a tasting at the end; for more money tack on a yummy lunch or dinner. There's more boozing in the municipality's main town of **Godby** on tours run between late June and mid-August at **Ställhagen Brewery** (☎018/48500, ⊛www.stallhagen.com; €14), Getavägen 196, set in a former Russian barracks. North, about 2km before the approach to Tjudö, is the fifteenth-century **St Michael's Church** (early May to mid-Sept Mon–Fri 10am–4pm), with walls bedecked with folksy paintings and a large twelfth-century carved wooden bust of a medieval saint. Godby has a barebones but fairly modern **youth hostel** (☎018/41555, ⊛www.idrottscenter.com; dorms €20, doubles ❸), Bärvägen 5, which is part of a large sports centre and swimming pool complex.

Geta and Saltvik

Starting barely 1km on from Tjudö, **Geta**, the northernmost municipality on the Åland mainland, combines a farming countryside of lush groves with a hilly coastline looking out onto the Norrhavet. From **Getabergen** hill, where a restaurant and café is set within a lookout tower, several hiking trails, each a couple of kilometres long, head out through the surrounding fields; the Grottstigen trail is the longest (5km) and most interesting, leading down to a small cave and the Djupviken bay. On Geta's west coast, a summertime **bicycle ferry** (€9) operates from Hällö to Skarpnåtö on Hammarland (departs Hällö mid-June to mid-Aug 11.30am, plus 5pm in July; departs Skarpnåtö 30min earlier).

Southeast of Geta, amidst a landscape of golden fields and emerald meadows is **Saltvik**, whose main town of **Kvarnbo** became well known for its saline exports. Today, the municipality's biggest claim to fame is its medieval church, **St Mary's** (Sankta Maria Kyrka), at the Kvarnbo harbour. Hewn out of red granite in the 1280s, it is likely to have served as the Åland diocese's cathedral – possibly for several hundred years. The church is best known for the sharp spire peeking out of its tower and for its small, colourful three-part Baroque altar cabinet. Åland's first *landsting*, or parliamentary assembly, was held in the field just south of the church.

There are a couple of **accommodation** options in the region worth considering. Most spectacular is ⚔ *HavsVidden* (☎018/49408, ⊛www.havsvidden.com; ❺), Åland's plushest place to stay. Set across 44 acres of land right at the sea on Geta's northern coast, this palatial resort feels something like a Finnish eco-architect's palace, with brushed-oak-wood rooms, an excellent restaurant, plus smoke sauna, jacuzzi and indoor pool. Less posh and pricey is *Kvarnbo Gästhem* (☎018/44015, ⊛www.kvarnbogasthem.com; ❸), 100m from the Saltvik church, with six rustic rooms in a wooden building that originally served as Åland's first bank. There is a sandy beach and swimming jetty a five-minute walk away.

Sund

Just southeast of Saltvik is the far more compelling municipality of **Sund**, which today holds one of the most archeologically important finds in western Finland. Sund also has its own **church**, whose limestone cross and runic lettering suggest that a tenth-century bishop may lie buried underneath.

Kastelholm and museums

Sund's main attraction – indeed possibly Åland's most popular, other than Mother Nature herself – is the fourteenth-century **Kastelholm Castle** (Kastelholm slot;

May to mid-Sept daily 10am–5pm, July until 6pm; €5), built on a tiny island in grounds formerly used for royal elk hunts. Intended to consolidate Swedish domination and monitor trade routes on the Baltic, the castle was occupied by numerous Swedish monarchs, including Duke Johan, son to Gustav Vasa, who imprisoned his brother King Erik XIV and his wife in the tower in 1571, and King Charles IX, whose armies severely damaged the castle while conquering it in the 1599 civil war. Once surrounded by a large moat, Kastelholm was mostly destroyed by fire in the mid-eighteenth century and an extensive renovation process has often kept entire wings closed to visitors; the five-story central tower and a newer outer ward are the areas you're most likely to visit on the English-language guided tours (mid-June to Aug Sat & Sun 2pm), which cover in much more intricate detail the history of the place, and provide background on the castle's role in Åland's history.

Just next to the castle is the open-air **Jan Karlsgården Museum** (May daily 10am–4pm; June–Aug daily 10am–5pm; first two weeks Sept Mon–Fri 10am–4pm; free), made up of buildings transported here from Finström in the 1930s, including an old windmill; a maypole (*midsommarstång*) stands just nearby the dance pavilion. Next door is the **Vita Björn Prison Museum** (Fängelsemuseet Vita Björn; May–Aug Mon–Fri 10am–5pm; €2), whose five cells functioned as the archipelago's sole prison for nearly two hundred years until being decommissioned in 1975 – crime is virtually unknown in the archipelago today. A few bare cells are on display, with some information on some of the prisoners once held here.

Bomarsund and Prästö island

Several kilometres east of Kastelholm just before the bridge over to Prästö island lie the fortress ruins of **Bomarsund**, one of the most important locations on the old post road. The fortress, a semicircular, double-brick-walled construction fronted by massive hexagonal granite blocks, was built by the Russians following the cession of Finland from Sweden after the Finnish War of 1808–09, and served as a key strategic outpost on Russia's new western border. The capacity was earmarked at five thousand men, but only three of Bomarsund's turrets could be completed before the Crimean War broke out and an Anglo–French force stormed the infant castle in 1854, reducing it to rubble with explosives. All that now remains are the scattered crumbling ramparts and redoubts and several skilful examples of rose-granite stonework, executed by some two thousand builders. After visiting you might fancy a walk up from the ruins to Djävulsberget Hill for some inviting vistas out to the sea. From here, look across over the channel to **Prästö island**, where a tiny **museum** (June–Aug daily 10am–4pm, plus weekends in July; free) displays pictures and finds from the fortress. The military hospital and cemeteries were also kept on this side of the water, now surrounded by forest; it's worth spending some time scurrying about the spongy moss and loose rocks to view the solemn graves of the Jewish, Lutheran, Muslim, Roman Catholic and Russian Orthodox soldiers and labourers who served the tsar – at the time, Russian garrisons were some of the most ethnically diverse in the world.

Right by the Bomarsund fortress ruins is *Puttes Camping* (☎018/44040; cabins €29), with a handful of well-kept cabins set across several acres of grass meadows 10m from a small beach.

Vårdö

Though officially considered part of Åland's outer archipelago, **Vårdö** is effectively part of mainland Åland, connected as it is to Prästö in Sund via a nonstop two-minute cable ferry. The island's name – "Guardian Island" – stems from the practice of pre-modern islanders who would clamber up to Vårdö's highest point and light bonfires warning other islands of danger. Today, though, the only island danger is missing a ferry further on; it's most often just used as a stepping-stone to the more remote islands. If you do get stuck here – or want to catch the first morning ferry east – **spend the night** at *Bomans Gästhem* (☎018/47821 or 0457/524 4260; May to mid-Sept; ❸), a recently restored farmhouse 5km from Hummelvik harbour whose woody rooms have quaint, folksy decor – think tiny paintings of rural scenes and pastel floral curtains – (❸), two small cottages (€65) with sauna and a hostel annex (doubles ❷, no dorms) that was awarded the best in the country in 2007. They also organize plenty of maritime activities, have a golf driving range out back and bicycles for hire. You can **camp** in a wooded pine setting near a beach at *Sandösunds* (☎018/47750 or 0457/379 9119, ⓦwww .sandocamping.aland.fi; mid-April to Oct; cabins ❷), where canoe excursions and fishing tours can also be arranged.

Lemland and Lumparland

Head due east out of Mariehamn along the road that lines the placid Slemmern Bay and you'll come to **Lemland**, a sizeable island separated from Jomala on mainland Åland by the Lemström Canal, dug by Russian prisoners in the 1880s. Lemland was the seafaring capital of the archipelago a century ago, and numerous sea captains' manor homes can still be seen in its main town of **Söderby**, though its large shipyards are long gone. The rest of the island has a few worthwhile sites, including the **Lemböte chapel ruins** (Lemböte kapellruin), near the west coast in Lemböte – all that's left of a tiny one-roomed granite seafarers' church built in the twelfth century. Some 270 silver coins were unearthed here a century ago, and are now held in Mariehamn's Åland Museum. Elsewhere, the medieval **St Birgitta Church** (Mon–Sat 10am–4pm), on the road departing Söderby to the east, contains fetching examples of Gothic wall paintings – expressive portraits of the apostles – that date from the 1300s and are some of the country's oldest. Surrounded by burial cairns from the late Bronze Age, the church is also known for its sculpted triumphal cruci-fixes, mint-condition votive ships hanging from the ceiling, and the so-called "Lemland Madonna," an oak-carved statue of the Madonna and Jesus from 1327, showing details in the clothing and very expressive faces. The **Pellas Shipmaster's Home** (Skeppargården Pellas; mid-June to mid-Aug 11am–4pm; €3), in **Granboda** before the bridge to Lumparland, is an 1880s-era example of a shipowner's homestead, revived following a fire a few years ago.

Northeast of Lemland, **Lumparland** has the archipelago's oldest surviving **wooden church** (Mon–Sat 10am–4pm), located in the main town of **Klemetsby**, with an altar painting by Victor Westerholm, but the island is more frequently visited for its harbour at **Långnäs**, whose ferries provide access to the southern reaches of the archipelago. If you're interested in hiking or kayaking to explore some of Lumparland's handsome hinterland, enquire with Get Out Adventures at the *Café Ingela* in Svinö, which runs several half-day nature trips from June to August (from €50, including picnic lunch).

Northeastern islands

Åland's northeastern islands are the least visited of any of the archipelago's settle-ments, and as ferry connections are as good as anywhere else, you'll be spoiled for choice if you're on the hunt for some real seclusion. A good hour away from Vårdö is **Kumlinge**, a solid choice for a lazy afternoon cycle out to its prepossessing medieval church. Northeast of here, fronting the mainland, is slender **Brändö**, whose undulating causeways span a dozen or so islands and offer some genuine backwater spots perfect for a hike, a paddle or a ride on some Icelandic stallions out on the tiny islet of **Jurmo**.

Kumlinge and Enklinge

The rocky outpost of **Kumlinge**, a collection of several small islands splayed between Vardö and Brändö, is best known for its fifteenth-century **St Anna's Church** (mid-June to mid-Aug Mon–Fri noon–5pm), whose walls and ceilings are plastered with sixteenth-century Byzantine-style paintings of angels, garlands and the Passion that consist almost exclusively of women and saints – only two paintings have men in them. The church's thirteenth-century French-style altar cabinet is the oldest in Finland.

Just to the north, the much smaller, and much greener, island of **Enklinge** holds one point of interest: the **Hermas Farm Museum** (Musiegården Hermas; June–Aug Mon–Fri 10am–5pm; €2). During the 1809 Finnish War, the Swedish king Charles XIII burned the village to prevent Russian soldiers from wintering on it, but islanders returned the following spring to rebuild the foundations of the houses. The present farmstead consists of two-dozen-odd buildings that include cow shed, windmill, smoke sauna and livestock courtyard, plus a small museum.

Ferries on the Hummelvik–Torsholma route arrive on the north coast of the island at Krokarna. Kumlinge has several small **guesthouses**: the best is *Remmarina Stugby* (T0400/529 199, W www.remmarina.com; €55), set in pine surroundings a few metres from the island's northern marina at Krokarna with a small terrace restaurant, *Kastören*.

Brändö

"Fire Island", or **Brändö**, designates a collection of slender, grassy islets, bays, creeks and straits that link up Åland with the furthest reaches of the Turku archipelago just off the Finnish mainland. The main dozen or so specks of land are connected via a series of long, curvaceous causeways, providing for some great journeying through a landscape that alternates between dense forest and lush grassy pasture. With more than two islands for every inhabitant – and fewer tourists than anywhere else in Åland – this is prime get-away-from-it-all territory.

Brändö town is dominated by a country store, a bank and the whitewashed **Church of St Jacob** (Sankt Jakobs Kyrka; late June to early Aug daily noon–5pm). There are signs from the main town road to an **observation tower** (follow the signs to *utsiktstorni*), a great spot for birders, especially come late summer. A kilometre south you'll find decent swimming, plus a waterslide and small trampoline, at the sandy **beach** at Korsklobbsrevet. North of town, the road branches to the left, a gravelly, blacktop road leading to the tiny wharfside settlement of Norrviken, one of the quietest and most remote places in the archipelago and perfect for catching unfettered sunset views over Labbholm and the Västerfjärden isles. North of the main town the road branches off to the right, stretching up to **Åva**, a community of several small towns. Here you can catch a ferry east to mainland Finland or to the island of **Jurmo**, a miniscule, very green island known for its highland cattle – brought to Jurmo in 2002 to graze and tidy up the island's mischievous weeds – and Icelandic horses, which can be ridden at Talli Perla (T040/562 0488, W www.talliperla.com). Jurmo also has a small folklore **museum** (daily late June to mid-Aug 4–6pm and 7–9pm; €2).

Practicalities

Ferries from mainland Hummelvik on Vårdö (via Kumlinge) arrive at Torsholma harbour at the southern tip of Brändö's main island, while those from Ösnäs on mainland Finland arrive at the northern end of the island at Åva. *Brändö Stugby* (☎018/56221, ⓦhome.åland.net/lameta) has a dozen or so log **cabins**, as well as small rowboats for hire, as well as a great restaurant serving large tasty burgers with meat sourced locally from Jurmo. Further north of Brändö Town in Björnholma is *Hotell Gullvivan* (☎018/56350 or 040/537 1777, ⓦwww.gullvivan.aland .fi; ➌) the island's nicest place to stay, with wood-dominated, modern hotel rooms and cabins (€49) set on well-trimmed lawns; it has the added advantage of being open year-round. *Granbergs Stugor* (☎018/31704 or 040/865 1010; ➌) in Åva has six sizeable cottages and two apartments that are ideal for larger groups, as well as access to great fishing. Jurmo island offers a small, red clapboard **youth hostel** (☎018/56477 or 040/506 4777, ⓔvandrarhem@jurmo.net; dorms €12), with four rooms of varying sizes housed in an old schoolhouse; kayaks are available for rent and it too is open year-round. *Trixies*, a friendly, family-run shop and **café** near the Brändö town church sells island handicrafts and serves cold cider and sandwiches.

Southeastern islands

Barely 5km from mainland Åland, **Föglö** feels more an extension of Lumparland than a discrete island, but explore and you'll find some lovely bridle paths (and horses to take you along them) as well as a couple of great places to stay. A short ride away is the teensy island of **Sottunga**, good for an afternoon hike but with rather few ferry connections, while much further east are the fields and inlets of captivating **Kökar**, a super place to hole up for a few days. Should that not be idyllic enough for you, the stark cliffs and rock sculptures out at **Källskär** were once home to a Swedish count and remain about as remote as you'd ever care to get anywhere.

Föglö

Of all the specks of land that comprise Åland's outlying islands, closest and easiest to reach from mainland Åland is **Föglö** ("Bird Island"). Ferries from Svinö arrive in **Degerby**, where you'll find a small **tourist information** shed (☎045/7342 5254, ⓦwww.foglo.ax/turism; mid-June to late Aug Mon–Sat 10am–5.30pm, Sun 10am–noon & 12.30–5.30pm). Three kilometres south of here is Karins Ridskola (☎018/51086 or 0457/569 2586), Björsboda Ringväg 136, which offers hour-long escorted **horseback rides** (€20) through Föglö's pines and pastures throughout the summer; ring ahead and they'll pick you up in Degerby. On Wednesdays and Saturdays at 1pm in the summer you can hop on an afternoon tour (€30) out to the island of **Björkör**; contact Coja (☎0400/947 502, ⓦwww .coja.nu), east off the road to the ferry harbour at **Överö** on Östersocknen, who can also rent you a small motorboat (€25 per day) if you want to explore the waters on your own.

Though open May to September only, Degerby's prized place to **overnight** is *Enigheten* (☎018/50 310 or 040/554 2937, ⓦwww.enigheten.ax; ➌), a beguiling inn founded in 1745, with twelve rooms and an old windmill. Though the atmosphere at *Föglö Wärdshus* (☎018/50 002, ⓦwww.wardshus.com; ➌) is slightly less idyllic – rooms are furnished in standard, not-quite-IKEA decor – there is home cooking, sauna and internet access. Northeast of Degerby along the road to Överö on Finholma island is *C&C Camping* (Ⓣ018/51440, Ⓦhome.aland.net/cc.camp; June–Aug; €8), with small cottages snuggled between some dense pines and a grassy slab of land on a small bay (€30); they can also rent out kayaks and canoes. Nearby is *Restaurang Seagram*, well known for its fish buffet and as good a place as any to try raw Föglö whitefish, pickled with onion, cream and black pepper. *Nina's Café*, about 1km south of the Överö ferry dock, is a good place to pick up pastries or sandwiches before hopping on a boat towards Sottunga and Kökar.

Sottunga

"They are the most handsome and the strongest people on Åland," observed visitor E.D. Clark in 1799 upon a visit to **Sottunga**, Åland's smallest municipality. Whether or not this holds true today, today's inhabitants should certainly be commended for sticking around; with a population of 118, this demarcates the smallest municipality in Finland – and possibly the EU. The name refers to a trio of inhabited islands – and many more uninhabited ones – though it is usually shorthand for the largest of them, Storsottunga, a largely desolate place that was burned to the ground during the Finnish War in 1809 in order that enemies would not occupy it.

Storsottunga's **Maria Magdalena Church** (mid-June to mid-Aug Tues–Fri 11am–4pm), set a few hundred metres from the ferry harbour, was built in 1661 but burnt down some 60 years later; the version that stands today is nonetheless one of the islands' prettiest. Though short on amenities, Sottunga is well known for its **walking trails**, containing three well-indicated paths of a few kilometres each, one of which begins right at the ferry harbour. Here also is *Strandhuggets Stugor & Café* (Ⓣ018/55255 or 0400/306 794), offering **accommodation** in small cottages, serving breakfast, lunch and dinner, and hiring out several bicycles. Sottunga is reached by ferry from Långnäs in Lumparland and Galtby in Korpo (Korppoo), though many ferries bypass the island without making a stop.

Kökar

Sweet, remote **Kökar** (pronounced "CHYOOK-air") is Åland's most southerly and outermost island, quite possibly its prettiest, and small enough that you can easily cover the entire place on bike in a day – though there is one real winner of a hotel in case you decide to stay the night. An oversized skerry of grey gneiss bedrock, the island is covered in small brushwood, with alder, birch and juniper bushes overrunning everywhere, through which small paths run out to the sea. Kökar was originally inhabited by sealers, but Franciscans built the first significant island structure in the early fourteenth century, a stone monastery that was disassembled a century later by King Gustav Vasa when he came to power. Set in a field at the sea's edge and flanked by a small graveyard and a cluster of sharp rocks, the current **St Anna's Church** (mid-June to mid-Aug Tues–Fri 11am–4pm), in the island's northeast at **Hamnö**, was erected on the same spot from its rubble in 1784. Inside the large, musty interior, the ship that hangs from the ceiling was donated by a local sailor captured by Turkish pirates; his votive is a facsimile of the Turkish vessel, complete with four dozen cannons. South of here at Munkvärvan a small hiking path along flat rocks, steep hills, pastures and dells leads south to Grönvik, and eventually back to **Karlby**, the main town, via Överboda (pick up the leaflet *Hiking Paths on Kökar Kalen* at *Brudhäll* en route; see p.176). Several kilometres east of Karlby near **Österbygge** is **Peders Aplagård** (late June to mid-Aug 10am–6pm; Ⓣ0407/362 498, Ⓦwww.aplagarden.ax), a family-run apple farm with a boutique and café that features home-produced ciders, juices, sauces and chutneys, as well as excellent island Ålandspannkakor.

Once you've exhausted Kökar's offerings, head out to the nearby tiny island of **Källskär**, known for its stone formations and undulating cliffs, long shaved smooth by rocks set in rotation by water from melting glaciers – most notably the *källskär-skannan*, a rounded, three-metre-high rock at the water's edge hollowed and carved in the shape of a kettle. The island was inhabited by a Swedish baron who commissioned the Finnish architect couple Reima and Raili Pietilä to build a series of remarkable buildings in the 1960s that are dead ringers for the homes of the Moomin characters; Tove Jansson visited on several occasions, making a series of sketches that later became models for the buildings in the books and at Naantali's Moominworld. Today, the buildings are mainly used by Nordic artists visiting the island on residence programmes. *Brudhäll* (see below) runs guided tours of the island departing at noon during July; at other times contact Kökar transport (℡040/836 4333).

Practicalities

Kökar is reached by **ferry** either via Långnäs or from Galtby on Korpo in the Turku archipelago. A few kilometres south of the main harbour in Karlby is ✯ *Brudhäll* (open May–Sept; ℡018/55955, ⓦwww.brudhall.com; ➎), a superb modern **hotel** run by two whiz-kid Finnish chefs, with comfy, well-appointed rooms that look right out to the harbour. Even if you're not planning on staying overnight on Kökar – though with somewhat sporadic ferry timings you might not have a choice – be sure to stop here for some of southern Finland's best food; their succulent leg of veal (€26) is outstanding. Northwest of here near the church at Munkvervan is *Sandvik* (℡018/55911 or 0457/342 9242, ⓦwww.sandvik.ax; May–Sept), a simple, slightly unkempt campsite on a grassy knoll (pitches €12) looking out onto a calm bay and small marina; they also have several cabins (€30) with wi-fi and a small shop for provisions, and kayak rental is just nearby.

Travel details

Buses

Mariehamn to: Eckerö (4–8 daily; 40min); Geta (4–6 daily; 50min); Hummelvik (3–8 daily; 55min–1hr 5min); Kastelholm (3–9 daily; 40min).
Torsholma to: Turku (summer only 1 daily; 2hr 50min–4hr).

Domestic ferries

Åva to: Jurmo (hourly; 10min); Ösnäs (6 daily; 35min).
Hummelvik to: Kumlinge (3–4 daily; 1hr 10min–1hr 20min); Snäckö (mid-April to Sept 5–6 weekly; 1hr); Torsholma (4 daily; 2hr 20min).
Kökar to: Galtby (1–3 daily; 2hr 20min); Långnäs (3–5 daily; 2hr 30min); Överö (2–4 daily; 1hr 40min).
Långnäs to: Galtby (1–3 daily; 5hr); Kökar (3–5 daily; 2hr 30min); Överö (5–9 daily; 30min); Snäckö

(2–3 daily; 1hr 30min); Sottunga (3–7 daily; 1hr–1hr 25min); Turku (2 daily; 5hr 20min).
Mariehamn to: Helsinki (4 daily; 10hr); Turku (2 daily; 5hr 30min).
Snäckö to: Hummelvik (mid-April to Sept 5–6 weekly; 1hr); Långnäs (2–3 daily; 1hr 30min).
Svinö to: Degerby (hourly; 25min).

International ferries

Eckerö to: Grisselhamn (2–3 daily; 3hr).
Långnäs to: Stockholm (2 daily; 5hr 30min).
Mariehamn to: Kapellskär (2 daily; 2hr); Stockholm (2 daily; 5hr 30min); Tallinn (1 daily; 9hr).

Air

Mariehamn to: Helsinki (4–5 daily; 50min); Stockholm (2 daily; 20min); Turku (2 daily; 30min).

Karelia and Kainuu

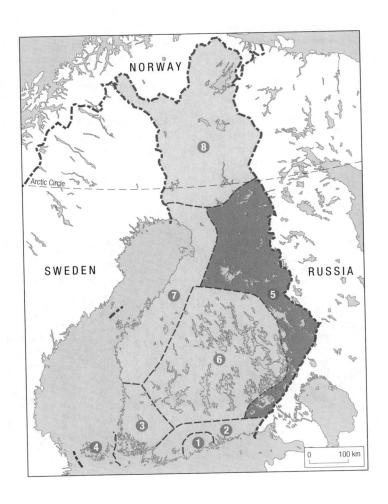

✳ **Lappeenranta Fortress** Stroll the cobbled streets and visit the fascinating museums of this eighteenth-century bulwark against the Russians. See p.182

✳ **North Karelian Museum, Joensuu** Delve into Finland's often uneasy relationship with neighbouring Russia at the best museum in Karelia. See pp.186–187

✳ **Koli National Park** Admire the cinemascope views from the Koli hills out over the island-studded expanse of Lake Pielinen – this is classic Finland. See pp.188–189

✳ **Old town, Nurmes** Small but perfectly formed, Nurmes' old town is a rare example of wooden architecture from Finland's Grand Duchy period within the Russian empire. See p.190

✳ **Paltaniemi Church** Ogle the ornate murals inside this stunning wooden church, one of Finland's largest. See p.194

✳ **Kalevala village, Kuhmo** Take a guided tour of a reconstructed Karelian village and try your hand at traditional tasks such as bread making and woodcarving. See p.196

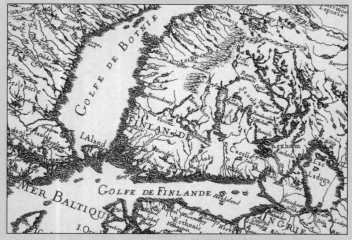

▲ North Karelian Museum, Carelicum, Joensuu

5

Karelia and Kainuu

With its appealing mix of birch forest and rolling farmland, studded with countless lakes and watercourses, **Karelia** (Karjala in Finnish) is one of Finland's most rewarding destinations. Readily accessible from the capital, this eastern province, which forms a good chunk of the border with Russia, offers a great introduction to the country beyond Helsinki: shimmering lakeside towns, such as charming Lappeenranta and Joensuu as well as vast, wild expanses of forest, notably around Lake Pielinen in the north of the province. Add in a generous dose of (often painful) history (see box, p.181) and it's clear why Karelia is a popular destination for home-grown tourists.

If you're looking for something altogether more untamed, head further north along the Russian border to **Kainuu**, a thinly populated rural province of traditional peasant lands and wild, unsullied tracts, ideal for off-the-beaten-track hiking. It not only serves as an eastern gateway to Lapland but also rewards visitors with some of Finland's most striking scenery: sweeping forests with great gorges and river rapids, and fells on which reindeer are as common as people. There's just one main town in these parts, Kajaani, which makes the best base from which to explore the surrounding countryside.

Getting around Karelia is best done by **train** since there's a dependable network of lines linking the main towns; services also run north into Kainuu. Getting around Kainuu, however, is best done by **bus** since rail services pretty much peter out at Kajaani.

Karelia

Today Karelia is dominated by two towns. Just 18km from the Russian border, the commercial, lakeside hub of **Lappeenranta**, with its sizeable fortress, is the most southerly of the Karelian towns and makes a superb introduction to the region. From here road and rail links skirt the Russian border, bound for tiny **Parikkala**, where there's a wealth of hiking and boating opportunities, before heading north to the region's second town, **Joensuu**, an easy-going place with a superb museum of Karelian history. There's serene Lakeland scenery north of here around **Lake Pielinen**, which is linked in turn with **Nurmes**, a modest, yet handsome wooden town with a reconstructed Karelian village.

Lappeenranta and around

Likeable **LAPPEENRANTA** provides an excellent first taste of South Karelia, conveniently sited on the main rail line between Helsinki and Joensuu and along all the eastern bus routes. It's a small, slow-paced town where summer evenings find most of the population strolling around the linden-tree-lined **harbour**, admiring one of the world's biggest sand castles, reconstructed here every year. Once holding a key position on the Russian border, Lappeenranta boasts historical features that its neighbouring towns don't share, including a rambling, old **fortress**, which sits above the harbour and provides an eye-opening introduction to political conflicts that not only affected medieval Finland but also shaped the country's current land borders. It's also a good jumping-off point for **boat trips** on Lake Saimaa and to Russia.

Founded by Queen Christina of Sweden under the Swedish name of Villmanstrand, the town was granted a charter in 1649 by the Kingdom of Sweden in order to profit from trade at the burgeoning local market and to secure its eastern border against an ever-encroaching Russia. With that aim, construction of a fortress began, but, following the bloody battle of Villmanstrand in 1741, the outnumbered Swedes were soon forced to retreat, losing the town to the Russians. The Peace of Turku in 1743 formalized the new border between Sweden and Russia, leaving Villmanstrand firmly inside Russian territory. Subsequently, a garrison of the tsar's army arrived and, by 1775, had erected most of the stone buildings of the fortress. Following the severing of ties with Sweden, Lappeenranta, as the town became to be known, remained in Russian hands until Finnish independence in 1917.

Arrival and information

It's a fifteen-minute walk from the **train** and **bus stations** on Ratakatu, northwest along Kauppakatu, to the thoroughly modern town centre, befuddled

The Karelia question

Mention the name Karelia to any Finn and it's likely to trigger a deep, melancholic sigh. Be under no illusion, though: this stirring of emotions is much more than misty-eyed nostalgia. Indeed, it borders on real bitterness towards Russia, felt by the entire nation, for the loss of these former Finnish lands to their powerful neighbour. Over sixty years on, the loss of parts of Karelia (which then included Finland's second city, Viipuri) is just as heartfelt as it was when Finland was forced to cede the territory to the Soviet Union following the Winter War and Continuation War. The Karelia question, as it's known, is always present in Finnish politics, albeit rarely occupying central stage since no political party supports the idea of regaining sovereignty over the lost areas. Finland has diplomatically stated that it has no territorial claims on Russia, though it is always ready to discuss the return of ceded lands should Russia desire to raise the issue. Borders have rarely been stable in this part of the country and the root of the problem can be traced back to the Treaty of Nystad in 1721 which divided Karelia in two: North Karelia was awarded to Sweden, whilst South Karelia joined Russia, a clear sign to local folk that they could no longer count on their colonial master to protect them against the colossal force of Russia.

at its heart by platoons of graceless concrete blocks, crowding around the *kauppatori*; you'll pass the **tourist office**, at Kauppakatu 40, en route (Mon–Fri 9am–4.30pm; ℡05/667 788, ⓦwww.gosaimaa.fi). There's also a small tourist booth open by the harbour in summer (daily June to mid-Aug 9am–8/9pm; ℡05/411 8853). The main tourist office has free internet terminals, and there's also gratis internet at the town library, Valtakatu 47 (Mon–Fri: June to mid-Aug 10am–6pm; mid-Aug to May 10am–8pm).

Accommodation

Given the large numbers of Russian tourists who regularly fill Lappeenranta's hotels and guesthouses, it's a good idea to book accommodation here well in advance, certainly in the summer months when holidaying Finns add to the fray.

Citi Motel Lappee Kauppakatu 52 ℡05/415 0800, ⓦwww.freewebs.com/citilappee. Popular with Russian backpackers and housed in a charmless 1950s concrete block in the town centre, this guesthouse wins no prizes for style, but it does represent good value for money for such a central location. There are just eighteen simply decorated rooms, plus a sauna. ❸

Cumulus Valtakatu 31 ℡05/677 811, ⓦwww .cumulus.fi. The cheapest of the chain hotels in town, this one has all the modern fittings you'd expect – wooden floors and well-appointed bathrooms – and a small swimming pool to boot. ❹/❻

Gasthaus Kantolankulma Kimpisenkatu 19 ℡05/0328 7575, ⓦwww.gasthauslappeenranta .com. This long-established guesthouse has everything from one-room studios to larger apartments (two-bed apartment €90) with a separate living room and bedroom. Cooking facilities in all rooms. ❸

Huhtiniemi Kuusimäenkatu 18 ℡05/451 5555, ⓦwww.huhtiniemi.com. Located 2.5km west

of the town centre and reached by bus #5 from the bus and train station, this hostel and campsite enjoys a superb lakeside setting. Dorms €10 (June–Aug only); apartments ❸, year-round.

Karelia-Park Korpraalinkuja 1 ℡05/453 0404, ⓦwww.karelia-park.fi. Located just 2km west of the centre, next to the airport, this summer-only hotel has good-value (if plainly decorated) budget rooms. There's a choice of double rooms or larger apartments with a kitchen (€80). It functions as student accommodation during the rest of the year. June–Aug only. ❸

Sokos Lappee Brahenkatu 1 ℡05/762 1000, ⓦwww.sokoshotels.fi. This massive, modern pile is the pick of several high-standard central hotels. The comfortable rooms all have wooden floors and minimalist Nordic decor. You may wish to time your arrival for breakfast carefully to avoid the bruising scrum of Russian tourists at the buffet table. ❹/❻

The Town

Easily covered in a day, Lappeenranta falls neatly into two main areas: the **town centre**, dominated by the market square, where the main activity is strolling and snacking from the numerous stands selling the local specialities – spicy meat pastries called *vetyjä* and *atomeja* – and the altogether more agreeable **fortress** area, down by the harbour, which is also where you'll find the town's museums. Incidentally, Finland's biggest **sand castle**, a mammoth structure containing three million kilos of sand and standing 10m high, stands proud below the fortress on Linnoitusniemenkärki every summer between June and August.

The fortress

Once you've had your fill of pastries and the gaggle of shops which line the streets leading east from the *kauppatori*, notably Valtakatu and Koulukatu, it's best to press on north up to the town's old ramparts and into the **fortress** area, where

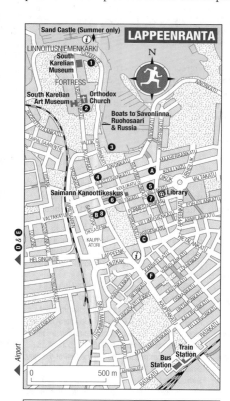

Lappeenranta's past soon becomes apparent. Its origins as a trading centre reach back to the late sixteenth century, but it was with the westward shift of the Russian border in 1721, especially, that the town found itself at the frontline of Russian–Swedish conflicts. Sitting squatly atop a rectangular earthen mound above the town and commanding views out over the Saimaa lake system, the fortress was completed by the Russians as part of a greater defence plan for St Petersburg. At its heart is the cobblestoned **Kristiinankatu**, which leads along the headland before descending to the shores of the lake, and is lined with the fortress's oldest surviving buildings, dating from the Russian fortification period of the 1770s. The **Orthodox Church** (June to mid-Aug Tues–Sun 10am–6pm; rest of the year by appointment; ☎05/451 5511), diagonally opposite, is Finland's oldest, founded in 1785. Inside the glow of beeswax candles helps illuminate some impressive icons.

The museums

From the Orthodox Church, step back across Kristiinankatu, and you'll find yourself before two low brick buildings, now painted yellow and joined at the hip,

ACCOMMODATION		EATING & DRINKING	
Citi Motel Lappee	F	Café Majurska	2
Cumulus	B	Old Cock	5
Gasthaus		Old Park	6
Kantolankulma	A	Olé	7
Huhtiniemi	E	Prinsessa Armada	3
Karelia-Park	D	Serra	1
Sokos Lappee	C	Tassos	8
		Wolkoff	4

Boat trips to Russia

Given Lappeenranta's proximity to Russia, it's tempting to tag on a trip to **Viipuri** to a visit to this part of Finland. Visa-free trips for all nationalities are now available providing travel in both directions is by boat from Lappeenranta via the Saimaa Canal, with both one-day minibreaks and overnight stays of up to two nights available. Between late June and mid-September there are almost daily departures, costing €49–59 return (plus a port fee of €4) depending on the date of travel. Boats leave the main harbour at 7.45am, arriving in Viipuri at 2.15pm Russian time, starting the return journey at 5.15pm with arrival into Lappeenranta at 9.45pm; contact Saimaa Matkaverkko (℡05/541 0100, www.saimaatravel.fi) for tickets; they charge an additional €15 service fee and will require a copy of your passport three working days before departure. Incidentally, a street plan of Viipuri is included in the excellent *Karjala* map produced by Karttakeskus, usually available at bookshops in Lappeenranta.

which once served as the town barracks. Inside is the **South Karelian Art Museum** (June to mid-Aug Mon–Fri 10am–6pm, Sat & Sun 11am–5pm; mid-Aug to May Tues–Sun 11am–5pm; €8 joint ticket with South Karelian Museum), which rotates its permanent stock of paintings with South Karelian connections – mostly a mundane, contemporary bunch of landscapes and portraits dating from the 1960s onwards. However, there are some important eighteenth-century Finnish artists also represented: look out, in particular, for Albert Edefelt's *Sorrow* from 1894, depicting a weeping wife, deep in the forest, grasping her grieving husband's hand, both figures visibly distressed over their homeland's fate within the Russian empire.

Continue northwards along Kristiinankatu, and close to its end at no. 15 you'll reach the **South Karelian Museum** (same hours; €8 joint ticket with South Karelian Art Museum), housed in a sturdy building of thick limestone once used as a storehouse for artillery and ammunitions. Surprisingly, it isn't collections from Lappeenranta that form the main displays here, but ceramics, souvenirs and sporting trophies from two former Finnish towns now within Russia: Käkisalmi (Priozersk in Russian) and, most significantly, **Viipuri** (Vyborg in Russian), a major centre 60km from Lappeenranta that was ceded to the Soviet Union after World War II (see box, p.181). Elsewhere in the museum, those of a cartographical bent are in for a treat as there are dozens of maps on display which help to chart the ever-shifting frontier, and frankly downright confusing, border disputes with Russia.

Eating and drinking

There are plenty of places to eat and drink in Lappeenranta, catering to the many Russian tourists keen to try out Finnish cuisine. To be sure of a table, though, especially in summer, call ahead to reserve.

Café Majurska Kristiinankatu 1. Reward yourself after a tour of the fortress area with coffee and a home-baked pie or cake at this colourfully decorated café in the fortress. Sit inside among the antiques or on the glass veranda at the side.

Old Cock Valtakatu 54. Instantly noticeable for the brightly coloured wooden cockerel plonked up on the roof, and complete with wood panelling – and

Beamish – this is the best British-style pub in Lappeenranta.

Old Park Valtakatu 36. A first-floor Irish-style bar, which, despite its lack of authenticity, is nearly always guaranteed to be full of well-oiled revellers.

Olé Raatimiehenkatu 18 ℡05/415 6004. A new and very popular brick-and-arcade-style Spanish restaurant that serves a solid range of *paellas*, *pescados* and *pechugas*. Mains begin at €16.80.

🏃 **Prinsessa Armaada** Satamatori. This open-decked, black-hulled boat moored down in the harbour is where locals gather during the late summer evenings to catch the last rays and sip on a pint (or six). Also has an open-air terrace on the quayside. Open May–Sept only.

Serra Satamatie 4 ☎05/541 1316. Rough brick walls, linen tablecloths and candles help set the scene for this cosy, upmarket fish restaurant down by the harbour. The quality of the fish is superb: the smoked salmon pastrami (€9) and the home-made bouillabaisse (€20) are particularly good.

Tassos Valtakatu 41 ☎05/762 1452. A very popular Greek restaurant complete with ornate fake columns and OTT statues. Mains from €17, including *souvlaki* (€22.50) and *stifado* (€18.50).

🏃 **Wolkoff** Kauppakatu 26 ☎05/415 0320. Lappeenranta's finest gourmet restaurant sits snugly inside one of the town's oldest wooden buildings, complete with creaky floorboards and bare timber walls. Cuisine is top-notch, with mains (from €19) including reindeer fillet with creamed mushrooms (€32) and fillet of smoked salmon (€25).

Boat trips on Lake Saimaa

Covering a whopping 4500 square kilometres, **Lake Saimaa** is not only the largest lake in Finland, but the fourth largest in Europe. Clearly, you're not going to get around very much of it under your own steam, but spending a day or two paddling the calm waters just off Lappeenranta and exploring the multitude of smaller islands and islets is a must. While there's very little to set one pine-clad isle apart from another, the larger **Ruohosaari island**, just off the *Huhtiniemi* campsite and youth hostel is a particular favourite, with plenty of secluded bays for swimming and sunbathing and even a barbecue site. Ask at the tourist office for their waterway excursion map, which will give you an idea of distances and possible routes. **Kayaks** and **canoes** can be rented in the centre of town from Saimaan Kanoottikeskus, Kirkkokatu 10 (☎05/411 7722; €30 per day, including life jacket and compass), who also rent camping equipment for longer trips. Alternatively, if you're feeling less energetic, M/S *Kristina Brahe* sails from the harbour across Lake Saimaa en route for **Savonlinna** on Thursdays at 10.45am between June and August (🌐www.kristinacruises.com; €70).

Parikkala

Heavily wooded with oak and maple trees, the dense forest around the railway junction town of **PARIKKALA** offers ample opportunities for hiking, boating and goggling at the numerous species of bird – over 280 at last count – that call this part of Finland home. **Tourist information** is a ten-minute walk from the station at Harjukuja 6 (☎05/68611). Your best choices for **accommodation** are two small places just outside of town. Run by a Finnish-born American, *Laatokan Portti* (☎05/449 282, 🌐www.laatokanportti.com; ❷), in a wonderfully idyllic lakeside setting 6km south of the centre, offers a range of double rooms and has a large wooden deck at the lake's edge; you can also rent boats and fishing gear for around €15 per day. There are slightly more comfortable rooms, as well as a lakeside sauna and indoor swimming pool, a couple of kilometres further south at the rustic *Karjalan Lomahovi* (☎05/657 7700, 🌐www.karjalanlomahovi.com; ❷). The friendly staff here can also arrange winter **horse-and-carriage** trips along the Russian border. Both of these guesthouses offer hearty **meals** to both guests and non-guests; bank on around €15. Otherwise, in town, you're pretty much limited to €12 lunchtime dishes like lasagne and potato gratin at *Kaakonranta*, Parikkalantie 19, which is also a **bar** hangout for local old-timers.

Joensuu and around

The capital of what remained of Finnish Karelia after the eastern half was ceded to the Soviet Union in 1944, **JOENSUU** has a history closely linked to that of Russia. The town was founded by Tsar Nicholas I in 1848 and grew into a busy trading centre, shipping goods via the Saimaa Canal to Russia. Today, though, the closure of several large industrial plants has reduced trading links with Russia and the city is, instead, becoming known as a centre of learning, with two universities to its name. Consequently, there's a lively buzz to the streets of Joensuu, a decent-sized city of 72,000 inhabitants and a great base from which to push on into the more rural reaches of northern Karelia and the Lake Pielinen area. This is also the place to get to grips with Karelia's history since the city is home to the best museum in the entire province, admirably explaining the turbulent past of this divided region. Thanks to its fast and plentiful train links, Joensuu is also readily accessible from other areas of Finland.

Arrival and information

Whether you arrive by **bus** or **train** (the terminals are adjacent to one another), the kilometre-long walk into the centre of Joensuu is one of the most enjoyable introductions to any Finnish lakeside town: crossing the broad Pielisjoki River and bridging Ilosaari island and the narrow Joensuu Canal, the route gives a clear idea of Joensuu's watery surrounds before reaching Eliel Saarinen's epic Art Nouveau City Hall and the wide *kauppatori*.

The cultural and tourist centre, **Carelicum**, in the centre of the city at Koskikatu 5, houses the **tourist office** (Mon–Fri 9am–5pm, plus mid-June to Aug Sat 10am–3pm, July Sun 10am–3pm; ☏0400/239 549, ⓦwww.kareliaexpert.fi); staff hand out maps and useful city guides. There's also free internet access, a **box office** (☏013/267 5222) selling tickets for all the city's theatrical and musical performances, and a decent café and gift shop.

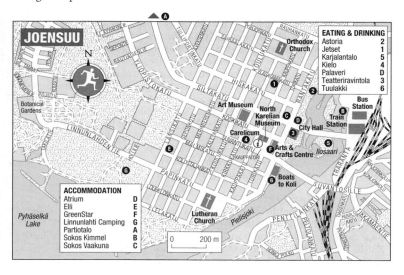

Accommodation

You shouldn't have too much trouble finding a bed for the night in Joensuu – there's enough capacity for the modest number of visitors the city receives and standards are generally good. Nevertheless, it's wise to book ahead during the summer months to ensure space is available.

Atrium Siltakatu 4 ☎013/255 888, ⓦwww
.hotelliatrium.eu. Boasting balconies and suites with
private sauna, rooms here certainly offer better
value for money than at the two *Sokos* hotels, for
example, though are less stylish and can be a little
fusty. Have a look at several before deciding –
rooms on the top floor are newly renovated. ❹/❺
Elli Länsikatu 18 ☎010/421 5600, ⓦwww
.summerhotelelli.fi. With prices similar to the
GreenStar (see below), this hotel operates from
June to Aug when the nearby university is closed. It
has comfortable if rather spartan rooms. ❸
🏃 **GreenStar** Torikatu 16 ☎010/423 9390,
ⓦwww.greenstar.fi. The city's newest
hotel, a simple and efficient, environmentally
friendly concept hotel that functions without a
reception; you book on the internet or at the
kiosk downstairs (breakfast €5). ❸
Linnunlahti Camping Linnunlahdentie 1 ☎013/126
272, ⓦwww.linnunlahticamping.fi. Operating

June–Aug only, this pleasant campsite beside
Pyhäselkä lake also has small cottages from €35.
Partiotalo Vanamokatu 25 ☎013/123 381,
ⓦwww.youthhostel-joensuu.net. Located 1km
north of the city centre, Joensuu's youth hostel is
run by the scouts and has rock-bottom prices. No
credit cards. Snug dorms sleeping four cost €12
per bed; double rooms with shared facilities. ❷
Sokos Kimmel Itäranta 1 ☎020/123 4663,
ⓦwww.sokoshotels.fi. Enjoying an enviable riverside
location and very handy for the station, this rambling
pile easily beats its more central sister hotel on
views. Rooms are modern and decked out in classic
modern Scandinavian style featuring subtle natural
colours and plenty of wooden fittings. ❺/❻
Sokos Vaakuna Torikatu 20 ☎020/123 4661,
ⓦwww.sokoshotels.fi. Joensuu's predictable chain
option with similar modern rooms to the *Kimmel*,
though right in the heart of the city centre, saving a
fifteen-minute walk. ❺/❻

The City

Pleasing first impressions apart, compact and modestly sized Joensuu doesn't have too much beyond the usual round of local museums and churches to fill your time – you can cover it in a day with ease. It's best to start your wanderings, though, at the **City Hall** (*kaupungintalo*), Joensuu's most imposing building by far, located at the corner of Rantakatu and Siltakatu. Designed by one of Finland's most distinguished architects, **Eliel Saarinen**, in 1914, this red-brick Art Nouveau beauty complete with sturdy tower, bears a striking resemblance to Saarinen's most well-known structure, Helsinki's main train station, albeit in smaller scale. Although the offices inside are not open to the public, you can get a glimpse at the sumptuous interior by wandering into the *Teatteriravintola* restaurant, also housed in the building, and gawping at the ornate ceiling decoration and soaring columns. Another fine building, though this time in wood, stands diagonally opposite the City Hall, at Koskikatu 1. Dating from 1870 and once the home of local bigwig and shipowner, Antti Juhaha, this handsome structure now houses the engaging **Arts and Crafts Centre** (Taitokortteli; Mon–Fri 9am–5pm, Sat 9am–1pm), where you can pick up a few handicrafts and other knick-knacks, try your hand at rug weaving, or simply savour a coffee and a slice of cake in the **café**.

The North Karelian Museum

Just one block on from the Arts and Crafts Centre, you'll find the well-organized **North Karelian Museum** (Mon–Fri 10am–5pm, Sat & Sun 10am–3pm; €4.50), inside the Carelicum at Koskikatu 5. Head upstairs first, where the fascinating "Karelia – both sides of the border" exhibition traces Karelia's historical position in the context of an East–West power struggle, with plenty of space given to the ever-changing borders between Russia and Finland. A timeline helps visitors make sense of the most significant events in the region's past, such as the Winter War and the Continuation War. There are also three detailed scale models, which chart development in the former Finnish town of **Sortavala** (see p.214), on the northwestern shores of Lake Ladoga, from the late eighteenth century to 1939. Now a decaying Russian settlement, Sortavala was once of great importance on account of its seminary and teachers' college, which served as early training grounds for Karelian intellectuals. Check out, too, the impressive horde of **silver coins**, including both Swedish kronor and Russian roubles dated 1664–1762, which was discovered in a potato field outside Joensuu in 1997. Elsewhere, diverting ethnographic pieces include a number of original Karelian women's costumes, whilst downstairs there's a brief section on Karelian pre-history, including a few earthenware pots, and, more interestingly, an old wooden ski, found in a local bog, which has been dated to the seventh century.

The Art Museum and the churches

Considering the devastation caused by World War II, Joensuu has a surprising number of intact nineteenth-century buildings. These include, at Kirkkokatu 23, the neo-Renaissance, red-brick former grammar school from 1894 that now holds the **Art Museum** (Tues & Thurs–Sun 11am–4pm, Wed 11am–8pm; €4.50). Inside is an impressive collection of Finnish modernism, including Albert Edelfelt's finely realized portrait, *The Parisienne*, and the gloriously sensual, wine-sipping male nude, *Drinking Bacchante* by Magnus Enckell, as well as a collection of Orthodox church icons donated to the museum in 2000. Leaving the Art Museum and glancing either way along the aptly named Kirkkokatu, you'll spot Joensuu's major churches standing at opposite ends. To the right, the neo-Gothic **Lutheran Church** (June to mid-Aug Mon 11am–7pm; rest of the year Mon–Thurs 4–6pm) can seat a thousand worshippers but, aside from Antti Salmenlinna's impressive stained-glass windows, is not wildly different from its counterparts in other towns. At the northern end of Kirkkokatu, the wooden **Orthodox Church of St Nikolaos** (mid-June to mid-Aug Mon–Fri 10am–4pm; other times by arrangement on ☎013/266 000 or 050/587 5066), built in 1887, is a few years older and much more deserving of a swift peek, with some excellent examples of gilded relief iconography on the altar screen, painted at the Alexander Nevsky monastery in St Petersburg.

Eating and drinking

Besides the tasty morsels which can be picked up for a few euro inside the *kauppahalli* (beside the *kauppatori*), Joensuu has a few good places to try out, including the chance to dine in style inside the elegant City Hall.

Astoria Rantakatu 32 ☎013/229 766. The most enjoyable restaurant in town by a long chalk, this gabled brick building by the riverside is the place to come for good Hungarian food: goulash soup (€9), pork cordon bleu (€21.50) and chicken paprika (€15). In warm weather you can eat outside overlooking the Pielisjoki.

Jetset Kauppakatu 35. Squeezed into small premises at the corner of Yläsatamakatu and Kauppakatu, this busy sports-bar regularly shows soccer matches on its big screen and is a locals' favourite.

Karjalantalo Siltakatu 1 ☎0400/880 881. *The* place to sample top-notch local specialities such as game stew, herring salad and barley blinis. Eat as much as you like from the buffet table for €29, or

go for a soup and starter (€20). Open daily 11am–2pm (till 3pm in June & Aug, 8pm in July).

Kielo Suvantukatu 12. Newly opened gourmet restaurant which serves traditional Finnish dishes such as roasted duck with cherry vinegar sauce (€22.50) and overnight-marinated beef with chanterelle sauce (€21).

Palaveri Siltakatu 4. Attached to the *Atrium* hotel, this popular two-storey drinking hole is both sports-bar (downstairs) and old-fashioned pub (upstairs), where there's plenty of brass lanterns and high-backed chairs for effect. Over a hundred different beers available.

Teatteriravintola Rantakatu 20 ☎013/256 6900. Forego the pricey main courses served in the evening and come to enjoy the

elegant Art Nouveau surrounds during a delicious, daily-changing buffet lunch (€10.50) instead.
Tuulakki Rantakatu. Housed in a wooden building at the passenger quay, this summer-only restaurant (with a glassed-in terrace) is a great place for a burger and fries, as well as a beer or two when evening comes.

Lake Pielinen region

From Joensuu, Route 6 strikes off through Karelia's northernmost reaches towards the old wooden town of **Nurmes**, skirting the western shores of **Lake Pielinen**, a vast, tear-shaped body of water dotted with islets and skerries which weighs in as Finland's sixth largest lake. Finns wax lyrical about the countryside in the **Koli National Park** hereabouts, claiming it contains everything that is quintessentially Finnish: lakes, ridges, hills, islands and forest all coming together to create picture-postcard-perfect views that are classic Finland. True enough, artists have long been drawn to this area, enchanted by the ever-changing light and interplay of lake and forest which is a reoccurring theme in Finnish landscape painting.

Getting to and from the Lake Pielinen region by public transport takes a little advance planning because connections are rather thin on the ground. Although **buses** between Joensuu and Nurmes all stop at the tiny settlement of **Ahmovaara**, 10km short of Koli National Park, it's a much better idea to book a **share taxi** (T 0100/9986; 4 daily; €14 per person) from Joensuu (they are not available from Nurmes) which will take you all the way to **Koli village**. Alternatively, **trains** run twice daily between Joensuu and Nurmes, calling at **Lieksa**, on the lake's eastern shore. During the summer months a car ferry links Koli and Lieksa (June to mid-Aug; 1hr 40min; €15), crossing twice a day. Buses meet ferry arrivals at Koli harbour and whisk passengers up to the top of Koli hill. The **ferry** service between Joensuu and Koli has now resumed though departures are rather irregular; check with the tourist office for the latest details.

Koli National Park

Tourists have been attracted to **Koli National Park**'s woody heights for over a hundred years and consequently the place thrills in billing itself as Finland's first tourist destination. Covering an area of 30square kilometres along the south-western shore of Lake Pielinen, the park, founded in 1991, can be divided into three main areas: the **central Koli hills** (the highest in southern Finland), which include the peaks Ukko-Koli (347m), Akka-Koli (334m) and Pieni-Koli (238m), offer views of some fine Lakeland scenery and is arguably the best area to base yourself; **Koli village**, to the north, where you'll find the tourist office (see below) and a super-market; and **Loma-Koli**, near the harbour, a sprawling area of cabins and holiday homes down on the lakeshore. The main road which leads to Koli from Ahmovaara links all three areas.

The most enjoyable thing to do at Koli is to take the short ten-minute walk from the car park at the top of the hill out to the twin peaks, **Ukko-Koli** and **Akka-Koli**, barely 200m apart, to enjoy the sweeping panorama across Pielinen to the Russian border, away in the distance. Whilst up here, it's also worth popping quickly into the **Luontokeskus Ukko** nature centre (mid-June to mid-Aug daily 10am–7pm; rest of the year Mon–Sat 10am–5pm, Sun 10am–3pm; €5), at the car park, where there are short photographic exhibitions on the geology and nature of the national park.

Practicalities

The **tourist office** (mid-Feb to Sept Mon–Fri 9am–5pm, plus July Sun 11am–5pm; T 050/408 1051, W www.kareliaexpert.fi) is located in Koli village at Ylä-Kolintie 2.

Cabins throughout the park can be rented from here – reckon on around €400 per week though prices vary greatly depending on the size and quality of the cottage. The one and only **hotel** at Koli, *Sokos Hotel Koli* (☎020/1234 662, ⓦwww .sokoshotelkoli.fi; ⑥) is located beside the nature centre up in Ukko-Koli at Ylä-Kolintie 39. Perched high on the hill, it has spectacular views of the lake, so be sure to ask for a room facing the water, rather than the car park. There's a free chairlift from the hotel down to the lakeshore, several hundred metres below. When it comes to **eating and drinking**, it's hard to beat the eagle's-nest location, overlooking the lake, of the restaurant inside the *Sokos*, where mains such as grilled salmon with marinated vegetables or chicken fillet in a chanterelle sauce go for €12.60–16.80. For self-catering, head for the supermarket opposite the tourist office.

Lieksa and around

A modest-sized village about 100km north of Joensuu, **LIEKSA** is known primarily as a summer watersports and winter dogsledding centre. Lieksa beats Koli in terms of accessibility since getting here is possible by train, and should you want to combine it with a visit to Koli, simply hop on the ferry across Pielinen (see opposite). Lieksa is also the location for one of Finland's biggest open-air museums, the engaging **Pielinen Museum** (Pielisen museo; mid-May to mid-Sept daily 10am–6pm; rest of the year Tues–Fri 10am–3pm; €5) at Pappilantie 2, a staggering collection of seventy or so Karelian buildings, grouped according to either the year of construction or their use. Photographic and ethnographic displays of Karelian country living are contained in the main entrance building – it's this part of the museum which stays open during the winter months.

Once you've perused the museum, there's little else in the village to detain you and it's best to scoot to the tourist office to make enquiries about **whitewater rafting** around **Ruunaa**, a small village about 30km east hard up against the Russian border; operators will collect you from Lieksa (€50 per person). In winter, Bearhill Husky (☎013/854 106, ⓦwww.bearhillhusky.com), Kontiovaarentie 207 in **Hattuvaara** (between Lieksa and the town of Ilomantsi), run **dogsled tours** out into the surrounding wilderness; prices depend on the length of the tour.

The **tourist office** (Mon–Fri 8am–4pm; ☎0400/175 323, ⓦwww.kareliaexpert .fi) is on the main street at Pielisentie 2–6. **Accommodation** choices in Lieksa are extremely limited and most visitors go for the modern and comfortable *Hotelli Puustelli* (☎013/511 500, ⓦwww.finlandiahotels.fi; ④/⑤), situated in parkland between the two bridges over the Lieksa River at Hovilerinkatu 3. For something much less expensive, however, there are good-value student apartments with kitchen facilities and laundry available at *Aikuisopiston asuntola* (☎050/328 4816, ⓔtuula.liimatta@pkky.fi; ②) at Oravatie 1. Don't get your hopes up as far as **food** is concerned – it's either the *Kebab ja Pizzahouse* at Pielsentie 2–6 by the tourist office, or the more pleasant *Paakarin Paja* bakery and café, a couple of doors down at no. 20, which also serves lunch. The hotel restaurant offers more substantial meals at higher prices in nicer surroundings.

Nurmes

Idyllically peaceful and with an appealing location between forest and saturated marshland, the small town of **NURMES**, at the end of the railway line, is quite simply a gem. Its old town occupies a narrow, steep, sandy ridge (glacial drift material left over from the ice age) and still contains some fine examples of historical wooden buildings from the late 1800s when the town was founded by Tsar Alexander II of Russia.

The Town

Arriving at the train station, make a stroll around the **old town**, Puu-Nurmes, your first priority: simply head left along the main street, Kirkkokatu, lined with hundreds of swaying birch trees, for five minutes or so, and then weave in and out of Harjukatu, Työväenkatu and Rajakatu, which all lead off Kirkkokatu. The original plans for this area were drawn up in 1897 and construction began once approval had been granted by the tsar. From Rajakatu, Kötsintie leads north past the library and towards the **old cemetery** where hundreds of local people were buried in mass graves in the 1860s after starving to death following a series of failed harvests; a series of black crosses still stands in their memory. From the cemetery, retrace your steps and head back into the town centre, where, once you've seen the sizeable Orthodox **church** (late June to early Aug daily 11am–5pm) from 1896 at Kirkkokatu 18 (inside there are models of earlier Lutheran churches), you've just about wrapped things up in the centre.

Nurmes' main attraction, **Bomba Village**, is a couple of kilometres east of the town centre, and easily reached on foot in about 45 minutes: from the train station, follow the railway line out of town, crossing the bridge at Mikonsalmi, and head all the way up to the roundabout in the distance, where you turn right into Esa Timosen tie and pick up signs for Bomba. A reconstruction of a traditional Karelian house originally built by the large Bombin family in 1855 in Suojärvi (now in Russia), this is another example of Finns clinging on to their heritage and bringing it home again. In 1976 the residents of Suojärvi formalized plans to rebuild the family's main house, the Bombantalo, on the Finnish side of the border, in Nurmes. Built of stout round pine logs and measuring about 25m in length, the structure is certainly impressive and includes all the features of the original – even the cattle ramp up to the first floor. In addition to the main house which includes a buffet restaurant, there is now a gaggle of other outbuildings, including a lakeside sauna, summer theatre and even a small *tsasouna* (wooden chapel).

Practicalities

There's a useful **tourist office** in the town centre at Kauppatori 3 (June & July daily 8am–10pm; Aug–May Mon–Fri 9am–5pm; ☎050/336 0707, ⓦwww.nurmes.fi).

▲ Wooden chapel, Bomba Village

You can see the town on your own by hiring a cycle (€5 per day) at Kesport Konesola, Kirkkokatu 16A (☎013/480 180). Budget **accommodation** in Nurmes can be found at the *Hyvärilä* (☎013/687 2500, Ⓦ www.hyvarila.com; dorms €10.50, doubles ❸; breakfast €8), Lomatie 12, which is also the location of the town's summer-only **campsite**. There's a choice of both modern and traditional-style accommodation at Bomba Village: cabin-style accommodation is available close to the Bombantalo itself, or there are well-appointed Nordic-style hotel rooms in the main hotel building, the ⚐ *Holiday Club Bomba* (☎020/1234 908, Ⓦ www.holidayclubhotels.fi; ❺), which also has a pool and sauna. There's also a very ordinary, central hotel, *Nurmeshovi*, Kirkkokatu 21 (☎013/256 2600, Ⓦ www .nurmeshovi.com; ❸).

Eating is best enjoyed at the restaurant inside the Bombantalo, where there's a traditional Karelian buffet every lunchtime. In town, the best restaurant is *Bella*, inside the Poronkylä shopping centre at Poronkylänkatu 18, just beyond the cemetery, which has pizzas, passable Italian pasta dishes and daily lunch specials, though there's also a more central café, *Kaarlo*, serving burgers and other fast food, at Kirkkokatu 18.

Kainuu

Stretching north of Karelia well off the beaten track along the wilds of the Russian border, the region of Kainuu, roughly the size of Belgium, supports a population of just 84,000 people. Until the nineteenth century Kainuu produced more tar than anywhere else in the world, shipping it and plentiful supplies of timber down the Oulujoki River to the coast for export. Today, though, the last of the region's paper mills has closed due to spiralling transport costs, spelling the end to centuries of traditional industry; indeed, life has always been tough, and money scarce, in this forgotten corner of the country.

The undisputed capital of Kainuu is **Kajaani**, a modest town with links to former president Urho Kekkonen. East of Kajaani, things start to get pretty isolated, though **Kuhmo**, barely 50km from the Russian border, offers a notable web of nature trails and hiking routes and a respectable Kalevala theme park. Further north, the little-visited hiking centres of **Suomussalmi** and **Hossa** offer blissful isolation, and it's not until **Kuusamo**, another 140km further north, that civilization returns in the form of a pleasant, if low-key town, whose main claim to fame is its proximity to one of Finland's leading ski resorts, **Ruka**, and the wilds of the **Oulanka National Park**.

Kajaani and around

Roughly half the people of Kainuu live in **KAJAANI** (pronounced kye-arnie), 230km northwest of Joensuu, a self-effacing place that could hardly be more of a contrast to the bold communities of Karelia. Though small and pastoral, Kajaani offers some insight into Finnish life in one of the country's less prosperous regions. Fittingly, it was here that Elias Lönnrot completed his version of the *Kalevala*, the nineteenth-century collection of Finnish folk tales and poems that extolled the virtues of traditional peasant life (see box below). During the first week of July, Kajaani also hosts Finland's biggest annual **poetry festival** (Ⓦwww.runoviikko.fi), during which the main street, Kauppakatu, turns into a bustling market. But whatever time of year you visit, be sure to head out to the nearby village of **Paltaniemi**, whose vast wooden church, replete with eighteenth-century murals, is one of the most impressive in the whole of Finland.

Arrival, information and accommodation

Kajaani's **train station** is located at the southern edge of the town centre on Vienankatu, whereas **buses** pull into the slightly more central terminal at the junction of Lönnrotinkatu and Sammonkatu. From either station, it's an easy walk to the **tourist office** (June–Aug Mon–Fri 9am–5.30pm, Sat 9am–2pm; Sept–May Mon–Fri 9am–4.30pm; ☏08/6152 5555, Ⓦwww.kajaani.fi), in the centre at Kauppakatu 21, which can offer assistance with finding **accommodation**, though there's rarely a pull on rooms here.

Kainuun Portti Mainuantie 350 ☏08/613 3000. Four kilometres south of town on Route 5, this rustic country hotel has regular doubles and a campsite (May–Oct only; €15); to get there, take bus #7 from the bus station. ❸

Kajaani Onnelantie 1 ☏030/608 6100, Ⓦwww .hotellikajaani.fi. The riverside location is a bonus but the rooms are a little on the small side and rather drably decorated. ❹

Karolineburg Karoliinantie 4 ☏08/613 1291, Ⓦwww.karolineburg.com. Undoubtedly the best choice in town, this proud manor house from

1836 sits on a hilltop just across the river and has opulent rooms to match the exquisite exterior. ❹
Scandic Kajanus Koskikatu 3 ☏08/616 41, Ⓦwww.scandic-hotels.fi/kajanus. Across the main bridge in pleasant riverside surroundings, this is a top-notch modern business hotel servicing the nearby congress centre; use the entrance on Puutavarantie. ❸/❹
Sokos Valjus Kauppakatu 20 ☏08/615 0200, Ⓦwww.sokoshotels.fi. Predictable chain hotel is stamped right across this modern pile on the town's main street; central but uninspiring. ❸/❺

The Town

On arrival, pause for a while to admire the Art Nouveau glory of the town's **train station** which was constructed in 1904. It's one of the finest railway buildings in

Lönnrot and the Kalevala

Hailed today as one of Finland's greatest heroes, **Elias Lönnrot** (1802–1884) is remembered for his compilation of the **Kalevala** (meaning "lands of Kaleva", the -la ending indicating "place" in Finnish), the collection of fifty Finnish folk poems widely regarded as one of the greatest works of Finnish literature and often associated with the national awakening, which ultimately led to the declaration of national independence from Russia in 1917. Lönnrot was a scholar from Sammatti near Helsinki, who lived during the uncertain years when Finland was a Grand Duchy within the Russian empire. In 1827 he began travelling across rural Karelia and neighbouring eastern areas, collecting and carefully recording Finnish folk poems – a form of poetry, sung to tunes based on a pentachord (a five-note scale), that had already died out in western Finland, where it had been replaced by regular European rhyme poetry. Once he began to assemble them into a coherent whole, Lönnrot soon began to suspect the poems were, in fact, part of a greater whole, telling the tale of the shamanistic Väinämöinen, and the colourful characters he meets on his travels. The first version of his compilation, known as the *Old Kalevala*, was published in 1835–36, but the version of the *Kalevala* read today is the second edition, containing new material, which was published in 1849.

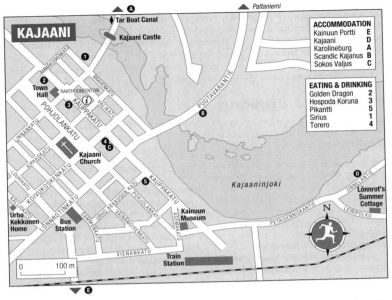

Finland and has been meticulously renovated over the years. Pressing for the centre along Kauppakatu, you'll come to the Carl Engel-designed **town hall** (*raatihuone*), occupying prime position at the junction with Linnankatu on Kajaani's main square, Raatihuoneentori. It was built in 1831 with financial support from the Russian authorities, who sanctioned Engel's harmonious design which includes a central rooftop clocktower and turret. The whole shebang was restored in 1990 and is now painted a fetching yellow ochre.

Elsewhere in the centre, you may wish to cast a cursory glance and reverential nod at Kalliokatu 7, near the bus station, where local boy made good, former prime minister and Finland's longest serving president, **Urho Kekkonen**, lived in a corner apartment until 1926; a commemorative relief on the outer wall marks the house in question. Having grown up and attended school in Kajaani, Kekkonen found work here as a journalist before moving to Helsinki. As president, Kekkonen was responsible for the controversial policy known as Finlandization which allowed the Soviet Union to exert power over Finland. Supporters of the policy claim it prevented a Soviet invasion of Finland, allowing the country to remain outside the Soviet bloc in stark contrast to other neighbours in central and eastern Europe; opponents claim it surrendered too much power to Moscow and strained relations with Finland's long-standing Scandinavian allies. Whatever the truth, a **statue** of Kekkonen, raised by a proud town, stands close to Kajaani church.

Kajaani Castle

More historically significant, perhaps, is the ruined **Kajaani Castle**. Built in 1604 to forestall a Russian attack, it later served as a prison where, among others, Johannes Messenius (1579–1636), the troublesome Swedish historian and university professor, was incarcerated. In 1716, during the Great Northern War between Sweden and Russia, however, the fortress was totally destroyed by its own store of gunpowder, and one of Kajaani's main roads now slices unceremoniously through the remaining heaps of stones as it crosses the river. Given the paucity of other sights in town, the ruins are worth a quick look, and, whilst you're here, it's worth pottering over the bridge to see the narrow **tar boat canal** and **lock keeper's cabin** on the far bank which were in use until 1915. Barges laden with tar regularly passed through the canal, thus avoiding the rapids, in order to gain access to Oulujärvi lake and onwards into the Oulujoki.

Eating and drinking

There aren't a huge number of decent places to eat and drink in Kajaani and what is on offer will barely set your taste buds tingling; most places are centrally located along the main drag, Kauppakatu.

Golden Dragon Kauppakatu 38. Choose from a good variety of Chinese mains from €12.50 or go for the €8 lunch buffet.

Hospoda Koruna Kauppakatu 30. A modern bar with a covered terrace out front with a good choice of foreign beers including Paulaner and Budweiser Budvar.

Pikantti Kauppakatu 10. Reassuringly old-fashioned lunch place with flowery tablecloths serving an all-you-can-eat lunch for €8.90, though the solid Finnish fare is anything but piquant. Closed Sun.

Sirius Brahenkatu 5 ☏08/612 2087. Kajaani's best restaurant is housed in a sturdy functionalist building which once played host to Soviet and Finnish presidents Leonid Brezhnev and Urho Kekkonen. The Finnish food here is not cheap but certainly tasty, and they do a really good buffet lunch for €14. There's a large terrace overlooking the river at the rear.

Torero Kauppakatu 20. Classy Spanish restaurant with stone walls and red table lanterns offering a wide choice of pasta (€8.90) and tapas (€11.90) as well as steaks (€20) and salads.

Around Kajaani: Paltaniemi

The hourly #4 bus from Kajaani winds its way to the well-preserved village of **PALTANIEMI**, 9km away on the shores of Oulujärvi lake. In contrast to rough-and-ready Kajaani, eighteenth-century Paltaniemi was home to Swedish-speaking aesthetes lured here by the importance of Kajaani Castle during the halcyon days of the Swedish empire. Their transformation of Paltaniemi into something of a cultural hotbed seems incredible given the place's tiny size and placid setting, but evidence of a refined pedigree isn't hard to find. Most obviously there's the massive wooden **Paltaniemi Church** (May–Aug daily 10am–6pm; Sept–April guided tours only, bookable in the tourist office in Kajaani), built in 1726, whose ornately painted interior is kept unheated in order to preserve its amazing ceiling **frescoes**. Painted by Emmanuel Granberg between 1778 and 1781, these include a steamy vision of hell in a gruesome *Last Judgement* just above the main door. Apparently, the locals were so shocked by the scenes that part of the fresco had to be painted over. Across the road, the **Eino Leino Talo** is a copy of the former home of the eponymous Finnish poet (1828–1926), whose poems captured the increasingly assertive mood of Finland at the beginning of the twentieth century. His life and the history of Kajaani Castle form the subject of a modest exhibition within (mid-June to mid-Aug daily except Sat 10am–6pm; €6).

Kuhmo

With belts of forests, hills and lakes, and numerous nature walks and hikes within easy reach – including the beginning of the arduous though rewarding UKK hiking trail – unassuming **KUHMO** makes a fine base for exploring the untamed land hereabouts. The terrain is in some ways less dramatic than that further north, but then again it's also far less crowded. If your route north to Kainuu missed out Karelia, Kuhmo offers a belated chance to submerse yourself in Karelian culture, since this pint-sized place likes to see itself as the Finnish "capital" of **White Karelia**, a region across the border in Russia which stretches as far east as the White Sea. Although the town is not officially part of Karelia, it was from Kuhmo that Elias Lönnrot set out for the nearby villages of Venehjärvi and Vuokkiniemi where he recorded poems and ballads that would later become part of the *Kalevala*. Indeed, links with White Karelia remain strong today and twice per week a bus rattles across the border to **Kostamus** (Kostomuksha in Russian; visas necessary), the nearest town on the Russian side and site of a strategic iron-ore mine. Kuhmo also boasts a superb information centre about the *Kalevala* as well as a theme park dedicated to the epic. The best time to be in town is during the fortnight-long **Chamber Music Festival** (Ⓦ www.kuhmofestival.fi), which begins around mid-July. More than seventy music concerts, dance performances and lectures are held in the town, attracting music lovers from across the region; tickets go on sale in February and are available online.

Arrival, information and accommodation

The **bus station** is located on Koulukatu, a five-minute walk away from the intersection with the other main street, Kainuuntie. You can get details of hiking routes, maps and other practical information from the **tourist office** on Väinömöinen at the Kalevala village theme park (June–Aug daily 8am–6pm; Sept–May Mon–Fri 8am–6pm, Sat 10am–4pm; Ⓣ 0440/755 500, Ⓦ www .kuhmo.fi); see p.196 for directions. Budget **accommodation** options are limited, though there are a couple of guesthouses in town.

Kainuu Kainuuntie 84 Ⓣ 08/655 1711, Ⓦ www .hotellikainuu.com. The only hotel option in town has rather tired, uninspiring rooms overlooking the main road. ❸/❹

Kalevala Väinömöinen 9 Ⓣ 08/655 4100, Ⓦ www.hotellikalevala.fi. Three kilometres from the town centre beside the Kalevala village with clean, modern rooms, set on a lake with great views. ❺

Kalevala Spirit Camping Väinämöinen 13 Ⓣ 0440/755 500, Ⓦ www.kalevalaspirit.fi. The town's campsite is located just before the Kalevala village about 3km from the centre; open late May to Sept.

Matkakoti Parkki Vienantie 3 Ⓣ 08/655 0271, Ⓔ ematkakoti.parkki@elisanet.fi. A good, friendly bed-and-breakfast choice, just off the main Kainuuntie, handy for the town centre. ❷

Matkustajakoti Uljaska Koulukatu 38 Ⓣ 08/655 0545. Well-established guesthouse in a blocky modern building about halfway to the Kalevala village. Have your Finnish phrasebook handy. ❸

The Town

Before heading out to the Kalevala village, Kuhmo's main attraction, there are a couple of things to check out in town. First of all, head off west down Kontionkatu, which runs parallel to Kainuuntie, to reach **Juminkeko** (Sun–Thurs noon–6pm, July also Fri & Sat noon–6pm; €4; Ⓦ www.juminkeko.fi), at no. 25, the town's authoritative information centre on all things *Kalevala* and Karelia, and an amazing example of modern Finnish wood architecture to boot. Inside, the largest collection of *Kalevala* books in Finland awaits your perusal, and with the aid of a multimedia programme you can listen to excerpts narrated in fifty or so different languages. Three English-language films are shown at regular intervals in the auditorium, dealing with the birth of the *Kalevala*, Kainuu during the Lönnrot period and the history of White Karelia. Across Kontionkatu from the centre, Kuhmo's imposing **wooden church** from 1816, used as a venue for the summer chamber-music festival, is also worth a quick peep.

It's a well-signposted walk of around 3km out from the town centre to the Kalevala village. En route, you'll pass the new **Orthodox church**, close to the junction with Peuranpolku (actually Route 912 towards Suomussalmi), which contains several rare eighteenth-century icons that once adorned the walls of the Valamo Monastery in Lake Ladoga in Russia.

Kalevala village

From here it's another 2km to the **Kalevala village** (Kalevankylä in Finnish; guided tours at noon and 2pm mid-June to mid-Aug; €20) itself, a theme park re-creation of a wooden Karelian village and an excellent place to pick up some interesting handicrafts and souvenirs. Perched on a hilltop and surrounded by traditional woven fencing, the village consists of a narrow street edged with sturdy wooden buildings built in traditional Karelian style with painted shutters and overhanging eaves. Two-hour-long tours led by knowledgeable guides dressed in period costume aim to give visitors an insight into how people used to live. As you wander around you'll encounter staff performing traditional duties such as tar making, bread making and woodcarving, precisely as people once did centuries ago in this part of the country; there's a chance to roll up your sleeves and try your hand at some of the activities yourself, too. It was traditional for people to gather together on Saturday evenings, after a long week of hard work, to take a sauna and wash away the grime of their labours: have a peep inside the traditional smoke sauna for an idea of how an original sauna was constructed with roughly hewn logs and a wood-burning stove to heat the structure. If you're around between mid-December and mid-January, the site opens as a Christmas Village (same times) with some traditional yuletide food to sample as well as a few Santa Claus knick-knacks for purchase.

Eating and drinking

Options for eating and drinking in Kuhmo are limited. However, there's a supermarket at the junction of Kainuuntie and Koulukatu with a wide range of provisions if all else fails.

Eskobar Kainuuntie 84. The best bet for something filling to eat in town: pizzas from €6.60, burgers from €3.90, pasta €9.50 as well as more substantial steaks and pork dishes from €11.70.

Kalevala Väinämöinen 9. An upmarket restaurant within *Hotelli Kalevala* serving a range of traditional Finnish dishes as well as more mainstream international fare such as steaks.

Känsäkoura Koulukatu 7. Locals pour in here to dine and dance the night away; there's

usually karaoke and a live band cranking out Finnish hits.

Lounas-Kahvila Neljä Kaesaa Koulukatu 3. Daytime restaurant and café with a range of lunchtime local specialities including the Kainuu potato and lingonberry pie, *rönttönen*. Closed Sun.

Villipeura Kainuuntie 84. A colourful local boozer's hangout just off the reception of *Hotelli Kainuu* – you won't be alone for long.

North to Hossa

About 200km north of Kuhmo, near the village of Pirttivaara off Route 843, the **Martinselkonen Nature Reserve** (Martinselkosen Eräkeskus) is a remote conservation area next to the Russian border, known locally as the "last wilderness". The forests in the area have stood untouched for over fifty years and support a wealth of wild animals, including bears, wolverines and elk, as well as birds like the capercaillie and black grouse. Between early May and early August, **bear-watching safaris** are available within the reserve from the **Martinselkonen Wilds Centre**

(☎08/736 160, ⓦwww.martinselkonen.fi) for €145 per person, including a night spent in a hide deep in the forest. The centre also provides **accommodation** in regular double rooms (❸) or cabins (from €25 per day) and full meals. The closest public transport to the park is the Suomussalmi–Hossa bus, which calls at Juntusranta, about 20km away.

Heading north from the Martinselkonen Nature Reserve along Route 843, it's roughly another 30km to **HOSSA**, a nature tourism centre on Kainuu's isolated northern fringe which provides ready access to some of northern Finland's most rewarding terrain. The village sits close to a ninety-kilometre network of hiking paths that pass through pine forest and over undulating ridges between steely lakes; the paths are graded according to difficulty and range in length from 1km to 25km. Around 5km north of Hossa is the **Hossa visitor centre** (daily: March–May 10am–4.30pm; June–Aug 9am–10pm; Sept & Oct 10am–4.30pm; ☎020/564 6041, ⓦwww.metsa.fi) at Jatkonsalmentie 6 beside Öllöri lake, which has a café, an information centre on the local area and an adjacent **campsite**, *Karhunkainalo* (☎020/344 122, ⓦwww.villipohjola.com), with cabins (€90) and camping. Canoe rental is available for €30 per day (reserve on ☎08/732 366). For more **accommodation** options, back in Hossa village at Hossantie 278 there's an all-year campsite (☎050/016 6377) and adjacent holiday village, *Hossan Lomakeskus* (☎08/732 322, ⓦwww.hossanlomakeskus .com) with double rooms (❹), cabins (from €27) and a **restaurant** serving Kainuu specialities. From Hossa, it's 80km north to Kuusamo and 200km south to Kajaani; **buses** run to both destinations (change at Suomussalmi for Kajaani).

Kuusamo and around

In all but name, **KUUSAMO**, 250km north of Kajaani, is part of Finnish Lapland. True, the provincial border between Kainuu and Lapland (Lappi in Finnish) is still a further 50km to the north, but the scenery hereabouts has more in common with the far north than the tamer tracts further south: bare, round-topped mountains, sweeping plains blanketed with impenetrable boreal coniferous forest and boundless, inaccessible marshland – not to mention omnipresent reindeer. Lapland, and Kuusamo in particular, suffered grievously during the latter stages of World War II as the German forces who were stationed in Finland withdrew to the north and implemented their infamous scorched-earth policy. In September 1944, they mercilessly torched the entire town, leaving just three buildings standing. Hardly surprising then that Kuusamo today has little of architectural note and is best used as a staging post on the way to Lapland or as a base from which to reach the nearby **Ruka** ski resort. However, with its population of 11,000, Kuusamo is a veritable giant in these parts and you'd be wise to lap up a bit of urban sophistication before pressing on into the wilds beyond.

Arrival, information and accommodation

Kuusamo's **bus station** is located on the northern edge of the tiny town centre on Kaarlo Hännisentie. The **airport**, 6km to the northeast of town, is linked by shuttle buses which operate in connection with scheduled plane arrivals. Annoyingly, the **tourist office** (early May to early Aug daily 9am–5pm; early Aug to mid-Sept Mon–Fri 9am–5pm; ☎03/0650 2540 or 08/860 0200, ⓦwww .kuusamo.fi) is a good 1.5km walk away up at Torangintaival 2, by the junction of Route 20 to Oulu and Route 5, the Kajaani–Rovaniemi road. **Accommodation** choices are rather limited.

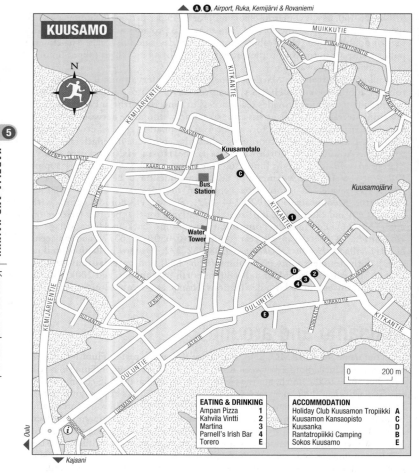

KUUSAMO

N

Kuusamotalo

Kuusamojärvi

Bus Station

Water Tower

0   200 m

EATING & DRINKING		ACCOMMODATION	
Ampan Pizza	**1**	Holiday Club Kuusamon Tropiikki	**A**
Kahvila Vintti	**2**	Kuusamon Kansaopisto	**C**
Martina	**3**	Kuusanka	**D**
Parnell's Irish Bar	**4**	Rantatropiikki Camping	**B**
Torero	**E**	Sokos Kuusamo	**E**

▲ Oulu

▼ Kajaani

Holiday Club Kuusamon Tropiikki Kylpyläntie
☎020/1234 906, ⓦ www.holidayclubhotels.fi.
Set in forest 6km north of town (accessible on
Kuusamo–Ruka buses; see opposite), this is a luxury
spa resort complete with sauna, pool and tropical
water funland. **⑤/⑥**
Kuusamon Kansaopisto Kitkantie 35 ☎04/08
608 715, ⓦ edu.kuusamo.fi/kansanopisto. Opposite
the bus station, the town's youth hostel is well kept
and independently run. You must book in advance
and arrive between 8am and 3.45pm Mon to Fri. **①**
Kuusanka Ouluntie 2 ☎08/852 2240, ⓦ www
.kuusanka.fi. A compact, family-run hotel in the

centre of town with twelve cosy, if rather cramped
rooms. Handy for the bus station. **③**
Rantatropiikki Camping Kylpyläntie ☎08/859
6000, ⓦ www.holidayclubhotels.fi. Adjacent to the
spa hotel, the high-end campsite (€15) also has fully
equipped cabins for €90.
Sokos Kuusamo Kirkkotie 23 ☎08/859 20,
ⓦ www.sokoshotels.fi. A soulless outpost of the
Sokos chain whose interlinking blocks lie a
ten-minute walk from the centre of town. Although
the rooms are unexceptional, the hotel boasts an
usually large, indoor swimming pool. **④/⑤**

The Town

Having stocked up with information at the tourist office, don't leave without checking out the sterling nature photography on display here by Hannu Hautala, a local man who trained as a car mechanic before realizing his hidden talent for taking some truly spectacular pictures of the region's wildlife. An **exhibition** of Hannu's work (same hours as tourist office; €4) is available for viewing in a separate hall within the tourist office complex; be sure to sit in the rocking chair and listen to the sounds of birdsong which play automatically as you sway back and forth admiring the photographs. From the tourist office, take a stroll back into town, heading for the **water tower** (June–Aug Tues–Sat 10am–6pm) off Oulangantie, which has a platform at the top offering impressive views of the lakes and hills which surround Kuusamo; there's also a nice café. From here, it's a short walk through the bus station to **Kuusamotalo**, the town's sleek concert hall and cultural centre at Kaarlo Hännisentie 2, where, if you're lucky, there may be something of distraction, since, sadly, there's little else to occupy your time in Kuusamo.

Eating and drinking

Before heading north, make the most of what Kuusamo has to offer to **eat and drink** – it's nothing exceptional, but it is the best choice for miles around.

Ampan Pizza Kitkantie 18. Run by a local actor, this place serves the best pizzas in Kuusamo, as voted by readers of the local newspaper.

Kahvila Vintti Ouluntie 1. This great local café is the best place in town to people-watch and enjoy some good local Finnish lunch dishes, too. Mon–Fri 8am–3.30pm.

Martina Ouluntie 3. The Kuusamo branch of this pan-Finland chain is a decent choice for pizzas, pasta and steaks and other fry-ups:

fried chicken, chips, salad and a beer will cost around €15.

Parnell's Irish Bar Ouluntie 5. Undoubtedly the best and most popular bar in town with a wide range of Irish and other international beers.

Torero Kirkkotie 23. Inside the *Sokos* hotel, this pseudo-Spanish place offers a good choice of steaks, pasta and tapas as well as the "Kuusamo Menu", a selection of local specialities including reindeer and vendace.

Ruka

Twenty-five kilometres north of Kuusamo along Route 5 to Kemijärvi, **RUKA** (www.ruka.fi) is locked in permanent battle with Levi in Lapland to be regarded as Finland's number-one ski resort. Planeloads of southern Finns are lured here every winter by the prospect of guaranteed snow and the chance to fling themselves down one or all of the 29 slopes located on **Rukatunturi**, the 500m-high fell which overlooks the centre; there are over two hundred skiing days per year here, the season generally running from October to June. There's also a whopping 500km of cross-country trails in the vicinity, as well as a special area set aside for snowboarding. A detailed price breakdown for ski passes (from €5) and equipment rental is available online.

Buses run every one or two hours from Kuusamo to Ruka; timetables can be found at www.matkahuolto.fi/en. There's plenty of **accommodation** in Ruka, though most of it doesn't come cheap. One of the best hotels is the well-appointed *Rantasipi Rukahovi*, Rukankyläntie 15 (08/859 1888, www.rantasipi.fi; ④/⑤), at the very heart of things in the resort, whilst *Royal Ruka*, Mestantie 1 (08/868 6000, www.royalruka.fi; ④/⑥), with bizarre fairytale castle-style turrets, is another good choice located right by the slopes. For something cheaper, *Willis West* (08/868 1712, www.williswest.com; ②), Rukkanriutta 13, by the turn-off from Route 5, is a pleasant motel offering regular doubles, while *Ruko-Ko* (08/866 0088, www.ruka-ko.fi), nearby at Rukkanriutta 7, is a central booking agency for **cabins** (from €50).

Eating and drinking in Ruka can be quite pricey, but two of the cheaper options are *Pizzeria Ruka* (☎08/868 1445) on Kelorrinne, its decent selection of pizzas including a reindeer option, and *Pitäjän-Pirtti* (☎08/868 1325) at Rukankyläntie 14, a café-cum-restaurant serving snacks, burgers and more substantial Lapland specialities. The most fun place to party is *Zone*, close by at no. 13, with regular karaoke and dancing on the tables, whilst *Suomi-Pop Bar*, Rukankyläntie 15, thrashes out crowd-pleasing Finnish hits all night long.

Oulanka National Park

Roughly halfway between Kuusamo and Salla and covering a vast area of remote upland terrain, **Oulanka** (ⓦwww.outdoors.fi) is one of Finland's most popular national parks. At its heart is the valley of the powerful **Oulankajoki River** which flows east into Russia's White Sea through a series of deep ravines, most notably at **Kiutaköngäs**, a 300m-long set of thundering rapids squeezed between rugged walls of dolomite and quartzite rocks. Much of Oulanka is covered in dense pine forest, though in the north there are sizeable areas of marshland which form an important nesting ground for whooper swans.

A total of four long-distance **hiking trails** wind their way through Oulanka, varying in length between 12km and 80km and accessible from late May to October. Details of all routes are available at two **visitor centres**, Hautajärvi (☎020/564 6870) in the north and Oulanka (☎020/564 6850) further south. The most notable of these trails – in fact the best-known hiking route in Finland – is the **Karhunkierros Trail** (also known as the Kuusamo bear circuit, though you're extremely unlikely to see one), for which Ruka is the southern starting point. It's an eighty-kilometre trek, which weaves over the summit of Rukatunturi, dipping into canyons and across slender log suspension bridges over thrashing rapids, ending up at Hietajärvi. There are some considerable climbs to contend with and, in the north, extensive marshland which is crossed on duckboard. The route can be made shorter by taking the bus from Kuusamo to **Ristikallio**, which gives secondary access to the hike; this path then joins the main trail at the Taivalköngäs rapids (crossed by suspension bridge). Wilderness huts are placed roughly at ten-kilometre intervals along the route. There's no shortage of places to pitch your own tent in the park, and about halfway along the route are three **campsites**: *Juuma* (☎08/863 212; late May to Sept), *Jyrävä* (☎050/361 4631; June to early Sept) and *Retki-Etappi* (☎08/863 218; June–Sept).

Travel details

Trains

Joensuu to: Lieksa (2 daily; 1hr 20min); Nurmes (2 daily; 2hr).
Kajaani to: Kuopio (5 daily; 2hr); Oulu (5 daily; 3hr).
Lappeenranta to: Joensuu (6 daily; 2hr 30min); Parikkala (6 daily; 1hr 5min).
Nurmes to: Joensuu (2 daily; 2hr); Lieksa (2 daily; 1hr 20min).

Kajaani to: Kuhmo (Mon–Fri 8 daily, Sat 5 daily; 1hr 40min); Kuusamo (3–5 daily; 3hr 35min–4hr 15min); Nurmes (3 daily; 2hr).
Kuhmo to: Kajaani (Mon–Fri 8 daily, Sat 5 daily; 1hr 40min).
Kuusamo to: Kuhmo (Mon–Fri 3–5 daily; 4hr); Oulu (5 daily; 3hr); Rovaniemi (5 daily; 3hr).
Nurmes to: Kajaani (Mon–Fri 6 daily; 1hr 40min).

Buses

Hossa to: Kajaani (4 daily; 4hr); Kuusamo (1 daily; 1hr 15min).
Joensuu to: Ahmovaara (6 daily; 1hr); Nurmes (6 daily; 2hr).

International buses

Joensuu to: Ladoga (1 daily in summer; 4hr).
Lappeenranta to: St Petersburg (1–2 daily; 5hr 30min); Viipuri (1–2 daily; 2hr 45min–3hr 40min).

6

The Lake District

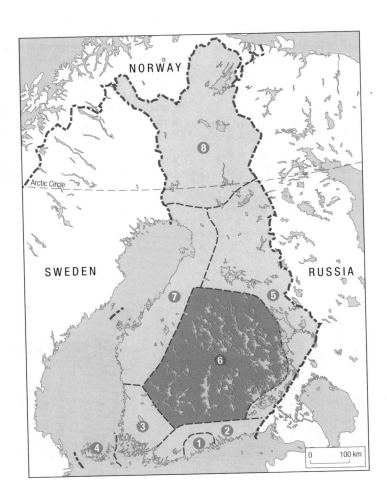

CHAPTER 6   # Highlights

* **Boat trips from Savonlinna** Cruise the serene waters around the Lake District's most delightful town for the best views of Olavinlinna Castle. See p.208

* **Punkaharju ridge** Enjoy classic Lakeland scenery on this narrow, pine-clad ridge, home to the engaging Lusto forestry museum, too. See p.208

* **Jätkänkämppä woodsmoke sauna, Kuopio** Steam to your heart's content in the world's biggest smoke sauna and get tips from the locals on the Finns' national pastime. See p.212

* **Valamo Monastery** Spend the night in this serene monastery at the heart of Finland's Orthodox faith. See p.214

* **Headquarters Museum, Mikkeli** Get to grips with the history of the tragic Winter War at this engrossing museum. See pp.216–217

* **Alvar Aalto, Jyväskylä** Learn all about one of the world's greatest architects in his home town and admire some of his finest buildings. See p.225

* **City living, Tampere** Sample some of Finland's most sophisticated restaurants and bars in the country's buzzing second city. See pp.234–236

▲ Olavinlinna

The Lake District

K nown unofficially as "the land of a thousand lakes" (*tuhansien järvien maa*), Finland boasts more than forty thousand waterways and lake chains, the majority of them – chiefly the Päijänne and Saimaa systems – located in the **Lake District**. It's a region unique not just to Scandinavia but to the whole of Western Europe – a third of it is taken up by water, with each of the lake chains featuring countless bays, inlets and islands interspersed with dense forests. The towns and cities in this part of the country, often laid-back places draped leisurely over several small islands, are some of Finland's most scenically alluring. Although many towns hereabouts grew up around paper mills which used the natural waterways to transport timber to pulping factories, the focus of lakeland life today is more on enjoying the water for leisure purposes than industrial exploitation. Indeed, waterborne exploration by canoe or scheduled boat is the main reason to come here, for which most people make a beeline for modestly proportioned **Savonlinna**, arguably the best base from which to discover the region. Time is rarely wasted, though, in larger **Kuopio**, **Jyväskylä** or Finland's lively and engaging second city, **Tampere**, each dominated by an extensive waterfront and offering plentiful opportunities for messing about in boats.

Although the western Lake District is mostly well served by **trains**, rail connections to – and within – the eastern part are awkward and infrequent. With daily services between the main towns and less frequent ones to the villages, **buses** are generally handier for getting around but to really explore the countryside, you'll need to rent a **car** or **bicycle**.

Eastern Lakeland

The eastern lakes, spanning an area roughly the size of the English region of East Anglia, are characterized by slender ridges furred with conifers which link the few sizeable areas of land. Consequently, travel around this part of the region can be circuitous and time-consuming. It's therefore best to base yourself in one of the two main regional centres, from where you can strike out to visit the surrounding area using a combination of buses and trains. The best of these two bases is **Savonlinna**, which is arguably the Lake District at its most perfect. Stretching delectably across

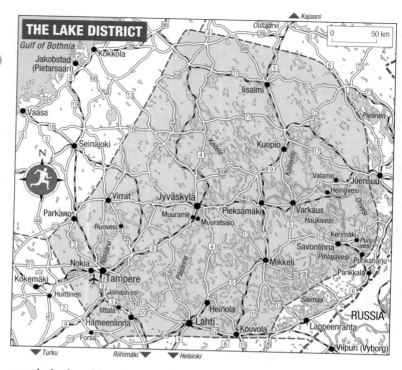

several islands and boasting a superbly preserved medieval castle which hosts an annual opera festival, the town is a great place to chill for a day or two. Savonlinna also provides ready access to historically significant **Mikkeli**, 100km to the west along Routes 14 and 5, which played a significant role during the Winter War. Routes north then lead to the region's second main centre, **Kuopio**, an altogether busier destination with an engaging museum and a raft of boat excursions to get you out onto the water.

Savonlinna and around

Draped across a series of tightly connected islands, **SAVONLINNA** is one of the most relaxing towns in Finland. Formerly sustained by the woodworking industries that grew up as consequence of its position at a major junction on the Saimaa lake network, the town nowadays prospers on the income generated from tourism, and the cultural kudos derived from its annual international **opera festival**. The main focus in town is the harbourside, where gleaming white steamers stand in neat lines, awaiting day-trippers keen to see Lake Saimaa. Indeed, visit Savonlinna in July (when the opera festival takes place) and early August and you'll find the quayside here packed to the gills with holidaymakers, but on either side of the peak season the town's streets and numerous small beaches are uncluttered. The easy-going mood, enhanced by a decent range of bars and restaurants, makes Savonlinna a superb base for a two- or three-day stay, giving ample time to soak up the mellow atmosphere and discover the local sights and curiosities. Chief among these is the medieval castle, **Olavinlinna**, which justifies a visit here in itself – a completely intact structure which has given the town its name, Savon*linna* in Finnish and Ny*slott* (literally, Newcastle) in Swedish.

Just east of Savonlinna, the remarkable modern arts centre at **Retretti**, the **Lusto forestry museum** (more interesting than the name might suggest), plus the slender pine-clad ridge of **Punkaharju** nearby, one of Finland's most hyped and photographed locations, make for a perfect day-trip destination. Alternatively, you could stop before you get to the ridge itself and take in one of Finland's most impressive wooden churches, the cavernous **Kerimäki kirkko**.

Arrival and information

Whether arriving by train from the north (Joensuu) or the south (Lappeenranta), connections for Savonlinna are made in Parikkala (see p.184), from where it's a glorious ride of around 60km or so on a winding single-track line. Although there are only half a dozen trains to Savonlinna, there is a choice of **train stations**: Savonlinna-Kauppatori is by far the most central, although if you're making straight for the *Malakias* youth hostel, get off at Savonlinna, 1km to the west. The **bus station**, too, is a ten-minute walk west of the centre, just off Olavinkatu, while the **tourist office**, Puistokatu 1 (June & Aug daily 9am–5pm; July daily 8am–8pm; Sept–May Mon–Fri 9am–5pm; ☏015/517 510, Ⓦwww.savonlinna.travel), faces the passenger harbour. Staff can point you in the right direction to **rent bicycles** and also supply useful route maps for cycling in the area; there are also two **internet** terminals here. For longer usage, try Herkku Pekka, an internet café at Olavinkatu 53.

Accommodation

Savonlinna has several budget accommodation possibilities and some good **hotels**, but don't expect the big discounts you might find elsewhere, as there's no shortage of summer business and prices soar during the opera festival.

Malakias Pihlajavedenkuja 6 ☏015/533 283 (advance bookings on ☏015/739 50 when closed), Ⓦwww.spahotelcasino.fi. A summer hotel, 2km west of the centre, offering basic but reliable studios sharing kitchens and bathrooms. A good choice for self-catering. Open July only. €95 for a twin-bed studio.
Opera Kyrönniemenkuja 9 ☏015/521 116 (advance bookings on ☏015/744 3440 when closed), Ⓦwww.savocenter.fi. Another of Savonlinna's summer-only hotels: this one is just past the castle near the road to Punkaharju. Rooms are pleasant and modern, though unexceptional. Open early June to late Aug only. ❹

Perhehotelli Hospitz Linnankatu 20 ☏015/515 661, Ⓦwww.hospitz.com. Excellent, classically decorated rooms with hardwood oak floors, classy striped wallpaper and views of either an apple garden or Lake Saimaa. Buffet breakfast is served on a boat. Be sure to book ahead as it's very popular. ❹
Savonlinnan Seurahuone Kauppatori 4–6 ☏015/5731, Ⓦwww.savonlinnanseurahuone.fi. Completely renovated in 2007, this 1956-era hotel is set smack on the *kauppatori*, while many of its 84 modern (ie blandly decorated) rooms look onto

The Savonlinna Opera Festival

Begun in 1912, and an annual event since 1967, Savonlinna's **Opera Festival** lasts for the whole of July. The major performances take place in the courtyard of the castle, and there are numerous spin-off events all over the town. **Tickets**, priced €39–190, go on sale the preceding November and sell out rapidly, although the tourist office keeps some back to sell during the festival. For further details contact the **Opera Office** (☏015/476 750, Ⓦwww.operafestival.fi), though it's easiest to buy your tickets directly from the tourist office.

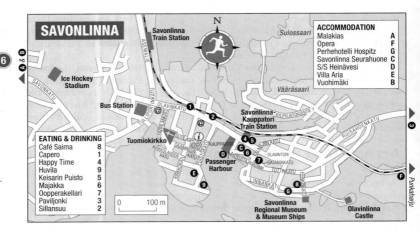

the lake. Prices nearly double during the festival. Has two decent restaurants. ④–⑤

🏃 **S/S Heinävesi** Savonlinna Harbour ☎015 517 510, ⓦ www.savonlinnanlaivat.fi. For an atmospheric summertime option, it's hard to beat the crew quarters of a working steamboat, moored in the harbour overnight once it returns from its day-trips to Punkaharju (see p.208). The shared-bath cabins are a bit cramped, but loaded with character, and evenings here during the festival are known for being some of the liveliest in town. ③

Villa Aria Puistokatu 15 ☎020/744 3447, ⓦ www.savocenter.fi. A score of very nice rooms in a renovated wooden building from 1896, originally built as a public hospital. Great location by the lakeside, just down the street from the tourist office, which makes this a good central choice. Mid-June to mid-Aug only. ⑥

Vuohimäki Vuohimäki ☎015/537 353; out of season ☎015/6138 3210. Savonlinna's campsite, beautifully located beside the lake, 7km west of the centre and served by bus #3. Open June–Aug only.

The Town

Although Olavinlinna Castle remains the key sight in Savonlinna and is likely to take up the lion's share of your time, the stroll out to it from the centre along the water's edge takes you past the town's other attractions, which it makes sense to take in on the way there.

The harbour and Regional Museum

Start your wanderings at the centrally placed **passenger harbour** and *kauppatori*, the prettiest part of town, and pleasant spots to mingle with the crowds and enjoy a snack from one of the numerous food stalls. Meander along the lakeshore, and you'll soon reach the **Savonlinna Regional Museum** (July to early Aug daily 11am–5pm; early Aug to June Tues–Sun 11am–5pm; €4), which occupies an 1852 granary at Rihisaari, just a stone's throw from the castle. Sadly, though, it's not one of Finland's greatest museums and the displays inside of spinning wheels, old wooden tools and black-and-white photographs of former steamboats fail to set the pulse racing. The bulk of the museum's collection charts hunting and farming techniques, and the birth of the area's tar and logging industries, although the upper level holds temporary art exhibitions. Much more interesting are the three c.1900 steamers known as the **Museum Ships** (June–Aug only, same times as regional museum; same ticket), docked outside at the end of a jetty, which earned their keep plying the Saimaa waterways, sometimes travelling as far as St Petersburg and Lübeck.

Olavinlinna Castle

Accessed across a pontoon bridge from beside the Regional Museum, Savonlinna's greatest possession now rises up before you: perched on a small island and looking like some great grey sea monster surfacing from the deep is the mighty **Olavinlinna Castle** (daily: June to mid-Aug 10am–6pm; mid-Aug to May Mon–Fri 10am–4pm, Sat & Sun 11am–4pm; €5, which includes an hourly English-language guided tour; ⓦ www.olavinlinna.fi), named after St Olaf. Although the town of Savonlinna was founded by the Swedish Crown in 1639, a mighty castle, its walls 5m thick, had already stood on this site for over one hundred and fifty years, founded in 1475 to secure this important lake-transport junction on Sweden's unstable eastern border against Russia. However, following the Swedish–Russian war of 1741–43, the castle and the town fell into Russian hands, in which it remained until 1812 when restored to Finland. It was the Russians who added the incongruous **Adjutant's Apartment** which, with its bright yellow walls and curved windows, resembles a large piece of Emmenthal cheese. With military importance lost when Finland became a Russian Grand Duchy in 1809, the castle ended its pre-restoration days rather ignominiously as the town jail, before standing empty for several decades. Repair work was begun in the 1870s following two major fires which ravaged large parts of the interior. Following much debate about its future use, the opera singer, Aino Ackté, hit upon the idea of holding a series of opera festivals in the castle in 1912, though it wasn't until 1967 that the annual opera festival was launched, in the midst of yet more restoration work. Sadly, the castle interior is rather less inspiring than the building's history and, although the entertaining guides do their best to bring the place to life, the structure remains best viewed from the outside.

Eating and drinking

For a town of modest proportions, Savonlinna has a respectable range of places to eat and drink. Be sure to book a table well in advance, though, if you're here during the opera festival.

Café Saima Linnankatu 11. The most atmospheric of all Savonlinna's cafés, with gloriously high ceilings and wooden floorboards, stuffed with old clocks, chandeliers and even an old upright piano.

Capero Olavinkatu 51. There's both booth seating and regular tables at this basic Italian place, serving lasagne (€7.20), tagliatelle dishes (€7.50) and pizzas (€7.20).

Happy Time Olavinkatu 36. The most popular pub in which imbibe towards midnight – a dark interior, though with classic paintings of Finnish landscapes adorning the walls.

Huvila Puistokatu 4 ☎015/555 0555. Housed in Savonlinna's former TB hospital, this atmospheric old wooden building down on the waterfront has top-notch Finnish cuisine, plus outdoor seating in summer: the frothy crab soup (€9.80) and lemon-glazed char in carrot butter sauce (€20.40) are superb. The on-site brewery makes its own beer and cider.

Keisarin Puisto Olavinkatu 33. Regular Chinese place with predictable decor, though with an extensive menu featuring all your favourites from €12.

Majakka Satamakatu 11 ☎015/531 456. A good and dependable choice for solid Finnish meals overlooking the harbour with fish speciali-ties such as fried vendace (€12.80) and breaded zander with beetroot risotto (€17.20), though tasty meat dishes, too, including pork noisettes with baked cheese (€13.80).

Oopperakellari Kalmarinkatu 10 ☎020/744 3445. Set menus of excellent Finnish cuisine start at around €60 in this elegant restaurant, replete with linen table-cloths and candles. Be ready for the waiters – many of them local opera students – to start bellowing out arias as they prance about the restaurant.

Paviljonki Rajalahdenkatu 4. Finland's top trainee chefs serve up their latest creations at this out-of-town restaurant, an easy 1.5km walk east of the centre along Route 14. The service is excellent, and the food imaginative and well prepared; lunch here costs around €13, which includes dessert and coffee.

Sillansuu Verkkosaarenkatu 1. Close to the *kauppatori* and train station, this excellent bar is known for its wide selection of beers with daily specials. The walls are covered with hundreds of business cards – add yours, and order another.

Boat trips and boat rental on Lake Saimaa

Between June and August, you're spoilt for choice when it comes to boat trips on Lake Saimaa. Over half a dozen vessels ply the serene waters, departing from the main passenger harbour, roughly every hour (2hr; €13), cruising amongst the countless pine-clad islands and skerries dotted in the lake. Precise departure times and details change from year to year but the main operators are **Vipcruise** (Ⓦwww.vipcruise.info), **Ieva** (Ⓦwww.ieva.fi) and **Lakestar** (Ⓦwww.lakestar.info). Undoubtedly, though, the best trip is aboard the atmospheric old steamer, **S/S Heinävesi**, which departs Savonlinna daily at 11am for Punkaharju, returning at 3.30pm (Ⓦwww.savonlinnanlaivat.fi; €32 return). Alternatively, it's also possible to move on from Savonlinna by boat: Kuopio is served on Mon, Wed and Fri at 9am by **M/S Puijo** (Ⓦwww.mspuijo.fi; €79) and departures for Lappeenranta are available on **M/S Kristina** (Ⓦwww.kristinacruises.com; €70) on Fri at 11am.

   Boat rental is available from the cabin marked Blue Outdoor, also down at the harbour (℡040/500 4888, Ⓦwww.blueoutdoor.fi) – they have motorboats (€100 per day) and canoes (€35 per day). Regular rowing boats can be rented from the *Vuohimäki* campsite – rowing past Olavinlinna, for example, is really quite spectacular.

Punkaharju ridge and around

From Savonlinna, the railway line and Route 14 head southeast towards the **Punkaharju ridge**, which, according to local belief, is the healthiest place to breathe in the world, thanks to an abundance of conifers that super-oxygenate the air. This narrow thread of land between lakes Puruvesi and Pihlajavesi begins 27km southeast of Savonlinna and accommodates both the road and the railway line as it snakes along for a distance of 7km; it's then another 6km or so from the southern end of the ridge to the tiny village of **Punkaharju** itself (see "Practicalities", p.209). Created by gravel deposits left behind when the ice sheet melted at the end of the Ice Age, the water here is never more than a few metres away on either side: quite simply, this is the Lake District at its most beautiful.

   Punkaharju has enchanted visitors for centuries; indeed, an early fan was none other than Tsar Alexander I of Russia, who decreed that the area should be protected for future generations to enjoy. The best views of it are from the northern end; stand with your back to the forest, looking past the reddish trunks of the pines growing along the water's edge out over the lakes and Punkaharju itself and you have a classic picture of Finland. Perhaps not surprisingly, it's heavily over-hyped in Finnish tourist literature, and, although you should make an effort to see the ridge, don't rule out other places hereabouts.

Lusto forestry museum

Along the ridge about 25km southeast from Savonlinna and 6km before Punkaharju village you'll find **Lusto**, the national forest museum (May & Sept daily 10am–5pm; June–Aug daily 10am–7pm; Oct–April Tues–Sun 10am–5pm; €10; Ⓦwww.lusto.fi). Designed, predictably, from wood, two inter connecting buildings showcase the Finnish forest in all its glory. The highlight of the museum is the fabulous Room of Silence, a **film theatre** with padded walls and floor, whose back wall is occupied by one large cinema screen. Clever computer graphics coupled with a sophisticated surround-sound system re-create a 3D lake scene somewhere deep in the forest: swans take off from the lake and seemingly fly right towards you, woodpeckers hack away in the pine trees and a great northern diver even pops up from under the water – all totally captivating. Elsewhere other exhibits trace the history of the forestry and log-floating industries, while the second building, reached by a connecting walkway, is given over to a collection of forest tractors and harvesters, as well as possibly the largest number of chainsaws you'll ever see in one place.

Retretti Arts Centre

Next door to Lusto, the main road passes the extraordinary **Retretti Arts Centre** (daily: June & Aug 10am–5pm; July 10am–6pm; €15; **W** www.retretti .fi), a place devoted to the visual and performing arts. The unique element is the setting – man-made caves gouged thirty metres into three-billion-year-old rock by the same machines that dug the Helsinki metro. Outside, in the large sculpture park, fibreglass human figures by Finnish artist Olavi Lanu entwine cunningly with the forms of nature: tree branches become human limbs, and plain-looking boulders transform slowly under your gaze into a pile of male and female torsos. Inside the caves, the exhibitions are changed every year, with artists developing site-specific projects to complement the dramatic setting. The interior also features underground streams, whose gushings and bubblings underpin the music piped into the air.

Practicalities

The easiest way to reach the ridge is by **train**: all services between Parikkala and Savonlinna run along it, calling at Lusto and Retretti stations, though trains only run at three-hourly intervals and there are none at all in the evening, so be sure you time your visit carefully and check timetables. For information about travelling here by **boat**, see the box on p.208. Should you want to **stay**, the most atmospheric hotel is *Punkaharjun Valtionhotelli*, Harjutie 596 (🕾015/739 611, **W** www .lomaliitto.fi/punkaharju; ❹–❺), an ornate wooden house close to the junction of Routes 14 and 4792 between Retretti and Punkaharju village that still summons up the tsarist era, despite an insipid restoration; their simple summer cabins (€49) are much more affordable than rooms inside the house. Another, much less attractive option is the dingy cabins at *Gasthaus Punkaharju* at Palomäentie 18 in the village of Punkaharju itself (🕾015/473 123, **W** www.naaranlahti.com; €100). Alternatively, next to the Retretti Arts Centre, is *Punkaharjun Lomakeskus* (🕾020 752 9800), an extensive **camping** area with simple cabins (€95) and larger, fully equipped cottages (€115) as well.

Kerimäki

Unlike Lusto and Retretti, which are both accessible by train, the village of **Kerimäki**, on the shores of Lake Puruvesi, can only be reached by bus from Savonlinna, from which there are several daily services (check the latest details at the tourist office) – though there is a train station called Kerimäki, it's located an inconvenient 10km or so from the village itself. The reason to come to this otherwise unremarkable village is to see the **Kerimäki church** (daily: May & mid- to late Aug 10am–4pm; June & early Aug 10am–6pm; July 10am–7pm), an immense wooden construction holding three thousand people, built in 1848 and claimed to be the largest wooden church in the world. Its remarkable scale was the brainchild of the charismatic local priest of the day who, keen for his entire flock to hear God's word, threw out the original plans for a modest church, urging the locals to build a veritable giant instead. It's a truly astonishing sight, complete with double-tiered balconies, and a yellow-and-white-painted exterior which shines through the surrounding greenery.

Kuopio

Located on a major inland north–south rail route and the hub of local long-distance bus services, **KUOPIO** has the feel – and, by day, much of the hustle and bustle – of a large city, despite being only marginally bigger than most of the other Lake District communities. Nonetheless, it's an important Finnish town and, especially if you're speeding north to Lapland, provides both a break in the journey and an enjoyable taste of the region. One of the best times to visit is mid-June, when the long-established **Kuopio Tanssii ja Soi dance festival** (Ⓦ www.kuopiodancefestival.fi) inundates the streets with a week of performances, workshops, classes and the like, turning the town into a veritable mecca of artistic activity. Soon after, early July sees the slightly more bacchanalian **wine festival** (Ⓦ www.kuopiowinefestival.com), where a world wine region is selected and fêted in restaurants, bars and other venues all over the city. Kuopio is also home to one of the best museums in the country – the engrossing **Orthodox Church Museum**, which is stuffed full of ornate icons and other rare religious finds, many of them rescued from Russia.

Arrival and information

Adjacent to one another at the northern end of Puijonkatu, Kuopio's **train and long-distance bus stations** are an easy walk from the town centre. **Boats** from Savonlinna arrive at the passenger harbour, 300m southeast of the train station, whilst the **airport**, 14km north of the centre, is linked to the city by bus (Ⓦ www.savonlinja.fi). The **tourist office** is located in the City Hall, which faces the *kauppatori* at Haapaniemenkatu 17 (June–Aug Mon–Fri 9.30am–5pm, plus Sat 10am–3pm in July; Sept–May Mon–Fri 9.30am–4.30pm; ☏017/182 585, Ⓦ www.kuopioinfo.fi).

Accommodation

Though Kuopio has no official HI youth hostel, there are a couple of rock-bottom budget accommodation options around the train station, while most of the pricier places are closer to the town centre.

Best Western Atlas Haapaniemenkatu 22 ☏017/211 2111, Ⓦ www.hotelliatlas.com. Standard, predictable, functional rooms look right onto the central market square. At least you know what you're getting. ❹/❺

Jahtihovi Snellmaninkatu 23 ☏017/264 4400, Ⓦ www.jahtihovi.fi. Pleasant family-run hotel close to the harbour that makes a nice change from the usual chain hotel offerings. Rooms are modern and neutrally decorated; two larger flats are also available for about €20 extra. ❹/❺

Matkustajakoti Rautatie Vuorikatu 35 ☏017/580 0569. Decent place with no-frills double rooms (and a few singles); reception is at the train station restaurant. ❸

Rauhalahti Katiskaniementie 8 ☏030/608 30 and 017/473 000, Ⓦ www.rauhalahti.com. Kuopio's hostel and campsite (May–Aug only) are located within a spa complex 5km south of the town centre. The doubles here are quite spacious and all have access to numerous pools, jacuzzis and saunas. Take bus #7 from the *kauppatori*. ❺

Retkeilymaja Virkkula Asemakatu 3 ☏040/418 2178, Ⓦ www.kuopionsteinerkoulu.fi/retkeilymaja _virkkula. Centrally located a block from the train station, with 30 dorm beds. Early June to early Aug only. Dorms €17.

Scandic Kuopio Satamakatu 1 ☏017/195 111, Ⓦ www.scandichotels.com. Unsurpassed views of the Kallavesi lake as well as a superb ground-floor sauna and pool offset the standard chain-style rooms here. ❹/❺

Sokos Puijonsarvi Minna Canthinkatu 16 ☏017/170 111, Ⓦ www.sokoshotels.fi. Stellar, luxurious rooms (some with lake views and private saunas) make this the most luxurious place to stay in town. Breakfast is served in the restaurant across the road, accessed by an underground tunnel. ❹/❻

KUOPIO

Kallavesi Lake

EATING, DRINKING & NIGHTLIFE

Apteekkari	8
Gloria	7
Harra Partanen	5
Intro	6
Isä Camillo	4
Kreeta	2
Musta Lammas	10
Pannuhuone	4
Sampo	3
Vanha Tuomari	9
Wanha Satama	1

ACCOMMODATION

Best Western Atlas	D
Jahtihovi	E
Matkustajakoti Rautatie	C
Rauhalahti	A
Retkeilymaja Virkkula	B
Scandic Kuopio	G
Sokos Puijonsarvi	F

The Town

Kuopio's broad **kauppatori**, overlooked by the nineteenth-century city hall, is very much the heart of the town, with live jazz and rock music issuing from its large stage in summer. Most things worth seeing in town, with the notable exception of the extraordinary Orthodox Church Museum, lie eastwards from here along Kauppakatu, which leads down towards the busy passenger harbour on the Kallavesi lake. However, before you head off down to the water, take a stroll past the atmospheric old wooden houses which line the narrow, pedestrianized shopping street known as **Pikku-Pietari** (June–Aug Mon–Fri 10am–5pm, Sat 10am–3pm), a great place to pick up arts and crafts. Get here from the *kauppatori* by heading three blocks west along Kauppakatu and then turning right into Hatsalankatu; the shopping alley runs between this street and Puistokatu, in the block behind.

Back in the main square, head east for a couple of minutes along Kauppakatu and you'll reach the **Lutheran Cathedral** (Mon–Thurs 10am–3pm, Fri 10am–midnight), a handsome creation erected in 1815 using local stone. Although spacious, the cathedral's interior could hardly be described as opulent, but years ago it did contrast dramatically with the cramped living quarters of most Kuopio folk. Just south of here, at Kuninkaankatu 14, the **VB Photographic Centre** (June–Aug Mon–Fri 10am–7pm, Sat & Sun 11am–4pm; Sept–May Tues–Fri 11am–5pm, Wed until 7pm, Sat & Sun 11am–3pm; €5 summer, €3 winter) is a small museum of local and international photography, some of it quite inspiring.

The Art Museum and the Kuopio Museum

Immediately north of the cathedral at Kauppakatu 35, the **Kuopio Art Museum** (Tues–Fri 10am–5pm, Wed until 7pm, Sat & Sun 11am–5pm; €3; guided tours Thurs 2pm from mid-July to early Sept) fills a sturdy granite building with an enterprising assortment of contemporary exhibitions and, on the upper floor, keeps a less stimulating stock of twentieth-century Finnish painting with local connections.

Further along the same street at no. 23, the **Kuopio Museum** (same hours; €5) comes in two parts: social and natural history. Collections on the upper floors chart the switch from rural to urban life with plenty of how-we-used-to-live paraphernalia. Much of the **social history** section is eminently missable, except for the giant fresco on the main staircase by local artist Juho Rissanen. A graphic study of eleven naked Nordic men levering a block of stone uphill, *The Builders* is a refreshingly no-nonsense portrayal of male nudity yet still turns many a conservative head. The second part of the museum, found on the first floor, is an extravaganza of **natural history**, housing, in particular, a spectacular, full-size reconstruction of a woolly mammoth, one of only a handful in the world. Musk-oxen hides have been used to simulate the beast's shaggy appearance, based on a real mammoth found in Siberia two hundred years ago. Mammoth remains have been found in ten locations in Finland, including near Kuopio: in 1873 a local man came across an upper molar from one that lived 20–30,000 years ago – hence all the museum excitement. The rest of the section is a taxidermist's dream, everything from elk and wolverine to lynx and bear: you name it, they've got it stuffed.

Orthodox Church Museum

Set on the brow of the hill at Kuopio's northwest corner, the enormously impressive **Orthodox Church Museum**, Karjalankatu 1 (May–Aug Tues–Sun 10am–4pm, Wed until 6pm; Sept–April Tues–Fri noon–3pm, Sat & Sun noon–4pm; €5), draws the Orthodox faithful from many parts of the world. You can walk here from the *kauppatori* in around fifteen minutes by heading west on Tulliportinkatu and then taking a right into Puistokatu which then becomes Karjalankatu, leading all the way to the museum. Even if the workings of the Orthodox religion are a complete mystery to you, there's much to be enjoyed, from elaborate Russian-made icons to gold-embossed bibles, gowns and prayer books. The placing of the museum in Kuopio is no accident. This part of Finland has a large Orthodox congregation, many of them (or their parents) from the parts of eastern Finland that became Soviet territory after World War II.

Most of the icons, chalices and tabernacles are contained in the exhibition rooms on the first floor, where many objects from the original Valamo Monastery (see p.214) are also on display. Look out, in particular, for the book of commemoration dating from 1610 which lists (in Russian) the names of all those whose executions were

Jätkänkämppä smoke sauna

One of Kuopio's highlights is an evening at the world's biggest **woodsmoke sauna** (€11), an enormous affair at the *Rauhalahti* hostel (see p.210) which can hold well over a hundred people. The **Jätkänkämppä sauna** and neighbouring restaurant were once part of a lumberjack camp, located at the tip of a promontory in Kallavesi Lake, perfect for a refreshing dip afterwards. The sauna is so large that it takes 24 hours just to heat up – consequently, it's only open on Tuesdays (year-round) and Thursdays (summer only). Unusually for Finland, the sauna is unisex so you should bring a swimming costume with you.

▲ Orthodox Church Museum, Kuopio

ordered by Ivan the Terrible and the equally eye-catching eighteenth-century altar cabinet which once adorned the cathedral in Viborg, richly decorated with scenes from the Old Testament. The museum also holds the original gloves and hat worn by Tsar Alexander II on the day he was killed in a bomb attack in St Petersburg in 1881; the tsar's wife donated them to Valamo Monastery in appreciation for its work.

Eating, drinking and nightlife

In addition to Kuopio's expertise in pies (see box, p.214), the city offers a number of solid options for more substantial **eating**, while several of the pubs serve good-value lunches, too. Kuopio's venues for evening **drinks** are central and mostly located on the same block of Kauppakatu just east of the *kauppatori*. The town also has a reputation for being the stamping ground of some of Finland's best rock musicians, and some pubs host **live music**.

Cafés and restaurants

Intro Kauppakatu 20. This lounge-bar-cum-restaurant is a dependable choice for pasta dishes (around €13), burgers (€12) and steaks (from €18.90). After dinner people tend to gravitate to the soft seats of the bar (to the left of the entrance).

Isä Camillo Kauppakatu 25–27 ☏017/581 0450. Set in the former 1912 premises of the Bank of Finland, this popular, casual restaurant serves a range of Mediterranean and world food, including Indian chicken, tuna steaks and grilled halloumi. Starters, including plenty of salads, from €6.30, mains from €15.50.

Kreeta Tulliportinkatu 46–48. Excellent new Greek restaurant with mains starting at a reasonable €8.40.

Musta Lammas Satamakatu 4 ☏017/581 0458. Bookings are essential at this gourmet cellar restaurant that's been in business since 1862 and is still Kuopio's finest. Try the excellent reindeer rillette with parsley root purée or the fillet of lamb in fennel sauce with deep-fried sweet pepper risotto; mains are in the range €24–34. Closed lunchtimes and all day Sun.

Sampo Kauppakatu 13 ☏017/261 4677. This long-established fish restaurant is the place to sample locally caught vendace fresh from the lake: either in a delicious soup (€11), or gracing a stew of potato and bacon (€13.50).

Wanha Satama Set in a former customs house at the harbour, this modern Finnish

www.roughguides.com

Kalakukko pies

While you're in Kuopio, look out for **kalakukko** – a kind of bread pie, baked with fish and pork inside it. While it's found all around the country, Kuopio is *kalakukko*'s traditional home and the town's bakeries generally sell it warm and wrapped in silver foil; a fist-sized piece costs about €2.50. You can also buy *kalakukko* hot from the oven at the *Hanna Partanen*, in a backyard at Kasarmikatu 15 (daily 5am–9pm); it's reckoned to be the best place in town, if not the whole of Finland, to sample it. A kilo loaf costs about €12.

restaurant is very popular on sunny summer evenings. The standard local-style mains are good, but the sandwich meals are less expensive and just as filling: try the *kanaleipä*, a delicious chicken club sandwich served with spicy fried potatoes, with plenty of bacon, cheese and red onions in there, too (€14). Open June–Aug.

Bars and clubs

Apteekkari Kauppakatu 18. An American-style bar that hosts popular jam sessions and a number of live bands.

Gloria Kauppakatu 16. Makes the most out of its real estate to offer bar, garden café, restaurant and disco all in one complex, though the disco here only gets hopping weekends after midnight.
Pannuhuone Kauppakatu 25–27. This basement bar, with a summer terrace, claims to offer over 200 varieties of whisky, though most of its youthful clientele go for the draught pints of Lapin Kulta.
Vanha Tuomari Käsityökatu 19. The closest thing Kuopio has to a British pub, with a semi-wood-panelled interior and comfy chairs. Popular with an older crowd.

Valamo Monastery

Situated amid some of the country's finest, undulating Lakeland scenery, the Orthodox **Valamo Monastery** (☏017/570 111, ⓦwww.valamo.fi), one of only two Eastern Orthodox cloisters in Finland, is the undisputed highlight of any trip between Kuopio and Savonlinna. Although the monastery is located just north of Route 23, which leads west from Joensuu (see pp.185–188), it is readily accessible with your own transport along Routes 471 and 477 heading north of Savonlinna, and Routes 17 and 477, southeast of Kuopio. Annoyingly, though, public transport hereabouts is poor, and visiting the Orthodox site without your own wheels can be fraught with difficulties. Full details can be found online at ⓦwww.matkahuolto.fi/en, but, in short, you will need to head first to industrial Varkaus, where you connect onto the bus to the monastery.

The original monastery, on an island southeast of Sortavala in Lake Ladoga, was the spiritual headquarters of Orthodox Karelia from the twelfth century onwards. In 1940, however, with Soviet attack imminent, the place was abandoned and rebuilt well inside the Finnish border, roughly 90km southeast of Kuopio. Consequently, today's structure is a potent symbol of Finland's lost territories and wounded pride and makes a moving place to imbibe the atmosphere of the country's religious past. True, there's little to do here other than eye up the ornate trappings of the Orthodox faith and enjoy the tranquility of the setting, but informative daily English-language guided **tours** (€4) are given on request during the summer, taking in the grounds as well as several churches and chapels housing original accoutrements from the earlier monastery. There are both dormitories (€25) and private rooms (❷) if you want to **stay** overnight; reservations are highly recommended.

Orthodoxy in Finland

Finnish Orthodoxy has its roots in Russia. During the twelfth century, monks and traders spread Christianity from the city of Novgorod to Karelia and eastern Finland, extending the circle of faith which already surrounded the religious power-houses of the day, namely the original Valamo Monastery in Lake Ladoga and its neighbour, Konevitsa; later, in the sixteenth century, a third Finnish monastery was founded at Petsamo on the Arctic Ocean. However, it wasn't until the early nineteenth century that the Orthodox religion became a credible alternative to the colonial religion, Lutheranism, introduced to Finland by the ruling Swedes. The reunification of the former Finnish province of Viipuri, which had been in Russian hands since 1710, with Finland proper in 1809 under the Treaty of Hamina saw Finland's Orthodox population increase tenfold. Gradually, Orthodoxy spread as believers moved from the eastern districts of Finland to live in other towns further west. With Finnish independence in 1917, the Orthodox church acquired the status of a national church alongside the Lutheran and became an autonomous bishopric of the Patriarchate of Constantinople. Today, although membership of the Orthodox church is proportionally greater in Karelia and other eastern districts, overall numbers remain small: just 1 percent of the Finnish population belongs to the church, compared with 82 percent of Finns who are members of the country's principal, Lutheran, church.

Mikkeli

The name **MIKKELI** is synonymous with just one thing in most Finnish minds, the Winter War, since it was from this unassuming Lake District town that General Mannerheim conducted Finland's military campaign against the Soviet Union. The presence of Finnish military headquarters here led the Soviets to heavily bomb the town, though Mannerheim's operations centre remained unscathed. Although military matters are still a strong local feature, you don't need to be a bloodthirsty warmonger to find interest in the town's museums – the insights they provide into Finland's recent history can be fascinating. More generally, Mikkeli also functions as a district market town (the daily crowds and activity within its *kauppahalli* seem out of all proportion to its size), while sporting a handsome cathedral and a noteworthy art collection.

Arrival, information and accommodation

The adjoining **train and bus stations** on Mannerheimintie are both just a block away from the *kauppatori*; simply walk up Hallituskatu from the terminals. The north-eastern corner of the square is home to the **tourist office**, at Porrassalmenkatu 23 (Mon–Fri 9am–5pm, Sat 10am–3pm; ☎010/826 0246, ⓦ www.travel.mikkeli.fi); on Sundays the office moves to the red cottage by the market square (10am–3pm). Free **internet** access is available at the library (Mon–Fri 10am–8pm, Sat 9am–2pm), opposite the tourist office at Raatihuoneenkatu 6.

There's no shortage of **accommodation** in Mikkeli, though most of the central hotels are characterless chain affairs. For more style, head out to the village of Ristiina, 15km to the south, where there's one of Finland's best youth hostels.

Cumulus Mikonkatu 9 ☎015/20 511, ⓦ www .cumulus.fi. A large hotel with 140 rooms aimed at the business end of the market. Rooms are modern and comfortable but rather bland. The hotel's best asset is its large swimming pool. ❸/❹

Löydön kartano Kartanontie 151, Löytö, 15km south of Mikkeli ☎015/664 101, ⓦ personal.inet.fi/yritys/kartano. This family-run hostel occupies a large, atmospheric wooden mansion, for two hundred years home to an aristocratic Russian general and his descendants: it's one of the most beautiful hostels in Finland. Take any bus bound for Kouvola. Generous breakfast (€5). As well as dorms, they also have pricier, stand-alone cottages. Dorms €16.50.

Sokos Vaakuna Porrassalmenkatu 9 ℡015/20 201, Ⓦwww.sokoshotels.fi. Another of the town's business hotels, though this one has attractive wall paintings of the Lake District to enliven the rooms. Excellent top-floor sauna suite with outside balcony. ④/⑤

Uusikuu Raviradantie 13 ℡015/221 5420, Ⓦwww.uusikuu.fi. This recently overhauled hotel,

1km west of the centre, is the best-value deal in town. Any of the 49 spacious, simply furnished rooms must be booked online or by phone between 9am and 3pm (a €6 fee is added to phone reservations); guests access all doors with a code. ③

Visulahti ℡015/18 281, Ⓦwww.visulahti.com. Mikkeli's campsite, next to the amusement park, 5km from the centre and a convoluted bus ride – get details of services at the bus station or tourist office. Camping for €17, plus cabins from €100. Mid-May to mid-Aug.

The Town

Mikkeli's modern town centre is composed of the familiar grid of streets, centred around the *kauppatori*. Distances are not great and it's an easy walk of around fifteen minutes from one side of town to the other. The Tuomiokirkko, Art Museum and Headquarters Museum all lie within a few blocks of each other on the western edge of the centre, whilst the Infantry Museum can be found to the south of the town centre.

The Headquarters Museum and around

Finns visiting Mikkeli tend to make a beeline for the school building on Ristimäenkatu, where the office used by **Carl Gustaf Emil Mannerheim** (see p.76) is preserved as the **Headquarters Museum** (May–Aug daily 10am–5pm; Sept–April Fri–Sun 10am–5pm; €6 including Communcations Centre Lokki). This is the best place in Finland to get to grips with the strategically significant **Winter War**, a 105-day campaign which Finland fought against the Soviet Union. It's not so much the exhibits that give the museum its significance but the fact that the Winter War, which effectively prevented a Soviet invasion of Finland in 1939 (see p.310), was waged and won from this most modest of rooms, the former school staffroom. The room still looks as it did during Mannerheim's day: his cigar and glasses are on his desk; a bust of the poet Runeberg gathers dust on the shelves behind, where

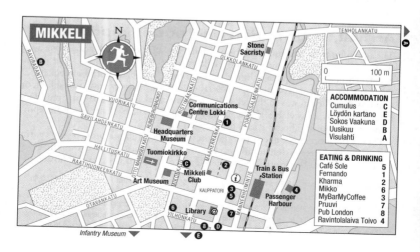

For more Mannerheim, peek through the windows of his vintage 1929 **saloon car** at the train station, which clocked up an impressive 78,000km during the war years when the General used it to travel around Finland. It was in this carriage that Mannerheim met Hitler in railway sidings near Immola in southeastern Finland; there are photographs of the event on display inside the carriage. Sadly, the interior is only open for viewing on Mannerheim's birthday (June 4, 10am–5pm).

there's even a stuffed snowy owl. A recording of Mannerheim's voice, recorded on his seventy-fifth birthday, plays on a loop; his pronounced Finnish-Swedish accent clearly stands out to the trained ear – his mother tongue was Swedish not Finnish. The Finns didn't expect the Winter War to last as long as it did, and a second room, upstairs, looks as equally temporary as Mannerheim's study; this former classroom functioned as the operations room for Finland's land forces and contains plenty of complicated-looking charts and maps plotting Finnish troop movements – quite a contrast set amid schoolchildren's chairs and benches. Elsewhere in the museum, there are poignant photo displays which recount the key events of the Winter War, including the evacuation of 400,000 people from the Karelian isthmus, and a not-to-be-missed English-language video which offers a first-class account of the predicament Finland found itself in during the conflict.

Just outside the Headquarters Museum, at the corner of Ristimäenkatu and Vuorikatu, the **Communications Centre Lokki** (May–Aug daily 10am–7pm; €6 when combined with the Headquarters Museum), is also worth a quick look. This underground bunker is where all telephone, teleprinter and Morse signals were transmitted on behalf of Mannerheim and his staff. Inside, there's a mock-up of how the communications centre looked during the Winter War, with dummies sitting obediently in front of rows of telephone exchanges.

Tuomiokirkko and the Art Museum

Raised in 1897, Mikkeli's red-brick Gothic Revival **Tuomiokirkko** (June–Aug daily 10am–6pm; Sept–May Mon–Fri 10–11am) sits primly on a small hill in the middle of Hallituskatu. Inside, Pekka Halonen's 1899 altarpiece attracts the eye, a radiant Christ against a dark, brooding background. Take a close look, too, at Antii Salmenlinna's stained-glass windows and you'll spot depictions of three Finnish towns – Viipuri (now Vyborg), Sortavala and Käkisalmi (now Priozersk), ceded to Russia after World War II. If you've ever wondered how vergers in eighteenth-century Finland kept their church congregations awake, the answer (a big stick) can be seen at the tiny **Stone Sacristy**, a detour to the north at Porrassalmenkatu 32A (late June to early Aug daily 10am–4pm; other times by appointment on ☏015/194 2424; free); the church which the sacristy served was demolished in 1776. Oddly, the sacristy now sits smack in the middle of Porrassalmenkatu, obliging all traffic to detour around its squat form.

Opposite the cathedral and housed in a sturdy granite building from 1912, the excellent **Art Museum**, at Ristimäenkatu 5A (Tues, Thurs, Fri & Sun 10am–5pm, Wed noon–7pm, Sat 10am–1pm; €4), stages some engaging temporary exhibitions of the latest Finnish art, and has two permanent displays of artworks bequeathed to the town. The Martti Airio Collection is a forceful selection of early twentieth-century Finnish Impressionism and Expressionism – Tyko Saalinen's *Young American Woman* and *On the Visit* are particularly striking. In addition, Airio collected Gustavian and Rococo furniture from Sweden and several of his pieces, including an elegant sofa and accompanying chairs, are on display. The museum's other benefactor was the Mikkeli-born sculptor Johannes Haapasalo, who bequeathed nearly three hundred finished works and over a thousand sketches.

One of Haapasalo's better works can be seen beside the cathedral: called *Despair*, it marks the graves of Mikkeli's Civil War dead.

Infantry Museum

A few minutes' walk south from the town centre is the **Infantry Museum**, Jääkärinkatu 6–8 (May–Sept daily 10am–5pm; Oct–April Fri–Sun 11am–4pm; €6), which records the key armed struggles that marked Finland's formative years as an independent nation. Assorted rifles, artillery pieces and maps of troops' movements provide the factual context, but it's the scores of frontline photos and display cases of troops' letters and lucky charms that reveal the human story. A second, substantially less interesting section of the museum concentrates chiefly on the Finnish role in the United Nations Peacekeeping Force.

Eating and drinking

In addition to the fresh breads, fish, fruit and other snacks available at the daily market in the *kauppatori*, Mikkeli has an unusually good range of **restaurants and bars** for a provincial city. In short, make the most of it before moving on.

Café Sole Porrassalmenkatu 19. Opposite the *kauppatori*, this café is popular with locals for its good-value, filling lunch specials (11am–3pm) which change daily. Closed eves & Sun.

Fernando Maaherrankatu 17. With fake shutters and curtains adorning the walls and tequila bottles in holsters strung from the ceiling, the scene is set for some excellent Mexican food (tacos €10.20, fajitas €15.90).

🏃 **Kharma** Porrassalmenkatu 18. Trendy, stone-walled café and lounge bar sporting black and gold wallpaper. A nice, modern contemporary feel, and a great place for a pre-dinner drink. Closed Sun.

🏃 **Mikko** Mikonkatu 1 ☏015/335 344. A stylish Finnish restaurant whose walls are adorned with brightly coloured Marimekko-style flowers, serving a good range of contemporary dishes such as bear-meat ravioli or oxtail soup en croûte; mains are €17–25.

MyBarMyCoffee Porrassalmenkatu 21. A bar-cum-café with a perfect location overlooking the main square, ideal for people-watching. The bar is in the front, the café at the rear, and there's outdoor seating in summer.

Pruuvi Raatihuoneenkatu 4 ☏015/214 613. There's good continental cuisine at this well-priced restaurant offering a wide range of European dishes such as gratinated chicken breast with pesto (€18.70) and Wiener schnitzel with grilled vegetables (€19.50).

Pub London Porrassalmenkatu 10. Just across from the *Sokos Vaakuna* and the place to find Mikkeli's youth drinking the night away.

Ravintolalaiva Toivo Laiturikatu ☏0440/752 453. The newest addition to Mikkeli's eating options: a traditional Finnish restaurant set within an 1870s triple-masted ship moored right in the harbour serving some excellent salmon dishes and some solid Finnish home-cooking. Reckon on €20 per main dish.

Central and western Lakeland

The land to water ratio is slightly greater in central and western Lakeland than in areas further east. That said, water abounds and remains the defining factor for the region's three main cities. In the south, **Lahti**, barely 100km from Helsinki, is the southern gateway to the Lake District and comes into its own as a winter sports resort, though during summer is comparatively quiet. From here, one of the

Lakeland's key bodies of water, Päijänne, stretches in a tear-shape north all the way to **Jyväskylä**, whose wealth of buildings by Alvar Aalto draws modern architecture buffs to what is otherwise a sleepy, yet friendly student town. However, the region is dominated by Finland's second city, **Tampere**, likeable as much for its lakeside setting as for its cosmopolitan cultural delights. It's also Ryanair's only destination in Finland, with flights here from half a dozen European cities.

Lahti

Gone are the days when **LAHTI** languished as a culturally starved outpost of the greater Helsinki region. Now, with a collection of interesting museums, a spectacular concert hall and some inviting wood-handicrafts shops, this lakeside settlement now very much holds its own against other Finnish cities of its size. The bulk of Lahti's growth took place in the twentieth century, when it developed and thrived as the "city of carpenters": two of Finland's largest furniture companies, Isku and Asko, were established here when timber transport on the lake was all the rage, and Alvar Aalto (see p.225) opened several furniture factories here to keep himself going between architectural commissions. Today, however, the town, which has a population of 100,000, is best associated with snow, and its importance in the winter cannot be overstated: for many Finns, very mention of the place is emblematic of the country's wild successes in competitive skiing. It is one of Scandinavia's best-known centres for competitive **winter sports**, with three enormous ski jumps hanging over the town, and offers some of the best cross-country skiing in the Nordic countries, as well as the renowned **Lahti Ski Games** (Ⓦ www.lahtiskigames.com) and **Finlandia ski marathon** (Ⓦ www.finlandiahiihto.fi). Given its proximity to **Lake Päijänne**, Lahti is also the gateway to the Lake District itself, with access to several harbours (such as Helsinki, Kotka, Hamina and Loviisa) and good rail and road connections to destinations further on.

Arrival, information and accommodation

Boats arrive at the **passenger harbour**, northwest of the centre. While the **bus station** is right in the centre of town at the end of Aleksanterinkatu, it's a ten-minute walk north of the **train station** to the town centre, where you'll find the very helpful **tourist office** (Mon–Thurs 9am–5pm, Fri 9am–4pm, plus June–Aug Sat 10am–2pm; ☏ 0207/281 750, Ⓦ www.lahtitravel.fi) at Rautatienkatu 22, offering plenty of information and occasional English-language guided **tours** of town (€8). Both the tourist office and the library, Kirkkokatu 31 (Mon–Fri 10am–6pm, Sat 10am–3pm), provide free **internet** access. Lahti doesn't have spectacular **accommodation**, but a few spots are fine for a night's stay.

Alex Park Aleksanterinkatu 6 ☏ 03/52 511, Ⓦ www.alexpark.fi. The basic rooms in this large, central hotel do an amazing job of hiding the fact that they were remodelled several years ago, though a few sport characterful hardwood floors. They do, however, serve very good breakfasts and there is a modestly sized swimming pool next to the sauna. ❹/❺

Kansanopiston Kesähotelli Harjukatu 46 ☏ 03/878 1181, Ⓦ www.lahdenkansanopisto.fi. Lahti's reliable summer hostel is centrally located halfway between the railway station and the market square, offering dorm beds in unmemorable rooms (€25), plus doubles, that are otherwise occupied by local vocational students. June to mid-Aug. ❸

Mukkula Ritaniemenkatu 14 ☏ 03/753 5380, Ⓦ www.mukkulacamping.fi. Lakeside campsite situated about 4km to the north of Lahti, with a range of lovely brand-new wooden cottages (€50) with full kitchens. The tent area, situated under a family of birch trees, offers views onto the Vesijärvi beach. Reached directly by bus #30 from the bus station.

NEXT Hotel Salpaus Vesijärvenkatu 1 ☏03/339 3911, ⓦwww.nexthotels.fi. The town's resident Best Western is a great example of what an ounce of inspiration can do in a chain hotel. Wedged into a corner just opposite the train station, the comfy lobby, very friendly staff and sprightly rooms – all of which have recently seen a thorough remodelling – make it Lahti's best place to stay. ➍/➎

Patria Vesijärvenkatu 3 ☏03/782 3783, ⓦwww .matkakotipatria.com. Budget guesthouse a few minutes' walk from the train station, with fifteen

double and single rooms in strikingly putrid colours, featuring shared baths and "modern" furniture that even IKEA wouldn't attempt to peddle. That being said, they're the cheapest single rooms in town. ➋

Sokos Lahden Seurahuone Aleksanterinkatu 14 ☏020/1234 655, ⓦwww.sokoshotels.fi. A warm welcome awaits at this chain spot, located just off the market square. Its 155 rooms tend towards the small side but are nevertheless done in brushed woods and (just about) acceptable pastels. Walk-in, last-minute room rates in summer can be as low as €55 per night. ➍/➎

The Town

From many angles, downtown Lahti's concrete blocks and predictable urban architecture make it appear rather dull and uniform, but a few structures in the centre have injected some style into the town's landscape.

Around the centre

North of the train station, at the foot of Radiomäki hill is Eliel Saarinen's distinctive red-brick **town hall**, which bears an unavoidable resemblance to Helsinki's railway station, which Saarinen also conceived. Built in 1912, many of its Art Nouveau features were considered immensely daring at the time, and although most of the originals were destroyed in World War II, careful refurbishment has re-created much of Saarinen's design. From Harjukatu, steep pathways wind up towards the **Radio and Television Museum** (Radio Ja TV museo; Mon–Fri 10am–5pm, Sat & Sun 11am–5pm; €5), inside the original radio transmitting station at the base of one of the twin masts atop Radiomäki hill. Here, a large room holds outmoded presentations of bulky Marconi valves, antiquated phonographs, ham radio stations and so on. Look out for the Pikku Hitler – the German-made "little Hitler", a wartime portable radio that forms an uncanny facsimile of the dictator's face.

Back at ground level, Lahti's other notable building is at the far end of Mariankatu, which cuts through the town centre from the town hall: the **Church of the Cross** (Ristinkirkko; Mon–Fri 10am–6pm, Sat & Sun 10am–3pm) at Kirkkokatu 4, whose white roof slopes down from the bell tower in imaginative imitation of the local ski jumps; its bright and open off-white interior is typical of many Finnish churches of the last century. Interestingly, this was the last church to be designed by Alvar Aalto, who died during its construction in 1976.

From here, head along Kirkkokatu for the somewhat space-starved **Art Museum** (Mon–Fri 10am–5pm, Sat & Sun 11am–5pm; €5), just around the corner at Vesijärvenkatu 11. Without any real permanent display, the museum puts on a number of modern as well as older art and graphic design exhibitions, both from Finland and from abroad. These include a few well-known Finnish nineteenth- and twentieth-century works, most notably by Gallen-Kallela and Edelfelt. Finally, near a hazardous web-like junction by the bus station and hidden behind a line of trees, is the wooden nineteenth-century **Lahti Historical Museum** (same hours; €5), Lahdenkatu 4. Housed in a pretty *fin-de-siècle* manor house, the permanent exhibition contains regional paraphernalia, numerous Finnish medals and coins, plus an unexpected hoard of French and Italian paintings and furniture.

The ski jumps and museum

Located a 1.5-kilometre-walk from the centre (the location is unmistakable), Lahti's three parallel **ski jumps** are a defining feature of the landscape, and a

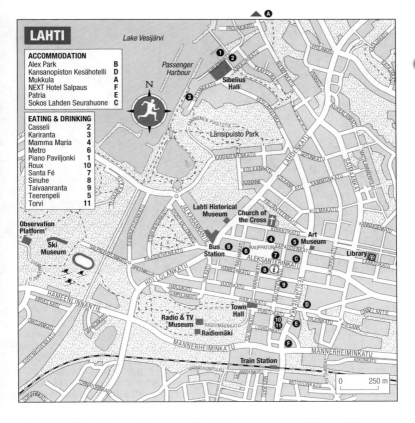

chairlift, followed by an elevator, will whisk you up to the highest of them – at 116m, it's the country's highest – which views out to Lahti and its environs from its **observation platform** (June–Aug Mon–Fri 10am–5pm, Sat & Sun 11am–5pm; at other times of the year reserve on ☎03/816 8223; €5 including the chairlift). From such a dizzying altitude the lakes and forests around Lahti stretch dreamily into the distance, and the large swimming pool below the jump resembles a puddle, which when frozen in winter is used as a landing zone.

Walk round the base of the platform to reach the slatted, slanting wooden **Ski Museum** (Hiihtomuseo; Mon–Fri 10am–5pm, Sat & Sun 11am–5pm; €5) at Salpausselänkatu 8, whose interior is filled with nostalgic exhibits, including some handsome outfits from the early years of competitive skiing and a display of several thousand-year-old skis, plucked from preservation in various swamps around the country – note the old wooden ski poles sporting bayonets, which doubled as harpoons for game foraging.

Sibelius Hall and Vesijärvi harbour

Spend any time at Lahti's passenger harbour, located 1km northwest of the centre (bus #17 from the north side of the market square), and you'll quickly see why locals call this their summer *olohuone* (living room). Dominating the harbour is the gorgeous modern **Sibelius Hall** (Sibelius Talo; 1hr tours late June to early Aug

▲ Sibelius Hall, Lahti

Tues & Thurs 2pm, including an organ recital; €10; ⓦ www.sibeliustalo.fi), home to Lahti's renowned Symphony Orchestra (☎ 03/814 4451, ⓦ www.sinfonialahti .fi), a complex that melds a 1900s-era brick factory with a striking new structure made of glass, steel and timber. The oval, 1250-seat Main Hall consists of several hundred electronically controlled doors opening to reverberation chambers to allow for fine tuning of the hall's acoustics, which have been ranked among the top ten in the world. Walk past the lovely wood sculptures to have a peek in at the mammoth Forest Hall, whose ceiling, supported by nine laminated spruce trusses, is illuminated with a constellation of tiny star-shaped lamps that mirror the alignment of the heavens on Sibelius's birthday.

The hall looks straight out onto the **Vesijärvi harbour**, where there are a number of floating and fixed restaurants and cafés, a handicrafts shop – try Pro Puu ("Pro Wood'"), immediately across from the concert hall – and a broad gravel promenade popular for evening walks that leads south to the Salpausselkä. In the winter the lake is frozen solid, but in the summer, paddle-wheel, steam and motor **boats** (mid-May to early Sept; €16.50–28.50; ⓦ www.paijanne-risteilythilden.fi or www.lahdenjarvimatkailu.fi) depart the harbour several times a day for cruises around the Vesijärvi and Päijänne lakes, as well as a ten-hour summer cruise to Jyväskylä departing on Tuesdays (€50).

Eating and drinking

Considering its relatively small size, Lahti does very well on the **restaurant** front. A few terrace **bars** on the market square, including *Santa Fé* and *Metro*, catch the setting sun until late in the evening.

Casseli Borupinraitti 4 ☎ 010/422 5950. Fine dining in a refashioned factory building at the harbour just next to the Sibelius Hall. The menu is modern Scandinavian, and includes a great peppered beefsteak and roast whitefish (most

mains from €20). Most tables give you views of the lakeside. Closed Sun.
Kariranta Satamakatu 9. Set down at the harbour in Lahti's first railway depot – rails once ran down to the water to support the thriving timber industry

in the early twentieth century – this wooden café now feels more like a conglomeration of old living rooms. It's perfect for an afternoon coffee along with either *juustosarvi* (€2) or *korvapuusti* – the biggest in town (€1.80).

Mamma Maria Vapaudenkatu 10. Run by a born and bred Roman, Gianni, this very familiar Italian spot does well over a hundred pastas, pizzas and salads (from €7.50); try the *penne alle salsiccia*, with home-made spicy Italian sausage. They also produce their own delicious ice cream.

Piano Paviljonki Borupinraitti 6. Designed by Swedish architect Gert Wingårdh in the image of Renzo Piano's work, this sleek new café smack at the waterfront is Lahti's most modern building, a sleek structure of glass and wood that stands out as clean, angular and bright. Easily the best spot for a sunset drink.

Roux Rautatienkatu 10. Pronounced "ruuks" by locals, this one-time pharmacy is now an excellent white-tablecloth eaterie with rattan chairs and Art Deco chandeliers. In addition to mains (from €25) such as pigeon, veal and reindeer, specialities include lobster soup with scallops, and snails with blue cheese and red wine sauce.

Sinuhe Mariankatu 21. Though heralded Finnish author Mika Waltari wasn't actually from Lahti, his family established this pastry shop here in 1957, bestowing upon it the name of one of his most beloved protagonists. They serve excellent chocolate muffins, apple cakes and *mansikkawiener*.

Taivaanranta Rautatienkatu 13. A great choice for lunch or dinner, this casual spot serves a lengthy menu that includes a few very good dishes: goat's cheese chicken, sided with sun-dried tomatoes and coconut chilli sauce; and a unique whisky pepper steak with chorizo-potato cake. They also serve locally produced beers and ciders from the Teerenpeli brewery.

Teerenpeli Vapaudenkatu 20. Very popular with young local professionals, this classy bar is great for kicking back in the afternoon or evening. They produce a dozen-odd beers, ciders and whiskies; try the Sauhusanttu, a light and smoky lager, or the tart Lempi cider, in blueberry, lingonberry or apple flavours. Sandwiches (€6) and nachos (€4.50) served until late.

Torvi Loviisankatu 8. With low ceilings, graffitied benches and the blackest of black paint everywhere, this is about as gritty and grotty a basement rock pub as you'll ever find in Finland, but for raw charm it's unbeatable.

Jyväskylä and around

JYVÄSKYLÄ (pronounced "YOO-ves-koo-leh") should be on every architecture lover's list of must-sees. The town (and particularly its university campus) is quite simply littered with buildings spanning the entire career of legendary Finnish architect, **Alvar Aalto**, who grew up here and opened his first office in 1923. Although there's not much more to Jyväskylä than Aalto's buildings – it's the most low-key and provincial of the main Lake District towns – the presence of its big university, which consumes one entire end of the place, does give it something of a youthful feel. If you feel like breaking your journey on the run north, this is a sound choice, plus there's the option of onward travel by **boat to Lahti** (mid-June to mid-Aug Wed at 9am; ⓦwww.paijanne-risteilythilden.fi; €55 one way), or a trip out to Aalto's summer retreat.

Arrival, information and accommodation

From the **train and bus stations**, right in the centre, it's a short walk to the **tourist office**, in a beautiful wooden building at Asemakatu 6 (June to mid-Aug Mon–Fri 9am–6pm, Sat 10am–3pm; mid-Aug to May Mon–Fri 9am–5pm, Sat 10am–3pm; ☏014/624 903, ⓦwww.jyvaskylanseutu.fi), which can supply a useful free leaflet on the local buildings designed by Aalto and has **internet** access. There's paid access available at Avatar, Puistokatu 1 (€4 per hr).

Finding somewhere **to stay** shouldn't be a problem, as there's plenty to go round. Sadly, the local campsite is closed indefinitely and the nearest option is roughly 30km away; check with the tourist office for the latest details on pitching tents or parking campers in the area.

Ada & Alex Samulinranta 5 ☎0400/597 072, ⓦwww.ada-alex.fi. A beautiful lakeside location 3km east of the centre is the draw for these tastefully decorated, stylish apartments (from €90), full of contemporary furnishings and fittings with their own kitchen and sauna. Stay for four nights or more and the price falls by €25 per night.

Alba Ahlmaninkatu 4 ☎014/636 311, ⓦwww.hotellialba.fi. Just by the Alvar Aalto Museum, this modern hotel with contemporary designer rooms is a fine choice. A roomy sauna suite adds to the feeling of well-being. ④/⑥

Laajari Laajavuorentie 15 ☎014/624 885, ⓦwww.laajavuori.com. The local youth hostel is a state-of-the-art affair, 4km from the centre; take bus #25 from Vapaudenkatu. Dorms €19.50, doubles ②

Milton Hannikaisenkatu 27–29 ☎014/337 7900, ⓦwww.hotellimilton.com. A great family-run hotel right by the train station, that's been drawing the crowds for over 50 years. Rooms have wooden floors and wall panelling, though can be a little too floral for some tastes. ④

Omena Vapaudenkatu 57 ⓦwww.omena.com. The Jyväskylä branch of this burgeoning modern, spartan, reception-less chain can be one of the cheapest and best stays if you book in advance. ②/③

Pension Kampus Kauppakatu 11A ☎014/338 1400, ⓦwww.kolumbus.fi/pensionkampus. Spartan and rather cramped rooms with few mod-cons, though all are en suite and there's a communal kitchen. All in all, good value if you're self-catering. ③

Scandic Jyväskylä Vapaudenkatu 73 ☎014/330 3000, ⓦwww.scandichotels.com. The place if you fancy a little pampering – rooms are well appointed and decked out in contemporary Scandinavian style with wooden floors and netural decor; some even have their own private saunas. A large pool and sauna suite are available to all guests. ④/⑥

The Town

Jyväskylä is small and compact, its centre covering just three blocks sandwiched between the train station on Hannikaisenkatu and Yliopistonkatu. At the heart of it all is the town's nineteenth-century **church** (Kaupungin kirkko; June–Aug Mon–Fri 11am–6pm; Sat & Sun 11am–2pm; Sept–May Wed–Fri 11am–2pm), in the small park one block west of the tourist office. The church was the centrepiece of town life a century ago, but declined in importance as Jyväskylä gained new suburbs and other churches. Despite recent restoration – when the interior was repainted in its original pale yellow and green – the church looks authentically dingy.

Across from the church at Kauppakatu 23, Jyväskylä holds an impressive **Art Museum** (Taidemuseo; Tues–Sun 11am–6pm; €4, free on Fri; ⓦwww.jyvaskyla .fi/taidemuseo), which is split into two exhibition sites: one houses changing,

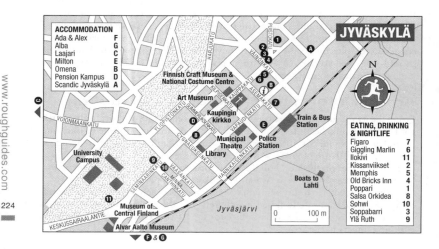

Alvar Aalto

Widely regarded as the Father of Modernism, **Alvar Aalto** (1898–1976) is undoubtedly one of Europe's greatest architects, with a list of works that can be seen in towns right across Finland, from Turku to Rovaniemi. Born in western Finland, Aalto was raised in Jyväskylä, living here until the age of 29. Inevitably, he then moved to Helsinki to explore the greater opportunities that the capital presented and soon began exhibiting at the World Trade Fairs of the 1930s, which brought him to worldwide attention. Praised as a genius by influential American critics, Aalto accepted an invitation to teach experimental architecture at the Massachusetts Institute of Technology and moved to the United States in 1941, returning to Finland a decade later.

Aalto's oeuvre features the creative use of wood, brick and glass – often in warm, natural colours and undulating forms – in a style that had its roots in Nordic classicism, a genre which had developed in reaction to the dominant Nordic romanticism of the period. In the late 1920s, however, he moved towards modernism with his design for **Viipuri Library** (1935), famous for the wave-shaped ceiling in its auditorium, and widely regarded as one of the architect's finest creations. Other key works include the critically acclaimed **Baker House** dormitory at Massachusetts Institute of Technology (1948), the first of Aalto's red-brick period, with a distinctive facade built in an undulating pattern, creating wedge-shape rooms in the interior. Several decades later followed the **Finlandia Hall** in Helsinki (1975); designed as a concert hall and congress centre at the behest of the City of Helsinki, the towering asymmetrical marble walls of the auditorium are one of the building's key features, accessed via a broad Venetian staircase leading from the foyer. In Jyväskylä, Aalto worked on around fifteen projects in all, including the main **university building** at Seminaarinkatu 15 (1956), the **police station** at Kilpisenkatu 1 (1970), and the **Municipal Theatre** (1964–82) at Vapaudenkatu 36.

Aalto also designed **furniture and glassware**, notably the Aalto vase (1936), inspired by the dress of a Sámi woman, which has become an iconic piece of Finnish design over the decades and is now reproduced in various forms by the Finnish design giant, Iittala (see p.237 and *Finnish design* colour section).

temporary shows reflecting the latest trends in modern art from Finland and the rest of the world whilst the other site is dedicated to creative Finnish photography and printmaking. Just next door at no. 25 (both Tues–Sun 11am–6pm; €5, free on Fri) are the **Finnish Craft Museum** (Suomen Käsityön museo), with displays ranging from bell-making to spectrolite jewellery, and the **National Costume Centre** (Suomen kansallispukukeskus), which holds a definitive collection of 26 complete Finnish and Karelian smocks, bodices and headdresses.

Two of the town's most important museums are situated close together on the western edge of the city on the hill running down from the university towards the edge of the lake, Jyväsjärvi. At the request of the town authorities (rather than through any vanity of his own), Aalto built the **Alvar Aalto Museum** at Alvar Aallon Katu 7 (Tues–Sun 11am–6pm; €6, free on Fri; W www.alvaraalto.fi). The architect's best works are obviously out on the streets, making this collection of plans, photos and models, which occupies the entire first floor, seem rather superfluous, but the Aalto-designed furniture, glassware and lamps make partial amends. Elsewhere in the museum, the Gallery section contains temporary art exhibitions and you'll also find a pleasant if unexciting café on the ground floor. Aalto also contributed to the exterior of the nearby **Museum of Central Finland** (Keski-Suomen Museo; same hours; €5, free on Fri; W www.jkl.fi/ksmuseo), which contains two separate well-designed exhibitions: one devoted to Middle

Finland – which traces regional history from prehistoric times to the Industrial Revolution, featuring rare finds such as part of a 4000-year-old sledge – and the other documenting the development of Jyväskylä itself – look out for the five scale models on display which give a clear idea of the town's impressive growth over the centuries.

Eating, drinking and nightlife

Jyväskylä's **eating** options range from the quotidian pizza establishments along the main streets to a few worthy upscale places. If you get tired of Finnish cuisine, you may want to explore the town's fetish for Tex-Mex restaurants. The town's student population ensures a good crop of **bars**, though things are somewhat sedate in the summer out of term-time. There is quite a strong **gay** scene; for information on local gay events, call in at SETA, Kilpisinkatu 8 (☎045/638 9540, Ⓦ www.jklseta.fi).

Cafés and restaurants

Figaro Asemakatu 14 ☎014/212 255. This central, comfy family-style restaurant matches fair-priced salads, pastas, steaks and fish dishes with a well-endowed wine list. A three-course meal won't run over €30, but they also offer a great lunch buffet for €8.90. It's justifiably busy, and reservations are recommended on weekends.

Kissanviikset Puistokatu 3. "The Cat's Whiskers" serves sizeable Finnish fish and meat dishes (most under €20) in an elegant, old-world setting.

Salsa Orkidea Kauppakatu 6. One of the town's better Tex-Mex restaurants, with tacos, tortillas, quesadillas, burritos and *chimichangas*, all for under €10.

Sohwi Vaasankatu 21. A popular, light and airy place serving inexpensive burgers, ribs, steaks and a number of tapas dishes. Evenings frequently feature live music, and the bar stays hopping until well after midnight.

Soppabarri Väinönkatu 26. The "Soup Bar" dishes out inexpensive, innovative soups, pastas and vegetarian mains.

Bars and clubs

Giggling Marlin Kauppakatu 32. The local branch of the ubiquitous Finnish chain disco is currently the place to be for local clubbers.

Ilokivi Keskussairaalantie 2. Located in the university grounds, this lively cultural space is a hot student destination on account of its live bands, art exhibitions, theatre and stand-up comedy performances.

Memphis Kauppakatu 30. This central restaurant-cum-bar has massive front windows and attracts younger Finns, especially on Thursday nights, when live rock bands take the stage. Less expensive beer is on offer downstairs at the *Ale Pub*.

Old Bricks Inn Kauppakatu 41. On sunny evenings, the outdoor seating at this popular pub really pulls in the crowds. There's a good selection of imported beers, great coffee and several scrumptious dinner dishes to boot.

Poppari Puistokatu 2–4. Live music (mostly jazz) several days a week, and open jam sessions on Tuesday nights.

Ylä Ruth Seminaarinkatu 19. This bar is often filled with lively characters, generally members of the university's philosophy and politics departments, who come here for a game of chess and/or some hard drinking.

Muuratsalo and the Sauna Village

Occupying a gorgeous spot on Lake Päijänne, about 15km south of Jyväskylä, the rocky island of **Muuratsalo** is where Alvar Aalto and his second wife Elissa built their summer retreat, known as the **Experimental House**, in 1957, in the red-brick style Aalto had pioneered in America and further developed in Helsinki on his return to Finland. The site contains several buildings, though the main one is the summer house itself, an L-shaped structure enclosing a central courtyard. It was here that Aalto developed many experimental ideas about future architectural projects, such as solar heating and construction without foundations. Two-hour **guided tours** (June to mid-Sept Mon, Wed & Fri 1.30pm; €17; advance booking necessary, ☎014/624 809) can be arranged through the Aalto Museum in

Jyväskylä and take in the house, lakeside sauna and the boatshed where Aalto kept his home-made motor launch, *Nemo propheta in patria* ("Nobody is a prophet in his homeland"). To get to the site in time for the guided tour, take **bus** #16 from Jyväskylä library at 12.19pm to its final destination. The house is a further 500m along the same road, on the right-hand side. The return bus leaves at 4pm.

Just west of Muuratsalo, the village of **Muurame**, 14km south of Jyväskylä along Route 9 towards Tampere, is home to a quintessentially Finnish attraction: the **Sauna Village** (Muuramen saunakylä; June–Aug Tues–Sun 10am–6pm; €4), a collection of 29 traditional smoke saunas now gathered together in an open-air museum. They come in all shapes and sizes and were culled from regional farmhouses across Finland. In addition to the saunas themselves, there's also an engaging exhibition of sauna culture in Finland. On Wednesdays (6–8pm), it's possible to have a smoke sauna here for just €5; bring your swimwear though, as it's open to both men and women. The Sauna Village is located by the water's edge on the right-hand side of the main road, Isolahdentie, when approaching from Jyväskylä, just after the turn for Rannankyläntie. Muurame is served by regular express **buses** running to both Helsinki and Turku.

Tampere and around

"Here it was as natural to approve of the factories as in Mecca one would the mosques," wrote John Sykes of **TAMPERE** in the 1960s – and you soon see what he meant. Although Tampere has long been Finland's biggest manufacturing centre and is currently Scandinavia's largest inland city, it's a highly scenic place, with leafy cobbled avenues, sculpture-filled parks and two sizeable lakes. The factories that line the Tammerkoski rapids in the heart of the city actually accentuate its appeal, their chimneys standing as bold monuments to Tampere's past. Its rapid growth began two centuries ago when Tsar Alexander I abolished taxes on local trade, encouraging the Scotsman James Finlayson to open a textile factory here, drawing labour from rural areas where traditional crafts were in decline. Metalwork and clothing factories soon followed (mobile-phone giant Nokia was founded here in 1865 as a wood-pulp manufacturer), their owners paternalistically providing culture for the workforce by promoting a vigorous local arts scene. Free outdoor rock and jazz concerts, lavish theatrical productions and one of the best modern art collections in Finland maintain such traditions to this day.

Arrival and information

Tampere's **airport** (ⓦ www.finavia.fi/airports/airport_tampere-pirkkala), Pirkkala, lies 15km southwest of the city centre. Buses (30min; €6) meet Ryanair arrivals at Terminal 2 and drop passengers at the central train station. All other airlines use Terminal 1 next door, from where bus #61 (€4.10) runs into town roughly every hour, stopping along Hatanpään valtatie and Hämeenkatu for the city centre. The **train station** is located at the eastern end of the centre along Rautatienkatu, whilst the **bus station** is just 300m to the southwest at Vuolteenkatu.

Tampere's friendly and helpful **tourist office**, Go Tampere, at the train station (Jan–May Mon–Fri 9am–5pm; June–Aug Mon–Fri 9am–8pm, Sat & Sun 9.30am–5pm; Sept Mon–Fri 9am–5pm, Sat & Sun 9.30am–5pm; Oct–Dec 9am–5pm, Sat & Sun 11am–3pm; ⓣ 03/5656 6800, ⓦ www.gotampere.fi), hands out maps, hiking itineraries and copies of the excellent free *Tampere* guide; there are also two free **internet** terminals. Between mid-June and August, the **Tampere**

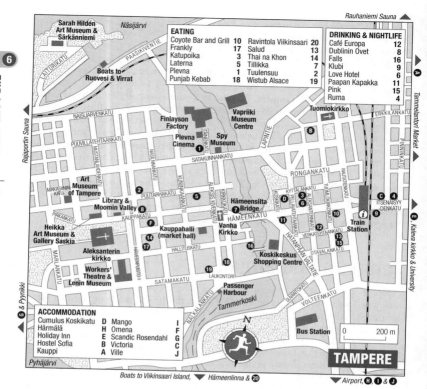

Card (24hr €25, 48hr €31), on sale at the tourist office, offers free entrance to most city museums and attractions. During the same period the office also organizes daily 90-minute sightseeing **tours** of the town; enquire for specifics.

Accommodation

Being one of Finland's most popular destinations, Tampere has plenty of central accommodation options to suit every taste and pocket, from elegant upmarket **hotels** with waterfront views to **youth hostels** and **campsites**. Still, many of these get booked up early, especially during the peak June–August period, so you'll want to book ahead if possible, lest you be left foraging for the more expensive leftovers. The city is well equipped with affordable **self-service hotels**, which represent good value for money; bookings must be made via the internet.

Cumulus Koskikatu Koskikatu 5 ☏03/242 4111, Ⓦwww.cumulus.fi. Excellent location for this chain favourite, set right on the rapids (request a room with a view). Staff are very friendly and there is a great lounge-bar and restaurant attached to the lobby. ❹/❺

Härmälä ☏03/265 1355 or 09/6138 3210, Ⓦwww.lomaliitto.fi/harmala. Lakeside camping facilities (€13 per tent) 4km south of the city at Härmälä. Small cabins are also available (€38) and

several that sleep up to five (€66); take bus #1. Mid-May to Aug only.

Holiday Inn Yliopistonkatu 44 ☏03/245 5111, Ⓦwww.restel.fi/holidayinn. Rooms are spacious and modern and inordinately popular, thanks to their sensible price, particularly at weekends. Excellent buffet breakfast makes this a sound choice if money's tight. Just a ten-minute walk from the train station. ❸/❺

Hostel Sofia Tuomiokirkonkatu 12A ☏03/254 4020, ⓦwww.hostelsofia.fi. These newly renovated dorm rooms breathe a bit of colour into Finland's institutional hostel look and feel, and they're the cheapest beds in town (€20). The doubles (❸) are also a comparatively good bargain though they get booked up early.

Kauppi Kalevan puistotie 2 ☏03/253 5353, ⓦwww.hotelli-kauppi.fi. This modern hotel, just 1km from the city centre, is good for simple self-catering, since all rooms have a microwave and a fridge. ❹/❺

🎿 **Mango** Hatanpään puistokuja 36 ⓦwww .mangohotel.fi. A fantastic self-service place whose quality rooms are decorated with Rococo-style furniture. Great style for little money and just twenty minutes on foot from the train station. ❸

Omena Hämeenkatu 28 ☏200/39 000, ⓦwww .omena.com. Central, post modern concept establishment that eschews human interaction. As with other self-service hotels, an electronic code grants you access to the very sleek, very modern rooms. ❷

Scandic Rosendahl Pyynikintie 13 ☏03/244 1111, ⓦwww.scandichotels.com. Lakeside luxury a couple of kilometres west of the city centre, right inside Pyynikki park. The hundred or so rooms are comfortable and tidy, and many have views to the lake. There's free use of the pool and several saunas, too. Bus #21. ❻

Victoria Itsenäisyydenkatu 1 ☏03/242 5111, ⓦwww.hotellivictoria.fi. Directly opposite the train station, the *Victoria*'s rooms are simple but spacious and well appointed, though lacking any real character. ❹/❻

🎿 **Ville** Hatanpään valtatie 40 ⓦwww .hotelliville.fi. Modern and cosy self-service hotel a twenty-minute walk from the train station, which represents exceptional value for money. Just €10 more gets a double room with a kitchen. Discounts for stays of seven days or more. ❷

The City

Tampere is a city on the water, occupying a narrow isthmus of land between the lakes, Näsijärvi and Pyhäjärvi. Almost everything of consequence lies within the central section of the city, bordered by the lakes to the north and south and Hämeenpuisto and Rautatienkatu to the west and east. Short, broad streets run off either side of **Hämeenkatu**, Tampere's main thoroughfare, which leads directly from the train station across Hämeensilta, the bridge over **Tammerkoski River**. You'll need to cross back over the river (most easily done by following Satakunnankatu) to reach Tampere's historic cathedral, as well as a couple of worthwhile museums, the cinema and several upmarket restaurants – and to get the best view of the superbly maintained Finlayson Factory, on which the city's fortunes were founded; it's now home to the editorial offices of the region's main newspaper as well as a couple of museums and restaurants.

Hämeenkatu

Cross Rautatienkatu from the train station, and the whole of Tampere stretches out before you. Long and straight, Hämeenkatu affords views all the way to the Tammerkoski River, and it's here, on the city's busiest street, that you'll find Tampere's commercial heart: restaurants and bars, shops and offices, and it's a favourite place for local people to stroll and peruse the windows. Just a couple of hundred metres from the train station, Hämeenkatu widens out as it meets **Hämeensilta Bridge**, notable for its weighty bronze sculptures by Wäino Aaltonen which represent four characters from local folklore. The road now runs through the wide-open space of Keskustori, dominated by the lovely, wooden **Vanha kirkko** (Old Church; daily: May–Aug 10am–3pm; Sept–April 11am–1pm), built in 1824 in Neoclassical style with a belfry atop its pastel-coloured walls designed by renowned German architect Carl Engel; unusually, the church hosts a service in English (Sun 4pm). Walking the full length of Hämeenkatu to its junction with Hämeenpuisto leaves you in front of another of Tampere's churches: the upwardly thrusting neo-Gothic **Aleksanterin kirkko** (daily: May–Aug 10am–5pm; Sept–April 11am–3pm), named after Tsar Alexander II. With a riot of red-brick walls and green spires outside and knobbly ceiling decorations inside, the

Nokia

The world's largest manufacturer of mobile phones, **Nokia** began life in 1865 as a paper mill and manufacturer on the banks of the Tammerkoski rapids. A second mill soon followed in neighbouring Nokia, a town 15km to the west of Tampere, where the production of hydropower was far superior; the town ultimately gave the company its name. In the early days, Nokia produced everything from Wellington boots and bicycle tyres to televisions and steel cables; indeed Nokia supplied the Soviet Union with vast amounts of cables as part of Finland's war reparations. It wasn't until the 1960s that the company began to specialize in electronics, producing its first car-based mobile phone in 1971 before finally divesting itself of its non-electronics divisions in 1992 and launching headlong into the burgeoning mobile-phone market. Today, as the largest company in Finland, Nokia accounts for around one quarter of the country's total exports.

effect is something like an ecclesiastical train station, with an unusually unpleasant, artexed altar.

The Lenin Museum

From Aleksanterin kirkko, following the line of greenery south down Hämeen-puisto, it's a five-minute stroll to no. 28, the Tampere Workers' Theatre and, on the second floor in the same building, the intriguing **Lenin Museum** (Mon–Fri 9am–6pm, Sat & Sun 11am–4pm; €5; Ⓦ www.lenin.fi), which, oddly, is the only permanent museum dedicated to Lenin anywhere in the world. After the abortive 1905 revolution in Russia, Lenin lived in Finland for two years (from November 1905 to December 1907) and chaired the Tampere conferences which were held in what is now the museum. Attended by around forty Russian Bolsheviks, the conferences addressed the general political situation in Russia and agrarian matters. It was here that Lenin first encountered Stalin, although this is barely mentioned in the displays, which consist of lots of old black-and-white photographs, copies of letters, old newspaper cuttings and various maps. The exhibition is divided into two sections, one of which concentrates on Lenin himself, the other on his relationship with Finland and on his visits to numerous Finnish cities – Lenin visited Finland a total of 26 times during his lifetime, on one occasion, in 1917, living underground for two months whilst in hiding from Russia's provisional government. For a detailed explanation, borrow one of the English-language mini-books from reception.

The art museums

Just around the corner at Puutarhakatu 34 is the **Art Museum of Tampere** (Tampereen Taidemuseo; Tues–Sun 10am–6pm; €5; guided tours by arrangement on Ⓣ 03/3146 6580, Ⓦ www.tampere.fi/taidemuseo), housed in a former granary from 1838 designed by Carl Engel, and containing a rotating display of around seven thousand pieces. The first floor holds powerful if staid temporary exhibitions featuring Finnish and international artists whilst contemporary local work by the likes of Kaarlo Vuori, Gabriel Engberg, Kalle Löytänä and Lennu Juvela is on show in the large basement galleries. Although the oldest works in the museum's collection are the Early Romantic paintings by Alexander Lauréus, most date from the late nineteenth century.

If you're looking for older Finnish art, head instead for the far superior **Hiekka Art Museum**, a few minutes' walk away at Pirkankatu 6 (Hiekan Taidemuseo; Tues & Thurs 3–6pm, Wed 3–7pm, Sun noon–3pm, other times by arrangement; €5; Ⓣ 03/212 3973, Ⓦ www.hiekantaidemuseo.fi). Kustaa Hiekka was a gold- and silversmith whose professional skills and business acumen made him a local bigshot around 1900. The art collection he bequeathed to Tampere reflects his interest in traditional lifestyles; amongst the most notable work (including sketches by Gallen-Kallela and Helene Schjerfbeck) are two of Hiekka's own creations: a delicately wrought brooch marking the completion of his apprenticeship, and a finely detailed bracelet with which he celebrated becoming a master craftsman. Borrow a catalogue from reception, since most pieces are identified only by numbers. Well worth the diversion, and free too, is the next-door **Gallery Saskia** (daily noon–6pm; Ⓦwww.tampereensaskiat.com), showing intriguing and unusual new work.

The library and Moomin Valley Museum

Nearby, at Pirkankatu 2, stands **Tampere library** (June–Aug Mon–Sat 10am–7pm; Sept–May Mon–Fri 10am–8pm, Sat 10am–4pm), an astounding feat of user-friendly modern architecture. The work of Reina and Raili Pietilä (who also designed the epic Kaleva kirkko – see p.232), and finished in 1986, the library's curving walls give it a warm, cosy feel; believe it or not, the building's shape was inspired by the capercaillie (a stuffed specimen of which sits in the reception area). Strolling around is the best way to take in the many small, intriguing features, and will eventually lead you up to the top-floor café, which gives a good view of the cupola, deliberately set eleven degrees off the vertical to match the off-centre pivot of the earth. In the basement of the library, with its own entrance at Hämeenpuisto 20, the **Moomin Valley Museum** (Mon–Fri 9am–5pm, Sat & Sun 10am–6pm; €4; Ⓦwww.tampere.fi/muumi) uses some two thousand dolls, models, dioramas, sets and interactive displays to re-create scenes from the incredibly popular children's books about the Moomin trolls by Tove Jansson; originally written in Swedish (Jansson was a Swedish-speaking Finn), the books have been translated into forty languages. Jansson claimed she found inspiration to write her first Moomin book, *The Moomins and the Great Flood*, during the war years when she longed to write something naïve and innocent.

▲ Tampere

Finlayson Factory and the Spy Museum

Cross to the eastern side of the Tammerkoski River along Satakunnankatu and you'll not only see – foaming below the bridge – the rapids that powered the **Finlayson Factory**, but also to the north the factory building itself, still standing and well worth a wander for its crafts shops. The six-storey building is named after its founder, Glasgow-born Quaker, James Finlayson (1772–1852), who moved to Tampere in 1820 with the backing of the Russian tsar and established his factory making textile machinery, later switching to cotton production. Also within the Finlayson complex is an absorbing addition to Tampere's museums, the **Spy Museum** (June–Aug Mon–Sat 10am–6pm, Sun 11am–5pm; Sept–May daily 11am–5pm; €7; ⓦwww.vakoilumuseo.fi) at Satakunnankatu 18 – it's best to enter the museum, though, from the main street as it's hard to find from within the factory complex. The range of gadgets, clothing, machines and documents – including a set of now-declassified KGB maps of the Baltic – attest to the rampant espionage on both sides of the Finnish and Russian border during the last century. Don't underestimate the kitsch value of all the gizmos on display here, which include night-vision goggles, James Bond-style semi-automatic pistols and even an ancient-looking tape recorder used by the Stasi at the East German embassy in Helsinki during the 1950s. However, the fifty-page folder containing the English translations of the items on display, available at reception, does require some dedication to get through.

Vapriikki Museum Centre

To learn more about Tampere's origins, visit the **Vapriikki Museum Centre** (Museokeskus Vapriikki; Tues & Thurs–Sun 10am–6pm, Wed 11am–8pm; €5, special exhibitions €7; ⓦwww.tampere.fi/vapriikki), housed in former engineering works just across the river from the Finlayson Factory at Alaverstaanraitti 5. Though the museum covers everything from archeology to handicrafts, its most interesting section, the Tampere 1918 exhibition, deals with the impact of the Finnish Civil War (see p.308) in moving black-and-white photographs. The Battle of Tampere which took place in March and April 1918 was the largest urban battle in the Nordic countries, with 300,000 soldiers involved. The right-wing private army known as the White Guard besieged and captured Tampere from the workers' Red Guards, taking 10,000 people prisoner and leaving parts of the city in ruins with corpses littering the streets. After independence the city became a Social Democratic stronghold, and was ruthlessly dealt with by the right-wing government in Helsinki following the Civil War – yet the municipal administration remains amongst the most left-leaning in Finland; to this day, the wounds of the war, which often pitted family members against each other, are still not fully healed.

Tuomiokirkko and Kaleva kirkko

Set in a grassy square at Tuomiokirkonkatu 3, the **Tuomiokirkko** (daily: May–Aug 9am–6pm; Sept–April 11am–3pm) is a picturesque cathedral in the National Romantic style, designed by Lars Sonck and finished in 1907. It's most remarkable for the gorily symbolic frescoes by Hugo Simberg – particularly the *Garden of Death*, where skeletons happily water plants, and *The Wounded Angel*, showing two boys carrying a bleeding angel through a Tampere landscape – which caused an ecclesiastical outcry when unveiled. So did the viper (a totem of evil) which Sonck placed amongst the angel wings on the ceiling; Simberg retorted that evil could lurk anywhere – including a church.

From the cathedral it's a short walk down Rautatienkatu to the train station, from where Itsenäisyydenkatu runs uphill to meet the vast concrete folds of the **Kaleva kirkko** (daily: May–Aug 10am–5pm; Sept–April 11am–3pm). Built in

1966, it was a belated addition to the neighbouring **Kaleva estate**, which was heralded in the 1950s as an outstanding example of high-density housing. Though initially stunning, the church's interior lacks the subtlety of the city library, despite being designed by the same team of Reima and Raili Pietilä, who this time based their plan on a fish rather than a capercaillie.

Näsijärvi lakeside

Just north of Tampere's central grid-plan streets, the tremendous **Sara Hildén Art Museum** (mid-Feb to April, mid-May to Aug & Oct to mid-Jan Tues–Sun 11am–6pm, plus Mon noon–7pm June–Aug; €4–7 depending upon exhibitions; Ⓦwww.tampere.fi/sarahilden), built on the shores of Näsijärvi, displays Tampere's premier modern-art collection by means of changing exhibitions. On display here are a number of works from 1960s Informalist painters, as well as modern masters such as Klee, Delvaux, Bacon, Lèger – there's even a Picasso. The museum is on the other side of the northern arterial road, Paasikiventie, from the city centre (take bus #16, or the summer-only #4 bus from the town centre or train station).

Occupying the same waterside strip as the Hildén collection is **Särkänniemi** (Ⓦwww.sarkanniemi.fi), Tampere's most popular tourist destination. A sizeable complex incorporating an adventure park, dolphinarium, aquarium, planetarium and an observation tower with rotating restaurant, the site is open year-round (daily 11am–9pm, often closes later during summer), though the zoo and theme park rides operate between May and August only. Seen from the **tower** (April–Sept daily 11am–11.30pm; Oct–March Tues–Sat 11am–11.30pm, Sun & Mon 11am–9.30pm; €8), itself an unmistakeable element of Tampere's skyline, the city seems insignificant compared to the trees and lakes that stretch to the horizon. The rapids that cut through them can be identified from afar by the factory chimneys alongside. The tower's admission charge is waived if you're eating at its restaurant; the other diversions cost €8 apiece and are usually crowded with families. To make a day of it, buy the €30 Adventure Key, valid for all parts of the complex except parasailing. Särkänniemi's café serves half-decent, inexpensive pizza, salads and the like.

Rajaportin and Rauhaniemi public saunas

A fifteen-minute walk west from Särkänniemi brings you to the atmospheric **Rajaportin public sauna** (Mon & Wed 6–10pm, Fri 3–9pm, Sat 2–10pm; Mon & Wed €4, Fri & Sat €6), opened in 1906 and Finland's oldest, at Pispalan valtatie 9. Sadly, public saunas like this are few are far between now, since most people have a sauna at home or they use the modern, electric ones at the local swimming pool. This wood-burning sauna, though, is the real McCoy and if you're looking for an authentic sauna experience, this is it. The rather primitive interior has changed little since the sauna opened – there are even troughs full of water for a quick sluice-down once the heat is over, whilst outside there's a courtyard where people congregate for a chat. Indeed, there's a real sense of local community amongst the friendly bathers, many of whom have been coming here for years. You can also walk here from the city centre by following Hämeenkatu west, which then turns into Pirkankatu and ultimately into Pispalan valtatie, or take any of the buses #1, #13, #22, #25, #26 or #27. If you fancy a dip in the lake after your sauna, head instead for the **Rauhaniemi sauna** (Mon–Fri 3–7.30/8pm, Sat & Sun 1–7/7.30pm; €4.50), Rauhaniementie 24, another place oozing character, built in 1929 right on the shores of Näsijärvi. Get here on bus #2 from the centre.

Boat trips and beaches

A few blocks south of Hämeenkatu, the passenger harbour is the departure point for Hopealinja summer **lake cruises** around Pyhäjärvi Lake (May–Aug Tues–Sun

12.30pm; 1hr 30min; €20 including buffet lunch; ⓦwww.hopealinja.fi). For something simpler, take a quick trip over to nearby **Viikinsaari** (June to mid-Aug Tues–Sun hourly, the last boat returning Mon–Thurs at 10.30pm, Fri & Sat at 12.30am and Sun at 7.30pm; 15min; €10). First known as Jomasaari ("Island of God"), this small wooded island served as a popular weekend destination for nineteenth-century Finnish nobility, but fell into some disrepute after local ne'er-do-wells claimed it as their private watering hole. Today, it houses a small chapel and a nature reserve, making it popular with many locals looking for some fresh air. At midsummer, Viikinsaari hosts evening fêtes, tango dancing and a traditional *kakko*, a large bonfire lit right on the banks of Lake Pyhäjärvi. The island also holds the *Ravintola Viikinsaari* restaurant (see opposite). Between June and mid-August, Hopealinja also operate a longer service to **Hämeenlinna**, departing from Laukontori in the passenger harbour at 9.30am (Wed–Sat), arriving into Hämeen-linna's harbour on Arvi Kariston katu at 5.45pm (one way €43); all these boats sail across Pyhäjärvi.

Operating in the opposite direction, across Näsijärvi, the old steamer S/S *Tarjanne* (ⓦwww.runoilijantie.fi), sails north for **Ruovesi** (€38; 5hr) and **Virrat** (€49; 8hr 30min) on Wednesday & Fridays (10.15am) from June to mid-August (also Mon in July), departing Mustalahti harbour, beside Särkänniemi. Once the boat arrives in Virrat, you can spend the night in a cabin onboard for an extra €34, including breakfast. This route, known as the Poet's Way, is one of the most enchanting in the entire Lake District, due to the ever-narrowing shape of the lake.

For the best **beaches** head west from the centre to the wooded expanses of **Pyynikki**, a hilly gravel ridge between Näsijärvi and Pyhäjärvi where there are two sandy strands either side of the tennis courts, just below the *Scandic Rosendahl* hotel; this area is known as Jalkasaari.

Eating

Tampere boasts an eclectic range of **restaurants** and **cafés** to suit all pockets. Several places in the Koskikeskus shopping mall, Hatanpään valtatie 1, offer cheap lunchtime specials. Across the city there are also numerous **supermarkets** at which to stock up on provisions. Three central options are the big Sokos store at Hämeenkatu 21, or the two significantly cheaper Lidl shops, at Rautatienkatu 21 and Hallituskatu 14–16. There's also a large **kauppahalli** (market hall) at Hämeenkatu 19 (Mon–Fri 8am–6pm, Sat 8am–4pm), and **open-air markets** at Laukontori (Mon–Fri 6am–2pm, Sat 6am–1pm) and Tammelantori (Mon–Fri 6am–2pm, Sat 6am–1pm).

Coyote Bar and Grill Hämeenkatu 3 ☏03/214 3911. A full-on retro dining affair with loads of young locals chowing down burgers (€11) and finger food, and sipping on bottles of imported beers against murals of Castro. Salads go for €7–9, steaks from €18 and roast meats such as kangaroo or lamb are around €20.

Frankly Hallituskatu 22 ☏03/212 0235. The best place in Tampere to sample traditional Finnish food given an international twist such as chicken breast stuffed with feta cheese (€17.40) or lamb tender-loin with thyme sauce (€19.80). Mains in the range €17–25.

Katupoika Aleksanterinkatu 20 ☏03/272 0201. A local institution, this fairly priced restaurant is popular with locals and visiting families. It's known for its tasty Finnish dishes, such as pork stew with potato purée (€11) but it's also a great place to try the local speciality *mustamakkara*, a rich blood sausage, or *lehtipihvi*, a succulent goat's cheese-stuffed "leaf" steak (€20.70).

Laterna Puutarhakatu 11 ☏03/272 0241. Tampere's oldest restaurant is full of Art Nouveau flourishes and rather grand oil paintings, and specializes in tasty Russian food, including various types of caviar and smoked salmon with mustard mayonnaise. Reckon on around €20 for a main course.

Plevna Itäinenkatu 4. This brewery-cum-restaurant within an old weaving mill inside the Finlayson complex makes fifteen varieties of its own beer and serves a wide range of Finnish and

German specialities, including various varieties of sausage.

Punjab Kebab Kirkkokatu 10. Cheap and cheerful place, one block up from the passenger harbour, serving the city's favourite kebabs (€5–6).

Ravintola Viikinsaari Viikinsaari island ☎010/422 5666. Under new management, this grand old place has been in operation since 1900 and is a wonderful venue for upscale dinners at reasonable prices. Most of the traditional Finnish dishes, such as the Tallqvist onion steak, cost around €15. Take the boat to get there (see opposite).

Salud Tuomiokirkonkatu 19 ☎03/233 4400. A lively Spanish restaurant serving mixed tapas plates (€8.40), and sizeable Iberian meat dishes such as pork ribs (€16.70) and a succulent guinea-fowl breast with mushrooms (€21). Mains are in the range €18–29, though the sprawling weekday lunch buffet (€9.50) is one of the best deals in town.

Thai na Khon Hämeenkatu 29 ☎03/212 1778. Genuinely tasty Thai food served in a typically ornate interior full of dark wood panelling (and fake flowers). Mains such as the excellent chicken mussaman curry go for €10.50–17.50, whilst starters, such as spring rolls, are around €5–7.

Tillikka Hämeenkatu 14 ☎03/254 4700. This very classy Parisian-style place, with terraces overlooking the Tammerkoski rapids, is appropriately dressed up with early twentieth-century flair featuring stuccoed ceilings and balloon chandeliers. The continental food includes interesting dishes like reindeer steak (€23.40) and chicken breast stuffed with Finnish cheese and basil served in a port sauce (€14.80).

Tuulensuu Hämeenpuisto 23 ☎03/214 1553. Top-notch gastropub with wooden tables and chairs serving a varied range of French and Belgian dishes such as Flemish meat stew, duck confit and a carrot and spinach lasagne for around €14–20. Also boasts a huge range of Belgian beers.

Wistub Alsace Laukontori 6B ☎03/212 0260. Excellent harbourside spot serving great Alsatian food in a charming, familial interior. Mains start at €21, and include salmon with puy lentils or braised lamb shank with root vegetables. Don't miss the excellent starter of *escargots à l'alsacienne* (€9.50).

Drinking, nightlife and entertainment

Tampere is very much alive and buzzing after dark, with numerous late-night bars, cafés and clubs – and many spots host **live music** acts, especially in the summer, often with little or no cover charge.

On warm nights the crowds head out to the Pyynikki area (see opposite). Tickets for the **Pyynikki Summer Theatre** (☎03/216 0300, ⓦ www.pyynikinkesateatteri .com) cost €27, but it's worth trekking out just to look at the revolving auditorium which slowly rotates the audience around during performances, blending the surrounding woods, rocks and water into the show's scenery. All theatre performances here are in Finnish only, but there are a number of orchestra concerts as well. Plevna, Itäinenkatu 4 (ⓦ www.finnkino.fi), is the city's largest **cinema**, with ten screens and frequent runs of English-language pictures.

Bars

Café Europa Aleksanterinkatu 29. More a bar and restaurant than a café, this bohemian place stuffed with red velvet sofas and soft antique furnishings is one of the best bets to meet Tampere's trendy young things who chill here beneath the paintings of the Madonna adorning the walls. One of the more international places in town in terms of clientele.

Dublinin Ovet Kauppakatu 16. True to its name ("Doors of Dublin"), this popular Irish theme pub features garishly painted green doors inside. Elsewhere the interior is equally lurid green but the Finns seem to love all the ersatz Hibernia and come here in droves.

Falls Kehräsaari. This former brick factory puts its original interior to good use with chandeliers and arty paintings adding to the industrial-urban style. However, most people come here for the great little terrace overlooking the rapids – it's undoubtedly one of the best places to sip a beer in the city.

Paapan Kapakka Koskikatu 9. With Guinness, Kilkenny, Carlsberg and Hoegaarden on tap, this pub-styled jazz bar attracts the more mature drinker. You don't even need to know the address: just follow your ears to the squealing sax, simmering snare and piano soloing of the swing-style groups that regularly hold session on the bar's intimate stage.

Clubs

Klubi Tullikamarin Aukio 2 ⓦ www.klubi.net. An extremely popular nightclub set in an old customs house just behind the train station off Itsenäisyydenkatu. Regular DJs spin and locals party until the sun rises. Also serves inexpensive lunches. Closed Sun.

Love Hotel Hämeenkatu 10A ⓦ www .lovehotel.fi. While there are no rooms at this large, provocatively named nightclub, many couples here often behave like they need to get one. Tricked-out lighting displays, a maze of corridors, a lone blackjack table do their best to draw your attention away from pricey

cocktails, an empty dancefloor and flirting *à la finlandaise*.

Pink Otavalankatu 9 ⓦ www.pinkclub.fi. One of the few gay bars in the country outside of Helsinki, this friendly and laid-back spot sports large mirrors and red sofas. Gets going after 12.30am. Open Fri & Sat only.

Ruma Murtokatu 1 ⓦ www.ruma.fi. Popular dance bar set a block away from the train station. The minimum age limit of 18 does little to deter teenagers who show up with fake IDs aplenty.

Hämeenlinna and around

Forty minutes from Tampere on the busy rail line to Helsinki, **HÄMEEN-LINNA** is one of Finland's most likeable towns and makes a perfect place to break the 190km journey between the two cities. The Swedes founded Hämeenlinna, or Tavastehus as it's known in Swedish, in 1649, making it Finland's oldest inland town, though they'd already harried the area in the thirteenth century when they built the fabulous Häme Castle (*linna* is Finnish for castle) which occupies a strategic position on the waterway snaking northwest into Vanajavesi Lake. Military matters apart, Hämeenlinna is also revered across the country as the birthplace of Jean Sibelius, though the town is typically modest in its praise of its most famous son and Finland's greatest composer. Nevertheless, it's a rewarding place to visit and one that can easily be combined with a trip to nearby **Iittala**, home of the famous designer glass-works. Thanks to plentiful train connections at Riihimäki, just down the line, it's also one of Finland's most easily accessible towns.

The Town

The centre of Hämeenlinna is a warren of pretty, cobbled streets, centred around the *kauppatori*. Whilst it's pleasant enough to wander around here taking in the comings and goings, you'll soon want to ogle the town's major attraction, **Häme Castle** (Feb–April & mid-Aug to Dec Mon–Fri 10am–4pm, Sat 11am–4pm; June to mid-Aug daily 10am–6pm; €5; free guided tours are available in English by appointment – call ☏03/675 6820), which lies an easy fifteen-minute walk north of the centre along Linnankatu. This mighty red-brick fortress began to take shape around 1260, constructed by the Swedes as a bulwark against the belligerent Russians of Novgorod, but in the event it never saw serious military action as the Russian–Swedish wars of later centuries were fought further east in Karelia and the eastern Lake District. After service as a prison until the 1980s, the castle underwent major renovation, and now the nearby **National Prison Museum**, housed in the former cell block just beside the castle, next to the moat, gives an insight into prison life. Inside, a couple of cells have been left pretty much as they were when the last inmates left. Remark-ably, prisoners were allowed to take a sauna without supervision by the warders, which often led to a violent settling of scores.

Hämeenlinna has a gaggle of low-key museums, though only two are worthy of your time. Start with the **Sibelius Museum**, located in the composer's childhood home (daily: May–Aug 10am–4pm; Sept–April noon–4pm; €4) back in the centre of town at Hallituskatu 11, where Sibelius was born in 1865 and began playing the piano at the age of nine. Although the house has been reverentially restored to how it was during the first years of his life, it offers only the briefest insight into the great composer's life and regrettably leaves many stones unturned. The other collection of note is just a few blocks away at Viipurintie 2 inside a former granary designed by Carl Ludvig Engel: the town's **Art Museum** (Tues–Thurs 11am–6pm, Fri–Sun 11am–7pm; €6) musters a mundane collection of nineteenth-and twentieth-century works by major Finnish names, among them Järnefelt, Gallen-Kallela and Halonen.

Practicalities

From the **train station**, a kilometre or so east of the town centre, it's an easy stroll south on Hämeentie and then right into Viipurintie, crossing the bridge, to reach the town's main street, Raatihuoneenkatu. Here, at no. 11, the **tourist office** is a useful source of leaflets and maps; there's also **internet** access. **Boats** from Tampere put in at the passenger harbour, a couple of blocks east of the *kauppatori*, at Arvi Karistonkatu.

Accommodation choices in the centre are limited to the excellent-value *Hotelli Emilia*, Raatihuoneenkatu 23 (☏03/612 2106, ⓦwww.hotelliemilia.fi; ❹/❺), and the more upmarket *Sokos Vaakuna* at Possentie 7 (☏020/123 4636, ⓦwww .sokoshotels.fi; ❺/❻), close to the train station. Otherwise, 4km south of Hämeenlinna and just across the river is *Katajistan Kartana* (☏03/682 8560, ⓦwww.aulanko.com; May to mid-Aug; dorms €14, doubles ❺), a youth hostel, campsite (June–Aug) and restaurant. For **eating** in the centre, head for either *Georgios*, an agreeable Greek place at Linnankatu 3, or *Popino*, behind the tourist office at Raatihuoneenkatu 11, for some good pasta dishes and pizzas. The best **bar** in town is *O'Maggie's*, Kirkkorinne 2, an Irish theme place housed in the former home of artist Albert Edelfelt.

Iittala

Just 20km north of Hämeenlinna and easily accessible by direct train, the otherwise unremarkable village of **Iittala** is renowned for its absorbing **glass museum** (May–Aug daily 10am–6pm; Sept–April Sat & Sun 10am–5pm; €3) where you can watch glassblowers at work. Instantly recognizable by its trademark white "i" logo set against a red circle, Iittala's stylish glassware can be found in homes across Finland and is one of Finland's best-known exports. The **museum** contains a wide range of Iittala creations over the years and provides a wider insight into Finnish design. Reduced-price seconds are sold in the adjoining shop.

Travel details

Trains

Hämeenlinna to: Helsinki (hourly; 1hr); Iittala (6 daily; 12min); Tampere (hourly; 45min).
Jyväskylä to: Kuopio (7 daily; 2hr); Tampere (11 daily; 1hr 20min).
Kuopio to: Helsinki (6 daily; 4hr); Jyväskylä (7 daily; 1hr 30min–1hr 45min); Kajaani (6 daily; 1hr 50min); Mikkeli (9 daily; 1hr 45min); Oulu (4 daily; 4hr); Tampere (7 daily; 2hr 50min–3hr 30min).

Lahti to: Helsinki (hourly; 1hr–1hr 30min); Joensuu (5 daily; 3hr 45min); Kuopio (8 daily; 3hr 45min); Lappeenranta (5 daily; 1hr 20min); Mikkeli (7 daily; 1hr 45min); Tampere (hourly; 2hr).
Mikkeli to: Kuopio (8 daily; 1hr 30min); Lahti (7 daily; 1hr 45min).
Parikkala to: Joensuu (5 daily; 1hr 15min); Lappeenranta (6 daily; 1hr).
Savonlinna to: Lusto (5 daily; 25min); Parikkala (5 daily; 55min); Punkaharju (5 daily; 30min); Retretti (5 daily; 22min).

Tampere to: Hämeenlinna (hourly; 40min–1hr); Helsinki (hourly; 1hr 45min–2hr 5min); Jyväskylä (12 daily; 1hr 20min); Kuopio (8 daily; 3hr 20min); Oulu (11 daily; 4hr 50min–7hr); Pori (6 daily; 1hr 30min); Turku (10 daily; 1hr 45min).

Buses

Kuopio to: Joensuu (9–12 daily; 1hr 50min–2hr 45min); Jyväskylä (4–7 daily; 2hr 15min–3hr 40min);.

Lahti to: Mikkeli (11–12 daily; 1hr 45min–2hr); Savonlinna (7–10 daily; 3hr 30min–5hr 5min).
Mikkeli to: Savonlinna (5–12 daily; 1hr 20min–2hr 15min).
Savonlinna to: Kuopio (3–7 daily; 2hr 45min–4hr 20min); Parikkala (1–5 daily; 1hr 15min–1hr 30min); Punkaharju (1–9 daily; 45min–1hr 15min).
Tampere to: Helsinki (hourly; 2hr 15min–3hr 50min); Pori (7–14 daily; 1hr 45min–3hr 5min); Turku (frequent; 2hr 10min–4hr 5min).

7

The Bothnian coast

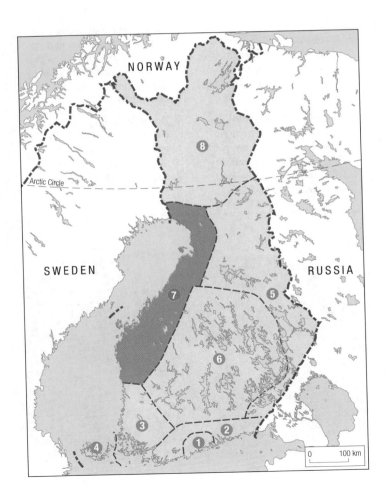

NORWAY

8

Arctic Circle

SWEDEN

7

RUSSIA

5

6

3

1   2

4

0   100 km

CHAPTER 7 # Highlights

✱ **Vaasa** The shoreline that fronts Vaasa's marine harbour – one of the most prepossessing in Finland – is the place to hang out with a beer on a summer's evening. See p.247

✱ **Jakobstad** Dip into Swedish-speaking Finland and discover one of the best-preserved wooden old towns in the country. See pp.250–253

✱ **Kalajoki beaches** Work on your tan on the golden strands of Finland's premier beach resort, renowned for long hours of sunshine and warm waters. See p.257

✱ **Eating out in Oulu** Sample the north's biggest choice of restaurants and bars and live it up with some big-city sophistication. See pp.263–264

✱ **Icebreaker tour, Kemi** Take a ride on an icebreaker out into the frozen reaches of the Gulf of Bothnia and float in the icy waters in a special wetsuit. See p.265

✱ **Border-hopping, Tornio** Join the locals in this riverside town on the border with Sweden and nip back and forth for a spot of shopping. See p.266

▲ The hard life, Kalajoki beach

The Bothnian coast

S tretching north along Finland's western shore from Kristinestad to the Swedish border at the head of the Gulf of Bothnia, the flat swathe of land that comprises the **Bothnian coast** takes up around a fifth of the country, but unlike the populous south or the more industrialized sections of the Lake District, towns here are predominantly rural, with small and widely separated communities. Instead, the Bothnian coast is a delightful jumble of erstwhile fishing villages, gently undulating, pastoral landscapes dotted with small farms and thick pine forest which backs the long sandy beaches for which this coast is justifiably known. Moreover, some of Finland's finest wooden town architecture can also be admired in a handful of towns up and down the coast. Socially, too, the region has a very individual feel: known as **Ostrobothnia**, it's home to many of the country's Swedish-speaking Finland-Swedes (see box, p.243), a small subsection of the national population, and towns hereabouts are known as often by their Swedish names as by their Finnish.

Kristinestad, with its pretty wooden architecture, makes a great place to begin explorations of the Bothnian coastline. Thankfully, it escaped the fires of the 1800s which ravaged many coastal communities and today presents a handsome face. Lively **Vaasa**, 100km to the north, couldn't be more different: a mish-mash of modern concrete structures with a handful of absorbing art museums, which can also be used as a jumping-off point for towns further up the coast. The architectural highlight of the coast lies a couple of hours north of Vaasa: small but perfectly formed, Swedish-speaking **Jakobstad** boasts one of the best-preserved wooden old towns in the entire country and is also home to an enlightening museum on all things Arctic. Next stop along the coast, **Kokkola** is a neat little town with a couple of interesting museums and some pleasant city parkland, and provides ready access to nearby **Kalajoki**, northern Finland's premier beach resort, blessed with miles of golden sand, and plenty of outdoor activities too.

The highlight of this stretch of coast, however, is **Oulu**, a major population centre that's full of lively bars and restaurants. It's easy to spend a couple of days here drinking up the urban sophistication and taking in some of the city's first-rate cultural offerings. Barely 100km north of Oulu, you'll cross into Finland's most northerly and enigmatic province, Lapland. The main town in these parts, **Kemi**, is a curiously agreeable sort of place, especially in winter when a giant snow castle is erected in the centre and there's the opportunity to take a ride on a genuine icebreaker out into the frozen expanses of the Gulf of Bothnia. At the very head of the gulf, **Tornio** is one of the few towns in the region that's actually expanding and is today busy transforming itself into a likeable cross-border retail centre.

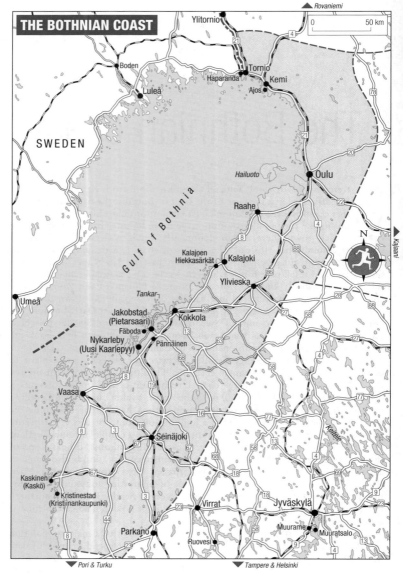

THE BOTHNIAN COAST

0   50 km

▲ Rovaniemi

Ylitornio

Boden

Tornio
Haparanda   Kemi
Luleå   Ajos

SWEDEN

Hailuoto   Oulu

▶ Kajaani

Raahe

N

Kalajoen   Kalajoki
Hiekkasärkät

Ylivieska

Umeå

Tankar

Jakobstad   Kokkola
(Pietarsaari)
Fäboda
Nykarleby   Pännäinen
(Uusi Kaarlepyy)

Vaasa

Seinäjoki

Kaskinen
(Kaskö)

Kristinestad
(Kristiinankaupunki)

Virrat   Jyväskylä

Parkano   Muurame   Muuratsalo
        Ruovesi

▼ Pori & Turku   ▼ Tampere & Helsinki

The easiest way to travel up and down the Bothnian coast is by **train**. Most services running between Helsinki and Oulu/Rovaniemi take this route, providing useful connections between the coast's major population centres. In Kalajoki and Kristinestad, both towns without train connections, **buses** fill in the gaps, providing services to the nearest railhead. The best places to base yourself if you're intent on seeing only part of the coast are Vaasa in the south and Oulu in the north, from where you can easily visit neighbouring towns.

Vaasa and around

Industrious, vibrant **VAASA**, once a bustling tourist centre patronized by middle-class Swedes who would cross the Gulf of Bothnia in search of little more than cheap drink, is today the de facto capital of the Ostrobothnia region. Its several museums, quiet, broad streets and collection of restaurants and watering holes make it one of the most pleasant places to spend a day or so along the Bothnian coast. It's also useful as a stopover for coastal travel both north to Oulu and south to Pori, and there's a very useful cross-country rail line connecting Vaasa directly with Jyväskylä (via Seinäjoki).

Vaasa has always been a centre for the arts, largely due to its sizeable population of wealthy Swedish burghers, many of whom developed a honed appreciation for fine works of art – today the city holds some two dozen museums and art galleries. With a relatively small population of 58,000, of whom around a quarter speak Swedish as a mother tongue, Vaasa is in fact one of the most bilingual towns in the country: Radio Vaasa is Finland's only bilingual radio station, and there is a high school, theatre and newspaper for each language. But it is also one of the most polarized places in the country, and it is not uncommon to meet members of the Finlandssvenska minority who don't (and, more crucially, don't want to) understand Finnish at all.

Though it proudly calls itself the sunniest destination in Finland – an arguable claim, anyway – Vaasa's past has not always been quite so bright. Established as the seat of Swedish power from the fourteenth to the early seventeenth century, Vaasa found its way into a catastrophic dispute between Sweden, Russia and Germany in 1715, during which the town was sacked, fleets of merchant ships were burned and most of the population fled overnight to Sweden. Trade soon returned though, after which wealth poured in from the export of tar, grain, butter, pelts and twine. A devastating fire in 1852 – known in Finnish as the *isoviha*, or "great wrath" – effected a rebuilding of the city on the Klementsö headland, 7km north of where it was originally founded, after which it was renamed Nikolaistad (Nikolainkaupunki in Finnish) to honour Tsar Nicholas I until 1917. Decades of steady income from trade – most notably seal skins, tar and maritime commerce – have given the town centre something of a staid, commercial countenance, but its wide avenues lead to an active passenger and freight harbour, through which the produce of southern Ostrobothnia's wheat fields is exported, and at which plenty of locals congregate on evenings and weekends.

Finland's Swedish-speaking minority

Making up just 6 percent of Finland's population, the Finland-Swedes, or Finlands-svenskar as they're known in Swedish, are concentrated in three main areas of Finland: along parts of the Bothnian coast, around Turku and the Åland islands. The term refers to Swedes who first began migrating to Finland in the twelfth century in search of increased wealth and prosperity. Many of the incomers were from old, aristocratic landowning families in Sweden and soon formed a new upper class within Finnish society. However, with every new generation, links with Sweden grew less and today Finland-Swedes tend to identify themselves as Finnish rather than Swedish, though remain proud of their links with their former motherland; consequently, some Finns find the Finlandssvenskar rather aloof and snobbish. To the visitor, cultural differences can be hard to discern, though the common use of Swedish in towns with larger Finland-Swede populations is perhaps the clearest indication of centuries of immigration.

Arrival, information and accommodation

Nearly all travellers to Vaasa arrive at the city's **train and bus stations**, next door to each other, from which it is a pleasant five-minute walk to the *kauppatori*. **Ferries** from Umeå in Sweden (Uumaja in Finnish) arrive at Vaasa's passenger harbour terminal on Vaskiluoto, from which buses #5 and #10 go to town. The **tourist office** is located inside the town hall at Raastuvankatu 30 (Mon–Fri 9am–4pm; ☎06/325 1145, ⓦwww.vaasa.fi). There's free **internet** access close by at the town library, Kirjastonkatu 13 (Mon–Thurs 11am–8pm, Fri 10am–6pm, Sat 10am–3pm).

The majority of Vaasa's best **hotels** are close to the train station.

Astor Asemakatu 4 ☎06/326 9111, ⓦwww.astorvaasa.com. Small, independently owned hotel just opposite the railway station with a good collection of charming, classy doubles and suites, some of which feature exposed hardwood floors and pretty, faux-antique furniture. For an extra €21 you can get a room with private sauna. Breakfast is served in the attached Gustavian-styled restaurant. ❹/❺

Best Western Silveria Ruutikellarintie 4 ☎06/326 7611, ⓦwww.hotelsilveria.com. The least chain-like of the city's hotels, the rooms here are spacious and have a smidgen of modernist charm to them, and there's access to a moderately sized pool as well. It's about 2km from the town centre, set next to a sprawling park. Bus #4 from town stops right in front of the hotel. ❺

EFÖ Rantakatu 21–22 ☎06/317 4913, ⓦwww.efo.fi. Located within a vocational school, the singles and doubles in this affordable summer hotel are simply furnished and decorated in IKEA-esque pale wood furnishings against white and off-white panelled walls. Open mid-June to mid-Aug. ❸

Kenraali Wasa Hostel Korsholmanpuistikko 6–8 ☎040/066 8521, ⓦwww.kenraaliwasahostel.com. Situated in an old army garrison building a ten-minute walk from the market square, this is the best budget accommodation in town, with a dozen homely doubles with shared bathroom. ❷

Omena Hovioikeudenpuistikko 23 ⓦwww.omena.com. This reception-free concept hotel offers great modern rooms done up in bright woods and comfy linens with amenities that include Web TV and coffee makers. Booking is via the internet or kiosk downstairs. ❷

🏃 **Sokos Vaakuna** Rewell Center 101 ☎040/066 8521, ⓦwww.sokoshotels.com. This great standby is miles above the city's other

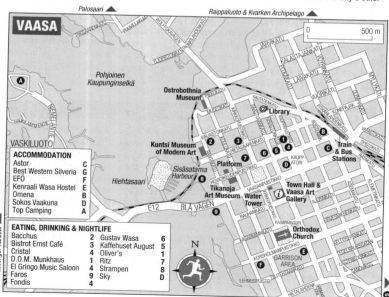

VAASA

Palosaari ▲   Raippaluoto & Kvarken Archipelago ▲

0 ——— 500 m

Pohjoinen Kaupunginselkä

Ostrobothnia Museum

ⓘ Library

Kuntsi Museum of Modern Art

Platform

Sisäsatama Harbour

Hiehtasaari

Train & Bus Stations

Tikanoja Art Museum

Town Hall & Vaasa Art Gallery ⓘ

Water Tower

Orthodox Church

GARRISON AREA

VASKILUOTO

ACCOMMODATION

Astor	C
Best Western Silveria	G
EFÖ	F
Kenraali Wasa Hostel	E
Omena	B
Sokos Vaakuna	D
Top Camping	A

EATING, DRINKING & NIGHTLIFE

Bacchus	2	Gustav Wasa	6
Bistrot Ernst Café	3	Kaffehuset August	5
Cristal	4	Oliver's	1
D.O.M. Munkhaus	1	Ritz	7
El Gringo Music Saloon	4	Strampen	8
Faros	9	Sky	D
Fondis	4		

N

chain hotels in terms of warmth, service and location, with light and airy rooms set smack on the market square; those on the top floor offer great views. If it's a weekend be wary of (or excited by) the prospect of the ever-popular rooftop nightclub. ❸/❺

Top Camping Niemeläntie 1 ☎06/211 1255, ⓦ www.wasalandia.fi. More than adequate camping facilities – including pine cabins (€65) – are 2km from the town centre right on the Vaskiluoto island waterfront near the ferry harbour; take bus #5. Open late May to mid-Aug.

The Town

Following Vaasa's devastation by fire in 1852, county architect Carl Axel Setterberg drafted a new plan for the town, buffering buildings with vast, planted boulevards and grand spaces. Today, Vaasa has a somewhat greener feel than most Finnish settlements of its size, with five spacious esplanades (*puistikko*) dividing the city into distinct quadrants and breaking up much of the drab modern architecture. A brief walk through the city streets turns up an interesting mixed bag of architectural styles, ranging from 1850s Empire-style to 1920s functionalist to early twenty-first-century postmodern.

The Ostrobothnia Museum

At Vaasa's central *kauppatori* stands Yrjö Liipola's revered "Statue of Liberty", a bronze image of two peasant soldiers – one wounded, the other waving his cap hoping to attract attention – cast to commemorate Finland's independence. But the pinnacle of local social and cultural development is represented by the **Ostrobothnia Museum** (Mon–Fri 10am–5pm, Wed until 8pm, Sat & Sun noon–5pm; €5; ⓦ www.museo.vaasa.fi) at Museokatu 3, a simply constructed complex of several collections that recount the history of the town and its reliance on tar burning, seal hunting and seafaring. The **main collection** here contains some 3600 examples of seal-hunting equipment, local glassworks, folksy furniture, tapestries, uniforms, ceramics and silverware bearing Nordic folk ornamentation; look out for the Luleå Sámi spoon, dating back to the early 1700s, and the pristine Gustavian wall clock, a gift from King Gustav III. A second part of the museum, christened **Terra Nova**, is an interactive nature centre popular with school kids, while the first floor of the old wing holds the **Hedman Collection**, containing all in all some ten thousand works of art, including fifteenth- and sixteenth-century Italian, Dutch and Flemish paintings and works from Finland's Golden Age (1870–1930). The pieces are grouped by period, and highlights include works by Edelfelt, Gallen-Kallela, Hugo Simberg, Schjerfbeck and Järnefelt.

The art museums

Topping the list of Vaasa's numerous art galleries is the **Tikanoja Art Museum** (Tikanojan taidekoti; Tues–Sat 11am–4pm, Sun noon–5pm; €5; ⓦ www .tikanojantaidekoti.fi), Hovioikeudenpuistikko 4, housed in the one-time home of Vaasa merchant and nobleman Frithjof Tikanoja, and containing the strong collection of international paintings he bequeathed to the city. You'll find works by Matisse, Picasso and Gauguin, as well as a good selection by Finnish painters, including several Vaasa-born artists – have a look at Toivo Talvi's doleful portrait, *Kansanelämää*. For modern art, try next across the street at **Platform** (Wed & Sun 2–6pm, Thurs 2–8pm; ⓦ www.platform.fi), Hovioikeudenpuistikko 3, which features the work of Vaasa artists who take part in a local residency programme. Much larger is the wide range of modern Finnish art on display down at the waterfront in the **Kuntsi Museum of Modern Art** (daily except Mon 11am–5pm, Thurs till 8pm; €6; ⓦ www.kuntsi.fi), occupying the former customs warehouse on Sisäsatama, where some nine hundred works are on display ranging from pop art to postmodernism, in addition to regular temporary shows.

7

Après-sauna

A ten-minute walk from the *kauppatori* is the small wooded islet of **Hiehtasaari** (Sandö in Swedish), accessed by road and footbridge at the western end of Vaasan-puistikko. Hiehtasaari is the headquarters of the **Vaasa Winter Penguin Club** (ⓦwww.vaasanpingviinit.com), a group of some 1000 older Vaasalaiset who get their kicks from indulging in that quintessentially Finnish ritual of having a broil in a sauna, then doing a two-step into freezing cold water. To try it out, you need to either be a Penguin Club member or befriend one, but as locals here are remarkably open to sharing the intricacies of Finnish culture with curious outsiders, try hanging around for long enough outside the building and you just might be invited in.

The water tower

Head southeast back towards the centre to suss out some of the city's older history. At Raastuvankatu 32 – but visible from pretty much anywhere in town – stands the fetching 49-metre Art Nouveau **water tower**, built in 1915 and used as an air defence unit during World War II. It's a two-hundred-step ascent to the top, from where you'll find the city's best panorama. Alternatively, try the climbing wall on the outside facade.

The Orthodox church and Russian garrison

Further south down Kirkkopuistikko, the elephantine brick **Orthodox church** (Mon–Fri 10am–2pm), one of Setterberg's creations, sits atop the city's highest point, 18m above sea level; it was built at the decree of Alexander II. A block further south is the town's **garrison area**, a collection of simple wooden buildings constructed in 1880 by Russia to house and shelter some five hundred Finnish soldiers, who remained until 1902, when the tsar installed his own Russian soldiers there. The area was decommissioned in 1997, and the buildings are now occupied by various organizations, societies and a youth hostel (see p.244), housed in the old garrison infirmary.

Eating, drinking and entertainment

Vaasa has a number of very good **dining** establishments, though they tend to be pricier than in other Finnish towns. A night's **drinking** in a multilingual town like Vaasa will often be divided along linguistic lines, with Finnish speakers visiting certain bars and Finlandssvenska frequenting others. For everyone though, Wednesdays and Saturdays tend to be the best nights to go out, while Fridays are often surprisingly quiet. For some interesting evening **entertainment**, try Ritz, Kirkkopuistikko 22A (Thurs–Sat; ⓦwww.ritz.fi), a new cultural centre featuring regular music concerts and an artsy bar, as well as regular off-the-cuff events such as Lindy Hop dance evenings, tapas tastings and open-mike nights. Otherwise, the Vaasa City Orchestra (☎06/325 3989, ⓦwww.vaasa.fi/kaupunginorkesteri) performs concerts several times a month on Thursdays and (occasionally) Fridays, offering great student discounts (€10 and under) as well as a "concert supper" (€26), which includes a concert and dinner at the *Fondis* restaurant.

Cafés and restaurants

Bacchus Rantakatu 4 ☎010/470 6200. Housed in the basement of a fetching seaside wooden building, this bright restaurant has some interesting takes on Finnish and Russian dishes, including blini served with whitefish roe and *smetana* (€15.20) and fillet of deer with a rich blackberry sauce and truffle potato (€32). If you're coming as a couple, make a reservation for the "German" table, wedged into a private nook in the corner of the cellar.

246

Faros Kalaranta. Soups, meat and veg dishes are served on this quaint floating restaurant, making it easily the best spot in town for a sunset meal. Mains from about €15.

Fondis Hovioikeudenpuistikko 15 ☏06/280 0400. Popular upscale restaurant serving traditional steaks, a good range of fish dishes (prepared in Finnish style) and some Mediterranean-style dishes such as beef casserole with garlic and red pepper stuffed with vegetable couscous. Have a pre-dinner drink at swanky *Cristal* in the same building as you wait for your table.

Gustav Wasa Raastuvankatu 24 ☏050/466 3208. Superb white-tablecloth restaurant set deep into an old coal cellar that reigns as Vaasa's classiest dining establishment. The simple menu offers excellently prepared Finnish and Scandinavian dishes – confit of pikeperch, fillet of moose, red deer with shiitake sauce and partridge on a potato pancake – each for around €30. The wine list (and the cellar it calls on) is legendary.

Kaffehuset August Hovioikeudenpuistikko 13. Set just across from the *kauppatori*, this dainty café-restaurant, done up in pastel blues and Art Deco lighting, is a great place for a casual but refined meal. They prepare several lovely seafood dishes, including a flame-grilled whitefish fillet with root vegetables (€19) and scampi *fritti* (€15), as well as a selection of smaller, savoury crepe plates.

Strampen Rantakatu 6. The simple meals at this waterside terrace restaurant – a Setterberg pavilion-style design from 1868 – include grilled chicken (€16.50) and garlic rosemary lamb (€24.50), plus a selection of decent salads and burgers. Open mid-April to late Dec.

Bars and clubs

Bistrot Ernst Café Hietasaarenkatu 7. Located in the same building as the town's Swedish-language theatre, this candlelit corner bistro is great for a civilized glass of wine; inexpensive nibbles (and pricey mains) are also served.

Cristal Hovioikeudenpuistikko 15. This sleek new lounge bar has a collection of comfy felt sofas and professional-looking bar staff, though the alcohol content of the cocktails could use a little work.

D.O.M. Munkhaus Hietasaarenkatu 14. This relaxed cellar bar is a good bet for meeting local students from the Finnish university.

El Gringo Music Saloon Hovioikeudenpuistikko 15. This down and dirty basement bar is still searching for its look – Tex Mex? Modern Rock? Greaser? Still, it's one of the city's least pretentious places to spend the night drinking and draught pints are €2.50 if you show a student ID. They also do a good burger and fries (€7), usually until midnight.

Oliver's Kauppapuistikko 8. This pub-themed bar offers darts, a jukebox and a good number of draught beers. It's the drinking establishment of choice for Swedish university students – Tuesdays and Saturdays are the most packed nights in town.

Sky Rewell Center 101, top floor of the *Sokos Vaakuna*. This rooftop disco spins loud Euro-pop, offers the best views of any drinking spot in the city, and is usually packed to the gills on weekends. Tends to be frequented by teens who make it past security, as well as the odd hotel guest who's come to see what all the racket is.

Finnish emigration to America

Between 1866 and 1930, a total of 361,020 Finns departed for foreign lands, nearly half of them coming from the then impoverished region of **Ostrobothnia** and many of them bound for the **United States**. Despite the onset of the industrial age elsewhere, the region's economy towards the end of the nineteenth century was still largely rural and agrarian, and as industrialization moved in fast, unemployment rose and wages reached an all-time low, many looked to the allure of riches across the Atlantic. The states of Michigan, Wisconsin and Minnesota were the most popular for Finnish settlements; most US farmland further south and east had already been claimed under Lincoln's 1862 Homestead Act and the landscape and climate suited them well. Finns worked in gold and copper mines, granite quarries, fisheries and in logging camps and in the forest industry, and once settled, became especially active in labour unions and the temperance movement. Only twenty percent ever made it back to Finland, although many more had planned to do so. In the 2000 US census, some 798,000 people claimed Finnish heritage, the largest Finnish community outside of Scandinavia today being in Lake Worth, Florida, just north of Miami.

Kristinestad

About 70km south of Vaasa, roughly halfway between Vaasa and Pori, is the coastal village of **KRISTINESTAD** (Kristiinankaupunki in Finnish), resting at the base of a peninsular arm on the Pohjoislahti bay. Amply referred to in local tourist brochures as "The Pearl of the Bothnian Sea", Kristinestad features a clutch of diminutive wooden houses, built on a surviving seventeenth-century layout of narrow alleys, that comprise one of the most beautifully preserved collection of homes in Scandinavia. It was the only town in Finland spared from the disastrous fires that liquidated nearly all of the country's pre-nineteenth-century architectural heritage.

The village

Kristinestad was established in the name of Sweden's Queen Kristina at a time when shipbuilding, sailing and fishing were the only industries in town, and built on a typical narrow-street grid plan, with a central square at the bay, and burgher's residences surrounding it. Start several hundred metres south of the market square at the atmospheric **Old Customs House**, Staketgatan, which was built in 1720 and did a roaring trade in taxation during the town's heyday as a busy tar-shipment port. Just opposite here is the eighteenth-century **Ulrika Eleonora Church**, with meticulously decorated model ships dangling from the ceiling and a western tower that now leans slightly after centuries of gusty squalls. Nearby at Rantakatu 51–53, the two-storey, log-built **Lebell Merchant House** (Lebellin kauppiaantalo; June–Aug Mon–Fri 11am–5pm, Sat 11am–3pm; €4) is worth a visit for its Baroque-style salon, adorned with ceiling frescoes, linen wallpapers and green ceramic-tile oven – reputedly the oldest in Finland. The house was built in 1762 by Casper Lebell (né Casimir Subkowski), a Polish prisoner of war who set up shop as a merchant of tar, salt and wood products after securing his freedom by marrying a local demoiselle.

Tucked into the upstairs of a large Empire-era house on the market square at Salutorget 1 is the **Maritime Museum** (June–Aug Tues–Sun noon–4pm; €4). The building served as a sail-making workshop in the early nineteenth century, and now boasts a reconstruction of a ship's deck, replete with a captain's cabin. Kristinestad's municipal museum, **Carlsro** (June–Aug Tues–Sun 11am–4pm; €4), is 5km out of town on the shores of Lake Suurjärvi, where the region's shipping magnates kept their summer homes. The building here contains an assortment of some eleven thousand ethnographic items amassed from surrounding towns, giving a good impression of the discrete, charmed life of the bourgeoisie in nineteenth-century Finland. As there is no bus out here, you'll need to arrive by car or bicycle; the latter can be hired from the tourist office (€10 per day).

Practicalities

Buses stop just outside the Sellari supermarket on Sjögatan 4, from where it's a minute's walk to the town's **tourist office** (June & Aug Mon–Fri 8am–4pm, Sat 10am–2pm; July Mon–Fri 9am–5pm, Sat Sun 10am–2pm; Sept–May Mon–Fri 8am–4pm; ☎06/221 2311, ⍟www.krs.fi), Östra Långgatan 53–55, which offers an internet terminal (€3 per hour) and free wi-fi. The town's homely feel might compel you to stay in a **bed and breakfast**, the most atmospheric of which is *Houneistomajoitus Krepelin* (☎040/066 1434, ⍟www .huoneistomajoituskrepelin.fi; ❸) at Östra Långgatan 47, with several charming, handsomely done-up apartments. More bare bones is *Eivor's Bed & Breakfast*

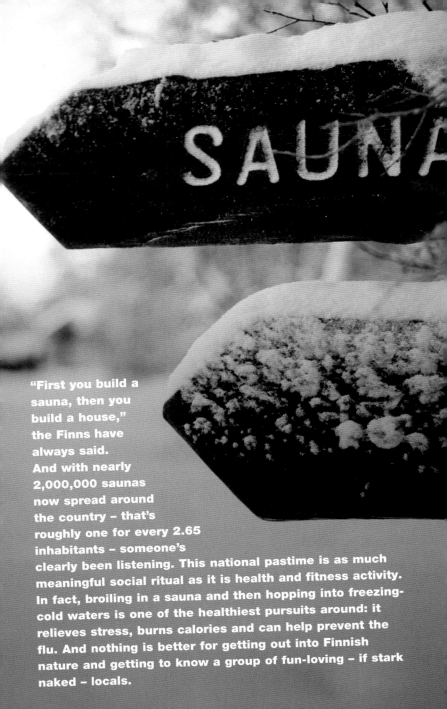

"First you build a sauna, then you build a house," the Finns have always said. And with nearly 2,000,000 saunas now spread around the country – that's roughly one for every 2.65 inhabitants – someone's clearly been listening. This national pastime is as much meaningful social ritual as it is health and fitness activity. In fact, broiling in a sauna and then hopping into freezing-cold waters is one of the healthiest pursuits around: it relieves stress, burns calories and can help prevent the flu. And nothing is better for getting out into Finnish nature and getting to know a group of fun-loving – if stark naked – locals.

Inhibitions – and clothes – are left at the sauna door ▲

Vista from sauna to lake ▼

Etiquette

For Finns, the sauna (pronounced "SOW-na" in Finnish, sow rhyming with how) remains a place free of cares, grudges, titles – and clothes. The first and perhaps most important thing to remember about the sauna experience is that you are at some point probably going to get your kit off. In fact, the sauna – and subsequent bathing in the nearest lake – is the one locale where nudity is commonly and publicly practised. In public spaces, however, Finns tend to wear a loose towel, but bear in mind that more die-hard Finnish hosts will probably remain *au natural*, which is equally acceptable. That being said, don't get confused: the sauna is not the place for sexual encounter or romance; behavioural codes are rather strict here and the sexes bathe separately. If ex-president Urho Kekkonen charmed Brezhnev at his private sauna in the Finnish woodlands, famously averting a Soviet invasion in the process, how racy can it be, right? In the end, the sauna should be about clearing your mind, refreshing your spirit and getting away from the world. Remember the popular Finnish adage: "One is most beautiful two hours after the sauna."

How it's done

In most saunas, the temperature is kept around 70°C, although the Finnish Sauna Society recommends a somewhat balmier 80–100°C (175–210°F) with the national sauna championships turning up the heat to over 110°C (230°F) – a temperature more commonly used for grilling meats or cauterising metal. Begin by showering outside the main sauna room, then enter the sauna with your skin still wet. To avoid scalding yourself, sit down on a towel on the lower platform – often reserved for children – where it will be slightly cooler (as low as 30°C, or 85°F), then breathe deeply and relax. Every few minutes, take the ladle from the bucket and pour water over the hot stones; the dry steam, *löyly*, that rises up will create a moist heat, raising the humidity to above twenty percent and causing you to perspire.

Some public saunas keep a hardy Finn or two on hand to swat you with a wet birch switch, the *vihta*, before scrubbing you down. This increases blood circulation, exfoliates the skin and helps to release toxins – a typical twenty-minute sauna session can extract roughly one litre of water from the body. If no professionals are on hand however, just ask the person next to you, *Voitko vihtoa minua?* ("Would you mind beating me with birch leaves?"). After about fifteen minutes, muster up all the chutzpah you can, step outside onto the terrace or porch, then venture to the nearest body of water, hopping in, feet first. If you're really brave, try this in the wintertime and roll into the snow or jump into a hole carved in the ice (an *avantouinti*) – it looks much more shocking than it actually is. Hopping from steamy sauna into bone-chilling lake is a great way to unwind both body and mind, and it'll give you a real rush.

Afterwards, rest and drink something refreshing, and get dressed only after you have stopped perspiring. A sauna is most spectacular if you visit while the bright, fiery tapestries of the aurora borealis or northern lights are glimmering up above – try a clear evening in September, October, February or March. If you're still unsure, Ⓦ www.sauna.fi has indispensable practical advice on sauna dos and sauna don'ts.

▲ Saunatytöt (sauna girls) dining

▼ Two Finnish traditions: a ladle and a lager

▼ Binding birch twigs for the *vihta* (whisk)

The sauna-on-a-boat, Åland ▲

A pre-sauna meal in a traditional smokehouse ▲

Après-sauna cooling off ▼

Super saunas

Great **saunas** aren't just found in private Finnish homes. There are some really wild and fetching places all over the country for visitors to experience this quintessentially Finnish ritual, including gondola saunas, mobile saunas – even saunas in rebuilt Viking castles. See Ⓦ www.gosauna.fi, or try our favourites:

▶▶ **Rastila Camping (Helsinki)** Take a bus out to this campsite come wintertime and join bands of certifiably loony Finns in that most savoury of après-sauna experiences: running stark naked from the steamy, sweaty heat into a hole carved in the ice (see p.61).

▶▶ **Rauhalahti (Kuopio)** The world's biggest woodsmoke sauna is this enormous unisex affair; it's best visited just before a hearty buffet meal and right after one of their lumberjack variety shows (see p.212).

▶▶ **Saunabussi (Tammela)** The really adventurous hire this sixteen-person tour bus retrofitted with a functioning sauna in the back, then pull over to the side of the road and jump in the nearest body of water. Ⓦ www.kala-apaja.fi /saunabussi.html

▶▶ **Sauna-on-a-boat (Åland)** Moored at the dock of the stellar Övernäsgården guesthouse, you can take this fully mobile, two-floor sauna out to the middle of the bay, grill some sausages on the roof, then dive into the cool water below (see p.163).

▶▶ **Tin Tin Tango (Helsinki)** Once you've had a coffee, a croque or a pint of Karjala, drop off your clothes at this hip café's on-site washing machine and retire to the group sauna out back (see p.85).

Tango in Finland

"Finns are very shy people. They're not very talkative. So, fifty years ago you couldn't find a woman. With tango, because the lady should say yes, you get the chance to share your feelings without talking. You can see if there's a connection between you. And if it works, you don't know – maybe one day you will marry that woman."

Frans Karki, 2005 winner, Snow Tango championships

The tiny town of **SEINÄJOKI**, inland from Vaasa and just as big in terms of population, often gets short shrift from visitors as it's mostly a hub for IT, metals, wood and foodstuffs. But for five long evenings in the summer, Finns flock to this two-horse town to let loose and dance tango. Troubadours brought the dance from Argentina to Europe at the end of the nineteenth century, and by the roaring twenties and thirties it had become all the rage in Finland; by the 1940s, nearly half of all songs on Finland's popular-music charts were tangos. Dire conditions during World War II led to lyrics that waxed about departure and longing, and the song and its dance had soon spread from city to countryside, settling into the national consciousness as a defining soundtrack of the Finnish soul. The tango did for Finns what no other ballroom dance had managed to accomplish: while marches were patriotic, polkas and schottisches were comic and foxtrots celebratory, Finnish tangos evolved as melancholic laments. They were played slowly, melding major and minor keys – "minor with joy and major with sorrow", as one musicologist has characterized them – that incorporated influences from Finnish folk tunes, German marches and Russian waltzes. These songs eventually evolved into deep, drawn-out melodies that evoked the emotions of nostalgia, love, loss, sorrow and a specific longing for the homeland – a poignant grace-note for many Finns, considering the nation's struggles at the time. Today, tango remains one of the most enduring and popular forms of musical expression in the country.

Seinäjoki's colossal **Tangomarkkinat festival** (Ⓦwww.tangomarkkinat.fi) rakes in some 100,000 visitors over five days in mid-July. It was founded – as many great Finnish ideas are – during the summer solstice in the 1980s when two Finns entered a sauna with several six-packs of beer, and made a drunken promise to give Finnish tango the recognition it deserves. It is now one of the biggest tango festivals on the planet, drawing dancers, singers, composers and fans from all over the world.

(Ⓣ050/529 8646; ❷), Strandgata 43, where the single apartment would be ideal for a study of early 1970s folk furnishings, though there are ample amenities for self-catering – you can even stoke your own fire in the small ceramic stove. About a ten-minute walk south of town at Salavägen 32, the austere *Bockholmens Camping* (Ⓣ06/221 1484; May–Sept) offers fifteen basic cabins (€39) with toilets in a separate building, while at the opposite end of the spectrum is the very well dressed up *Alma* (Ⓣ06/221 3455, Ⓦwww.hotelalma.info; ❹), Pakkahuoneentori, in grassy grounds right at the water's edge. When Finnish president Tarja Halonen stayed here she took the upstairs suite, with satin sheets, French windows and antique furniture, but the second-floor room, with its own balcony and large bath, would have more than sufficed. They also operate a summer hostel (❷). Hotel reception is at the *Café Alma*, where you can sit down for a great lunch buffet for under €10. From May to August, locals regularly dine at *Pavis* (Ⓣ050/554 1570, Ⓦwww.pavis.fi), a swish-meets-rustic **restaurant** 2km south of town on Korkeasaari; jazz evenings are also scheduled there several times a summer.

Jakobstad and around

A mildly scenic journey of around 100km up the coast from Vaasa (change at Seinäjoki if travelling by train), passing the odd fishing hamlet along the shore, inconsequential **Pännäinen** is the railhead for the Bothnian coast's best-preserved wooden town: **JAKOBSTAD**; buses quickly mop up straggling passengers disgorged from the train and trundle the 10km or so into Jakobstad. Once in the centre, it's clear that this is another of the Bothnian coast's Finnish-Swedish towns: all signs and advertisements, street names and chatter in the street is in Swedish. Indeed, links with Sweden have always been strong and for forty years, until 1999, the town's ferry operator, Jakob Lines, ran regular, inordinately popular crossings over the Gulf of Bothnia to several Swedish cities, which attracted equal numbers of day-tripping Swedes, so furthering the use of Swedish in day-to-day affairs. Despite the continued majority role Swedish plays in the town, Finnish Railways still insist on referring to Jakobstad by its Finnish name, Pietarsaari (attracting the ire of many local people), so be sure to look under "P" not "J" when hunting for train times and connections. We have followed local usage and have employed the town's Swedish name and Swedish terms for all references.

Jakobstad is named after Jacob de la Gardie, a statesman and military commander of the Swedish realm, who was married to Countess Ebba Brahe. Despite bearing him fourteen children, Ebba, a noblewoman of great energy and drive, was also having a less-than-secret extramarital affair with the Swedish king, Gustavus Adolphus. Following the death of her husband, she successfully petitioned Swedish Queen Kristina I to found Jakobstad in his honour, and in 1652 she set about planning the town, ordering the construction of a town hall and customs house.

Arrival, information and accommodation

Rail shuttle buses from Pännäinen drop passengers at the former train station, which now serves as the town's **bus station**. The friendly **tourist office** (June–Aug Mon–Fri 8am–6pm, Sat 9am–3pm; Sept–May Mon–Fri 8am–5pm; ☏06/785 1208, ⓦwww.jakobstad.fi) is perfectly located close to the main square at Köpmansgatan 12, where there's also an **internet** terminal for use.

Due to its historical links with Mother Svea across the Gulf of Bothnia, Jakobstad receives plenty of Swedish visitors during the short summer months. Hence, if you're visiting at this time, you should be sure to book **accommodation** well in advance. Otherwise, there shouldn't be a problem in finding a bed as things are pretty quiet out of season.

Epoque Jakobsgatan 10 ☏06/788 7100, ⓦwww.hotelepoque.fi. The town's elegant former customs house, built in National Romantic style, has been lovingly restored with minimalist interiors of wood and white stone and stylish bathrooms: the last word in Nordic chic. ❻

Hostel Lilja Storgatan 6 ☏06/781 6500, ⓦwww.aftereight.fi/hostellilja. Housed in a former stable building, this snug hostel, with tasteful wooden wall panelling and wooden flooring throughout, is a real find. Shared facilities and no dorm beds. Bike hire available. ❷

Jugend Skolgatan 11 ☏06/781 4300, ⓦwww.visitjugend.fi. Offering both stylish, modern hotel rooms and cheaper, plainer guesthouse rooms with access to a shared kitchen, all options representing excellent value for money. Hotel rooms ❹ (€15 cheaper at weekends), guesthouse rooms ❷

Stadshotellet Kanalesplanaden 13 ☏06/788 8111, ⓦwww.stadshotellet-jakobstad.fi. In town for over 100 years, this handsome pile has individually decorated rooms which reek of grandeur. Cheaper budget rooms (❹) are also available – perfectly functional though without the flourishes. ❹/❻

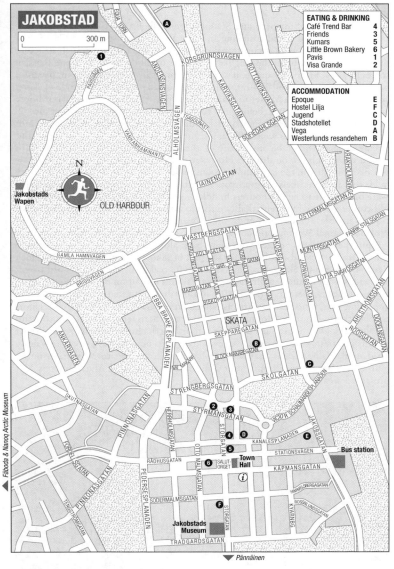

JAKOBSTAD

0   300 m

EATING & DRINKING
Café Trend Bar	4
Friends	3
Kumars	5
Little Brown Bakery	6
Pavis	1
Visa Grande	2

ACCOMMODATION
Epoque	E
Hostel Lilja	F
Jugend	C
Stadshotellet	D
Vega	A
Westerlunds resandehem	B

Jakobstads Wapen

OLD HARBOUR

N

SKATA

Town Hall

Bus station

Jakobstads Museum

Fäboda & Nanoq Arctic Museum

Pännäinen

Vega Alholmsvägen 9 ☎06/781 6850, ⓦwww
.hotelvega.net. No-nonsense Finnish-speaking hotel
with rather boxy rooms and old-fashioned fittings.
Nevertheless, the atmosphere is homely and it's
the cheapest of all the town's hotels. ❸/❹
Westerlunds resandehem Norrmalmsgatan 8
☎06/723 0440, ⓦwww.multi.fi/westerlund.

Housed in a charming old wooden building in the
heart of the old town, *Westerlunds* has been
providing accommodation since 1923 and has a
long list of regulars. Rooms are a little small
and rather dowdily dressed, but the price is
unbeatable. ❷

The Town

At the junction of Storgatan and Stationsvägen, Jakobstad's turreted **town hall**, built with plentiful wood-panelling in New Renaissance style in 1875 (by the town's unemployed as an occupational project), is in fact the fourth such structure to grace the main square; the original *rådhus* was burnt down by invading Russian forces in 1714. From the square, it's a two-minute walk down Storgatan, passing a wealth of pretty, wooden 1840s Empire-style houses painted a multitude of pastel colours, to **Jakobstads Museum** (daily noon–4pm; €2), housed in a manor house and farm buildings once belonging to local worthy, Peter Malm, at no. 2. Naturally, the town's seafaring past takes up a large proportion of the museum; around a thousand ships were built in Jakobstad, including the first Finnish boat to circumnavigate the globe, and many of the rare blueprints which were used to design the vessels are on display. However, it's the collection of late 1800s New Rococo furniture in the large public room, where concerts and lectures were once held, that is more likely to grab your attention. Outside, wooden houses which were once home to farm labourers huddle around the courtyard, together with an old corner shop, which remarkably only closed in 1960 and still today contains a riotous jumble of odds and ends which were once for sale, including some of Nokia's original Wellington boots.

From the museum, retrace your steps back along Storgatan, continue through the square northwards, and head for the part of Jakobstad known as **Skata**, which lies to the north of Skolgatan, and is the town's real gem. Here, in the **old town**, a glorious knot of uneven dirt streets, you'll find row upon row of low, roughly hewn timber houses from the 1780s, around three hundred in total, painted in appealing reds, mustards and greens, which were once home to the town's sailors and workers. Though Holmgatan, at the northern edge of Skata, contains Jakobstad's oldest houses, it's the long run of Norrmalmsgatan where the district is at its prettiest, with gloriously uneven dwellings nestling eave to eave. Wholly residential, it's admirable that the area has not succumbed to conversion into a glut of cutesy tourist shops; after Rauma (see p.147), it's the country's best preserved area of old wooden architecture.

▲ Entering the old town, Jakobstad

From Skata, you're now within easy reach of **Jakobstads Wapen**, a full-scale replica of a twin-masted eighteenth-century galleon, which was built, like the original, in the old harbour, just to the northwest of Skata. The replica made her maiden voyage in 1994, six years after the keel was laid, though recent concerns over her seaworthiness have halted the public sailings she made a couple of times a year; check with the tourist office for the latest information. Although the ship is not open to the public, you can gawp at her from the harbourside.

Eating and drinking

With the exception of one notable place in the old harbour, all Jakobstad's **eating and drinking** options can be found in the compact town centre, though they're unlikely to be the highlight of your visit.

Café Trend Bar Storgatan 13. Airy, corner café and bar with huge glass windows, ideal for people-watching. Serves light snacks as well as a good selection of cakes and sandwiches.

Friends Alholmsgatan 6. With tartan curtains in the windows, dartboard and heavy wood panelling, this is the closest Jakobstad comes to a traditional British pub, and the locals love it.

Kumars Storgatan 11. Try to ignore the fake brick walls inside because the pizzas (from €7.60), schnitzel (€14), and Indian dishes such as Balti gosht (€18), served up here are surprisingly authentic.

Little Brown Bakery Rådhusgatan 4. An intimate and tastefully designed café and bakery with

brown walls and wooden floors. Wonderful home-made chocolates and cakes.

Pavis Pavisvägen 2 ☏06/723 1687. Open May–Aug only, this is the town's best restaurant, located by the water's edge in a 100-year-old yachting pavilion. Sit on the open-air terrace and enjoy a plate of shrimps or fresh fish. Live music on Fri & Sat.

Visa Grande Storgatan 20. Fun, American-style bar that greets its customers with a sign reading "Clothing optional beyond this point". A good choice for burgers, steaks and other bar snacks for around €15. Huge open-air terrace at the rear.

Fäboda and the Nanoq Arctic Museum

On a sunny day, you'll find the population of Jakobstad sunning themselves on the sandy beaches at **Fäboda**, an agreeable little seaside hamlet 7km or so southwest of the town centre. There are plenty of secluded, craggy inlets hereabouts, too, ideal for the most solipsistic of souls, should you wish to escape the crowds on the main beach. Although there is no public transport here, Fäboda is an easy cycle ride from town down a narrow country lane which sees little traffic; **bike hire** is available in Jakobstad from *Hostel Lilja* (see p.250).

Fäboda is also the location for one of Finland's most unusual museums: the **Nanoq Arctic Museum** (June–Aug daily noon–6pm; €7; ⓦ www.nanoq.fi) at Pörkenäsvägen 60, a couple of hundred metres beyond the turn into Fäboda itself. Run by the endearing Pentti Kronqvist, who's made no fewer than twelve exploration trips to the Arctic, the remarkable collection is a homage to all things polar (*nanoq* is Inuit for polar bear). The museum, which fills a large version of a typical Greenlandic turf-roofed house, partly built into the hillside, covers two floors. Collections on the entrance level include: several *tupilak*, ancient Greenlandic fantasy figures carved of bone used to ward away evil spirits; fearsome weapons for slaughtering walrus and seals; and a series of oil paintings by Vladimir Goichman, an internationally renowned artist of Arctic landscapes, who painted in extreme weather conditions in situ. Upstairs, rare original artefacts such as logbooks and skis help bring to life the expeditions of Amundsen, Nansen and the ill-fated attempt by Sweden's Andrée to cross the North Pole by hydrogen balloon in 1897. Outside the main building, also have a quick peep in the cramped trappers' cabin from Spitsbergen for an idea of the spartan living conditions in the Arctic.

When nibbles strike, make for the beach, where on Lillsandsvägen you'll find the sturdy log cabin, *Café & Restaurant Fäboda* (May–Aug daily from 10am; Sept eves and weekends only), serving up tasty fish dishes.

Kokkola and around

Back in Pännäinen again, heading north on the coastal train line between Helsinki and Oulu, it's barely another 30km to the regional centre, the low-key port town of **KOKKOLA** (Karleby in Swedish), where Finnish resumes its dominant roll as the majority language. Although you'll still hear Swedish spoken in the streets here, only around one fifth of local people have the language as their mother tongue. Twice the size of its southerly neighbour, there's more of a buzz to Kokkola than Jakobstad, and it also has some pleasant parkland perfect for a picnicking stroll down to the sea. That said, the town is never going to win any beauty contests, and the diminutive **old town**, by far its most attractive part, is not a patch on Jakobstad's Skata. Unless you're an aficionado on maritime warfare – the town had a role in Britain's attack on Finland during the Crimean campaign – Kokkola is perhaps worth just a whistle-stop tour before pressing on further north. Incidentally, Kokkola lies roughly halfway between Helsinki (478km) and Rovaniemi (420km).

Arrival, information and accommodation

From the **train** and **bus stations**, diagonally opposite each across the main street, Rautatienkatu, it's a walk of around 500m into the *kauppatori*, following any of the straight parallel streets north; Isokatu and Rantakatu are as good as any. The welcoming **tourist office**, in the former fish market at the *kauppatori* (June–Aug Mon–Fri 8am–5pm, Wed till 8pm, Sat 9am–1pm; Sept–May Mon–Fri 8am–4pm; ☏06/828 9402, ⓦwww.visitkokkola.fi), can help with maps and has plentiful brochures about the town. **Accommodation**, too, is rarely in short supply. In addition to the options below, you can also stay on the island of Tankar (see p.256).

Best Western Kokkola Rantakatu 14 ☏06/824 1000, ⓦwww.hotelkokkola.fi. Modern, uninspired, yet comfortable chain hotel right in the centre of town. The extensive breakfast buffet and decent sauna suite are both plus points. ④/⑥

Brink Old Vicarage Opettajankuja 4 ☏040/825 5955, ⓦpp.kpnet.fi/brinkinpappila. Characterful nineteenth-century wooden vicarage 2km away from the centre surrounded by swaying birch trees, which now runs as a B&B. The taste-fully decorated rooms, in keeping with the period, share facilities. Walk or take a taxi. ②

Finlandia Seurahuone Torikatu 24 ☏020/795 9600, ⓦwww.seurahuone.com. Though one of Finland's oldest hotels – dating from 1894 –this

venerable place enjoys a perfect central location and tasteful rooms that beat the *Best Western*'s in contemporary style. ④/⑥

Kaupunginkartano Lumitähti Pakkahuoneenkatu 5 ☏050/016 2302, ⓦwww.citymansion.net. Old-fashioned 1840s charm and elegance are the key to this great old-town B&B, housed in a restored wooden house which was once a local school. Breakfast is available (€7) but not included in the room rate. ④

Kokkola Camping Vanhasatamanlahti ☏06/831 4006, ⓦwww.kokkola-camping.fi. Occupying a nice harbourside location, this campsite also has 2–4 person cabins (from €40) and youth-hostel doubles (②) available.

The Town

First of all, make for the *kauppatori* to check out the **Krunni**, a twin-masted sailing ship now plonked unceremoniously in the square to mark the isostatic uplift of the Finnish west coast that has occurred since the last Ice Age; as the ice melted, the land, no longer weighed down by ice up to 3km thick, began to rise. In 1800, the square was under water – now, owing to this geological process, the sea is a full 2km away. Check out the notches on the vessel's bow which denote the extent of the uplift.

Neristan
From the square, Pormesterinkatu heads west towards the old-town district known as **Neristan**, literally "lower town" (confusingly in Finnish-speaking Kokkola, it is the Swedish term, rather than its Finnish counterpart, that is used). Arranged along a handful of residential streets, dominated by pretty Itäinen Kirkkokatu, the pastel-coloured wooden houses here date mostly from the nineteenth century (older seventeenth-century ones were lost to successive fires) and were home to craftsmen and sailors when Kokkola was proud to be Finland's biggest tar-exporting town. During Neristan's heyday in the eighteenth and nineteenth centuries, the narrow sound, **Sunti**, which runs up from the present old harbour, was navigable all the way to the market square where ships would unload their goods for sale.

The English Park
Continuing north along Itäinen Kikkokatu and then taking a right into Härnösand-inkatu, you'll soon reach the **English Park** (Englantilainen puisto), the beginnings of an attractive ribbon of parkland which winds either side of Sunti down to the harbour. Here, in a glass-fronted boathouse (not open to the public) beside Isokatu, you can view a British landing boat, captured by the Finns during the Crimean campaign in 1854. Dispatched by the British Crown to destroy Russian tar stores and harbours in the Gulf of Bothnia (Finland was a Grand Duchy of Russia at this time), two British boats met resistance in Kokkola and were fired upon by Finnish volunteer forces waiting in hiding at Halkokari beach (just east of the present-day campsite); 17 British sailors were killed and 39 wounded, whilst the Finns lost nothing more than a horse which suffered a broken leg. The people of Kokkola haven't forgotten this victory and celebrate it with pomp every year on June 7 with a parade through the town in historical costumes, and a ball.

The museum complex
The full story of what's known as the Halkokari skirmish is told in pictures inside Kokkola's **museum complex**, back in town at Pitkänsillankatu 26 (June–Aug Tues–Sun 11am–4pm; Sept–May Tues–Fri noon–3pm, Thurs until 8pm, Sat & Sun noon–5pm; €4). Although there are actually four museums in one here, you can easily dispense with the mind-numbing displays of rocks in the Mineral Collection and the stuffed birds and animals in the Natural History section. Concentrate instead on the Historical Museum, which traces Kokkola's trading history, and the Art Museum, which features the sizeable collection of Karl Herman Renlund, who donated his paintings from the golden era of Finnish art to the town on his death.

Eating and drinking
Thanks to its relative size, there's a fairly decent choice of **places to eat and drink** in Kokkola. Things are busiest between June and August when you should book in advance, otherwise you shouldn't have a problem finding a table.

Corner's Torikatu 24, at the corner with Rantakatu. The fake stained-glass windows at the *Seurahuone* hotel's popular pub are a hint of what's to come inside: fake Britannia *in extremis*.

Kokkolinna Isokatu 1 ☎06/825 2025. Opposite the train station, this stylish Art Nouveau building from 1908 is not what you'd expect from a restaurant for trainee chefs. The food (two modern

Finnish classics to choose from Mon–Fri, or buffet on Sat) is good when it comes, but the wait can be a little annoying. Open lunchtime only Mon–Sat.

🏃 **Krunni** Kauppatori. The former Danish sailing ship in the main square has to be the best and most unusual place for a beer in town. Either sit up on deck or take a table beside the keel in the square itself.

Rafla Torikatu 24 ☎ 06/865 3111. Another of the *Seurahuone*'s options, this accomplished restaurant is a good-value choice for lunch when an ever-changing (and extensive) buffet table goes for around €10 – dessert and coffee included.

Schönes Fräulein Rantakatu 9 ☎ 020/775 9888. Fake it may be, but this German-style *Bierstube* with stone walls and over-the-top lanterns is

tremendous fun and really draws the crowds. The food, *Wurstplatte* and other Teutonic classics, is not great – go for the beer instead.

🏃 **Vanhankaupungin Ravinotola** Isokatu 28 ☎ 06/834 9030. Elegant candle-lit dining in the heart of the old town. Starters such as crayfish soup go for €10; mains are in the range €18–32, though the lamb rack marinated with garlic and whisky is worth every cent. The cuisine is modern Finnish with a hint of French.

Wanha Lyhty & Kellari Pitkänsillankatu 24 ☎ 06/868 0188. Opposite the museum complex, this cosy little place with window boxes is a local favourite for its tasty Finnish home-cooking: smoked reindeer soup with sherry (€7.20) and the fried salmon steak in wild mushroom sauce (€18.90) are particularly good.

Around Kokkola: Tankar Island

For centuries, the red-and-white lighthouse on the tiny rocky island of **Tankar**, 15km off Kokkola, has warned shipping of the approaching danger of dozens of even smaller islands and skerries on the way into Kokkola harbour. Tankar Island was until the mid-twentieth century home to a working fishing hamlet, and is a now a popular summer day-trip. In addition to nosing around the **chapel**, built in 1754, where the fishermen carved their initials in the back of the cramped pews, and the humble former **fishermen's cabins**, you can explore the rest of the island on foot along a 1.5km **nature trail** which winds along the shore. It's also possible to **spend the night** on the island in double rooms with shared facilities in the former pilot station (❺) or the lighthouse master's cabin (❹); contact the tourist office in Kokkola for bookings. **Boats** sail for Tankar from near the campsite at the old harbour in Kokkola (mid-June to mid-Aug Tues–Fri 1 daily, Sat 2 daily; 1hr 30min; €17 return).

Kalajoki

Continuous sunny days spent lazing on the beach is the image most Finns have of **KALAJOKI**, northern Finland's premier beach resort, located roughly one-third of the way between Kokkola and Oulu. A stereotypical image perhaps, especially since Vaasa, 175km to the south, holds the record as the sunniest place in Finland, yet this is still one of the region's most popular holiday resorts – and with good reason. Thanks to its enviably long sandy strands and shallow waters, which warm up quickly during the long days of summer, Kalajoki attracts a wide range of visitors – though almost all of them are Finnish – and consequently the variety of accommodation available caters to all tastes and pockets, running from a luxury spa hotel to self-catering cabins. Once you've tired of dozing on the beach, there are plenty of activities to enliven your stay, too: from catching (and eating) your own salmon to boat trips out to the offshore islands, seemingly everything is on hand.

The geography of Kalajoki is straightforward, dividing neatly into two centres: the **town** itself, which straddles the banks of the Kalajoki River, is where you'll find the bus station and other services such as banks and shops, whilst 7km to the south along Route 8 towards Kokkola are the **beaches** at **Kalajoen hiekkasärkät**; the latter is where the action is and makes a much better place to stay.

Arrival and accommodation

Buses between Kokkola (70km) and Oulu (130km) call at both Kalajoen hiekkasärkät and Kalajoki Town. To get here by **train**, head for either Kokkola, or better **Ylivieska**, which is just 37km from Kalajoki and connected by regular bus. For **accommodation**, the swankiest choice is *Spa Hotel Sani* (℡08/469 2500, ⓦwww.hiekkasarkat.fi; ❺), a harmonious structure at Jokupolku 5 whose sand-coloured walls are faced with wooden planking to blend effortlessly into the natural surroundings; the modern rooms enjoy superb sea views and there's any number of spa treatments on hand. *Fontana Rantakalla*, at Matkailutie 150 (℡08/466 642, ⓦwww.rantakalla.fi; ❺), is another good choice, though rather less luxurious; while at the junction of Route 8, *Tapion Tupa* at Matkailutie 3 (℡08/466 622, ⓦwww.tapiontupa.com) rents out fully equipped cabins (from €85) and has simpler youth hostel dorm beds (€20). For more **cabin** accommodation, contact the tourist office, which keeps an extensive list.

The Town

You're unlikely to spend much time in Kalajoki town, but if you do pop in, it's worth having a nose around the nineteenth-century wooden shacks of the former **marketplace**, or Plassi – once the commercial heart of the town, where a brisk trade in fish secured most people's livelihoods from the 1500s onwards; it's by the riverside and immediately left as you cross the bridge arriving from the beaches. Here, too, you'll find a modest fisheries **museum** (open on request; contact the tourist office), charting the town's connections with the sea, which once included sealing. The graceful Art Nouveau residence behind the market-place is the 1912 **Havula manor** (guided tours: late June to early Aug Tues & Thurs 6 & 7pm; €4.50), the former home of a local sawmill owner stuffed with original furnishings and deserving of a quick peek, even if you don't fancy the obligatory guided tours of the sumptuous interior. The rest of the town is modern and anodyne in the extreme, though it does have a decent restaurant you may want to check out (see p.258).

The beaches

From Route 8, Matkailutie makes a loop out towards the sea, running parallel to the **beaches**, before rejoining the main road a kilometre or so further on; most things of interest lie beside this loop road. A total of around 1.5km of sandy beach extends below the road, divided by an expanse of shops and restaurants into two main sections. The main and widest stretch of sand lies between the **tourist office** (June–Aug daily 11am–7pm; ℡08/466 655, ⓦwww.kalajoki.fi) and the *Fontana* hotel and restaurant (see above), within easy reach of the two main attractions: the **Juku water park and amusement centre**, next to the tourist office, and the **golf course**, about 500m to the south, just off Tiitaival road. Next to the water park at Merisärkäntie 10, the Safaritalo shop (℡045/111 6633, ⓦwww.hsop.fi) rents out **jet skis** and **quad bikes** in summer, as well as snowmobiles in winter; there's also a smoke sauna here out back.

At the northern end of the beach, off Tahkokorvantie road, keep an eye out for ⚓ **Lohilaakso** (℡08/466 645, ⓦwww.lohilaakso.fi), a fun **fishing** activity centre, beer garden and restaurant all rolled into one. Run by the ebullient Englishman John and his Finnish partner, Marja, this is the place to come to catch your own salmon (a day-licence costs €2, or €5 to also hire your fishing equipment) and have it grilled for dinner (see p.258). Should all the fun and excitement have left you with a desire to know more about this area of the Finnish west coast, head for the informative **Sea Life Centre** (Tues–Sun

11am–6pm), where there's an exhibition about the nature and cultural heritage of the northern Gulf of Bothnia; it's attached to the *Spa Hotel Sani* (see p.257), beside the tourist office at Jukupolku 5.

Eating and drinking

Eating and drinking is best enjoyed by the beaches, though in Kalajoki itself *Mamma Leone*, Kalajoentie 8 (☎08/462 820), opposite the town hall, has good-value pizzas and Italian-style meat dishes. At the beach, the freshest choice is *Lohilaakso* (see p.257), where you pay per kilo for any salmon you catch yourself (reckon on around €20), plus side orders of potatoes or salad. Alternatively, the juicy steaks at *Pihvitupa* (☎08/466 608), Tuomipakkaintie, are worth seeking out, whilst for sea views and hearty Finnish dishes, the restaurant at the *Fontana* hotel (see p.257) is hard to beat. Following a day on the beach, late-night revellers head for the *Dyyni* **nightclub**, Tuomipakkaintie 59 (ⓦwww.hiekkadyyni.fi), beside the *Spa Hotel Sani*, with its sea-view terrace.

Oulu and around

From Ylivieska, it's an hour and a quarter up the rail line to **OULU** (pronounced OH-loo), which, with its 135,000 inhabitants, is not only the biggest centre north of Tampere, but also the largest city in the entire north of Scandinavia. Oulu, or Uleåborg as it's known in Swedish, is also one of the north's most likeable destinations, particularly so since its transformation in recent years into a kind of Finnish Silicon Valley. The driving force behind Oulu's revitalization has been its **university**, whose computing expertise has lured dozens of IT companies to set up in science and technology parks on the outskirts of the city, confirming Oulu's role as national leader in the **computing and microchip** industries; many of Nokia's mobile phones, for example, are designed here and the city is at the cutting edge of ever-developing wireless internet techniques. Attracting highly skilled employees from across the world as well as local graduates, Oulu has boomed and the wealth has percolated through the city, resulting in the busy, cosmopolitan and prosperous population centre of today – no mean achievement for a city located smack on the 65th parallel.

That said, Oulu still has sufficient remnants from the past to remind visitors of its nineteenth-century status as a world centre for **tar**. International demand for use of the black stuff in ship- and road-building helped line the pockets of Oulu's merchants. Their affluence and quest for cultural refinement made the town a vibrant centre, not only for business, but also for education and the arts. A handsome series of islands, several highly conspicuous old buildings, and a nightlife fuelled by the university's fun-hungry students add colour to an already energetic city. And though it has its share of faceless office blocks in common with many other Finnish cities, there's an ancient feel to Oulu, too, as seen in tumbledown

---

Oulu's music festivals

Undoubtedly, a great time to visit Oulu is during the summer months, particularly August, when the city is abuzz with festivals. Both the **Oulu Music Video Festival**, which features the weird and wonderful World Air Guitar Championships (ⓦwww .airguitarworldchampionships.com), and **Elojazz and Blues** (ⓦwww.elojazz.com), a great weekend music event, draw people from across the country. Full details are available online.

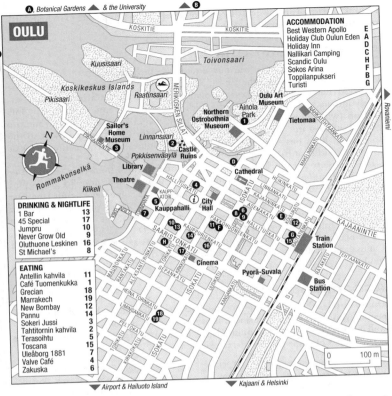

OULU

Ⓐ, Botanical Gardens ▲ & the University ▲ ▲ Ⓑ

Ⓒ

KOSKITIE   KOSKITIE

Kuusisaari

Toivonsaari

Koskikeskus Islands

Pikisaari   Raatinsaari

Oulu Art Museum

Ainola Park

Northern Ostrobothnia Museum ❶

Tietomaa

Sailor's Home Museum ❸

Linnansaari

Castle Ruins ❷

Rommakonselkä

Pokkisenväylä

Library

Kiikeli

Theatre

Cathedral Ⓓ

ACCOMMODATION

Best Western Apollo	E
Holiday Club Oulun Eden	A
Holiday Inn	D
Nallikari Camping	C
Scandic Oulu	H
Sokos Arina	F
Toppilanpukseri	B
Turisti	G

Rovaniemi

KAJAANINTIE

DRINKING & NIGHTLIFE

1 Bar	13
45 Special	17
Jumpru	10
Never Grow Old	9
Oluthuone Leskinen	16
St Michael's	8

EATING

Antellin kahvila	11
Café Tuomenkukka	1
Grecian	18
Marrakech	19
New Bombay	12
Pannu	14
Sokeri Jussi	3
Tähtitornin kahvila	2
Terasoihtu	5
Toscana	15
Uleåborg 1881	7
Valve Café	4
Zakuska	6

KAUPP-ATORI

City Hall

Kauppahalli

Train Station

Cinema

Pyörä-Suvala

Bus Station

0   100 m

▼ Airport & Hailuoto Island   ▼ Kajaani & Helsinki

wooden shacks around the intricately carved *kauppahalli*. What's more, the city is readily accessible from outside Finland thanks to its international air connection to Riga on the Air Baltic network: it's possible to fly into Oulu without passing through Helsinki on the way – a rare opportunity which helps make air fares here more competitive than many other places in the country.

Some history

Founded by Swedish king Karl IX in 1605, Oulu is believed to take its rather unusual name from the Sámi word for "floodwater", no coincidence since the city is located at the estuary of the Oulujoki River, which was once an important trading site for the local indigenous population. The city's Swedish name, Uleåborg, gives further clues to the past: a *borg* or castle once stood here beside the Ule River (its Swedish name includes the component "å", meaning "river") to offer protection from Russia, since the Oulujoki/Uleå River was formerly a major waterway between east and west. Due to its strategic location on both river and sea and the granting of trading rights in 1765, Oulu grew into a tar-exporting centre, shipping out the black gold after arrival by barge from the inland forests of Kainuu. Following a disastrous fire in 1822, which laid the city to waste, the German architect Carl Ludwig Engel was enlisted to redesign the city centre in Empire (Neoclassical) style, and several of his impressive structures, including the cathedral, can still be seen. Today, Oulu is the fastest-growing city outside

Helsinki, boasting an unusually large number of young people due to its high birth rate; the average age here is just 36.

Arrival and information

Oulu receives trains from various directions, including direct services from Helsinki and Tampere to the south, Kajaani to the east and Rovaniemi in the north. Arriving here, you'll find the platforms of the **train station** feed conveniently into an underground walkway with two exits: one runs to the nearby **bus station** (with regular services to and from Kalajoki and Kuusamo), while the other leads towards the compact city centre. From the **airport**, 15km to the southwest, local bus #19 runs every twenty minutes into town (timetables at ⓦwww.koskilinjat.fi), dropping off at the central Torikatu.

Here, close to the city hall at no. 10, the **tourist office** (mid-June to mid-Aug Mon–Fri 9am–6pm, Sat 10am–3pm; mid-Aug to mid-June Mon–Fri 9am–4pm; ⓣ08/5584 1330, ⓦwww.visitoulu.fi) arranges summertime free English-language **tours** of the city, departing Kirkkokatu 11 (late June to mid-Aug Wed 6pm & Sat 1pm) as well as providing a wealth of other information about the city. The entire centre of Oulu is a free **wi-fi** zone: there's no user ID or password needed.

The market square is the pick-up point for **canoes** and **kayaks** rented through Oulusafarit, though you must ring them first on ⓣ040/556 7533. For **bike hire** in Oulu, see p.264.

Accommodation

Oulu's **hotels** are busy throughout much of the year, due to the high number of people who come here on business. It pays, therefore, to book somewhere to stay well in advance. Low-cost accommodation is, unfortunately, limited, though there are a number of respectable mid-range options.

Best Western Apollo Asemakatu 31–33 ⓣ08/374 344, ⓦwww.hotelapollo.fi. This chain hotel fortunately doesn't feel too much like one, with spacious rooms and 1970s-meets-the-future decor. Rooms with their own sauna run about €20 more. ④/⑤

🏃 **Holiday Club Oulun Eden** Holstinsalmentie 29, Nallikari Island, 5km northwest of the centre ⓣ08/884 2000, ⓦwww.holidayclub.fi. If you're after luxury, this place hits the spot – it's got a superb pool and offers spa treatments and steam rooms, and there's a fine restaurant serving tasty fish dishes. Take bus #5. ⑤

Holiday Inn Kirkkokatu 3 ⓣ08/883 9111, ⓦwww.restel.fi/holidayinn. Opposite the cathedral and Ainola Park, rooms at the world's northernmost Holiday Inn are individually decorated and some even have their own sauna and jacuzzi. Definitely worth considering at weekends when prices are fantastic value. ③/⑥

Nallikari Camping Leiritie 10, Hietasaari Island ⓣ08/5586 1350, ⓦwww.nallikari.fi. Set on an island 4km from town (bus #17) and near to a sliver of sand that locals call a beach, with a range of cabins (from €36) – some rickety and traditional, others modern and filled with amenities – as well as pitches (€11).

🏃 **Scandic Oulu** Saaristonkatu 4 ⓣ08/543 1000, ⓦwww.scandichotels.com. Opened in 2007, this central *Scandic* has quickly become one of the chain's favourite outposts. The 214 rooms are spacious, with comfortable beds, heated bathroom floors, and free access to a fitness centre and several saunas. The same building also houses a large movie-theatre complex. ④/⑥

Sokos Arina Pakkahuoneenkatu 16 ⓣ08/312 3111, ⓦwww.sokoshotels.fi. One of the city's larger hotels ranges over seven floors with 260 classy rooms right in the pedestrian centre. Although it's a chain hotel, the feel is more in keeping with a contemporary design establishment with plenty of nice Nordic minimalist touches. ④/⑥

Toppilanpukseri Satamatie 13 ⓣ08/554 3335, ⓦwww.toppilanpukseeri.fi. A small and cheery guesthouse, with a few simple beds in an old house a few kilometres north of the centre across from Toppilansaari Island; take bus #1 or #30. ①

Turisti Rautatienkatu 9 ⓣ08/563 6100, ⓦwww.hotellituristi.fi. Placed above a convenience store, this lovely, very central pile offers Oulu's cheapest year-round hotel rooms, decked out with exposed pine flooring, crisp modern furnishings, and florals and pastels. ③/④

The City

Leaving either the bus or train station, it's a fifteen-minute walk straight ahead to the *kauppatori*, an appealing place busy with commercial activity. Oulu has one of Finland's nicest market squares, dotted with red-ochre wooden shacks and store-houses, which now serve as chi-chi restaurants or knick-knack shops, and backed by the sleekly modern **library** and **theatre** which rise on stilts from the water. The library has an extensive selection of foreign-language newspapers and magazines and sometimes also stages art and craft exhibitions, which are usually worth a look. In the square, you'll also find the ornate **kauppahalli** (Mon–Thurs 8am–4pm, Fri 8am–5pm, Sat 8am–3pm), whose indoor stalls are good for cheap eats. From the market hall, Kiikelinsilta leads to a small but sandy **beach**, known as Kiikeli, from which you can swim in summer.

The city hall

At Kirkkokatu 2A, four blocks east of the square back towards the train station, the Neo-Romantic **city hall** is well worth seeking out. Built of stone in 1887 to the plans of renowned Swedish architect J.E. Stenberg, it was originally used as a luxury hotel, clubhouse and restaurant, symbolizing the affluence and cosmopolitan air of this nouveau-riche tar-rich town. A contemporary local newspaper called it "a model for the whole world. A Russian is building the floor, an Austrian is doing the painting, a German is making the bricks, an Englishman is preparing the electric lighting, the Swede is doing the masonry, the Norwegian is carving the relief and the Finn is doing all the drudgery." Today, painted in a subtle mustard-rich yellow, the building retains much of its late nineteenth-century grandeur, though the interior is now occupied by local government officials, who've become accustomed to visitors stepping in to gawp at the wall paintings and enclosed gardens that remain from the old days. While inside, venture up to the second floor, where the **Great Hall** still has its intricate Viennese ceiling paintings and voluminous chandeliers.

The cathedral

Further along Kirkkokatu, at the junction with Kajaaninkatu, the hand of German architect Carl Ludwig Engel, who designed much of Senate Square in Helsinki, is clear to see on the copper-domed, yellow-stuccoed **cathedral** (Tuomiokirkko; May–Aug daily 11am–8pm; Sept–April Mon–Fri noon–1pm; free), built in 1832 following the great fire ten years earlier. Precious little escaped the flames and even the wooden structures of the previous church, which had stood here since 1777, fell victim to the inferno. The present structure underwent a full and successful restoration in 1996. Within the cathedral is a portrait of Swedish historian Johannes Messinius, supposedly painted in 1612. Hanging above the door to the vestry, restored and slightly faded, it's believed to be the oldest surviving oil painting in Finland, despite the efforts of the Russian Cossacks, who lacerated the canvas with their sabres in 1714.

Ainola Park and the museums

Cross the small canal behind the cathedral to reach **Ainola Park**, a pleasantly wooded space which makes a nice spot for a picnic or a late evening stroll. In the park, the **Northern Ostrobothnia Museum** (Pohjois-Pohjanmaan Museo; Tues–Sun: June–Aug 10am–6pm; Sept–May 10am–5pm; €3, free on Fri) does its utmost to present regional history in an engaging manner – but fails. You can safely ignore the tedious collections of prehistory on the ground floor and head straight for the numerous tar-stained remnants and collections from Oulu's past which are moderately interesting, though, to be honest, the history of tar is never going to be an audience grabber.

If the future does more to excite your imagination than the past, head for **Tietomaa** (the Science Centre), a few minutes' walk away at Nahkatehtaankatu 6 (May, June & Aug daily 10am–6pm; July daily 10am–7pm; Sept–April Mon–Fri 10am–4pm, Sat & Sun 10am–6pm; €13; Ⓦ www.tietomaa.fi). Housed in an old power station, Finland's oldest and best science museum is a great place to explore the bounds of technological possibility, with several floors of gadgets to test mental and physical abilities as well as video games, holograms, a ski-jump simulator, a giant-screen IMAX cinema and a glass elevator that takes you to the top of a tower from which you can get unparalleled views of Oulu.

Just around the corner, **Oulu Art Museum** (Tues–Sun 10am–5pm; €3, free on Fri; Ⓦ www.ouka.fi/taidemuseo), Kasarmintie 7, is located in a renovated glue factory and a newer, postmodern glass structure. One of the largest galleries in Finland, its exhibitions change on a frequent basis, though it generally houses visiting international and Finnish contemporary art collections. There's also a particularly good café (see opposite).

The city islands

A pleasant way to pass an afternoon is to explore the four small islands which stretch north of the *kauppatori*, collectively known as **Koskikeskus**. From the market square the first island, **Linnansaari**, is reached by a footpath beginning at the northern end of Torinranta which crosses the narrow inlet of Pokkisenväylä. The island holds the somewhat inconsequential remains of Oulu's sixteenth-century **castle**, most of which was destroyed when lightning struck the gunpowder store during a particularly ferocious thunderstorm in 1793. The observatory now built on the ruins carries a summer café and a small exhibition about the castle in the basement.

Continuing along the footpath, **Raatinsaari** comes next, home to Oulu's **swimming pool** (due to reopen in autumn 2010 after renovations), followed by **Toivonsaari**, beyond which lie the rapids that drive a power station designed by Alvar Aalto, with twelve fountains added by the architect to prettify the plant.

▲ Drinking in Oulu

Pikisaari, the fourth island, is much the best to visit, reached by a short road bridge from Raatinsaari. A number of tiny seventeenth-century wooden houses here have survived Oulu's many fires, the oldest of which, Matila House, at Pikisaarentie 6, dates from 1737. It now houses the **Sailor's Home Museum** (mid-June to mid-Aug Wed–Sun 10am–4pm; €3, free on Fri), which replicates the modest home of an average sailor in the late nineteenth century. In addition, Pikisaari has become the stamping ground of local artists and trendies, with several **art galleries** and **craft shops**.

Eating, drinking and nightlife

Oulu and its outlying islands boast some delightful **cafés** for lunch or a snack. One of the best is located inside the Art Museum (closed Mon) and is known across the city for its sumptuous pastries. The *kauppahalli*, too, can be a good place to find a bite to eat. For something more substantial, you shouldn't have a problem finding a good place for a sit-down meal, as the city's **restaurants** run the full gamut from basic to upscale. With an active Finnish and international student population, Oulu's lively nightlife revolves around its numerous **pubs** and **bars**, most within a block or two of the centre; after hours, several **clubs** provide all-night entertainment.

Cafés

Antellin kahvila Kirkkokatu 17, entrance on Rotuaari. This small patisserie on the pedestrian walkway smack in the centre of town makes the best apple pies in Oulu and has its own bakery.

Café Tuomenkukka Ainola Park. Sip a coffee amid the leafy surrounds of Oulu's city park and don't leave without sampling the doughnuts for which the café is justifiably famous.

Tahtitornin kahvila Linnansaari Island. Set high up in a century-old observation tower within the castle ruins, this summer café is one of Oulu's most picturesque options for a coffee or tea. Mid-June to mid-Aug.

Terasoihtu Storehouse 24, Kauppatori. A wildly attractive place for a cuppa inside one of the old wooden storehouses in the *kauppatori*. It doesn't get much better than this for atmosphere, though there's also an outdoor terrace if you've been pipped to the post for a seat inside.

Valve Café Hallituskatu 7 @www .kulttuurivalve.fi. Cultural centre for the town's youth, with a laid-back courtyard café that's a great place to lounge about on a Sunday. Movies are shown every evening at the Oulu Film Centre in the same building.

Restaurants

Grecian Kirkkokatu 55 ☎08/311 1555. A hearty Greek-Cypriot restaurant in Oulu's backstreets whose interior is a dazzling array of whites and blues. The well-prepared food includes classics such as grilled halloumi cheese (€6.50) and

moussaka (€17.50), as well as less common dishes like lamb sausages (€8.50).

Marrakech Kirkkokatu 55 ☎08/311 9113. Next door to *Grecian*, this North African restaurant is deservedly popular with Oulu's expat community. Plenty of sensual colours and smells please the senses while you peruse the menu of Moroccan specialities, including a whole range of couscous and tajine dishes (around €16) which rarely disappoint.

New Bombay Asemakatu 39 ☎08/331 237. Perfectly located for the train station, here's a rare taste of India in the Finnish north. All your favourites are on the menu, such as chicken *masala* and *aloo gobi*, and the prices are quite reasonable: €13 for a main course.

Pannu Kauppurienkatu 12. Oulu's most popular pizzeria, with a family-restaurant feel. The menu offers standard Finnish dishes like fillet of wild boar (€19.50) but the deep-pan pizzas (€10–15) are the best in town. Usually full, even at lunchtime, but they don't take reservations.

Sokeri Jussi Pikisaarentie 2, Pikisaari Island. Set in a low-ceilinged old salt warehouse just over the bridge from the market square, and great for a traditional Finnish lunch or just a drink outside on the terrace.

Toscana Hallituskatu 35 ☎08/332 133. A grown-up Italian restaurant with a nice brick-walled interior serving delicious mains such as grilled tuna in lemon sauce (€18.90), porcini risotto (€14.50) and salmon tagliatelle (€14.50). Mercifully, there are no pizzas.

Uleåborg 1881 Aittatori 4–5 ☎08/881
1188. The pick of Oulu's restaurants, set at
the waterside in a nineteenth-century granary, and
offering mains such as scallops au gratin with
salsa verde and breast of guinea fowl with
sage-nut butter and serrano ham; it also has a
sizeable wine menu. The waterfront terrace out
back makes for excellent sunset/moonlit meals.
Reckon on around €25 for a main course.

Zakuska Hallituskatu 20 ☎08/379 369.
This authentic, mid-priced Russian place
was Oulu's first "ethnic" restaurant, and it's very
popular for its spot-on tsarist-period decor. The
extensive menu features scrumptious selections
like the "Vladimir in Sheep's Clothing", tasty chops
of garlic pork with creamy gratin potatoes and
beetroot (€22). Closed Sun.

Bars, clubs and live music

1 Bar Kauppurienkatu 5. Sleek new place with
irreverent bartenders and relaxed clientele. Oulu's
current it-bar.

45 Special Saarisonkatu 12 ⓦwww.45special
.com. A legendary rock club whose three floors
each has a different atmosphere and clientele.
Frequent live bands, and the Sunday jams are
very popular.

Jumpru Kauppurienkatu 6 ⓦwww.jumpru.fi.
Popular bar and nightclub, with a decor chock-full
of early twentieth-century charm: opulent leather
armchairs, dark wood detailing and heavy velvet
drapery. Pub food is available.

Never Grow Old Hallituskatu 13–17. Oulu's
boho, dreadlocked crowd has finally found its
home. Swinging wicker bungalow chairs, a
painted Caribbean beachscape and reggae
music all night long bring in Finns by the
camperload.

Oluthuone Leskinen Isokatu 30. With a
wide selection of European beers, this is
Oulu's rather cramped bar of choice for international students and expat workers.

St Michael's Hallituskatu 13–17. Oulu's best Irish
pub, with 240 types of whisky, plus Guinness,
Murphy's and Kilkenny on draught.

Around Oulu: Hailuoto Island

Oulu's best **beaches** are to be found on pristine **Hailuoto** (Karlö in Swedish), a
horseshoe-shaped island, about 20km wide, off the coast of Oulu and linked to the
mainland in summer by a free ferry and in winter by an official road across the ice.
The weather on Hailuoto is often sunnier than on the mainland, perfect for beach
bumming, or exploring the quiet country lanes by bicycle. Indeed, a perfect way
to get here is to hire a **bike** in Oulu from Pyörä-Suvala, Saaristonkatu 27
(☎08/375 467), and then cycle out to the ferry in Oulunsalo, a distance of around
27km. The **ferry** runs all day at roughly hourly intervals and takes half an hour to
make the crossing. Departure times (in Finnish only though easy to work out) are
posted at ⓦwww.tieliikelaitos.fi/lautat/aikataulut/hailuoto.htm.

Once ashore, orientation is easy since there's only one main road which leads to
the only village, **Kirkonkylä**, in the centre of the island, so it's simply a matter of
stopping wherever you choose and wandering down to the shore. Should you
want to **stay**, the best choice is *RantaSumppu Camping* (☎08/555 4025, ⓦwww
.luontokeskus.fi) on the island's sunny west coast in Marjaniemi, which has tent
pitches, dorm beds in the former pilot station (€20) and cabins (€85), as well as a
licensed restaurant; they also rent bikes. **Bus** #66 (ⓦwww.koskilinjat.fi) runs
between Oulu and Hailuoto; it accepts bikes, making it possible to bike one way
and bus it back.

Kemi

Travelling north, the train finally rattles into gritty **KEMI**, 110km northwest of
Oulu, a small, low-key industrial place of barely 23,000 people on the rail route
to Rovaniemi that is **Lapland**'s most southerly town and only deepwater port.
Although undistinguished, Kemi is likeable for its no-messing, northern down-to-
earth quality, as attested to by the stench of wood pulp issuing from the nearby

paper mills; locals, however, insist it's money you can smell in the air, and they're not wrong – a whole ten percent of Finland's exports pass through the harbour here. Your impressions of Kemi will, however, probably depend on when you choose to visit, because the town has a split personality: in summer the streets are all but deserted as local people escape to their summer cottages in the forest; during the dark winter months, however, things ratchet up several notches and Kemi really comes to life. From late December to late April, hundreds of people pour into town to experience one of Finland's most alluring winter attractions: a tour on the only private **icebreaker** in the world.

Arrival, information and accommodation

From the **train station**, head two blocks north of the city hall (in front of you as you exit) to Kauppakatu, where you'll find the welcoming **tourist office** at no. 16 (Mon–Fri 8/9am–4/5pm; ℡040/568 2069, ⓦwww.kemi.fi/matkailu). If you want to **stay**, and can't afford the *Snow Castle* (see below), rooms at the *Merihovi*, Keskuspuistokatu 6–8 (℡016/458 0999, ⓦwww.merihovi.fi; ❹/❺), are pure 1950s functionalism, full of plush and stylish furniture. The modern *Palomestari* (℡016/257 117, ⓦwww.finlandiahotels.fi; ❹/❺) at Valtakatu 12 and the *Cumulus* (℡016/228 31, ⓦwww.cumulus.fi; ❹/❺), Hahtisaarenkatu 3, are very similar, though the latter is less fusty.

Icebreaker tours

Built in 1960 in Helsinki, the **Sampo icebreaker**, kept 11km south of town at Ajos harbour, kept shipping lanes open in the northern Gulf of Bothnia for nearly thirty years until she became too narrow for the new generation of larger, wider freighters and was forced into retirement. Today, between late December and late April, the ship departs once daily at noon for a four-hour "**cruise**" through the icefields off Kemi, breaking ice over one metre thick (the ice is at its thickest in February and March). During the tour, which includes lunch onboard, there's also an unmissable opportunity to don a bright-orange rubber survival suit and float in the icy waters off the ship's stern – all this costs €225, but is undoubtedly worth the expense. The icing on the cake, however, is to depart by **snowmobile** from the centre of Kemi, travelling out over the ice to join the ship at its parking position out in the icefield. This seven-hour tour doesn't come cheap – upwards of €365 per person – but, if you can afford it, is a once-in-a-lifetime experience. For more information, contact Sampo Tours at Kauppakatu 16 (℡016/256 548, ⓦwww.sampotours.com).

The Snow Castle

In an attempt to lure winter tourists away from Sweden's famous *IceHotel* near Kiruna, Kemi built its first **Snow Castle** (Lumilinna in Finnish) in 1996, using snow made from frozen seawater after natural snow proved too soft for construction purposes. The venture was an instant hit and every winter since a castle carved entirely of snow and ice has been erected by Kemi's **inner harbour** at the foot of Meripuistokatu, though the exact design and appearance changes slightly from year to year depending on the architects' whim. Generally though, the castle contains a restaurant, chapel, hotel rooms and children's play area, and is open daily (10am–7pm; €7) from the end of January, when the winter chill is at its most extreme, to the middle of April. Should the inside temperature of 5°C not deter you, double **rooms** are available for €260 per night (℡016/259 502, ⓦwww.snowcastle.net); guests are guaranteed warmth, though, inside special thermal sleeping bags. Room rates include breakfast (in the warmth) and a shower and sauna in one of the nearby hotels; a set three-course menu in the **restaurant** starts at €35 and includes Lapland delicacies such as reindeer.

The rest of the town

Kemi's other attractions, if they can be called such, are subtle. From the train station on Rautatiekatu, head two blocks west on Kemi's main street, Meripuistokatu, to the **city hall** at the junction of Valtakatu. Unremarkable the building itself may be, it's nevertheless worth stepping inside to ride the lift up to the top floor for some impressive panoramic views across the northern Gulf of Bothnia from the outdoor terrace; there's also a simple café here (Mon–Fri 8am–3pm).

Continue down Meripuistokatu towards the inner harbour, keeping an eye out for the ornate **School of Music** at the junction with Sankarikatu (no. 19), a richly ornamented structure typical of the wooden architecture of the early 1900s. At the quayside, the **Gemstone Museum**, at Kauppakatu 29 (Mon–Fri 9/10am–4/5pm, plus late Jan to mid-April & mid-June to mid-Aug Sat & Sun 9am–5pm; €7), has an extraordinary collection of three thousand rare stones and jewellery items, including the crown intended for the King of Finland, the fabulously named Friedrich Karl Ludwig Konstantin von Hessen-Kassel, who reigned for a paltry two months in 1918. The museum also holds replicas of the lavish necklace of Marie Antoinette, containing no fewer than 647 diamonds, and an exact copy of Britain's imperial state crown. And be sure to check out the museum's other *pièce de résistance*: a piece of fossilized dinosaur dung on the ground floor. Next door at no. 27, Kemi's former **customs storehouse**, from 1883, contains a rather good craft shop, ideal for picking up a knick-knack or two.

Between June and September, **M/S Helena** sails from the nearby marina out into the Kemi archipelago or down to the main harbour at Ajos for a glimpse of the icebreaker. **Trips** last around three hours and cost €35, which includes a snack and coffee onboard; ring ☏ 040/038 5580 for departures times. Just beyond the marina on Rantamakasiini you'll find a pleasant sandy **beach**, perfect for catching a few rays if the weather is playing along.

Eating and drinking

Aside from the **restaurant** inside the *Snow Castle* which is open to non residents (see p.265), the best food in town is to be found at the restaurant inside the *Merihovi*, with solid Finnish mains for around €20. For good food and great views, *Puistopaviljonki*, the former courthouse overlooking the harbour at Urheilukatu 1, has a dependable lunch buffet and excellent pizzas, whilst back in town, the café at the top of the city hall tower has equally inspiring views, though only serves simple snacks. *Pizzeria Roma*, Valtakatu 12, was one of Finland's first Italian restaurants and has tasty meat mains as well as pizza and pasta dishes. Later on in the evening, *Olutravintola Kukko*, a hotel **pub** attached to the *Palomestari* with a wide range of whisky and beers, and the *Corner Inn* at Kauppakatu 10, are both popular hangouts.

Tornio

Sitting snugly at the extreme northern tip of the Gulf of Bothnia and hard on the border with Sweden, **TORNIO** (Torneå in Swedish), 24km northwest of Kemi, once made its living by selling booze to fugitives from Sweden's ruinously expensive alcohol prices. However, the difference in cost between Finland and Sweden is now much less, and the border checks against spirits smuggling between Tornio and its Swedish neighbour, **Haparanda**, are long gone. Instead, the flow of traffic today is in the opposite direction as flat-pack-loving Finns flood over the border to shop at the world's most northerly outlet of **IKEA**, opened in 2006. The decision to locate at such a strategic position in northern Scandinavia has paid dividends for the Swedish furniture giant: its store now regularly attracts shoppers from as far afield as Tromsø in Norway and Murmansk in Russia, and has led to a veritable commercial boom for both Haparanda and Tornio. A new shopping centre known as **Rajalla/På Gränsen** (literally "on the border") opened on the Finnish side of the frontier in 2008 and construction is now well underway to extend the retail area across into Sweden and build a conjoining market square right on the border line itself.

Arrival, information and accommodation

Buses from Kemi terminate at the bus station on the northern edge of the town centre. Though there is a train station, Tornio Itäinen, services are so infrequent as to be of little use. The friendly, helpful **tourist office** is located a ten-minute walk away in the Green Line Centre at Pakkahuoneenkatu 1 by the Swedish border (June–Aug Mon–Fri 8am–8pm, Sat & Sun 10am–6pm; Sept–May Mon–Fri 9am–6pm; ☏016/432 733, ⓦwww.haparandatornio.com).

In keeping with Tornio's modest proportions, there's not a whole load of **accommodation** available, though demand for beds remains pretty low throughout the year.

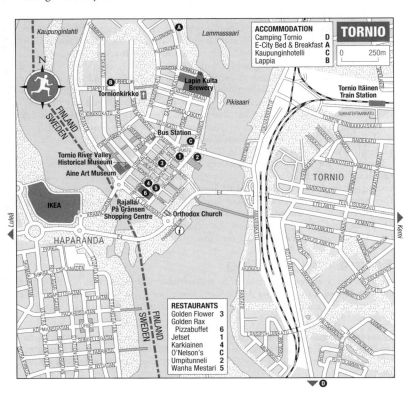

Camping Tornio Matkailijantie ☎016/445 945,
Ⓦ www.campingtornio.com. Located 2.5km from
the town centre and open mid-May to Aug with
fifteen cottages (from €36) as well as pitches (€10).
E-City Bed & Breakfast Saarenpäänkatu 39
Ⓦ www.ecitybedandbreakfast.com. A homely,
family-run establishment with twelve rooms, four
with private facilities. Free wireless internet. ❸
Kaupunginhotelli Itäranta 4 ☎016/433 11,
Ⓦ www.tornionkaupunginhotelli.fi. Serving the city

for over seventy years, this is the largest hotel in
town with around 100 rooms, recently renovated in
an agreeable, modern Nordic designer-style. In
addition, there's a restaurant, bar, nightclub, three
saunas and a swimming pool. ❹/❻
Lappia Urheilukatu 6 ☎010/192 049. This
vocational school has sparkling doubles with
private bath, available from June to early Aug.
You must ring ahead during the week to
reserve. ❶

The Town

Having had your fill of Tornio's newly expanded retail offerings, set off in search of
the town's other attractions, notably the ornate, wooden **Orthodox church** at
Lukiokatu 1, close to the Finnish customs station. Surrounded by a low wooden
fence and swaying birch tress, its Oriental onion domes and rooftop crosses sit in
rude juxtaposition to the brash shopping emporium across the road. Commissioned
by Tsar Alexander I, the present church dates from 1884 and is open for viewing in
summer only (June–Aug Tues–Sat 10am–6pm). The town's other wooden church,
the **Tornionkirkko** (late May to Aug Mon–Fri 9am–5pm, Sat & Sun 9.30–6pm)
predates its Orthodox counterpart by two centuries and is widely regarded as one of
the most beautiful churches in Finland because of its eye-pleasing symmetry; it's
located just beyond the bus station at the junction of Seminaarinkatu and Vapaudenkatu, and has impressive views all around from the top of the **observation tower**
(June to mid-Aug Mon–Fri 10am–4pm; €1) which is accessed by a rather rickety lift.

Trace your steps back to the bus station, follow Torikatu back down towards the
shopping centre and you'll soon reach the **Aine Art Museum** (Aineen Taidemuseo; Tues–Thurs 11am–6pm, Fri–Sun 11am–3pm; €4), inside the library at
Torikatu 2. The museum was founded by local couple Eila and Veli Aine and
showcases contemporary northern Finnish art alongside occasional exhibitions of
international artists of mild renown. Close by, the **Tornio River Valley Historical Museum** (Tornionlaakson Maakuntamuseo; Tues–Fri 11am–5pm, Sat & Sun
11am–3pm; €4), near the corner of Torikatu and Keskikatu, contains a small but
well-organized display on the region's past, with an interesting section on the role
played by Finnish Lapland in World War II.

Elsewhere, the **Lapin Kulta brewery**, Finland's largest, runs interesting free
one-hour tours of its premises at Lapinkullankatu 1, which includes sample
tastings of the brew (☎020/717 151; June & July Tues & Thurs 1pm). Although
the brewery was established in 1873 as plain Torneå Bryggeri, Finnish copyright
law prevented the use of the considerably catchier Lapin Kulta name (literally
"Lapland gold") until 1963 when the concern was obliged to acquire a gold-
mining company operating under the same name.

Eating and drinking

A dominant feature of Tornio is its **restaurants** and **bars**, which still attract
countless Swedes from across the border, cheesed off with Haparanda's miserable
offerings. All these places are close by one another in the town centre so there's
never far to go if you fancy a beer after dinner.

Golden Flower Eliaksenkatu 8. A decent Chinese
place that cooks up great seafood dishes – try the
spicy curried jumbo shrimp (€12.75). There's a
filling lunch buffet, too.

Golden Rax Pizzabuffet Länsiranta 10. A popular
stop for the as-much-as-you-can-eat pizza buffet
which also includes salad, chicken wings and
lasagna. The quality is low, but so, too, is the price.

Jetset Satamakatu 3. A small sports-bar, attracting the few jetsetters who haven't yet boarded the fast boat out of town.

Karkiainen Länsiranta 9. A trendy café handily located opposite the shopping centre that's good for a wide range of coffees, as well as fresh breads and cakes.

O'Nelsons Itäranta 4. Attached to the *Kaupunginhotelli*, this fresh and airy bar with its black-marble bar is the latest addition to Tornio's drinking scene.

Umpitunneli Hallituskatu 15. This unusually named restaurant-cum-bar-cum-disco boasts a nice riverside location and one of the largest outdoor terraces in the country. On the menu there's a range of fried and grilled meats and fish, including salmon and chicken, for around €15. A half litre of Lapin Kulta is €4.

Wanha Mestari Hallituskatu 5. One of Tornio's busiest (and most drunken) pubs, which gets quite crowded in the evenings: a pub crawl around Tornio always calls in here.

Travel details

Trains

Kemi to: Oulu (6 daily; 1hr); Rovaniemi (6 daily; 1hr 30min).

Kokkola to: Oulu (9 daily; 1hr 40min); Pännäinen (9 daily; 20min); Rovaniemi (3 daily; 5hr 30min).

Oulu to: Helsinki (5 daily; 6–9hr); Kajaani (5 daily; 2hr 10min); Kemi (6 daily; 1hr); Kokkola (9 daily; 1hr 40min); Rovaniemi (6 daily; 2hr 20min); Tampere (10 daily; 4hr 30min).

Vaasa to: Helsinki (via Seinäjoki; 10 daily; 4hr–4hr 30min); Oulu (via Seinäjoki; 5–7 daily; 4hr 55min–6hr 10min); Pännäinen (via Seinäjoki; 5 daily; 2hr); Tampere (9–10 daily; 2hr 30min).

Ylivieska to: Iisalmi (for Kajaani and Kuopio; 2 daily; 1hr 30min); Kokkola (9 daily; 1hr); Oulu (9 daily; 1hr).

Buses

Jakobstad to: Kokkola (5–13 daily; 35–55min); Vaasa (13 daily; 1hr 35min).

Kalajoki to: Oulu (8 daily; 2hr); Ylivieska (10 daily; 40min).

Kokkola to: Kalajoki (every 2hr; 1hr 30min).

Kristinestad to: Vaasa (10 daily; 1hr 40min).

Pännäinen to: Jakobstad (16 daily; 15min).

Vaasa to: Pori (7–8 daily; 2hr 45min–5hr 15min); Turku (10–13 daily; 5–8hr).

Ferries to Sweden

Vaasa to: Umeå (June & July 1 daily; Aug–May 5–6 weekly; 4hr).

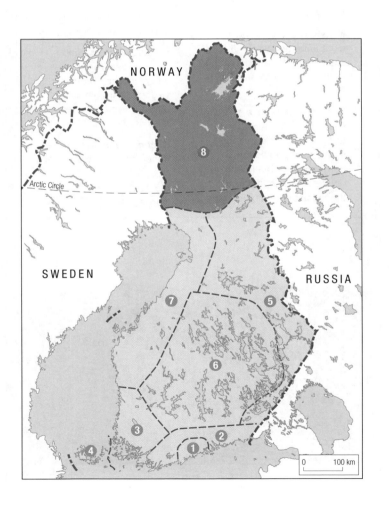

8

Finnish Lapland

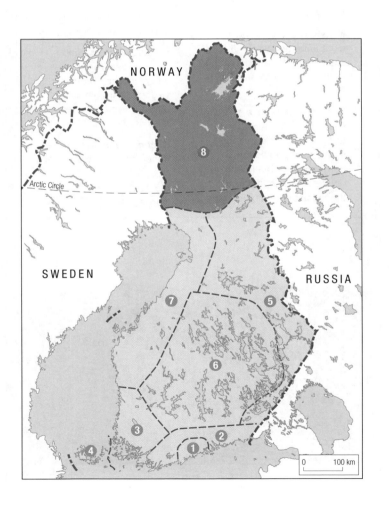

NORWAY

Arctic Circle

SWEDEN

RUSSIA

8

7

5

6

3

2

1

4

0   100 km

CHAPTER 8

Highlights

* **The Arctic Circle** Cross the Arctic Circle on a snowmobile safari or even by reindeer, but don't forget to visit Santa Claus and beat the Christmas rush. See p.279

* **Kakslauttanen** Spend a night snug and warm in a log cabin – or why not brave the Arctic chill in a glass igloo. See p.286

* **Inari** Visit Siida, one of Finland's best museums, to mug up on the country's indigenous population, before getting the lowdown on reindeer husbandry at the fascinating reindeer farm

just outside town. See p.289 & p.290

* **Levi** Hit the slopes before enjoying the fun après-ski scene – renowned across Finland – at the country's leading ski resort. See p.294

* **Husky safari, Muonio** Scud across frozen lakes and discover the Lapland wilderness from a sledge pulled by your own team of huskies. See p.297

* **Hiking, Kilpisjärvi** Tackle the peaks around this pretty mountain village or hike out to the border with Sweden and Norway. See p.299

▲ Hiking in Lapland

8

Finnish Lapland

One of Europe's last great wilderness areas, **FINNISH LAPLAND** is very different to the rest of the country. This vast province at the very tip of the European continent is equal in size to the whole of Portugal or the US state of Kentucky, yet barely four percent of Finland's population lives here. Instead of people, you'll find cinemascope panoramas of rounded hills and immense swathes of coniferous forest, punctuated only by steely lakes, impenetrable areas of marshland and tracts of desolate upland rising high above the treeline. Towns and villages are few and far between and often so small that you'll miss them if you blink on the way through. Indeed, if you're looking for architectural gems in this part of the country, you'll leave sadly disappointed, since the majority of buildings in Finnish Lapland were burnt to the ground by retreating German forces at the end of World War II. Rebuilding was fast though uninspired, and consequently, the region's charm is to be found in its glorious natural landscapes rather than its towns which tend to be apologetic, self-effacing types of places. To fully understand what Lapland is really all about, you should take the trouble to do some hiking.

The whole region is home to several thousand indigenous **Sámi** (for more on whom, see the box on p.291), who have lived in harmony with this special, often harsh environment for millennia. Discovering their culture and way of life can be as exciting as experiencing the Arctic north itself. Despite serious threats from a number of sources, including modernization, tourism and – most dramatically – the fallout from Chernobyl, a fair number of Sámi still herd their reindeer and maintain their traditions in these uncompromising latitudes.

Most visitors make a beeline for **Rovaniemi**, the undisputed capital of Finnish Lapland and home to the famous **Santa Claus Village**, which lures families with small children from across Europe every winter. However, this flashy, commercial town is totally unrepresentative of the rest of the province and once you've handed your Christmas present list to Santa it's a good idea to head out of town. From Rovaniemi, two main roads lead north, though it's the Arctic Highway, **Route 4/E75**, which sees most traffic and functions as the province's main artery. This route services the **northeast**, linking the isolated communities of Sodankylä, Ivalo, Inari and Utsjoki. The most appealing destination is **Inari**, a remote village in the far north with a superb Sámi museum, remote wilderness church and boat trips on the local lake. At the very top of Finland, minuscule **Utsjoki** is hard to beat for splendid isolation, complete with views into Norway across the mighty Tenojoki River. If you don't want to venture so far north, **Sodankylä** is worth a quick look for its old wooden church and interesting Sámi art museum; it's also the only place to cut across to the region's other main road, **Route 79/E8**, which serves the **northwest**. In

8

this corner of the province, the places to seek out are the ski resort at **Levi**, near Kittilä; the dog-sledding centre at Harriniva, near **Muonio**; and far-flung **Kilpisjärvi**, right on the border with Norway, where some superlative hiking trails, including a route to the geographical point where Finland, Sweden and Norway all meet, await discovery.

Beyond Kemijärvi, **transport** within Finnish Lapland is by bus; most long-distance routes radiate from Rovaniemi and follow the two main roads north, bound for Sodankylä/Inari/Utsjoki and Kittilä/Muonio/Kilpisjärvi respectively. The only way to cross from one trunk route to the other, without first backtracking to Rovaniemi, is between Sodankylä and Kittilä.

The Arctic Circle and around

At just over 66° north, the **Arctic Circle** is arguably Finland's most magical destination. For children and adults alike, there's an elemental sense of satisfaction in crossing this imaginary line, which marks the southernmost extremity of the midnight sun, and, conversely the polar night, the period in winter when the sun never rises above the horizon; on the Arctic Circle, each phenomenon can be observed one day per year. Due to the tilt of the earth, the Arctic Circle is not static and is currently moving 15m north every year which means that the marker posts denoting the circle are not exact.

Although the Arctic Circle streaks across the entire width of Finnish Lapland, it is most readily accessible from **Rovaniemi**, where it also supports the **Santa Claus Village**. No matter what time of year you choose to visit this Christmas theme park, the big fat man in the red cape is always here – just like the adjacent souvenir and factory shops, who're also vying for your cash. There are plenty of other diversions here however, including **husky and reindeer safaris**. Whereas Rovaniemi is a brash sort of a place, full of restaurants, bars and shopping opportunities, **Kemijärvi**, 85km to the east, couldn't be more different. A quiet lakeside town at the end of the train line, it can make a good alternative base once the bright lights of its western neighbour begin to pale. However, it's shy and retiring **Salla**, another 64km to the east, where rural charms finally win over; there's good skiing and hiking around here, plus a bus connection to the Russian town of **Kandalaksha** (Kantalahti in Finnish), 200km away on the White Sea.

Rovaniemi and around

Easily accessible by train or bus, **ROVANIEMI** is touted as the capital of Lapland. Just south of the Arctic Circle it may be, but anyone arriving with an expectation of sleighs and reindeer will be disappointed: Rovaniemi's soulless administrative buildings, busy shopping streets and *McDonald's* (the most northerly in the world) are a far cry from the surrounding rural hinterland. Like many places in Finnish Lapland, the elegant wooden houses of old Rovaniemi

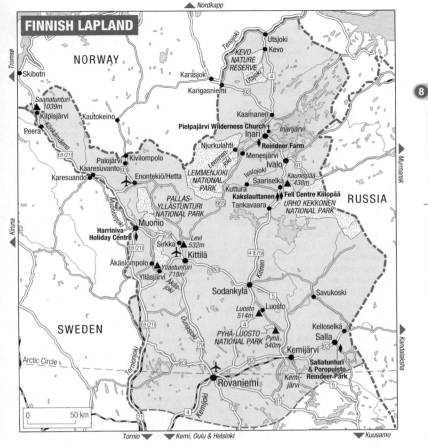
were razed to the ground by departing Germans at the close of World War II, and the town was completely rebuilt during the late 1940s. Alvar Aalto's bold but impractical design has the roads forming the shape of reindeer antlers, though the centre of town is based on a familiar grid pattern. Although Rovaniemi can be quite dismal in summer, with its uniform greyish-white buildings and an unnerving newness to everything, during the cold months the city really comes into its own, with the neutral colour of the buildings working in perfect harmony with the snow and ice that cover the streets for almost six months of the year. During the winter, the town plays host to busloads of nervous southern Europeans swathed from head to toe in the latest cold-weather gear, heading out on snowmobile safaris (see p.278) or simply stumbling around the icy streets as proof that they have endured an Arctic winter.

Arrival and information

Rovaniemi's **bus and train stations** are just a couple of minutes' walk from each other, located on the western edge of the city centre. From either terminus, the best route into town is to take the subway under Valtatie (Route 4/E75) and to walk down Hallituskatu. From the **airport**, 10km northeast of the city, a shuttle bus (€5) meets scheduled arrivals and runs into town, dropping off at the main hotels. The very organized and helpful **tourist office** (June–Aug Mon–Fri 9am–6pm, Sat & Sun 9am–1pm; Sept–May Mon–Fri 9am–6pm; ☎016/346 270, ⓦ www.visitrovaniemi.fi), Maakuntakatu 29–31, is a tremendous source of local information and has free wireless internet access.

Accommodation

Budget accommodation in Rovaniemi is not hard to find as the city has several good **guesthouses** – but booking ahead, especially around midsummer and Christmas, is recommended.

Aakenus Koskikatu 47 ☎016/342 2051, ⓦ www .hotelliaakenus.net. A new and welcome addition to the Rovaniemi scene. Rooms at this homely, family-run place are tastefully decorated and excellent value for money. All are en-suite and have free wireless internet access. ❸

Borealis Asemieskatu 1 ☎016/342 0130, ⓦ guesthouseborealis.com. Great-value, family-run guesthouse with cheery en-suite rooms, close to the train station and very popular with InterRailers. The price includes breakfast and the staff are very knowledgeable about local goings-on. ❷

City Pekankatu 9 ☎016/330 0111, ⓦ www .cityhotel.fi. Although the modern, plainly decorated rooms are a little on the small side, the combination of city-centre location and a great in-house restaurant is unbeatable; the *Monte Rosa* (see p.279) also doubles as the hotel's breakfast room. ❻

Clarion Santa Claus Korkalonkatu 49 ☎016/321 321, ⓦ www.hotelsantaclaus.fi. If you can get over the name, this hotel is one of the city's best places to stay, with well-appointed rooms and great deals in the summer. The very chic Santa Claus Suite has its own sauna, though at €490 the bragging rights may not be worth it. ❹

Niemeläntalo Pappilantie 75A ☎0400/791 560, ⓦ www.niemelantalo.fi. A rare

opportunity in Lapland to stay in an atmospheric old timber house from the 1800s; there's access to the kitchen, too. Two kilometres south of the centre; take bus #4 or #14. Breakfast is an extra €6. ❷

Ounaskoski Camping Jäämerentie 1 ☎016/345 304. The city's only camping facility, located on the far bank of the Ounasjoki River; facilities include a kiosk, café and sauna. Open late May to Aug.

Outa Ukkoherrantie 16 ☎016/312 474, ⓦ www .guesthouseouta.com. A long-established if rather eccentrically run guesthouse on a very quiet street a block from the tourist office: the seven rooms here are comfy and cosy and feature microwaves, TVs and electric kettles. Washing machine also on the premises. ❸

Rudolph Koskikatu 41. The rooms at Rovaniemi's all-year youth hostel are spacious, spotless and devoid of any soul, but you're nearly always guaranteed one to yourself. There is no reception here so you book via the *Clarion Santa Claus* hotel (see opposite). Dorms beds are €30, singles ❷, doubles ❸.

Sokos Vaakuna Koskikatu 4 ☎020/123 4695, ⓦ www.sokoshotels.fi. The modern rooms here are saturated with designer throughout, and overall this is the swankiest hotel in town. Sits close to the Ounasjoki River. ❹/❺

The City

If you have any interest in Lapland culture, make your first call to the fascinating **Arktikum**, built on the banks of the Ounasjoki River at Kantatie 74 (mid-Jan to mid-June & mid-Aug to Sept Tues–Sun 10am–6pm, plus Mon in Aug; mid-June to mid-Aug daily 9am–7pm; Oct–Nov Tues–Sun 10am–5pm; Dec to mid-Jan daily 10am–6pm; €12; ⓦ www.arktikum.fi). Its great arched atrium emerges from the ground like a U-boat, with almost all the exhibition areas submerged beneath banks of stone. The lower level of the complex contains the **Provincial Museum of Lapland** which canters through a century or so of local history. There are pictures of the horrific devastation caused by German soldiers in 1944, when they were forced to retreat, burning every building in sight – look out for the two scale models from 1939 and 1944

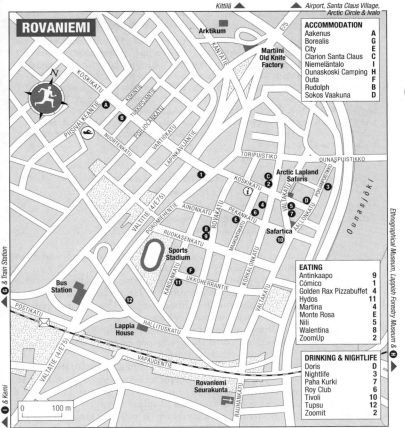

ROVANIEMI

Kittilä

Airport, Santa Claus Village, Arctic Circle & Ivalo

Arktikum

Martiini Old Knife Factory

ACCOMMODATION

Aakenus	A
Borealis	G
City	E
Clarion Santa Claus	C
Niemeläntalo	I
Ounaskoski Camping	H
Outa	F
Rudolph	B
Sokos Vaakuna	D

& Train Station

Bus Station

Sports Stadium

Lappia House

Rovaniemi Seurakunta

& Kemi

0   100 m

Arctic Lapland Safaris

Safartica

Ethnographical Museum, Lappish Forestry Museum & ▲

Ounasjoki

EATING

Antinkaapo	9
Cómico	1
Golden Rax Pizzabuffet	4
Hydos	11
Martina	4
Monte Rosa	E
Nili	5
Walentina	8
ZoomUp	2

DRINKING & NIGHTLIFE

Doris	D
Nightlife	3
Paha Kurki	7
Roy Club	6
Tivoli	10
Tupsu	12
Zoomit	2

showing the city before and after, and be sure to take in the poignant video footage that compares the heady life in Rovaniemi before the war, when loggers and lumberjacks would pour into the city's hotels and bars at weekends, with the sharply contrasting scenes of total devastation just a couple of years later – the people of Lapland have clearly still not forgiven the Germans for what happened. Elsewhere in the hall there's a rather disappointing section dedicated to local nature, containing stuffed examples of bear, elk and reindeer. Upstairs, the recently overhauled **Arctic Centre** provides a varied insight into the history and present-day lives of the peoples of the Arctic and includes a stylized show of the northern lights; lie down on the mattresses on the floor and gaze up at the computer-generated images of animals sweeping across the simulated night sky.

Opposite the Arktikum is the **Marttiini Old Knife Factory** (Mon–Fri 10am–6pm, Sat 10am–2pm, plus Sun noon–4pm in summer; ⓦwww.marttiini .fi), Vartiokatu 32. In the kingdom of the sharp edge, the Marttiini multipurpose knife reigns supreme and traces its history back to 1928. In addition to perusing the knives for sale (from €20 plus seconds at knockdown prices), check out the

Activities around Rovaniemi

Due to the massive influx of Santa-seeking visitors in winter, Rovaniemi has learnt to gear itself up to the needs of tourists and now provides a wide range of outdoor activities that are the envy of many other towns in the region. In winter, **snowmobile tours** and **husky safaris** are particularly popular, though there's also the possibility to visit a local **reindeer farm**. In summer, the emphasis shifts to the water with boat and fishing excursions on offer. In general, you should reckon on around €110 for a snowmobile trip from Rovaniemi to the Santa Claus Village; €120 for a husky safari and €105 for a tour by reindeer; most trips last around 3hr. The bewildering range of activities varies from year to year and prices change accordingly but the latest details are always available online.

Activity operators

Arctic Lapland Safaris Koskikatu 6 ☏020/786 8700, ⓦwww.arcticsafaris.fi.

Enonvene Napapiirintie 20 ☏016/356 0190, ⓦwww.enonvene.com.

Eräsetti Safaris Santa Claus Village ☏016/362 811, ⓦwww.erasetti.fi.

Safartica Valtakatu 20 ☏016/311 485, ⓦwww.safartica.com.

---

unexpectedly interesting video which recounts the company's history and the Finnish obsession with knives, the key to survival in the forest.

Back in the town centre, **Lappia House**, an Aalto-designed building from 1965 a short distance from the bus and train stations at Hallituskatu 11, contains a theatre and concert hall, plus an excellent **library** (Mon–Thurs 11am–8pm, Fri 11am–5pm, Sat 11am–4pm) with several free internet terminals. There's also a **Lapland Department** (turn immediately left as you enter the building), housing a staggering hoard of books, magazines and newspaper articles in many languages covering every conceivable Sámi-related subject.

Other points of interest in Rovaniemi are few. At Rauhankatu 70, **Rovaniemi Seurakunta** (daily 9am–4pm), the parish church, repays a peek on account of its jumbo-sized altar fresco, *Fountain of Life* by Lennart Segerstråle, an odd work that pitches the struggle between good and evil into a Lapland setting. If you're here in winter, ask about the concerts that are staged here. If you have more time to kill consider visiting the **Ethnographical Museum** in Pöykkölä (June–Aug Tues–Sun noon–6pm; €3), 3km southeast of town and accessible by bus #6. It's a collection of farm buildings that belonged to the Pöykkölä family between 1640 and 1910, and forms part of a potpourri of objects pertaining to reindeer husbandry, salmon fishing and rural life in general.

Eating

While Rovaniemi has a few pleasant **cafés**, its opportunities for fine or exotic dining leave a lot to be desired – though dishes featuring reindeer are very easy to find. Most numerous are the standard kebab and pizza joints around Koskikatu, nearly all of which offer late-night snacks to bar-hoppers.

Antinkaapo Rovakatu 13. Rovaniemi's best café, serving a lavish range of delicious cakes and butter cookies. Opens at 7.30am during the week. Closed Sun.

Cómico Koskikatu 25. Jumping on the Tex-Mex bandwagon, this place is a big hit with younger locals, and the burritos (€9.90), fajitas (€14.80)

and greasy Cajun *gambas* (€7.90) are all quite tasty. In the evenings it turns into a popular place for a drink, with student bands occasionally taking to the stage.

Golden Rax Pizzabuffet Koskikatu 11. The eat-as-much-as-you-can pizza buffet, complete with salad bar for €8.70, really draws the crowds and it's consistently one of the busiest places in town. The quality of the food isn't great, but at prices like this it's hard to complain.

Hydos Kansankatu 10. The interior of this Turkish restaurant is done up in a mixture of 1980s kitsch and Ottoman-style chintz, making it one of the more eccentric local finds. The €7 lunch specials are popular with local workers and dinners are well priced, too. Don't mistake the entrance with that of the erotic showbar immediately next door.

Martina Koskikatu 11. Pizza and pasta dishes from €10.90, salads from €7 and steaks around €18 at this predictable chain restaurant, though the decor here is a bit warmer than most places in town.

Monte Rosa Pekankatu 9. Rovaniemi's best Italian restaurant serves a few Finnish dishes, too. The interior is supposed to be modelled on the *Little House on the Prairie* – a similarity lost on most diners. Excellent pan pizzas for €10.90, sautéed reindeer for €19.90, and pasta dishes at

€12.80. The plate of Lappish antipasti including local cheese, salted reindeer, whitefish roe and salmon and mushroom pie (€11.60) is excellent.

Nili Valtakatu 20 ☎0400/369 669. If you haven't yet tried reindeer or any other Lappish specialities, this is a great place to take the plunge. Prices are a tad high but the food is excellent, and you're likely to find everything from bear tenderloin (€52.30) and sautéed reindeer (€18.90) to snowgrouse breast (€38.50) and chargrilled Inari trout (€19.60). The decor is equally appealing – plenty of Sámi handicrafts and even reindeer leather furniture. Evenings only from 5pm.

Walentina Rovakatu 21. Very good coffee, great sticky buns and a full collection of deliciously tooth-rotting pastries and sweets. Closed Sun.

ZoomUp Koskikatu 10. Venetian blinds and fake stone adorn this new trendy bistro above the *Zoomit* bar, serving burgers, salads and pasta dishes from €13.50.

Drinking and nightlife

With a sizeable university population during term-time and thousands of tourists visiting throughout the year, Rovaniemi offers a lively nightlife for every school of libation. The most popular places for a **drink** are just off the pedestrian walkway of Koskikatu, and there are several places for a **dance**, some set within the hotels.

Doris *Sokos Vaakuna*, Koskikatu 4. Set in the hotel basement, this is the most popular club in town and as such gets away with charging a €5–10 cover. The young and beautiful of Lapland come to dance, drink and play the €1 minimum casino tables at the back.

Nightlife *Hotel Rantasipi Pohjanhovi*, Pohjanpuis-tikko 2. Three bars in one, aimed at a mature crowd. Upstairs is a meat-and-potatoes Finnish bar that at times has the vague sense of a forty-something pick-up joint; at the back, there's a relaxed dance-floor, and downstairs an ever-popular karaoke bar.

Paha Kurki Koskikatu 5. Small, dark, dingy and extremely popular rock club that fills up with hardcore hipsters from all over the Arctic.

Roy Club Maakuntakatu 24. A somewhat relaxed atmosphere pervades upstairs, while downstairs

the floor is beer-sticky and the DJs have a thing for the dry-ice button. Usually less drunken than most other places.

Tivoli Valtakatu 19. Great, unpretentious bar popular with students and other locals not into the disco scene. Closed Sun–Tues.

Tupsu Hallituskatu 24. This favourite local hangout is as authentic a Finnish bar as you'll probably find. Because it's a bit out of the way near the bus station, the atmosphere is somewhat tranquil though it sometimes puts on impromptu theatre performances. Be especially wary, though, of the all-weekend karaoke fetes.

Zoomit Koskikatu 10. Popular chrome- and glass-fronted place often stuffed with trendy young things from the Lapland university.

The Arctic Circle and Santa Claus Village

Most people are lured to Rovaniemi solely for the thrill of crossing the **Arctic Circle** (*napapiiri* in Finnish). While the "Circle" itself doesn't remain constant, slipping northwards every year, its man-made markers do – 8km north of town along Route 4 bang in front of the Santa Claus Village and generally heralded by a crowd of visitors taking photographs of each other with one foot either side of the line. The first sign marking the Arctic Circle was erected in the 1920s, though it wasn't until the visit here in 1950 by former American First Lady, Eleanor Roosevelt, that local tourist bosses realized the money-spinning potential of the line and came up with the idea of a Santa Claus Village, which began to take shape a decade later. Bus #8 goes to the Circle from the train station every hour (€6.40 return), and also calls at several stops in town including those on Hallituskatu and Valtakatu.

On the Circle and served by the same bus, the **Santa Claus Village** (daily: June & Aug 9am–6pm; July & Dec 9am–7pm; rest of the year 10am–5pm; free; Ⓦ www.santaclausvillage.info) is a gaggle of around a dozen timber buildings. Considering its tourist pitch, the main structure – a very large log cabin – is quite within the bounds of decency: two floors of souvenir shops selling everything from T-shirts and mugs to cuddly reindeer and bottle openers made of reindeer horn. There's also a useful **tourist information office** (same hours; ☎016/356 2096, Ⓦ www.arcticcircle-information.fi) here by the main entrance. Behind this building, the Santa Claus office is the place to meet Father Christmas (he's been here all year round since 1985) and you can leave your name for a Christmas letter from Santa (€7) in the adjacent post office. Beyond here, the Christmas House contains an eminently missable exhibition about Christmas traditions in various parts of the world (daily 8am–6pm; €5), whereas the two neighbouring buildings are factory outlets for glass and crockery manufacturers, Iitala, Arabia and Marimekko, where prices are generally less than in Rovaniemi itself.

Ice Park Finland (Dec to mid-March daily noon–5pm; Ⓦ www.iceparkfinland .fi), next to the village, is the latest attraction on the Arctic Circle: a theme park dedicated to ice which contains a series of buildings, sculptures, stage and ice rink. Once the winter is over and temperatures start to rise, all the structures will melt and be rebuilt the following season. The park is still in its infancy but organizers claim it will become a showcase for ice construction techniques.

Kemijärvi and around

The railway reached **KEMIJÄRVI**, the northernmost station on the Finnish train network with daily services, in the 1930s and still today transports most foreign visitors here, keen to see what lies at the end of the ribbon of iron that stretches all the way up from Helsinki. In addition to the direct train to and from the capital, the rail line has been used for decades to transport logs from the surrounding forests down to the port in Kemi for export, though the town now faces an uncertain future following the recent closure of its last functioning timber factory. Nevertheless, Kemijärvi remains a pleasant, if low-key, lakeside town that offers welcome respite from the commercialism and Santa Claus mania that grips Rovaniemi during the winter months. It also provides easy access to the border village of **Salla**, known for its hiking and skiing opportunities and its **bus link to Russia**.

The centre of town, modest in the extreme, is composed of a handful of short, stubby streets, and lies within five minutes' walk of the train station. Although there are no specific sights in town, keep your eyes peeled for the unusual **wooden sculptures** dotted around the place which are leftovers from the annual **sculpture week** which takes place just after the midsummer holiday attracting woodcarvers from across the world who work alfresco on their submissions. Having wandered around the centre, the best bet is to get out onto **Lake Kemijärvi**, a vast tooth-shaped body of water, actually part of the Kemijoki River, beautifully surrounded by low hills and deep evergreen forest. M/S *Ahti* operates a four-hour Arctic Circle-crossing trip (June–Sept; days vary; €20), departing from the quay beside the church on Sallantie. The *Mestarin Kievari* hotel (see opposite) can book these tours and also rents **rowing boats** for €10 for four hours.

Practicalities

From the **train station** on Asematie, turn left and walk along the main Rovaniementie towards the town, before turning right into Luusantie to reach the centre. **Buses** use the car park behind the main **hotel**, *Mestarin Kievari* (℡016/320 700, Ⓦwww.mestarinkievari.fi; ❹/❺) at Kirkkokatu 9, which has functional, plainly decorated rooms overlooking the lake in a building dating from 1889. Close by, at Vapaudenkatu 4, *Hotelli Kemijärvi* (℡016/458 2200, Ⓦwww.hotellikemijarvi .com; ❹) is the other central option though its rooms are more dated and dowdy. For **campers**, there's the lakeside *Heitaniemi Camping* (℡016/813 640) at Hietaniemenkatu, whilst next door, *Lohen Lomakeskus* (℡040/581 2007, Ⓦwww.lohen lomakeskus.fi), Lohelenkatu 1, has simple **youth hostel** double rooms (❷) and **cabins** (from €80); both are located between the centre and the train station.

For **eating and drinking**, it's hard to beat the restaurant in the *Mestarin Kievari* which has an excellent lunch buffet as well as local specialities such as Arctic char. Otherwise, try the *Wanha Mestari* pub at Jaakonkatu 4, which also serves bar meals. Kemijärvi is known as the karaoke capital of Finland and most locals love to belt out the hits in the town's drinking holes after a beer or six; the *Mestarin Kievari* is the only place to escape the crooning.

Salla and trips to Russia

SALLA, a peaceful village 64km east of Kemijärvi, has paid the ultimate price for Russia's security paranoia. In 1940, the Peace Treaty of Moscow obliged the Finns to extend the train line east of Kemijärvi to the border in order to provide the Soviets with direct rail access, across Finnish territory, from the White Sea to the Gulf of Bothnia. The line, however, was blown up during the final stages of World War II by retreating German forces who also destroyed eighty percent of Salla's houses. Then, in 1945, Finland was forced to cede half of the Salla municipality to the Soviet Union following claims by Moscow that the existing Finnish border ran too close to the (militarily sensitive) Leningrad–Murmansk rail line; at one point the border came to within 80km of the Soviet rail network. As a result, eight settlements (now collectively known as Old Salla, or Vanha Salla in Finnish) were reluctantly handed over to the Soviet Union and a new centre was created just over 20km west of the new borderline. The former village of Märkäjärvi changed its name to Salla and life started all over again. As part of the postwar reconstruction programme, the railway line was relaid, and, until the late 1960s, passenger services operated to Salla. Although it's not presently possible to take the train to Salla, or indeed on to Russian **Kandalaksha** (75km of track is now missing on the Russian side of the border), there are plans to reopen the route as part of ongoing cross-border initiatives to increase links between Finland and Russia. For the time being, buses run twice weekly (Mon & Thurs) across the Russian border east of Kelloselkä, passing the handful of dilapidated villages in Old Salla that were Finnish property before World War II en route for Kandalaksha; timetables are at Ⓦwww.goldline.fi. You'll need to have organized your visa beforehand.

Activities around Salla

Although there's little to hold your attention in Salla itself, the surrounding area is well worth exploring. The little-known 35-kilometre **Six Fells Hiking Route**, more commonly known by its tongue-twisting Finnish name Kuudentunturinkevelyreitti and actually part of the UKK trail, begins 6km south of Salla village at the *Sallan Maja* roadside café, and includes some stiff climbs up the sides of spruce-covered fells, with spectacular views from their bare summits.

Varpulahti Lake, 4km south of Niemelä, on the road between Salla and Kuusamo (Route 950), marks the other end of the trail.

Four kilometres south of *Sallan Maja*, the compact ski resort of **Sallatunturi** at the foot of the twin peaks of Sallan Pyhätunturit (477m) has four downhill slopes as well as a good cross-country network of trails; there's also a decent sports centre and swimming pool here. Incidentally, the much higher mountain you can see to the east in the distance is the original Sallatunturi (658m), which was separated from its smaller siblings when the border was shifted westwards. The **Poropuisto Reindeer Park** (daily 9am–4pm; closed May, Oct & Nov; €7.50), a further 4km south of the ski resort on the Kuusamo road at Hautajärventie 111, makes another good stop for its herd of around 35 reindeer. It's possible to get relatively close to

Hiking in Finnish Lapland

The best way to experience Finnish Lapland is to get off the bus and explore slowly, which means on foot. The rewards for making the physical effort are manifold. There's a tremendous feeling of space here, and the wild and inhospitable terrain acquires a near-magical quality when illuminated by the constant daylight of the summer months (the only time of year when hiking is feasible).

Many graded **hiking routes** cover the more interesting areas; most of the more exhilarating are distributed among the region's four national parks: **Pyhä-Luosto**, southeast of Sodankylä; **Urho Kekkonen** and **Lemmenjoki**, further north off the Arctic Highway; and **Pallas-Yllästunturi**, near Muonio in the northwest. There are challenges aplenty for experienced hikers, though novices need have nothing to fear provided they employ basic common sense. The more popular hikes can become very busy and many people find this an intrusion into their contemplation of the natural spectacle – others enjoy the camaraderie. If you're seeking solitude you'll find it, but you'll need at least the company of a reliable compass, a good-quality tent, and emergency supplies.

We've included broad introductions to some of the major hikes throughout this chapter, and described the type of terrain you'll find on them. Bear in mind, though, that these aren't definitive accounts as conditions and details often change at short notice; always gather the latest information from the nearest tourist centre or park information office. Most tourist offices hand out free trail descriptions in English and also sell excellent 1:10,000 hiking maps. For copious information on hiking in Finland, visit the Finnish Forest Service's comprehensive, expertly written English-language web site, ⓦ www.outdoors.fi.

Hiking rules and tips

Obviously you should observe the **basic rules** of hiking, and be aware of the delicate ecology of the region: never leave litter, don't start fires in any old place (most hikes have marked spots for this), and don't pitch your tent out of specified areas on marked routes. You should always check that you have maps and adequate supplies before setting out, and never aim to cover more ground than is comfortable. Bathe your feet daily to prevent blisters, and carry some form of mosquito repellent – the pesky creatures infest the region and will descend en masse anytime after noon.

Hiking accommodation

To be on the safe side, you shouldn't go anywhere without a good-quality tent, although the majority of marked hikes have some form of basic shelter, and most have a youth hostel and campsite (and at times even comfy hotels) at some point on the trail. These fill quickly, however, and few things are worse than having nowhere to relax after a long day's trek – so make advance reservations whenever possible. See ⓦ www.hostellit.fi and www.outdoors.fi site for more details.

the animals by taking one of the short walking trails around the park, or you can arrange reindeer or husky safaris out into the surrounding wilderness.

Practicalities

Buses link Salla village with both Kemijärvi and Kuusamo several times a day. Services to and from Kuusamo operate via Sallatunturi, pulling up at *Hotel Revontuli* (☎016/879 711, ⓦsalla.fi; ❺), a great **place to stay** is lit up beautifully at night; adjacent to the sports centre, there are also some comfortable and well-appointed cabins (☎016/837 766, ⓦwww.tunturimokit.com; €85). For eating and drinking, try the excellent *Kelo* **restaurant** beside the hotel, which does a good range of local specialities as well as steaks and pizzas.

Northeast Lapland

Leaving the rail network behind in Rovaniemi, Route 4 (also known as the E75 and the Arctic Highway), the main artery of **Northeast Lapland**, streaks north towards the tiny village of Utsjoki, over 460km away, at the very top of Finland. The elemental landscapes the route traverses are classic Lapland: sweeping coniferous forest; distant, dusky hills with low, rounded tops; and curiously shaped tarns of steely grey, which reflect the expansive skies of the Arctic north. In common with other eastern areas of Finland, this part of Lapland has also suffered several border shifts, most painfully in 1944 when war reparations required the coastal Petsamo area (Pechenga in Russian) in the far north to be ceded to the Soviet Union; Finland once had direct access to the Barents Sea via an arm of nickel-rich land which stretched northeast from Saariselkä and Ivalo. Distances in this part of the province are huge and it's important not to underestimate how long it will take to travel from one town to the next: Rovaniemi to Ivalo, for example, is 300km, a journey of around four hours. People who live here are accustomed to several hours' travel just to get to the shops or go out for dinner, though they always plan ahead, checking opening times and bus schedules in particular. You should do the same since buses tend to run at infrequent intervals and a quick look at ⓦwww.matkahuolto.fi/en can save you getting stranded in the middle of nowhere.

Northbound, **Sodankylä**, a small, pleasant town on the Kitinen River, is the first settlement of any significance after Rovaniemi and makes a good first stop; in a province where half of all buildings were razed to the ground in 1944, the town's seventeenth-century wooden church is all the more remarkable. Further north minuscule **Kakslauttanen**, 120km north of Sodankylä, is the access point for challenging wilderness treks through the whopping **Urho Kekkonen National Park**. Kakslauttanen is also the site of a fun winter ice hotel and igloo village as well as year-round cabins, which can make a good base for skiing in the resort of **Saariselkä**. North of here, workaday **Ivalo** is the service centre for the whole of northernmost Lapland and people travel from miles around to stock up at the village's supermarkets and shops. The shores of Lake Inari, the north's greatest expanse of water, make a picture-perfect setting for the neighbouring village of **Inari**, a Sámi settlement at heart, whose considered museum offers the most comprehensive introduction to Scandinavia's indigenous population you'll find anywhere in Lapland. Beyond Inari, there's precious little sign of human settlement: crossing the treeline, it's another 125km scudding over barren tundra to tiny **Utsjoki**, a strangely likeable, if remote, Sámi settlement close to the raw beauty of the stunning **Lemmenjoki National Park**. At Utsjoki Finland expires at a rare bridge across into Norway – come here secure in the knowledge that everywhere else lies south.

Sodankylä and around

North of Rovaniemi, it's an uneventful 130-kilometre drive along Route 4 to **SODANKYLÄ**, a modest, comfortable town whose modern appearance belies its ancient foundation. From the late seventeenth century, Finnish settlers and Sámi gathered here on high days and holidays to trade and to celebrate religious festivals. Unusually, their wooden **church** (June–Aug daily 10am–6pm) of 1689 has survived intact, its rough-hewn timbers crowding in upon the narrowest of naves and with the pulpit pressing intrusively into the pews. The old church nestles beside the Kitinen River, in the shadow of its uninspiring nineteenth-century counterpart and a stone's throw from the **Alariesto Art Gallery** (Mon–Fri 10am–4pm, Sat 10am–4pm; €3), which features the work of Andreas Alariesto, a twentieth-century Sámi artist of some renown. Each canvas is an invigorating representation of traditional native life and custom, notably the crystalline *View from the Arctic Ocean* embellished with chaotic boulders, predatory fish jaws and busy Sámi. Nearby activities include the **horseback rides** at Laphorse, Mantovaarantie 17 (€25; ☎0400/683 417, ⓦwww.laphorse.com), and outdoor activities like **paintball** with Nature X-Ventures (€25 per person; ☎040/867 1786, ⓦwww.naturex-ventures.fi).

Practicalities

Sodankylä is little more than an elongated main street: Jäämerentie. The **bus station**, post office and petrol stations are within a few metres of each other along here, while the **tourist office** (Mon–Fri 9am–5pm, plus Sat June–Aug; ☎040/746 9776, ⓦwww.sodankyla.fi) is in the centre of the village at Jäämerentie 3, a ten-minute walk from the bus station.

There are just two **hotels** in the village: the bear-themed *Karhu* (☎0201/620 610, ⓦwww.hotel-bearinn.com; ④), a five-minute walk from the bus station at Sodankyläntie 10, and offering rooms with either sauna or hydromassage shower and extremely gregarious and helpful reception staff; and the less inspiring *Hotelli Sodankylä*, Lapintie 21 (☎016/617 121, ⓦwww.meteli.net/hotellisodankyla; ④/⑤) – both are open year-round. The *Kolme Veljestä* **guesthouse**, north of the bus station at Ivalontie 1 (☎0400/ 539 075, ⓦwww.majatalokolmeveljesta.fi; ③), has comfortable rooms – breakfast and use of the kitchen and sauna are included.

Sodankylä's Midnight Sun Film Festival

Accommodation is especially hard to come by in Sodankylä during the **Midnight Sun Film Festival**, which draws film-loving Finns – and a remarkable number of top directors and their latest cinematic offerings – to the tiny town for a week each June. The event is the brainchild of local film producers, brothers Mika and Aki Kaurismäki, whose aim is to showcase the best of Finnish and European cinema. For more information about the event, visit ⓦwww.msfilmfestival.fi.

There's also a **campsite** right on the river (☎016/612 181, ⓦwww.naturex
-ventures.fi; June–Sept; cabins €36; rooms ❸), which rents cheap canoes and
inexpensive jet skis.

As for **meals**, *Annabella*, Jäämerentie 13, is a new Turkish pizza-and-kebab
place in the centre of town that's popular with everyone. Elsewhere, *Pizza
Paikka à la Riesto*, Jäämerentie 25, has pizzas from €6, and *Ravintola Revontuli*,
Jäämerentie 9, offers Finnish meat and fish dishes for around €10 and is also a
popular place for a drink.

Around Sodankylä: Pyhä-Luosto National Park

Sandwiched between Routes 4 and 5, some 40km southeast of Sodankylä, lies
Pyhä-Luosto National Park, and the steep slopes and deep ravines of the most
southerly Finnish fells, Pyhä (540m) and Luosto (514m). Here, the 45-kilometre
Pyhätunturi hiking trail rises from marshlands and pine woods and round five
fell summits, connecting the holiday resorts of **Pyhä** and **Luosto** which lie on
Route 962 between Sodankylä and Kemijärvi. Five kilometres from the start is the
impressive waterfall of the Uhrikuru gorge, after which the track circles back for
a short stretch, eventually continuing to Karhunjuomalampi ("The Bear's Pool").
There's a *päivätupa* (cabin) here, but the only other hut on the route is by the pool
at Pyhälampi.

Near the hike's starting point at Pyhä are a **nature centre** (June–Sept daily
9am–5pm; Oct–May Mon–Fri 10am–4pm; ☎020/564 7302, ⓦwww.outdoors
.fi), a **campsite** (☎016/852 103, ⓦwww.lapinorava.fi; cabins €55), and two
reasonably priced **hotels**: the *Pyhätunturi* (☎016/856 111, ⓦwww.pyha.fi; ❸) and
Pyhän Asteli (☎016/852 141, ⓦwww.pyhanasteli.fi; ❷), both of which are incidentally well placed for skiing in the winter. The hike ends in the village of Luosto,
where accommodation includes the upmarket *Scandic Hotel Luosto* (☎016/624 400,
ⓦwww.scandichotels.com; ❹/❺) and the popular *Hotel Luostotunturi* (☎016/620
400, ⓦwww.luostotunturi.com; ❹), as well as the more basic *Luostonhovi*
(☎020/1620 660, ⓦwww.luostonhovi.fi; ❷). The daily **bus** between Sodankylä
and Kemijärvi stops close to both ends of the trail.

Saariselkä and around

From Sodankylä, a pleasant drive north of 130km along Route 4 brings you to the
purpose-built holiday village of **SAARISELKÄ**, a grouping of a few modest
hotels and restaurants at the foot of the fells, Kaunispää (438m) and Iisakkipää
(454m), which claims to be the most northerly ski resort in the world. Impressive
the boast may be, but in reality the place is lacklustre and disappointing and if
you're intent on skiing in Finnish Lapland, you'd be wiser to head for Levi (see
p.294) or Ruka (see p.199) where the skiing is altogether more challenging, the
après-ski scene much livelier and the clientele more international; Saariselkä is
extremely popular with Finnish families looking for a winter break. Rather than
basing yourself here, Saariselkä is better used as a quick stop on the trip north to
take in the impressive panoramic views from the top of **Kaunispää** which stretch
out across the tundra and well beyond the Russian border in the distance, or as a
starting point for canoeing on the Ivalojoki River (see box, p.286).

There's no real centre to Saariselkä and all accommodation and eating options are
located on Saariseläntie, the road which runs through the village; buses use the
Tunturihotelli as their stop. As you swing off Route 4 into Saariselkä, you'll come

Canoeing the Ivalojoki river

From its source high in the fells east of Hetta, the graceful **Ivalojoki river** flows across the barren tundra of northern Lapland into Lake Inari. With justification, the river is regarded as the finest **canoeing** route in the whole of Finland, since it offers the chance to explore pristine wilderness areas which are otherwise inaccessible. Despite its many rapids, the Ivalojoki is suitable even for beginners and during the summer months is relatively shallow, even rocky in parts. The best section of the river for canoeists stretches over 70km from **Kuttura**, a small hamlet west of Saariselkä and reached via a minor road just north of *Kakslauttanen*, to **Ivalo**. There's a full description of the route at Ⓦ www.luontoon.fi/page.asp?Section=5569&Item=9156, including details of the unlocked wilderness huts along the way for overnight accommodation. Canoes can be rented from Lapin Luontolomat (Ⓣ 016/668 706; €45 per day) beside the *Tunturihotelli* in Saariselkä.

first to the Pohjois-Lapin Matkailu travel agent which functions as the **tourist office** (Mon–Fri 9am–5pm; Ⓣ016/668 402, Ⓦwww.saariselka.fi) and which also has **internet** access. Although you're better off staying in *Kakslauttanen*, just to the south, there are a couple of **accommodation** options here: the rambling *Tunturihotelli* (Ⓣ016/681 501, Ⓦwww.tunturihotelli.fi; ❹/❺) is the best of the hotels with a range of comfortable doubles as well as apartments with their own sauna, whilst *Holiday Club Saariselkä* (Ⓣ020/123 4907, Ⓦwww.holidayclub.fi; ❻) is a modern spa hotel offering the last word in pampering and luxury. For **eating**, it's hard to beat *Pirtti* inside the *Tunturihotelli* which serves up local specialities including a delicious reindeer pepper steak (€25.90) and a filling bowl of reindeer and bacon pasta in cream (€13.50). The best place for a **drink** is *Panimo*, the local pub, which also serves light snacks.

Kakslauttanen

Just 12km south of Saariselkä, ⚴ **Hotel Kakslauttanen** (Ⓣ016/667 100, Ⓦwww.kakslauttanen.fi; ❻) is one of the most enjoyable destinations in the whole of the Finnish north. Located beside Route 4, this dot on the map is not only the location for Lapland's best **log cabin accommodation**, but it's also home to its only **igloo village**. It makes a much more agreeable base from which to explore the surrounding countryside than pallid Saariselkä, offering ready access to the Urho Kekkonen National Park, just 7km away, and a selection of **adventure safaris** by reindeer or snowmobile out into the forests beyond.

An idyllic collection of log cabins and igloos, *Kakslauttanen* is beautifully located either side of a small river, where, in winter, a hole is kept open in the ice for the courageous few prepared to submerse themselves in the chilly waters. What makes this place such a find is the quality of the accommodation: the spacious **cabins**, for example, are placed a respectable distance from each other offering much more privacy than is usually the norm and are constructed of entire trunks of Russian dead standing pine, which measures over half a metre in diameter and affords a superbly sturdy yet cosy look. The cabins (from €118 per night for two) vary in size, sleeping between two and six, but each one has a fully fitted kitchen, open fireplace, private sauna and generous terrace. Beyond the cabins, the **igloo village** stands proud every winter between December and April. It's composed of one large igloo, akin to Sweden's famous *IceHotel* though on a smaller scale, and contains nine bedrooms, a restaurant, gallery and chapel whose nippy inside temperature ranges between -3°C and -6°C. Immediately outside, half a dozen individual **snow igloos** (from €276 for two) are also built each year, providing accommodation for up to five people: thermal sleeping bags and assorted woolly apparel are provided. *Kakslauttanen* also offers the unique opportunity to spend a night in a heated **glass igloo** (€322 for two) specially constructed of thermal glass; privacy is assured since the glass functions like a one-way mirror allowing you to see outside but no one to see in. A night spent here offers a perfect chance to watch the northern lights through the glass roof from the comfort of your remote-controlled reclining bed; each glass igloo also has a private toilet and shower. It's also home to the world's largest **smoke sauna**, with ample space for up to one hundred people (minimum: twenty). For **eating and drinking**, there's an on-site restaurant (open to non-residents) which offers half-board (€26).

Outdoor activities can be booked through the reception: husky, reindeer and snowmobile tours are all available. One popular excursion is the trip to the nearby reindeer farm in Purnumukka (€100). Safaris lasting a couple of hours by husky or snowmobile are available costing €138 and €118 respectively; an evening snowmobile tour to see the northern lights costs €130.

Kakslauttanen provides a pick-up service from Ivalo **airport**, about 40km away, by snowmobile (€216) and regular car (€24); any **bus** between Sodankylä and Ivalo will pass by.

Fell Centre Kiilopää and Urho Kekkonen National Park

Just 7km down the minor road from *Kakslauttanen* is the **Fell Centre Kiilopää** (daily 8am–10pm, closed May & Oct; ☏016/670 0700, ⓦwww.kiilopaa.fi), a popular and well-equipped fell-walking centre on the edge of the **Urho Kekkonen National Park**. The park is one of the country's largest, incorporating the uninhabited wilderness that extends to the Russian border – pine moors and innumerable fells scored by gleaming streams and rivers. With regular bus connections to north and south, the Fell Centre (also known by its Finnish name, Tunturikeskus) is easily the most convenient base for exploring the park. It's at the head of several walking trails, which range from the simplest of excursions to exhausting expeditions using the park's chain of wilderness cabins. As well as providing park information, selling detailed trail maps, renting mountain bikes and organizing guided walks, staff can arrange accommodation in the adjoining year-round **youth hostel**, *Ahopää* (same phone number; dorms €33, breakfast not included); the centre also has some en-suite rooms (❹/❺), a good restaurant and a smoke sauna.

Ivalo

The gruelling 300km journey from Rovaniemi finally ends in **IVALO**, 23km north of Saariselkä and the biggest place for miles around, though sadly with little to recommend it. However, given the vast expanses of wilderness which emanate from here in all directions, it would be churlish not to stop and make the most of the relative urban sophistication offered by the handful of shops and eateries which line Route 4 as it streaks through town; particularly useful are the supermarket, S-Market, stocked with a large selection of fresh fruit and vegetables (which are hard to find the further north you venture) and the local Alko store which is located in the same building. Before you head off make sure you pop inside the surprisingly good Sámi **souvenir shop**, Lahjatalo Ivalo, which sells everything from reindeer hides (from around €40) to candlesticks. It's located on the main road, Ivalontie, close to the *Luaran Grilli* restaurant, and is one of the largest you will find in the whole of Finnish Lapland.

Buses call at the new **bus station** on Petsamontie (the Murmansk road) behind the Siwo supermarket. The travel agent at Ivalontie 7 in the Inarilainen newspaper building (June–Sept Mon–Fri 9am–6.30pm, Sat & Sun 9am–3pm; Oct–May Mon–Fri 9am–5pm; ☎03/0624 4120, ⓦwww.readytogo.fi) offers friendly smiles along with helpful **information** about the region; they also organize a range of husky, reindeer, snowmobile and skiing excursions. For **accommodation**, at either end of the tiny centre ⵊ *Hotel Kultahippu* (☎016/320 8800, ⓦwww.kultahippuhotel.fi; ❹), Petsamontie 1, and *Hotelli Ivalo* (☎016/688 111, ⓦwww.hotelivalo.fi; ❹), Ivalontie 34, both enjoy good riverside locations, while the much cheaper *Näverniemen Lomakylä* (☎016/677 601), just south of town, has **camping** spots and a few simple summer cabins (€25).

Ivalo's uninspiring **eating** options amount to the hotel restaurants, of which *Pankkila*'s is the best, closely followed by the filling lunch buffet at the *Kultahippu*, whose restaurant is decked out with bank notes and gold pans, and a few pizza places. For a **drink**, try the new pub in town, *pubi.fi*, at Ivalontie 12.

Inari and around

The road heading north to Inari winds around the southern shores of **Lake Inari-järvi**, the third largest in Finland, which is transformed into a vast ice sheet between November and early June ahead of the late spring thaw – it's a spectacular route at any time of year, though, particularly so if you can time your trip with the glorious Lapland *ruska*, a season that takes in late August and early September, when the trees take on brilliant citrus colours that are reflected in the still waters. **Inari** itself, 40km north of Ivalo, is quite a bit more amenable than Ivalo, straggling along the bony banks of the Juutuanjoki River as it tumbles into the freezing-cold waters of the lake, studded with over three thousand islets. There's nothing remarkable about the village itself, but it's a pretty little place with several appealing diversions and it buzzes in the summer season with transitory visitors taking a break from the Rovaniemi–Nordkapp beaten path. As the seat of Sámediggi, the Finnish **Sámi Parliament**, Inari is the centre of Sámi culture in Finland and makes a great place to get to grips with the history and traditions of Scandinavia's indigenous population.

Arrival, information and accommodation

Inari's new **tourist office** (June–Sept daily 9am–8pm; Oct–May Tues–Sun 10am–5pm; ☎016/661 666, ⓦwww.inarilapland.org) is located within the Siida museum, on the one and only main road, where helpful staff can advise on accommodation, trips to Russia and organize a fishing licence (from €10 for one week).

Many travellers pass through Inari during the summer, so it's best to reserve **accommodation** during this period. One of the most enjoyable places to stay is

---

Getting to Nordkapp

Between June and late August a daily bus runs between Rovaniemi and Nordkapp (North Cape) in **Norway** – generally regarded as Europe's northernmost point – routing via Sodankylä, Ivalo and Inari. The bus leaves Rovaniemi at 11am, arriving in Inari at 5pm and finally reaching Nordkapp at 10.20pm, in time to see the midnight sun. The bus then returns for the southbound journey around 1am. Detailed timetable information is available at ⓦwww.eskelisen-lapinlinjat.com.

Villa Lanca (☎040/748 0984, ⓦwww.villalanca.com; ❹), run by an effusive Finnish-Sámi couple who rent out charming apartments across several floors just off the main drag, as well as a nearby cottage on a secluded peninsula. Elsewhere in the village, the newly renovated *Inarin Kultahovi* hotel (☎016/671 221, ⓦwww .hotelkultahovi.fi; ❸), Saarikoskentie 2, offers comfortable rooms with river views (those in the new wing have their own sauna) and an excellent, reasonably priced restaurant; the *Lomakylä Inari* (☎016/671 108, ⓦwww.saariselka.fi/lomakylainari), Inarintie 26, has well-kept wooden cabins (€50); while the **campsite**, *Uruniemi Camping* (☎016/671 331, ⓦwww.uruniemi.com; June–Sept), 3km away on the southern outskirts of the town, has smaller cottages (❶).

The Town

The place to make for is **Siida**, the Sámi museum and nature centre (June–Sept daily 9am–8pm; Oct–May Tues–Sun 10am–5pm; €8; ⓦwww.siida.fi), located beside the main road and on the banks of the river. This considered museum, with its professional, no-nonsense presentation of the Sámi's intimate bond with the delicate nature of the far north, is the best in Scandinavia. From the reception, take the ramp up to the first floor where you'll find the principal exhibition, which includes a timeline tracing the Sámi from pre history to the present day, detailing all the social, cultural and political changes which have affected them: whilst the world watched with bated breath as Gorbachev and Reagan met in the mid-80s, for example, the Sámi were rejoicing over the publication of *Donald Duck* in their own language, a key milestone in the official recognition of their minority tongue. The walls of the main exhibition hall are bound by a series of floor-to-ceiling photographs measuring an impressive 10m wide by 5m high, portraying the landscapes of Lapland throughout the seasons, whilst a subtle soundtrack conjures up the sounds of trickling streams, rustling birch trees and the enigmatic *joik*, a form of melodic throat-singing known, and widely appreciated, throughout the Sámi community. Back on the ground floor, an exhibition hall occasionally hosts displays of local photographic work, whilst the excellent outdoor section features a re-sited nineteenth-century village and various reconstructions illustrating aspects of Sámi life – principally hunting and fishing techniques. Across the road is the Sámi handicraft store, **Sámi Duodji** (July–Aug daily 10am–6pm; Sept–June Tues–Sat 10am–5pm), a good place to pick up a souvenir or two.

Eating

The *Siida Ravintola* **restaurant** at the Siida museum is very good – go for the scrumptious hollandaise Lake Inari trout and whitefish platter with boiled potatoes (€18). If money's tight, stick to the popular restaurant known for its generous portions inside *Hotelli Inari* (opposite *Villa Lanca*), where a mixed fish platter of salmon and whitefish, for example, costs €14.90, though be prepared to share the place with drunken locals at weekends.

Pielpajärvi wilderness church and Inarijärvi cruises

Beginning at the car park located 2.5km northeast of the museum (take the road towards Sarviniemi from behind Siida; maps available at the museum), a worthwhile **hiking trail** of a further 4.5km leads through ancient pine forest to the isolated **Pielpajärvi wilderness church** from 1752, surrounded by whispering birch trees beautifully sited in a flower meadow on the shores of Iso Pielpajärvi lake. Although the trail is well signposted you should take extra care if it's wet underfoot since the path can be extremely slippery, especially around the halfway point where it crosses a narrow isthmus between two lakes. Services are still held in the church at Easter and Midsummer and every summer when volunteers cut and dry hay here, in keeping with age-old traditions. If you don't fancy expending any energy to see some scenery, head for the bridge over the Juutuanjoki, from where, in summer, you can take a two-hour **lake cruise** (early June to late Sept daily 2pm or 6pm; €16; ☎0400/879 203) out to **Ukko island**, a former Sámi sacrificial site; there are good views out across the lake from the island's hillock. On the way to the island the boat calls at Peinovuopio Bay from where you can also walk to the wilderness church. **Fishing trips** (all year) are also available, though a twelve-seat boat and a guide for three hours costs €300, so the per-person price depends on the total number in the group. In the winter, popular guided **snowmobile trips** (from €90 per person), bookable via the tourist office, set out over the frozen lake.

Inari reindeer farm

Thirteen kilometres southwest of Inari along Route 955 towards Kittilä, the **Inari reindeer farm** in Solojärvi (☎016/663 005, ⓦwww.reindeerfarm.fi) offers the chance to learn about reindeer husbandry and its importance to the Sámi, whilst getting up close to this Lapland icon. Visits, which last two hours and include the opportunity to feed the animals, are best booked in advance and cost €65 per person, which includes transfer from Inari. However, without booking, it's also possible to make a visit to the farm every weekday at noon (€20), providing you can make your own way there (it's signed from the main road) and be at the entrance gate on time. During the winter months, reindeer **safaris** (€100 per person) are also available.

Lemmenjoki National Park

About 40km southwest of Inari, **Lemmenjoki National Park** is a vast tract of birch and pinewood forest interrupted by austere, craggy fells, marshland and a

▲ Inari reindeer farm

Reindeer husbandry and land rights in Finnish Lapland

There is only one animal that truly encapsulates the spirit of Finnish Lapland: the reindeer. For thousands of years this hardy creature has been the lifeblood of the Sámi, providing them with food, clothing, shelter, and even shamanistic inspiration. On Europe's northernmost fringe winter lasts for over seven months of the year, yet for millennia **reindeer herding** has enabled the far north's indigenous people to survive in the harshest of climates, following ancient patterns of calf marking in the high fells between June and August, and herd separation in November or December.

Today's globalized society, however, has increasingly threatened traditional lifestyles in Finnish Lapland, and now only one in ten Sámi families still earns its living from reindeer husbandry. Many Sámi claim that the practice is no longer economically viable, blaming the Finnish government's controversial policy on the recognition of **indigenous rights**. Unlike neighbouring Sweden and Norway, Finland does not recognize the Sámi's exclusive claim to herd reindeer – indeed, in the Finnish north any European Union citizen can legally tend reindeer.

Sámi leaders are also locked in bitter dispute with the Finnish state over **land rights**; the Finnish government is reluctant to grant the Sámi unique rights over land usage, even in traditional Sámi herding areas, for fear of alienating the powerful forestry industry, responsible for a significantly large proportion of Finland's exports, which claims that reindeer grazing decimates newly planted saplings. The result is an uneasy standoff and a mounting distrust between the state and its indigenous population. True, outside arbitration, such as that offered by international human rights organizations, has helped ease matters, but the particularly thorny issue of land ownership in the Finnish north remains unresolved.

For more information on the Sámi in Finland, check out the website of the Finnish Sámi Parliament at ⓦwww.samediggi.fi.

---

handful of bubbling rivers. The area witnessed a short-lived gold rush in the 1940s, and a few panners remain, eking out a meagre living. The park's most breathtaking scenery is to be found on its southeastern side along the Lemmenjoki river valley. To get there, take the daily bus from Inari to **Njurku-lahti**, a tiny settlement on the edge of the park about 12km off Route 955 to Kittilä (the district's main road), which is where the 55-kilometre, two-day hike down the river valley begins; taking the twice-daily boat (June–Aug; €15 one way) from Njurkulahti to Kultasatama cuts 20km off the hike's full distance. At **Härkäkoski**, hikers cross the river by a small boat, pulled by rope from bank to bank; the track then ascends through a pine forest to **Morgamoja Kultala**, the old gold-panning centre, where there's a big unlocked hut. There are a couple of other huts set aside for those walking the trail, but the snuggest accommodation, *Hotel Korpikartano* (☎040/456 0457, ⓦwww.menesjarvi.fi; ❹), is back on the main road at Meneskartanontie 71 in **Menesjärvi**. For organized gold-panning and camping trips – and interesting day-long Sámi felt-making workshops – plump for those offered by Kaija and Heikki Paltto (☎016/673 542, ⓦwww.lemmenjoki.org), a very welcoming Sámi family in the hamlet of **Lemmenjoki** who also rent out several comfortable **cabins** (€46) with free use of a rowing boat and sauna. Just across the river, *Ahkun Tupa* (☎016/673 435, ⓦwww.ahkuntupa.fi; ❷), has similar-priced but less intimate accommodation in smaller cottages. For more information on the park, ask at the Lemmenjoki nature hut (June–Sept daily 9am–5pm; ☎020/564 7793) at the park entrance, which is well signposted from Inari.

North to the Norwegian border

Although Inari may feel like the end of the road, a quick look at the map will soon clarify matters: there's still another 125km to go before Finland finally expires her last breath in remote **Utsjoki**, a small border village beside the Tenojoki River. There's a certain masochistic pleasure to be gained from continuing north to the end of the road where you can finally take stock of your position at the very tip of the European Union's most northerly country – and claim the T-shirt.

Kaamanen and Karigasniemi

From Inari, Route 4 continues first to dreary **Kaamanen**, though on the way, 2km past the *Kaamasen Kievari* year-round **campsite** (☎016/672 713, ⓦwww .kaamasenkievari.fi), is a bold, stark and deeply evocative **World War II memorial** in rusty red metal. It states simply "the battles of these light infantrymen in the wilds of Lapland were brought to an end in Kaamanen, Inari, towards the end of October 1944. 774 killed, 262 missing, 2904 wounded". There is now a parting of the ways: Route 92 swings westwards on its way to Nordkapp, exiting Finland at **KARIGAS-NIEMI**, an unprepossessing hamlet with a **restaurant**, *Soarve Stohpu*, which serves a yummy smoked reindeer-and-cheese soup for around €10, and pleasant rooms in the small and basic *Kalastajan Majatalo* **hotel** next door (☎016/676 171, ⓦwww.kalas tajanmajatalo.com; ❸); Route 4 meanwhile continues stubbornly across a lonely tundra plateau northwards bound for Utsjoki.

Utsjoki and around

Dominated by its suspension bridge across the Tenojoki River to Norway, tiny **UTSJOKI** marks the end of Route 4 which began 1300km away in Helsinki. The bridge's completion in 1993 transformed this remote village from a dead-end last place into a mini-cross-border shopping destination for Norwegians intent on beating their own country's ruinous prices; count how many Norwegian cars you see coming over the bridge to fill up with significantly cheaper fuel and food at the supermarket by the foot of the bridge.

Other than chilling out on the banks of the salmon-rich Tenojoki or exploring the river by rowing boat (see below for rental details), the main activity here is hiking. An enjoyable trail of around 10km begins opposite the supermarket and leads south over Vuolleseavtetvárri fell (300m) to **Mantojärvi Lake** where a roughly hewn timber church stands on the shores, surrounded by a dozen or so attendant cabins, which once served as overnight accommodation for churchgoers who had trekked here from surrounding villages; buses to and from Inari also pass by the church. A second, more challenging route of 64km begins 20km south of the village at Kenespahta, leading through the Kevo canyon inside the **Keno Nature Reserve** which is located between Routes 4 and 92. The trail terminates at **Suttesjärvi**, a lake 10km east of Karigasniemi on Route 92, though you will need your own tent as there is only one overnight cabin; buses from Inari to Utsjoki pass the starting point, whilst services to Karasjok in Norway call at the end of the trail.

Utsjoki also offers the rare chance to head up on to the surrounding high fells with a family of traditional Sámi **reindeer herders** to see their animals; transport is by 4x4 and the entire trip costs €400 for a total of four people. For bookings, and rowing boat rental (€30 per day), contact *Poronpurijat* (see below).

Practicalities

The best **place to stay** in Utsjoki is in one of the cosy riverside cabins at ⅄ *Poronpurijat* (☎0400/948 210, ⓦwww.poronpurijat.fi; €90), located 2km from the village along the road to Karigasniemi; the unusual Finnish name derives from the age-old practice of castrating reindeer by biting off their testicles. All the cabins here have river views and their own private sauna; meals are available on request. Alternatively, *Hotel Luossajohka* (☎016/321 2100, Ⓦwww.luossajohka.fi; ❺), close to the bridge at Luossatie 4, has comfortable modern rooms overlooking the river and a decent restaurant. Opposite the supermarket, *Camping Lapinkylä* (☎040/559 1542; mid-June to late Aug) also has cabins (€30). Other than the hotel restaurant, **eating** choices are limited to *Giisá*, a simple Sámi-run café near the campsite, and *Rastigaisa*, opposite the supermarket, which serves pizzas and other snacks.

Northwest Lapland

The thumb-shaped chunk of Finland that sticks out above the northern edge of Sweden is mostly uninhabited, a hostile arctic wilderness whose tiny, isolated settlements are strung along the **E8** (also known as Route 21), which scuds through the valley formed by the trio of rivers, Könkämaeno, Muonionjoki and Tornionjoki, which drain languidly into the Gulf of Bothnia. It's only here, in the southernmost reaches of the valley, that the land can be described as vaguely pastoral; the further north you venture, the more desolate the landscapes become, supporting a handful of untidy and uneventful villages. Northwest Lapland is at its most animated around frightfully ugly **Kittilä**, burnt beyond recognition during World War II, which serves as the gateway to the nearby ski resorts of **Ylläs** and **Levi**, the big winter crowd-pullers. Beyond here, **Muonio**, a shy and retiring place, is *the* spot in Finland for dog sledding: the *Harriniva Holiday Centre* here offers a variety of excellent, professionally run tours out into the frozen wilderness every winter. Though generally quiet in the summer – most people route via northeast Lapland en route to Nordkapp – this is the perfect time for hiking in the Finnish fells: **Kilpisjärvi**, in the far northwest of the province, is a long-established hiking centre surrounded by dramatic snow-covered peaks, more akin to the scenery over the border in Norway than the bumpy uplands further south.

Kittilä and around

Heading northwest from Rovaniemi, Route 79 sticks close to the banks of the Ounasjoki River before it reaches the straggling settlement of **KITTILÄ**, a distance of 150km. There's little in the way of sights to detain you in Kittilä itself – the departing German army burnt the place to the ground in 1944, and the rebuilding has been uninspired. However, as the service centre for this part of the province, the town does have a well-stocked supermarket and a few other shops and places to eat (all located on the main road, Valtatie) which are worth exploring before moving on. If you're travelling by bus in Lapland, it's good to know that Kittilä is the only place to transit between the province's two main routes north; there's a handy bus link (Mon–Fri at 12.20pm) from the petrol station on the main road across to Sodankylä, giving access to Route 4 and the northeast.

If you're coming here for winter skiing in nearby Ylläs or Levi, there's a good chance you'll arrive directly at the town's **airport**, 6km north of the minuscule centre, which handles direct charter flights from several European cities, including London, Birmingham and Manchester in the UK; shuttle services then operate to the ski resorts. There's just one **hotel** in town, the predictably named *Hotel Kittilä*, Valtatie 49 (℡016/643 201, Ⓦwww.hotellikittila.fi; ❸), easily pinpointed along the main road by the life-size red Spitfire plane, plonked at a jaunty angle on a huge plinth outside the main entrance. Inside, the rooms are nothing to write home about, but there is a pool and an inexpensive restaurant which serves a decent buffet lunch for €8; there's also a popular bar here, *Pilot's Pub*. A few doors down at no. 42, *Guesthouse Golden Goose* (℡016/642 043, Ⓦwww.goldengoose.fi; ❸) is a good choice for cosy, nicely appointed rooms whilst the **campsite**, Sodankyläntie 65 (beside the junction of Route 80 to Sodankylä), offers a cheaper, though less central option. Other than the hotel restaurant, the only place to grab anything else to **eat** is the bakery and small café, *Kahvila Herkkutupa*, at Valtatie 27.

Around Kittilä: Ylläs

Fifty kilometres west of Kittilä off Route 80, the ski resort of **YLLÄS** is composed of the 718m high Yllästunturi fell and the twin villages of **ÄKÄSLOM-POLO** and **YLLÄSJÄRVI**, to the north and south of the peak respectively, themselves linked by a road which winds around the foot of the mountain. Ylläs is locked in permanent battle with nearby Levi for the lucrative winter **ski** market which provides the main source of income for the settlements – indeed, Ylläs is the highest fell in Finland with ski lifts, twenty-nine of them in fact at the last count, and has a skiing tradition which dates back to the 1930s. Although both places contain plenty of top-end hotels and restaurants, it is larger Äkäslompolo which enjoys the prettier setting, squeezed around a small island in the Äkäsjoki River. Although most people come here in the winter season to sample some of the sixty-odd ski slopes and the 330km of cross-country trails, it's also a great place for some challenging summer **hiking** in the vast Pallas-Yllästunturi National Park (see pp.298–299).

For somewhere **to stay** in Ylläs, call in at the Ylläs Travel booking centre (℡030/650 2580, Ⓦwww.yllaksenmatkailu.fi), Sivulantie 8 in Äkäslompolo; they have access to a wide range of hotel rooms and cabins and can often better the prices offered directly by the hotels. Of the Äkäslompolo hotels, *Lapland Hotel Äkäshotel* (℡016/553 000, Ⓦwww.laplandhotels.com; ❺), Äkäsentie 10, built in the shape of a Sámi hut, and *Holiday Centre Seita* (℡016/569 211, Ⓦwww.seitahotelli.fi; ❺), Tiurajärventie 36A, both have modern, double rooms as well as cabins. In addition to the hotel **restaurants**, *Taiga* at Vaeltajantie 2 is a good steakhouse with a popular **bar**, whilst *Selvä Pyy* at Tunturitie 16 is a popular bistro-bar with solid Finnish fare.

Levi

Although Kittilä is the major town in these parts, it's the posh ski resort of **LEVI**, 20km further north, that is the real magnet. Attracting over half a million visitors every year with its numerous downhill trails, several dozen lifts, gondolas and ample après-ski attractions, Levi is every bit as stylish and cosmopolitan as you might imagine and, to be honest, is a more agreeable destination than Ylläs, even though the main hill here is around 200m lower than its nearby rival. Since the

1980s, Levi has experienced a remarkable rate of growth and now ranks as one of Finland's top ski destinations. Today, it's still wintering Finns who make up the biggest proportion of visitors, though the numbers of foreign skiers are growing – currently around a third of people are from abroad, many of them from Russia. On the way here, road signs give directions for the town of **Sirkka**, which, to be strictly accurate, is the name of the town where you'll find the tourist office and all other facilities – Levi is only the name of the mountain (532m). However, the distinction is lost on most people and, in general, the whole shebang is known simply as Levi.

Arrival, information and accommodation

From Kittilä **airport**, 14km to the south, buses meet all scheduled flights and run into Levi; private shuttle buses meet charter flights. Service **buses** to and from Rovaniemi stop outside *Spa Hotelli Levitunturi* on the main road, Levintie. Opposite, at Myllyjoentie 2, the helpful **tourist office**, Levin Matkailu (June–Aug Mon–Fri 9am–7pm, Sat & Sun 11am–5.30pm; Sept–May Mon–Fri 9am–4.30, Sat & Sun 11am–4pm; ☎016/639 3300, ⓦwww.levi.fi), has a wealth of maps and local information and can also assist with finding **accommodation**. During winter, rooms cost roughly double the summer prices and advance booking is absolutely vital.

Hullu Poro Rakkavarantie ☎016/651 0100, ⓦwww.hulluporo.fi. A vast restaurant and hotel complex which offers the cheapest place to stay in Levi if you opt for their "basic double rooms", which include private facilities. ❷

K5 Levi Kätkärannantie 2 ☎016/639 1300, ⓦwww.k5levi.fi. Stylish, decent-sized rooms decorated in natural colours with wooden floors and generous balconies. ❹/❻

Sirkantähti Levintie ☎016/323 500, ⓦwww .laplandhotels.com. One of the best choices of apartments in Levi, some boasting their own sauna and sun terrace, though there are

regular double rooms, too. Apartments from €120, rooms ❻

Sokos Levi Tähtitie 5 ☎016/321 5500, ⓦwww .sokoshotels.fi. The two hundred rooms over three buildings in this new hotel at the heart of the buzz are the last word in luxury, tastefully decorated in a range of warm Lapland colours from autumn russets to summer blues. ❻

Spa Levitunturi Levintie ☎016/646 301, ⓦwww .levihotelli.fi. Long-established luxury spa hotel with swimming pool, saunas and gym as well as courts for badminton, tennis and squash. Rooms are modern though not as stylish as those at the *Sokos*. ❹/❻

Activities in Levi

With forty-seven slopes and twenty-eight lifts, **downhill skiing**, clearly, is what most people come to Levi for in winter. However, **cross–country** is also popular and the resort has no fewer than 230km of tracks, some of which are illuminated. The season runs from November to May. A full set of equipment (€25.50 per day) can be rented from Zero Point on Hissitie at the foot of the Levi North ski lift in the centre (☎0207/960 206). **Snowmobile** rental is also available from €70 for two hours; contact PerheSafarit (☎016/643 861, ⓦwww .perhesafarit.fi) at Leviraitti near the *Sirkantähti* hotel, whilst for **husky safaris** you should speak to Polar Speed Tours (☎016/653 447, ⓦwww.levi.fi /polarspeed), who're based 11km away in Köngäs, and run tours over several days with accommodation in wilderness huts.

Outside of winter, there is relatively little going on here, though the surrounding hills boast seven **hiking** routes, including the enjoyable eighteen-kilometre Levi Fell trail, though **mountain biking** (rental from PerheSafarit) is also popular. All the routes begin in or near the centre of Sirkka and route maps are available from the tourist office.

Eating and drinking

In line with the number of visitors Levi attracts, there's a plethora of **eating and drinking** options in the centre of the village, though be sure to book a table during the height of the winter season.

Restaurants

Ämmilä Rakkavarantie ⓣ016/651 0100. Part of the *Hullu Poro* complex, this is the place to enjoy huge portions of traditional Finnish home-cooking, such as reindeer meatballs, served up in a fake country farmhouse stuffed with olde-worlde furniture. Mains around €15–22.

Árran Hissitie 3 ⓣ016/641 888. In keeping with its name (*árran* is Sámi for fireplace), a cosy fire burns here, creating a welcoming atmosphere to enjoy some traditional Lapland dishes such as creamy smoked-reindeer soup with chanterelle mushrooms. Mains cost around €20.

Bistro Hissitie 13 ⓣ016/644 125. A decent, brightly decorated place with large windows offering a good choice of pizzas (€9) and burgers (from €12) as well as more substantial meat dishes (around €22).

Pihvipirtti Rakkavarantie 5 ⓣ016/651 0100. A solid, dependable steakhouse for juicy cuts of meat in various forms; reindeer is also on the menu.

Bars

Hullu Poro Rakkavarantie. Legendary karaoke bar attracting a middle-aged crowd that's less than shy about letting rip.

V'inkkari Hissitie. Located at the foot of the Levi North ski lift, this is the most (in)famous après-ski bar in Finland, and sells more alcohol than any other place in the country. With DJs cranking out feel-good hits on the large open-air terrace, there's much drunken dancing on the tables.

Muonio and around

Sleepy **MUONIO** lies 60km northwest of Levi/Sirkka beside the fast-flowing Muonionjoki River that separates Finland from Sweden. What passes for the town centre falls beside the junction of the E8, the main north–south highway, and Route 79 from Kittilä. There's precious little to do in Muonio itself other than ogle the handsome, wooden **church** from 1822, which miraculously escaped the earth-scorching German soldiers of World War II, or pop into the Kiela Naturum **nature centre** (same times as tourist office; see opposite), opposite, where there are passable displays of the local flora and fauna. Otherwise, the village is best used to stock up on provisions if you're bound for the *Harriniva Holiday Centre* (see opposite) just to the south along the E8. Incidentally, Muonio is regarded as a reliable place to see the northern lights (see box below); there's a 55 percent chance of seeing them in the winter here, though it must be a clear night.

Northern lights

Also known by their Latin name, aurora borealis, the **northern lights** are visible all across northern Finland during the dark months of winter. These spectacular displays of green-blue shimmering arcs and waves of lights are caused by solar wind, or streams of particles charged by the sun, hitting the atmosphere. The colours are the characteristic hues of different elements when they hit the plasma shield which protects the Earth: blue is nitrogen and yellow-green oxygen. Although the mechanisms which produce the aurora are not completely understood, the displays are generally more impressive the closer you get to the poles – low temperatures are also rumoured to produce some of the most dramatic performances. Although displays can range from just a few minutes to several hours, the night sky must be clear of cloud to see the northern lights from Earth. **Forecasts** for displays of the northern lights are available at ⓦcc.oulu.fi/~thu/Aurora/forecast.html.

▲ Huskies out on Villa Lanca's cottage

The Esso petrol station at the E8/Route 79 crossroads functions as the **bus station**, where you'll also find the **tourist office** (daily 10am–6pm except Sun Oct & Nov; ☏016/532 141, Ⓦwww.muonio.fi). For **accommodation**, head for the superbly located year-round hostel *Lomamaja Pekonen* (☏016/532 237, Ⓦwww.lomamaja pekonen.fi; ❷), on a small hilly site overlooking a lake at Lahenrannantie 10. They also have simple, well-equipped cabins (€60); the ones at the top of the hill have their own saunas (€65). **Canoes** can also be hired here for €21 per day. For snacks, the woodsy *Naapuro*, Kosotuskeino 1, has fresh cakes, coffee and beer, while solid **meals** can be found next door at *Uncle Laban*, run by a friendly Palestinian family who dish up pizza and reindeer dishes for around €10.

Around Muonio: Harriniva Holiday Centre

Some 3km south of Muonio along the E8 lies the well-organized and well-equipped ⚑ **Harriniva Holiday Centre** (☏016/530 0300, Ⓦwww.harriniva.fi), where you can pitch a tent, hook up your camper van or stay in a range of **accommodation** that runs from cabins (€90) and double rooms (❺) to fully equipped apartments (€140). What makes this place special is the range of summer and winter activities on offer. A haven for dog lovers, *Harriniva* has around four hundred huskies – making it the biggest husky centre in Finland – and if you're here in winter and thinking of a **husky safari**, this is the place to do it. Although safaris are quite pricey – a week-long round-trip from Muonio up towards Hetta, covering a daily distance of around 40km, costs upwards of €1350, the price includes all food, your huskies and sledge plus overnight accommodation in log cabins – and, of course, the experience of riding across frozen lakes, winding through Lapland's silent snow-covered forests and ending the day with a roll in the snow after a genuine smoke sauna. The centre's **other activities** in winter include a six-hour snowmobile safari (€190), a four-hour reindeer safari (€180), and a dog sled day-trip (€200). In summer, the centre offers such things as whitewater rafting (€28; 1hr 30min), salmon fishing and quad-bike excursions to a reindeer farm (€165), and canoe trips (€60).

Hetta (Enontekiö) and around

Around 75km northeast of Muonio, **HETTA** (also known administratively as **Enontekiö**) is for most of the year possibly the dullest place in the whole of Finnish Lapland: outside of the Christmas rush, when daily charter flights flood the town with thousands of Santa-seeking Brits, there isn't much going on at all, though the place is useful as a jumping-off point for exploring the Finnish outdoors, notably the **Pallas-Yllästunturi National Park** which lies right on the village's doorstep. Things become slightly more animated when the festive celebrations of **Marianpäivä** (St May's Day festival; March 25) are well attended by people from all over the region and make a satisfactory introduction to the traditions and pastimes of the Sámi. Held in Hetta since the end of the fourteenth century, the annual festival is the most important date in the local Sámi calendar and marks the feast of the Annunciation with theatre productions, concerts, a market, reindeer races and lassoing competitions. Otherwise the only focus of interest in town is the **Fell Lapland Nature Centre** (mid-June to Sept daily 9am–5pm; Oct to mid-June Mon–Fri 9am–4pm; ☎020/564 7959, ⓦ www.outdoors.fi), with its black-and-white photographic displays of formerly commonplace Sámi summer migrations to the Arctic Ocean. Incidentally, from Hetta it's just 37km to the Norwegian border at Kivilompolo (Route 93 towards Kautokeino), whereas there's still a grinding 180km to cover along the E8, routing via Kaaresuvanto, to reach Kilpisjärvi, and ultimately the Norwegian border south of Skibotn.

Practicalities

The Fell Lapland Nature Centre functions as a **tourist office** of sorts, selling maps and making reservations for a host of cottages in the Pallas-Yllästunturi National Park, while **buses** use *Hotelli Hetta* as their main stop. For **accommodation** in Hetta, try the well-appointed, modern cabins, cottages and rooms at the *Hetan Lomakylä* (☎016/521 521, ⓦ www.hetanlomakyla.fi; ❶/❸) or the rustic-chic fireplace-outfitted cabins at *Ounasloma* (all year, but call ahead on ☎016/521 055, ⓦ www.ounasloma.fi; €60), both of which also have **camping** facilities. Among the settlement's hotels, a good choice is the *Hetan Majatalo* (☎016/554 0400, ⓦ www.hetan-majatalo.fi; ❹), which offers excellent, rustic-style en-suite rooms as well as cheaper and more basic options. In winter they organize a host of **activities**, from ice fishing, reindeer safaris and dog sleigh tours to summer fishing trips, as well as offering boat and bike rental, the latter year-round, while the hotel restaurant cooks up highly recommended traditional Lappish dinners. The *Hotelli Hetta* (☎016/521 361, ⓦ www.hetta-hotel.com; ❸/❹) offers a plush alternative, with several rooms overlooking the lake.

If you're looking for splendid isolation, it's hard to beat *Galdotieva* (☎016/528 630, ⓦ www.harriniva.fi; ❸), a collection of ten log cabins (some with their own sauna) in **Palojärvi**, 6km before the Norwegian border on Route 93, where camping is also available in summer.

Pallas-Yllästunturi National Park

Finland's third largest, the **Pallas-Yllästunturi National Park** is an elongated mountain plateau of bare peaks and coniferous forests stretching from Hetta, passing east of Muonio, all the way down to Ylläs. Lake Ounasjärvi, just outside Hetta, marks the start of the **Hetta–Pallas hiking route**, an arduous 55-kilometre trail of three to four days that crosses a line of fell summits; there are several overnight unlocked huts and camping areas en route. The trail's highest point is the summit of Taivaskero (807m), just north of the finish at **Pallastunturi** fell from where there are buses to Muonio, Kittilä and Rovaniemi; check times at ⓦwww .matkahuolto.fi/en. There's a **visitor centre** at Pallastunturi (Jan to mid-Feb, May, Oct & Nov Mon–Fri 9am–4pm; rest of the year daily 9am–5pm; ☎020/564 7930) and a posh **hotel**, *Lapland Hotel Pallas* (☎016/323 355, ⓦwww.lapland hotels.com; ❻).

Kilpisjärvi and around

Around 175km northwest of Hetta along the E8, and just 5km short of the Norwegian border, the isolated lakeside hamlet of **KILPISJÄRVI** is little more than a huddle of accommodation options and a supermarket, all located beside the main highway. The main reason for coming to this remote outpost is to tackle some of Finland's most dramatic fells – most of them over 1000m high. The most popular destination is **Saanatunturi**, which bears down on tiny Kilpisjärvi from a height of 1029m. A brace of ten-kilometre **trails** runs to the top of the peak, though the main way up (and down) is the track on the steep north side, whilst another route runs behind the fell to the northern shore of **Saanijärvi Lake**, where there's a *päivätupa* (cabin). Another hiking option is the 24-kilometre loop trail, beginning and ending at Kilpisjärvi, which runs north through the **Malla Nature Reserve** to the **Three Countries Frontier** cairn where Finland, Norway and Sweden meet. The hike can be shortened to just 3km by taking a **boat ride** across Kilpisjärvi Lake on board M/S *Malla* (late June to early Aug 10am, 2pm & 6pm; 45min; €16 per person return, minimum four passengers); for information ask at the visitor centre or call ☎0400/669 392. For more expensive adventure, Heliflite (☎016/532 100, ⓦwww.heliflite.fi), in the harbour 1.5km south of town, offers **helicopter tours** of the region between late July and September – though at €250 for a ten-minute flight, you might be more content with an aerial-view postcard from the visitor centre.

Practicalities

The **Kilpisjärvi visitor centre** (March–Sept daily 9am–5pm; ☎020/564 7990, ⓦwww.kilpisjarvi.fi), located at the southern end of the village, sells maps and offers helpful information on the local area, including the numerous hiking options. You'll find a **campsite** at the visitor centre (June–Sept), too, and, nearby on Käsivarrentie, a pleasant **guesthouse**, *Saananmaja* (☎016/537 746; ❷). Perched beside the coldest of lakes in the shadow of a string of stark tundra summits, the *Lapland Hotel Kilpis* (☎016/537 761, ⓦwww.laplandhotels.com; ❹) has a gorgeous location which means it gets booked up months ahead for the March to mid-June period. For year-round accommodation, try the excellent new cabins at *Kilpisjärven Lomakeskus* (☎016/537 801, ⓦwww.kilpisjarvi.net; €110). They also offer a full range of winter adventure activities. For **eating and drinking**, the best bet is *Tuula's Restaurant & Café* on Käsivarrentie, which serves local specialities like Arctic char as well as pizzas and burgers. About 25km south of Kilpisjärvi, the welcoming *Peeran Retkeilykeskus* **youth hostel** (☎016/532 659, ⓦwww.peera.fi; open March–Sept; dorms €25) also serves good food.

Travel details

Trains

Rovaniemi to: Helsinki (5 daily; 13hr); Kemi (6 daily; 1hr 15min); Kemijärvi (1 daily; 1hr 15min); Oulu (6 daily; 2hr 20min).

Buses

Inari to: Ivalo (3–6 daily; 40min); Rovaniemi (3–6 daily; 5hr15min); Utsjoki (2–3 daily; 1hr 30min).
Ivalo to: Inari (3-6 daily; 40min); Saariselkä (6 daily; 30min).
Kittilä to: Levi (6 daily; 15min); Muonio (3 daily; 1hr 15min); Sodankylä (Mon–Fri 1 daily; 1hr 15min); Ylläs (1 daily; 50min).
Muonio to: Hetta (3 daily; 1hr 15min); Kilpisjärvi (2 daily; 2hr 30min); Kittilä (3 daily; 1hr 15min); Levi (4 daily; 1hr).

Rovaniemi to: Hetta (2 daily; 4hr 45min–5hr 15min); Inari (3–6 daily; 5hr 15min); Ivalo (4–6 daily; 4hr 45min); Kilpisjärvi (2 daily; 6hr 15min); Kittilä (4 daily; 2hr); Muonio (3 daily; 3hr 20min); Saariselkä (6 daily; 3hr 30min); Sodankylä (3–10 daily; 1hr 40min).
Saariselkä to: Ivalo (6 daily; 30min); Rovaniemi (6 daily; 3hr 45min).
Sodankylä to: Inari (3 daily; 4hr); Ivalo (3 daily; 3hr45min); Kemijärvi (2 daily; 1hr 40min); Kittilä (Mon–Fri 1 daily; 1hr 15min); Rovaniemi (3–10 daily; 1hr 40min); Saariselkä (4 daily; 1hr 30min).
Utsjoki to: Inari (2–3 daily; 1hr 30min); Rovaniemi (2 daily; 7hr).

Air

Rovaniemi to: Helsinki (4 daily; 1hr15min).

Contexts

Contexts

History

L ong juggled like a hot potato between the medieval superpowers of Sweden and Russia, and later tacked on nearly as an afterthought to the Soviet Union, Finland's **history** is a captivating tale of a small country's struggle – and eventual triumph – against what have often seemed unsurmountable odds. Theirs is also a story full of powerful contemporary resonances – the Finns' battle to regain their independence did not go unnoticed on the other side of the Baltic Sea, having served as a model for the three ex-Soviet Baltic states of Latvia, Lithuania and Estonia in their fight for sovereignty and, more recently, EU membership. Wherever modern-day Finland progresses, its intricate, often turbulent history will remain a reminder of how dark times can get – and how Finns can beat the odds.

First settlements

As the ice sheets of the last **Ice Age** retreated, parts of the Finnish Arctic coast were settled by tribes from Eastern Europe. They hunted bear and reindeer, and fished the well-stocked rivers and lakes: relics of their existence have been found and dated to around 8000 BC. Pottery skills were introduced around 3000 BC, and trade with Russia and the east flourished. At the same time, other peoples were arriving and merging with the established population. The **Boat Axe** culture (1800–1600 BC), which originated in central Europe, spread as Indo-Europeans migrated into Finland. The seafaring knowledge they possessed enabled them to begin trading with Sweden from the Finnish west coast, as indicated by Bronze Age findings (around 1300 BC) concentrated in a narrow strip along the seaboard. The previous settlers withdrew eastwards and the advent of severe weather brought this period of occupation to an end.

The arrival of the Finns

The **Finns** were a race from central Siberia, who migrated in two directions. One tribe went south, eventually to Hungary, and the other westwards to the Baltic, where it mixed with Latgals, Lithuanians and Germans. The latter, the "Baltic Finns", were migrants who crossed the Baltic around 400 AD to form an independent society in Finland. In 100 AD the Roman historian Tacitus described a wild and primitive people called "the Fenni". This is thought to have been a reference to the earliest Sámi, who occupied Finland before this. With their more advanced culture, the Baltic Finns absorbed this indigenous population, although some of their customs were maintained. The new Finns worked the land, utilized the vast forests and made lengthy fishing expeditions on the lakes.

The main Finnish settlements were built up along the west coast facing Sweden, with whom trade was established, until the Vikings' opening up of routes further to the east forced these communities into decline. Meanwhile, the Finnish south coast was exposed to seaborne raiding parties and most Finns moved inland and eastwards, a large number settling around huge **Lake Ladoga** in Karelia. Eventually the people of Karelia were able to enjoy trade in two directions: with the Varangians to the east and the Swedes to the west. Groups from Karelia and the more northern territory of Kainuu regularly ventured into Lapland to fish and hunt. At the end of the pagan era Finland was split into three regions: Varsinais-Suomi ("Finland proper") in the southwest; Häme in the western part of the lake region; and Karelia in the east. Although they often helped one another, there was no formal cooperation between the inhabitants of these areas.

The Middle Ages and Swedish rule

At the start of the tenth century, pagan Finland was caught between two opposing religions: **Catholicism** in Sweden on one side and the **Orthodox Church** of Russia on the other. The Russians wielded great influence in Karelia, but the west of Finland began to gravitate towards Catholicism on account of its high level of contact with Sweden. In 1155 King Erik of Sweden launched a "crusade" into Finland – although its real purpose was to strengthen trade routes – which swept through the southwest and established Swedish control, leaving the English Bishop Henry at Turku to establish a parish. Henry was killed by a Finnish yeoman, but became the patron saint of the Turku diocese and the region became the administrative base of the whole country. Western Finland generally acquiesced to the Swedes, but Karelia didn't, becoming a territory much sought after by both the Swedes and the Russians. In 1323, under the Treaty of Nöteborg (or Pähkinäsaari), an official border was drawn up, giving the western part of Karelia to Sweden while the Russian principality of Novgorod retained the eastern section around Lake Ladoga. To emphasize their claim, the Russians founded the Orthodox Valamo Monastery on an island in the lake.

Kalmar Union

Under the Swedish crown, Finns still worked and controlled their own land, often living side by side with Swedes, who came to the west coast to safeguard sea trade. Finnish provincial leaders were given places among the nobility and in 1362 King Håkon gave Finland the right to vote in Swedish royal elections, though the 1397 **Kalmar Union** brought sovereignty over all of Sweden (Finland included) to Margrethe, Queen of Denmark and Norway. While most Finns were little affected by the constitution of the Union, there was a hope that it would guarantee their safety against the Russians, whose expansionist policies were an increasing threat. Throughout the fifteenth century there were repeated skirmishes between Russians and Finns in the border lands and around the important Finnish Baltic trading centre of Viipuri (now Russian Vyborg).

The election of King Charles VIII in 1438 caused a rift in the Union and serious strife between Sweden and Denmark. He was forced to abdicate in 1458 but his support in Finland was strong, and his successor, Christian I, sent an armed column to subdue Finnish unrest. While Turku Castle was under siege, the Danish noble Erik Axelsson Tott, already known and respected in the country, called a meeting of representatives from every Finnish estate where it was agreed that Christian I would be acknowledged as king of the Union. Tott went on to take command of Viipuri Castle, and he further strengthened Finland's eastern defences by erecting the fortress of Olavinlinna (in the present town of Savonlinna) in 1475, as a response to a revival of Russian claims on Karelia. After an alliance with Denmark was signed in 1493, the technically inferior Finns miraculously successfully fended off a Russian attack on Viipuri on November 30, 1495.

The Swedish empire

By the time the Kalmar Union collapsed and **Gustav Vasa** took the Swedish throne in 1521, many villages had been established in the disputed border regions.

Almost every inhabitant spoke Finnish – despite a largely Swedish-born nobility – but there was a roughly equal division between those communities who paid taxes to the Swedish king and those who paid them to the Russian tsar. In the winter of 1555, a Russian advance into Karelia was quashed at Joutselkä by Finns using skis to travel speedily over the icy roads, a victory that made the Finnish nobility confident of success in a full-scale war. While hesitant, Vasa finally agreed to their wishes: 12,000 troops from Sweden were dispatched to eastern Finland, and an offensive launched in the autumn of 1556. It failed, with the Russians reaching the gates of Viipuri, and Vasa retreating to the Åland Islands, asking for peace.

In 1550 Gustav Vasa founded the town of **Helsingfors** (whence, "Helsinki"), though it remained little more than a fishing village for the two centuries that followed. In 1556 Vasa made Finland a Swedish Grand Duchy and gave his son, Johan, the title "Duke of Finland". Johan was pro-Finnish, and Finland was divided between loyalty towards the friendly duke and the need to keep on good terms with the Swedish crown, now held by Erik XIV. The Swedish forces sent to collect Johan – who had been sentenced to death after breaching protocol by invading Livonia, but then pardoned – laid siege to Turku Castle for three weeks, executing thirty nobles before capturing the duke and imprisoning him.

The war between Sweden and Denmark over control of the Baltic took its toll on Erik. He became mentally unbalanced, slaying several prisoners who were being held for trial and, in a moment of complete madness, releasing Johan from detention. The Swedish nobles were incensed by Erik's actions and rebelled against him – with the result that Johan became king in 1568.

The Three Wraths

In 1570 Swedish resources were stretched when hostilities again erupted with Russia, now ruled by the aggressive **Tsar Ivan** ("the Terrible") **IV**. The conflict was to last 25 years, a period known in Finland as **"The Long Wrath"**. It saw the introduction of a form of conscription instead of the reliance on mercenary soldiers, which had been the norm in other Swedish wars. Able-bodied men aged between 15 and 50 were rounded up by the local bailiff and about one in ten selected for military service. Russia occupied almost all of Estonia and made deep thrusts into southern Finland. Finally the Swedish-Finnish troops regained Estonia and made significant advances through Karelia, capturing an important eastern-European trading route.

Sweden was established as the dominant force in the Baltic, but under Gustav II, crowned king in 1611, Finland began to lose the special status it had previously enjoyed. Conditions continued to decline until 1637, when Per Brahe was appointed governor general. Against the prevailing mood of the time, he insisted that all officers should study Finnish, selected Turku as the spot for a university – the country's first – and instigated a successful programme to spread literacy among the Finnish people.

But things were not looking up for the country. A terrible harvest in 1696 caused a **famine** that killed a third of the Finnish population, while a decade later Viipuri fell to the Russians. Under their new tsar, Peter ("the Great"), the Russians quickly spread across the country, causing the nobility to flee to Stockholm and Swedish commanders to be more concerned with salvaging their army than saving Finland. In 1714, eight years of Russian occupation – **"The Great Wrath"** – began. Descriptions of the horrors of these times have been exaggerated, but nonetheless the events confirmed the Finns' longtime dread of their eastern neighbour. The Russians saw Finland simply as a springboard to attack Sweden, and laid waste to anything in it which the Swedes might attempt to regain. After two more treaties and another occupation in 1742 – **"The Lesser Wrath"** – the Russians had succeeded in moving their border west.

The Russian era

In an attempt to force Sweden to join Napoleon's economic blockade, **Russia**, under Tsar Alexander I, attacked and occupied Finland in 1807. The Treaty of Hamina, signed in September of that year, legally ceded all of the country to Russia. The tsar had been in need of a friendly country close to Napoleon's territory as a reliable ally in case of future hostilities between the two leaders. To gain Finnish favour, he guaranteed beneficial terms at the Porvoo-based Swedish Diet, which at the time still exercised control (the Finns had yet to establish their own Diet and Senate), and subsequently Finland became an autonomous **Russian Grand Duchy**. There was no conscription and taxation was frozen, while realignment of the northern section of the Finnish–Russian border gave additional land to Finland. Finns could freely occupy positions in the Russian empire, although Russians were denied equal opportunities within Finland. The long period of peace that ensued saw a great improvement in Finnish wealth and well-being.

After returning Viipuri to Finland, the tsar declared Helsinki the capital in 1812, deeming Turku too close to Sweden for safety. The "Guards of Finland" helped crush the Polish rebellion and fought in the Russo-Turkish conflict. This, along with the French and English attacks on Finnish harbours during the Crimean War, accentuated the bond between the two countries. Many Finns came to regard the tsar as their own monarch.

Linguistic nationalism

There was, however, an increasingly active Finnish-language movement. A student leader, the future statesman **Johan Vilhelm Snellman**, had met the tsar and demanded that Finnish replace Swedish as the country's official language. Snellman's slogan "Swedes we are no longer, Russians we cannot become, we must be Finns" became the rallying cry of the Fennomen. The Swedish-speaking ruling class, feeling threatened, had Snellman removed from his university post and he retreated to Kuopio to publish newspapers espousing his beliefs. His opponents cited Finnish as the language of peasants, unfit for cultured use – a claim undermined by the efforts of a playwright, Aleksis Kivi, whose works marked the beginning of Finnish-language **theatre**. In 1835, the collection of Karelian folk tales published in Finnish by Elias Lönnrot as the Kalevala became the first written record of Finnish **folklore**, a solidifying force for standardization of the language and a focal point for Finnish nationalism. In 1858 Finnish was declared the official language of local government in areas where the majority of the population were Finnish-speaking, giving native-tongued Finns equal status with Swedish speakers.

The increasingly powerful Pan-Slavist contingent in Russia was horrified by the growth of the Finnish timber industry and the rise of trade with the west. They were also unhappy with the special status of the Grand Duchy, considering the Finns an alien race who would contaminate the eastern empire by their links with the west. Tsar Alexander III was not swayed by these opinions but, after his assassination in 1894, Nicholas I came to power and instigated a **Russification** process. Russian was declared the official language, Finnish money was abolished and plans were laid to merge the Finnish army into the Russian army. To pass these measures the tsar drew up the unconstitutional February Manifesto.

Nationalist stirrings

Opposition came in varying forms. In 1899, a young composer called **Jean Sibelius** wrote his majestic and dynamic *Finlandia*. The Russians banned all performances of it "under any name that indicates its patriotic character", causing Sibelius to publish it as *Opus 26 No. 7*. The painter Akseli Gallen-Kallela ignored international art trends and depicted scenes from the Kalevala, as did the poet Eino Leino. Students skied to farms all over the country and collected half a million signatures against the manifesto, and over a thousand of Europe's foremost intellectuals signed a document called "**Pro-Finlandia**". The leaders of the mass civil disobedience that followed went underground in Helsinki, entitling themselves the **Kagel** – borrowing a name used by persecuted Russian Jews.

In 1905 the Russians suffered defeat in their war with Japan, and the general strike that broke out in their country spread to Finland, the Finnish labour movement being represented by the Social Democratic Party. The revolutionary spirit that was moving through Russia encouraged the conservative Finnish Senate to reach a compromise with the demands of the Social Democrats, and the result was a gigantic upheaval in the Finnish parliamentary system. In 1906, the country adopted a single-chamber parliament, the **Eduskunta**, elected by national suffrage – Finnish **women** being the first in Europe to get the vote. In the first election under the new system the Social Democrats won eighty seats out of the total of two hundred, making it the most left-wing legislature seen so far in Europe.

Any laws passed in Finland, however, still needed the ratification of the tsar, who now viewed Finland as a dangerous forum for leftist debate (the exiled Lenin met Stalin for the first time in Tampere). In 1910 Nicholas II removed the new parliament's powers and reinstated the Russification programme. Two years later the Parity Act gave Russians in Finland status equal to Finns, enabling them to hold seats in the Senate and posts in the civil service. The outspoken anti-tsarist parliamentary speaker P.E. Svinhufvud was exiled to Siberia for a second time.

As World War I commenced, Finland was obviously allied with Russia and endured a commercial blockade, food shortages and restrictions on civil liberties, but did not actually fight on the tsar's behalf. Germany promised Finland total autonomy in the event of victory for the Kaiser and provided clandestine military training to about two thousand Finnish students – the **Jäger** movement who reached Germany through Sweden and later fought against the Russians as a light infantry battalion on the Baltic front.

Towards independence

When the tsar was overthrown in 1917, the Russian provisional government under Kerensky declared the measures taken against Finland null and void and restored the previous level of autonomy, so making Finland an **independent nation-state**. Within Finland there was uncertainty over the country's constitutional bonds with Russia. The conservative view was that prerogative powers should be passed from the deposed ruler to the provisional government, while socialists held that the provisional government had no right to exercise power in Finland and that supreme authority should be passed to the Eduskunta.

Under the Power Act, the Eduskunta vested in itself supreme authority within Finland, leaving only control of foreign and military matters residing with the Russians. Kerensky refused to recognize the Power Act and dissolved the Finnish parliament, forcing a fresh election. This time a bigger poll returned a conservative majority.

Around the country there had been widespread labour disputes and violent confrontations between strikers and strike-breaking mobs hired by landowners. The Social Democrats sanctioned the formation of an armed workers' guard, soon to be called the Red Guard, in response to the growing White Guard, a right-wing private army operating in the virtual absence of a regular police force. Within several months, Finland issued a de facto statement of independence and, shortly thereafter, an independent constitution approved by the Eduskunta and recognized by the Soviet leader, Lenin.

The civil war

In asserting its new authority, the government repeatedly clashed with the labour movement. The Red Guard, who had reached an uneasy truce with the Social Democratic leadership, were involved in gun-running between Viipuri and Petrograd, and efforts by the White Guard to halt it led to full-scale fighting. A vote passed by the Eduskunta on January 12, 1918, empowered the government to create a police force to restore law and order. On January 25 the White Guard was legitimized as the Civil Guard.

In Helsinki, a special committee of the Social Democrats took the decision to resist the Civil Guard and seize power, effectively pledging themselves to **civil war**. On January 27 and 28, a series of occupations enabled leftist committees to take control of the capital and the major towns of the south. Three government ministers who evaded capture fled to Vaasa and formed a rump administration. Meanwhile, a Finnish-born aristocrat, C.G.E. Mannerheim, who had served as a cavalry officer in the Russian army, arrived at the request of the government in Ostrobothnia, a region dominated by right-wing farmers, to train a force to fight the Reds.

The Whites were in control of Ostrobothnia, northern Finland and parts of Karelia, and were connected by a railway from Vaasa to Käkisalmi (Russian: Priozersk) on Lake Ladoga. Although the Reds were numerically superior they were poorly equipped and poorly trained, and failed to break the enemy's line of communication. Tampere fell to the Whites in March. At the same time, a German force landed on the south coast, their assistance requested by White Finns in Berlin (although Mannerheim opposed their involvement). Surrounded, the leftists' resistance collapsed in April.

Throughout the conflict, the **Social Democratic Party** maintained a high level of unity. While containing revolutionary elements, it was led mainly by socialists seeking to retain parliamentary democracy, and believing their fight was against a bourgeois force seeking to impose right-wing values on the newly independent state. Their arms, however, were supplied by the Soviet Union, causing the White taunt that the Reds were "aided by foreign bayonets". Many of the revolutionary socialists within the party fled to Russia after the civil war, where they formed the Finnish Communist Party. The harsh treatment of the Reds who were captured – 8000 were executed and 80,000 were imprisoned in camps where more than 9000 died from hunger or disease – fired a resentment that would last for generations. The Whites regarded the war as one of liberation, ridding the country of Russians and the Bolshevik influence, and setting the course for an anti-Russian Finnish nationalism. Mannerheim and the strongly pro-German Jäger contingent were keen to continue east, to gain the whole of Karelia from the Russians, but the possibility of direct Finnish assistance to the Russian White Army – who were seeking to overthrow the Bolshevik government – came to nothing thanks to the Russian Whites' refusal to guarantee recognition of Finland's independent status.

Later that year, a provisional government of independent Karelia was set up in Uhtua. Its formation was masterminded by Red Finns, who ensured that its claims to make Karelia a totally independent region did not accord with the desires of the

Finnish government. The provisional government's congress, held the following year, also confirmed a wish for separation from the Soviet Union and requested the removal of the Soviet troops; this was agreed, with a proviso that Soviet troops retained a right to be based in eastern Karelia. The eventual collapse of the talks caused the provisional government and its supporters to flee to Finland as a Finnish battalion of the Soviet Red Army moved in and occupied the area. Subsequently the Karelian Workers' Commune, motivated by the Finnish Communists and backed by Soviet decree, was formed. Their claims were ignored by the subsequent Treaty of Tartu, which gave Finland the Petsamo area, which led to a valuable ice-free harbour on the Arctic coast, but rejected the Karelians' demands for self-determination.

The republic

The White success in the civil war led to a right-wing government with a pro-German majority, which wanted to establish Finland as a monarchy rather than the republic allowed for under the 1917 declaration of independence. Although twice defeated in the Eduskunta, Prime Minister J.K. Paasikivi evoked a clause in the Swedish Form of Government from 1772, making legal the election of a king. As a result, the Finnish crown was offered to a German, Friedrich Karl, Prince of Hessen. Immediately prior to German defeat in World War I, the prince declined the invitation. The victorious Allies insisted on a new Finnish government and a fresh general election if they were to recognize the nation's independent status. Since the country was now compelled to look to the Allies for future assistance, the request was complied with, sealing Finland's future as a **republic**. The first president was the liberal **Ståhlberg**.

After years of rapidly increasing prosperity and great social reform including compulsory schooling, religious freedom and improved social services, Finnish economic development halted abruptly following the world slump of the late 1920s. A series of strikes culminated in a dock workers' dispute which began in May 1928 and continued for almost a year – a symbolic ideological clash that was a harbinger of events to come.

The government obtained a two-thirds majority in the elections of October 1930 and amended the constitution to make communist activity legal. This was expected to placate the extreme and violent communist youth movement known as the **Lapuans** but instead they issued even more extreme demands, including the abolition of the Social Democrats. In 1932, a coup d'état was attempted by a Lapuan group who prevented a socialist member of parliament from addressing a meeting in Mäntsälä, 50km north of Helsinki. They refused to disperse, despite shots being fired by police, and sent for backup assistance from Lapuan bases around the country. The Lapuan leadership took up the cause and broadcast demands for a new government. They were unsuccessful due to the loyalty of the troops who surrounded the town on the orders of the then prime minister, Svinhufvud. Following this, the Lapuans were outlawed, although their leaders received only minor punishments for their deeds. Several of them regrouped as the Nazi-style Patriotic People's Movement. But unlike the parallel movements in Europe, there was little in Finland on which Nazism could focus mass hatred and, despite winning a few parliamentary seats, the movement quickly dwindled into insignificance.

The Finnish economy recovered swiftly, and much international goodwill was generated when the country became the only nation to fully pay its war reparations to the USA after World War I. Finland joined the League of Nations hoping for a guarantee of its eastern border, but by 1935 the League's weakness was apparent and the Finns looked to traditionally neutral Scandinavia for protection as Europe moved towards war.

World War II

The Nazi–Soviet Non-Aggression Pact of August 1939 put Finland firmly into the **Soviet sphere**. Stalin had compelled Estonia, Latvia and Lithuania to allow Russian bases on their land, and by October was demanding a chunk of the Karelian isthmus from Finland to protect Leningrad, as well as a leasing of the Hanko peninsula on the Finnish Baltic coast. Russian troops were heading towards the Finnish border from Murmansk, and on November 30 the Karelian isthmus was attacked – an act that triggered the Winter War.

Stalin had had the tsarist military commanders executed, and his troops were led by young communists well versed in ideology but ignorant of war strategy. Informed that the Finnish people would welcome them as liberators, the Soviet soldiers anticipated little resistance to their invasion. They expected to reach the Finnish west coast within ten days and therefore carried no overcoats, had little food, and camped each night in open fields. The Finns, although vastly outnumbered, were defending their homes and farms as well as their hard-won independence. Familiarity with the terrain enabled them to conceal themselves in the forests and attack through stealth – and they were prepared for the winter temperatures, which plunged to -30°C (-18°F). The Russians were slowly picked off and their camps frequently surrounded and destroyed.

The **Treaty of Moscow** ceded eleven percent of Finnish territory to the Soviet Union – a mass exodus of nearly half a million people to the new boundaries of Finland soon followed – and the period immediately after the Winter War left Finland in a difficult position. Before the war, Finland had produced all its own food but was dependent on imported fertilizers. Supplies of grain, which had been coming from Russia, were halted as part of Soviet pressure for increased transit rights and access to the important nickel-producing mines in Petsamo. Finland became reliant on grain from Germany and British shipments to the Petsamo coast, which were interrupted when Germany invaded Norway. In return for providing arms, Germany was given transit rights through Finland. Legally, this required the troops to be constantly moving, but a permanent force became stationed at Rovaniemi.

The Continuation War

The Finnish leadership knew that Germany was secretly preparing to attack the Soviet Union, and a broadcast from Berlin had spoken of a "united front" from Norway to Poland at a time when Finland was officially outside the Nazi sphere. Within Finland there was little support for the Nazis, but there was a fear of Soviet occupation. While Finland clung to its **neutrality**, refusing to fight unless attacked, it was drawn closer and closer to Germany. Soviet air raids on several Finnish towns in June 1941 finally led Finland into the war on the side of the Nazis. The ensuing conflict with the Russians, fought with the primary purpose of regaining territory lost in the Winter War, became known as the **Continuation War**. The bulk of the land ceded under the Treaty of Moscow was recovered by the end of August. After this, Mannerheim, who commanded the Finnish troops, ignored Nazi encouragement to assist in their attack on Leningrad. A request from the British prime minister, Winston Churchill, that the Finns cease their advance, was also refused, although Mannerheim didn't cut the Murmansk railway which was moving Allied supplies. Even so, Britain was forced to acknowledge the predicament of its ally, the Soviet Union, and declared war on Finland in December 1941.

In 1943, the German defeat at Stalingrad, which made Allied victory almost inevitable, had a profound impact in Finland. Mannerheim called a meeting of inner-cabinet ministers and decided to seek a truce with the Soviet Union. The US stepped forward as a mediator but announced that the peace terms set by Moscow were too severe to be worthy of negotiation. Germany, meanwhile, had learned of the Finnish initiative and demanded an undertaking that Finland would not seek peace with Russia, threatening to withdraw supplies if it was not given. (The Germans were also unhappy with Finnish sympathy for Jews – several hundred who had escaped from central Europe were saved from the concentration camps by being granted Finnish citizenship.) Simultaneously, a Russian advance into Karelia made Finland dependent on German arms to launch a counterattack. An agreement with the Germans was signed by President Risto Ryti in June 1944 without the consent of the Eduskunta, thereby making the deed invalid when he ceased to be president.

Ryti resigned the presidency at the beginning of August and Mannerheim informed Germany that the agreement was no longer binding. A peace treaty with the Soviet Union was signed in Moscow two weeks later. Under its terms, Finland was forced to give up the Pestamo region and the border was restored to its 1940 position. The Hanko peninsula was returned but instead the Porkkala peninsula, nearer to Helsinki, was to be leased to the Soviet Union for fifty years. There were stinging reparations, and the Finns had to drive the remaining Germans out of the country within two weeks – easily accomplished in the south, much less so in Lapland, where bitter fighting caused the total destruction of many towns. As the German forces retreated they employed a scorched-earth policy in retaliation for the betrayal of their former colleagues in arms, the Finns. The Germans burnt the provincial capital Rovaniemi to the ground, leaving just thirteen percent of the buildings remaining. It is estimated that half of all structures in Finnish Lapland were **destroyed** during the retreat, which accounts for why the architecture of so many northern Finnish towns these days feels so bland: everything was completely rebuilt from scratch in the 1950s and 1960s. In total, 100,000 refugees fled the province at this time, half of them crossing into Sweden, as fighting flared between the two armies; particularly fierce battles were fought south of Ivalo as the Germans prepared to exit Finland.

The postwar period

After the war, the Communist Party was legalized and, along with militant socialists expelled from the Social Democratic Party, formed a broad leftist umbrella organization – the Finnish People's Democratic League. Their efforts to absorb the Social Democrats were resisted by that party's moderate leadership, who regarded Communism as "poison to the Finnish people". In the first peace-time poll, the Democratic League went to the electorate with a populist rather than revolutionary manifesto – something that was to characterize future Finnish Communism. Both they and the Social Democrats attained approximately a quarter of the vote. Bolstered by two Social Democratic defections, the Democratic League narrowly became the largest party in the Eduskunta. The two of them, along with the Agrarian Party, formed an alliance ("The Big Three Agreement") that held the balance of power in a coalition government under the premiership of Paasikivi.

To ensure that the terms of the peace agreement were adhered to, the Soviet-dominated Allied Control Commission stayed in Finland until 1947. Its presence engendered a tense atmosphere both on the streets of Helsinki – there were several incidents of violence against Soviet officers – and in the numerous clashes with the Finnish government over the war trials. Unlike the Eastern-European countries under full Soviet occupation, Finland was able to carry out its own trials, but had to satisfy the Commission that they were conducted properly. Delicate manoeuvring by the Chief of Justice, Urho Kekkonen, resulted in comparatively short prison sentences for the accused, the longest being ten years for Risto Ryti.

After Finland had pledged to not join any alliance hostile to the Soviet Union, the postwar economy was dominated by the reparations demand. Much of the bill was paid off in ships and machinery, which established **engineering** as a major industry. The escalating world demand for timber products boosted exports, but inflation soared and led to frequent wage disputes. In 1949 an attempt to enforce a piece-work rate in a pulp factory in Kemi culminated in two workers being shot by police, a state of emergency being declared in the town, and the arrest of Communist leaders. Economic conflicts reached a climax in 1956 after right-wingers in the Eduskunta had blocked an annual extension of government controls on wages and prices. This caused a sharp rise in the cost of living, and the trade unions demanded appropriate pay increases. A general strike followed, lasting for three weeks until the strikers' demands were met. Any benefit, however, was quickly nullified by further price rises.

The Kekkonen years

In 1957 a split occurred in the Social Democrats between urban and rural factions, the former seeking increased industrialization and the streamlining of unprofitable farms, the latter pursuing high agricultural subsidies. By 1959 a group of breakaway ruralists had set up the Small Farmers' Social Democratic Union, causing a rift in the country's internal politics that was to have important repercussions in Finland's dealings with the Soviet Union. Although the government had no intention of changing its foreign policy, the Social Democrat's chairman, Väinö Tanner, had a well-known antipathy to the Soviet Union. Coupled with a growing number of anti-Soviet newspaper editorials, this precipitated the "night frost" of 1958. The Soviet leader, Khruschev, suspended imports and deliveries of machinery, causing a rise in Finnish unemployment. **Kekkonen**, elected president in 1956, personally intervened in the crisis by meeting with Khruschev, so angering the Social Democrats, who accused Kekkonen of behaving undemocratically; meanwhile, the Agrarians were lambasted for failing to stand up to Soviet pressure.

Throughout the early 1960s there was mounting dissatisfaction within the People's Democratic League towards the old pro-Moscow leadership, and the election of May 1966 resulted in a "popular front" government dominated by the Social Democrats and the People's Democratic League.

This brought to an end a twenty-year spell of centre-right governments in which the crucial pivot had been the Agrarian Party. In 1965, the Agrarians changed their name to the Centre Party, aiming to modernize their image and become more attractive to the urban electorate. A challenge to this new direction was mounted by the Finnish Rural Party, founded by a breakaway group of Agrarians in the late 1950s, who mounted an increasingly influential campaign on behalf of "the forgotten people" – farmers and smallholders in declining rural areas. In the election of 1970 they gained ten percent of the vote, but in subsequent years lost support through internal divisions.

The Communists retained governmental posts until 1971, when they too were split – between the young "reformists" who advocated continued participation in government, and the older, hard-line "purists" who were frustrated by the failure to implement socialist economic policies, and preferred to stay in opposition.

Modern Finland

Throughout the postwar years Finland promoted itself vigorously as a neutral country. It joined the United Nations in 1955 and Finnish soldiers became an integral part of the UN Peace-Keeping Force.

The stature of Kekkonen as a world leader guaranteed continued support for his presidency. But his commitment to the Paasikivi–Kekkonen line ensured that nothing potentially upsetting to the Soviet Union was allowed to surface in Finnish politics, giving – as some thought – the Soviet Union a covert influence on Finland's internal affairs. Opposition to Kekkonen was simply perceived as an attempt to undermine the Paasikivi–Kekkonen line. Equally, the unchallenge-able nature of Kekkonen's presidency was considered to be beyond his proper constitutional powers. A move in 1974 by an alliance of right-wingers and Social Democrats within the Eduskunta to transfer some of the presidential powers to parliament received a very hostile reaction, emphasizing the almost inviolate position Kekkonen enjoyed. Kekkonen was re-elected in 1978, although forced to stand down due to illness in 1981.

Because Finland is heavily dependent on foreign trade, its well-being has closely mirrored world trends. The international **financial boom** of the 1960s enabled a range of social legislation to be passed and created a comparatively high standard of living for most Finns – albeit not on the same scale as the rest of Scandinavia. The global recession of the 1970s and early 1980s was most dramatically felt when a fall in the world market for wood pulp coincided with a steep increase in the price of oil. Although the country tackled the immediate problems of the recession, industry remained heavily concentrated in the south, causing rural areas further north to experience high rates of unemployment and few prospects for economic growth – save through rising levels of tourism.

Towards the EU

In 1992 celebrations to mark 75 years of Finnish independence were muted by the realization that the country was entering a highly critical period, facing more problems (few of its own making) than it had for many decades. The end of the Cold War had diminished the value of Finland's hard-won neutrality, the economic and ethnic difficulties in Russia were being watched with trepidation, while another global recession hit Finland just as the nation lost its major trading partner – the Soviet Union – of the last fifty years.

Throughout the early 1990s Finland's **economic depression** was among the worst in the industrial west. Its banking system was in crisis and unemployment figures were almost the highest in Europe, while the country's growing number of asylum seekers meant they became scapegoats for social problems; there was a spate of anti-immigrant violence during the mid-1990s. Such economic and societal strife forced Finland to pin its hopes on closer links with Western Europe. On January 1, 1995, the country became a full member of the **European Union** and, in the same year, the Social Democratic Party's Martti Ahtisaari was elected as president, with the general election resulting in a coalition win for the Social

Democrats, their chairman Paavo Lipponen forming a majority government that included conservatives, socialists, the Swedish Folk Party and the Green Party.

By the millennium, as Russia descended into farce, Finland had become more firmly linked to the EU and its economy had recovered sufficiently for it to be accepted into the first wave of countries to join the European Monetary Union. In 1999, for the first time, Finland assumed the presidency of the European Union, while President Ahtisaari established himself as an important international statesman through his interventions in the war in Kosovo.

The new millennium

On the eve of 2000, Finland's standing post the depression was uncertain. It fell to the Finnish governments over the next decade to reform the country's economic system through privatization, deregulation and tax cuts. When Ahtisaari decided not to seek re-election in 2000, long-standing member of parliament and then foreign minister Tarja Halonen ran a victorious campaign and became Finland's first **female president**. The independent-minded Halonen took an active role in leading the country, while maintaining a 95 percent approval rating in opinion polls; in 2004, she was nominated one of ten *suuret Suomalaiset* ("greatest Finns") – the only living person on the list.

The 2006 presidential campaign sparked a nationwide discussion over limiting the president's powers – an issue which brought to light Finnish concern over the degree of "democratic" decision-making effected by current heads of government. It also dredged up talk over the age-old issue of NATO membership and its link to threats of terrorism (most Finns are concerned that joining NATO would increase Finland's risk of terrorist attacks, though they aren't nearly as vocal about it as their continental neighbours). On January 29, 2006, Halonen was re-elected by a tiny margin for a second six-year presidential term. The future of Finland's long-standing neutrality in Europe was the campaign's focal issue, and Halonen's second win suggests that Finland will remain outside NATO until at least 2012.

Technology and the economy

Economically, Finland's highly educated populace and technological expertise have made it a powerful player in the world IT market, and it consistently ranks among the top countries in the world for **technological innovation**, as it does an outstanding job of investing in technology. It is the first country in the world to create laws guaranteeing broadband access, for example; in 2009, one-megabit broadband internet access was made a legal right for all Finns. Helsinki's technological infrastructure ranks among the most sophisticated anywhere, and it has proportionally more experts in science and technology than any other capital city in the world. Even among the hoi polloi, Finns are the second most active internet users in the world – over fifty percent of the country go online on a daily basis. Furthermore, thanks to Finnish government assistance available to small- and medium-sized overseas firms, many foreign entities doing business in Helsinki often grow at a quicker rate than native Finnish companies.

Finland's other industrialized sectors have helped it to maintain a per-capita output on a par with those of the UK and Germany, and while the country boasts the highest prices in the EU – a whopping 23 percent above the average for EU member states – Finns have been earning money at an unprecedented rate since the turn of the millennium. The Finnish economy has been growing steadily to become one of the wealthiest, heathiest and **most competitive** in the world – it's regularly rated as *the* most competitive by the Global Competitiveness Report

– with an estimated 2008 GDP of €192 billion. And all of this despite the general global economic downturn and a slowdown in GDP growth from 4.9 percent in 2006 to 2.5 percent in 2008. But business-wise the Finnish capital is thriving: Helsinki serves as headquarters to thousands of businesses, the largest of which trade in **paper manufacturing** (there's a good chance that the paper these words are printed on was made in Finland), **shipbuilding** (every fourth cruise-ship in the world sails out of a Finnish port on its maiden voyage) and **information technology** (make a phone call from Dublin to Delhi and you're likely to ring through Finnish networks, hubs and routers).

Much of this achievement was propelled by the jettisoning of the markkaa, the Finnish Mark, and the adoption of the euro as Finland's currency in 2002. This move brought a new pride to the Finnish nation after years of living in the shadow of the Soviet Union; political and economic freedom had finally and tangibly been won. And with neighbouring Estonia now a full member of the EU, a former foe has emerged from behind the Iron Curtain to establish itself as a trade and tourism ally on an equitable, if not entirely equal, footing.

Social and environmental problems

But while EU membership has provided a new sense of security and confidence, the contemporary picture is not entirely rosy: the age-old issue of alcoholism and the chaos of Russia's gangster economy on the doorstep provide major worries, as do continuing debates around the role of the welfare state. The dark memories of hot potato Karelia have also crept steadily into public debate as Halonen has endeavoured to strengthen cultural and economic ties with Putin's Russia – though Finland has made it clear that it is in no way asking for the territory back. Other pressing issues include the need to diversify an economy that is over-reliant on the Nokia phone company, and the means by which to continue development in rural areas without the support of big government subsidies. Thankfully, unemployment has been on the decline for nearly a decade, with the 2008 rate of 6.2 percent over half what it was just ten years prior. But as the baby-boomers of the early postwar period near retirement age, the labour force will need to be further empowered if Finland hopes to continue to provide adequate levels of care for its elderly and poor.

How these issues are addressed remains Finland's major concern heading into the second decade of the new millennium. However, general economic concerns notwithstanding, it's the role of the **environment** that's likely to grab the headlines in the coming years. For one, while Finland manages all its forests for timber production and is the largest wood-pulp producer in the EU, some 700 forest species are currently classified as endangered due to fallout from forestry, including allocation of very small areas for natural habitats and the prevention of trees from growing old and naturally decaying.

On the **nuclear** front, Finland is at the front of the race. After numerous delays, construction of Finland's fifth nuclear power station is slated to finish in late 2011 (at which point it will be more than fifty percent over budget). Once completed, nuclear energy will provide well over thirty percent of the country's total energy needs – Finland is one of the highest energy consumers in the world per capita due to frigid winters and the needs of the paper and wood industries, and at the moment, the country is totally dependent on Russia for natural gas, as well as for eighty percent of its oil. All this development comes at a time when most of the rest of Europe – and neighbouring Sweden – is scaling down nuclear power because of excessive cost, increasing fears of pollution and the possibility of terrorist attacks. While Finland does currently spend close to €1 billion annually on environmental protection, and is considered the most successful of all EU members in its efforts to achieve sustainable development, questions are being raised about the security and efficacy of the government's energy projects, not least by the vocal Green Party, which fled the government coalition in 2002 when approval for construction of the new nuclear plant, Okiluoto 3, was approved. Groups such as Greenpeace are regularly lobbying Finnish ministers for increased energy efficiency, reduced power consumption and the introduction of eco-friendly measures such as improved public transport and the use of bicycles. Meanwhile, there are already talks in government of plans for proposing an additional three nuclear reactor plants. A heated public debate on these very sensitive issues is looking to put further pressure on the tradition of Finnish consensus politics.

Finnish film

Finland's **cinematic traditions**, while far from widely known outside the country, have been integral to the development of a distinct national identity. Outside the country, Finnish film is effectively only known for the quirky, chimerical – and nearly silent – motion pictures of Aki Kaurismäki, as good an introduction as any to Finland's bizarre sense of humour, and the understandably fractured sense of self of the natives.

Cinematic beginnings

The **first feature film** made in Finland was the Swedish-directed *Salaviinanpolttajat* (*Bootleggers*), which premiered in 1907 and resulted from a national scriptwriting project. Since any particularly Finnish film had been repressed during the Grand Duchy, film production post-independence had become a nationalist project, intended to reinforce the identity and character of the Finnish people. Early films tended to be short newsreel-style documentaries about nature and industry in the country, though **Erkki Karu** (1887–1935), an early pioneer in Finnish filmmaking, managed to direct a handful of successful rural melodramas. At the end of the silent era, many films produced were dramatized adaptations of Finnish plays and novels, including *Koskenlaskijan Morsian* (1923), *Kihlaus* (1922) and the urban comedy *Kaikki Rakastavat* (1931). Successful foreign films – often Swedish – were adapted for Finnish-language audiences and, for the first time, domestic films were able to hold their own against foreign productions – though they didn't exactly export well.

Wartime production surged despite the obstacles of horrendous conditions, a lack of film stock, the bombing of Helsinki and many film technicians being called to the front. But as commercial embargoes meant fewer cinema imports, Finnish distributors were crying out for new films to release. A cinematographer, **Erik Blomberg** (1913–1996), directed *Valkoinen Peura* (*The White Reindeer*, 1952), one of the country's few internationally acknowledged productions, which won the International Prize at the Cannes Film Festival in 1953 and the Golden Globe in the United States in 1957. The state introduced a series of government film grants and awards during the 1940s, continuing the legacy of protectionism of a nationalist cinema, but by the 1960s, film in Nordic countries – as in much of Europe – had become an art in its own right. Disillusionment after World War II meant filmic themes shifted from romance and comedy to deep, dark social drama depicting the problems of industrialization, including *Ristikon Varjossa* (*Hunting Shadows*, 1945) and *Tuntematon Sotilas* (*The Unknown Soldier*, 1955), the first realistic account of the war and the most popular Finnish film ever made. By the late 1960s, auteur theory was the style *du jour*, and many smaller companies – often run by the filmmakers themselves – took over production of most Finnish films.

The Kaurismäkis and new Finnish directors

During the 1970s, pan-Nordic cooperation in cinema arose to combat the relatively small audience numbers and difficulty in exporting beyond Scandinavia. At this time, a new generation of film directors emerged, led by brothers **Aki** and **Mika Kaurismäki**, who made small films with a not small dose of quintessentially Finnish humour (and very little dialogue). Their 1989 movie *Leningrad Cowboys Go America*, which follows nine members of a Finnish rock band on their tour of the United States, had an offbeat, wry humour that was to characterize their films for the next two decades. Aki went on to become the better known and most productive of the

Filmic Finland

Given its handsome neoclassical facades, broad boulevards and excellent infrastructure, it comes as little surprise that the Finnish capital has served as a set piece for numerous Hollywood films. But **Helsinki** hasn't just been shot as Helsinki in the cinema. The city has often been a body double for **St Petersburg**, most notably before the breakup of the Soviet Union in Western movies set during the Russian Revolution and the Cold War. Of course, that Carl Engel effectively designed both cities didn't hurt the visual similarities between them. But Finland and Russia share a bit more in common – not just in looks but in popular perceptions in the Western imagination: a stark landscape, harsh seasons, and laconic people with a tradition of hard drinking.

Hollywood first brought Finland to the silver screen in David Lean's **Doctor Zhivago** (1965), when Joensuu played the role of Siberia, not least because it still had a fully functioning steam railway line. Omar Sharif memorably had a tryst with a local tavern waitress at the city's *Wanha Jokela* hotel. Later, the rickety cobblestone streets and iconic architecture of Helsinki served the city well as a double for both St Petersburg and Moscow in Warren Beatty's **Reds** (1981), a three-and-a-half-hour epic love story about anti-American intellectual socialists, and a film shot at a time when Ladas were still commonplace in Helsinki. The city was again stand-in for Moscow on Michael Apted's thriller **Gorky Park** (1983), though few Finns could have been too happy about seeing the red star mounted on top of the National History Museum for the months of filming. **White Nights** (1985), starring Mikhail Barishnikov, Isabella Rossellini and Helen Mirren, largely used shots from Helsinki largely out of fear that Barishnikov, who had defected to Canada in the 1970s, would be abducted by the KGB and returned to the mother country. And most recently, Christian Carion's French-produced **Farewell** (2009) used various parts of Finland to play the roles of Moscow, Austria and Washington.

two, making a series of critically acclaimed works that play on the common Finnish themes of nostalgia and loss, such as *Tulitikkutehtaan Tyttö* (*The Match Factory Girl*, 1990) and *Mies Vailla Menneisyyttä* (*The Man Without a Past*, 2002).

Klaus Härö's debut film, *Näkymätön Elina* (*Elina: As If I Didn't Exist*, 2002), won the Silver Bear at the Berlin Film Festival. His second film, meanwhile, *Uusi Ihminen* (*The New Man*), was made in Sweden using a Finnish camera and sound crew but with principally Swedish funding. These days, somewhere between ten and fourteen films are released annually, though funding is still a problem, and some Finnish directors go abroad to realize their projects.

Popular films nowadays tend to deal a lot with contemporary Finnish society, such as Johanna Vuoksenmaa's *Nousukausi* (*Upswing*, 2003), which looks at the role of family, and Petri Kotwica's *Koti-ikävä* (*Homesick*, 2005), a dirge on disturbed youth. Another popular genre is social commentary; Aleksi Salmenperä's second film *Miehen Työ* (*A Man's Job*, 2007) follows a man who turns to prostitution to provide for his family after he loses his job. Humour, of course, is never very far away. One of the funniest films to come out of Scandinavia in a while, Joona Tena's *FC Venus* (2006) is based around a Finnish guy who plays lower-league football. When he puts his sport before his girlfriend, she challenges his team to a match against her and her friends; it's a most predictable setup but a masterful execution.

Other postmodern directors include Timo Koivusalo and Pekka Lehto, and while drama and comedy fare fairly well domestically, films made about the struggles of Finland for its **independence**, such as Pekka Parikka's *Talvisota* (*The Winter War*, 1989), *Äideistä parhain* (*Mother of Mine*, 2005), Finland's entry for Best Foreign Language Film Academy Award, and Lauri Törhönen's 2008 *Jaya 1918* (*Border 1918*), which follows a national guard captain's sojourn along the newly created Finnish border, somehow always seem to come out on top.

Music

W hile the **music** of the Finns is, for better or worse, best known for the stage antics and heavy sounds of the 2006 Eurovision award-winners Lordi, the country has for centuries been producing interesting melodies and rhythms deeply rooted in its rural traditions. It's well worth checking out several modern Finnish pop or rock acts, too; in any case, you'll find their sounds hard to avoid if you spend even just one night out in one of Finland's larger cities.

Folk music

Long before the days of amplifiers, distortion and latex face makeup, Finnish music was played by bards who performed **runonlaulanta**, a chanting of memorized folk poems, usually without instruments, in rural communities across the country. Finland's musical traditions today draw some amount of influence from traditional Karelian tunes, which – despite their proximity to Russia – have existed largely without Germanic and Slavic influences. These early forms made extensive use of the *kantele*, a Finnish chordophone instrument used by the Kalevala's hero, Väinämöinen. In the seventeenth century, Nordic folk dance music, or *pelimanni*, evolved to replace this tradition of singing storytelling. These more mainstream Nordic folk musics make use of fiddles, clarinet, accordions, horns and whistles, and the tradition now prevails in the west of the country. Up in the north, meanwhile, the Sámi people maintain their own musical tradition of *joik*, a highly spiritual song that has made a remarkable transition to being integrated into modern Scandinavian pop music.

Finnish folk music has seen something of a roots revival in recent decades, not least by the smart folk-pop of **Värttinä**, a group of female singers who have managed to cross over to the world beat market and do amazingly well outside of Finland with their modern interpretations of classical folk songs. In 2003 Värttinä composed the score for a world-wide musical production of *Lord of the Rings*. And leave it to the Finns to pioneer a loud, thrashing interpretation of the genre called **folk metal**, a dynamic melodic concoction that melds the distorted guitars and synthesizers of heavy metal with traditional folk instruments and melodies. The genre's lyrics typically address themes of mythology, nature, paganism and, of course, death.

Classical music

Interest in **classical music** in Finland began a rapid growth after Russia annexed the country in 1809, and Helsinki became a cultural centre with several choirs, an opera and, in 1883, a philharmonic orchestra. Around the same time, Finnish nationalism was on the rise, and **Jean Sibelius** (see box, p.100) began studying the singers of Kalevaic poetry in Karelia, composing his vocal symphony *Kullervo* and, in 1899, *Finlandia*, which played no small role in ushering Finland forth to an era of independence. As Sibelius was composing his nationalistic tunes, a national romanticist movement gave birth to a number of other composers – Heino Kaski, Yrjö Kilpinen and Toivo Kuula, among others – who worked towards a specifically Finnish type of music. In 1924, Leevi Madetoja composed *Pohjalaisia*, an opera on the dark memory of Russian oppression in Finland. From the 1950s onwards, Finland began to experience some success in exporting its classical music traditions, and today important contemporary composers include Kalevi Aho, Kaija Saariaho and Jouni Kaipainen, figures that are joined by equally famous conductors, including Mikko Franck, Jukka-Pekka Saraste, Sakari Oramo OBE and Esa-Pekka Salonen, the latter holding a reputation rivaling only that of Sibelius.

Today when it comes to music, classical reigns supreme. Finland has fourteen professional **orchestras** – including the Helsinki Philharmonic, the first permanent orchestra in the Nordic countries – and two dozen semiprofessional and countless other smaller orchestras and ensembles. Finland is serious about music, and its success in producing outstanding musicians is due in large part to its numerous music institutes (around a hundred) all over the country, including seven conservatories and the celebrated Sibelius Academy in Helsinki; instruction at all is free. An astonishing 60,000 Finns study music professionally, making up more than one percent of the entire population of the country. Famously, the country puts on scores of annual music festivals (see pp.40–44), which draw both domestic and foreign artists.

Rock and pop

A few years ago, Finnish **popular music** barely existed save for a handful of heavy metal groups such as Apocalyptica, Nightwish and Hanoi Rocks, a kitschy, hard rock band that came together in 1985 and was then Finland's best-known music ensemble abroad. The deep, harsh power-chords of heavy metal music seemed to be emblematic of much about the country during and just after the Cold War: disaffected youth, confused society and bleak prospects. In 2004, heavy rockers HIM released their hit single "Funeral of Hearts," about as Finnish a song as you can get, but little else of note was happening on the music scene until Lordi won the 2006 Eurovision song contest, much to the consternation of conservative Finns weary of the country's image abroad. Though ultimate success was bolstered somewhat by predecessors Nightwish, Children of Bodom and Sonata Arctica, Lordi managed to do in Eurovision what Finland as a country had been doing for a long time: looking different and being proud of it.

It's not all Marshall stacks and face paint, of course. While Sweden has been astoundingly more successful at churning out popular rock and pop groups that crossover well outside of the country, this is not because Finland has not been trying. Early on in the 1990s, satirical group the Leningrad Cowboys fared well in central Europe and toured widely, even performing at the 1994 MTV Music Awards. But, famous as they were for their dry countenances and rock-a-billy looks, they never quite made it abroad. More recently, The Rasmus has gone gold eight times and platinum five across Europe, surpassing the sales of any other Finnish band abroad. Groups to follow in their success include Entwine, Lullacry and Poisonblack, among others. Hip-hop has never been strong, though Bomfunk MCs did fairly well in Scandinavia with their album *In Stereo* and single "Freestyler". Pop and rock groups often sing largely in Finnish, an admirable decision that reflects a strong sense of national pride, but not one that has made success abroad any easier.

Books

The number of English-language books about Finland is nowhere near that of many other European countries, but we've compiled some of the better titles out there. Culture-wise, there's plenty to choose from, especially when it comes to **design** and **architecture**. In terms of **history** and **society**, a number of releases in recent years have touched on some of the more idiosyncratic aspects of the country and its people. **Historical fiction**, meanwhile, has always been a popular genre for Finnish books in translation, while **literary fiction** has experienced a marked rise in commissioned translations in the past few years, with a concomitant rise in sales among the North American and British public – as well as reissues of some of the Finnish classics. The most recent information on who's been published where in English translation can be found at ⓦwww.booksfromfinland.fi or ⓦwww.finlit.fi.

Not every work we've listed will be on the shelves of your local bookshop, though if you can't order it there, you can on ⓦwww.amazon.com, or, failing that, through the publishers themselves, some of which are in Finland. Nearly all of the books we've listed are currently in print and readily available (the publisher is listed in parentheses) while the few that are no longer in print are indicated with "o/p". These still shouldn't be too difficult to track down, either at larger libraries or through online secondhand resellers. Those marked with a 🏃 indicate titles that are particularly recommended.

History and society

Robert Edwards *The Winter War: Russia's Invasion of Finland, 1939–40* (Pegasus Books). The Russian invasion of Finland in November 1939 was a critical turning point in world history. This excellent and popular account of the Finns' resistance and final defeat by overwhelming numbers of Soviet troops during the Winter War gives an excellent context for understanding the events, set against the rest of the war and against modern world history in general.

🏃 **Neil Kent** *Helsinki: A Cultural and Literary History* (Signal Books). This book, part of a popular series, looks at the creation of tradition in Helsinki through the city's architecture, art and literary production. Though the prose can be somewhat dry at times – this is not travelogue – it's a well-informed account of the historical development and evolution of the city into the cultural powerhouse it is today.

Veli-Pekka Lehtola *The Sámi People: Traditions in Transition* (University of Alaska Press). A well-written, fully illustrated contemporary history of the Sámi across Scandinavia, which details the social changes experienced by these once fully nomadic reindeer-herders, and explains how they are currently forging a delicate path between the traditional and the modern.

Richard Lewis *Finland, Cultural Lone Wolf* (Intercultural Press Inc). This interesting book attributes Finland's immense success at the end of the twentieth century not to business acumen or political savvy, but to Finnish culture. The eminently qualified Lewis looks at communication styles, dominant cultural values and image, and does it with great aplomb – and a great collection of humourous anecdotes along the way.

Alan Palmer *Northern Shores: A History of the Baltic Sea and Its Peoples* (John Murray). A fascinating history of this tumultuous body of water and the nations whose survival has depended on it, from the Baltic's role as a basin for Viking warships through to its present function in transport and tourism. The focus is on the people – from St Bridget to Lech Walesa – whose lives have become intertwined with the historical ebb and flow of the countries that border the Baltic.

Nikki Rajala *Some Like It Hot: The Sauna, Its Lore and Stories* (North Star Press). History of the most famous social institution in Finland, plus lots of interesting and funny stories, anecdotes, insights and factoids about the ritual and its role in the nation's development over the years. Features a hundred-odd black-and-white photographs.

Mayme Sevander *They Took My Father: Finnish Americans in Stalin's Russia* (University of Minnesota Press). This fascinating tale of loyalty, identity, and moral ideals is a compelling personal drama spread across Russia, Finland and rural Michigan. At age 11, Sevander and her family joined 6000 other Finnish-Americans during the Depression and emigrated to the Soviet Union in 1934 – almost unfathomably – in the belief that they were going to help build a workers'

paradise. They discovered instead something very, very dark. Touches upon tensions between Finns and Russians, the spirit of cooperation and rural family life.

🏃 **Fred Singleton** *A Short History of Finland* (Cambridge University Press). A very readable and informative account of Finland's past, including lengthy sections on Finnish land, people, nationalism, spirit, and the postwar achievements of the second republic, among other topics. It lacks the detail of most academic accounts – and somewhat awkwardly crams cultural history into a single chapter – but is an excellent starting point for general readers. Updated in 2005 from the original 1989 edition.

Linus Torvalds & David Diamond *Just for Fun: The Story of an Accidental Revolutionary* (HarperCollins). The autobiography of the twentysomething Finn who revolutionized modern computer technology with his innovative Linux operating system, while remaining true to his deeply religious belief in open-source computing. Filled with irreverent banter and off-the-cuff, email-like entries, this reads somewhat choppily but is enjoyable and insightful all the same.

Historical fiction

Laila Hietamies *Red Moon over White Sea* (Aspasia Books). An engaging historical novel exploring the experience of a family during the Russian Revolution of 1917 and Finland's Civil War of 1918. After striking gold in Canada, a Finnish emigré returns to develop the area and build a house in Karelia near the White Sea, while his granddaughters become caught up in, very disparate ways, in the turbulent, bleak aspects of war.

Leena Lander *Cast a Long Shadow* (Second Story Press). Set during Northern Europe's most infamous

witch hunt in seventeenth-century Sweden, this story of power and religious fanaticism stars Nils Psilander, an intellectual circuit-court judge who seeks to make sense of the beheading and burning of seven innocent witches, exploring notions of xenophobia, misogyny and scapegoating. A deft mélange of historical research and fanciful characterization.

🏃 **Väinö Linna** *The Unknown Soldier* (o/p). Based on his experiences fighting in the Winter War, Linna's novel triggered immense controversy for how it depicted

Finnish soldiers – not as "heroes in white" but as drunks and womanizers. Deals extensively with the uniquely Finnish concept of *sisu* (courage or tenacity). Less well known but equally poignant is *Under the North Star* (Aspasia Books), the first tome in a trilogy about a late nineteenth-century rural Finnish community, highlighting the seminal historical events which helped to mould the Finnish national character.

Elias Lönnrot *Kalevala* (Harvard University Press). Finland's fifty-chapter national epic is a conglomeration of ancient folk tales, creation myths, journeys, duels, spells and fables, transcribed over twenty years by nineteenth-century scholar and doctor Elias Lönnrot. Set in an unspecified point in the past, the plot centres on a state of war between the mythical regions of Kalevala and Pohjola over possession of a talisman called the Sampo. Given the linear course of the plot and length (22,750 lines) it's not an easy read, but its influence on Finnish literature is huge, and it became a linchpin of the Finnish nationalist and language movements. Essential for understanding the country's psyche.

Oscar Parland *The Year of the Bull* (Peter Owen). Absorbing look at the civil-war-torn Finland of 1918 through the eyes of a 6-year-old boy. The prize-winning author, a German-Russian-Ukranian émigré to Finland in the early twentieth century, worked in his early life as a military surgeon then as a music critic, and has ended up winning the National

Prize for Literature three times. One of Swedish-speaking Finland's greatest literary achievements.

Richard Rayner *The Cloud Sketcher* (HarperCollins). British-born Rayner penned this lyrical war novel in which protagonist Esko Vaananen fights for the White Army – in part out of his love for a woman, in part to defy his Bolshevik father – then emigrates to New York, where he becomes caught up in the gangsters, speakeasies and jazz of prohibition-era America. Very Gatsbyan and very good.

Runar Schildt *The Meat-Grinder and Other Stories* (Norvik). An intriguing collection of tales set mostly in Helsinki before and during the Finnish civil war. Contains *The Weaker One*, a gorgeously constructed, melancholic tale of deception and adultery. The Finlandssvenska Schildt (1888–1925) was long regarded as Finland's finest short-story writer. A consummate perfectionist, he suffered from an immense sense of insecurity and at the age of 37 entered a clinic on Unioninkatu, only to shoot himself.

Mika Waltari *The Egyptian: A Novel* (Chicago Review Press). Arguably the most translated work of Finnish literature after the *Kalevala* and the *Moomins*, this historical novel follows Sinuhe, the royal physician to Akhenaten's court, who narrates his travels through Syria, Babylon and Minoan Crete after Akhenaten's fall from power. Translated into English in 1949, it topped the bestseller lists in the US in part due to the many parallels with the various struggles of World War II.

Literary fiction

Elina Hirvonen *When I Forgot* (Portobello). One of the most widely read of all Finnish historical novels, this early 2009 English translation resulted in glowing reviews. An insightful book with a fractured postmodern narrative, it follows two young people – one Finnish and one American – each coming to terms with their own dark and tragic pasts following 9/11. A deep, piercing study of love, family, mental illness and memory.

Anselm Hollo *Braided River* (Salt Publishing). A self-professed Beat poet, Hollo has written and translated (into English) more than thirty books, and this anthology of his poetry reflects a complex twentieth-century existence between both Europe and America.

Tove Jansson *A Winter Book: Selected Stories* (Sort Of Books). Though best known for her magical Moomins – enduring children's tales offering subtle morality lessons and evocative descriptions of Finnish nature – Jansson's adult stories are no less engaging. This anthology contains rare archive photographs from the author's family album. Also pick up its predecessor, *The Summer Book* (Sort Of Books), and *Moomin: The Complete Tove Jansson Comic Strip* (Drawn and Quarterly).

Matti Joensuu *To Steal Her Love* (Arcadia Books). Joensuu, once a Finnish policeman, is Finland's greatest crime writer, and Sergeant Harjunpää Helsinki's finest detective. This time, he's on the hunt for Tweety, a mentally disturbed man who fondles young women while they sleep, as Harjunpää attempts to figure out the deranged man's psychology. Positively haunting. A second work, *Harjunpää and the Stone Murders*, is set in contemporary Helsinki during a bout of teenage gang warfare.

Aleksis Kivi *Seven Brothers* (Aspasia Books). Kivi's only novel is widely regarded as the first important modern novel published in Finnish, ending the reign in the nineteenth century of Swedish-speaking authors. As the title suggests, the book concerns a band of ne'er-do-well brothers and their struggle to survive following their parents' death. They escape their cloying village for rural Impivaara, where they begin their lives anew, change their ways and transform from scared, young boys into noble men and pillars of their new community. Required reading for most Finnish students.

Anita Konkka *A Fool's Paradise* (Dalkey Archive Press). One of Finland's most important contemporary writers, Konkka has come up with this wry, humorous narrative that is in many ways semi-autobiographical. The story describes a woman whose married Russian lover has recently left her and who becomes obsessed with astrology, omens and the paranormal as she attempts to put her life back together.

Rosa Liksom *Dark Paradise* (Dalkey Archive Press). This collection of visceral short stories perfectly encapsulates life in the modern-day, disaffected West through sharp and wry, penetrating prose. In one, a woman kills her recently wedded husband over his inability to depart from their bed; in another, a man murders a grocer over fifteen cents. The unpredictable narratives are very short – rarely longer than four or five pages – and rendered in clean, crisp English by expert translator David McDuff.

Arto Paasilinna *The Year of the Hare* (Peter Owen). Finland's most well-known author, Paasilinna has published forty-odd books that have been translated into dozens of languages. His keen eye for the Finnish character and sense of humour made this 1977 novel his best known, an inventive and satirical work that offers profound insight into late twentieth-century Western society. The story concerns a Finnish journalist who, after running over a rabbit and then nursing it back to health, pursues his own rebellion against social mores, politics and relationships. Also try *The Howling Miller* (Canongate).

Maria Peura *At the Edge of Light* (Maia Press). This award-winning novel, a modern-day *Romeo and Juliet* set far up in the permafrost, tells the coming-of-age story of a girl in rural Lapland. Her dysfunctional family, teenage angst and curiosity lead to her befriending a neighbouring misfit and experimenting with sex, drugs and death. Contains a good amount of absurdish humour. Deftly translated by the award-winning David Hackston.

Kirsti Simonsuuri (ed) *Enchanting Beasts* (o/p). A slender but captivating tome containing the works of eleven female Finnish poets including Arja Tiainen, Anne Hänninen, Eeva-Liisa Manner and Sirkka Turkka, this was one of the first – and remains one of the best – English translations of Finland's best modern poets.

Johanna Sinisalo *Troll: A Love Story* (Grove Press). Sodankylä native Sinisalo's debut novel received critical acclaim in Finland and abroad, capturing the prestigious Finlandia Prize. In this account, a young gay photographer is viscerally influenced by a curious find from his courtyard: a small troll which comes to awaken dark desires within him. Merging folklore with psychology, the book fuses an engaging mythological love story with subtly astute insight into modern human relationships. Also check out *Not Before Sundown* (Peter Owen).

Jarkko Sipila *Helsinki Homicide: Against the Wall* (Ice Cold Crime). Sipila is a Finnish journalist who has covered crime news for *Helsingin Sanomat* and Finnish TV, and his novel – which won the 2009 Crime Fiction

of the Year award – follows an undercover policeman who infiltrates a gang of criminals. The book has been hailed for its innovative use of dialogue and deft construction of plot, though the distinct lack of character detail has been criticized by some.

Antti Tuuri *A Day in Ostrobothnia* (Aspasia Books). Irony and wit run through this classic Finnish novel released in 1983, covering a day in the life of the Hakala brothers and including no shortage of historical dramatization of Finland's turbulent past. The book won the Nordic Prize for Literature, and has drawn comparisons to the work of Faulkner and Hemingway. Captivating stuff.

Kjell Westö *Lang* (Carroll & Graf Publishers; Harvill Press). Westö is one of the country's leading Finlandssvenska authors living today, and his first crime/suspense novel is based around Lang, a twice-divorced novelist and TV-talk-show host who has been living a self-obsessed and pretentious life for some time. He begins to fall apart after meeting Sarita, a distant woman with whom he develops a complicated and tortuous personal relationship.

Culture, cuisine, design and architecture

Marianne Aav *Iittala: 125 Years of Finnish Glass* (Arnoldsche Verlagsanstalt). This survey of some of the best designs in Finnish glassware looks at the history and development of the form through the lens of the world-renowned Iittala company. Focuses chiefly on the 1950s and 1960s, and includes a full catalogue with all glass designs by many famous designers. Aav's other design-related titles include *Marianne Marimekko: Fabrics, Fashion, Architecture* and *Finnish Modern Design: Utopian Ideals and Everyday Realities, 1930–97* (both Yale University Press).

Arthur Alexander *The Helsinki Chronicles of Dr Louise C. Love and*

Mr Poika: Six Adventures in Finland's Capital (Author House, 2005). Learn about Helsinki sights and Finnish history, personalities and language in this Sherlock-Holmes-meets-Rough-Guides romp that entertains and informs. Poika's "Notes" follow each mystery, adding interesting factoids and references.

Tim Bird *Living in Finland* (Flammarion). A gorgeous photographic coffee-table book that elucidates just how well many Finns live, with sections on landscape, interiors, artisan work and cuisine. Shot by one of Finland's foremost photojournalists – a Brit living in Helsinki – the book contains gorgeous imagery of lakeside cottages, rural traditions, culinary creations, and modern design and architectural pizzazz.

Harri Hautajarvi *Villas/Saunas in Finland* (Rakennustieto Publishing). This fascinating, full-colour book provides 44 detailed examples of Finnish summer homes and sauna architecture, ranging from the most basic of log cabins to spacious, modern villas. Each property is detailed and presented by the architects themselves.

Anja Hill *The Food & Cooking of Finland* (Aquamarine). This full-colour recipe book contains some sixty recipes that span all of modern Finnish cooking. Comprising dishes that meld traditional Finnish tastes with influences from the Mediterranean, Scandinavia and Russia, highlights include crayfish soup, Baltic herring with caper butter, reindeer *pot au feu* and Estonian salmon soup.

Jari Jetsonen *Finnish Summer Houses* (Princeton Architectural Press). Twenty villas, cottages and cabins by Finnish architect from Aalto to Saarinen are detailed via a series of photographs, drawings and blueprints, demonstrating the diversity of Finnish construction methods and designs throughout the late twentieth century.

Tero Kallio and Kimmo Saira *Simply Scandinavian: Travelling Through Time with Finnish Cuisine and Nature* (Raikas Publishing). Traditional Finnish meals made modern is the spin of this new cookbook by two famous domestic chefs, and the dishes are very international. The book organizes recipes according to month of the year they're best made in, and features some really spectacular photography of the Finnish landscape.

Tessa Kiros *Falling Cloudberries* (Murdoch Books). Written by a Finnish-Cypriot chef, this is an impossibly gorgeously shot cookbook, with anecdotes about the author's family and what it was like growing up as a multinational food lover. Recipes cover dishes from Finland, Greece, South Africa and Italy, and include salt-baked fish with lemon and parsley salad, veal loin with mustard, pancetta and cabbage, and baklava with nuts and dried apricots.

Beatrice Ojakangas *Finnish Cookbook* (Crown). Originally published in 1964, these timeless, all-round recipes shed light on one of Scandinavia's least known cuisines – everything from fish stew to prune tarts, as well as short stories about the Finnish way of life. The book definitely shows its age, but it's one of the few Finnish cookbooks out there, and includes most of the nation's classical dishes.

Micha Ramakers *Dirty Pictures: Tom of Finland, Masculinity, and Homosexuality* (St Martin's Press). An excellent account of the social and cultural issues in the work of gay-themed comic-strip artist Touko Laaksonen (aka Tom of Finland), who once memorably stated "If I don't have an erection when I'm doing a drawing, I know it's no good." Offers ample examples of the often graphically sexual penmanship of Finland's most well-known pictorial artist, alongside enlightening prose. Also have a peek at *Tom of Finland: The Art of Pleasure* and *Tom of Finland: The Comic Collection* (both Taschen).

Richard Weston *Alvar Aalto* (Phaidon). Excellent overview of Aalto's life and work, with beautiful photographs and unpretentious language. It's a solid introduction to one of Finland's most beloved artistic geniuses, and the standard monograph on the man who so helped make a name for modern Finland. The book is affectionate, but critical in its interpretation of Aalto's production, and explores the dialogue between nature and culture he sought to create, and the varying roles of the individual and the collective.

Language

Language

Finnish

It was like discovering a wine-cellar filled with bottles of amazing wine of a kind and flavour never tasted before. It quite intoxicated me.

J.R.R. Tolkien

Intoxicating though the **Finnish language** might be, sadly not all of us have the linguistic fascination (or acumen) of Tolkien. Finnish, simply put, is a very difficult language, and it's going to pose a problem to anyone whose mother tongue is an Indo-European language such as English. There's very little common ground between Finnish and any other mainstream Western European language, and this can frustrate basic understanding and communication – simple tasks like deciphering a menu are often fraught with difficulty.

Finnish also has nothing in common with the other Scandinavian languages – something that has led to considerable misunderstanding of the Finns, particularly in neighbouring Sweden. A member of the **Finno–Ugric** group of languages, Finnish is closely related to Estonian, Sámi and much more distantly to Hungarian, and its grammatical structure is complex, with fifteen cases to grapple with. Unlike Indo-European German, for example, which uses prepositions to determine the case of a noun, Finnish employs a set of complex suffixes, which, although straightforward to learn, are further complicated by a slew of vowel and consonant elision rules and, to a lesser extent, a process of obligatory vowel harmony. For instance, *autossa* means "in the car", *autooon* "to the car", whereas *autosta* is "from my car".

The language has some real **linguistic oddities**, too. It makes rich use of juxtaposed and double vowels, for example *riiuuyöaie*, "the intention to spend a night wooing women" (not to be confused with *hääyöaie*, "wedding-night plans"). Consonant doubling is a favourite trait of many Finnish words, as in *Emmäkä rääkkääkkään* ("I'm not tormenting it") – a defensive response to the command *Älä rääkkää sitä kääkkää!* ("Stop tormenting it!"). Another trait is the tendency to fit an entire sentence into one word, an example being *tehdäkseen* ("He did it in order to have done it"), and applying grammatical declensions to numbers; one version of the word for "29" is *kahdenneksikymmenenneneksiyhdeksänneksi.*

If the idea of learning Finnish makes you weak at the knees, at least have a go at memorizing the longest known palindrome in the world, Finnish *saippuakivikauppias* – the extremely useful "soapstone salesman", and a popular children's tongue-twister, *Kokooko Kokko kokoon koko kokon?* ("Will Kokko gather up the whole bonfire?")

Thankfully, in the large cities and main towns, **English** is spoken by the younger generation with amazing fluency – many have spent a school year abroad in an English-speaking country – but second-language ability drops significantly once you head to smaller, more remote areas and start conversing with older Finns. Swedish is a common second language, although many Finns are reluctant to use the language of their former colonial masters. It is, of course, the mother tongue of the Finland-Swedes, who live mainly in the western parts of the country, and the only language spoken on Åland.

If you're really turned on by the notion of attempting to crack Finnish, Routledge's *Colloquial Finnish: The Complete Course for Beginners* is a great start as it's sold with an accompanying audio CD. Fred Karlsson's *Finnish: An Essential Grammar* is the most accessible and comprehensive reference. Of the few available phrasebooks, *Finnish For Travellers* (Berlitz) is the most useful for practical purposes, also with CD; the best Finnish–English dictionary is *The Finnish Standard Dictionary* (Continuum International Publishing Group).

Pronunciation

Now the good news: in Finnish, words are **pronounced** exactly as they are written, with the stress always on the first syllable. In a compound word the stress is on the first syllable of each part of the word. Each letter is pronounced individually, and doubling a letter lengthens the sound: double "kk"s are pronounced by lingering somewhat on the "k" sound and the double "aa" pronounced as long as the English "a" in "car". The letters b, c, f, q, w, x, z and å are only found in words derived from foreign languages, and are pronounced as in the language of origin.

a as in father but shorter

d as in riding but sometimes so soft as to be barely heard

e like the a in late

g (only after "n") as in singer

h as in hot

i as in pin

j like the y in yellow

np like the m in mother

o like the aw in law

r is rolled

s as in said, but with the tongue a little further back from the teeth

u like the oo in cool

y like the French u in "sur"

ä like the a in hat

ö like the u in fur

Basics

Do you speak English?	Puhutteko englantia?	Good evening	Hyvää iltaa
I don't speak Finnish	Minä en puhu suomea	Good day (usually shortened to päivä)	Hyvää päivää
Yes	Kyllä/joo	Goodnight	Hyvää yötä
No	Ei	Goodbye	Näkemiin/hei hei
I don't understand	En ymmärrä	Yesterday	Eilen
I understand	Ymmärrän	Today	Tänään
Please	Olkaa hyvä/ole hyvä	Tomorrow	Huomenna
Thank you	Kiitos	Day after tomorrow	Ylihuomenna
Excuse me	Anteeksi	In the morning	Aamulla/Aamupäivällä
Hello	Terve/Moi	In the afternoon	Iltapäivällä
Good morning	Hyvää huomenta	In the evening	Illalla
Good afternoon	Hyvää päivää	At night	Yöllä

Some signs

Entrance	Sisään	Cold	Kylmä
Exit	Ulos	Open	Avoinna
Gentlemen	Miehille/Miehet/Herrat	Closed	Suljettu
Ladies	Naisille/Naiset/Rouvat	Push	Työnnä
Hot	Kuuma	Pull	Vedä

Arrival	Saapuvat	No trespassing	Läpikulku kielletty
Departure	Lähtevät	No camping	Leiriytyminen kielletty
Police	Poliisi		
Hospital	Sairaala	Danger	Vaara
No smoking	Tupakointi kielletty	No parking	Ei pysäköintiä/ Pysäköinti kielletty
No entry	Pääsy kielletty		

Questions and directions

Where's...?	Missä on...?	It's too expensive	Se on liian kallis
When?	Koska/milloin?	How much?	Kuinka paljon?
What?	Mikä/mitä?	How much is that?	Paljonko se maksaa?
Why?	Miksi?		
How do you say... in Finnish?	Miten sanotaan... suomeksi?	I'd like	Haluaisin
		Here	Täällä
How far is it to...?	Kuinka pitkä matka on... n?	There	Siellä
		Left	Vasemalla
Where is the railway station?	Missä on rautatieasema?	Right	Oikealla
		Go straight ahead	Ajakaa suoraan eteenpäin
Train/bus/boat/ship	Juna/bussi (or) linja auto/vene/laiva		
		Is it near/far?	Onko se lähellä/ kaukana?
Where is the youth hostel?	Missä on retkeilymaja?		
		Ticket/ticket office	Lipputoimisto
Can we camp here?	Voimmeko leiriytyä tähän?	Train/bus station	Rautatieasema/ linja-autoasema
Do you know anyone who could put us up for a night?	Tiedätkö ketään, joka voisi maijoitaa meidät yöksi?	bus stop	bussipysäkki
		Eastern	Itä-
		Western	Länsi-
Do you have anything better/ bigger/cheaper?	Onko teillä mitään parempaa/isompaa/ halvempaa?	Southern	Etelä-
		Northern	Pohjois-

General terms

		Traffic	Liikenne
Cheap	Halpa	Bus station	Linja-autoasema
Good	Hyvä	Castle	Linna
Lake	Järvi	Ticket office	Lipputoimisto
River	Joki	Tourist office	Matkailutoimisto
Expensive	Kallis	Museum	Museo
Canal	Kanava/Kanaali	Hill	Mäki
Street	Katu	Cabin	Mökki
Market hall	Kauppahalli	Information	Neuvonta
Market square	Kauppatori	Sight, attraction	Nähtävyys
Town hall	Kaupungintalo	Bad	Paha/Huono
Town centre	Keskusta	Bank	Pankki
Recycling	Kierrätys	Reindeer	Poro
Church	Kirkko	Gate	Portti
Village	Kylä	Post office	Posti
Airport	Lentokenttä		

Park	Puisto	Square	Tori
Bicycle	Pyörä	Tower	Torni
Coast	Rannikko	Roadside church	Tiekirkko
Beach	Ranta	Lappish mountain	Tunturi
Train station	Rautatieasema	Cathedral	Tuomiokirkko
Island	Saari	Hotel/guesthouse reception	Vastaanotto
Hospital	Sairaala		
Harbour	Satama	Boat	Vene/Laiva
Art museum	Taidemuseo	University	Yliopistoy
Road	Tie		

Numbers

0	nolla	10	kymmenen
1	yksi	11	yksitoista
2	kaksi	12	kaksitoista
3	kolme	13	kolmetoista
4	neljä	14	neljätoista
5	viisi	15	viisitoista
6	kuusi	16	kuusitoista
7	seitsemän	17	seitsemäntoista
8	kahdeksan	18	kahdeksantoista
9	yhdeksän	19	yhdeksäntoista

Helsinki slang

Like many urban centres, Helsinki has developed its own **slang** over the years. Known as *stadin slangi*, it's an argot rather distinct from standard Finnish and from the dialects of the rest of the country, and you'll hear a lot of it around the city, particularly after hours. Additionally, Finns tend to use a good deal of profanity in everyday speech, especially when under the influence. Hang out around the Central Railway Station in the wee hours and you're bound to hear some pretty lyrical swearing. Here are a few of the commonly heard words and phrases about the capital:

Bisse	Beer	Pussata	Kiss
Darra	Hangover (as in *Mulla on darra*, "I'm hung over")	Rööki	Cigarette
		Saatana	Satan, often used as *Saatanan helvetti* ("Oh F**k")
Dokata	To drink alcohol		
Dösä	Bus	Safka	Food
Flinda	Bottle	Siisti	Cool
Helvetti	Hell (as in *Mitä helvetti*, or "What the hell?")	Skoude	Policeman
		Snagari	Sausage stand
		Spora/Raitsikka	Streetcar
Hima	Home	Stenkku	Lighter
Kännissä	Drunk	Stoge/toge	Train
Paska	The "S" word	Suudella	French kiss
Perkele	Devil	Söpö	Cute
Pistä stobe	A pint	Vittu	The "C" word

20	kaksikymmentä	90	yhdeksänkymmentä
21	kaksikymmentäyksi	100	sata
30	kolmekymmentä	101	satayksi
40	neljäkymmentä	151	sataviisikymmentäyksi
50	viisikymmentä	200	kaksisataa
60	kuusikymmentä	1000	tuhat
70	seitsemänkymmentä	2000	kaksi tuhatta
80	kahdeksankymmentä		

Days and months

(Days and months are never capitalized)

Monday	maanantai	**March**	maalisku
Tuesday	tiistai	**April**	huhtikuu
Wednesday	keskiviikko	**May**	toukokuu
Thursday	torstai	**June**	kesäkuu
Friday	perjantai	**July**	heinäkuu
Saturday	lauantai	**August**	elokuu
Sunday	sunnuntai	**September**	syyskuu
January	tammikuu	**October**	lokakuu
February	helmikuu	**November**	marraskuu
		December	joulukuu

Food and drink terms

Basics

Hampurilainen	Hamburger	**Maito**	Milk
Hot dog	Hot dog	**Makeiset**	Sweets
Juusto	Cheese	**Makkara**	Sausage
Kakku	Cake	**Perunat**	Potatoes
Keitto	Soup	**Piirakka**	Pie
Keksit	Biscuits	**Riisi**	Rice
Leipä	Bread	**Voileipä**	Sandwich

Meat (*lihaa*)

Hirvenliha	Elk	**Lihapyörykät**	Meatballs
Häränfilee	Fillet of beef	**Maksa**	Liver
Jauheliha	Minced beef	**Nauta**	Beef
Jänis	Hare	**Paisti**	Steak
Hanhi	Goose	**Peura**	Venison
Kalkkuna	Turkey	**Poro**	Reindeer
Kana	Chicken	**Sianliha**	Pork
Kaniini	Rabbit	**Vasikanliha**	Veal
Kinkku	Ham		

Seafood (*äyriäisiä*) and fish (*kala*)

Ankerias	Eel	Sampi	Sturgeon
Graavilohi	Salted salmon	Sardiini	Sardine
Hauki	Pike	Savustettu lohi	Smoked salmon
Hummeri	Lobster	Savustetut silakat	Smoked Baltic
Karppi	Carp		herring
Katkaravut	Shrimp	Siika	Large, slightly
Lohi	Salmon		oily, white fish
Makrilli	Mackerel	Silakka	Baltic herring
Muikku	Small whitefish	Silli	Herring
Mäti	Roe	Taimen or forelli	Trout
Punakampela	Plaice	Taskurapu	Prawns
Rapu	Crayfish	Tonnikala	Tuna

Egg dishes (*munaruoat*)

Hillomunakas	Jam omelette	Munakokkeli	Scrambled eggs
Hyydytetty muna	Poached egg	Paistettu muna	Fried egg
Juustomunakas	Cheese omelette	Pekonimunakas	Bacon omelette
Keitetty muna	Boiled eggs	Perunamunakas	Potato omelette
Kinkkumunakas	Ham omelette	Sienimunakas	Mushroom omelette
Munakas	Omelette		

Vegetables (*vihannekset*)

Artisokka	Artichoke	Peruna	Potato
Herneet	Peas	Pinaatti	Spinach
Kaali	Cabbage	Porkkana	Carrot
Kukkakaali	Cauliflower	Riisi	Rice
Kurkku	Cucumber	Salaatti	Lettuce
Linssit	Lentils	Selleri	Celery
Maissintähkät	Corn on the cob	Sieni	Mushroom
Paprika	Green pepper	Sipuli	Onion
Parsa	Asparagus	Tilli	Dill
Pavut	Beans	Tomaatti	Tomato
Persilja	Parsley	Valkosipuli	Garlic

Fruit (*hedelmä*)

Ananas	Pineapple	Luumu	Plum
Appelsiini	Orange	(Kuivatut) Luumut	Prunes
Aprikoosi	Apricot	Mandariinit	Tangerines
Banaani	Banana	Mansikka	Strawberry
Greippi	Grapefruit	Meloni	Melon
Karhunvatukka	Blackberries	Mustikka	Blueberries
Kirsikka	Cherries	Omena	Apple

Persikka	Peach	Rusinat	Raisins
Päärynä	Pear	Sitruuna	Lemon
Pähkinä	Nuts	Vadelma	Raspberries
Raparperi	Rhubarb	Viinirypäleet	Grapes

Sandwiches (*voileipä*)

Kappelivoileipä	Fried French bread topped with bacon and a fried egg	Oopperavoileipä	Fried French bread with a hamburger patty and egg
Muna-anjovisleipä	Dark bread with slices of hard-boiled egg, anchovy fillets and tomato	Sillivoileipä	Herring on dark bread, usually with egg and tomato

Finnish specialities

Kaalikääryleet	Cabbage rolls: cabbage leaves stuffed with minced meat and rice	Läskisoosi	Crispy fried pork gravy
		Makaroonilaatikko	Macaroni casserole with milk and egg sauce
Kaalipiirakka	Cabbage and minced meat	Maksalaatikko	Baked liver purée with rice and raisins
Karjalanpaisti	Karelian stew of beef and pork with onions	Merimiespihvi	Casserole of potato slices and meat patties or minced meat
Kurpitsasalaatti	Pickled pumpkin served with meat dishes		
		Moska	Fried pork and potatoes
Lamasee	Jelly of vanilla, lemon and cocoa	Mämmi	Finnish Easter pudding
Lammaskaali	Mutton and cabbage stew or soup	Piparjuuriliha	Boiled beef with horseradish sauce
Lapskoussi	Karelian hot-pot stew of veal, pork, mutton and vegetables	Pirru	Reindeer and potato stew
		Porkkanalaatikko	Casserole of mashed carrots and rice
Lasimestarin silli	Pickled herring with spices, vinegar, carrot and onion	Poronkäristys	Sautéed reindeer stew
Lihakeitto	Soup made from meat, potatoes, carrots and onions	Sekali	Heavy stew with pork, beans and sauerkraut
Lindströmin pihvi	Beefburger made with beetroot and served with a cream sauce	Sianlihakastike	Gravy with slivers of pork
		Silakkalaatikko	Casserole with alternating layers of potato, onion and Baltic herring, with an egg and milk sauce
Lohilaatikko	Potato and salmon casserole		
Lohipiirakka	Salmon pie		
Lummuusi	Cow's head and hoof stew		

Stroganoff	Beef with gherkins and onions, browned in a casserole and braised in a tomato and sour cream stock	**Tunka**	Blood sausage
		Venäläinen silli	Herring fillets with mayonnaise, mustard, vinegar, beetroot, gherkins and onion
Suutarinlohi	Marinated Baltic herring with onion and peppers		
Tilliliha	Boiled veal flavoured with dill sauce	**Wieninleike**	Fried veal cutlet

Drinks

Appelsiinimehu	Orange juice	**Tomaattimehu**	Tomato juice
Kahvi	Coffee	**Tonic vesi**	Tonic water
Kivennäisvesi	Mineral water	**Vesi**	Water
Kuuma kaakao	Hot chocolate	**Gini**	Gin
Limonaati	Lemonade	**Konjakki**	Cognac
Omenamehu	Apple juice	**Olut**	Beer
Punainen maito	Full fat milk	**Tuontiolut**	Export beer
Sininen maito	Semi-skimmed milk	**Viini**	Wine
Tee	Tea	**Viski**	Whisky

One real draw of spending time in **Swedish-speaking Finland** is the respite it allows you from the often frustratingly complex Finnish language. Compared to Finnish, Swedish is a cakewalk: it's one of the easiest languages for English-speakers to learn, with a strikingly similar lexicon and grammar. Finlandssvenska (or Finland's Swedish, the tongue spoken by six percent of the Finnish population that is linguistically and culturally Swedish in background), differs from standard Swedish only slightly in pronunciation and a few expressions, so if you know even a bit of Swedish (or any of the Scandinavian languages, for that matter), you should be able to make your way around fairly well.

Useful words and phrases

Basic **words** include **ja** "yes" and **nej** "no". When you greet people you say simply **hej** "hello" or **god dag** "good morning". When someone hands you something they will usually say **var så god** "here you are", to which you'd usually respond **tack** "thanks", or maybe, **tack så mycket** "thank you very much". Other useful words and phrases include:

Var	Where?	**Talar du Engelska?**	Do you speak English?
När/hur dags	When?		
Vad?; varför?	What?; Why?	**Jag förstår inte**	I don't understand
Hur (mycket)?	How (much)?	**Hur mycket kostar det?**	How much is it?
Jag vet inte	I don't know		
Förlåt; ursäkta	Sorry; excuse me	**Jag tar det**	I'll take it
Varifrån kommer du?	Where are you from?	**Det är för mycket, jag**	It's too expensive
Vad heter du?	What's your name?	**Har du något billigare?**	Have you got anything cheaper?
Vad heter det Här på Svenska?	What's this called in Swedish?	**Får jag/vi tälta här?**	Can I/we camp here?

Numbers

ett	1	**sex**	6
två	2	**sjö**	7
tre	3	**åtta**	8
fyra	4	**nio**	9
fem	5	**tio**	10

Other terms

Bastu	Sauna	**Restaurang**	Restaurant
Berg	Mountain	**Rådhuset**	Town hall
Biljett	Ticket	**Sjö**	Lake
Bro	Bridge	**Slott**	Palace/castle
Båt	Boat/ferry	**Smörgåsbord**	Spread of different dishes
Cyckelstig	Cycle path		
Dagens rätt	Dish of the day	**Strand**	Beach
Färja	Ferry	**Stuga**	Cottage
Gata (g.)	Street	**Torg**	Square/market place
Hamn	Harbour	**Turistbyrå**	Tourist office
Kyrka	Church	**Tältplats**	Campsite
Muséet	Museum	**Vandrarhem**	Youth hostel
Öppettider	Opening hours	**Väg**	Road

Glossary of famous Finns

Alvar Aalto (1898–1976) Mastermind architect and designer who single-handedly changed the landscape of the country with his ground-breaking modernist buildings and sleek, organically designed furniture and glassware.

Wäinö Aaltonen (1894–1966) Cubist and futurist sculptor known for his war memorials and likenesses of national heroes, including Paavo Nurmi, Aleksis Kivi and Jean Sibelius.

Per Brahe the Younger (1602–1680) Swedish Governor General who introduced a postal system to Finland, founded new towns and developed commerce, agriculture and education.

Albert Edelfelt (1854–1905) Portraitist who was one of the first to achieve international acclaim, and greatly influenced younger artists such as Akseli Gallen-Kallela.

Carl Ludwig Engel (1883–1944) German architect whose stately Neoclassical buildings moulded the look and feel of much of downtown Helsinki.

Akseli Gallen-Kallela (1865–1931) Renowned painter best known for his Kalevala illustrations, who was also commissioned by Mannerheim to design the flags, decorations and uniforms for a newly independent Finland.

King Gustav Vasa (1496–1560) One of the most powerful and ruthless of Swedish kings and the founder of modern Sweden who, in Finland, centralized government, introduced Protestantism and founded the city of Vaasa.

Pekka Halonen (1865–1933) Celebrated painter and student of Gauguin whose work celebrates Finland's people and nature – especially in snow-swept winter landscapes.

Tove Jansson (1914–2001) Finlandssvenska illustrator and novelist whose adorable Moomin trolls have become some of the most recognizable cartoon characters in the world.

Eero Järnefelt (1863–1937) Realist painter and colleague of Akseli Gallen-Kallela and Jean Sibelius, with a vast body of work depicting nature and agriculture.

Urho Kekkonen (1900–1986) Iconic journalist, policeman, lawyer and high-jump champion who was elected president in 1956 and has since become the country's most beloved statesman.

Carl Gustaf Emil Mannerheim (1867–1951) Beloved soldier who served in the Imperial Russian Army for twenty years, became president from 1944–1946 and was given the unique title Marshal of Finland.

Eliel Saarinen (1873–1950) Finnish architecture's second son is best known for the Art Nouveau (Jugendstil) and National Romanticist buildings he designed in Helsinki, such as the iconic Central Railway Station.

Eero Saarinen (1910–1961) Son to Eliel, he studied at Yale and settled in the US, where he designed chairs with Eames and built the timeless Gateway Arch in St Louis and the TWA Terminal at JFK International Airport.

Helene Schjerfbeck (1862–1946) Swedish-speaking oil painter who created haunting portraits and scenes of rural Finland which are strongly evocative of the national character.

Jean Sibelius (1865–1957) Possibly the best-known Finn outside the country, his melodic, Romantic-period compositions were important in developing Finland's sense of national identity.

Hugo Simberg (1873–1917) Symbolist artist whose images depict the macabre, the supernatural, and naked pre-pubescent boys.

Lars Sonck (1870–1956) This architect's neo-Romanesque style fused traditions from medieval stone and later wood-based architecture, visible in his Tampere Cathedral and Kallio Church.

Mika Waltari (1908–1979) The country's most prolific and famous novelist penned *The Egyptian*, an allegory of World War II that became the best-selling Finnish novel of all time.

Travel store

More of Finland by train

Travelling by train is the best way to see Finland. Modern trains enable you to travel quickly and comfortable to anywhere in Finland.

Restfully on the night train to Lapland

When you want to discover the enchantment of Lapland, take the train. You can get to Rovaniemi and Kemijärvi comfortably in modern and well-equipped double-deck sleeping cars. You can also take your car on the train.

Connections to Russia

It is also very easy to travel to Russia from Finland. There are two daily departures by train from Helsinki to St. Petersburg and one to Moscow. Border formalities take place conveniently while the train is moving, and you can exchange currency during the trip.

Environment

VR has worked for a cleaner environment for a long time. In the coming years VR promises to offer passengers even more environmentally friendly transport services. The 12 environmental commitments were published in December 2007 and VR intends to make good on its promises by end of its jubilee year 2012. For more information on the environmental commitments: www.vr.fi. Environmentally friendly travelling by train in Finland www.ecopassenger.org.

Further information and booking

VR Ltd, Finnish Railways · Helsinki Railway station
www.vr.fi · contactcenter@vr.fi

Shortest travel times between Hel and major cities are shown on the

7 = number of Pendolino services per day on the line s
8 = number of InterCity services per day on the line se
4 = number of Express and Regional train services per
    day on the line section

Getting there together

HELSINKI STUDIO
www.helsinkistudio.fi

DOWNTOWN TERRACE STUDIO FLATS
Rent for a night – Rent for a month

HelsinkiStudio hires out a recently-built, ultra modern attic studio flat located in the trendy Punavuori district in a century-old Jugendstil carriage house. The flat features a living room with a double bed, fold-out sofa, kitchenette, bathroom, as well as a terrace with superb views over the rooftops of Helsinki. The décor is clean, sleek Scandinavian Modern, with furnishings by Alvar Aalto and other Finnish designers.

The living space has been featured in the pages of Finnish design magazines, and is few minutes' walk from many cosy cafés, restaurants and bars, and reachable from the railway station via trams 3B and 3T. Included is free high-speed wi-fi, plus coffee, tea and a complimentary bottle of wine. Our nightly rate is more affordable than most city hotel rooms, and we also rent other flats around Helsinki – just ask us!

www.helsinkistudio.fi
Tel: +358 (0)40 771 7034

Small print and
Index

A Rough Guide to Rough Guides

SMALL PRINT

Published in 1982, the first Rough Guide – to Greece – was a student scheme that became a publishing phenomenon. Mark Ellingham, a recent graduate in English from Bristol University, had been travelling in Greece the previous summer and couldn't find the right guidebook. With a small group of friends he wrote his own guide, combining a highly contemporary, journalistic style with a thoroughly practical approach to travellers' needs.

The immediate success of the book spawned a series that rapidly covered dozens of destinations. And, in addition to impecunious backpackers, Rough Guides soon acquired a much broader and older readership that relished the guides' wit and inquisitiveness as much as their enthusiastic, critical approach and value-for-money ethos.

These days, Rough Guides include recommendations from shoestring to luxury and cover more than 200 destinations around the globe, including almost every country in the Americas and Europe, more than half of Africa and most of Asia and Australasia. Our ever-growing team of authors and photographers is spread all over the world, particularly in Europe, the US and Australia.

In the early 1990s, Rough Guides branched out of travel, with the publication of Rough Guides to World Music, Classical Music and the Internet. All three have become benchmark titles in their fields, spearheading the publication of a wide range of books under the Rough Guide name.

Including the travel series, Rough Guides now number more than 350 titles, covering: phrasebooks, waterproof maps, music guides from Opera to Heavy Metal, reference works as diverse as Conspiracy Theories and Shakespeare, and popular culture books from iPods to Poker. Rough Guides also produce a series of more than 120 World Music CDs in partnership with World Music Network.

Visit www.roughguides.com to see our latest publications.

www.roughguides.com

Rough Guide credits

Text editors: Edward Aves, Helena Smith
Layout: Nikhil Agarwal, Pradeep Thapliyal,
Sachin Gupta
Cartography: Rajesh Chhibber, Ed Wright
Picture editor: Emily Taylor
Production: Rebecca Short
Proofreader: Diane Margolis
Cover design: Dan May, Chloë Roberts
Photographers: Roger Norum, Elina Simonen
Editorial: **London** Ruth Blackmore, Andy Turner,
Keith Drew, Alice Park, Lucy White, Jo Kirby,
James Smart, Natasha Foges, Róisín Cameron,
James Rice, Lara Kavanagh, Emma Traynor,
Emma Gibbs, Kathryn Lane, Monica Woods, Mani
Ramaswamy, Harry Wilson, Lucy Cowie, Alison
Roberts, Joe Staines, Peter Buckley, Matthew
Milton, Tracy Hopkins, Ruth Tidball; **Delhi**
Madhavi Singh, Karen D'Souza, Lubna Shaheen
Design & Pictures: **London** Scott Stickland, Dan
May, Diana Jarvis, Mark Thomas, Nicole Newman,
Sarah Cummins; **Delhi** Umesh Aggarwal, Ajay
Verma, Jessica Subramanian, Ankur Guha, Sachin
Tanwar, Anita Singh

Production: Liz Cherry
Cartography: **London** Katie Lloyd-Jones;
Delhi Ashutosh Bharti, Rajesh Mishra, Animesh
Pathak, Jasbir Sandhu, Karobi Gogoi, Alakananda
Roy, Swati Handoo, Deshpal Dabas
Online: **London** Faye Hellon, Jeanette Angell,
Fergus Day, Justine Bright, Clare Bryson, Aine
Fearon, Adrian Low, Ezgi Celebi; **Delhi** Amit
Verma, Rahul Kumar, Narender Kumar, Ravi
Yadav, Debojit Borah, Rakesh Kumar, Ganesh
Sharma, Shisir Basumatari
Marketing & Publicity: **London** Liz Statham,
Jess Carter, Vivienne Watton, Anna Paynton,
Rachel Sprackett, Laura Vipond; **New York** Katy
Ball, Judi Powers; **Delhi** Ragini Govind
Reference Director: Andrew Lockett
Operations Assistant: Becky Doyle
Operations Manager: Helen Atkinson
Publishing Director (Travel): Clare Currie
Commercial Manager: Gino Magnotta
Managing Director: John Duhigg

Publishing information

This first edition published June 2010 by
Rough Guides Ltd,
80 Strand, London WC2R 0RL
14 Local Shopping Centre, Panchsheel Park,
New Delhi 110017, India
Distributed by the Penguin Group
Penguin Books Ltd,
80 Strand, London WC2R 0RL
Penguin Group (USA)
375 Hudson Street, NY 10014, USA
Penguin Group (Australia)
250 Camberwell Road, Camberwell,
Victoria 3124, Australia
Penguin Group (Canada)
195 Harry Walker Parkway N, Newmarket, ON,
L3Y 7B3 Canada
Penguin Group (NZ)
67 Apollo Drive, Mairangi Bay, Auckland 1310,
New Zealand
Cover concept by Peter Dyer.

Typeset in Bembo and Helvetica to an original
design by Henry Iles.

Printed in Singapore

© Roger Norum and James Proctor 2010

Maps © Rough Guides

No part of this book may be reproduced in any
form without permission from the publisher except
for the quotation of brief passages in reviews.

352pp includes index

A catalogue record for this book is available from
the British Library

ISBN: 978-1-84836-257-4

The publishers and authors have done their best
to ensure the accuracy and currency of all the
information in **The Rough Guide to Finland**,
however, they can accept no responsibility for
any loss, injury, or inconvenience sustained by
any traveller as a result of information or advice
contained in the guide.

1   3   5   7   9   8   6   4   2

Help us update

We've gone to a lot of effort to ensure that the
first edition of **The Rough Guide to Finland** is
accurate and up-to-date. However, things change
– places get "discovered", opening hours are
notoriously fickle, restaurants and rooms raise
prices or lower standards. If you feel we've got it
wrong or left something out, we'd like to know,
and if you can remember the address, the price,
the hours, the phone number, so much the better.

Please send your comments with the subject
line "**Rough Guide Finland Update**" to
® mail@roughguides.com. We'll credit all
contributions and send a copy of the next edition
(or any other Rough Guide if you prefer) for the
very best emails.
  Have your questions answered and tell others
about your trip at ® www.roughguides.com

www.roughguides.com

Acknowledgements

Roger Norum This book would never have happened without the absurd amounts of patience, and pedantry shown by my editor and friend, Ed Aves, who suffered pushback after botched deadline and still sifted through my wordy copy with the punctiliousness and resoluteness of a monastic scribe. James Proctor was a knowledgeable and lightening quick co-author and Helena Smith swiftly edited final finals. Photo editor Emily Taylor graciously brought me on to shoot the book, while colleague Mark Thomas helped with tips on composition and reminders to look out for colourful mittens. Ed Wright came up with some crackerjack maps for the books; Nicole Newman, Lucy White and Jo Kirby made sure everything was out the door in time, several times. On the ground in Finland, I'd have been lost, confused and up a creek without the hospitality, knowledge and smiles of my close friends at the Helsinki City Tourist Office, especially the lovely Mari Lihr and Mrs. Hanna Porvari, who never once said Älä! when I rapped on their doors, and their wonderful colleagues Laura Itävaara (who conjured up a rolodex to rival that of Tyler Brûlé), Tiina Piipponen (who knew all the velvet ropes in town) and Jenny Taipale (who diplomatically tolerated my Karaoke voice at least once). Annica Grönlund (Visit Åland) ensured ample access to beach volleyball games, island guesthouses and expert cyclists; Berit Mariani-Cerati (Visit Southpoint Finland) single-handedly organized the most comprehensive three days of the summer; Virpi Hakkarainen (Kuopio) and Tarja Harinen (Joensuu) swiftly ferried me around Karelia and the Lake District from monastery to lumberjack community; and Mirka Syvänen and Janna Mylläri (Lahti Travel) pulled together a research trip to Lahti. Thanks too to Riitta Balza, Marika Finne, Eija Ahlberg, Anne Harju, Erkki and Satu Natunen, Margit Sellberg, Carola Ingman, Maija-Liisa Lähteenmäki, Taina Grönqvist, Marjukka Kauppinen-Heino, Teija Rantapero, Ulla Antola, Pekka Oivanen, Jenna Ylipuranen,

Leena Venho, Leena Suominen, Riitta Suominen, Marc Skvorc, Aino Collan, Roni Saari, Robert Laine, Marjo Kalliola, Teija Kirjavainen, Erja Ahteela, Salla Taurianen, Anna Ruohonen, Mika Ihamuotila, the Välimäkis and Juha Huttunen at Europcar in Ivalo. And to my Finn and HKI friends, especially Vasseli, Mona, Javi, Elena, Sacha, Vernari, Petra, Anna, Annika, Päivi, Maya, Jenni Kouri, who offered insight into language issues, and fellow writer Katja Pantzar, who was an inspiration and confidante over burgers at Bali Hai. Deep thanks, too, to friends/visitors/models Wei-Li Tjong and Lyle Kane and Sara Murphy, who generously lent me kitchen, couch and companionship in Brixton as months of scribblings somehow became a book. This guide, which has been some six years in the planning, I offer to my parents and my sister, who for some reason never said No when I wanted to go away.

James Proctor would like to thank John and Marja in Kalajoki for their great company and one too many beers; wonderful Tarja in Joensuu whose whistlestop tour of Karelia totally hit the spot; Johanna in Tampere for her all-round expertise on all things T; Tuula in Kemi for her sauna towels and also Eija-Sinikka for taking me to Haparanda; Anne in Inari whose knowledge of the far north is second to none; Jussi in Levi who, thankfully, never saw the pink longjohns I had to buy to prevent hypothermia; Päivi in Savonlinna and her encouragement about Luosto; Aila in Kajaani for opening up Paltaniemi; Dutch Bart for his warm welcome and tour of Salla on a dark, snowy day; Kirsti and Jari in Kuusamo for making me feel at home; Matti in Mikkeli for information on the Winter War; Heikki in Koli for enthusing about his favourite part of Finland; Matti in Oulu for a superb lunch and tips on everything to do with the best city in the north; thanks, too, to Nan and Jouni in Helsinki, whose tales of A Year in Addingham made me long for Yorkshire. Above all, thanks to Lance for supporting the long campaign to get this book into print.

Photo credits

All photos © Rough Guides except the following:

Introduction
Northern Lights © Konrad Wothe/Photolibrary
Rally car © Kuhmo/Lotus PR
Lutheran Christian cathedral in winter snow, Helsinki © Gavin Hellier/Photolibrary

Things not to miss
02 Husky Safari © Janne Ahvo/iStock Pictures
06 Kakslauttanen, Glass Igloo © Visitfinland.com
07 Wife Carrying Festival © Visitfinland.com
09 Pihlajasaari © Kalle Kataila/Visitfinland.com
11 Snow Castle, Kemi © Tiina Itkonen/Visitfinland.com
16 Ice Breaker Tour, Kemi © Visitfinland.com
18 Kiasma Museum of Modern Art, Helsinki © Elan Fleisher/PhotoLibrary
21 Savonlinna, Olavinlinna Castle, Opera Festival © Visitfinland.com
23 Hiking in the Forested Uplands © Pekka Antikainen/Visitfinland.com

Finnish design colour section
Aalto Poster © http://materialbank.iittala.com
Marimekko design patterns © Markku Ulander/Rex Features
Ivana Helsinki Fashion Design © Courtesy of lizparrypr.co.uk
Monarch Stool by Janne Kyttanen for FOC © Courtesy of Freedom Of Creation

Sauna colour section
Snow-covered sauna sign, Finland © Anna Watson /Axiom

Black and whites
p.202 Savonlinna Castle © Visitfinland.com
p.231 Tampere © Sylvain Grandadam/PhotoLibrary
p.272 Mountains around Kilpisjarvi © Bjorn Wiklander/PhotoLibrary

Index

Map entries are in colour.

Map symbols

maps are listed in the full index using coloured text

-------	International boundary	⊞	Hospital
——-··	Province boundary	⊠	Post office
——■——	Railway	♦	Museum
= = = =	Unpaved	ⓘ	Tourist information
═══════	Road	@	Internet access
═══════	Pedestrianized street	Ⓜ	Metro station
------	Footpath	✈	International airport
— —	Ferry route	✍	Skiing
———————	Waterway	♜	Castle
▬▬▬▬▬	Wall	⊛	Swimming pool
▲	Mountain peak	⊙	Statue
∴	Ruins	▮	Building
♦	Point of interest	⊡	Church (town maps)
🏛	Stately home	⬭	Stadium
♦	Church (regional maps)	▨	Park/National park/forest
)(	Bridge	⊞	Christian cemetery
⇟⇟	Swamp	⬚	Beach

So now we've told you
about the things not to
miss, t
stay, th
the live
most sp
it only seems fair to tell
you about the best travel
insurance around

WorldNomads.com
keep travelling safely

Recommended by Rough Guides